P9-CJF-228

# *How to Use*

# MICROSOFT WORKS FOR WINDOWS 95

A

# *How to Use*

# MICROSOFT WORKS FOR WINDOWS 95

VICTOR WRIGHT

Ziff-Davis Press
Emeryville, California

| | |
|---|---|
| Editor | Margo R. Hill |
| Technical Reviewer | Heidi Steele |
| Proofreaders | Nicole Clausing and Jeff Barash |
| Cover Design and Illustration | Regan Honda |
| Book Design | Dennis Gallagher/Visual Strategies, San Francisco |
| Screen Graphics Editor | P. Diamond |
| Technical Illustration | L. Blake |
| Word Processing | Howard Blechman |
| Page Layout | Janet Stephens, Rita Riley, and Meredith Downs |
| Indexer | Valerie Robbins |



Ziff-Davis Press imprint books are produced on a Macintosh computer system with the following applications: FrameMaker®, Microsoft® Word, QuarkXPress®, Adobe Illustrator®, Adobe Photoshop®, Adobe Streamline™, MacLink® *Plus*, Aldus® FreeHand™, Collage Plus™.

If you have comments or questions or would like to receive a free catalog, call or write:
Macmillan Computer Publishing USA
Ziff-Davis Press Line of Books
5903 Christie Avenue
Emeryville, CA 94608
800-688-0448



ISBN 1-56276-350-4

Manufactured in the United States of America
10 9 8 7 6 5 4

*To my wife, Stacy*

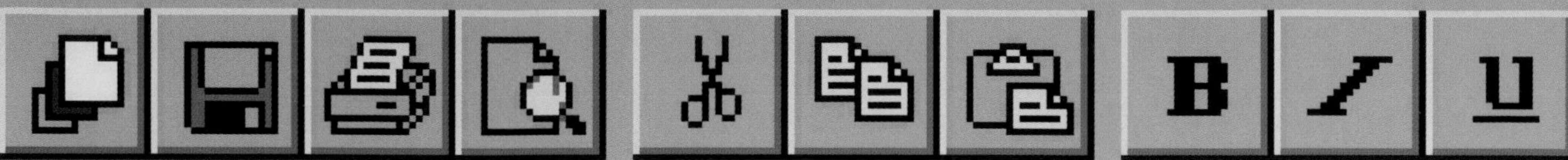


# TABLE OF CONTENTS

# TABLE OF CONTENTS

# ACKNOWLEDGMENTS

Never having written a book before, I had no idea how many people it took to publish one. Now that I know, it seems rather unfair that I get top billing when so many others contributed so much. I hope to include the names of all who made this book possible—if I don't, it's purely inadvertent.

My first acknowledgment goes to Suzanne Anthony, my acquisition editor. She gave me this opportunity and to her I am forever grateful.

I was particularly fortunate to have such an able project team. Each member performed his or her job flawlessly. Thanks to Cheryl Holzaepfel (editor in chief) for approving my schedules and watching over my work. Many thanks to Margo Hill, my copy editor, for taking my raw ideas and words and making them better. Heidi Steele (technical editor) tested each spread for accuracy. Thanks to L. Blake for creating the beautiful illustrations, and to Janet Stephens, Rita Riley, and Meredith Downs for balancing my text with the illustrations in layout. Pipi Diamond (systems administrator) made uploading files a cinch—thanks again Pipi. Assistant editor, Nicole Clausing, among other things, made sure my manuscript got to the right people. Word processing was skillfully performed by Howard Blechman. Finally, Lysa Lewallen kept me on schedule and made sure I was paid—very special thanks to you Lysa.

Thanks also to my wife Stacy for her many contributions, especially for entertaining our two youngest children so I could have a quiet house in which to write this book.

Special thanks to my mentor, Robert (Bob-O) Weink. His contributions to this project are too numerous to list. Thank you Bob-O, for your advice, help, and friendship—I couldn't have done this without you.

# INTRODUCTION

You're a beginning user of Microsoft Works for Windows 95. Maybe you're not quite sure what you can do with Works. Maybe you've never even used a computer. You're not looking to produce a work of art. You don't need hot shortcuts. You just need to get this thing to work.

*How to Use Microsoft Works for Windows 95* is for you. In this concise, colorful book, you will see what Works can do, step by step, task by task. When done reading, you'll be a comfortable, confident user of the most important features Microsoft Works offers. From letters and mailing lists to mathematical calculations and communications, a wide variety of computer resources will be right at your fingertips.

Each chapter of this book presents up to nine related topics. Because each topic spans two facing pages, everything you need to know about a topic is in front of you at one time. Just follow the numbered steps around the pages, reading the text and looking at the pictures. It's really as easy as it looks!

Colorful, realistic examples are included to help you understand how you might use each feature of Microsoft Works. You may wish to type and work with the samples as you learn, but doing so is not at all mandatory. If you want to stay focused on your own work and use this book as a reference, you will find it well suited for that purpose.

Even experienced computer users occasionally stumble into unfamiliar territory. Read the "Tip Sheet" accompanying each topic to learn more about the occasional pitfall, quirky feature, or clever tip, trick, or technique.

You will find special sections called "Try It" at strategic spots in this book. A Try It section is a hands-on exercise that gives you valuable practice with the skills you've acquired to that point. As you read a Try It section, be sure to follow each step at your computer.

To get the most out of this book, read it in sequence. If you have any experience with Microsoft Windows or Microsoft Works, you may already be familiar with the information in some of the chapters. However, skimming those chapters will provide a useful refresher on major concepts and terminology.

Welcome aboard.

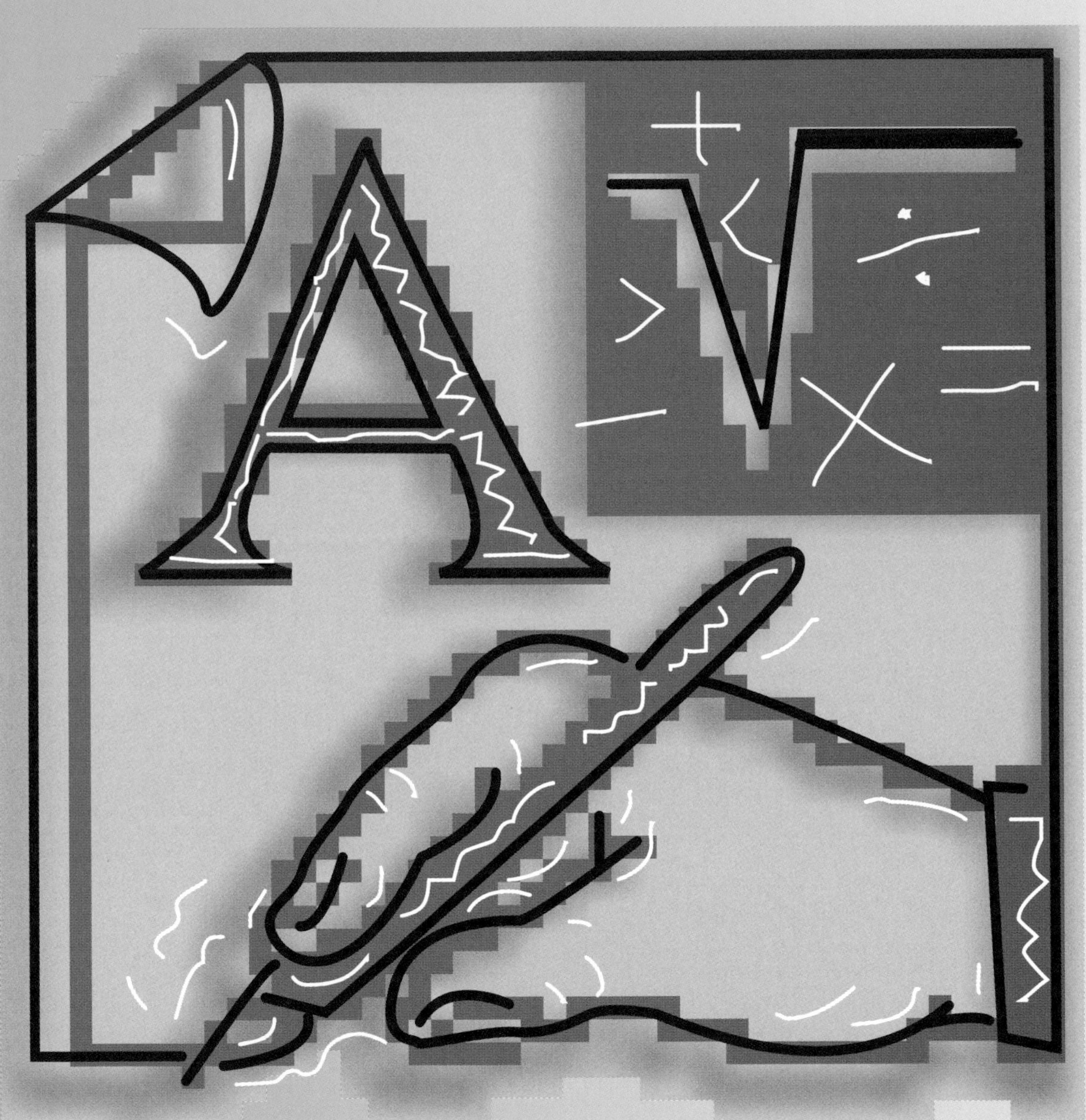

## CHAPTER 1

# What Is Microsoft Works?

Microsoft Works is a software package that helps you do many of the most popular and important tasks you can perform on your computer.

Microsoft Works, or just plain "Works," is an *integrated software* package. It combines the features of the most widely used software packages into a neat and easy-to-use bundle.

The part most people want to use first is the word processor. A word processor is software that helps you create documents. A document is simply anything written. It can be a note to a friend, a manuscript for a book, or anything in between.

The second part is a spreadsheet, which is a tool to help you perform and record mathematical calculations. You might use it to calculate your company's quarterly earnings, your personal budget, or even the returns you'll receive from the investment of your lottery winnings.

The third part is a powerful electronic database. A database is any collection of information. Mailing lists, address books, and compilations of baseball players' statistics are all databases.

The fourth part, and the last one we'll cover in this book, is a communications program for exchanging information with other computers.

Separately, these programs help you accomplish all of the basic computer tasks. Together in Microsoft Works, they form one of the most powerful and versatile software packages around.

# How to Put Microsoft Works to Work

Microsoft Works holds an unusual position in the world of software. Its true power lies not in any one of its parts, but in the ease with which you can combine them to fit your needs. Here are just a few simple examples of what Microsoft Works can do for you.

**1** With just a little experience, you'll discover that word processors can be the easiest way of creating documents. Word processors let you do your own writing, formatting, editing, revising, and printing without ever leaving your chair.

**5** Connecting PCs to bulletin boards and information services is becoming a very popular and important means of communication. The communications feature in Microsoft Works lets even a computer novice get started easily.

**4** With the help of the database and the word processor, you can create personalized letters to a large number of people.

**TIP SHEET**

- **This book is about version 4.0 of Microsoft Works. If you don't have version 4.0, some of the material in this book may not apply to you. Check your Microsoft Works packaging or documentation if you're not sure.**
- **Chapter 2 of this book is for first-time computer or Windows users. If you can start Microsoft Windows, use the mouse, choose commands from a menu, and make selections in a dialog box, skip ahead to Chapter 3. If you can't do all of these things (or if you don't even know what they mean!), Chapter 2 is just for you.**

**2** Spreadsheets are useful for performing calculations. The more numbers you have to manipulate, or the more repetition in your calculations, the greater the benefit.

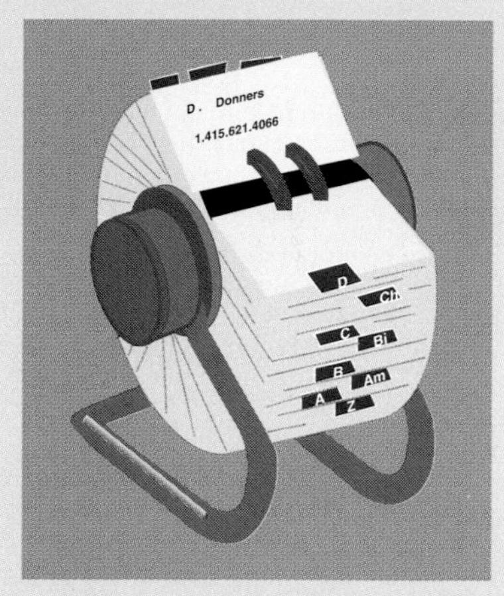


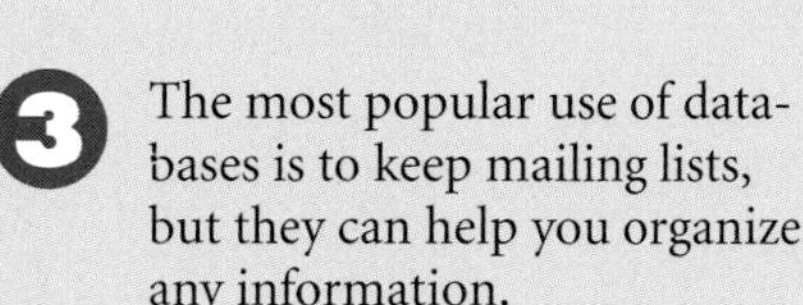

**3** The most popular use of databases is to keep mailing lists, but they can help you organize any information.

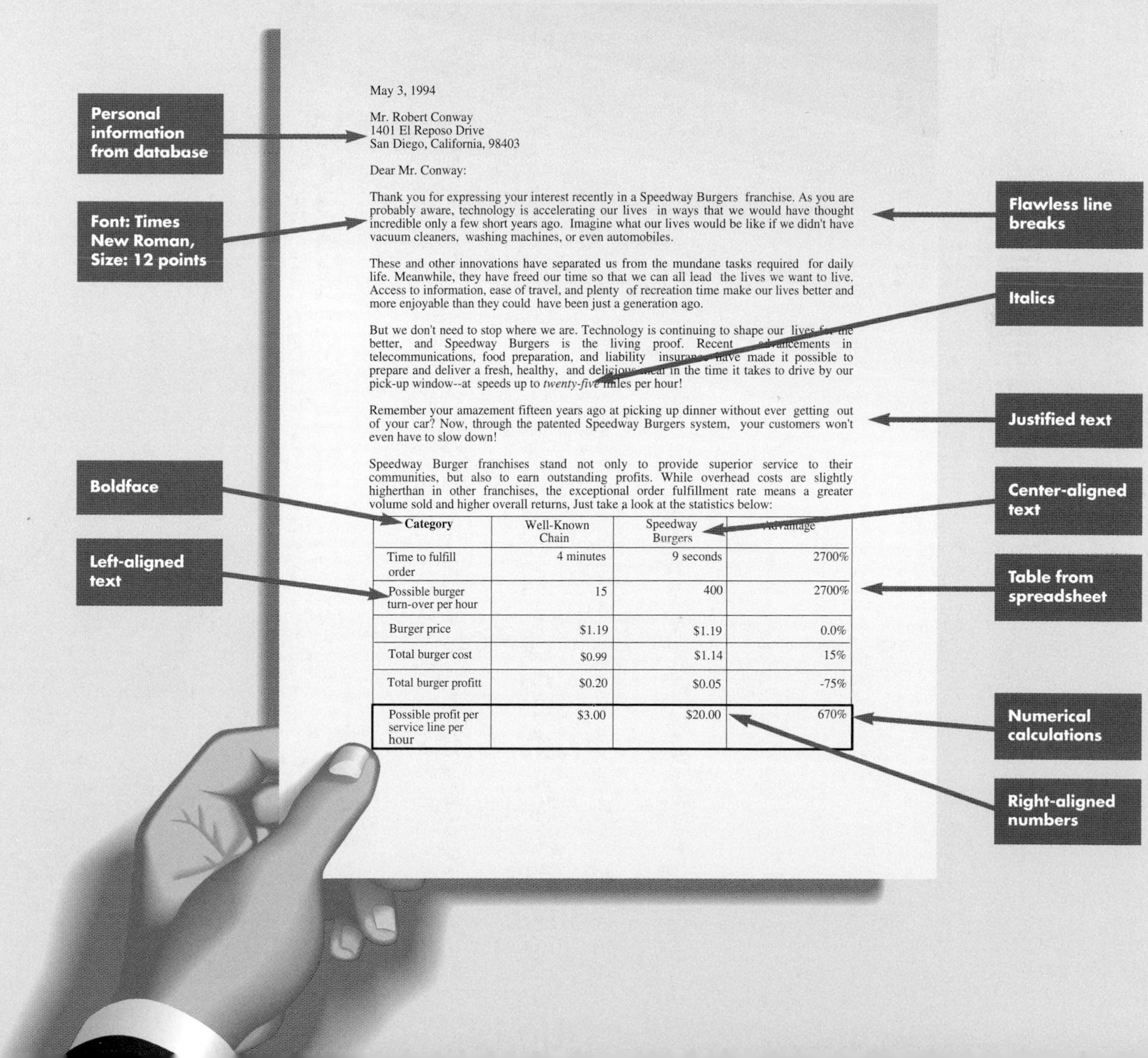

May 3, 1994

Mr. Robert Conway
1401 El Reposo Drive
San Diego, California, 98403

Dear Mr. Conway:

Thank you for expressing your interest recently in a Speedway Burgers franchise. As you are probably aware, technology is accelerating our lives in ways that we would have thought incredible only a few short years ago. Imagine what our lives would be like if we didn't have vacuum cleaners, washing machines, or even automobiles.

These and other innovations have separated us from the mundane tasks required for daily life. Meanwhile, they have freed our time so that we can all lead the lives we want to live. Access to information, ease of travel, and plenty of recreation time make our lives better and more enjoyable than they could have been just a generation ago.

But we don't need to stop where we are. Technology is continuing to shape our lives for the better, and Speedway Burgers is the living proof. Recent advancements in telecommunications, food preparation, and liability insurance have made it possible to prepare and deliver a fresh, healthy, and delicious meal in the time it takes to drive by our pick-up window--at speeds up to *twenty-five* miles per hour!

Remember your amazement fifteen years ago at picking up dinner without ever getting out of your car? Now, through the patented Speedway Burgers system, your customers won't even have to slow down!

Speedway Burger franchises stand not only to provide superior service to their communities, but also to earn outstanding profits. While overhead costs are slightly higherthan in other franchises, the exceptional order fulfillment rate means a greater volume sold and higher overall returns, Just take a look at the statistics below:

| **Category** | Well-Known Chain | Speedway Burgers | Advantage |
|---|---|---|---|
| Time to fulfill order | 4 minutes | 9 seconds | 2700% |
| Possible burger turn-over per hour | 15 | 400 | 2700% |
| Burger price | $1.19 | $1.19 | 0.0% |
| Total burger cost | $0.99 | $1.14 | 15% |
| Total burger profitt | $0.20 | $0.05 | -75% |
| Possible profit per service line per hour | $3.00 | $20.00 | 670% |

Personal information from database

Font: Times New Roman, Size: 12 points

Boldface

Left-aligned text

Flawless line breaks

Italics

Justified text

Center-aligned text

Table from spreadsheet

Numerical calculations

Right-aligned numbers

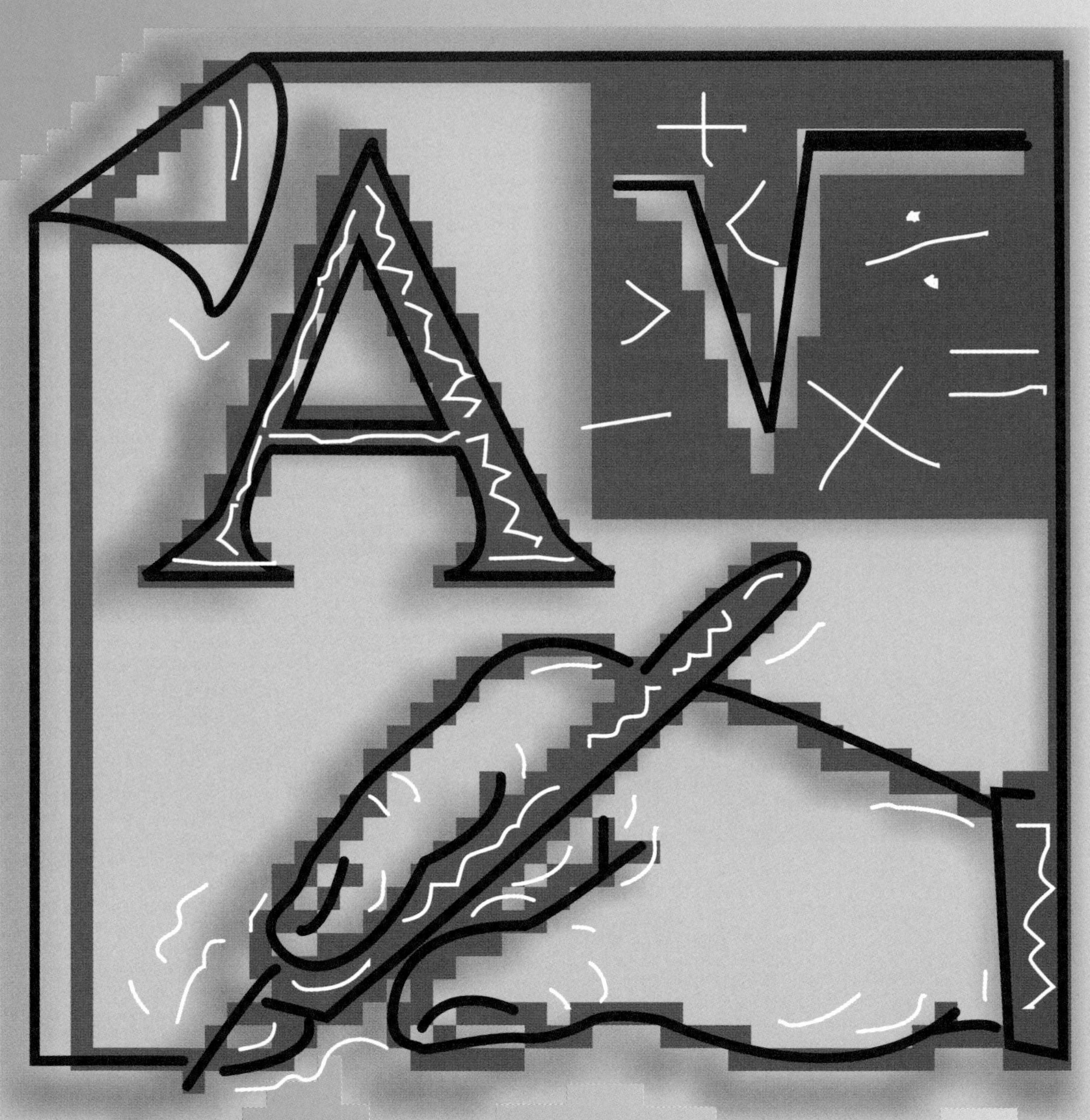

# CHAPTER 2

# What Is Windows 95?

Windows 95, or just plain *Windows*, is a program that enables you to run all the programs you really want to run: your database, your communications program—all of which are included in Microsoft Works—your games, and so on.

Windows, your computer's operating system, copies information to and from the disks in your computer. Without an operating system, your computer cannot do anything useful for you. You cannot run a program like Microsoft Works unless you tell Windows to copy it temporarily from the disk into *random-access memory (RAM)*, a temporary holding place. Likewise, you cannot electronically store and later reuse a document unless you have Windows copy it from RAM onto a disk.

Windows can simplify your role in directing these and many other affairs on your computer. It also provides a consistent and fairly appealing backdrop for Windows-based programs such as Microsoft Works. Windows-based programs look comfortingly similar on the screen, and there are many similarities in the ways you work with them. If you've used any Windows-based program, certain Microsoft Works operations will be familiar to you.

You don't need to "start" Windows. It starts automatically when you turn on your computer. After Windows is running, you can use Microsoft Works or any other Windows-based program. This chapter helps you start and run Windows.

# How to Start Windows 95

To start Windows, simply turn on your computer. Windows will automatically load into your computer, and when it's finished loading it will display the *desktop* from where you start a program, open a document, browse your PC hardware, manage your files, or do whatever it is you want to do using your computer.

**1** Switch on your computer. You may need to flick switches on several components of your computer system, including the main box containing the hard-disk and the floppy-disk drives, the monitor (screen), and the printer. Give the computer a minute or so to go through its wake-up ritual.

Shortcut icons

Taskbar

- **You can disable the "Welcome to Windows 95" screen by removing the checkmark in the checkbox next to the message "Show this Welcome Screen next time you start Windows." However, we recommend that you leave this feature enabled. The tips that appear in the Welcome screen will prove valuable in learning the many features available in Windows.**
- **The desktop can be customized to meet your particular needs. For instructions on how to customize the desktop, click on the Start button, click on Help, select the Find tab, and type Desktop. Many of the topics that now appear in the Help window will tell you how to customize your desktop.**
- **If you're a DOS diehard, a path to the DOS prompt can be found by choosing the "Shut Down" option from the Start button and then selecting "Restart the computer in MS-DOS mode?"**

**2** When the computer completes its wake-up ritual it loads Windows automatically into your computer. After Windows loads and is ready to accept your commands a desktop appears. On the desktop you'll find a variety of objects including *windows*, *icons*, and a *Taskbar*.

**3** In the center of the desktop is the Welcome window. The Welcome window provides "What's new" information and helpful tips for both experienced and new users. An online registration feature allows users with modems to electronically register their new software.

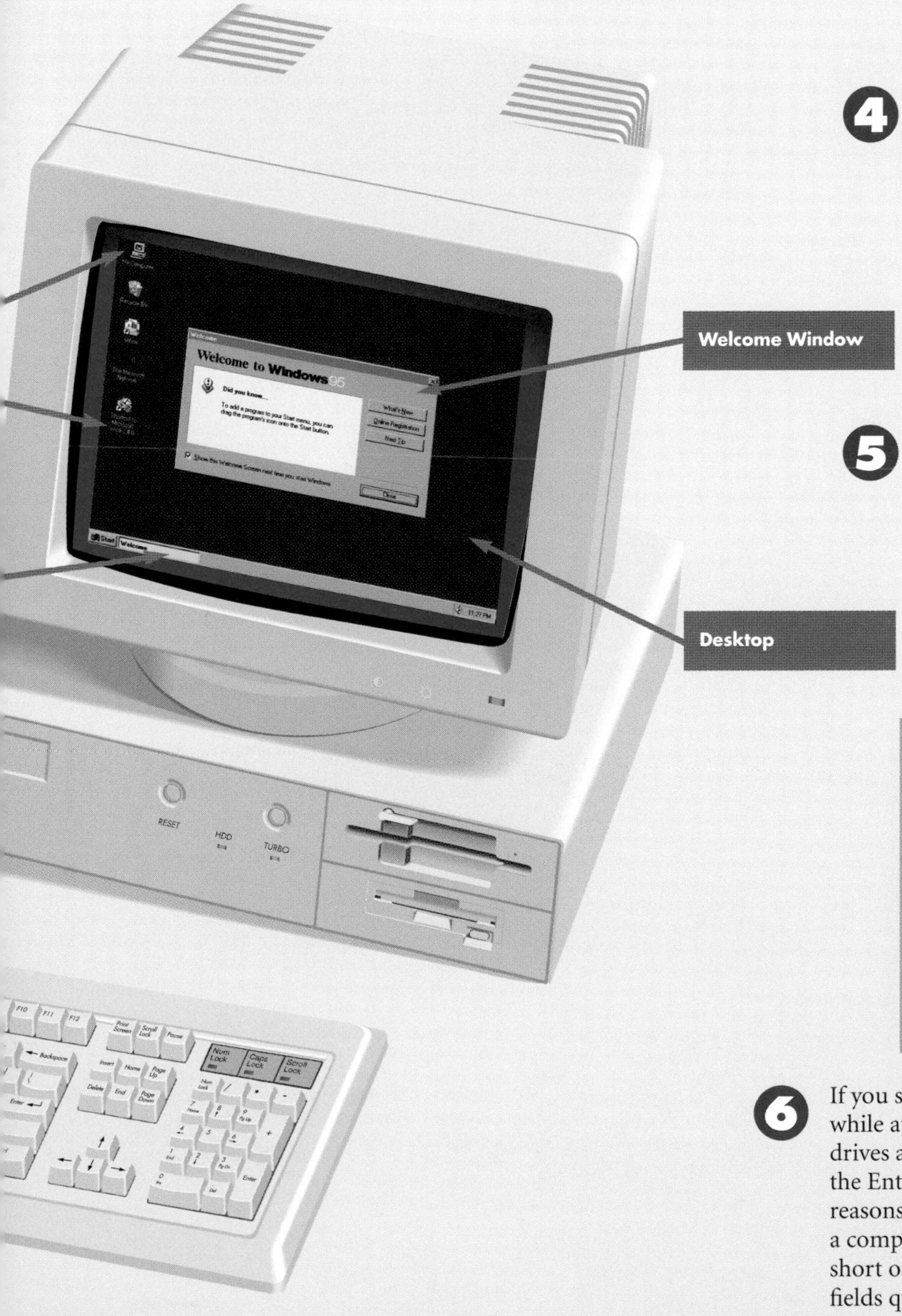

**4** Along the left side of the desktop are various *icons*. The icons provide shortcuts to favorite applications, file maintenance, or browsing your computer or network.

Welcome Window

**5** The *Taskbar*, which normally appears along the bottom row of the desktop, is used to start a program, open a document, or switch easily between running programs.

Desktop

**6** If you see the message "Non-System disk or disk error…" while attempting to start Windows, check your floppy-disk drives and remove any disks you find in them—then press the Enter key. Still can't start Windows? Well, the possible reasons and solutions are too many to enumerate here, but a computer-savvy colleague should be able to help you in short order. Or call Microsoft technical support, which fields questions like yours routinely.

# How to Use the Mouse in Windows

An *input device* is a means of giving instructions to the computer. You're probably familiar with the keyboard as the most common input device. A *mouse*, so named for its hunched-over appearance and tail-like cable, is a hand-held input device that, along with the *keyboard*, is one of the two input devices most people use routinely in Windows. Although it's possible to get by without a mouse and do all your work from the keyboard, it's not too wise. The Windows interface was designed with the mouse in mind. Keyboard alternatives can be awkward—and it's not always easy to find out what they are. Take a few minutes to learn the major mouse moves, and you'll be rewarded with smoother computing.

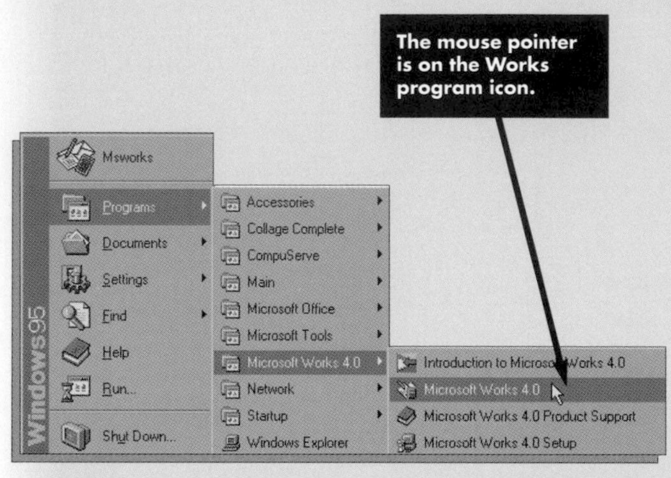


**1** As you roll the mouse along the table top, the mouse pointer on the screen moves in the same direction. You roll the mouse only to point to something on the screen as a prelude to another action.

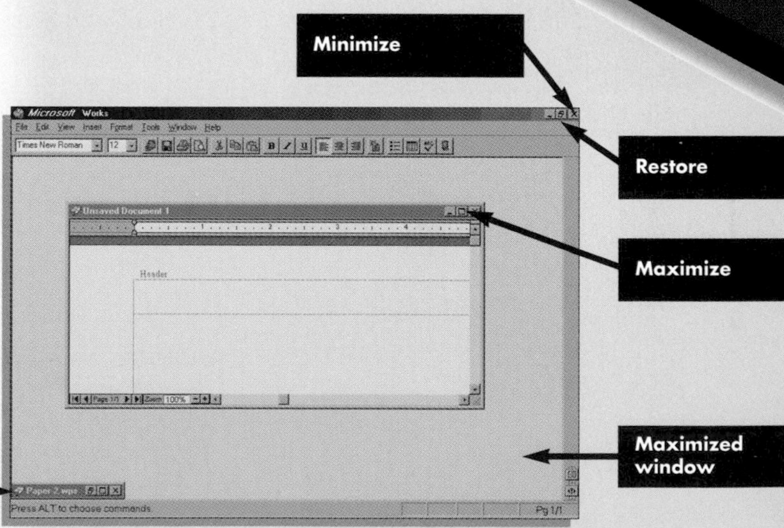


**6** To *maximize* a window (enlarge it so an application window fills the screen or so a document window fills its application window), click on its maximize button. To *restore* a maximized window to its original size, click on its restore button. To *minimize* a window so it's merely an icon with a title, click on its minimize button. To restore a minimized window to its original size, double-click on its title or icon.

**TIP SHEET**

- **Unless told otherwise, use the left mouse button.**
- **Some mice have two buttons, and others have three. In Windows 95 and many new applications like Works 4.0, the right mouse button is used to display shortcut menus. Take some time to read about how the right mouse button can save you time and trouble. Conversely, the middle button on the three-button mouse is almost never used.**
- **For keyboard alternatives to the scroll bars and the maximize/minimize/restore buttons, turn the page.**

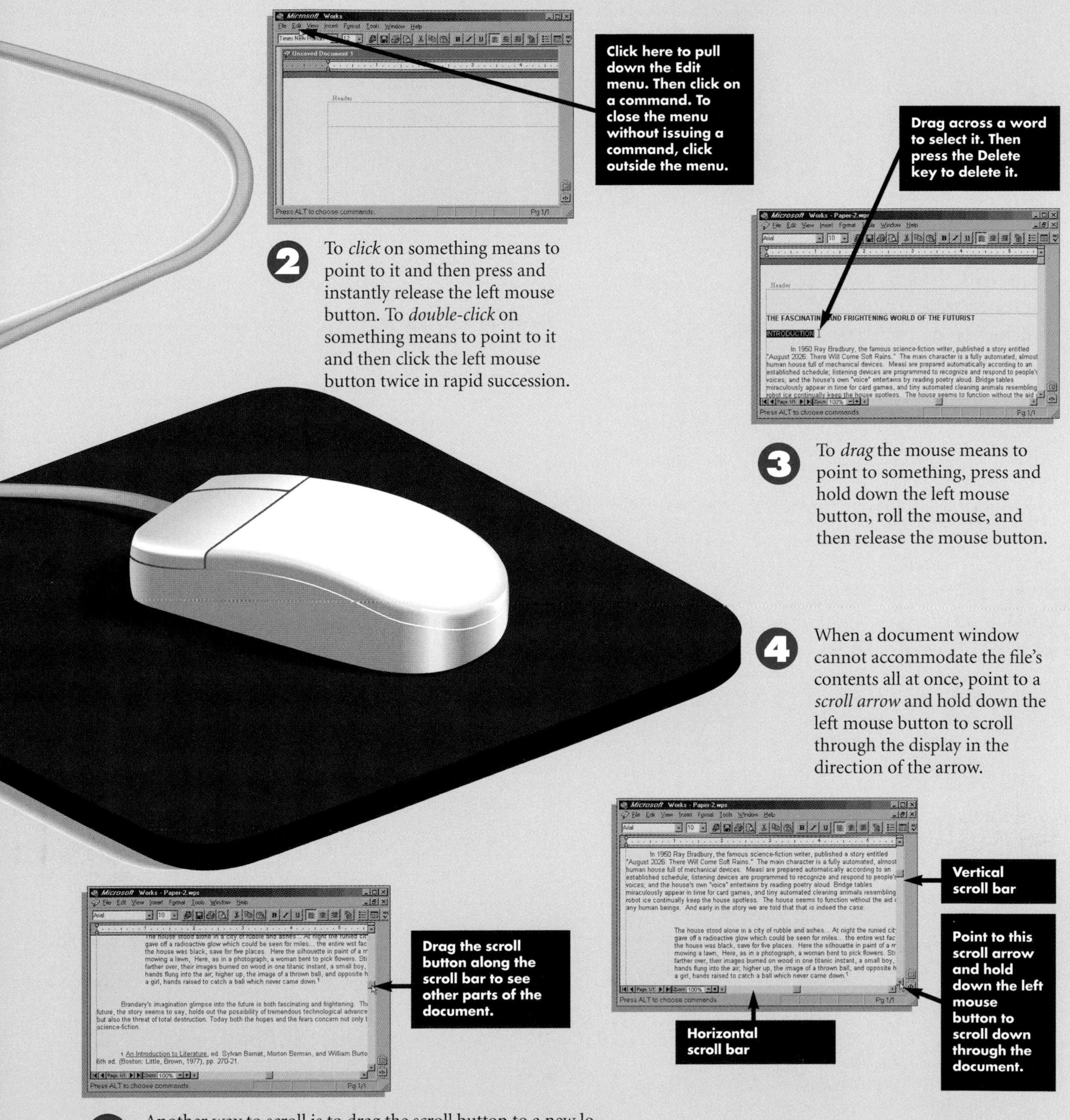

Click here to pull down the Edit menu. Then click on a command. To close the menu without issuing a command, click outside the menu.
Drag across a word to select it. Then press the Delete key to delete it.
Drag the scroll button along the scroll bar to see other parts of the document.
Vertical scroll bar
Point to this scroll arrow and hold down the left mouse button to scroll down through the document.
Horizontal scroll bar


**2** To *click* on something means to point to it and then press and instantly release the left mouse button. To *double-click* on something means to point to it and then click the left mouse button twice in rapid succession.

**3** To *drag* the mouse means to point to something, press and hold down the left mouse button, roll the mouse, and then release the mouse button.

**4** When a document window cannot accommodate the file's contents all at once, point to a *scroll arrow* and hold down the left mouse button to scroll through the display in the direction of the arrow.

**5** Another way to scroll is to drag the scroll button to a new location on the scroll bar. The position of the scroll button suggests what part of the contents you are viewing. For example, when the scroll button is about one-third of the way down the vertical scroll bar in a document window, you are one-third of the way from the top of the document.

# How to Use the Keyboard in Windows

In Windows and in most Windows-based programs, you don't have to use the keyboard for much of anything—except, of course, to type text. But if you type quite a bit, you may be interested in optional ways to move through documents, issue commands, and perform other routine functions without having to reach for the mouse. The more experience you get in a Windows-based program, the more likely you'll hanker for keyboard alternatives to the mouse actions you perform most often. Even if you're a true mouse-o-phile, you should be aware of the major keyboard techniques in case your mouse ever malfunctions.

**1** The Shift, Alt, and Ctrl keys always work in combination with other keys. No doubt you know that pressing the Shift key along with a letter key types a capital letter. The other available combinations vary by program.

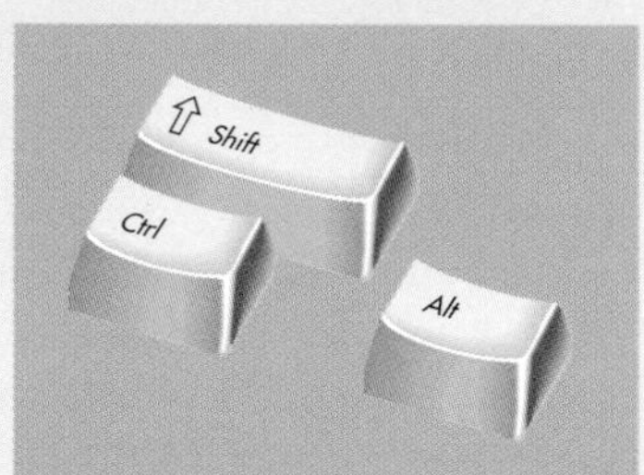

**6** Not surprisingly, the *Escape* key (Esc on most keyboards) lets you slam the door on possible hazards. If you pull down a menu but decide not to issue a command, press Esc twice to deactivate the menu bar. If you issue a command and a dialog box appears but you don't want to proceed, press Esc to close the dialog box.

**TIP SHEET**

- **In many programs, the PgUp and PgDn keys scroll the window contents in large increments, Ctrl+Home moves to the top of the window contents, and Ctrl+End moves to the bottom.**
- **Your function keys may be across the top of the keyboard or along the left side. Function keys along the side are easier for touch typists to reach and may make it worthwhile to memorize some keyboard shortcuts in your favorite programs.**

**2** Most often, Shift, Alt, and Ctrl combine with the function keys—labeled F1 through F10 or F12—as an alternative way to issue a command. For example, in most Windows programs, press Alt+F4 (hold down Alt, press and release F4, and release Alt) to close the program. The function keys can also work alone.

**3** When you don't want to reach for the mouse to scroll through the contents of a window, use the ↑, ↓, ←, and → keys instead. If the arrows on the numeric keypad don't work, press the Num Lock key and they should work fine.

**Control menu of the Works document window**

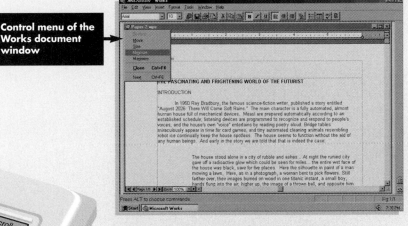

**4** To maximize, minimize, restore, or close a window, first open its *Control menu.* Press Alt+spacebar to open the Control menu of an application window; press Alt+hyphen to open the Control menu of a document window. Use the key to highlight the command you want: Maximize, Minimize, Restore, or Close. Then press Enter.

**Type the underlined character to issue the command.**

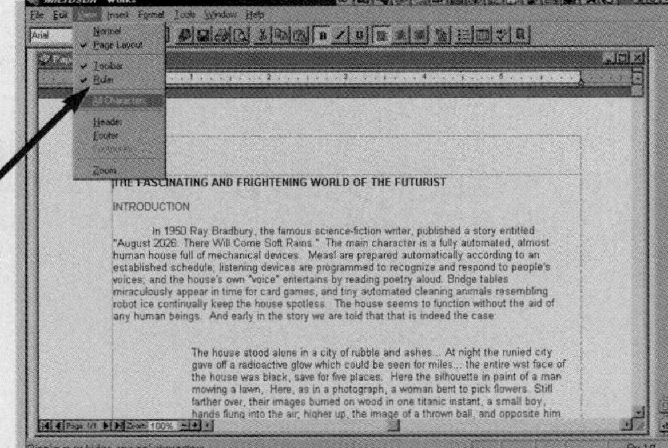

**5** To pull down a menu from the menu bar, press Alt and then type the underlined character in the menu name. Then, to issue a command from the menu, type the underlined character in the command name.

# How to Start a Program from Windows 95

There are many ways to start a program in Windows. The standard way is to start a program using the Start button on the Taskbar. The Taskbar is usually located on the bottom of the screen. But because Windows is highly customizable, you could find it at the top of the screen or on either side of the screen.

Once you have started several programs you'll need a way to move from one running program to another. This section also covers two techniques for switching between running programs. The first technique uses the mouse, while the second technique is for keyboard lovers.

**TIPS SHEET**

- **When you install an application in Windows 95 you'll be given the option to create a shortcut icon on the desktop. This provides a quick way to run applications that you use frequently.**
- **You can create a program icon in the Start menu by dragging the program file from its folder onto the Start button.**
- **For more information on creating shortcuts or modifying your Start menu, select the *Help* feature in the Start menu and enter "Shortcuts" or "Start menu."**

**1** The Taskbar appears along the bottom of the screen and is the starting point for launching a program. Position the mouse pointer over the Start button and click once.

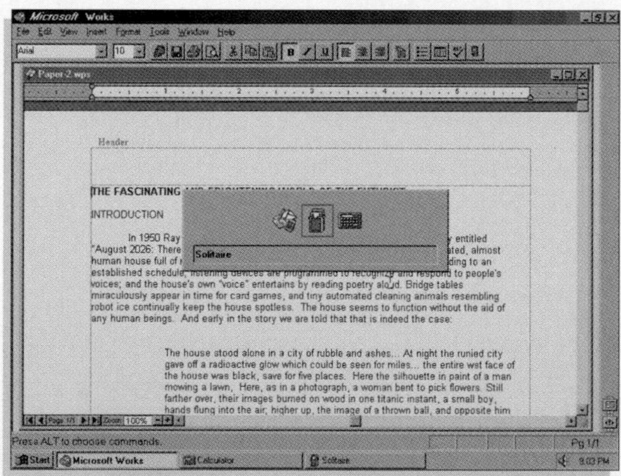


**5** Here are two ways to switch between running programs. On the Taskbar you'll find the names of running programs. To switch to a program, simply click on its name in the Taskbar. If you prefer using your keyboard, press and hold the Alt key and touch the Tab key. A list of running programs will appear in the center of your screen. When the program you want to switch to is highlighted, release the Alt key.

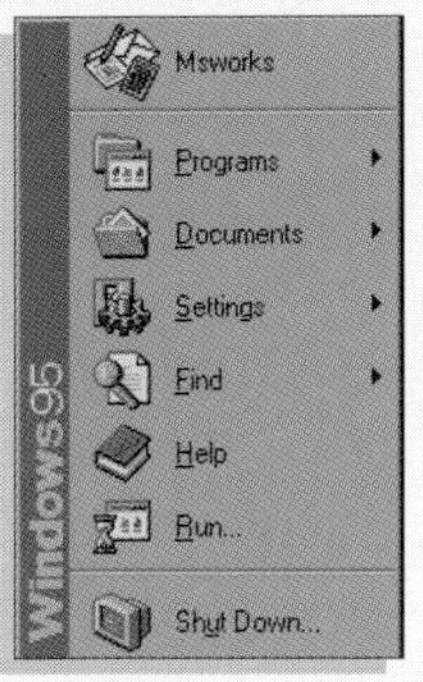


**2** A pop-up menu appears when you click on the Start button. Among the options that appear in the Start menu is the Programs submenu.

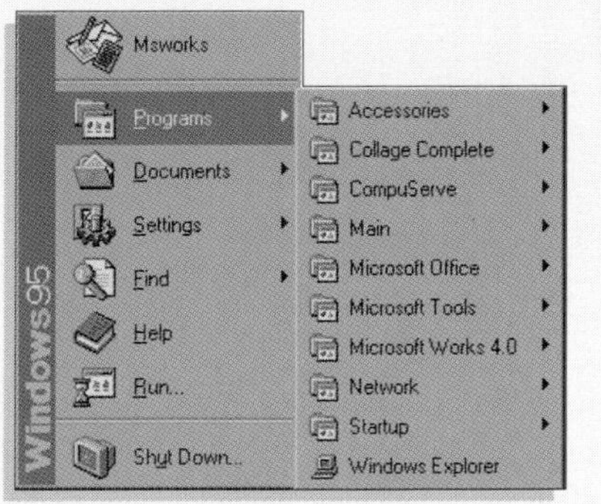


**3** To view the contents of the Programs submenu, position the mouse pointer over the word "Programs." A list of program folders is displayed to the right of the Start menu. The program you're looking for will be in one of these program folders.

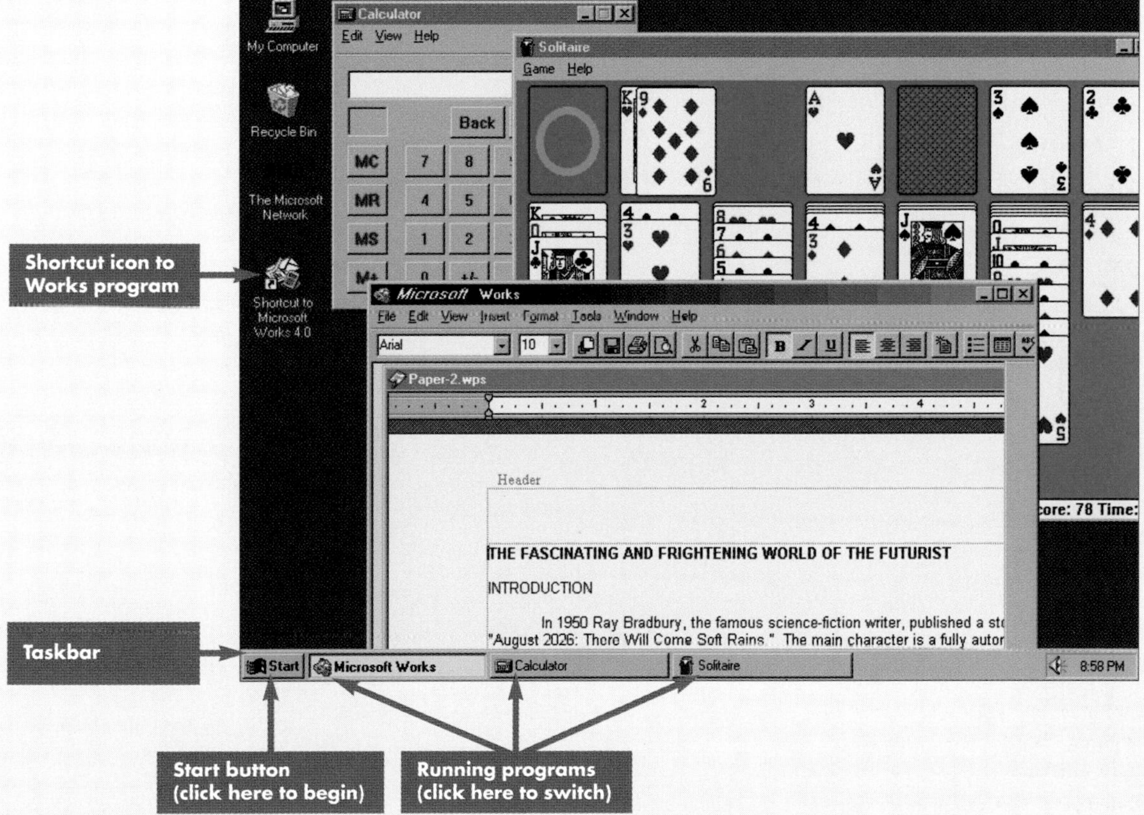

As you move the mouse pointer through the list of program folders, the programs that are stored in each folder are displayed. To launch a program, position the mouse pointer over the program name and click once. In the example we've selected Microsoft Works 4.0 to run.

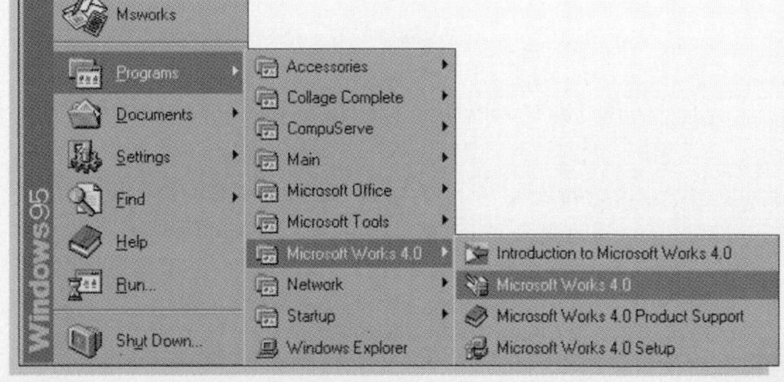

# How to Talk to a Dialog Box

A *dialog box* is where you give Windows (or a Windows-based program) the information it needs to carry out a command you have issued. Say you issue a command called *Print*, a command found in many programs. Before doing any printing, the program may present a dialog box to ask you how much of the window contents to print, how many copies to print, what printer to print it on, and so forth. Once you answer, the Print command takes effect. The name "dialog box" is just slightly misleading. In a human dialog, the participants take turns speaking. In a computerized dialog, the program asks all its questions at once, and then you give all your answers. It's more like a questionnaire than a dialog.

**TIP SHEET**

- **To choose a dialog box option from the keyboard, hold down Alt and type the underlined character in the option name. If the dialog box lacks underlined characters, press Tab to move from option to option. Then, to mark or clear a check box, press the spacebar. To mark the desired radio button within a group, use the arrow keys. To drop down a list, press the down arrow key; then press the down arrow to highlight your choice, and press Tab. To edit the contents of a text box, use the arrow keys, Backspace, Delete, and ordinary typing keys.**
- **If you need to see what's behind a dialog box, move the box by dragging its title bar.**
- **To close a dialog box without issuing the command, click on the Cancel button (available in most dialog boxes), double-click on the box's Control Menu box, or press Esc.**

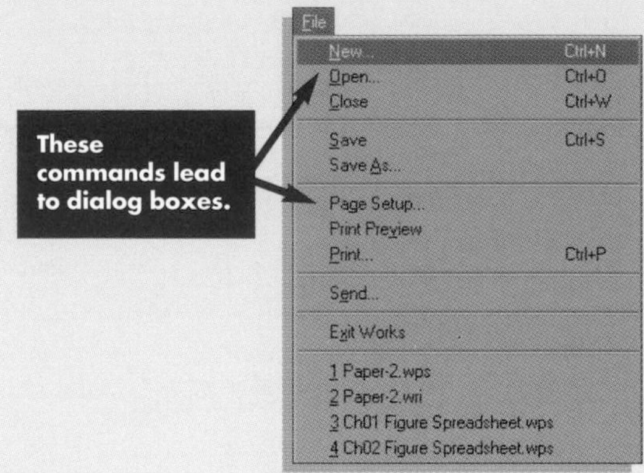


**1** In Windows menus, the presence of three dots after a command name means that a dialog box will appear when you issue the command.

OK

**6** When you've provided all the information requested, issue the command by clicking on the button labeled OK or on another appropriately named button. (The button name might be Print or Find or something else related to the command.)

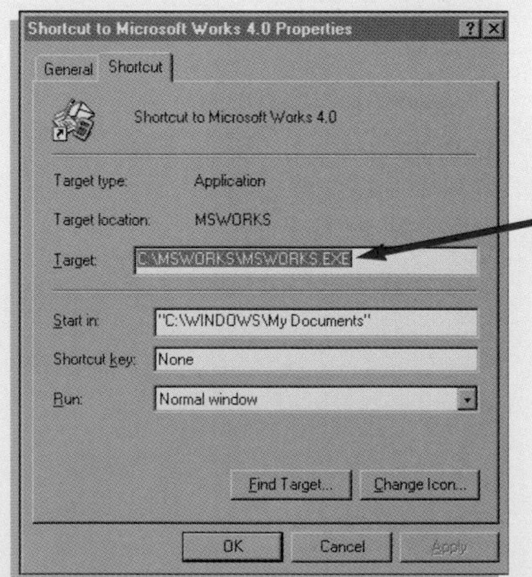


**5** To change the entry in a text box, first click anywhere in the box. Then use the arrow keys to position the cursor, use the Backspace and Delete keys to delete text as needed, and type new text from the keyboard.

Style
Bold
Italic
Underline
Strikethrough
Marked
Cleared

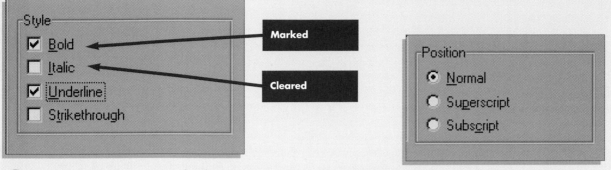

**2** One way to answer a question in a dialog box is to mark or clear a square check box. Click in an empty check box to mark it, accepting the option; click in a marked check box to clear it and reject the option.

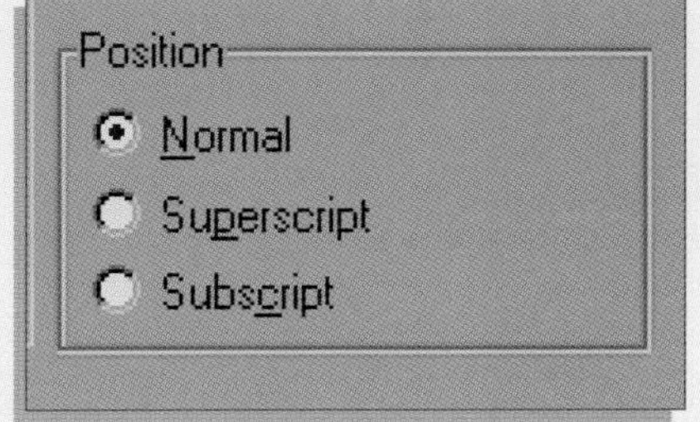


**3** Sometimes options are grouped in radio buttons. You can select only one option at a time in the group. Select an option by clicking in the round button; the previously selected button is cleared. It's just like the station-selector buttons on old-time car radios—hence the name.

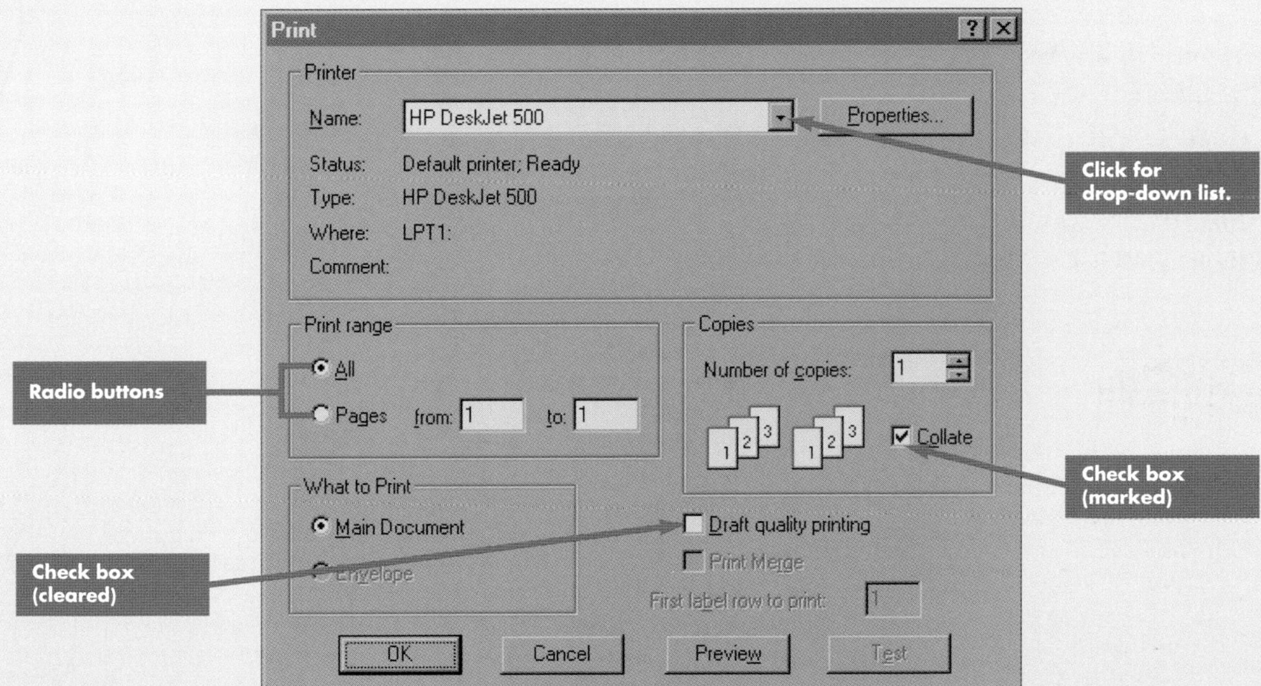


**4** A downward-pointing arrow with a horizontal line below it means you can click on the arrow to see a drop-down list of options. When you spot the option you need, click on it.

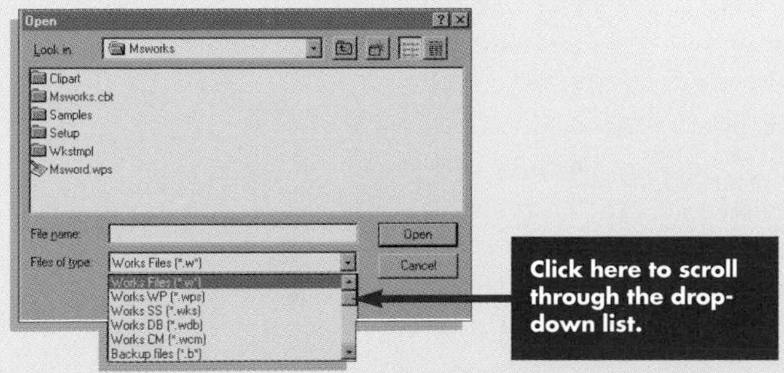

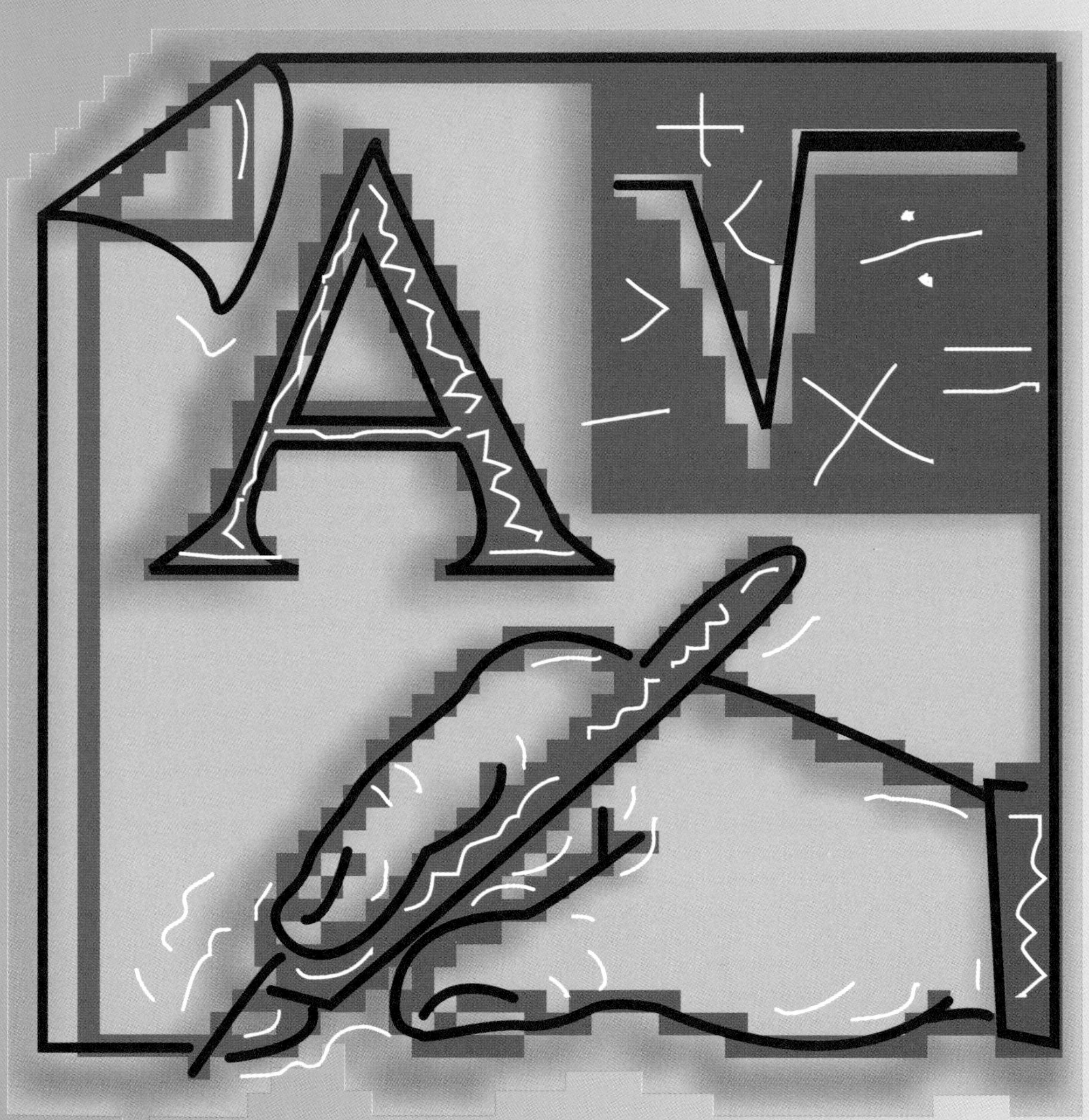

# CHAPTER 3

# Welcome to Microsoft Works

Now that you're familiar with the basics of Windows, it's time to step into the world of Microsoft Works. If you're new to Works, the number of controls on the screen might make it look to you like the instrument panel of a jet airplane. Don't worry. This chapter will introduce you to the most important tools and groups of tools on the screen, so that you will recognize them in the following chapters when it's time to use them. While you won't be learning to fly through the air, by getting you started with the most useful tools, this book will have you flying through your work in no time.

# How to Get Started in Microsoft Works

Whenever you start Microsoft Works, one of the first things you'll see is the Works Task Launcher window. After you select the part of Works you want to explore, you'll see a screen much like the one in the large illustration to the right. It shows the word processor with a new document window. If you're working with only one document, as you will be throughout most of this book, you'll have a little more elbow room if you maximize both the document and application windows. If you see a Restore button in the upper-right corner of either window, then it is already maximized. (See Chapter 2 if you need help maximizing your windows.) Most of the illustrations in this book, including the ones in this chapter, have maximized application and document windows.

## TIP SHEET

- **The *status bar* gives you helpful clues about what you can do in your document. As you try typing, highlighting menu items, or moving the mouse over buttons in the toolbar, the status bar will display different messages.**
- **If you need more space in the work area, you can hide the toolbar by opening the View menu and then clicking on Toolbar to remove the checkmark next to it. Beginners and experts agree, however, that using the toolbar is often the most efficient way to work. If the toolbar doesn't appear on your screen and you want it to, you can show it the same way you hide it: Click on the View menu, and then on Toolbar, this time to check the menu item.**
- **Help is always available in Microsoft Works when you need it. If necessary you can make selections from the Help menu just like any other menu, but you'll see more on help in the next chapter.**

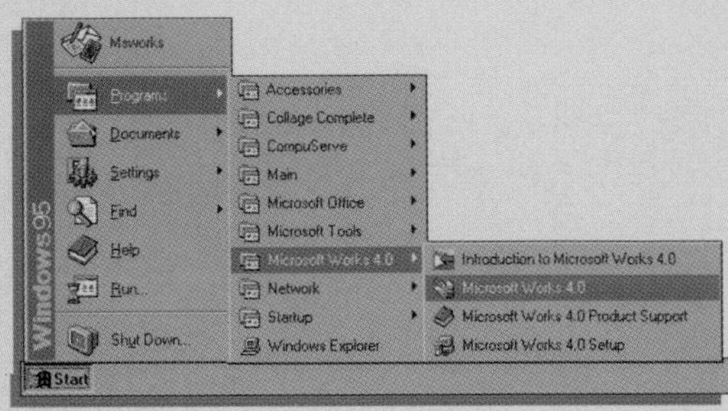


**1** To start Works, click on the Start button and point to Programs. From the list that appears on the right, point to the Works program folder. Then point and click on Microsoft Works 4.0.

**7** You can perform routine actions quickly and easily by clicking the buttons on the toolbar. The icon on each button gives a graphical representation of what the button does. If you move your mouse button over any of the buttons without clicking, a small box will appear below the pointer to show you the button's name.

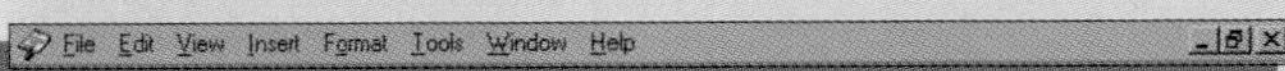


**6** The menu bar in Works shows these eight menu names except while you're in the communications package. Click on the menu name to pull down the menu. You can then either select an item in the menu by clicking on it or close the menu without making a selection by clicking outside it.

**5** When the document window is maximized, the title bar shows both the name of the application running in the window, "Microsoft Works," and the name of the maximized document active in that program. When you create a new document (either word processor, spreadsheet, database, or communications), Works will call it "Unsaved" until you save and name it.

**2** If you have chosen to skip the tour, you'll see the Works Task Launcher with three tabs to choose from. Click the Works Tools tab to enable you to select the part of Works you wish to use.

Works Task Launcher
TaskWizards
Existing Documents
Works Tools
Click the TaskWizard you want to begin
Common Tasks
Address Book
Letter
Letterhead
Newsletter
Resume (CV)
Start from Scratch
Correspondence
Envelopes and Labels
Business Management
Names and Addresses
Household Management
Click a category to show or hide a list of TaskWizards.
List categories in different order
Exit Works
OK
Cancel

Works Task Launcher
TaskWizards
Existing Documents
Works Tools
Click one of the Works tools
Word Processor
Create letters, memos, form letters, and mailing labels
Spreadsheet
Do budgeting and calculations, create charts and graphs
Database
Create address books, lists and reports
Communications
Send and receive documents with your modem
Exit Works
OK
Cancel

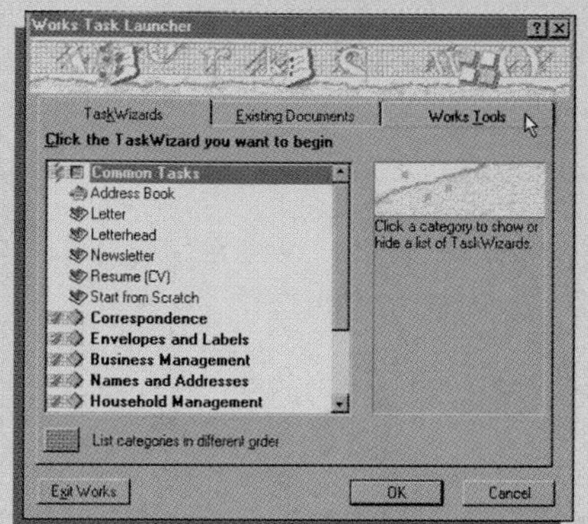

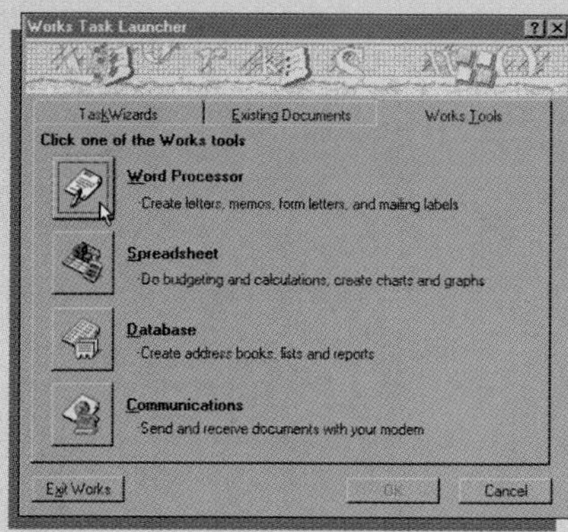

**3** You can now launch the Works tool you wish by clicking on one of the large square buttons.

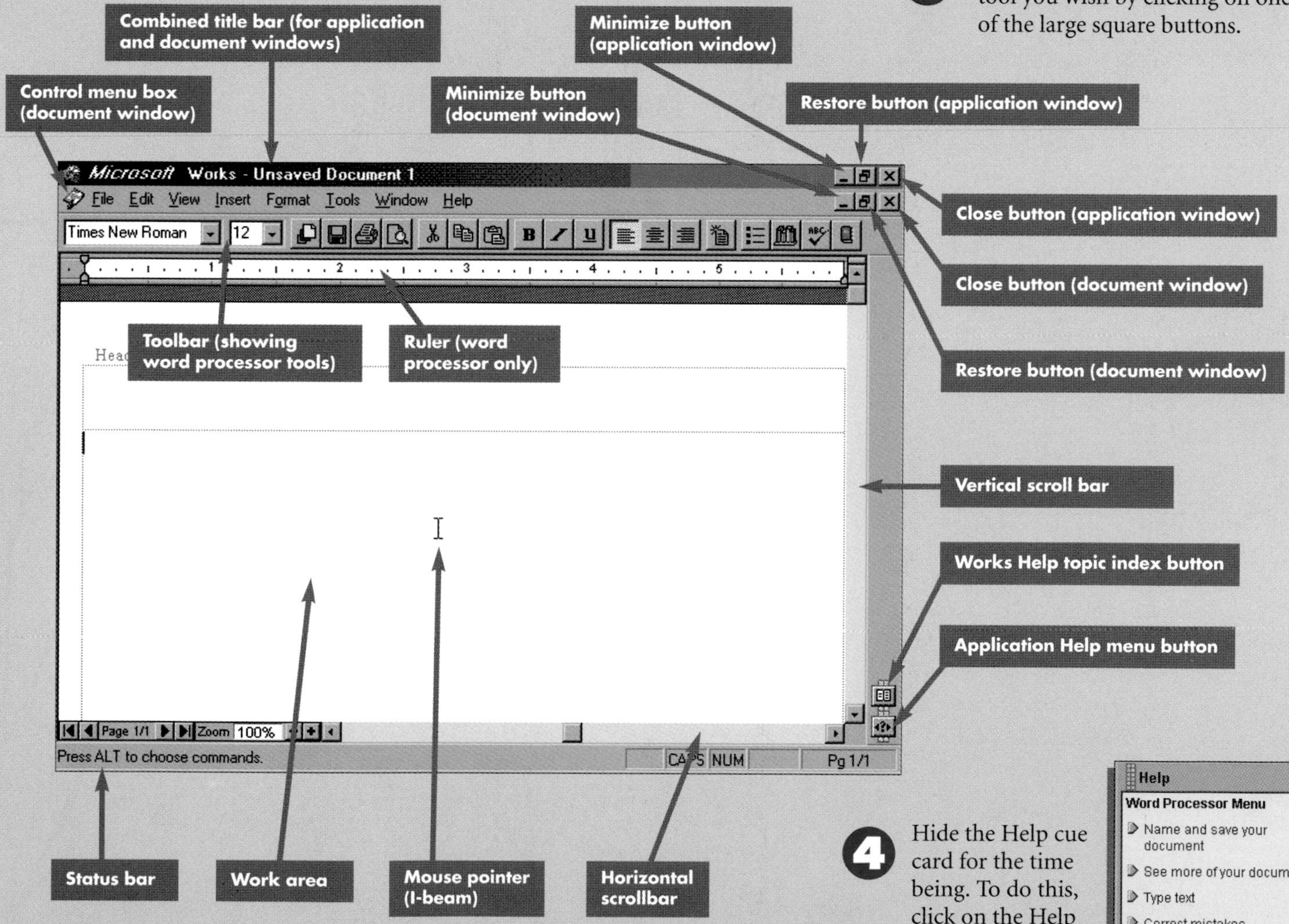

Combined title bar (for application and document windows)
Minimize button (application window)
Control menu box (document window)
Minimize button (document window)
Restore button (application window)
Microsoft Works - Unsaved Document 1
File Edit View Insert Format Tools Window Help
Times New Roman
12
Close button (application window)
Close button (document window)
Toolbar (showing word processor tools)
Ruler (word processor only)
Restore button (document window)
Vertical scroll bar
Works Help topic index button
Application Help menu button
Page 1/1
Zoom 100%
Press ALT to choose commands.
CAPS NUM
Pg 1/1
Status bar
Work area
Mouse pointer (I-beam)
Horizontal scrollbar

**4** Hide the Help cue card for the time being. To do this, click on the Help name located on the menu bar. Then select "Hide Help" by clicking on it.

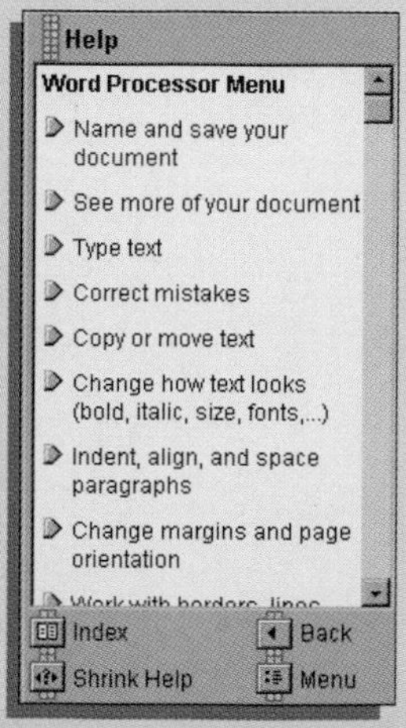

Help
Word Processor Menu
Name and save your document
See more of your document
Type text
Correct mistakes
Copy or move text
Change how text looks (bold, italic, size, fonts,...)
Indent, align, and space paragraphs
Change margins and page orientation
Index
Back
Shrink Help
Menu

## CHAPTER 4

# Creating a Document with the Word Processor

By now you should be familiar with Microsoft Windows and have a basic idea of what you can do with Microsoft Works. Of all the things Works can do, word processing will probably be the most important to you. You can use the word processor for jotting down your ideas, organizing them, formatting them, and showing them off. You can use the spreadsheet, the database, and other tools for their specialized purposes, but when it comes time to put all the pieces together, the word processor is the place you'll do it.

In this chapter you'll learn the basics of word processing. Creating new documents, saving them, retrieving saved documents, and printing them out are covered here, too, since these skills are necessary and useful throughout Windows. Finally, you'll see the proper way to shut down Works and your computer when you're finished. When you finish this introduction to the word processor, you'll know enough to complete much of your computer work, so turn the page!

# How to Create a New Word Processor Document

When you write a letter or other document, you'll have to begin somewhere. You've already taken the hardest step by sitting down in front of your computer, so the next step of creating a new document window in Works should be a little easier. The new document window looks blank, but there's really quite a bit there that you can't see immediately. Works starts your document with default settings for everything from the font, or typeface, to the tab stops. You'll learn to change these settings in later chapters, but for now it will be easier to take advantage of what Works has already set up for you.

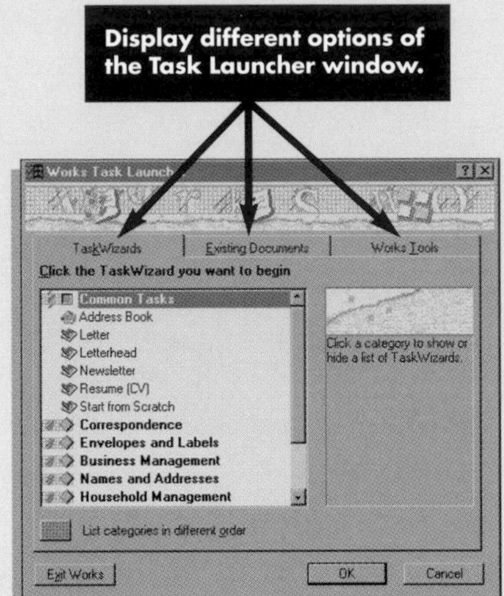


**1** The first window you'll see after Works starts is the Task Launcher. A list of TaskWizards appears which allow you to create professional looking documents quickly and easily. We'll show you how to use TaskWizards later in the book, but for now let's continue with the basics.

**TIP SHEET**

- **Microsoft apparently believes that you can have too much of a good thing, since they limit the number of documents you can open at one time to eight. This is plenty for doing just about anything you can imagine. Besides, too many open windows can be confusing and may slow down your computer.**
- **If you don't see the toolbar on your screen, you can still create a new document with the Task Launcher window. Simply click on the File menu name to pull down the menu, and click again on New to display the Works Task Launcher window, then click on the Word Processor button.**

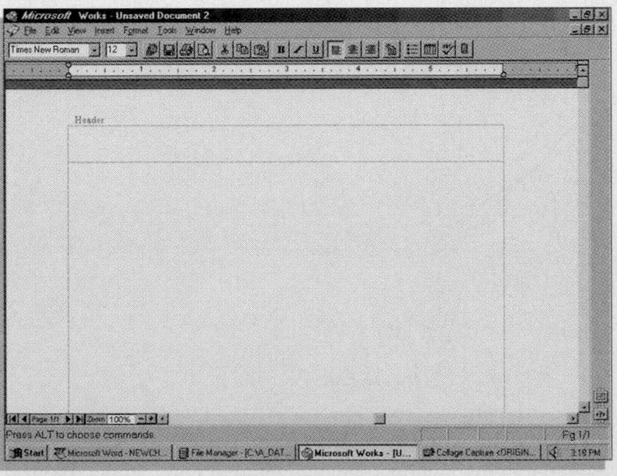


**5** Once you've started and maximized your second document window, your screen should look like this. Notice that the document is named Document 2, since it was the second new word processor document created in this session of Microsoft Works.

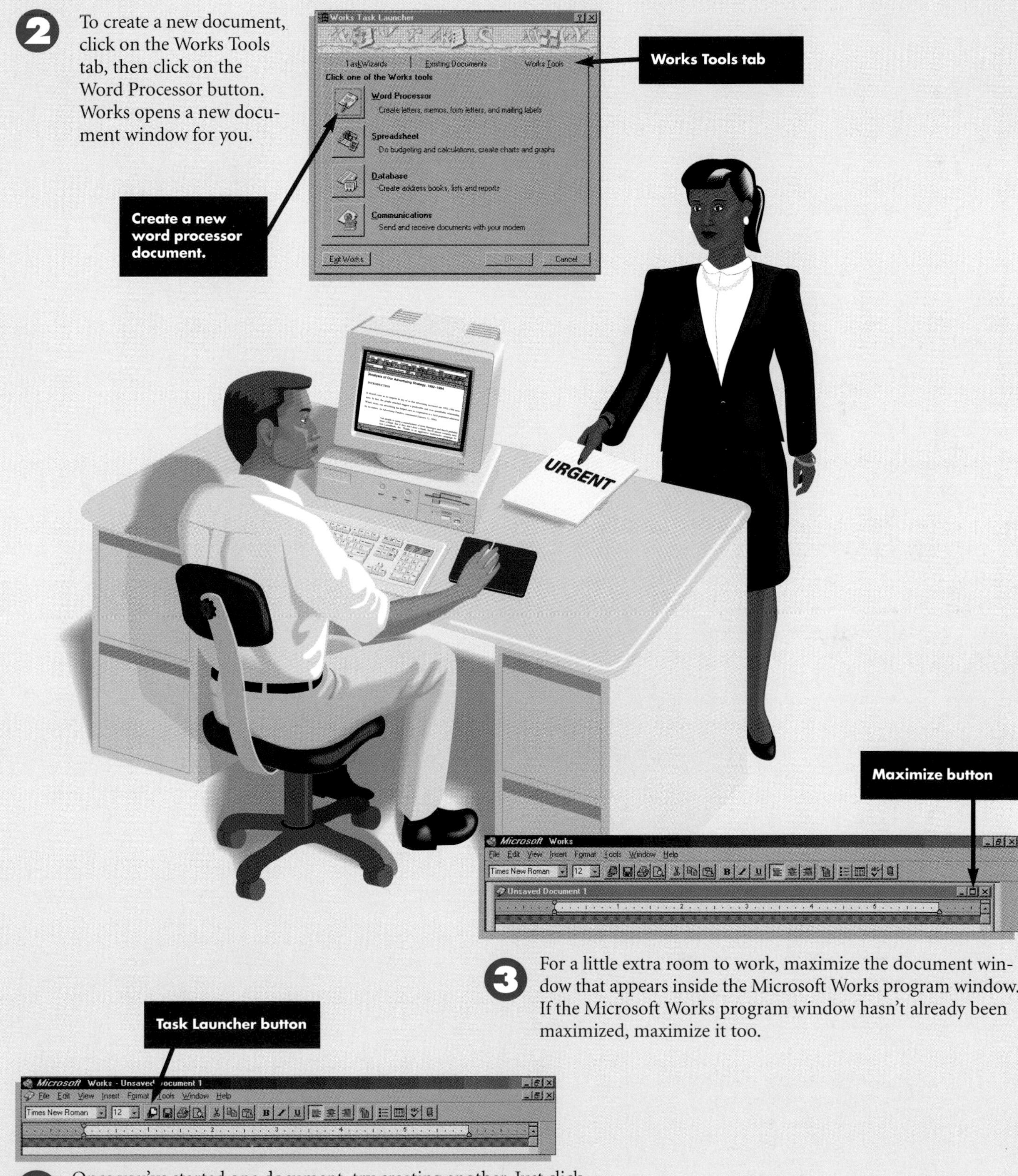


**2** To create a new document, click on the Works Tools tab, then click on the Word Processor button. Works opens a new document window for you.

**3** For a little extra room to work, maximize the document window that appears inside the Microsoft Works program window. If the Microsoft Works program window hasn't already been maximized, maximize it too.

**4** Once you've started one document, try creating another. Just click on the Task Launcher button on the toolbar, and the Task Launcher Window will open without affecting your first document. Click on the Word Processor button again to create your second document.

# How to Type in Text

Typing with the word processor of Microsoft Works is very similar to working with a typewriter. But in addition, the word processor handles many little typing tasks for you, such as figuring out if another word will fit at the end of a line. There are slight differences between typing on a typewriter and a word processor. Once you know them, though, you'll be on your way to proficient word processing.

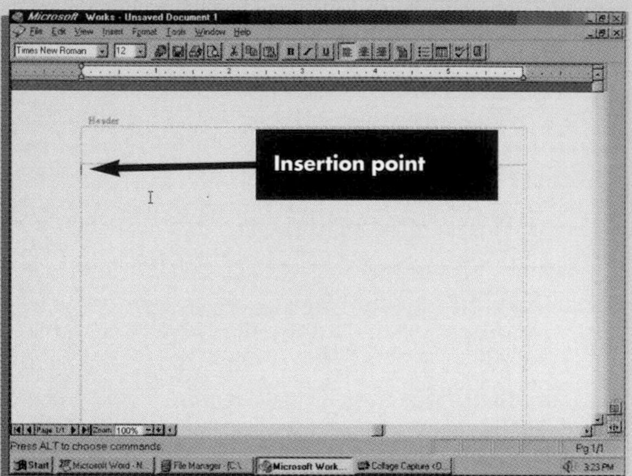


**1** Start by creating a blank document in Microsoft Works. When you do this, you will see an insertion point (a blinking vertical bar) in the upper-left corner of the document window.

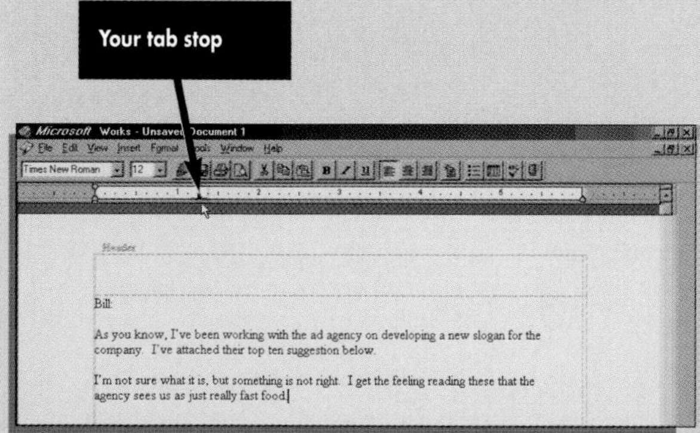


**5** Tab stops are adjusted on a typewriter with the Tab Set and Tab Clear keys. In Works, you set a tab stop by clicking the mouse on the bottom half of the ruler. To move a tab stop, click on it and drag it to the desired position. To clear a tab stop, click on it and drag it off of the ruler.

## TIP SHEET

- **If you type something incorrectly, you can erase it quickly and easily. Just back up with the Backspace key and type the correct letter or word.**
- **If you're accustomed to using a typewriter, you'll soon discover that the Caps Lock button on your computer keyboard doesn't work like you might expect. On a typewriter, you lock capital letters with the Caps Lock key and unlock them with the Shift key. On most word processors, including the one in Microsoft Works, you lock capital letters in the usual way, but you unlock them by pressing the Caps Lock key a second time.**
- **There are two kinds of tab stops in Works: default and user-defined. If you don't set your own tab stops, Works sets default tab stops at every half inch mark (0.5", 1.0", 1.5", and so on). If you look closely you'll see little vertical lines under each half-inch mark indicating a default tab. On the other hand, user-defined tab stops look like an L. Both behave in pretty much the same way as tab stops on a typewriter. As you set your own tabs, notice that there are no default tab stops to the left of your user-defined stops. That's because Works assumes that the tabs you set are the first ones you want to stop at.**
- **Custom tab settings are a type of paragraph formatting which works on only one paragraph at a time. As a result, you might notice that the tabs you set in one paragraph disappear when you click in another paragraph.**

**2** The insertion point shows you where the next letter you type will appear in the document window. Think of the work area of the document window as a sheet of paper. The letters you type on the keyboard will appear in the work area just like letters you type on a typewriter appear on your paper.

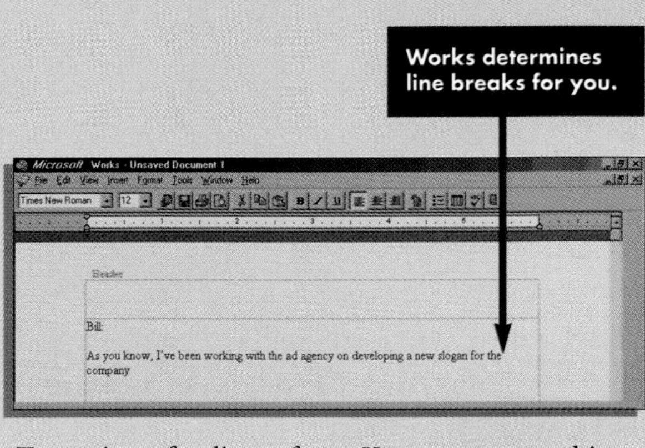


**3** Try typing a few lines of text. You can type anything you want, but if your imagination isn't in high gear right now, you are welcome to copy the text in the central graphic. Notice how Works determines what words will fit on a line and which word should start the next line. With Works, you'll never have to strain to hear the end-of-line bell, only to discover when it rings that you can't finish the word you've just started.

Bill:

As you know, I've been working with the ad agency on developing a new slogan for the company. I've attached their "top ten" suggeestions below.

I'm not sure what it is, but something isn't quite right. I get the feeling reading these that the agency sees us as just really fast food. I don't think that just being the fastest will lure in customers like our franchises deserve. Something seems to be missing. Maybe it's me, but I don't get from the slogans the feeling of warmth that I get after eating at Speedway. They don't call to mind the hard work, the comraderie, the smiling faces... I get the feeling that they really wanted to say: "Speedway: Wham, bam, thank-you ma'am," but didn't dare after all the bad press on our prototype safety systems.

These people are the pros, though, and really seem to know what they're doing. Let me know what you think.

-Marcie

Suggestions:

Speedway Burgers: Great food, low prices, highway speeds.

Speedway Burgers: Where the burger meets the road.

Speedway Burgers: It just doesn't get any faster.

Speedway Burgers: Dinner faster than you can read this.

Speedway Burgers: You should have stopped to say "Thank you," but we wouldn't let you.

How do they do it? I couldn't tell, light doesn't travel that fast.

Speedway Burgers: I'm hungry- That was great, wasn't it.

The only choice when you don't have time to taste it.

Speedway Burgers: Didn't we just eat?

**4** Your computer keyboard doesn't have a carriage return key like the one on a typewriter. Instead, it has an Enter key, which works somewhat differently. You won't need it to end every line at the right margin, but when you want to end a line early and start a new one, as at the end of a paragraph, the Enter key is just what you need.

# How to Save and Retrieve a Document

As mentioned in Chapter 2, your computer has two types of memory. It has short-term memory, called random-access memory (RAM), and it has long-term storage, generally a hard disk. When you create a document in Microsoft Works, you are creating it in RAM. You do this because RAM remembers and recalls information very quickly. The trouble is, when you turn off your computer, RAM forgets everything you told it. Everything.

For Works to remember your document when you turn off your computer, you first need to save it to your hard disk. Saving documents to disk ensures that your computer will be able to recall them for you days, weeks, or even years later, so that they can be retrieved to the faster RAM when you need them again.

## TIP SHEET

- After you have saved a document, you won't be asked to name it again when you use the Save button.
- If you want to rename a document after saving it, select the Save As command in the File menu. Works will open the Save As dialog box again for you so you can type in a new name.
- There's an alternative for reopening documents, too. Click on the File menu then select Open. You'll see the Open dialog box, which is much like the Save As dialog box. Open the file folder that contains your file and then double-click on the name of the file you want to open.

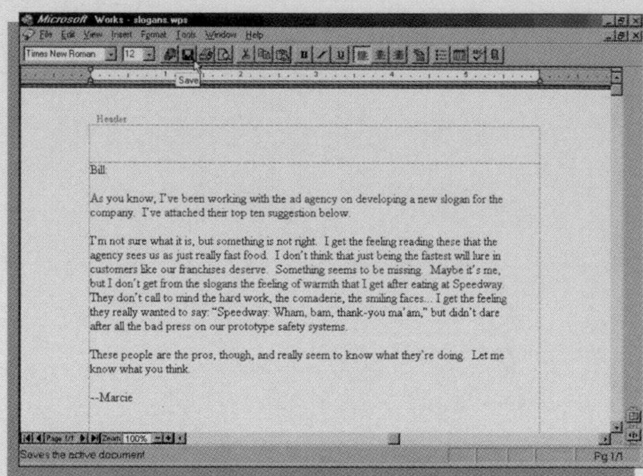

**1** The easiest way to save a document is to use the Save button on the toolbar. Move the mouse pointer over it and click the left mouse button once.

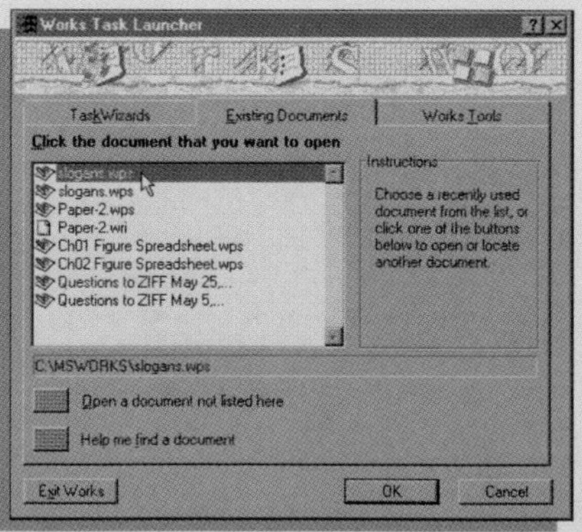

**6** Near the top of the Task Launcher window is the Existing Documents tab. When you click on that tab you'll see the file name you just saved at the top of the list. Double-click on the file to reopen it.

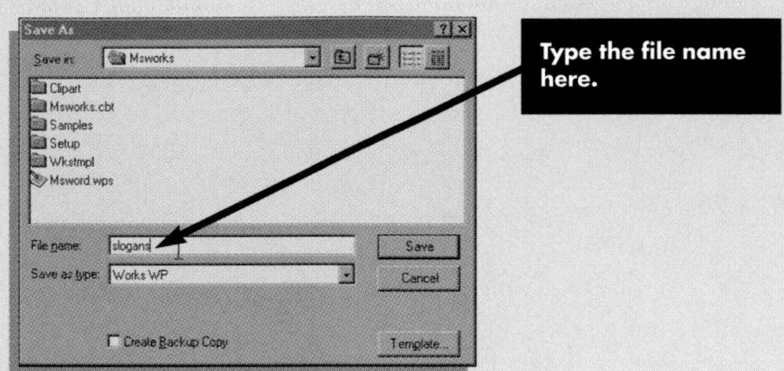


**2** If this is the first time you're saving this document, the Save As dialog box will open next. Click once in the File Name box in the bottom half of the dialog box. Type in a file name. You do not need to include the DOS file extension ".WPS" in the file name. Works automatically saves the file as a "Works WP" type file for you.

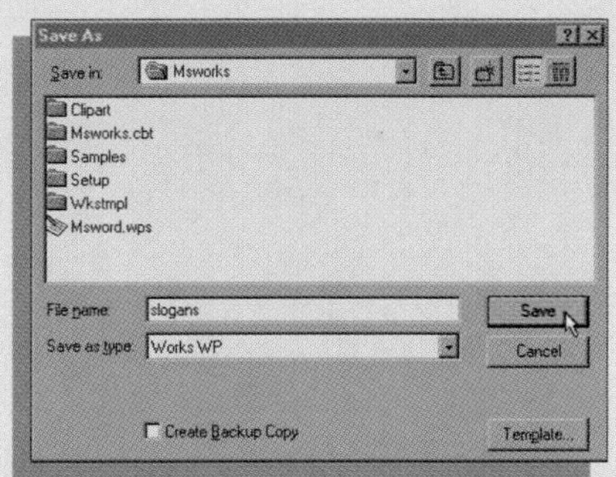


**3** Click on the Save button. Your document will be saved to your hard disk where you can retrieve it whenever you want.

**4** Close your document by clicking twice on the document Control Menu box.

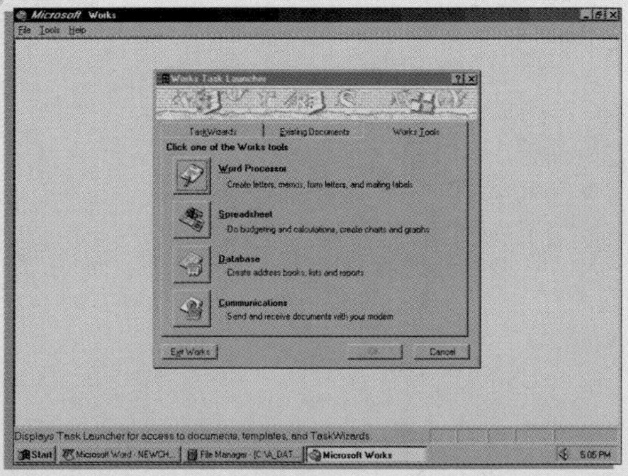

**5** If you don't have any other documents open, you'll see the Works Task Launcher window. If you do have another open, click once on the Task Launcher button in the toolbar.

# How to Print a Document

It would be nice if you could type in your document, save it to your hard disk, and then electronically mail it to everyone who needed to see it. It would be nice, too, if the text on a monitor were as clean and crisp as text on paper, and were as enjoyable to read and manipulate as a good book. This all may be possible someday, but unfortunately, it isn't yet.

Since the paperless office is still a long way off, you'll occasionally want to show your boss why he or she's paying you and print the document that appears on your screen.

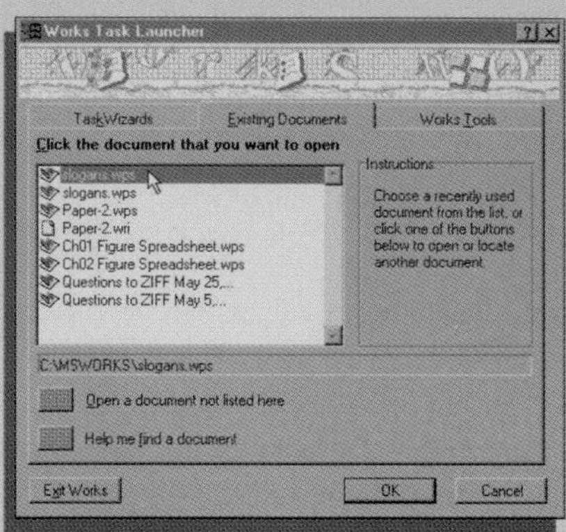


**1** To print the document, you'll first need to have it on your screen. Start by retrieving an old document or creating a new one.

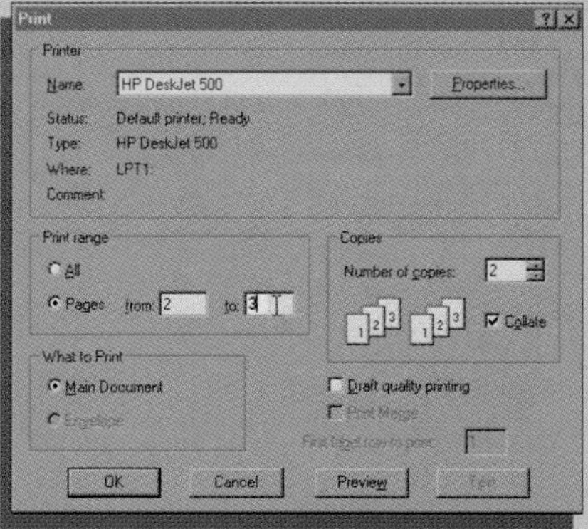


**7** Click in the To box just to the right and type in the number of the last page you want to print. Send the pages to the printer by clicking the OK button.

## TIP SHEET

- If you aren't getting a good feel for what your printout will look like by just scrolling through it, use the Print Preview button on the toolbar (or Print Preview command in the File menu). Print Preview will show you a reduced-size copy of your document just as it will appear on paper. You can scroll through the pages with the Next and Previous buttons, print with the Print button, and exit to the regular document window with the Cancel button.
- Like all Windows applications, Works lets you print "in the background." That means once you start printing you can go on to other functions, while the computer takes care of the printing for you.

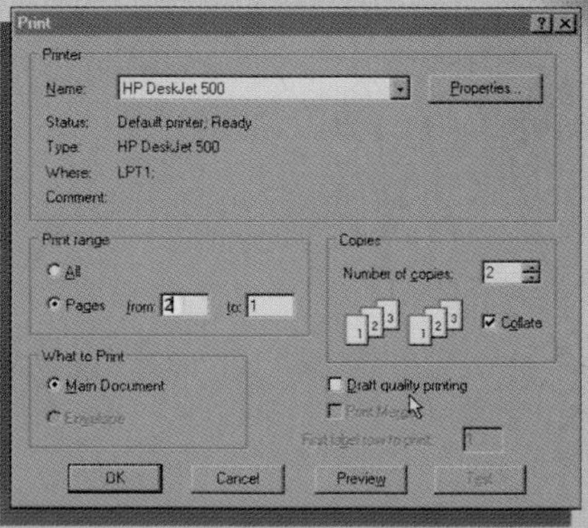


**6** In the Print Range box, click on the Pages option button. The cursor will move to the From box, where you type in the first page you want to print out.

**2** Review the document, first, so that you won't waste paper by having to print it again, and second, to be sure you won't be embarrassed if the wrong person gets to the printer before you do. When you're ready, click on the Print button.

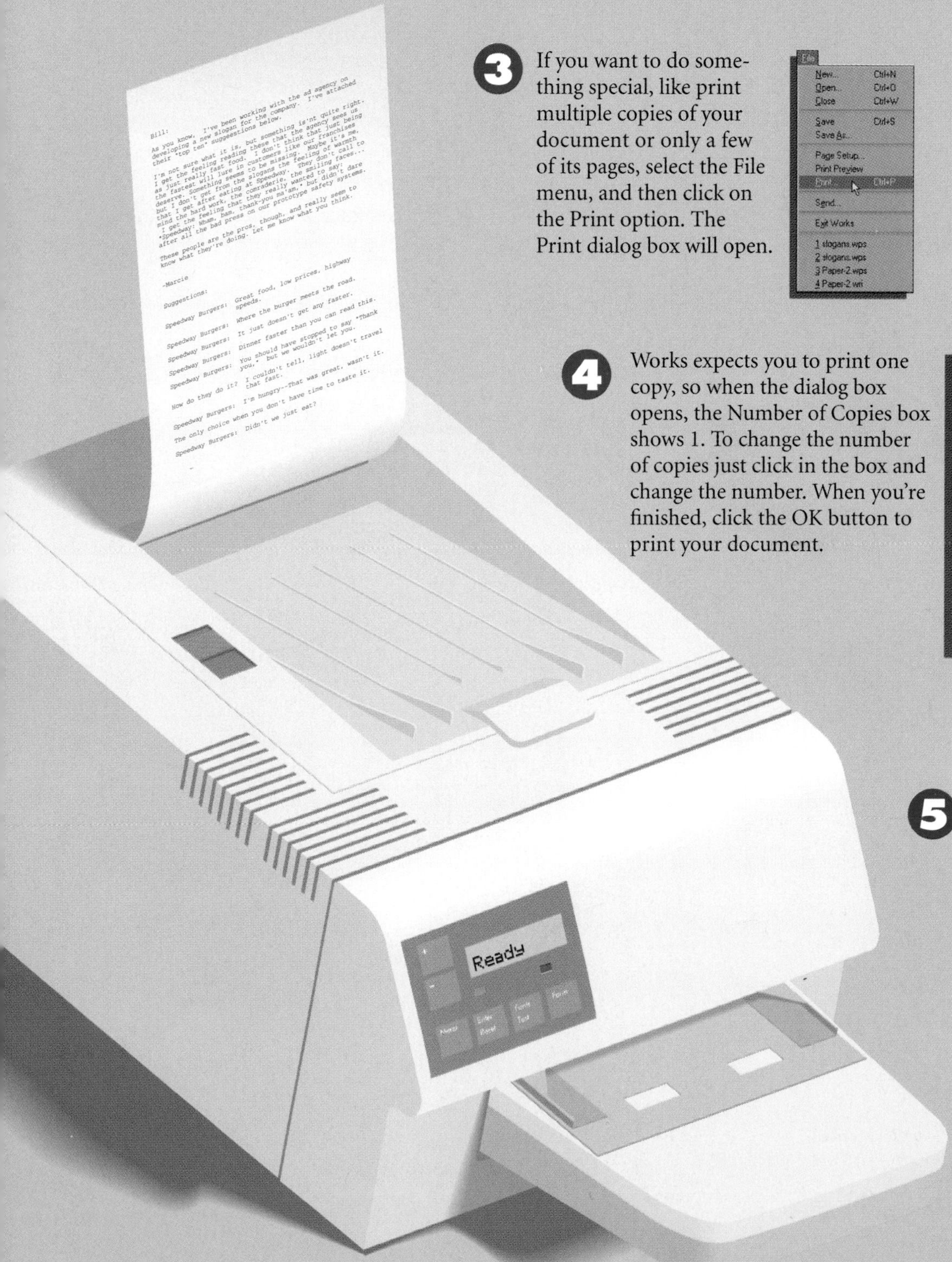

**3** If you want to do something special, like print multiple copies of your document or only a few of its pages, select the File menu, and then click on the Print option. The Print dialog box will open.

**4** Works expects you to print one copy, so when the dialog box opens, the Number of Copies box shows 1. To change the number of copies just click in the box and change the number. When you're finished, click the OK button to print your document.

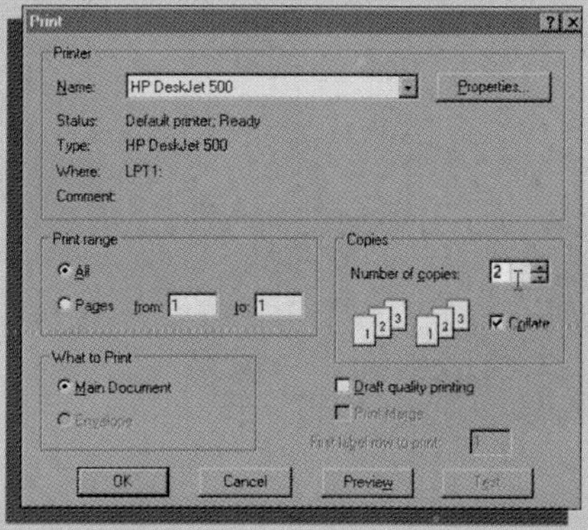

**5** To print just a few of the pages in your document (a handy feature if you've just corrected a mistake), you must first decide what range of pages you need to print. With that in mind, open the Print dialog box as you did in step 3.

# How to Get Help

Perhaps the most comforting feature of Works is its extensive help library. It contains answers to almost every question you can think up. While many of the help features aim at getting beginning users up and running, you'll never outgrow the help library. For many people, just the opposite is true: The more experience they have with Works, the more things they want to tweak to get a desired effect.

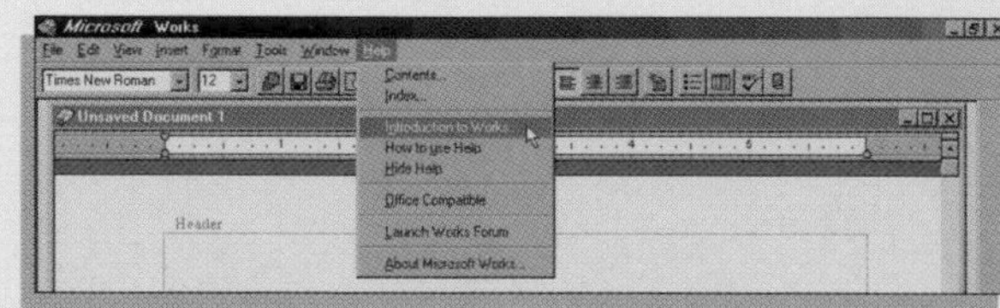

**1** If you're new to Windows or Works, and the thought of learning a new feature makes you anxious—even if it's learning how to get help—then start with the Introduction to Works. Start Works, and click on Help in the menu bar to open the Help menu.

**5** To quickly find information about a word or term use the Index option. From the Help menu select Index. In the text box, type a word or term. As you type, a list of applicable help folders and topics will appear just below the text box. Use the same technique described in step 4 to get the help.

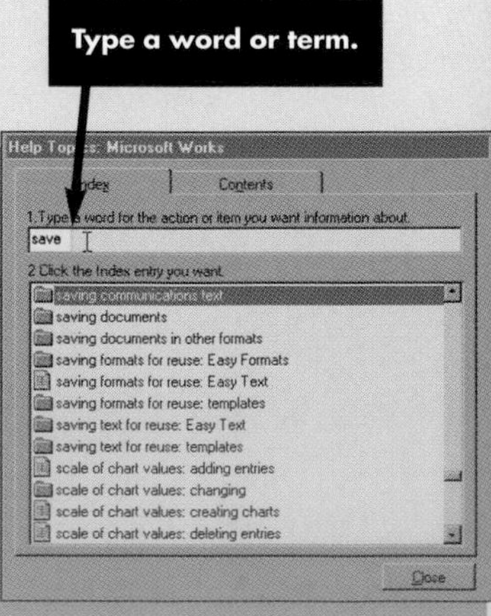


**6** The Help window remains open until you shrink or hide it. To shrink it, click on the Shrink Help button at the button of the Help window or select Hide Help from the Help menu.

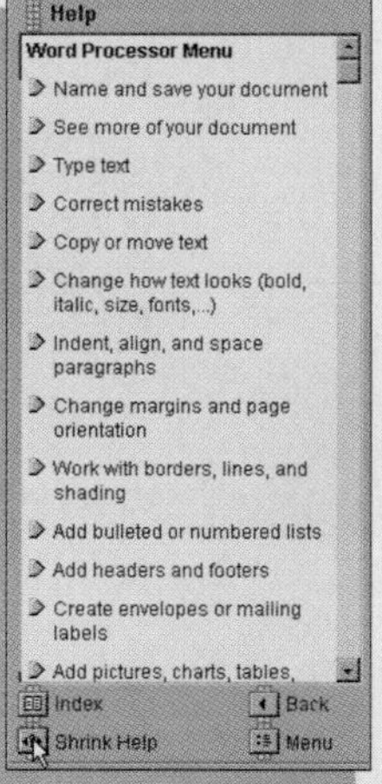


## TIP SHEET

- **You can print help information. Select a topic, then using the scroll bar in the help window, move to the bottom of the help information and click the Print this topic button.**
- **Pressing the F1 function key quickly opens the help window.**
- **The Help Topics window which opens when you select the "Contents..." or "Index..." option from the Help menu can be closed by pressing the Escape (Esc) key or by clicking on the Close button at the bottom of the Help Topics window.**
- **Dialog boxes are equipped with a special help buttons. To get help, click the ? button in the top right corner of the dialog box. When the ? cursor appears, point-and-click on the item in the dialog box that you need help with.**

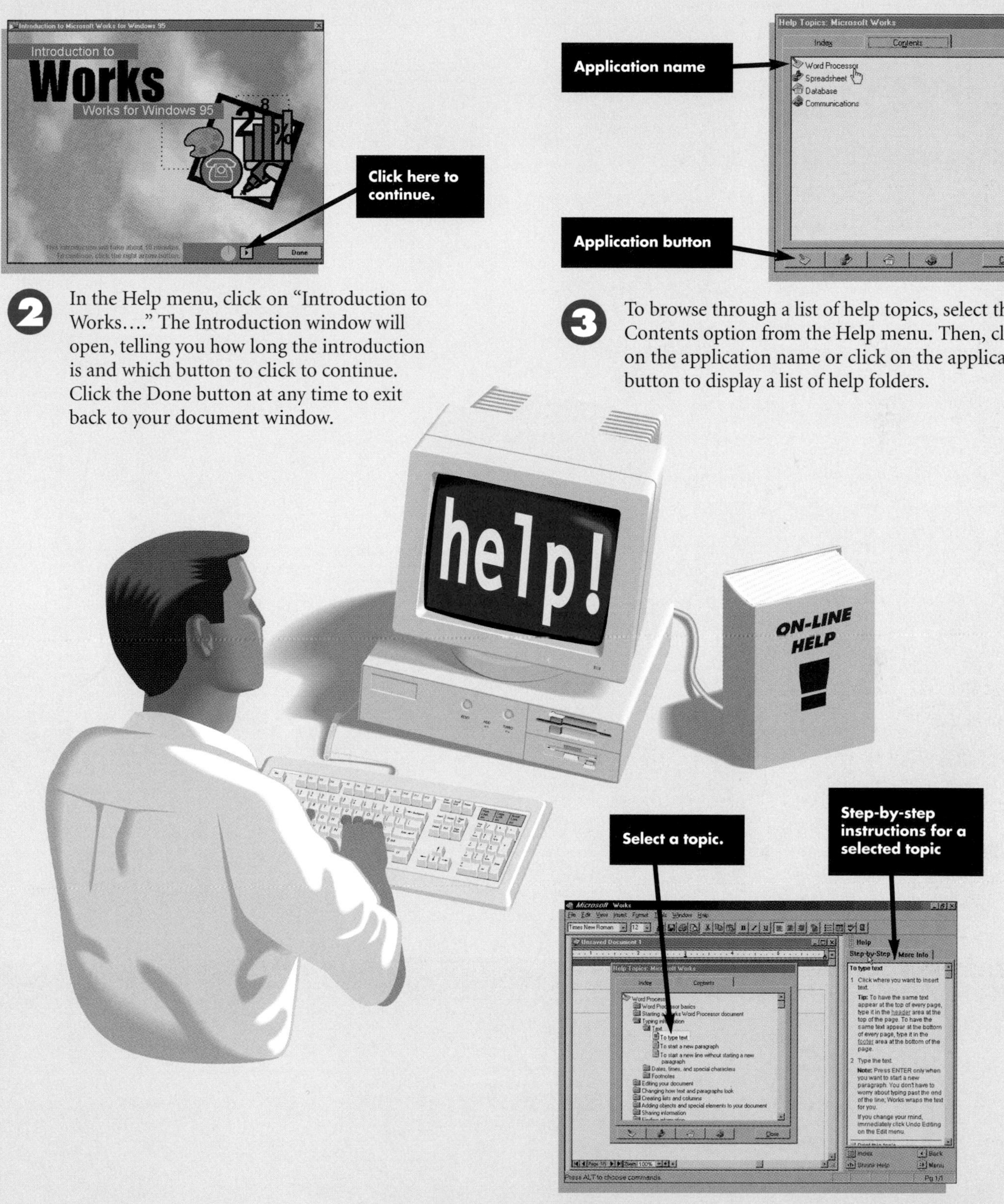


**2** In the Help menu, click on "Introduction to Works…." The Introduction window will open, telling you how long the introduction is and which button to click to continue. Click the Done button at any time to exit back to your document window.

**3** To browse through a list of help topics, select the Contents option from the Help menu. Then, click on the application name or click on the application button to display a list of help folders.

**4** Using the "point-and-click" technique discussed in Chapter 2, move through the help folders to select the topic you need help with. Step-by-step instructions for the topic you select appear in the Help window on the right.

# How to Exit Microsoft Works

It's the end of the day, you've been working hard and been extremely productive with your newly learned word processing skills. It's time to shut down the computer, but panic seizes you as you realize that you don't know how to exit Works! This is a joke, of course. You could just turn your computer off and go away, but there's a better, safer solution. Just turning off the computer would be like getting ready for bed by just turning out the light. You'll sleep better if you do a few things first.

**1** The first step is to save your work. Clicking on the Save button on the toolbar is the easiest way to do that.

**TIP SHEET**

- **The end of the day is a good time to create a backup (or second copy) of the document you're working on. Select the Save As command in the File menu and give your document a name you'll understand, like "MemoVer1." That way, if you accidentally save changes that you don't want to keep, you'll have an earlier version to fall back on.**
- **Chances are the next time you start Works you'll want to work on a document you saved the last time you left Works. If you click on the File menu you'll find the names of the four most recently saved files at the bottom of the menu. Just point to file you want to open and click.**

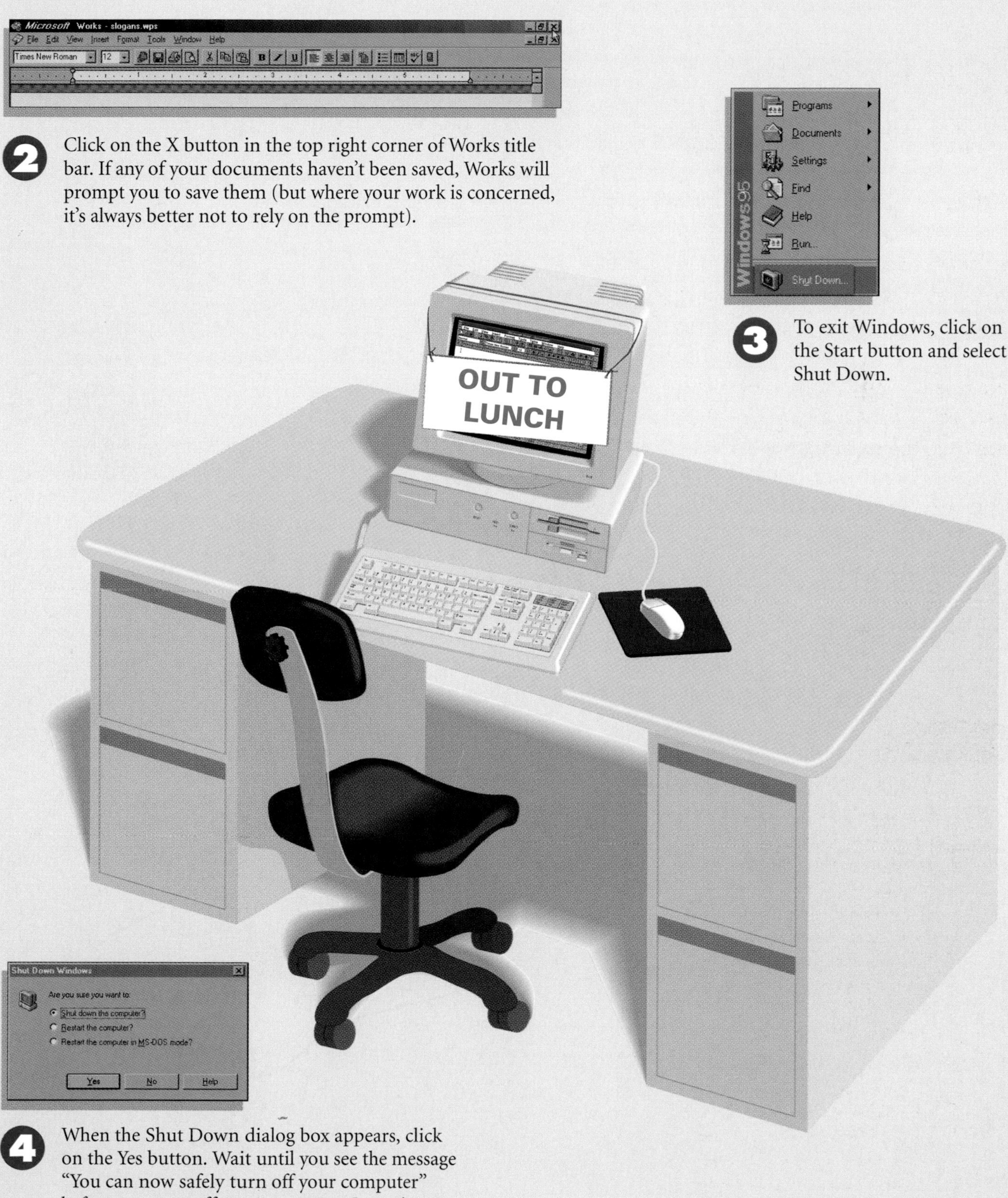


**2** Click on the X button in the top right corner of Works title bar. If any of your documents haven't been saved, Works will prompt you to save them (but where your work is concerned, it's always better not to rely on the prompt).

**3** To exit Windows, click on the Start button and select Shut Down.

**4** When the Shut Down dialog box appears, click on the Yes button. Wait until you see the message "You can now safely turn off your computer" before you turn off your computer. Impatience here could cause you to lose changes you've made in Windows and could litter your hard drive over time with temporary files that were never deleted.

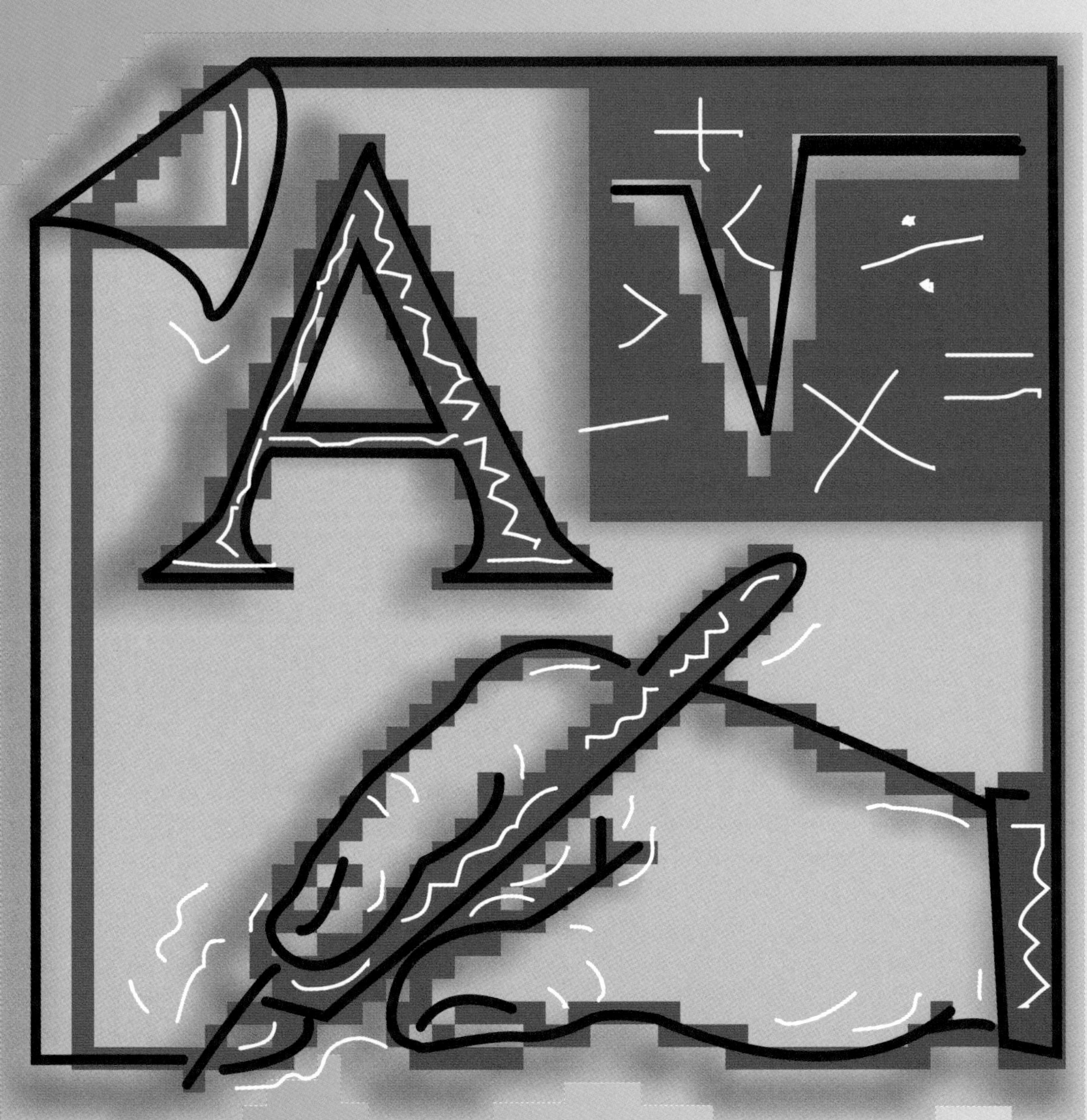
A
+
>
=

## CHAPTER 5

# Editing Text in a Document

In its most basic form, editing is simply correcting mistakes in your document. Perhaps you have misspelled a word and need to correct it, or maybe you have typed a word twice or left one out. Either way, you probably need to go back and retype a little.

In a slightly elevated form, editing can mean reorganizing and rearranging the text you have typed. Perhaps you need to explain one idea before introducing another. Maybe you omitted a concept or wrote it in a redundant fashion. In these cases, you may need to make substantial revisions, often by moving blocks of text from one location to another in your document.

Editing can get far more complex, but at these levels, the changes you need to make don't have to be difficult or time-consuming. If you were working with a typewriter, you might have to start from scratch and retype your entire document! With a word processor, however, changes that might otherwise take hours can be done with just a few simple mouse movements. With Microsoft Works, the only difficult part of editing is deciding what changes to make.

# How to Select Text

To select text is to mark one or more characters for action. What kind of action? After selecting text you can delete it, move it, format it—the list goes on. This page explains how to select text. Starting on the next page and continuing throughout this book, you will learn about the many actions you can perform on text and other objects after selecting them.

**1** Locate the text you want to select. If possible, scroll the document so that the entire block to be selected is in view. If you need a quick reminder on scrolling, see "How to Use the Mouse in Windows" in Chapter 2.

## TIP SHEET

- **To select text using the keyboard, first use the arrow keys to position the insertion point at one end of the text block. Then, hold down the Shift key and use the arrow keys to move toward the other end of the block, highlighting text as you go. Release the Shift key when the complete block is selected.**
- **To select a complete line or paragraph, position the mouse pointer in the left margin next to the line or paragraph you want to select. The mouse pointer becomes a right-pointing arrow. Then click once to select the line, or double-click to select the paragraph.**
- **To select just one word, position the mouse pointer over the word and double-click.**
- **To deselect text without performing an action on it, click anywhere in the work area of the window. Or, with the keyboard, release the Shift key and then press any arrow key.**
- **When you drag to select text, Works automatically selects whole words. If you want to select only parts of words, click on the Tools menu, select the Options command, click the Editing tab, and then click in the Automatic Word Selection check box to remove the check mark and turn off the feature. Click OK to close the dialog box.**

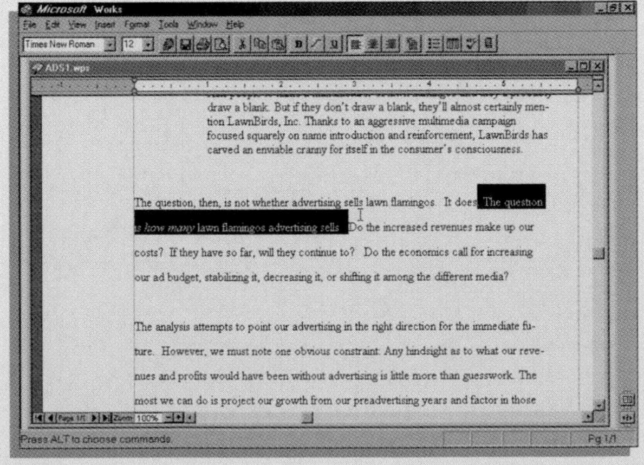


**5** Release the mouse button. The text remains selected. Now you can issue commands that affect only this text.

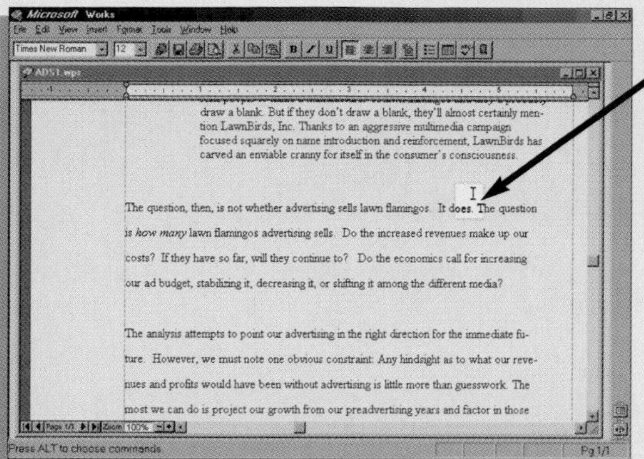


**2** Position the mouse pointer at one end of the block.

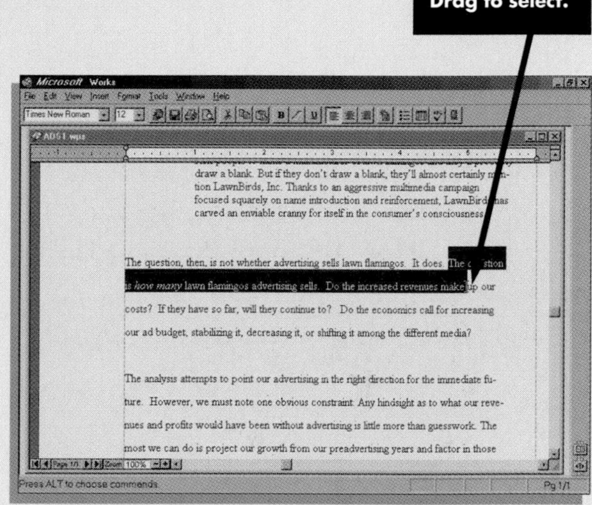


**3** Holding down the left mouse button, drag the mouse toward the other end of the block. As you drag over text, it becomes highlighted, indicating that it is selected. Remember to keep your finger on the left mouse button and don't let up—not just yet anyway.

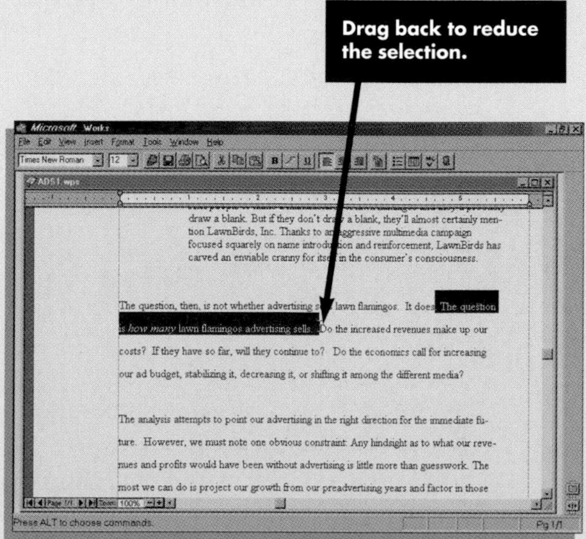


**4** If you select too much text, drag the other way to unselect it.

**LawnBirds, Inc.**

ANALYSIS OF OUR ADVERTISING STRATEGY, 1992–1994

INTRODUCTION

It should come as no surprise to any of us that advertising increased our 1992–1994 revenues. In fact, the graphs attached suggest a predictable and even quantifiable relationship. What's more, our advertising has helped earn us a reputation in a field populated otherwise by no-names. As *Advertising Punditry* commented (January 12, 1994):

> Ask people to name a manufacturer of lawn flamingos and they'll probably draw a blank. But if they don't draw a blank, they'll almost certainly mention LawnBirds, Inc. Thanks to an aggressive multimedia campaign focused squarely on name introduction and reinforcement, LawnBirds has carved an enviable cranny for itself in the consumer's consciousness.

The question, then, is not *whether* advertising sells lawn flamingos. It does. The question is *how many* lawn flamingos advertising sells. Do the increased revenues make up our costs? If they have so far, will they continue to? Do the economics call for increasing our ad budget, stabilizing it, decreasing it, or shifting it among the different media?

This analysis attempts to point our advertising in the right direction for the immediate future. However, we must note one obvious constraint: Any hindsight as to what our revenues and profits would have been without advertising is little more than guesswork. The most we can do is project our growth from our preadvertising years and factor in those marketplace changes that we understand and that are quantifiable.

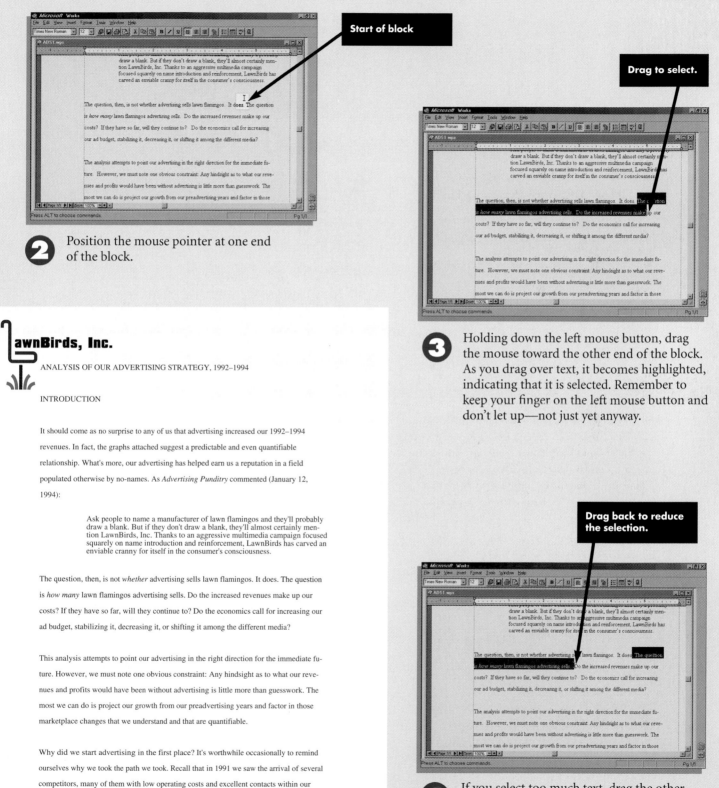

Why did we start advertising in the first place? It's worthwhile occasionally to remind ourselves why we took the path we took. Recall that in 1991 we saw the arrival of several competitors, many of them with low operating costs and excellent contacts within our

# How to Delete Text

To make changes to text in Microsoft Works, you'll often have to delete the old text first. You can delete one character at a time or make a mass deletion by selecting text first. Text to the right of the deletion point shifts left to fill the vacated space, and line breaks adjust automatically.

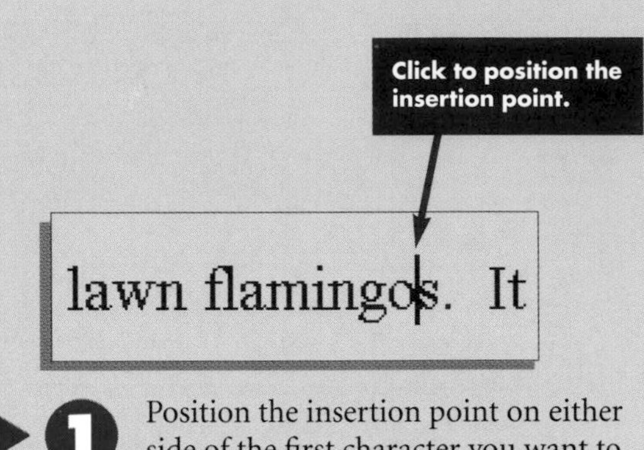


**1** Position the insertion point on either side of the first character you want to delete. Or, select a block of text (see preceding page) if you want to delete the whole block.

**TIP SHEET**

- **Most system setups allow you to delete the selected block and immediately start replacing it with other text by simply typing. If this feature does not work on your computer and you want to use it, click on Tools in the menu bar and then click on Options. Click on the Editing tab, then click on the Typing Replaces Selection check box. Then click on the OK button to return to your document.**
- **If you simply want to replace text, you can type over it. Move the cursor to the beginning of the text you want to replace, and press the Insert key (labeled *Ins* on some keyboards). You'll see the letters OVR appear near the right end of the status bar, meaning Works is in overtype mode. Each character you now type will replace the next character to the right of the insertion point. When you are through, be sure to press the Insert key again to return to insert mode.**

**2** To delete the character to the right of the insertion point, press the Delete key (labeled *Del* on some keyboards).

Backspace key

lawn flamings. It

**3** To delete the character to the left of the insertion point, press the Backspace key.

LawnBirds, Inc.

ANALYSIS OF OUR ADVERTISING STRATEGY, 1992–1994

INTRODUCTION

It should come as no surprise to any of us that advertising increased our 1992–1994 revenues. In fact, the graphs attached suggest a predictable and even quantifiable relationship. What's more, our advertising has helped earn us a reputation in a field populated otherwise by no-names. As *Advertising Punditry* commented (January 12, 1994):

> Ask people to name a manufacturer of lawn flamingos and they'll probably draw a blank. But if they don't draw a blank, they'll almost certainly mention LawnBirds, Inc. Thanks to an aggressive multimedia campaign focused squarely on name introduction and reinforcement, LawnBirds has carved an enviable cranny for itself in the consumer's consciousness.

The question, then, is not *whether* advertising sells lawn flamingos. It does. ~~The question is *how many* lawn flamingos advertising sells.~~ Do the increased revenues make up our costs? If they have so far, will they continue to? Do the economics call for increasing our ad budget, stabilizing it, decreasing it, or shifting it among the different media?

This analysis attempts to point our advertising in the right direction for the immediate future. However, we must note one obvious constraint: Any hindsight as to what our revenues and profits would have been without advertising is little more than guesswork. The most we can do is project our growth from our preadvertising years and factor in those marketplace changes that we understand and that are quantifiable.

Why did we start advertising in the first place? It's worthwhile occasionally to remind ourselves why we took the path we took. Recall that in 1991 we saw the arrival of several competitors, many of them with low operating costs and excellent contacts within our

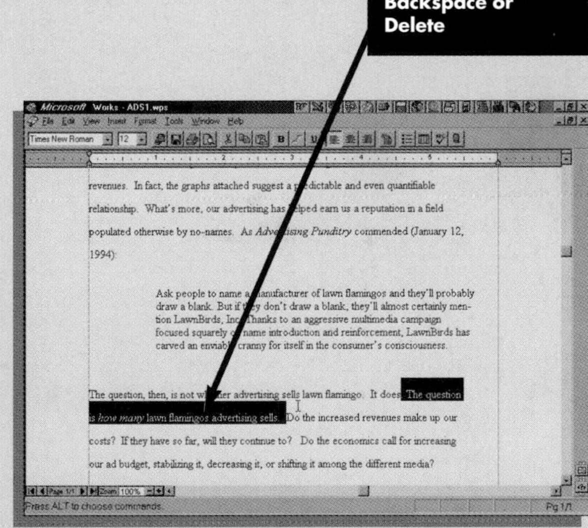

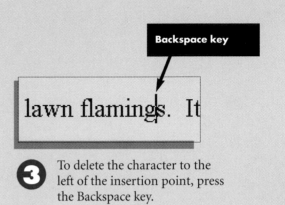

**4** To delete the selected block, press the Backspace key or the Delete key.

**5** If you delete text accidentally, immediately press Ctrl+Z to activate the Undo feature. Some or all of the deleted text may return so you don't have to retype it.

# How to Navigate through a Document

Most documents are too long to display on your screen all at once. To work with large documents, Works gives you two basic methods to move, or navigate, through them. The first way to navigate is to move the insertion point (see steps 1 through 4). The insertion point, of course, is where you add and delete text.

The second way to navigate is to show different parts of the document in the document window (see steps 5 through 7). Try thinking of the Works document window as just that: a window that lets you see a part of your document. You can't move the window around in front of the document, but you can move the document around behind the window to let different parts show through.

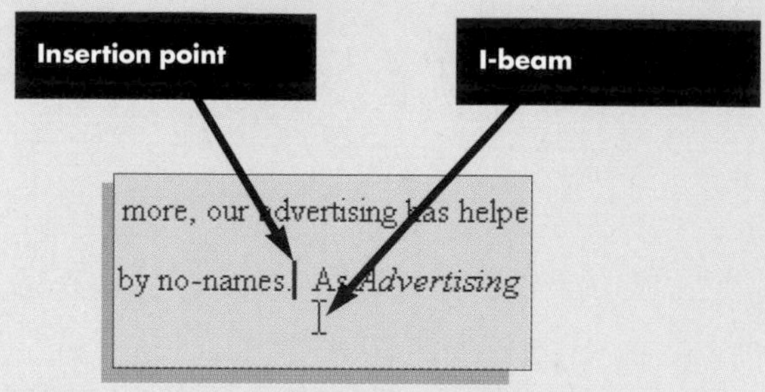


1. The easiest way to move the insertion point in a window is to point with the I-beam mouse pointer where you want to put the insertion point, and then click.

7. Click and drag the scroll box to move the document view anywhere in the document. The length of the vertical scroll bar represents the length of your document, so if you drag two-thirds of the way down the scroll bar and let go of the mouse button, Works will move you two-thirds of the way through your document.

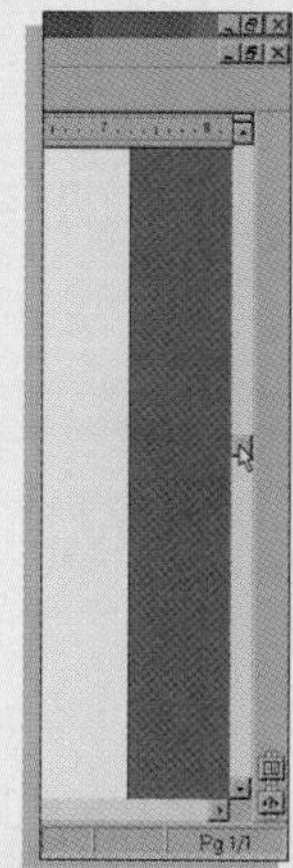

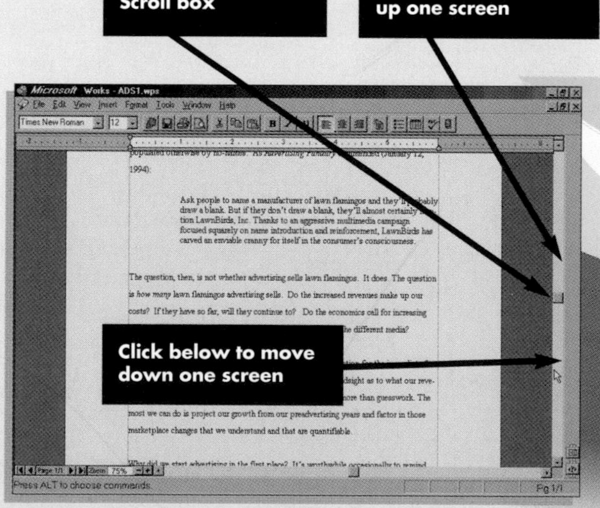


6. Click on the vertical scroll bar between the scroll box and either of its ends to move the view up and down by the amount you can see in the document window. (Use the horizontal scroll bar to move left and right one window width at a time.)

## TIP SHEET

- **To go directly to a page in your document press the F5 function key, type the page number in the Go To box, and then click the OK button. Works will take you and the insertion point to the top of the page. This "Go to" feature is also available in the Edit menu or you can press Ctrl+G to start the Go To process.**
- **Hold down the Shift key while you use any of the navigation keys on the keyboard, and you'll select text as you move. For example, the Shift+End key combination selects all of the text from the insertion point to the end of its line.**

**2** The arrow keys on the keyboard let you move the insertion point one step in any direction. The up and down arrows move one line at a time, while the left and right arrows move one character at a time.

**3** The Home and End keys move the insertion point to the beginning and end of the current line. The PgUp and PgDn keys move both the insertion point and the window view up and down by the amount you can see in the document window. If you change the size of the document window, you'll change the distance that these keys move you as well.

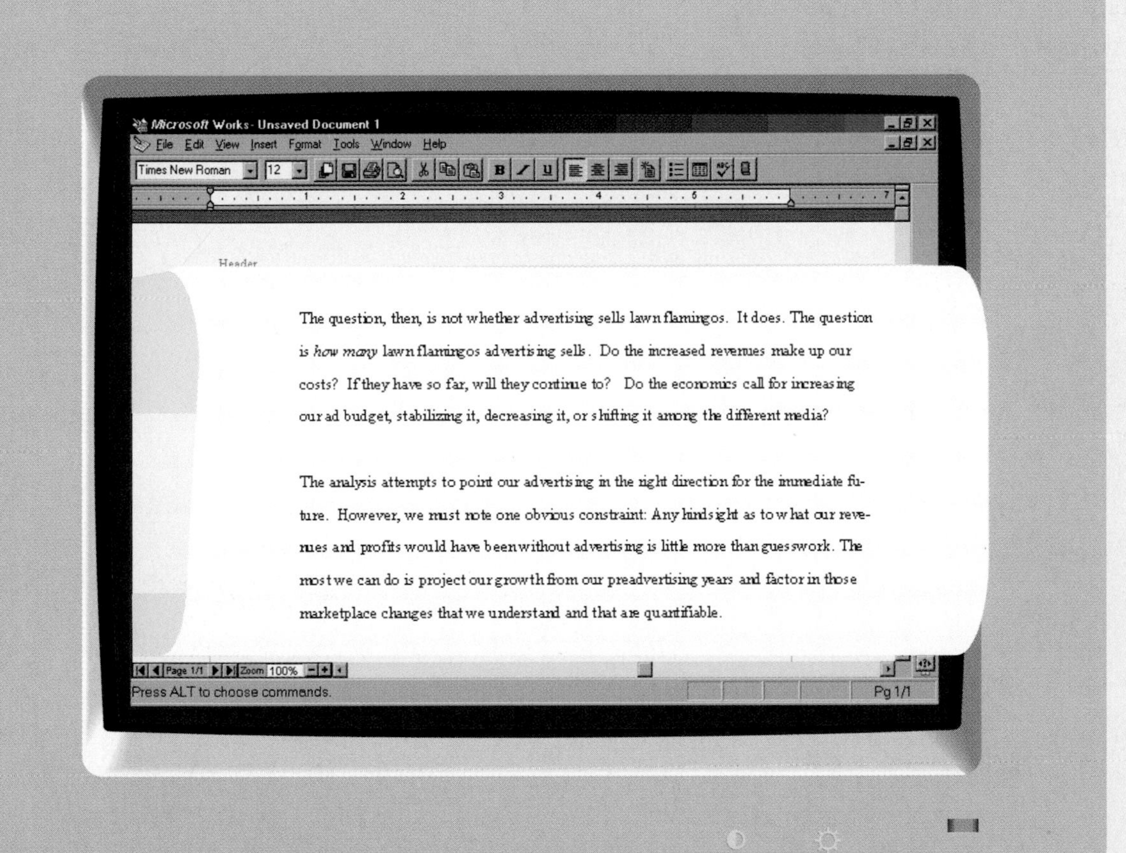

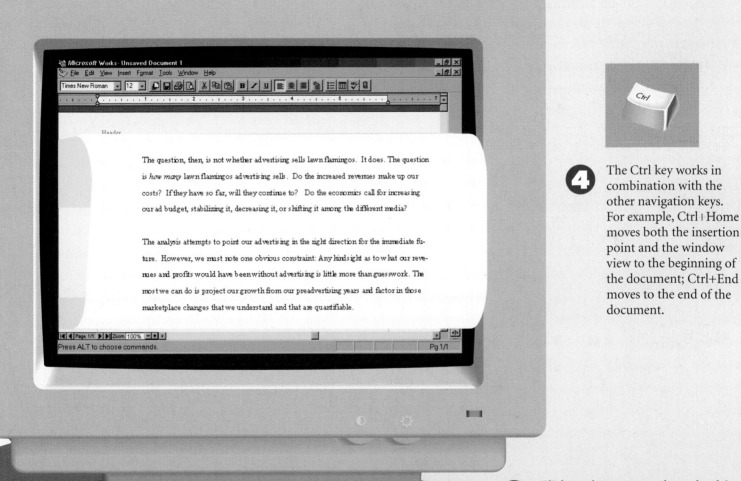

**4** The Ctrl key works in combination with the other navigation keys. For example, Ctrl+Home moves both the insertion point and the window view to the beginning of the document; Ctrl+End moves to the end of the document.

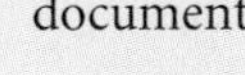

**5** Click on the arrows at the ends of the vertical scroll bar to move the document view up and down one line at a time. (Use the arrows on the horizontal scroll bar to move the document view small distances left and right.)

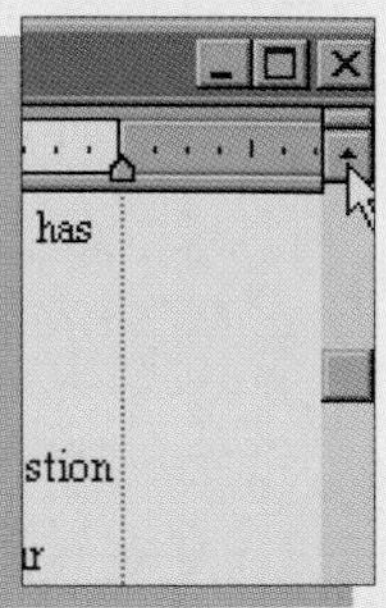

# How to Move Text

You'll sometimes find that you've typed in exactly what you intended to say, but in the wrong order. The next time this happens to you, don't bother retyping everything. Works gives you two ways to move blocks of text from one location in your document to another: *drag and drop* and *cut and paste.* Drag and drop is the easiest way to move blocks of text short distances in your document. Cut and paste, on the other hand, takes advantage of the Windows Clipboard, making it easier to move text long distances in your document, or even between the four main parts of Works (see Chapter 20).

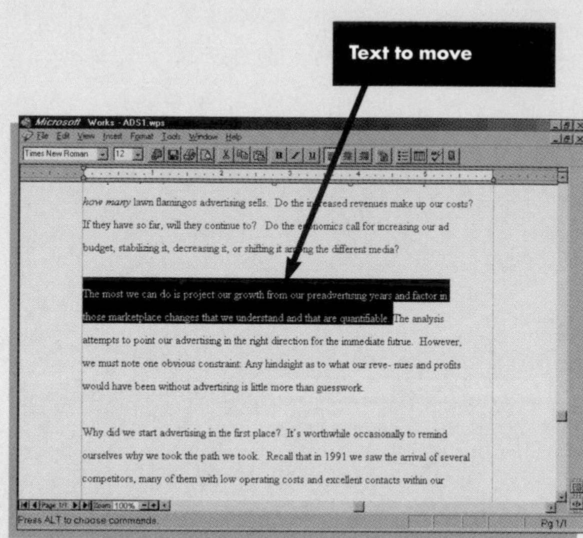


**1** To move a block of text using drag and drop, you first need to tell Works which block you want to move. Click and drag to highlight it.

**6** Move the insertion point to the text destination by clicking once. Now from the Toolbar, select the Paste tool (Clipboard icon). Works will insert the cut text from the Clipboard into the new location.

## TIP SHEET

- **If drag and drop isn't working on your computer, you can turn it on in the Options dialog box. Click on the Tools menu, and then select the Options command. Click on the General tab in the Options dialog box. Place a check mark in the "Enable drag-and-drop editing" check box. Click OK to close the dialog box.**
- **If you want to copy text with drag and drop, hold down the Ctrl key as you drag you'll see the COPY pointer instead of the MOVE pointer. When you are finished, Works will leave the original block of text unaltered.**
- **If you want to copy text by using the Clipboard, use the Copy command in the Edit menu instead of Cut. When you are finished, Works will leave the original block of text unaltered.**
- **After you paste text from the Clipboard, a copy of it remains there. This means that you can paste it again and again. Windows won't alter the Clipboard contents until you perform a new Cut or Copy.**

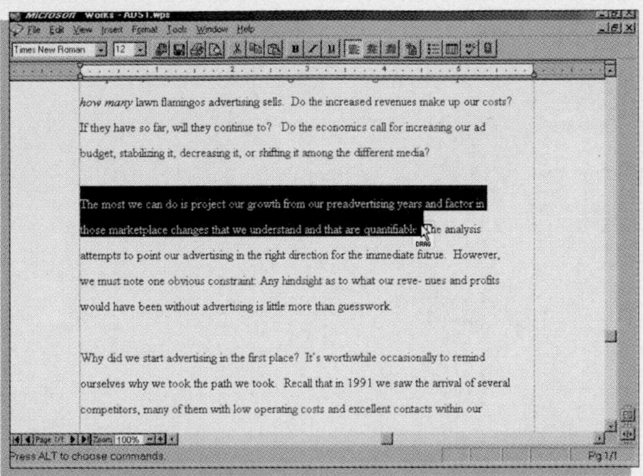

**2** To move the text, click once on the highlighted text and hold down the mouse button. The standard I-beam pointer will change to the *DRAG pointer.*

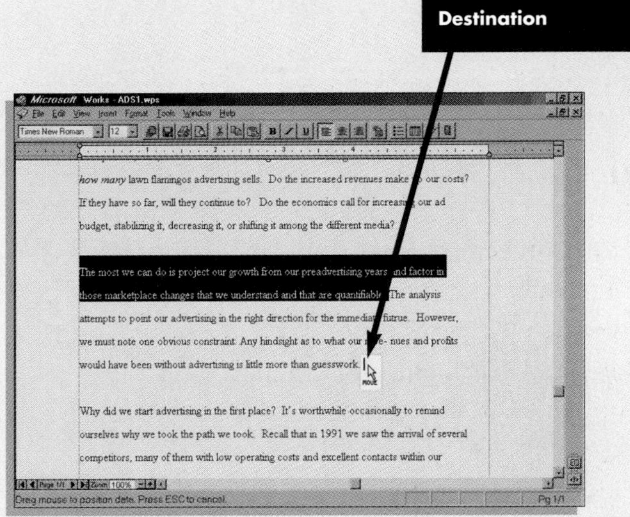


**3** Without letting go of the button, drag the mouse pointer and the attached insertion point to the new location for the text. The DRAG pointer will change to the *MOVE pointer.* When you reach the right spot, release the mouse button, and Works will move the text for you.

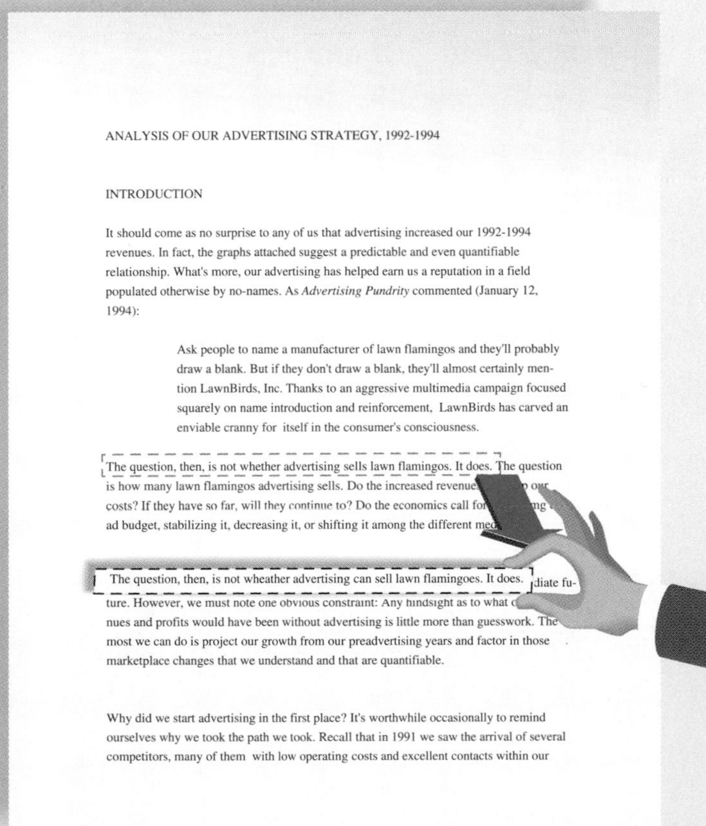

ANALYSIS OF OUR ADVERTISING STRATEGY, 1992-1994

INTRODUCTION

It should come as no surprise to any of us that advertising increased our 1992-1994 revenues. In fact, the graphs attached suggest a predictable and even quantifiable relationship. What's more, our advertising has helped earn us a reputation in a field populated otherwise by no-names. As *Advertising Pundrity* commented (January 12, 1994):

> Ask people to name a manufacturer of lawn flamingos and they'll probably draw a blank. But if they don't draw a blank, they'll almost certainly mention LawnBirds, Inc. Thanks to an aggressive multimedia campaign focused squarely on name introduction and reinforcement, LawnBirds has carved an enviable cranny for itself in the consumer's consciousness.

The question, then, is not whether advertising sells lawn flamingos. It does. The question is how many lawn flamingos advertising sells. Do the increased revenue... costs? If they have so far, will they continue to? Do the economics call fo... ad budget, stabilizing it, decreasing it, or shifting it among the different me...

The question, then, is not wheather advertising can sell lawn flamingoes. It does. ...diate future. However, we must note one obvious constraint: Any hindsight as to what ... nues and profits would have been without advertising is little more than guesswork. The most we can do is project our growth from our preadvertising years and factor in those marketplace changes that we understand and that are quantifiable.

Why did we start advertising in the first place? It's worthwhile occasionally to remind ourselves why we took the path we took. Recall that in 1991 we saw the arrival of several competitors, many of them with low operating costs and excellent contacts within our

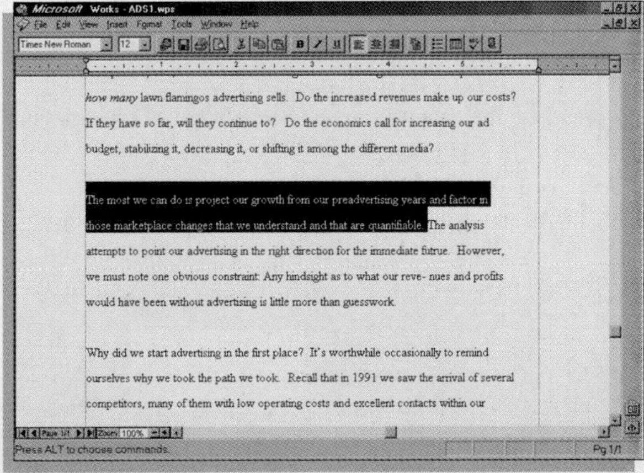

**4** To move a block of text using cut and paste, first select the block of text to move.

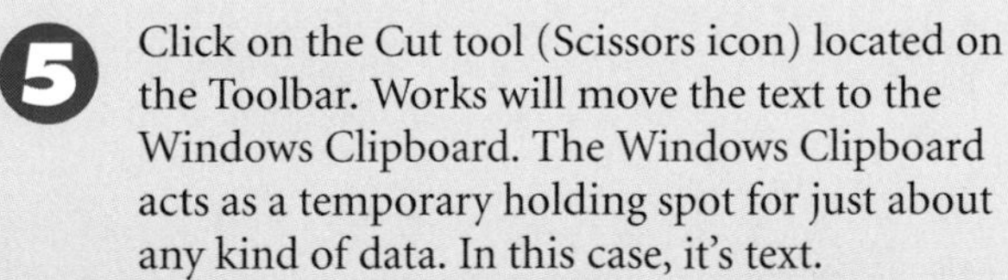

**5** Click on the Cut tool (Scissors icon) located on the Toolbar. Works will move the text to the Windows Clipboard. The Windows Clipboard acts as a temporary holding spot for just about any kind of data. In this case, it's text.

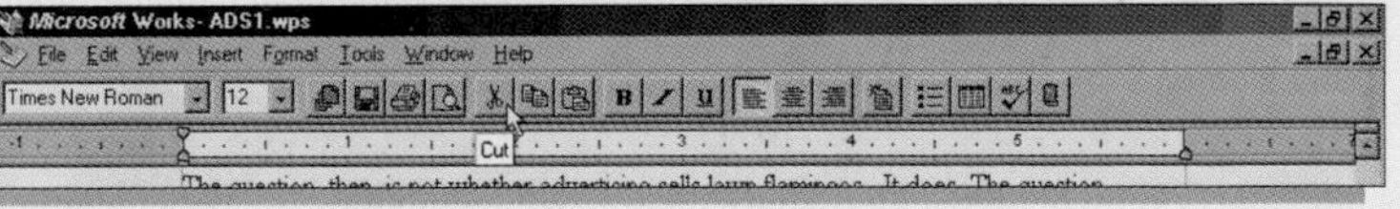

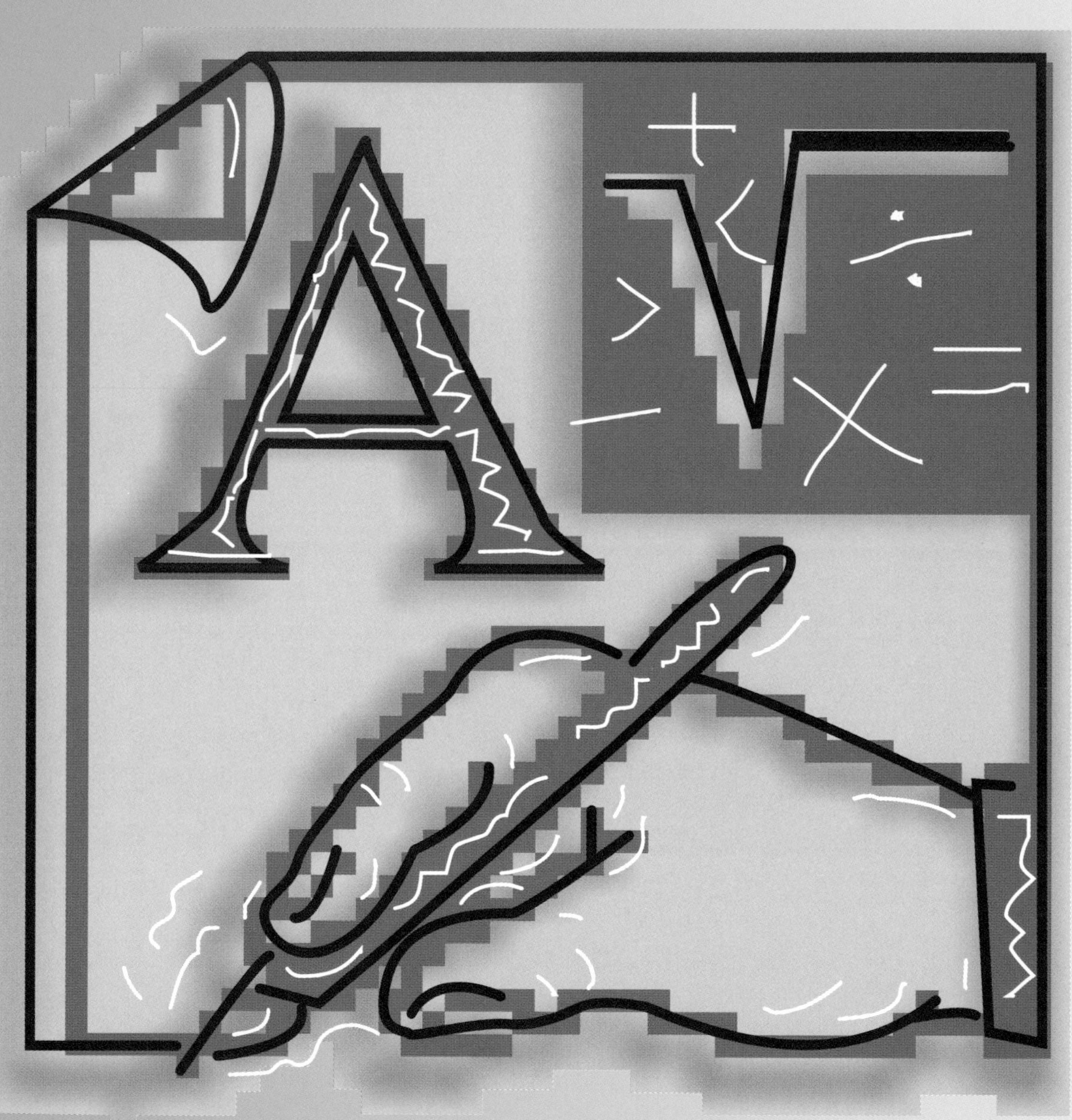

# CHAPTER 6

# Text Enhancement

Give your characters some character and watch your documents shine. Boldface, italics, font changes, and other text enhancements can make important text stand out and give your documents a more professional look.

Not that character formatting has aesthetic value only; sometimes convention demands it. For example, by convention, references to foreign-language words are printed in italics.

This chapter and the next cover Works' major character, paragraph, and page formatting features, so some advice is in order: Don't overformat your documents. A page crowded with text styles, margin changes, different type sizes, and other attention-getters is likely to backfire by becoming unattractive and difficult to read. Tinkering excessively with the formatting of an unimportant document is a real time-waster, too. Apply formatting judiciously when and where it will have an impact.

# How to Boldface, Italicize, and Underline Text

**Boldface** is probably the best way to emphasize a short block of text. Most headlines you see in publications are in boldface.

*Italic* type usually indicates new vocabulary, foreign-language words, and publication titles.

Underline substitutes for italics in handwriting and in type where italic type is unavailable.

The procedures for applying boldface, italic, and underline require the use of the Toolbar. If your Toolbar is not displayed, select the View Menu then click on the Toolbar option.

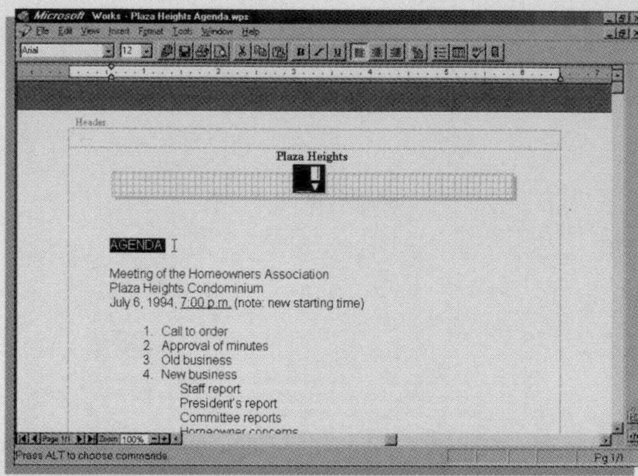


1. Type the text you want to boldface, and then select it. It can be any amount of text, from one character to an entire document.

## TIP SHEET

- **To remove any of these text formats, select the text, and again follow the steps shown here. This time, however, the styles are removed rather than applied.**
- **You can combine features such as boldface, italics, and underlining, though not all printers can print all possible combinations. Simply follow the specific procedure for each text style as described in this chapter.**
- **You can also apply and remove boldface, italics, or underlining using the Format Menu. After selecting the text, choose the Font and Style option from the Format Menu, then check the styles you want to apply or uncheck the ones you want to remove.**
- **The keyboard shortcut for applying or removing styles uses the Ctrl key. To apply or remove boldface press Ctrl+B, for italic press Ctrl+I, and for underline press Ctrl+U.**

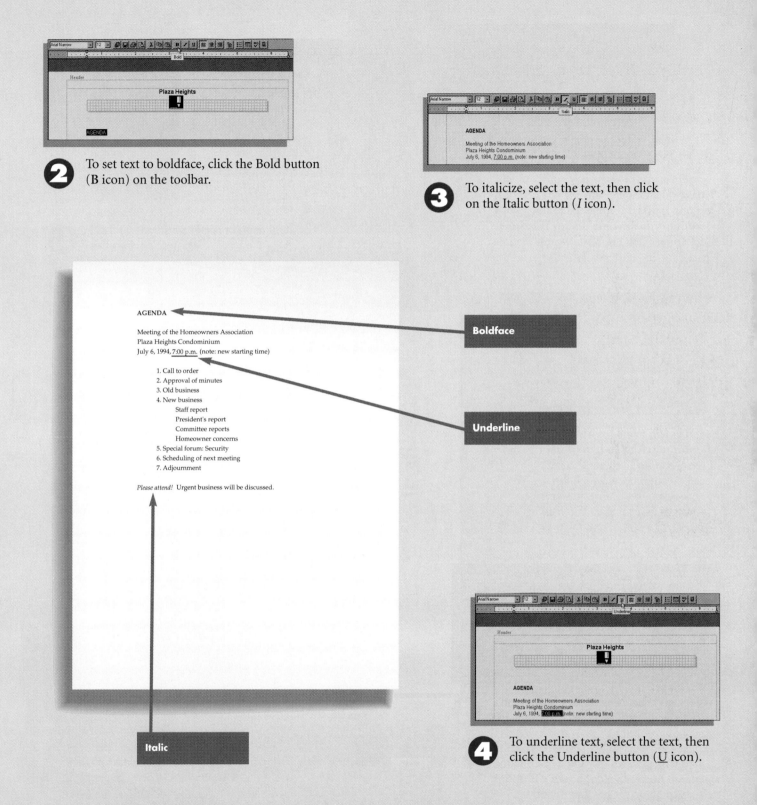


**2** To set text to boldface, click the Bold button (B icon) on the toolbar.

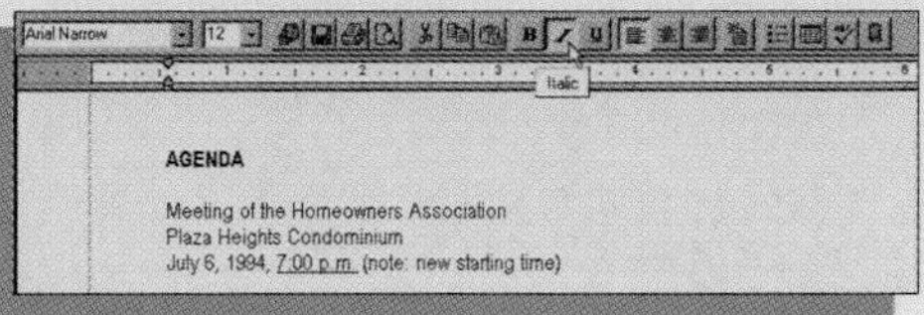


**3** To italicize, select the text, then click on the Italic button (*I* icon).

**AGENDA**

Meeting of the Homeowners Association
Plaza Heights Condominium
July 6, 1994, <u>7:00 p.m.</u> (note: new starting time)

1. Call to order
2. Approval of minutes
3. Old business
4. New business
   - Staff report
   - President's report
   - Committee reports
   - Homeowner concerns
5. Special forum: Security
6. Scheduling of next meeting
7. Adjournment

*Please attend!* Urgent business will be discussed.

**Boldface**

**Underline**

**Italic**

**4** To underline text, select the text, then click the Underline button (<u>U</u> icon).

# How to Change Fonts

The fonts you have available depend on such factors as your printer and your version of Windows. No matter, Works knows exactly what fonts you have and makes it easy for you to choose among them. Prudent use of fonts can make for truly handsome documents. Most type experts advise sticking to two fonts per document, perhaps one font for heading and one for body text. Then apply other text styles such as boldface and size changes to make other distinctions. For example, you might pick one font for all the headings in your document, and use different type sizes to show different heading levels.

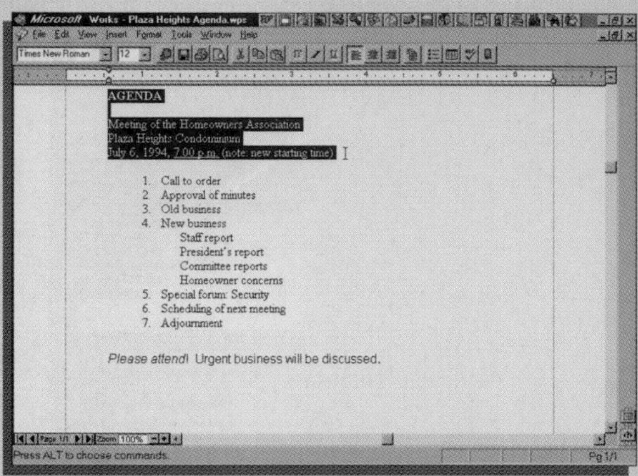

1. Type and select the text whose font you want to change. It can be any amount of text, from one character to an entire document.

5. Click on the desired font and then click on the OK button.

**TIP SHEET**

- **Technically, a font is a set of characters in one typeface, size, and style (such as bold, italic, or regular). However, most people use font as a synonym for typeface; this book follows the same convention.**
- **Works offers a command to instantly select the whole document for an operation such as a font change. Click on Edit in the menu bar and click on the Select All command. Then change the font as described on this page.**

2 Click on the drop-down list of fonts in the toolbar. Select the font you wish to apply. Notice that the font names are displayed in their own typeface, which takes the guesswork out of selecting a font.

File Edit View Insert Format Tools Window Help
Arial
Arial MT Black
Arial Narrow
Arial Rounded MT Bol
Arnold Boecklin
Aurora BdCn BT
AvantGarde SWA
Background Font 2

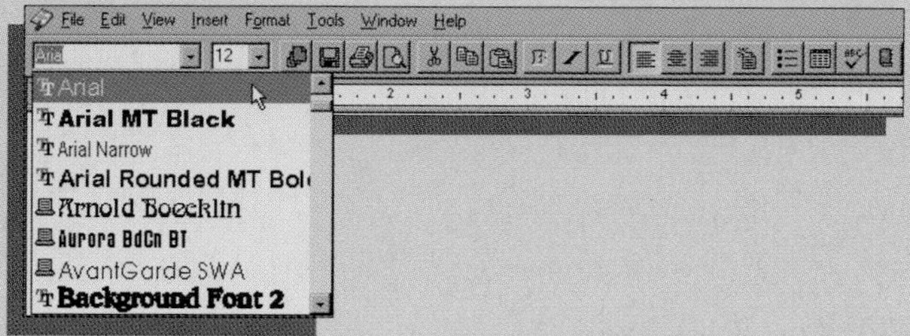

3 Here's another way to change fonts. Click on Format in the menu bar and then click on the Font and Style command.

Microsoft Works - Plaza Heights Agenda.wps
File Edit View Insert Format Tools Window Help
Arial
Font and Style...
Paragraph...
Tabs...
Borders and Shading...
Bullets...
Columns...
Easy Formats...
Text Wrap...
Picture...

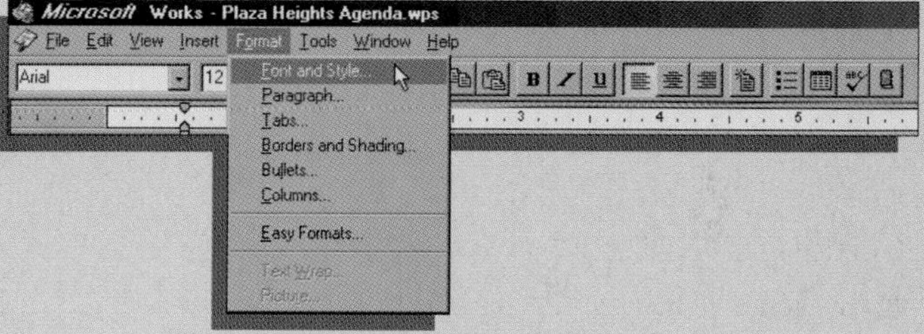

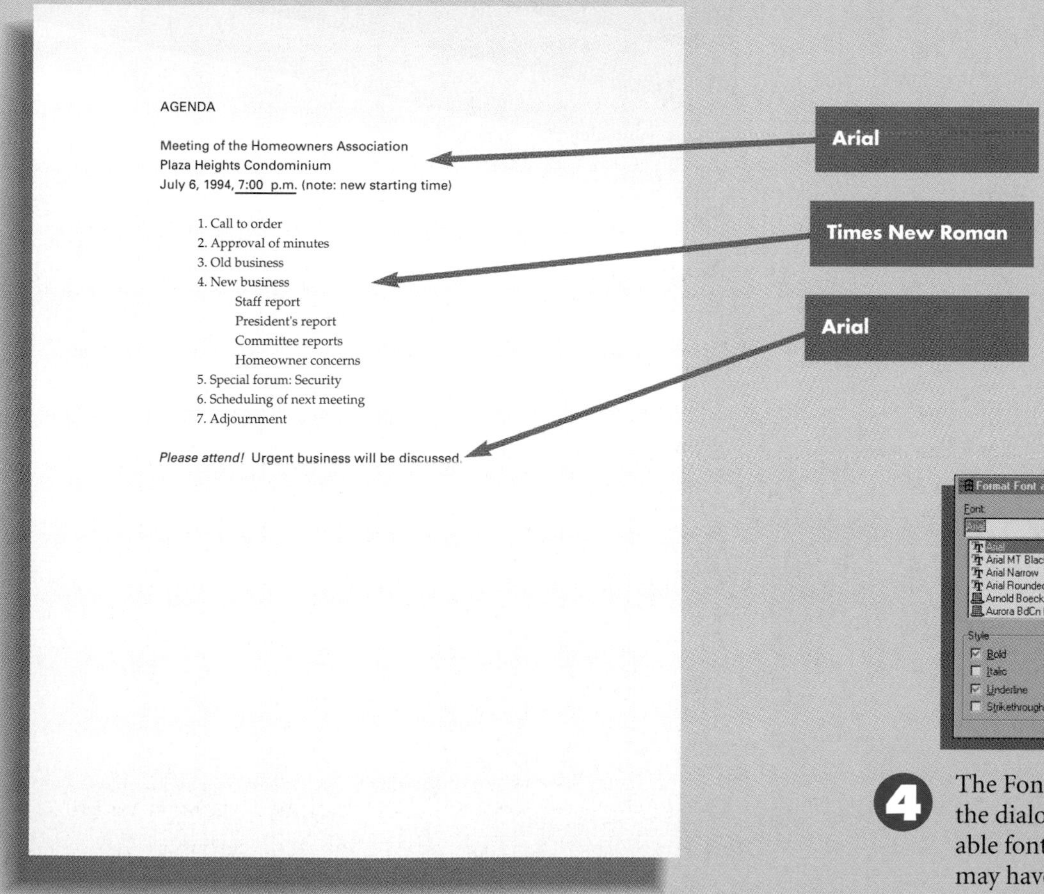

AGENDA
Meeting of the Homeowners Association
Plaza Heights Condominium
July 6, 1994, 7:00 p.m. (note: new starting time)
1. Call to order
2. Approval of minutes
3. Old business
4. New business
Staff report
President's report
Committee reports
Homeowner concerns
5. Special forum: Security
6. Scheduling of next meeting
7. Adjournment
Please attend! Urgent business will be discussed.
Arial
Times New Roman
Arial

Format Font and Style
Font:
Size:
Color:
Auto
OK
Cancel
Set Default
Arial
Arial MT Black
Arial Narrow
Arial Rounded MT Bold
Arnold Boecklin
Aurora BdCn BT
Position
Normal
Superscript
Subscript
Style
Bold
Italic
Underline
Strikethrough
Sample
AaYyZz

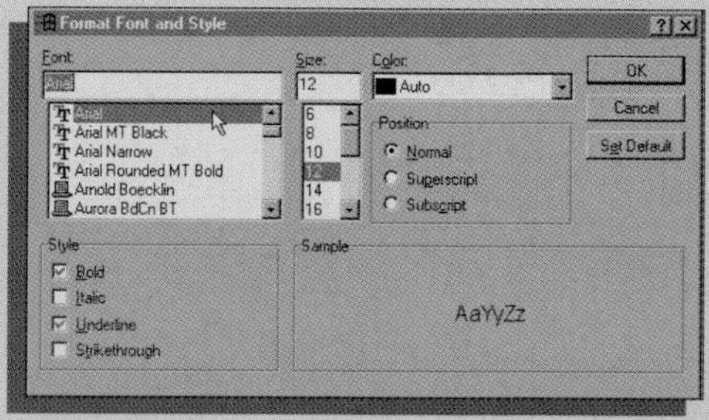

4 The Font list in the upper-left corner of the dialog box shows you all of your available fonts. Locate the font you need. You may have to scroll the list.

# How to Change Text Size

Most of the type you read in books and periodicals is 10, 11, or 12 points high. (There are 72 points to an inch.) Large type—especially when combined with boldface—is ideal for headlines and announcements. Small type is available for the proverbial "fine print."

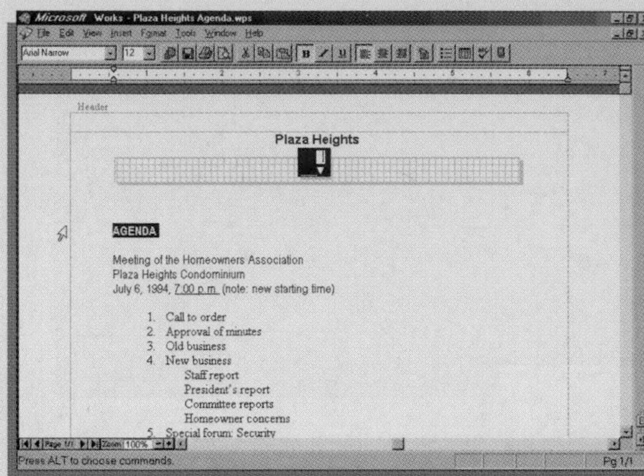

1. Type and select the text whose size you want to change. You can select any amount of text, from one character to an entire document.

## TIP SHEET

- **If you change your mind but don't remember what the old size was, don't panic: Select the Undo Editing option in the Edit menu or press Ctrl+Z.**
- **Different printers support different font sizes. Works automatically displays only the font sizes available for your printer.**
- **You can change the default font size that Works uses for new documents. To change the default font settings, open the Format Font and Style dialog box and select your font settings (see steps 3 and 4). Before you click on OK, click on Set Default.**
- **Beware that small variations in type size often go unnoticed by the reader, while extreme variations may be considered overstatements. Check your printouts carefully to make sure your size variations have the intended impact.**

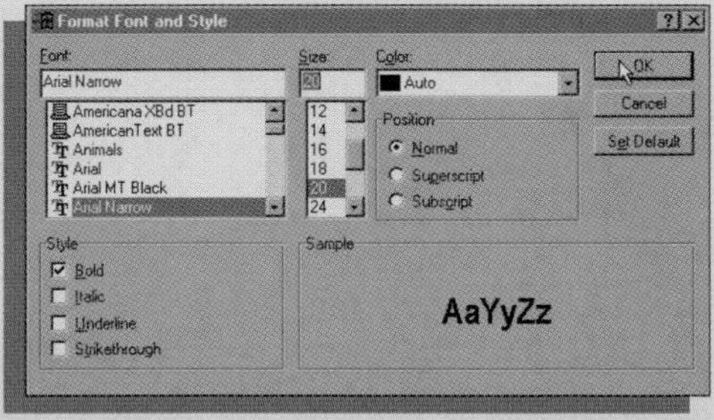

5. Click on the desired type size, then click on the OK button.

2 In the toolbar next to the font types is the font size drop-down list. Click on the down arrow to list the available sizes. From the list choose the size you want to apply to the selected text.

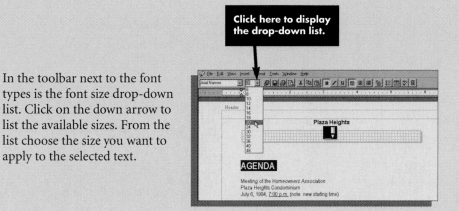

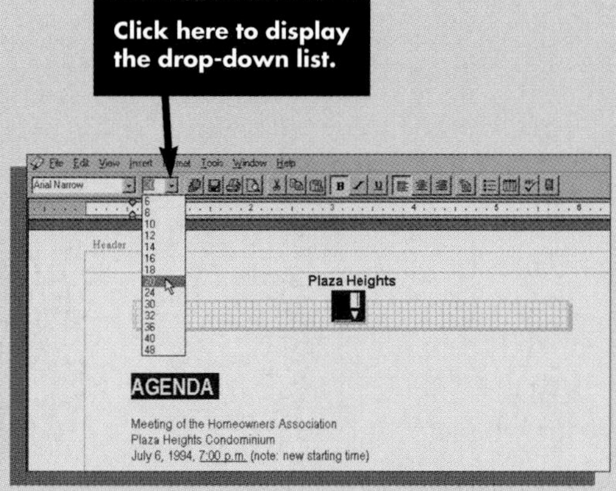


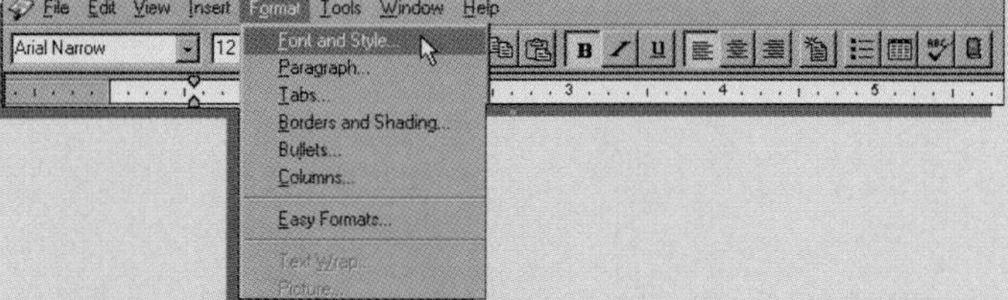


3 You can also use the Format menu to change text size. Select the Font and Style option from the Format menu.

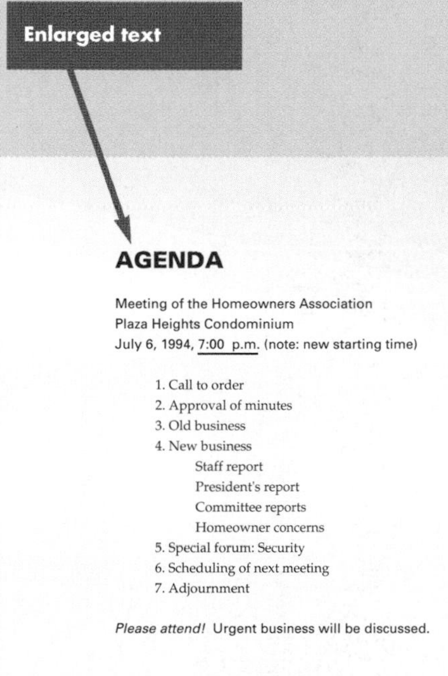


**AGENDA**

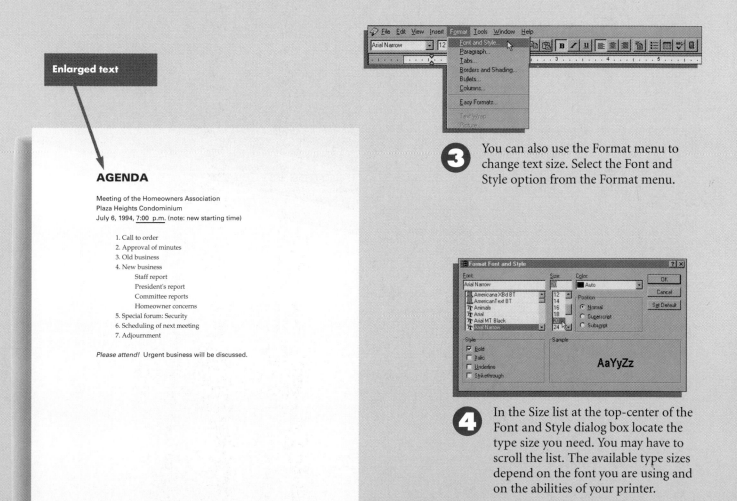

Meeting of the Homeowners Association
Plaza Heights Condominium
July 6, 1994, 7:00 p.m. (note: new starting time)

1. Call to order
2. Approval of minutes
3. Old business
4. New business
   - Staff report
   - President's report
   - Committee reports
   - Homeowner concerns
5. Special forum: Security
6. Scheduling of next meeting
7. Adjournment

*Please attend!* Urgent business will be discussed.

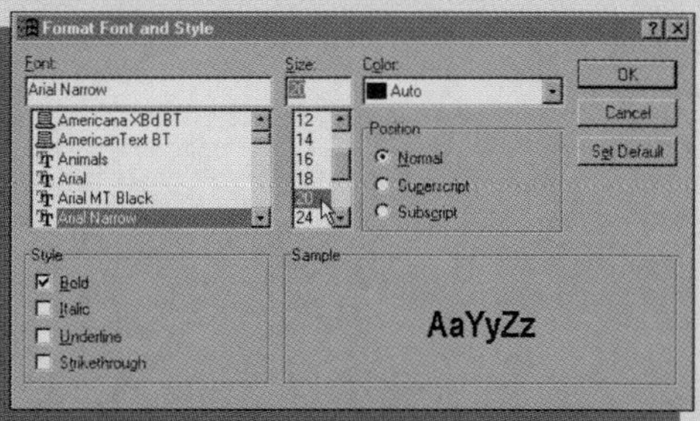


4 In the Size list at the top-center of the Font and Style dialog box locate the type size you need. You may have to scroll the list. The available type sizes depend on the font you are using and on the abilities of your printer.

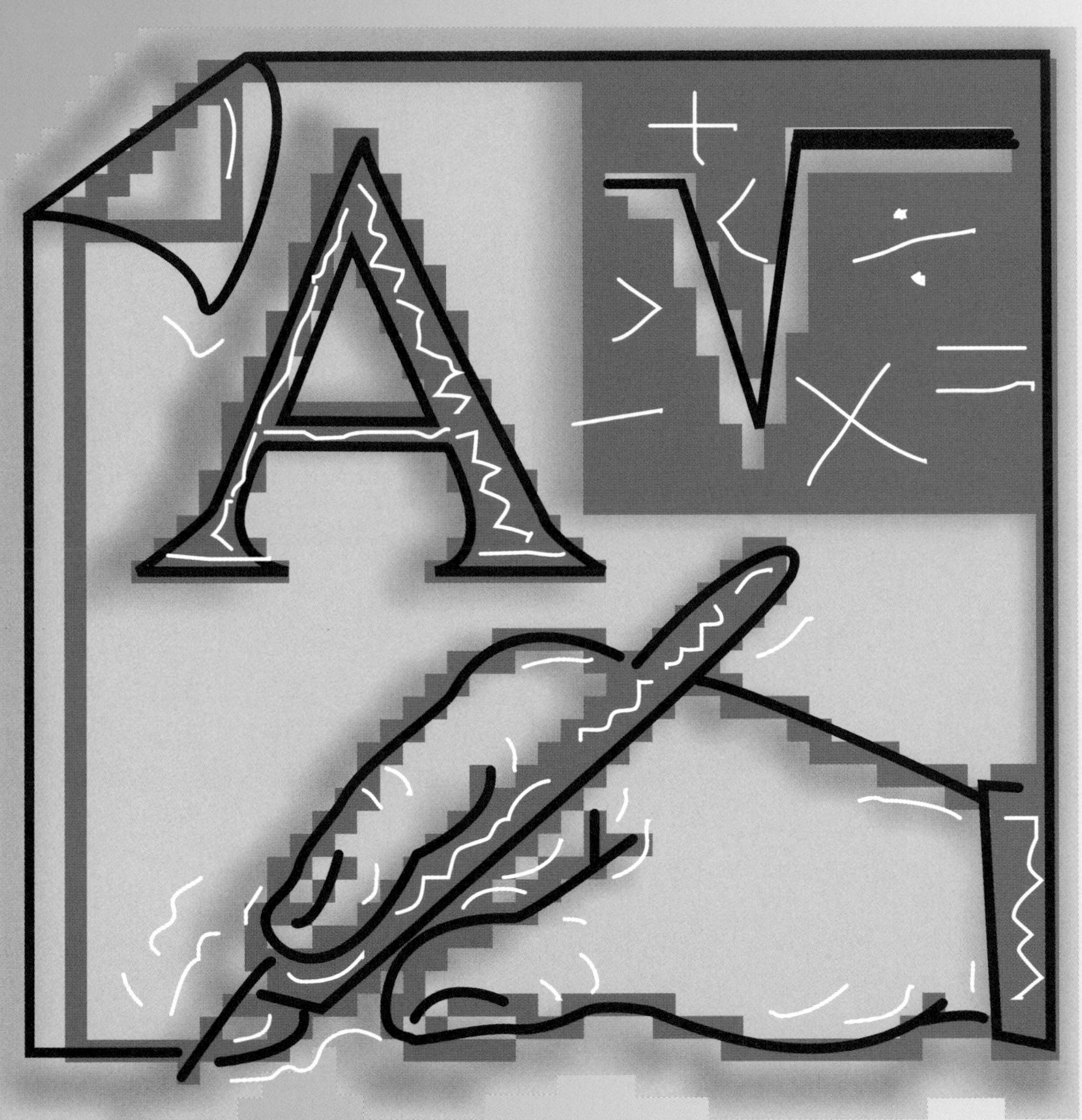

# CHAPTER 7

# Formatting

Formatting your document can serve two important purposes. First, it can improve the attractiveness of your document, drawing people in to read it. Using wide margins, for example, can make a document appear less dense and less intimidating to the casual reader. Second, good formatting can improve the readability of your document. For example, centering a heading at the top of a page can make it stand out and catch the reader's attention.

This chapter covers two types of document formatting: paragraph and page. Paragraph formatting affects your document on a paragraph-by-paragraph basis. For example, one paragraph may be single-spaced, and the next might be double-spaced. Line spacing, indents, and alignment are all forms of paragraph formatting. Page formatting, on the other hand, affects all of the pages of your document together. When you set the page margins, you do so for all of the pages in your document, and of course, all of the paragraphs on those pages.

# How to Change the Line Spacing

Line spacing is the amount of space between lines within a paragraph. In single-spaced text, there is no extra space between lines—just enough space so that letters don't overlap. Double-spaced text puts a blank line between lines of text. One-and-a-half spacing is a popular choice that makes text easier to read by separating lines of text with an extra half a line of blank space.

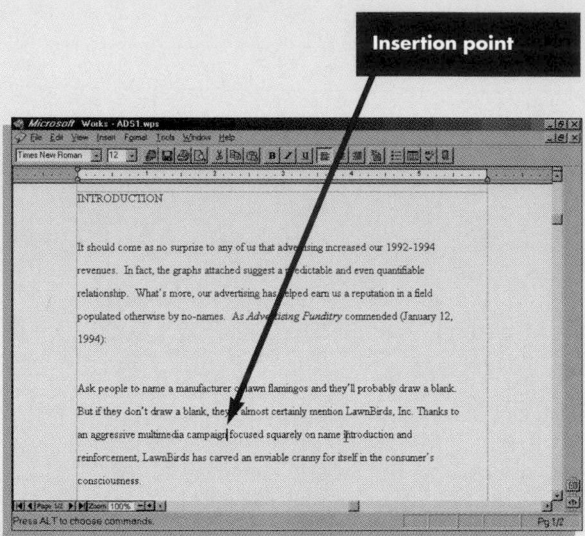


**1** Place the insertion point anywhere in the paragraph whose line spacing you want to change. It can be a blank paragraph—one you have just started by pressing Enter. Alternatively, select adjacent paragraphs to specify the same line spacing for all of them.

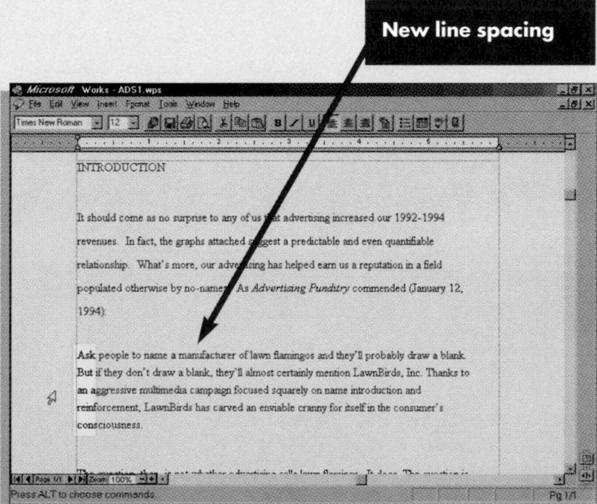


**6** The new line spacing is applied to the paragraph or to all the selected paragraphs.

### TIP SHEET

- **To change the line spacing for the whole document, click on Edit in the menu bar and then click on the Select All command. The whole document is selected. Then continue with step 2.**
- **You can enter any line spacing in the Line Spacing text box. If the spacing you enter isn't a whole or half space, Works will convert it to points. (There are 72 points in an inch.)**
- **A new paragraph takes on the formatting of the preceding one. Therefore, if you are typing in a double-spaced paragraph and you press Enter to start a new paragraph, the new paragraph too will be double spaced. You can change the line spacing of the new paragraph—or of any paragraph—by following the steps on this page.**
- **In Works, any text leading up to a paragraph mark is considered a paragraph. A paragraph mark is placed in your document every time you press the Enter key. To see the paragraph marks in your documents, click on View in the menu bar, and then click on All Characters in the drop-down menu. This will display all the hidden characters that Works uses to format your documents.**

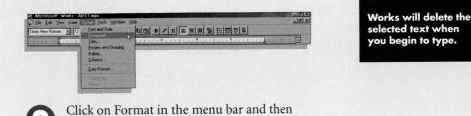

**2** Click on Format in the menu bar and then click on the Paragraph command.

**Works will delete the selected text when you begin to type.**

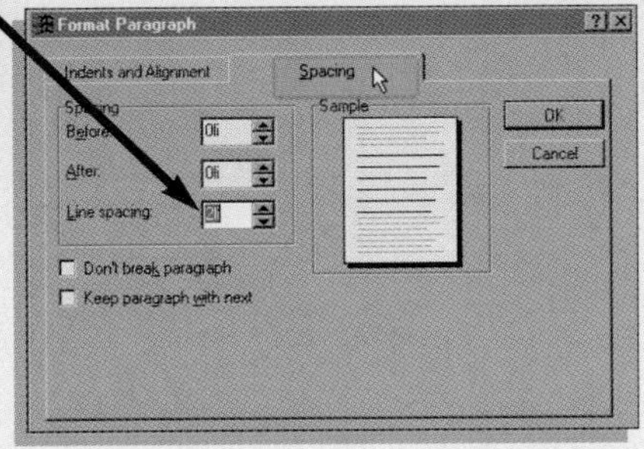


**3** At the top of the Paragraph dialog box, click on the Spacing tab if it is not already active. In the Spacing group, double-click in the Line Spacing text box to highlight all the text inside it.

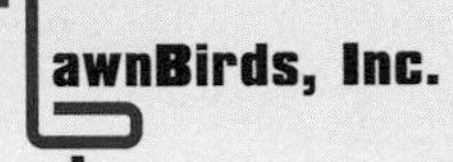


**Analysis of Our Advertising Strategy, 1992–1994**

**INTRODUCTION**

It should come as no surprise to any of us that advertising increased our 1992–1994 revenues. In fact, the graphs attached suggest a predictable and even quantifiable relationship. What's more, our advertising has helped earn us a reputation in a field populated otherwise by no-names. As *Advertising Punditry* commented (January 12, 1994):

Ask people to name a manufacturer of lawn flamingos and they'll probably draw a blank. But if they don't draw a blank, they'll almost certainly mention LawnBirds, Inc. Thanks to an aggressive multimedia campaign focused squarely on name introduction and reinforcement, LawnBirds has carved an enviable cranny for itself in the consumer's consciousness.

The question, then, is not *whether* advertising sells lawn flamingos. It does. The question is *how many* lawn flamingos advertising sells. Do the increased revenues make up our costs? If they have so far, will they continue to? Do the economics call for increasing our ad budget, stabilizing it, decreasing it, or shifting it among the different media?

This analysis attempts to point our advertising in the right direction for the immediate future. However, we must note one obvious constraint: Any hindsight as to what our revenues and profits would have been without advertising is little more than guesswork. The most we can do is project our growth from our preadvertising years and factor in those marketplace changes that we understand and that are quantifiable.

**Why did we start advertising in the first place?** It's worthwhile occasionally to remind ...rselves why we took the path we took. Recall that in 1991 we saw the arrival of several ...ompetitors, many of them with low operating costs and excellent contacts within our

**One-and-a-half spacing**

**Double spacing**

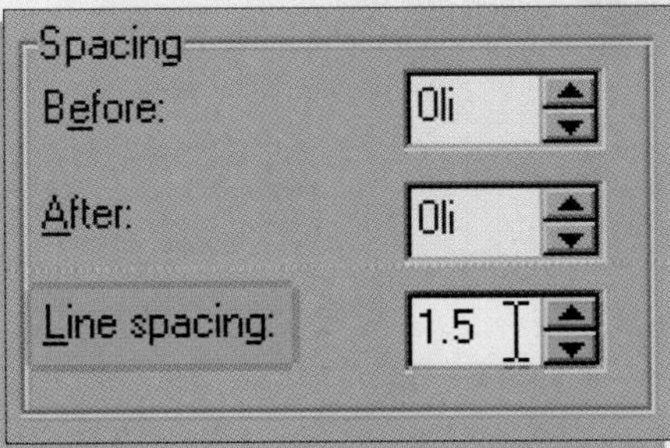


**4** Type in the desired spacing: 1, 1.5, or 2 for single, one-and-a-half, or double-spacing, respectively. (Typing the lines indicator, "li," is optional.)

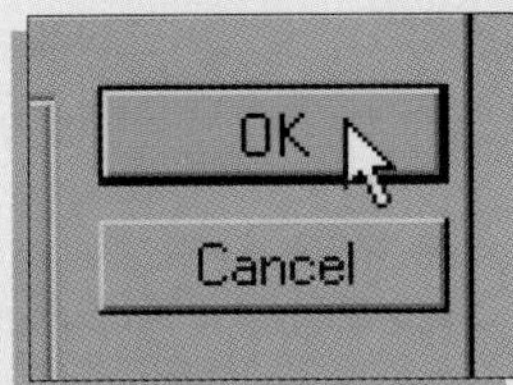


**5** Click on the OK button.

# How to Indent a Paragraph

Indentation is an effective way to call attention to a paragraph. It is also occasionally required by convention. For example, long quotations are by convention indented from the left (see the one in the sample document on this page). Microsoft Works lets you indent from the right, the left, or both.

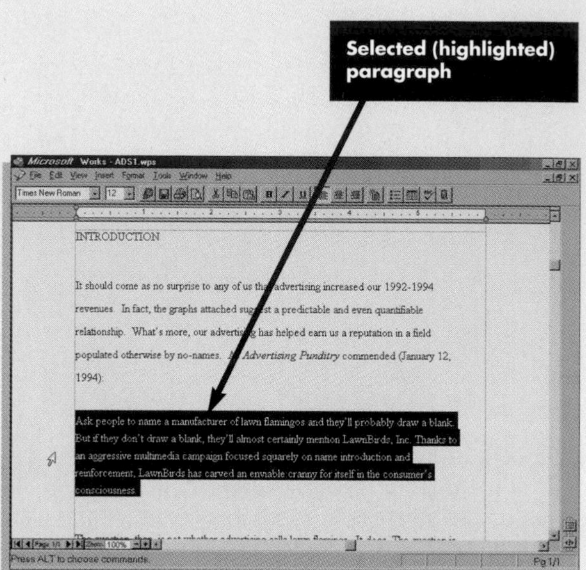


**1** Place the insertion anywhere in the paragraph you want to indent, or you can select (highlight) the entire paragraph. Recall that to select an entire paragraph, position the mouse pointer in the selection area to the left of the paragraph—the mouse pointer turns into a right-pointing arrow—now double-click. If you want to include adjacent paragraphs just drag the mouse pointer to include them too.

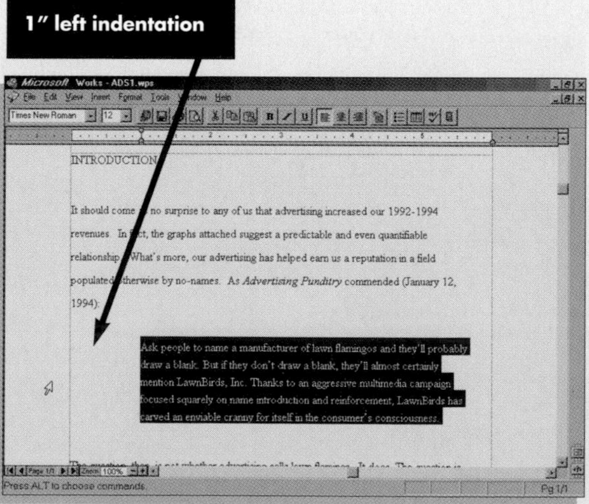


**6** Works applies the indentation to the paragraph or to all of the selected paragraphs.

**TIP SHEET**

- **To cancel indentation, repeat the steps shown here. In steps 3 and 4, specify indentations of 0.**
- **Microsoft Works measures indentation from the left or right margin (depending on whether you are assigning a left or right indent). Works uses default left and right margins of 1.25 inches each. So, for example, under the default margins, a left indent of 1 inch starts a paragraph 2.25 inches (1.25 inches for the margin, plus 1 inch for the indent) from the left edge of the paper. Indents remain the same relative to the margins. So, using the same example, if you change the left margin to 2 inches (explained later in this chapter), the paragraph will start 3 inches (2 inches for the margin, plus 1 inch for the indent) from the left edge of the paper.**

**2** Click on Format in the menu bar, and then click on the Paragraph command.

**3** At the top of the Paragraph dialog box, click on the Indents and Alignment tab if it is not already active. Then observe the Indentation area. If you want to specify a left indent, double-click in the Left text box, and type the indent amount in inches. Typing the inch sign (") is optional.

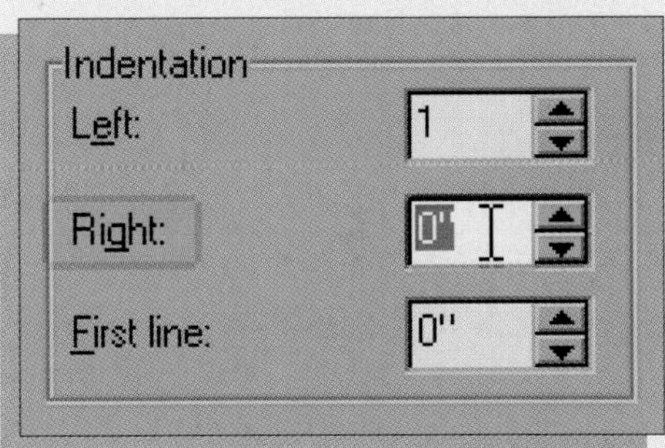


**4** If you want to specify a right indent, double-click in the Right text box to select all of the text in it. Type the indent amount in inches.

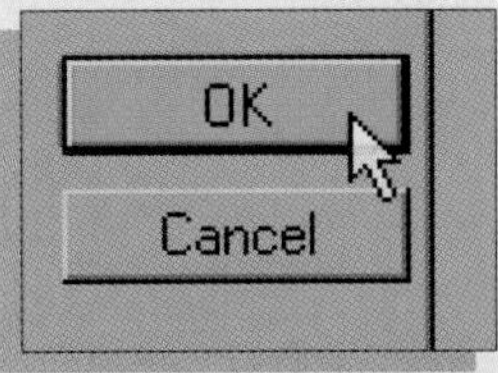


**5** Click the OK button.

Left indent

LawnBirds, Inc.

Analysis of Our Advertising Strategy, 1992–1994

INTRODUCTION

It should come as no surprise to any of us that advertising increased our 1992–1994 revenues. In fact, the graphs attached suggest a predictable and even quantifiable relationship. What's more, our advertising has helped earn us a reputation in a field populated otherwise by no-names. As *Advertising Punditry* commented (January 12, 1994):

Ask people to name a manufacturer of lawn flamingos and they'll probably draw a blank. But if they don't draw a blank, they'll almost certainly mention LawnBirds, Inc. Thanks to an aggressive multimedia campaign focused squarely on name introduction and reinforcement, LawnBirds has carved an enviable cranny for itself in the consumer's consciousness.

The question, then, is not *whether* advertising sells lawn flamingos. It does. The question is *how many* lawn flamingos advertising sells. Do the increased revenues make up our costs? If they have so far, will they continue to? Do the economics call for increasing our ad budget, stabilizing it, decreasing it, or shifting it among the different media?

This analysis attempts to point our advertising in the right direction for the immediate future. However, we must note one obvious constraint: Any hindsight as to what our revenues and profits would have been without advertising is little more than guesswork. The most we can do is project our growth from our preadvertising years and factor in those marketplace changes that we understand and that are quantifiable.

**Why did we start advertising in the first place?** It's worthwhile occasionally to remind ourselves why we took the path we took. Recall that in 1991 we saw the arrival of several competitors, many of them with low operating costs and excellent contacts within our

# How to Change Paragraph Alignment

Alignment refers to the way each line in a paragraph interacts with the margins. Paragraphs of ordinary body text are typically either left-aligned (sometimes called "ragged-right"), like the paragraph you are reading now, or justified, which means that word-wrapped lines are stretched out with extra space to span from margin to margin, producing a squared-off look. Centering and right alignment are rarely used in ordinary paragraphs, but can be helpful in short paragraphs such as headlines. Notice that the sample document to the right includes right-aligned, centered, and justified paragraphs.

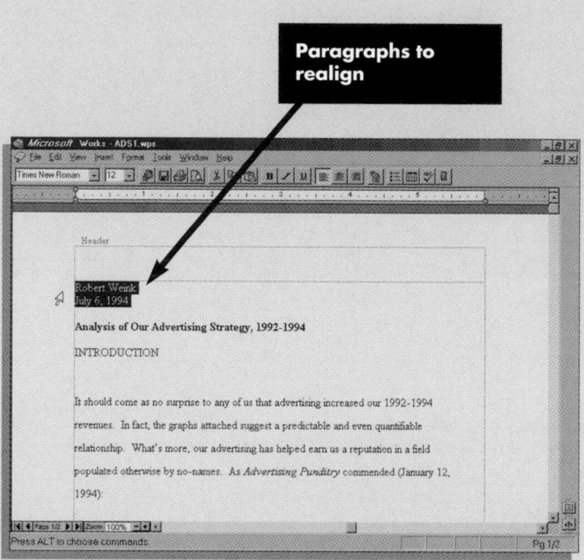


**1** Place the insertion point anywhere in the paragraph whose alignment you want to change. Or, select any portion of adjacent paragraphs to specify the same alignment for all of them.

## TIP SHEET

- **Justification alignment generally looks better with long lines than with short lines. With short lines, Works sometimes has to add extreme amounts of space between words to square-off the right margin. In a document that is otherwise justified, you may prefer to left-align heavily indented paragraphs or paragraphs typed in large type (because larger type produces correspondingly fewer characters per line). Notice that in this book, the chapter introductions—which have long lines—are justified, but narrower paragraphs—such as the one you are now reading—are left-aligned.**
- **Works treats all of its paragraph formatting as if it is stored in the paragraph marks. If you delete a paragraph mark, the preceding lines will take on the format of the next following paragraph mark. You can also copy formatting to your current paragraph by copying and pasting the paragraph mark of the paragraph you want to emulate. See the Tip Sheet under "How to Change the Line Spacing" in this chapter if you need help displaying paragraph marks.**

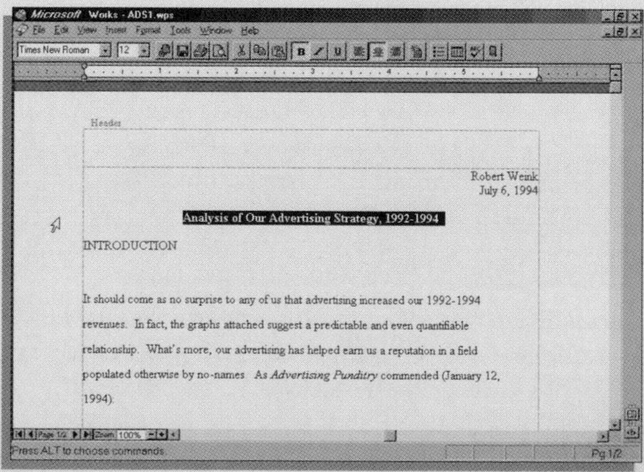


**6** The selected alignment is applied to the paragraph or to all of the selected paragraphs.

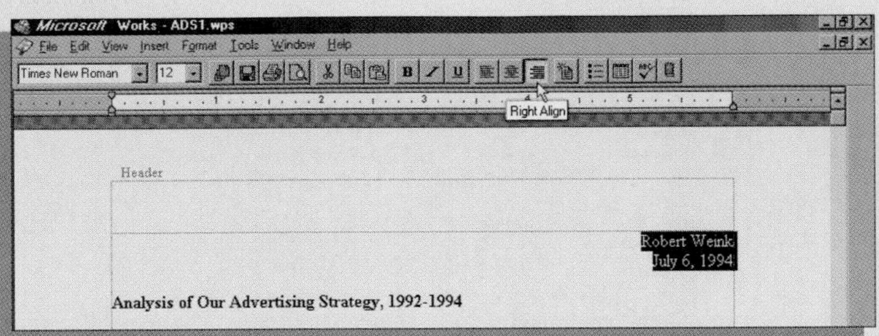

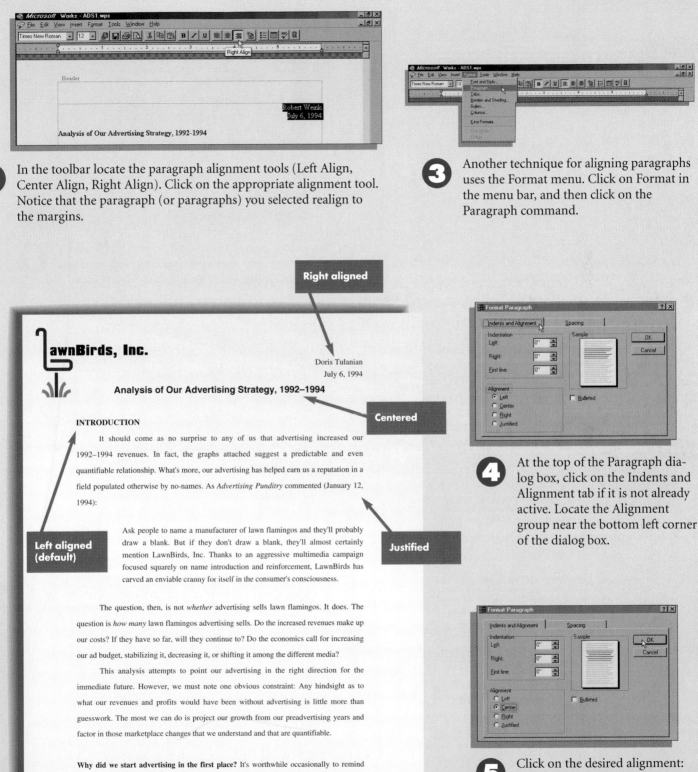

**2** In the toolbar locate the paragraph alignment tools (Left Align, Center Align, Right Align). Click on the appropriate alignment tool. Notice that the paragraph (or paragraphs) you selected realign to the margins.

**3** Another technique for aligning paragraphs uses the Format menu. Click on Format in the menu bar, and then click on the Paragraph command.

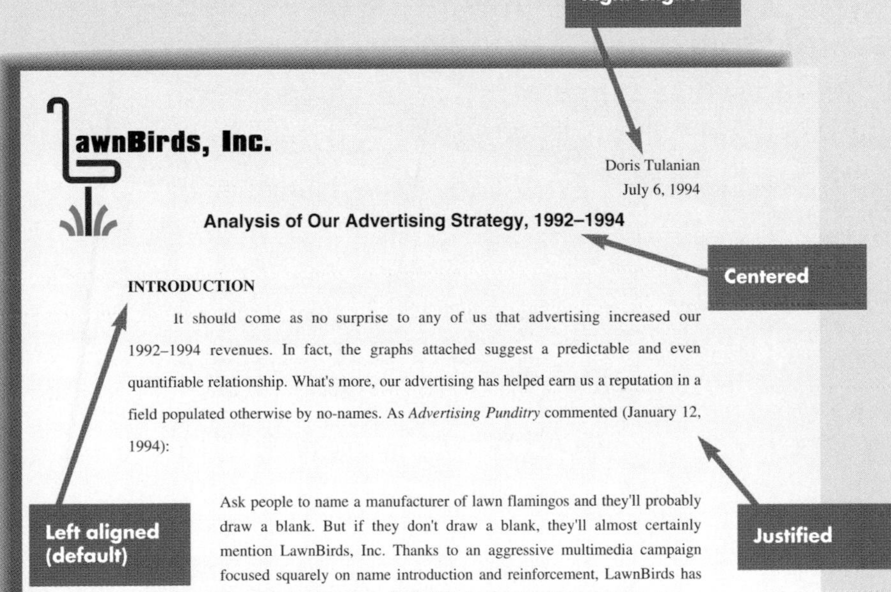


LawnBirds, Inc.

Doris Tulanian
July 6, 1994

Analysis of Our Advertising Strategy, 1992–1994

INTRODUCTION

It should come as no surprise to any of us that advertising increased our 1992–1994 revenues. In fact, the graphs attached suggest a predictable and even quantifiable relationship. What's more, our advertising has helped earn us a reputation in a field populated otherwise by no-names. As *Advertising Punditry* commented (January 12, 1994):

> Ask people to name a manufacturer of lawn flamingos and they'll probably draw a blank. But if they don't draw a blank, they'll almost certainly mention LawnBirds, Inc. Thanks to an aggressive multimedia campaign focused squarely on name introduction and reinforcement, LawnBirds has carved an enviable cranny for itself in the consumer's consciousness.

The question, then, is not *whether* advertising sells lawn flamingos. It does. The question is *how many* lawn flamingos advertising sells. Do the increased revenues make up our costs? If they have so far, will they continue to? Do the economics call for increasing our ad budget, stabilizing it, decreasing it, or shifting it among the different media?

This analysis attempts to point our advertising in the right direction for the immediate future. However, we must note one obvious constraint: Any hindsight as to what our revenues and profits would have been without advertising is little more than guesswork. The most we can do is project our growth from our preadvertising years and factor in those marketplace changes that we understand and that are quantifiable.

**Why did we start advertising in the first place?** It's worthwhile occasionally to remind ourselves why we took the path we took. Recall that in 1991 we saw the arrival of several competitors, many of them with low operating costs and excellent contacts within our

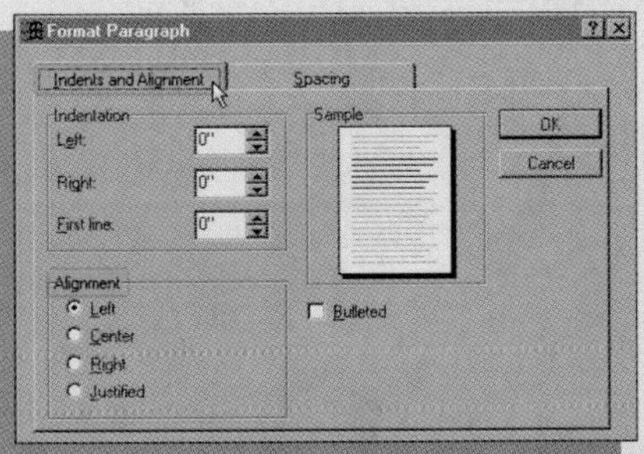


**4** At the top of the Paragraph dialog box, click on the Indents and Alignment tab if it is not already active. Locate the Alignment group near the bottom left corner of the dialog box.

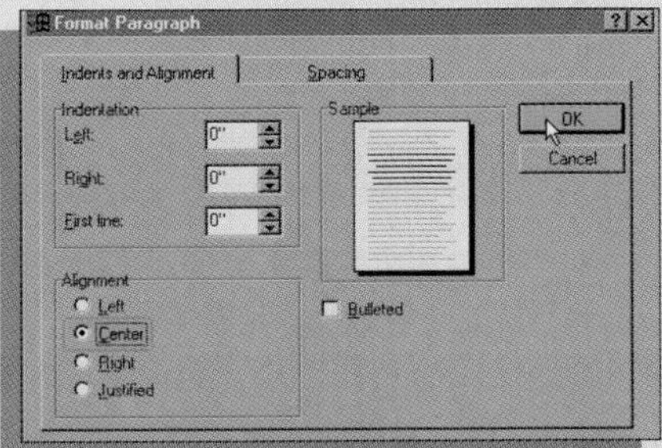


**5** Click on the desired alignment: Left, Center, Right, or Justified. Notice the Justified option—this option is not include in the toolbar. To apply the new alignment, click on the OK button.

# How to Reset the Page Margins

Works uses default margins of 1 inch on the top and bottom of the page and 1.25 inches on the left and right. These margins are fine for most documents, but like all features in Works, they are by no means mandatory. Larger margins can give the page a gentler, more spacious feel, and (attention students) can increase the page count of a document. Narrower margins (attention resume writers) can come in handy when you're trying to fit text onto one page. For example, in the document on this page, all the introductory text of a business report fits neatly on one page thanks to customized margins.

**1** Click on File in the menu bar and then click on the Page Setup command. (It does not matter where the insertion point is resting or whether text is selected.)

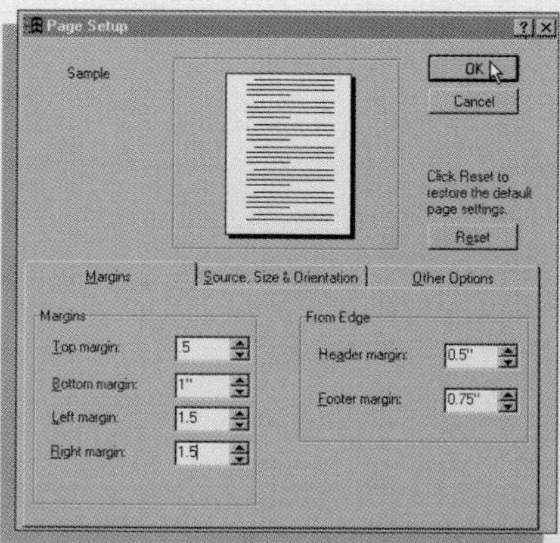


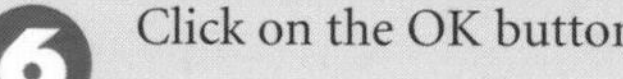

**6** Click on the OK button.

TIP SHEET

- **Remember, in Microsoft Works, the term *margins* refers to the overall margins applied to every page. To change the margins of a paragraph or two, as in the second paragraph of the sample document on this page, use indentation as described earlier in this chapter.**
- **Because indents are added to margin settings, you occasionally get more than you bargained for. Let's say you assign a 1-inch left indent to a paragraph in a document with a 2-inch left margin. You get a whopping 3-inch indent with respect to the left edge of the page. Consider the effect of the margin setting when deciding whether and how much to indent a paragraph.**
- **Margin jargon can be slightly confusing. Note that "narrow" margins produce long lines of text, and "wide" margins produce short lines of text.**

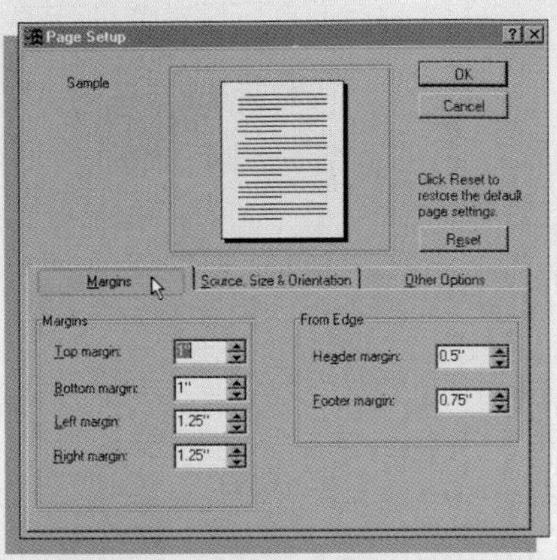


**2** In the Page Setup dialog box, click on the Margins tab if it is not already active.

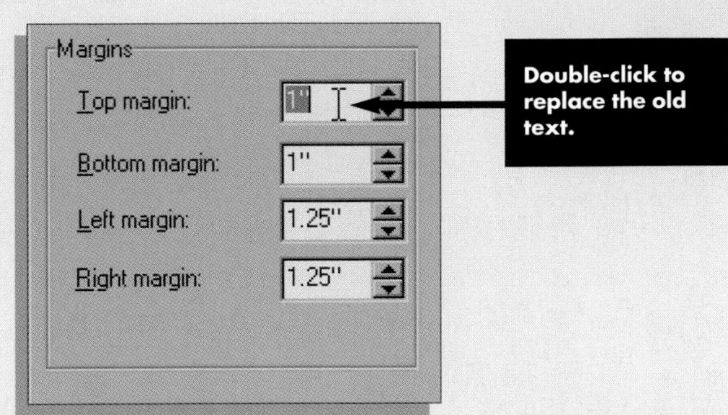


**3** Double-click to select everything in the text box for the first margin you want to change: Top Margin, Bottom Margin, Left Margin, or Right Margin.

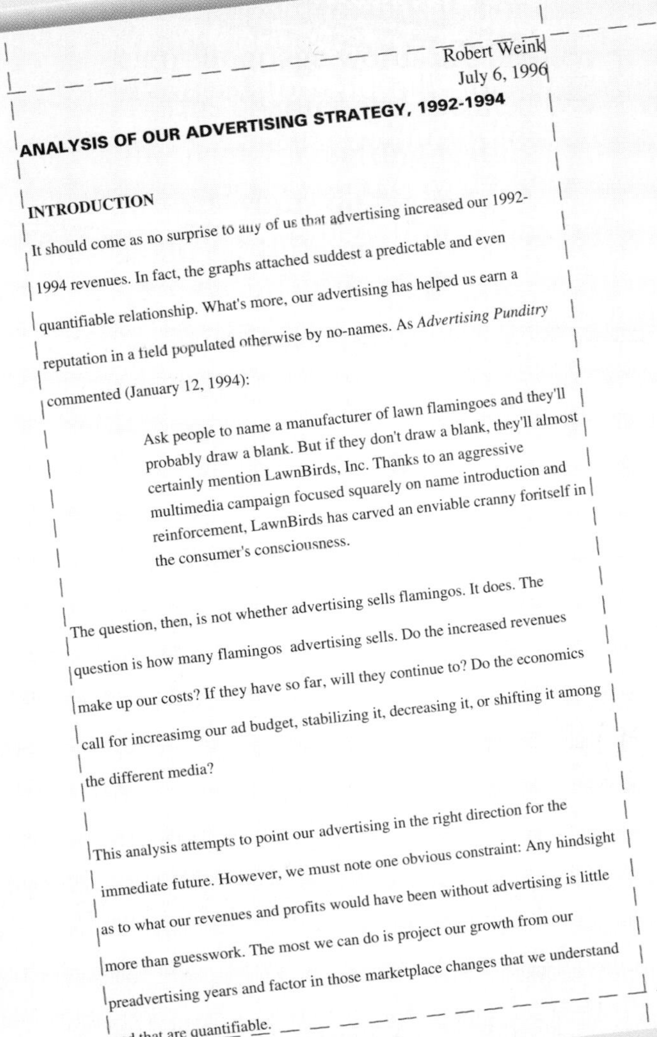

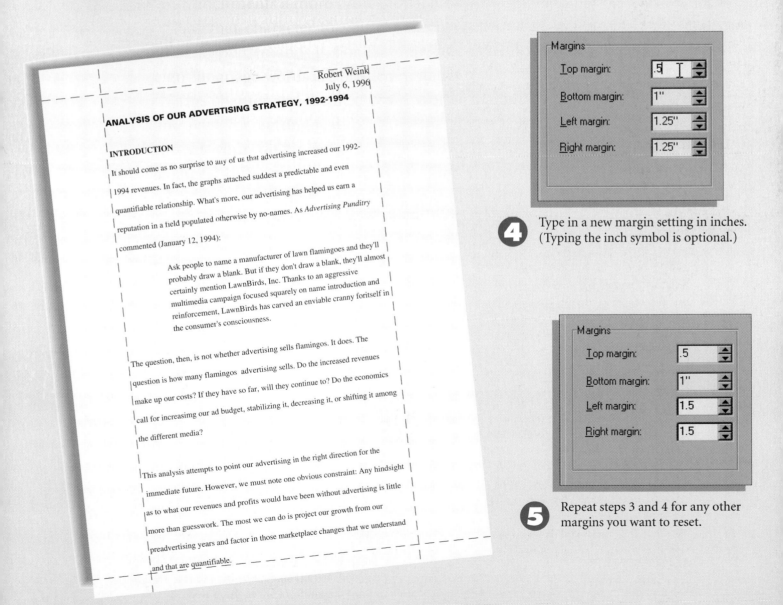

Robert Weink
July 6, 1996

**ANALYSIS OF OUR ADVERTISING STRATEGY, 1992-1994**

**INTRODUCTION**

It should come as no surprise to any of us that advertising increased our 1992-1994 revenues. In fact, the graphs attached suddest a predictable and even quantifiable relationship. What's more, our advertising has helped us earn a reputation in a field populated otherwise by no-names. As *Advertising Punditry* commented (January 12, 1994):

> Ask people to name a manufacturer of lawn flamingoes and they'll probably draw a blank. But if they don't draw a blank, they'll almost certainly mention LawnBirds, Inc. Thanks to an aggressive multimedia campaign focused squarely on name introduction and reinforcement, LawnBirds has carved an enviable cranny foritself in the consumer's consciousness.

The question, then, is not whether advertising sells flamingos. It does. The question is how many flamingos advertising sells. Do the increased revenues make up our costs? If they have so far, will they continue to? Do the economics call for increasing our ad budget, stabilizing it, decreasing it, or shifting it among the different media?

This analysis attempts to point our advertising in the right direction for the immediate future. However, we must note one obvious constraint: Any hindsight as to what our revenues and profits would have been without advertising is little more than guesswork. The most we can do is project our growth from our preadvertising years and factor in those marketplace changes that we understand and that are quantifiable.

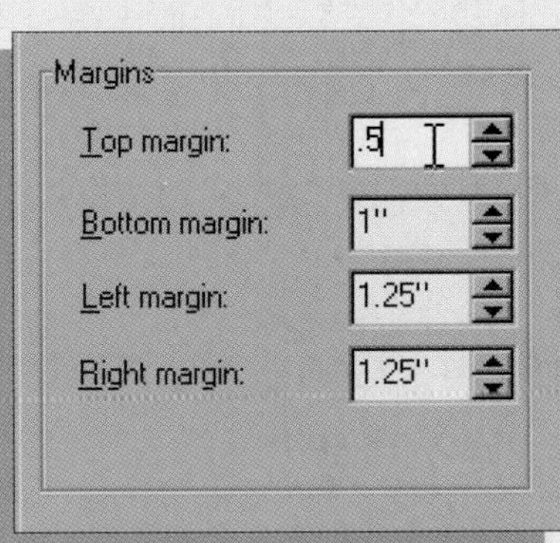


**4** Type in a new margin setting in inches. (Typing the inch symbol is optional.)

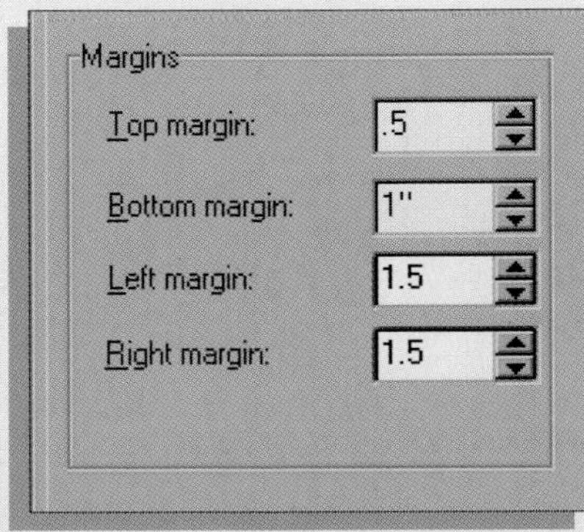


**5** Repeat steps 3 and 4 for any other margins you want to reset.

# TRY IT!

Here's an opportunity to try out the many skills you have learned in the first seven chapters of this book. Follow these steps to type, format, and print the document pictured here. Chapter numbers are included in italics to help you find more information on the skills required. Don't worry if your font looks different from the one shown here or if your lines break in different places. Factors like these can vary from one computer and printer to the next.

If necessary, switch on your computer and start Microsoft Works. *Chapters 2 & 3*

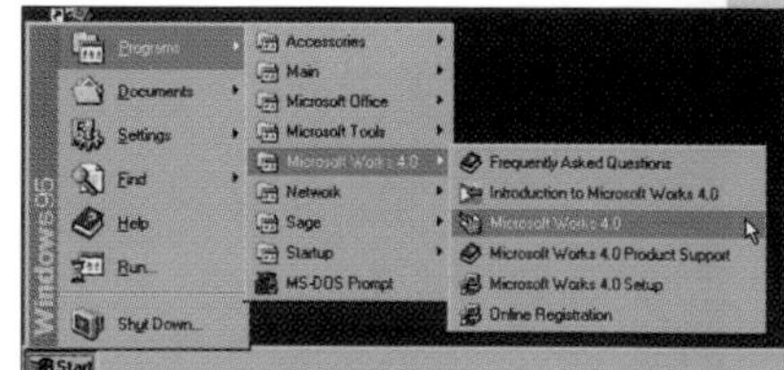

In the Works Task Launcher window, click on the Word Processor button to create a new word processor document. *Chapter 4*

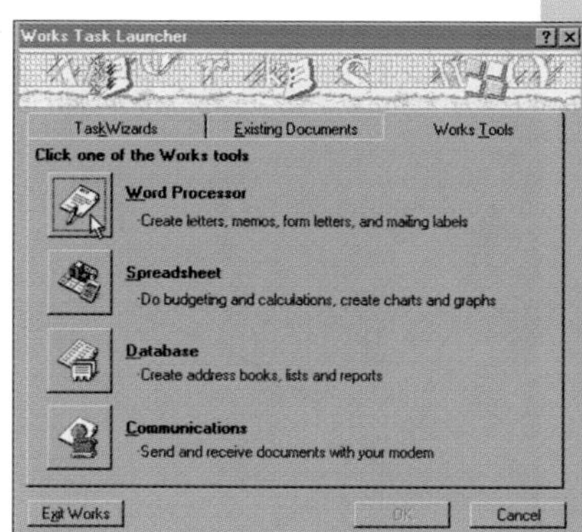


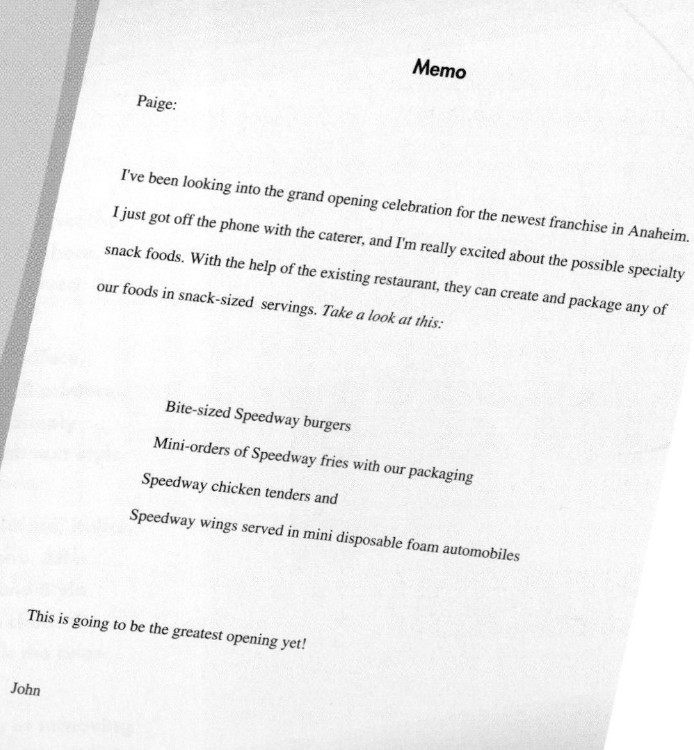

**Memo**

Paige:

I've been looking into the grand opening celebration for the newest franchise in Anaheim. I just got off the phone with the caterer, and I'm really excited about the possible specialty snack foods. With the help of the existing restaurant, they can create and package any of our foods in snack-sized servings. *Take a look at this:*

Bite-sized Speedway burgers

Mini-orders of Speedway fries with our packaging

Speedway chicken tenders and

Speedway wings served in mini disposable foam automobiles

This is going to be the greatest opening yet!

John

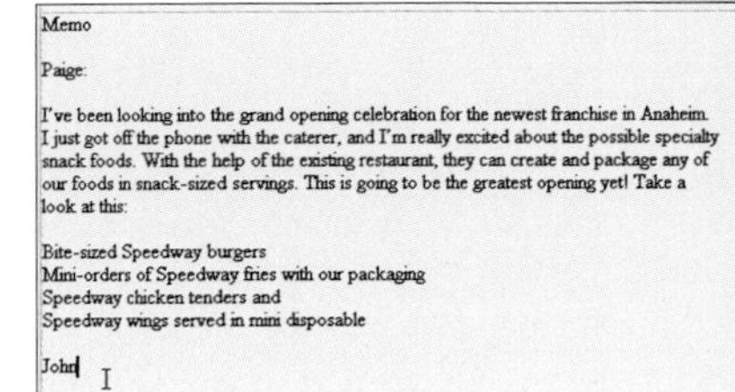


Type the text of the memo. Don't worry about any of the formatting yet. Press Enter once to end a short line, twice to skip a line. *Chapter 4*

Select the last full sentence in the main paragraph (This is going…). Be sure to select the space after the exclamation point. *Chapter 5*

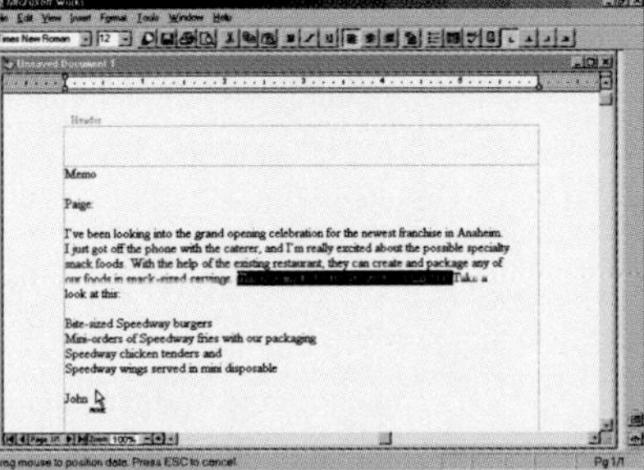

Click and hold down the mouse button on the selected text and drag it down to the line before John. Release the mouse button. *Chapter 5*

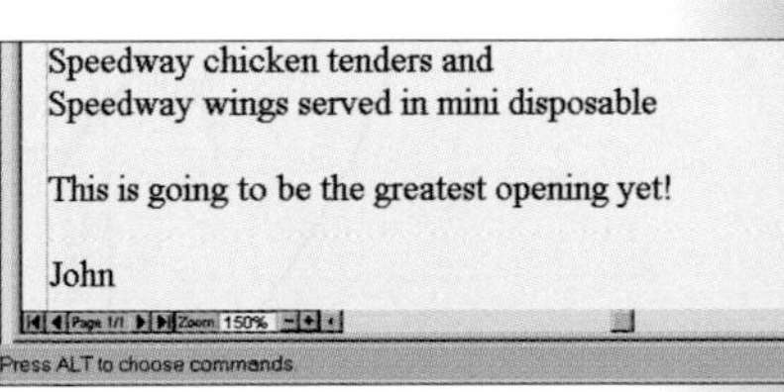


Place blank lines both before and after this new paragraph. To do this, click at the beginning of each of the last two lines (This is going…and John) and press Enter.

Select the text "Take a look at this:" at the end of the first main paragraph. *Chapter 5*

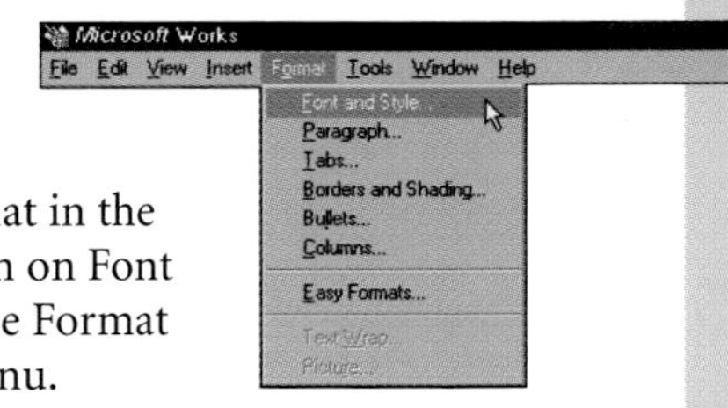


Click on Format in the menu bar, then on Font and Style in the Format pull-down menu. *Chapter 6*

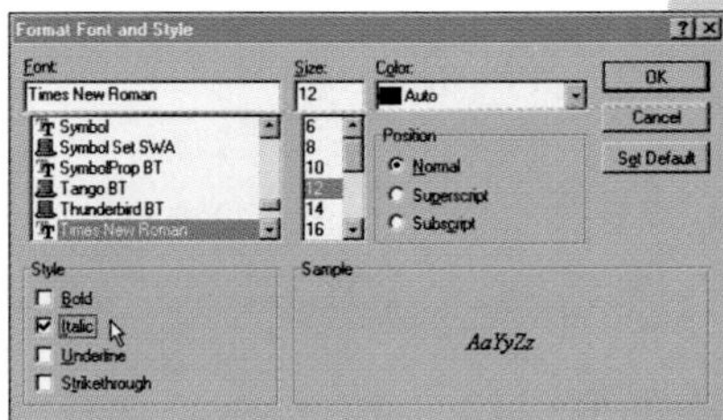


Click on the Italic check box to select it, and then click on the OK button. *Chapter 6*

Select the text, Memo, at the top of the page. *Chapter 5*

Click on Format in the menu bar, then on Font and Style in the Format pull-down menu. *Chapter 6*

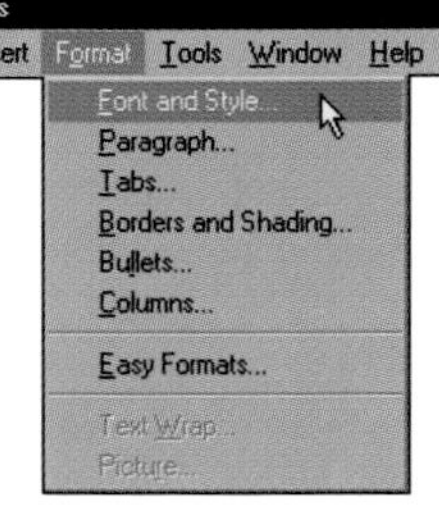


**Continue to next page ▸**

# TRY IT!

Continue below

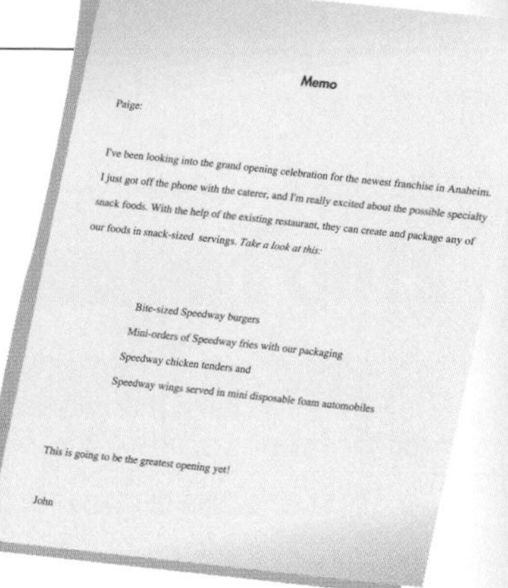
Memo

Paige:

I've been looking into the grand opening celebration for the newest franchise in Anaheim. I just got off the phone with the caterer, and I'm really excited about the possible specialty snack foods. With the help of the existing restaurant, they can create and package any of our foods in snack-sized servings. *Take a look at this:*

Bite-sized Speedway burgers
Mini-orders of Speedway fries with our packaging
Speedway chicken tenders and
Speedway wings served in mini disposable foam automobiles

This is going to be the greatest opening yet!

John

Click on the Bold check box to select it. *Chapter 6*

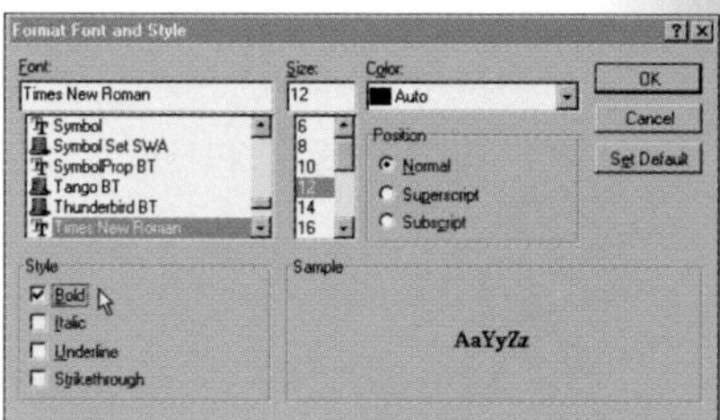

With the Font and Style dialog box still open, click once on Arial in the Font list box. You may have to use the scroll bar to find it. *Chapter 6*

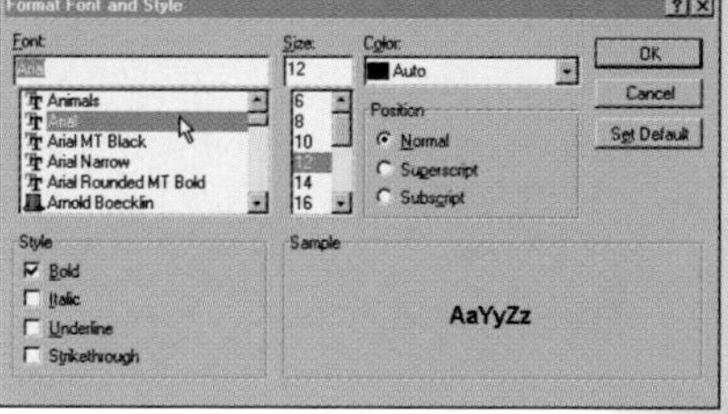

With the Font and Style dialog box still open, click once on 18 in the Size list box. You may have to use the scroll bar to find it. *Chapter 6*

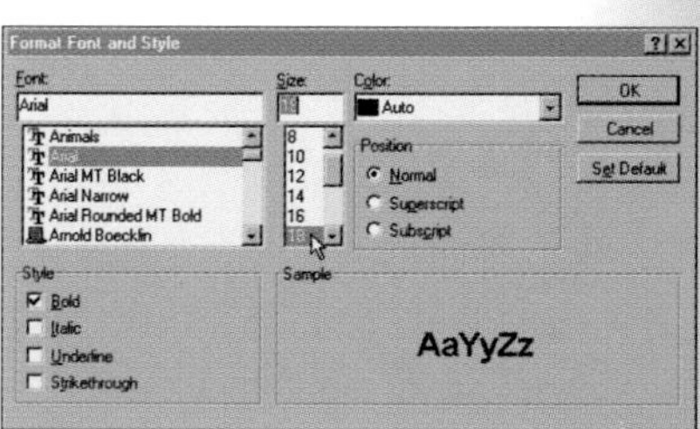

Click on the OK button to close the dialog box and make all of the changes you have selected.

With Memo still selected, click on Format in the menu bar, then on Paragraph. In the Paragraph dialog box, click on the Indents and Alignment tab to activate it. *Chapter 7*

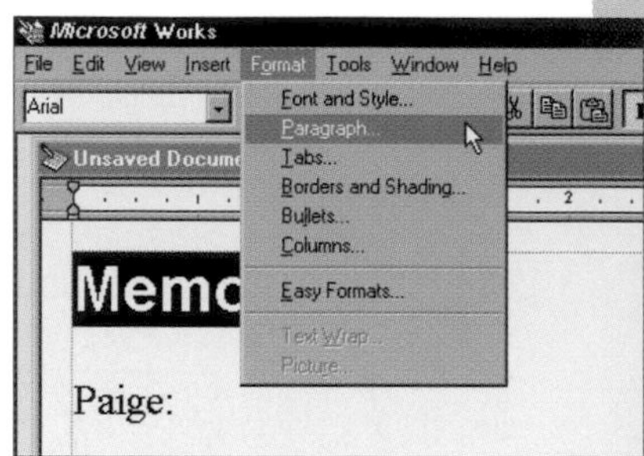

Click on the Center option button, and then click on OK to center this heading on the page. *Chapter 7*

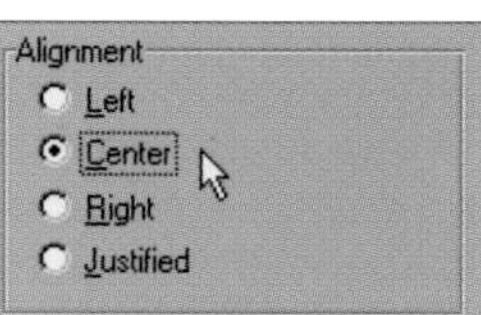

Select the four lines starting Bite-sized.... Click on Format in the menu bar, and then click on Paragraph. The Indents and Alignment tab should still be active. *Chapter 7*

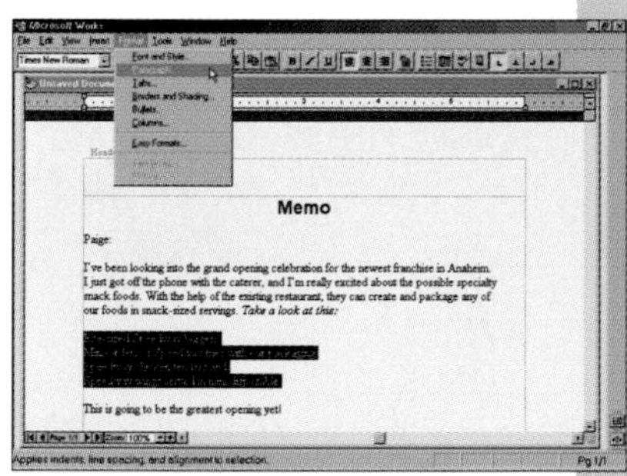

Double-click in the Left text box under Indents and type the number 1. Click on OK to indent these four lines 1 inch from the left margin. *Chapter 7*

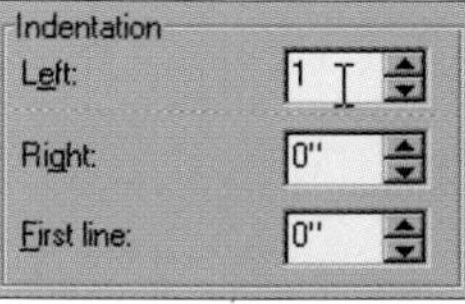

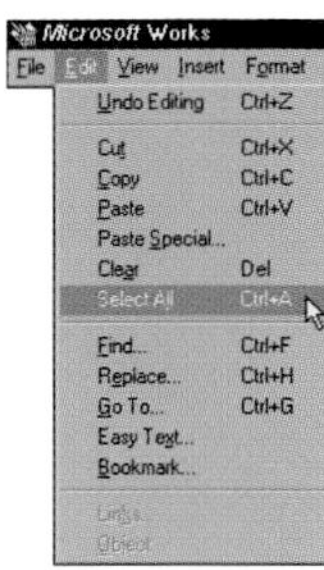

Click on Edit in the menu bar, and then click on Select All to highlight the entire document.

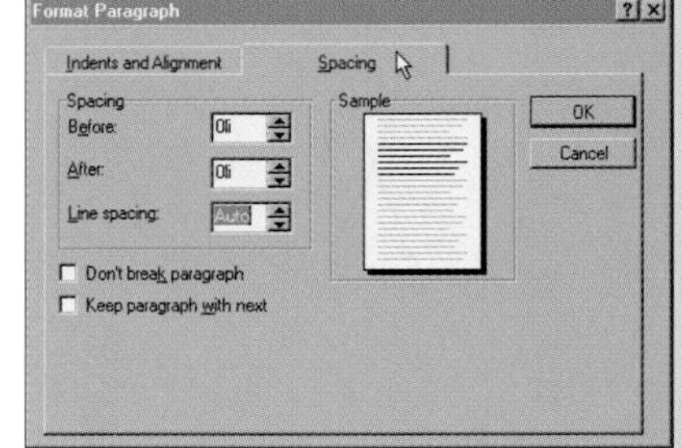

Click on Format in the menu bar, and then click on Paragraph. In the Paragraph dialog box, click on the Spacing tab to activate it. *Chapter 7*

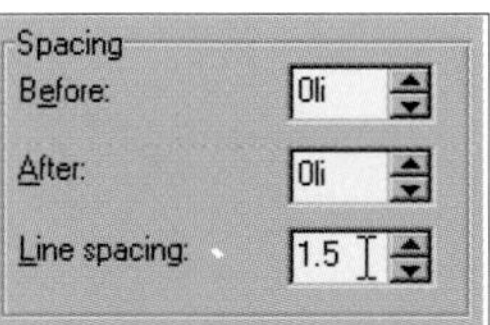

Double-click in the Line Spacing text box and type the number **1.5**. Click on OK to close the dialog box and one-and-a-half-space your entire document. *Chapter 7*

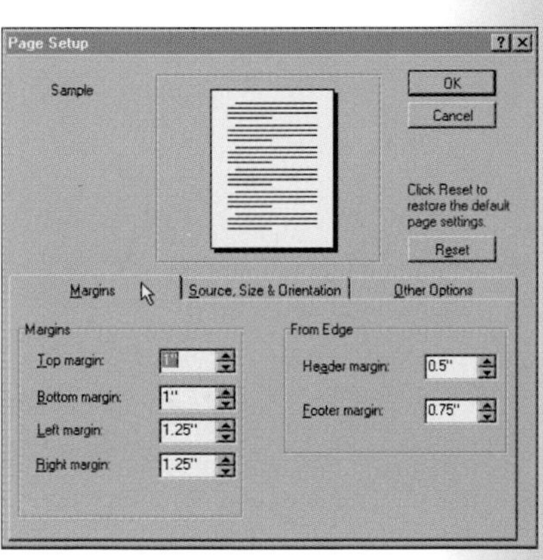

Click on File tool in the menu bar, then on Page Setup. In the dialog box, click on the Margins tab to activate it. *Chapter 7*

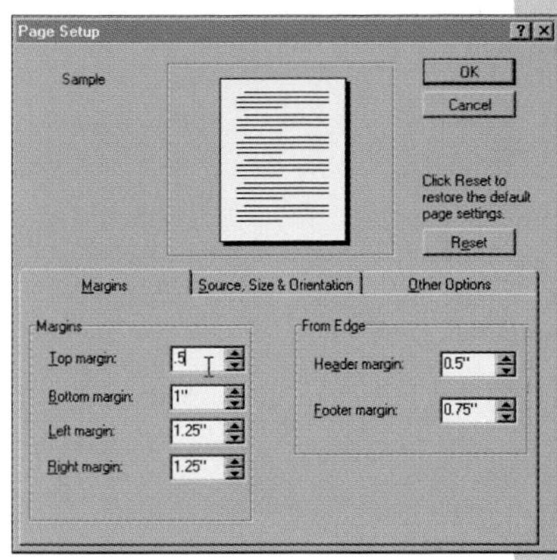

Double-click in the Top Margin text box and type the number **.5**. Click on OK to create a narrow top margin to prominently display the word Memo. *Chapter 7*

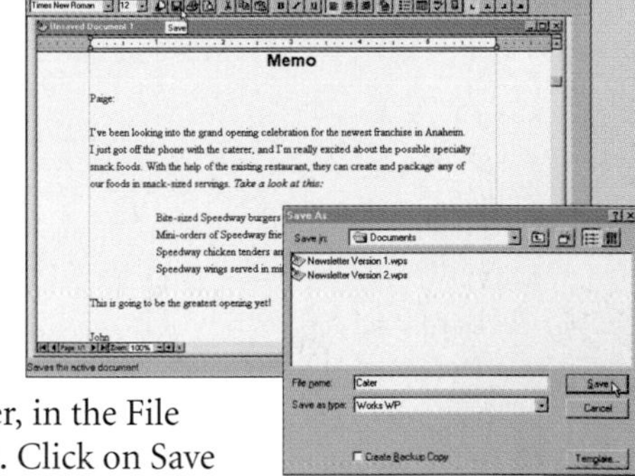

Click on the Save button to save your document. If you have not already saved it, type a name, like cater, in the File Name text box. Click on Save to save the memo. *Chapter 4*

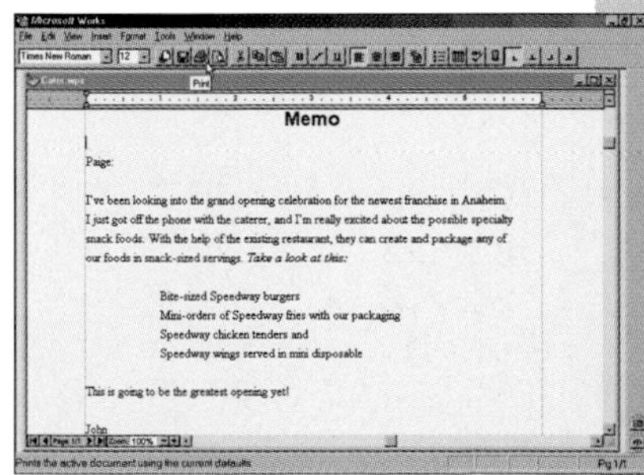

Click on the Print button to print the new memo. It should appear on paper just as it does on your screen. *Chapter 4*

## CHAPTER 8

# More Advanced Word Processing Techniques

Now that you've mastered the basics of word processing, it's time to turn your attention to more advanced word processing techniques—techniques that will give your documents that polished professional look. In addition, many of the techniques presented in this chapter will simplify how you create your documents and perform routine tasks—and best of all they'll save you time and trouble.

In the first sections of this chapter you'll learn how to create your own letterhead, include headers and footers containing page numbers, dates, and document titles, print individual envelopes, and create labels for a variety of needs like mass mailings, labeling file folders, and producing name tags.

The middle sections illustrate how to insert special characters like "©" into your documents, set custom tabs to organize your information into tables, and work with columns to create multiple-column documents like newsletters.

The last section in this chapter shows you how to use the spell checker to identify misspelled words, and the thesaurus to list alternative words.

# How to Use a TaskWizard to Create Letterhead

Works provides *TaskWizards* that make it easy to create common documents like letterhead. (Letterhead refers to professionally designed stationery used in business or personal correspondence.) While creating your letterhead, the TaskWizard will give you options to tailor your document to meet specific needs. And if you suffer from "writers block," the TaskWizard will provide sample text from over 100 common documents to get you started.

As you'll see in the following steps, using a TaskWizard is easy. Just pick the document you want to create, answer a few questions, fill out a few forms, then sit back and let the TaskWizard do its thing. In moments you'll have what you need—it's that easy.

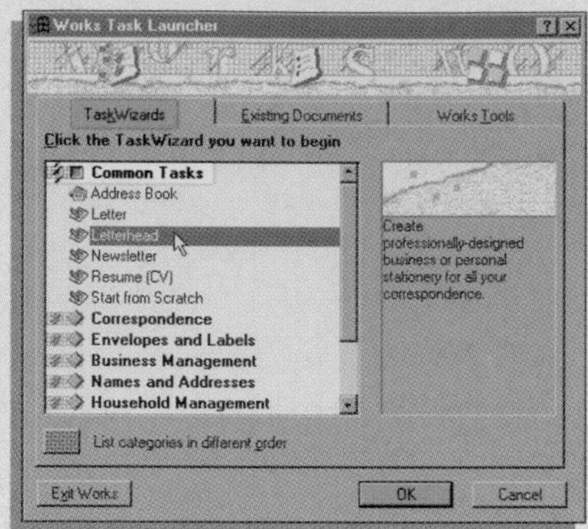


**1** If the TaskWizards are not displayed in the Task Launcher window, click on the TaskWizard tab, then click on the Common Tasks category. From the list of common tasks, double-click on Letterhead (or click once on Letterhead and then click the OK button).

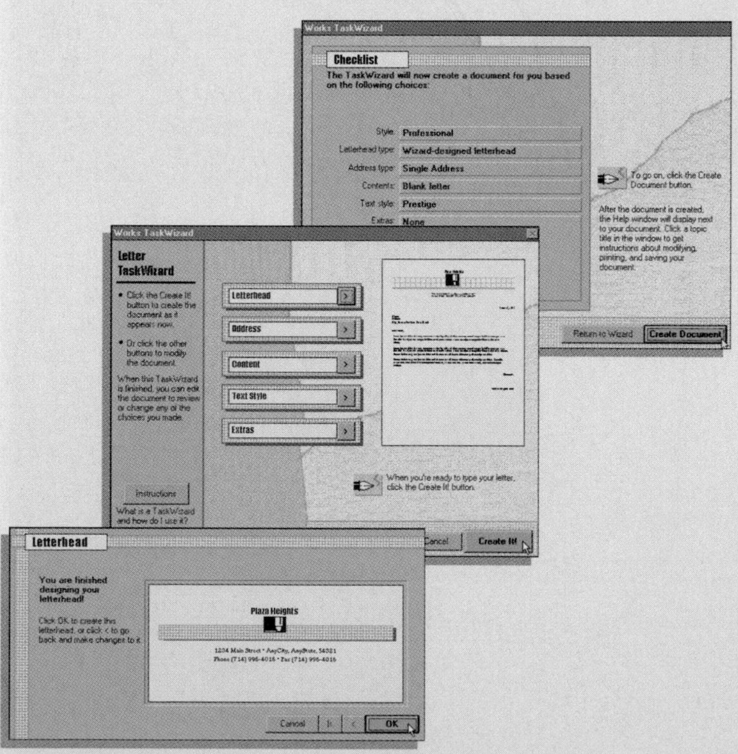


**8** You can complete the process by selecting OK, Create It, and Create Document on the next three forms—or you can go back and make changes.

## TIP SHEET

- **When you create letterhead, the TaskWizard includes either sample text or instructional text (e.g. "Start typing here."). If you just want a blank sheet of letterhead and nothing else, just delete the unwanted text and save the document as a template file. (See HELP for instructions on how to create a template file.)**
- **There are over 30 TaskWizards supporting a wide variety of needs. Take some time to discover the many documents and tasks performed by these little guys—you'll soon realize you don't have to live in the Land of Oz to appreciate a Wizard!**

**2** To create new letterhead, click on the "Yes, run the TaskWizard" button. (If this window does not appear, skip this step and go to step 3.)

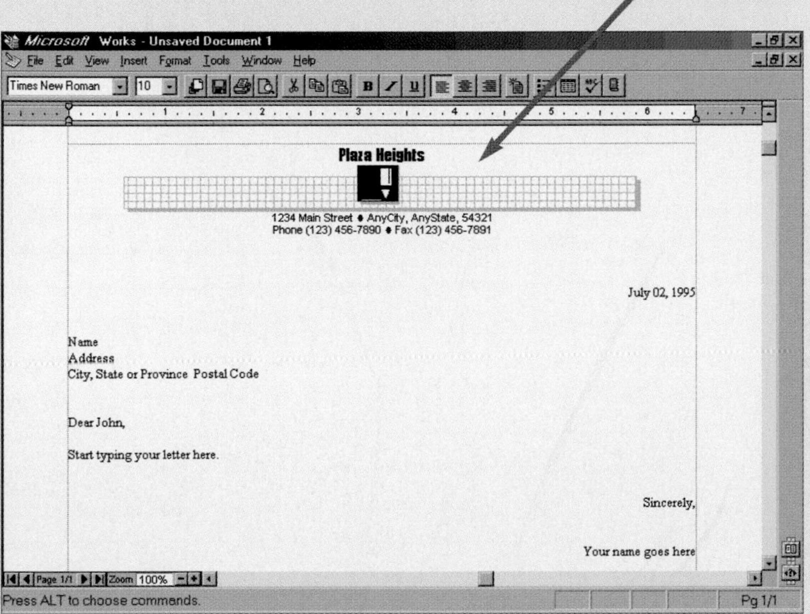

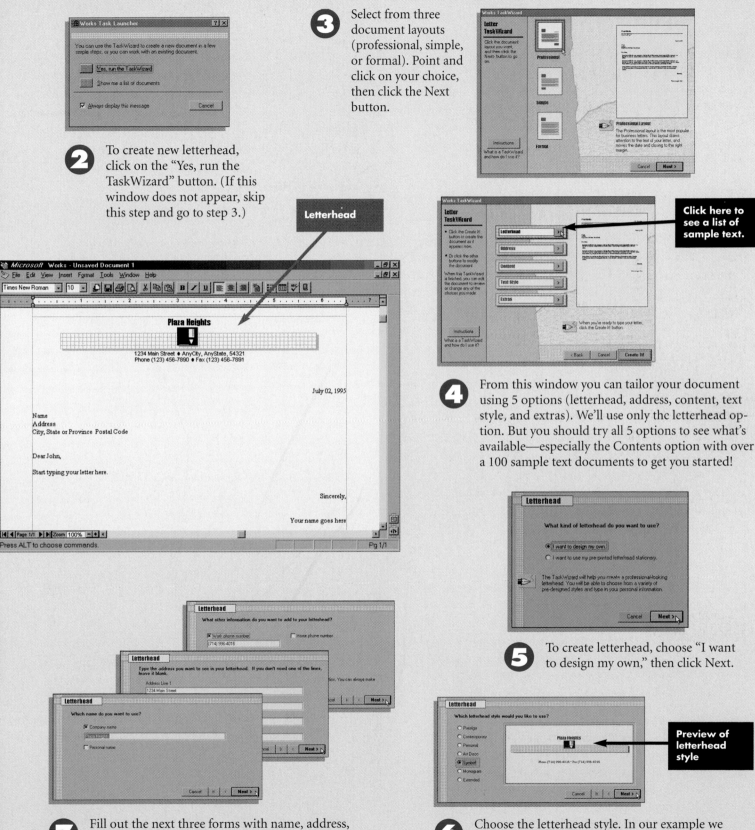

**3** Select from three document layouts (professional, simple, or formal). Point and click on your choice, then click the Next button.

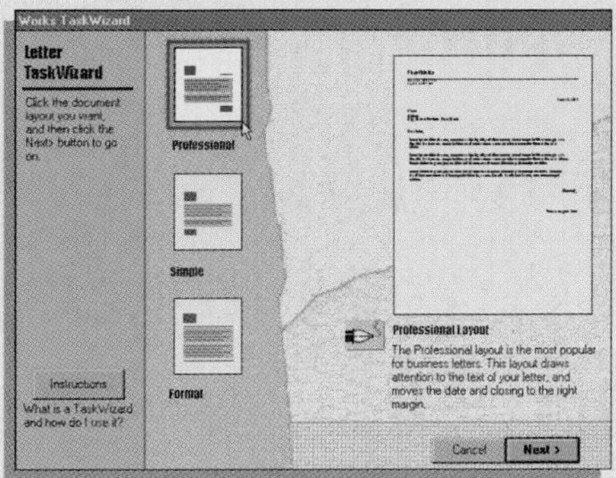


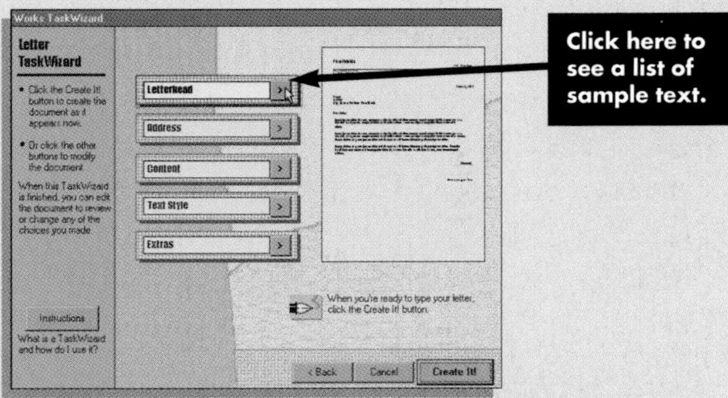


**4** From this window you can tailor your document using 5 options (letterhead, address, content, text style, and extras). We'll use only the letterhead option. But you should try all 5 options to see what's available—especially the Contents option with over a 100 sample text documents to get you started!

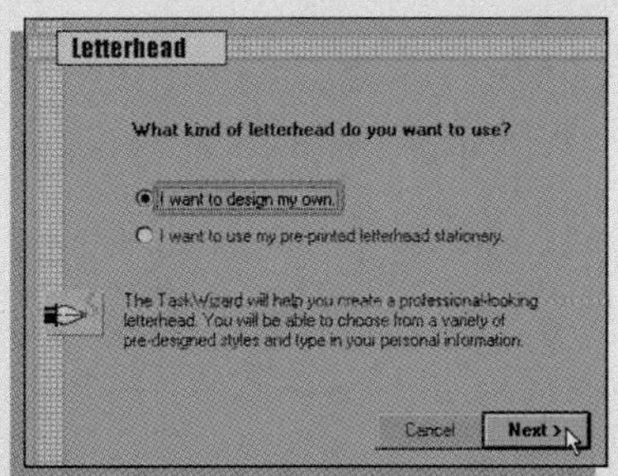


**5** To create letterhead, choose "I want to design my own," then click Next.

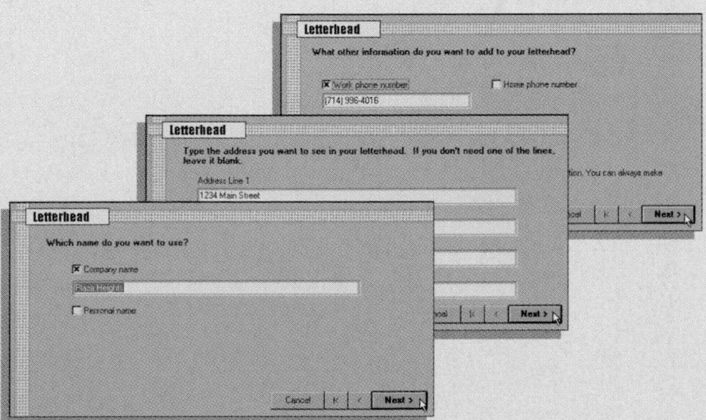


**7** Fill out the next three forms with name, address, and phone information. Click the Next button to move from form to form.

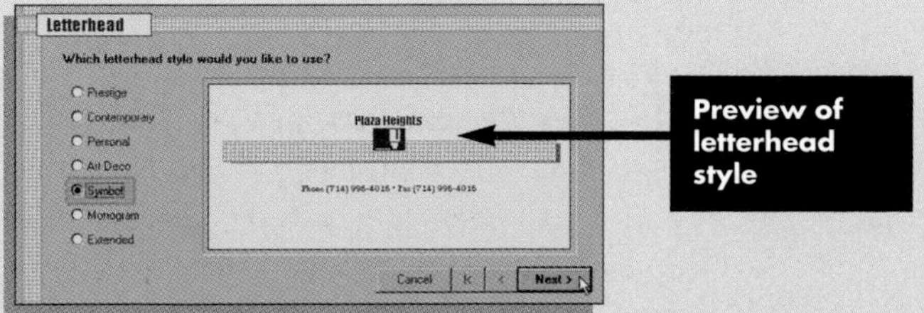


**6** Choose the letterhead style. In our example we picked Symbol. Go ahead and browse through the options. A preview of the option is displayed in the view box to the right. To continue on, click Next.

# How to Create Headers and Footers

A header is text that appears at the top of every page and a footer is text that appears at the bottom of every page. You can use headers and footers to add titles, page numbers, dates, or any words you want to display on every page, for example, "Draft." Headers and footers can also include art work—like a company logo.

Because the process to add a header and a footer is identical, our example focuses on creating a header only. To create a footer, substitute the word footer for header in any of the following steps.

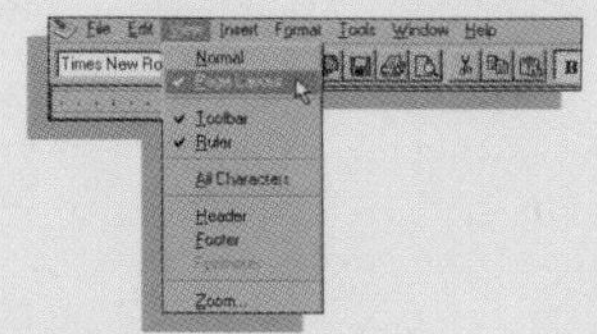

1. Your best view for creating a header is in Page Layout. To switch to Page Layout view, open the View menu and click on the Page Layout option.

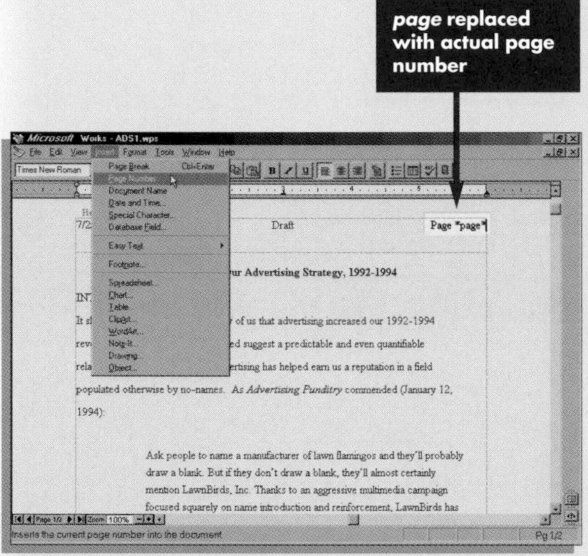


7. To enter a page number in the header, select a position, enter the word "Page" followed by a space, then from the Insert menu select Page Number. The place holder "*page*" appears and will be replaced with the appropriate page number when you print or preview your document.

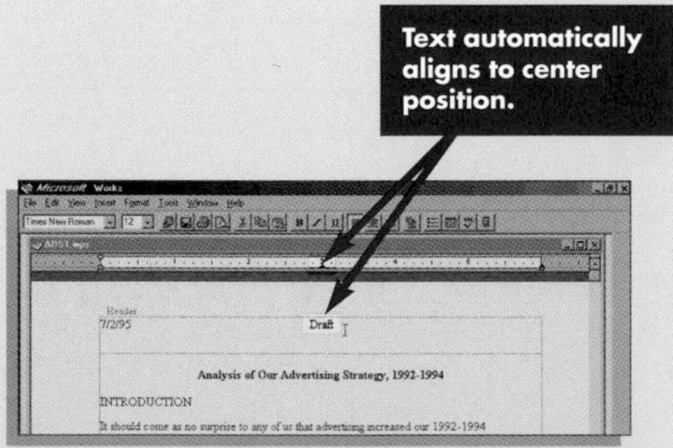


6. To enter text in the header, tab to a position and type the text. The text you type automatically aligns to the position you selected.

## TIP SHEET

- **Headers and footers are displayed differently in Page Layout view and Normal view. In Page Layout view, the header is displayed at the top of the page and the footer at the bottom—just the way you see them when you print your document. On the other hand, in Normal view, they're displayed at the beginning of the document. Works identifies the header with an "H" and the footer with an "F."**
- **You may not want headers and footers printed on the first page of your document; for example, if your first page is a cover page. To disable the header or footer on the first page of a document, select Page Setup from the File menu. In the Other Options box, check the No Header on First Page and No Footer on First Page boxes.**
- **You can add borders to headers and footers. Position the insertion point in the header or footer, then select the Format menu and click on Borders and Shading. Pick the type of border characteristics you want and click OK to apply them. Borders and shading enhance the look of your header and footer—try it.**

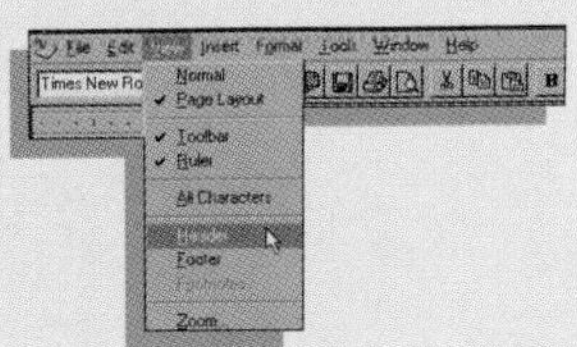

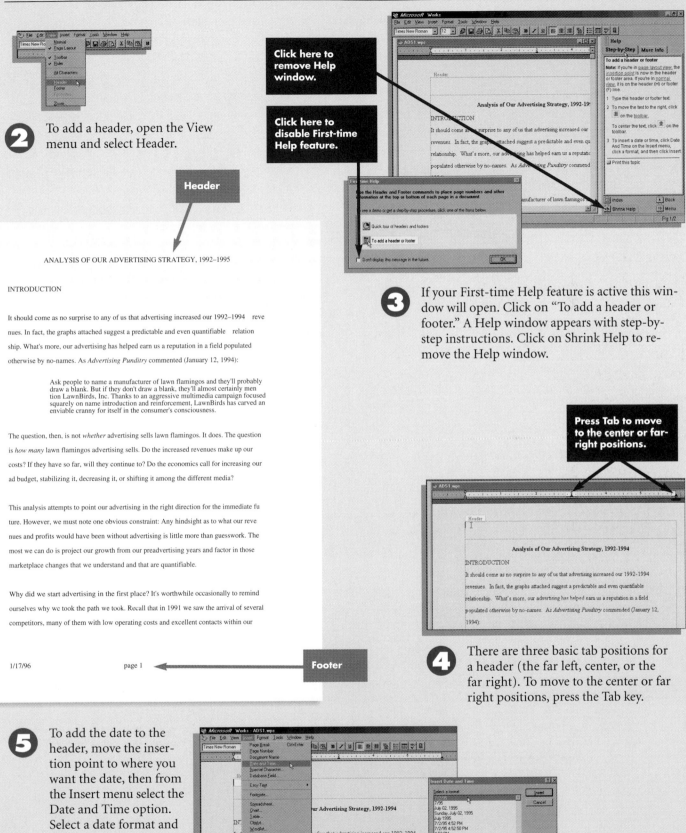

**2** To add a header, open the View menu and select Header.

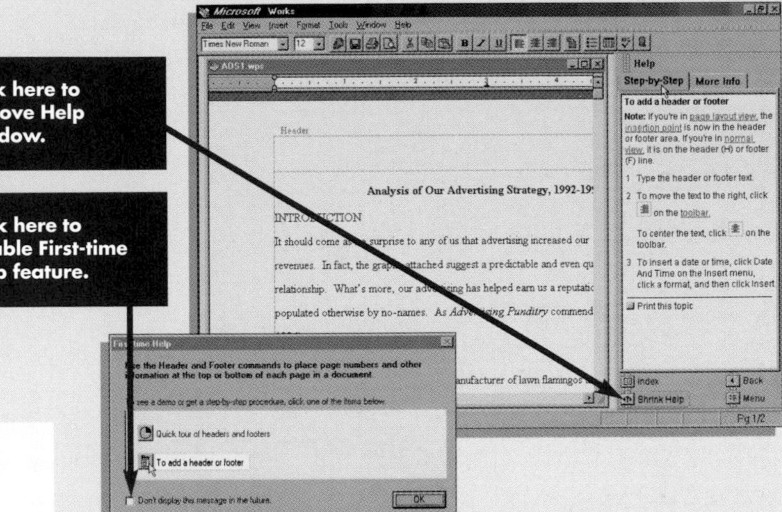


Click here to remove Help window.

**3** If your First-time Help feature is active this window will open. Click on "To add a header or footer." A Help window appears with step-by-step instructions. Click on Shrink Help to remove the Help window.

Header

ANALYSIS OF OUR ADVERTISING STRATEGY, 1992–1995

INTRODUCTION

It should come as no surprise to any of us that advertising increased our 1992–1994 revenues. In fact, the graphs attached suggest a predictable and even quantifiable relationship. What's more, our advertising has helped earn us a reputation in a field populated otherwise by no-names. As *Advertising Punditry* commented (January 12, 1994):

> Ask people to name a manufacturer of lawn flamingos and they'll probably draw a blank. But if they don't draw a blank, they'll almost certainly mention LawnBirds, Inc. Thanks to an aggressive multimedia campaign focused squarely on name introduction and reinforcement, LawnBirds has carved an enviable cranny for itself in the consumer's consciousness.

The question, then, is not *whether* advertising sells lawn flamingos. It does. The question is *how many* lawn flamingos advertising sells. Do the increased revenues make up our costs? If they have so far, will they continue to? Do the economics call for increasing our ad budget, stabilizing it, decreasing it, or shifting it among the different media?

This analysis attempts to point our advertising in the right direction for the immediate future. However, we must note one obvious constraint: Any hindsight as to what our revenues and profits would have been without advertising is little more than guesswork. The most we can do is project our growth from our preadvertising years and factor in those marketplace changes that we understand and that are quantifiable.

Why did we start advertising in the first place? It's worthwhile occasionally to remind ourselves why we took the path we took. Recall that in 1991 we saw the arrival of several competitors, many of them with low operating costs and excellent contacts within our

1/17/96 page 1

Footer

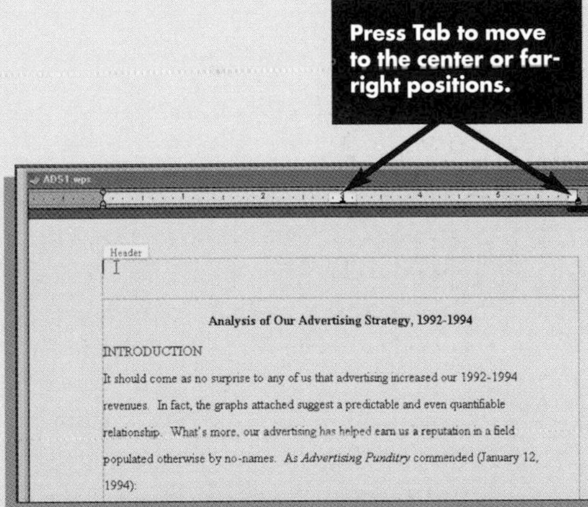


**4** There are three basic tab positions for a header (the far left, center, or the far right). To move to the center or far right positions, press the Tab key.

**5** To add the date to the header, move the insertion point to where you want the date, then from the Insert menu select the Date and Time option. Select a date format and click Insert. The date will appear at the insertion point.

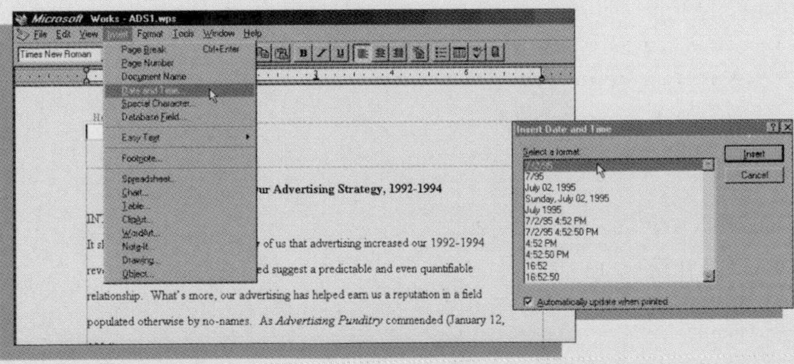

# How to Use the Envelopes and Labels Tools

Works makes it easy for you to print a return and recipient address on an individual envelope. Works also provides the capability to print sheets of return mailing labels that you can stick on business flyers, form letters, or holiday cards. And if you're using a Works database to manage your address book, you can easily create sheets of recipient labels.

You can use many of the popular Avery printer labels or specify a custom label. Either way, using your computer and printer to produce mailing labels makes short order of an otherwise tedious task.

When you complete this section you'll know how to print an individual envelope and a sheet of return addresses. For information on creating an address database that you can use to create recipient mailing labels, see Chapter 17.

## TIP SHEET

- **Be prepared to waste a few envelopes. This is not an exact science, so you'll need a few extra envelopes to get things right.**
- **A clever technique for aligning addresses and saving a few sheets of labels is to print your labels on a regular piece of paper. Then place the regular piece paper over a label sheet and hold them up to a light. You'll be able to see how well your names and addresses align and save yourself some label sheets.**

**1** To print a single envelope, open the Tools menu and select the Envelopes option.

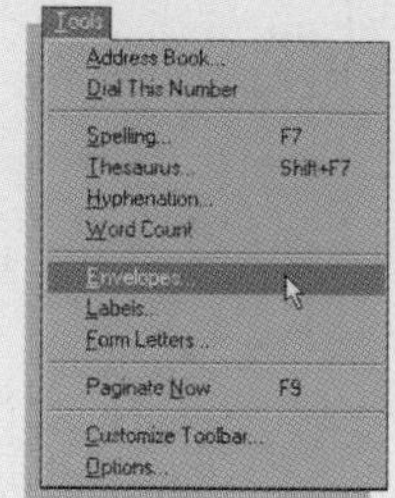

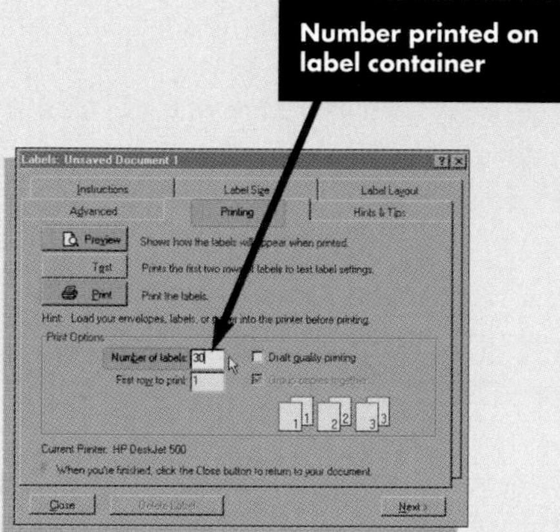


**8** To preview or print the labels click on the Printing tab. Enter the number of labels on one sheet. This number is usually printed on the box or container the labels were sold in. To check the printer alignment use the Test option to print a few rows of labels. If the alignment is off, adjust your printer, then test again. If that doesn't work go back to step 6 and adjust the alignment using the Custom

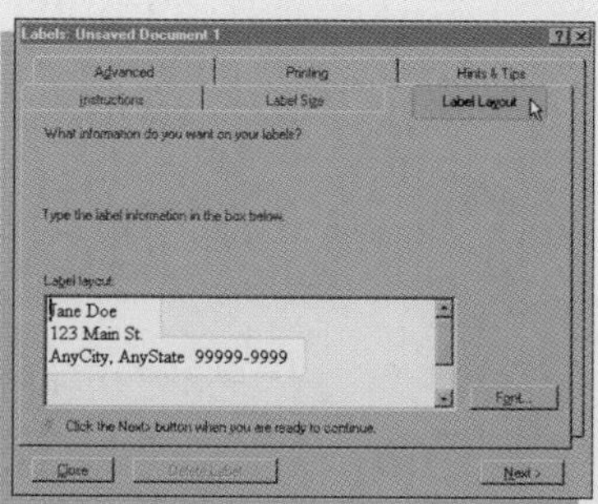

**7** Click the Label Layout tab, and enter the label content. For our example the content is the return name and address.

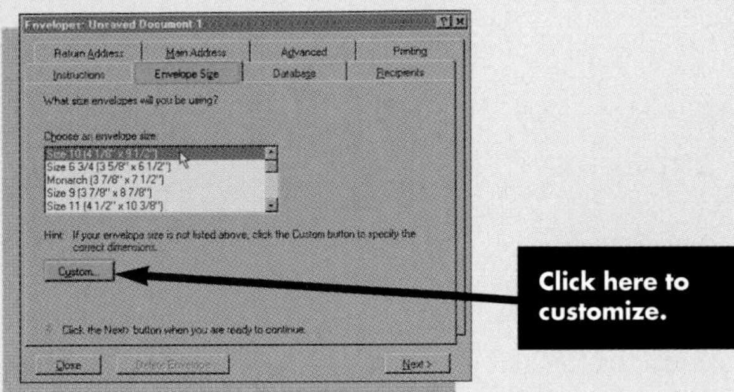


**2** Specify the envelope size. First click on the Envelope Size tab. In the Envelopes dialog box select the envelope size from the available list. To adjust the dimensions to a nonstandard envelope size click on Custom.

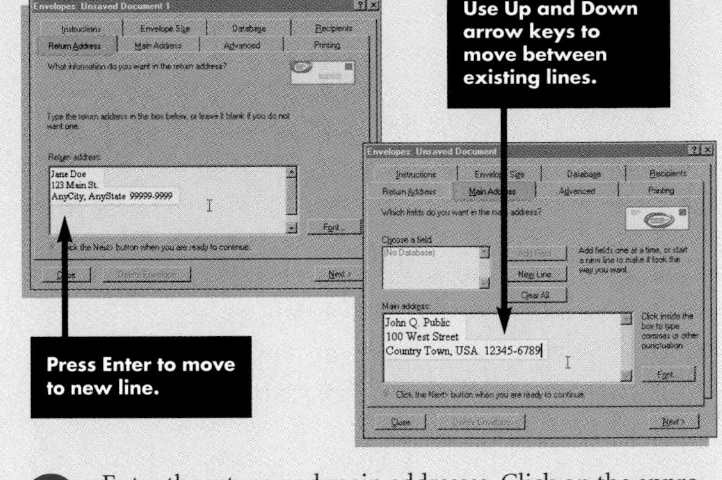


**3** Enter the return and main addresses. Click on the appropriate tab, click in the address field and type. Press Enter to move to a new line. Use the Up and Down arrow keys to move between existing lines.

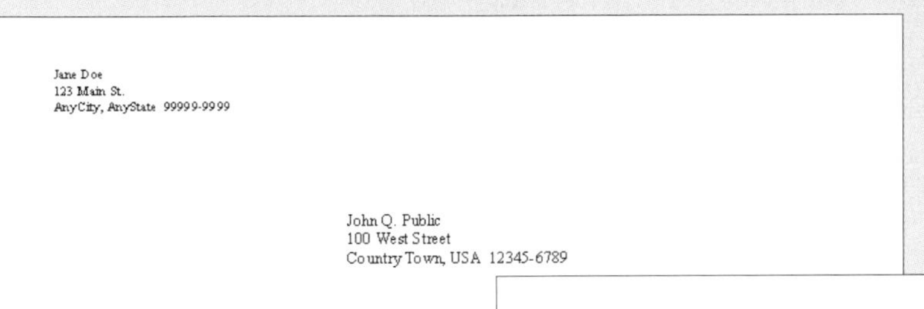

Jane Doe
123 Main St.
AnyCity, AnyState 99999-9999
John Q. Public
100 West Street
Country Town, USA 12345-6789

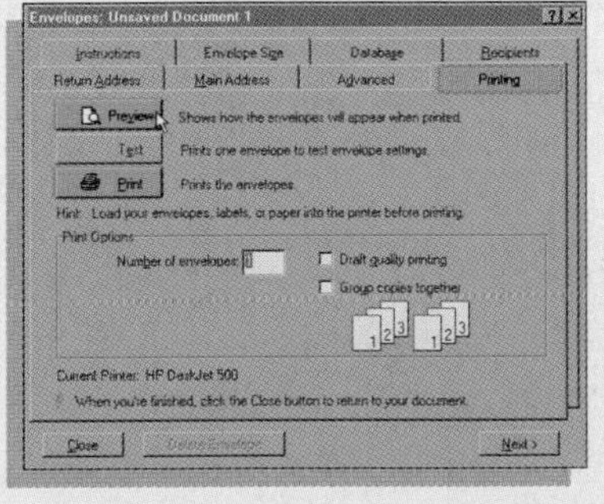

**4** It's good practice to preview your work before you print. That way you can make corrections and save printing time and cost.

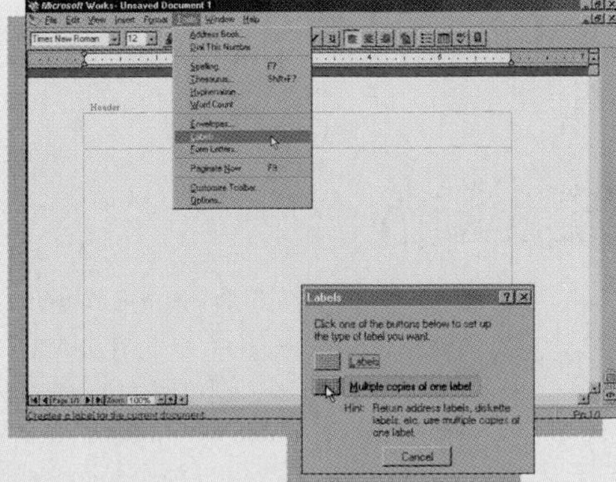

**5** To create return mailing labels, open the Tools menu and select the Labels option. In the Labels dialog box click on Multiple Copies of One Label.

**6** Choose the label type. From the Labels dialog window click on the Label Size tab. Select a label type from the list of available labels listed in the Choose a Label Size list box. Use the scroll bar to browse the list. To customize the label sizes, click on the Custom button.

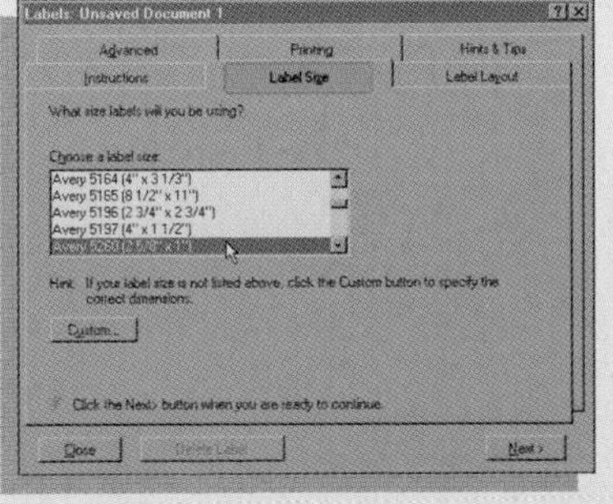

# How to Insert Special Characters

If you've ever wanted to insert a special character like "©" into your document, or start a new page, or add non-breaking hyphens to words—then you're in the right place!

Some of the steps in this section use the Character Map program provided with Windows 95. Unless someone moved it, you'll find the Character Map program in the Accessories folder. If you're confused, hang in there; it's not as hard as it sounds.

## TIP SHEET

- For other clever symbols to jazz up your documents, check your list of fonts for Wingdings and Zapf Dingbats.
- If the symbol is too small, select it and change the font size to something larger.
- If you have a color printer, add flair to your symbols (or any characters for that matter). Select the characters you want to apply color to, open the Format menu, select the Font and Style option, and from the Color drop-down list select a new color.
- The best place to insert a page number or a date is in the header or footer.

**1** To insert a special character into your document, position the insertion point to where you want the special character to appear.

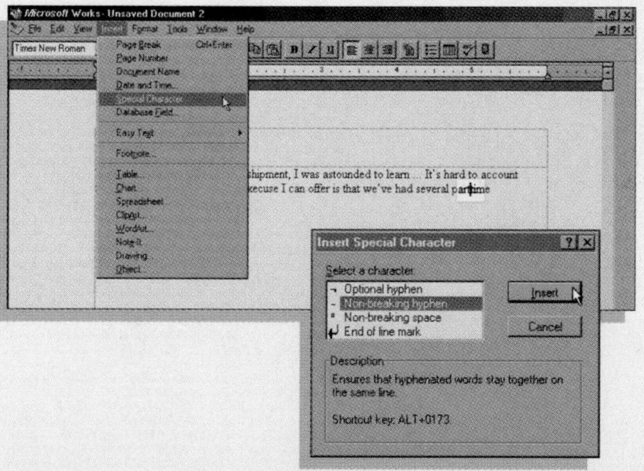


**6** You can keep hyphenated words like "part-time" on the same line by inserting a non-breaking hyphen. It's easy. Start by typing the word with no hyphen, place the insert point where you want the non-breaking hyphen, open the Insert menu, select Special Characters, and double-click on Non-breaking Hyphen. As you type and your text word-wraps, the non-breaking hyphenated words stay on the same line.

**2** Start the Character Map program. Click on the Start button, point to Programs, point to the Accessories folder, and then click on the Character Map program.

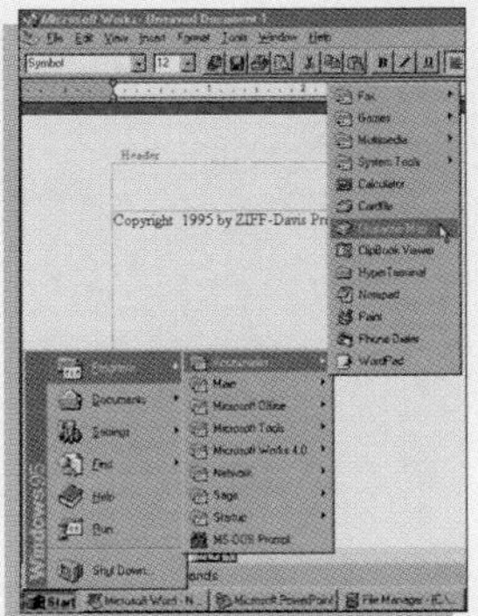

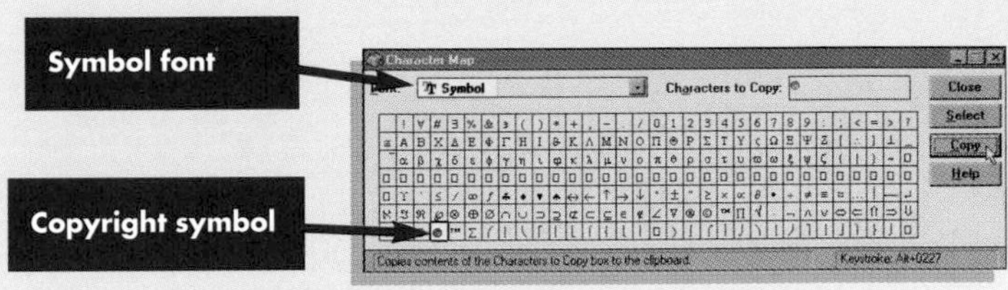


**3** From the Character Map window, ensure that the Symbol font is selected (top-left corner), click on the character you want to insert, click the Select button, click on the Copy button, and then click on the Close button to exit the Character Map program.

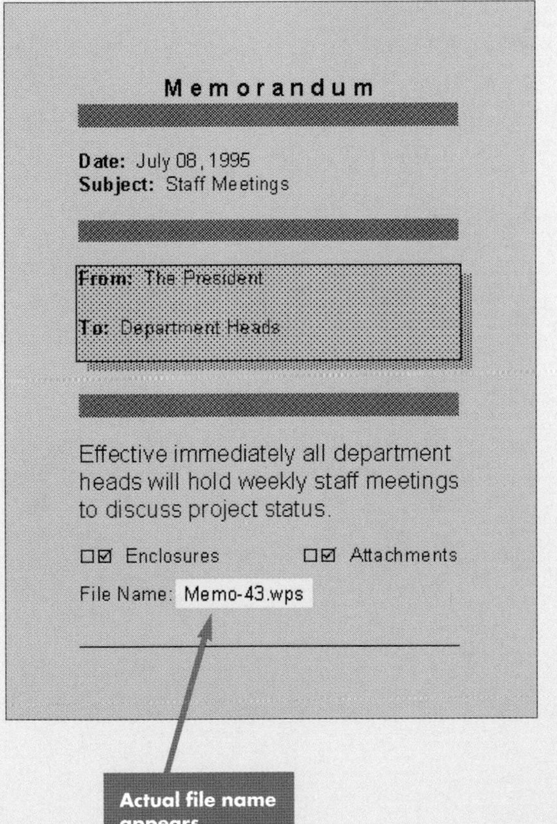

**Memorandum**

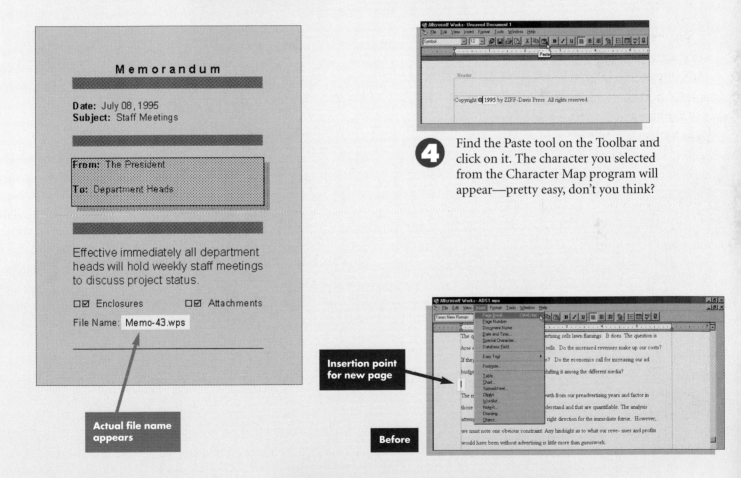

**Date:** July 08, 1995
**Subject:** Staff Meetings

**From:** The President

**To:** Department Heads

Effective immediately all department heads will hold weekly staff meetings to discuss project status.

☐☑ Enclosures ☐☑ Attachments

File Name: Memo-43.wps



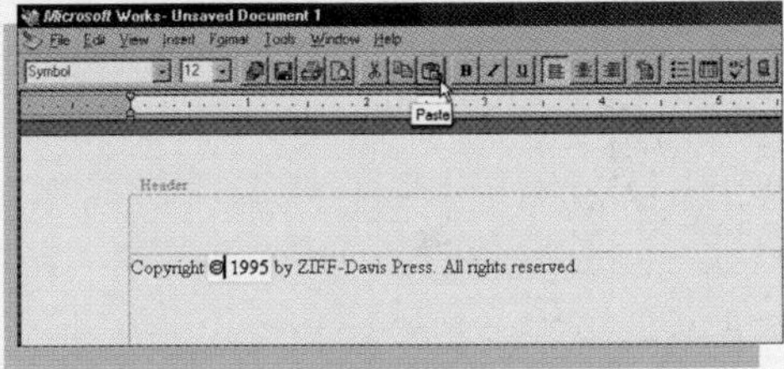


**4** Find the Paste tool on the Toolbar and click on it. The character you selected from the Character Map program will appear—pretty easy, don't you think?

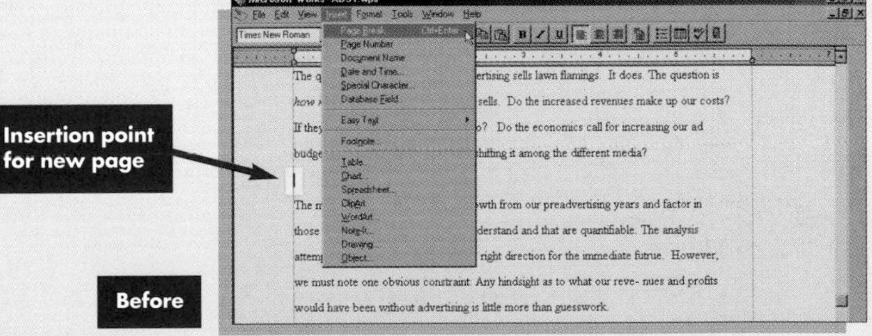


**5** To insert a new page, position the insert point where you want the new page to begin. From the Insert menu select Page Break. Make a mistake? No problem—just open the Edit menu and select Undo page break.

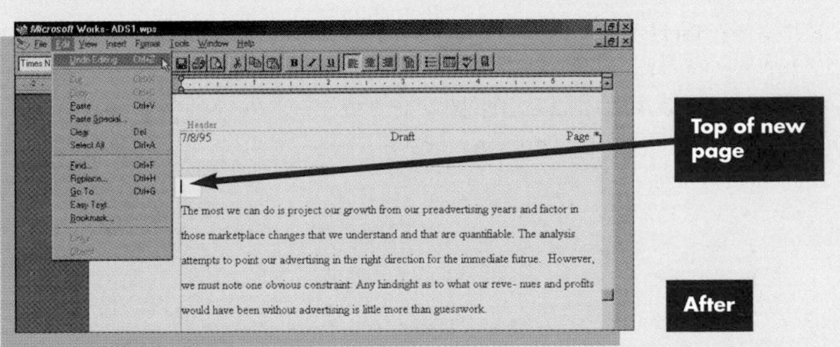

# How to Set Custom Tabs

Setting custom tabs allows you to align words to give your document that organized professional look. In Works you can use four different tab stop settings for each paragraph: left-, center-, right-, or decimal aligned

In this section we'll show you how to set tab alignments. We'll also show you how to include leader characters along with your tab setting. Leaders are great for keeping your reader's eye on the right line.

The steps in this section require the Toolbar and Ruler. If yours are not in view, open the View menu and click on Toolbar and Ruler.

- To open the Customize Works Toolbar window from the Tools menu, select the Customize Toolbar option.
- You can use the Format menu to set tabs. Select the Tab option and from the Format Tabs window type the tab stop setting and click clear. Repeat this process to add other tab stops. Click OK to return to your document.
- To clear all custom tab settings from your document, select the entire document by opening the Edit menu and choosing Select All. From the Format menu, select Tabs, and then click the Clear All button and then the OK button.

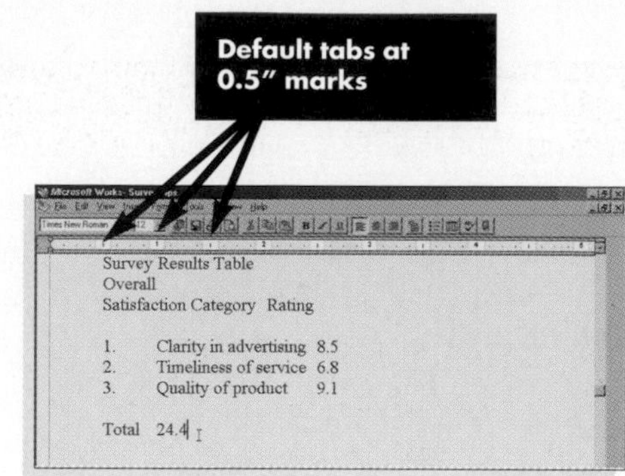


**1** Before setting custom tabs, type your text and insert default tab marks between the words you want to align. Default tab settings are at every 0.5" mark (0.5, 1.0, 1.5, etc.).

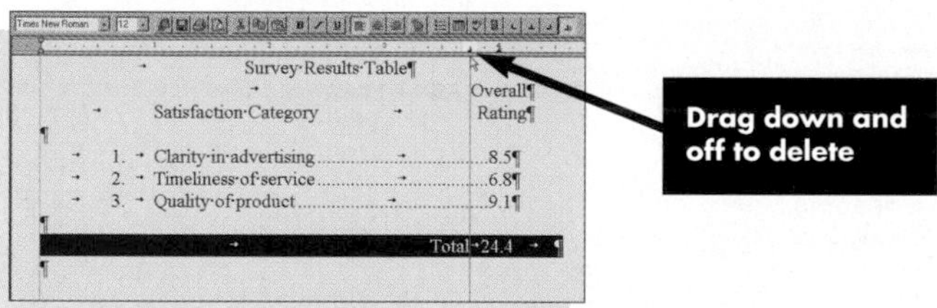


**7** To delete a tab setting, select paragraphs containing the tab setting you wish to delete, click and hold on the tab symbol in the Rule, then drag the tab symbol down off the Ruler.

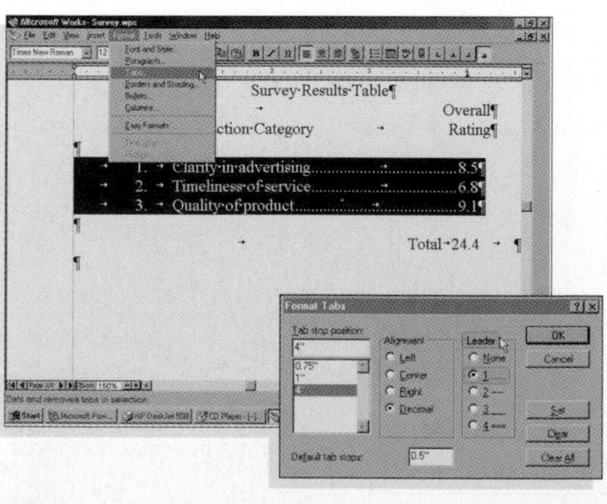

**6** To add leader characters to your tab setting, select the paragraphs you want to add leader characters to, then open the Format menu and select Tabs. From the list of tab stop positions select a setting. To complete the process select one of four leader patterns and click OK to apply.

**Tab marks**

**Paragraph mark**

❷ Works provides a visual aid to see your tab marks (➔). From the View menu select All Characters. The ¶ symbol indicates the end of a paragraph.

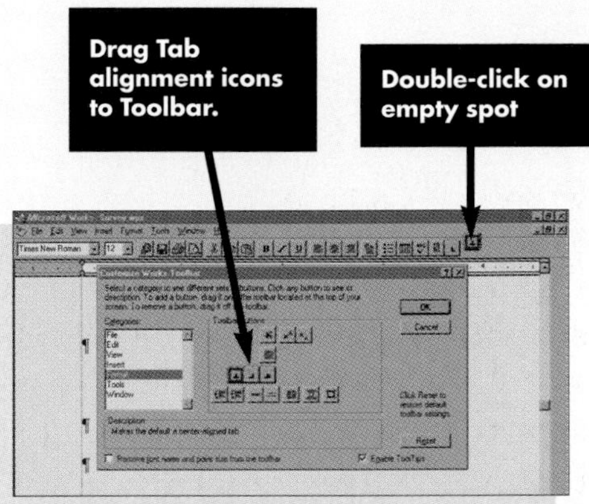


❸ Here's a Power User technique for setting tabs: Add the four tab alignment icons to your Toolbar. Double-click on an empty spot along the Toolbar—somewhere on the far right side will do. From the Customize Works Toolbar window select the Format category. Click and drag the tab alignment icons onto the Toolbar. Click OK to continue.

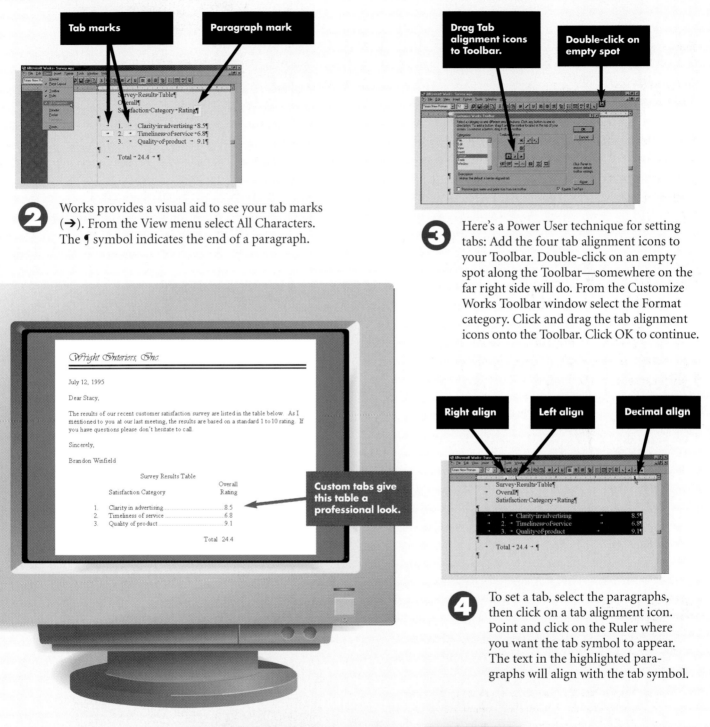

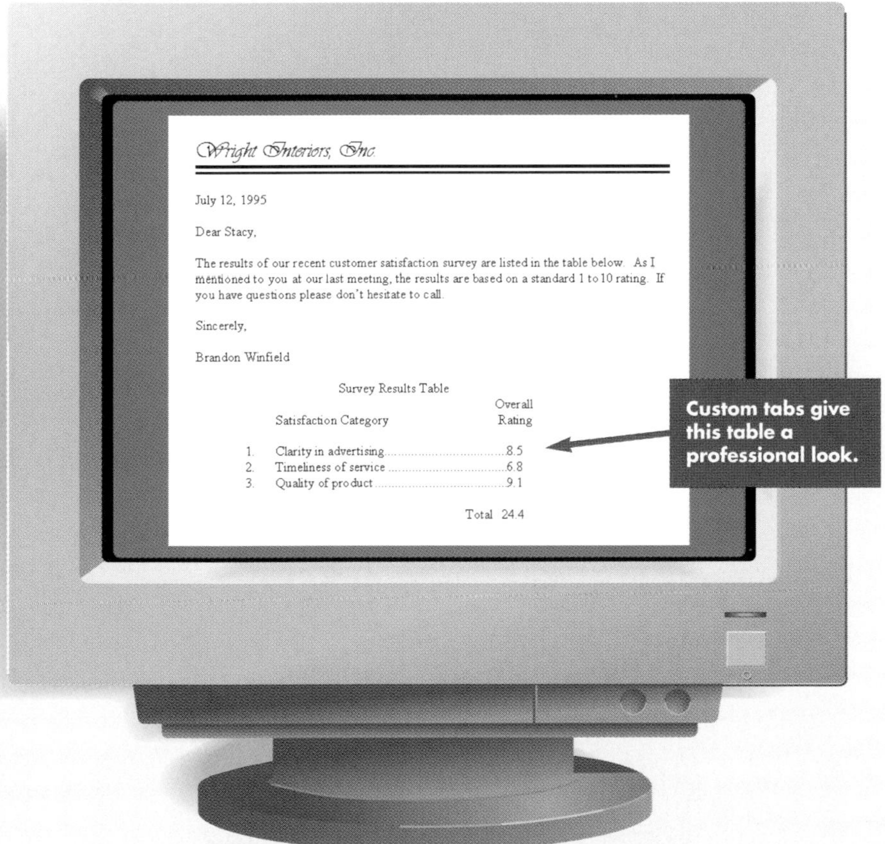


Wright Interiors, Inc.

July 12, 1995

Dear Stacy,

The results of our recent customer satisfaction survey are listed in the table below. As I mentioned to you at our last meeting, the results are based on a standard 1 to 10 rating. If you have questions please don't hesitate to call.

Sincerely,

Brandon Winfield

Survey Results Table

| | Satisfaction Category | Overall Rating |
|---|---|---|
| 1. | Clarity in advertising | 8.5 |
| 2. | Timeliness of service | 6.8 |
| 3. | Quality of product | 9.1 |
| | Total | 24.4 |

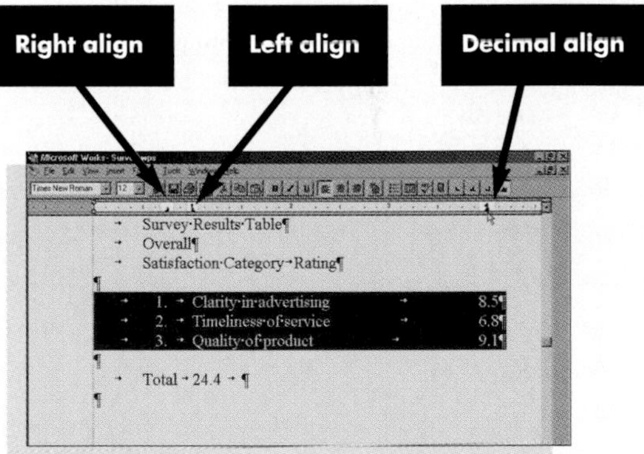


❹ To set a tab, select the paragraphs, then click on a tab alignment icon. Point and click on the Ruler where you want the tab symbol to appear. The text in the highlighted paragraphs will align with the tab symbol.

❺ To move a tab, click and hold on the tab symbol then drag to the new location and release.

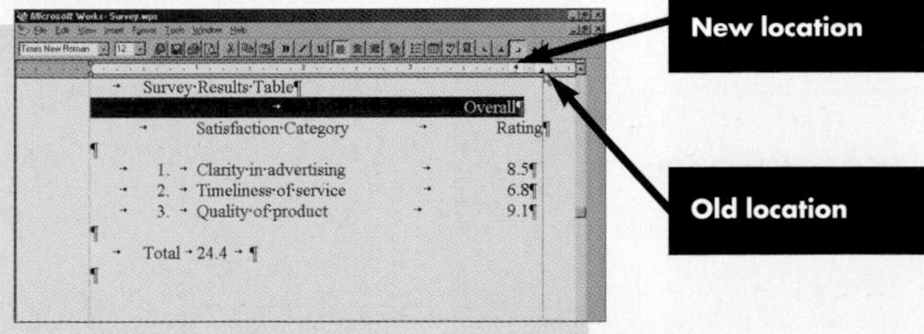

# How to Work with Columns

If you're looking to publish your own newsletter or other multiple-column document, then you'll want to use Works' column feature.

When you create multiple columns, your entire document, except the headers and the footers, has the same number of columns on each page. Be sure you're in Page Layout view, otherwise Works displays your document in one narrow column. In case you've forgotten, the Page Layout option is in the View menu.

**TIP SHEET**

- **You can place a headline across several columns. For instructions, click on Help in the menu bar, select Index, and type "headlines across columns."**
- **If you're creating a multiple-column newsletter, decrease the left and right margin sizes to 0.75". This will give your newsletter a more professional look and allow you to print more information per page.**
- **Add borders and shading to your headers to enhance the look of your multiple-column documents. Select the header, then from the Format menu select Borders and Shading.**
- **Use the Insert menu options to add pictures and charts to your multiple-column documents. Works will automatically size the pictures and charts to fit column widths.**

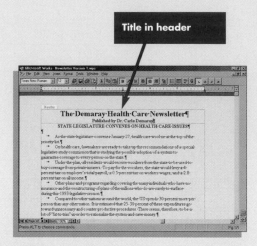

Title in header

1 Begin by typing in the text of your document. Enter the document title in the header. Apply style and alignment characteristics to your header.

6 You can return to a single-column document by entering a 1 in the Number of Columns box in the Format Columns window.

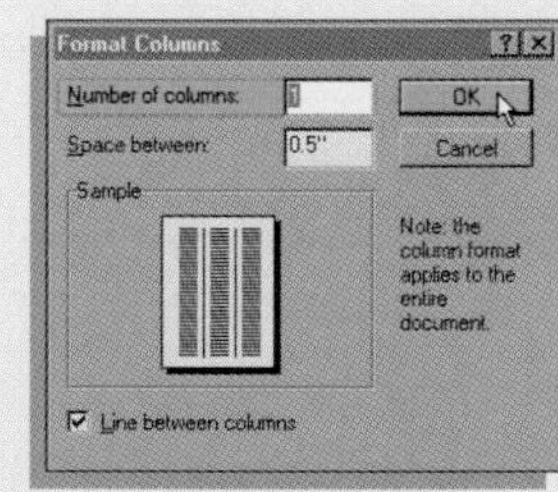


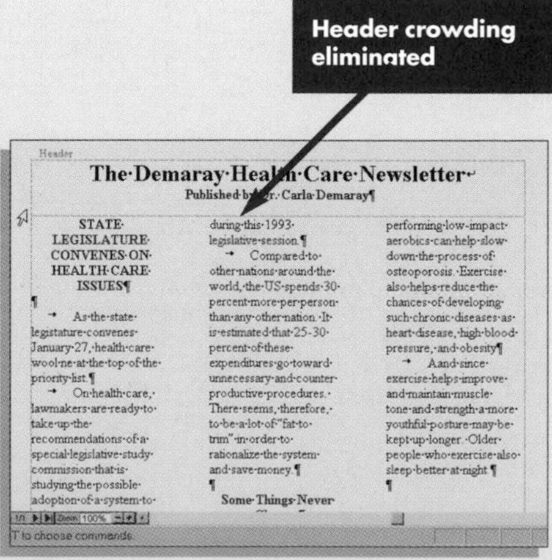


5 Adding a line after the header eliminates header crowding and gives your document a more professional look.

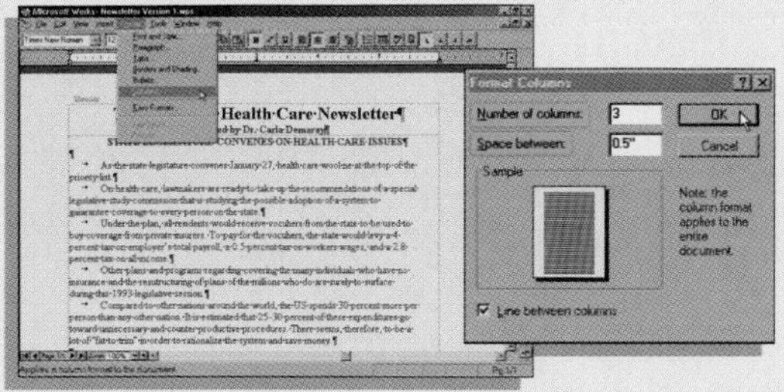

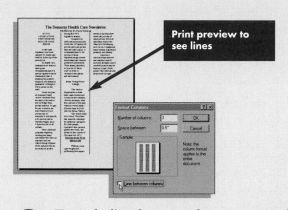

**2** To change the number of columns, open the Format menu and click on Columns. In the Number of Columns box, type the number of columns you want, then click the OK button. You can also change the spacing between columns.

Print preview to see lines

**3** To see the lines between columns you must be in print preview mode. From the toolbar click on the Print Preview tool or open the File menu and select Print Preview. To remove the lines between columns, remove the check mark in the Lines Between Columns check box.

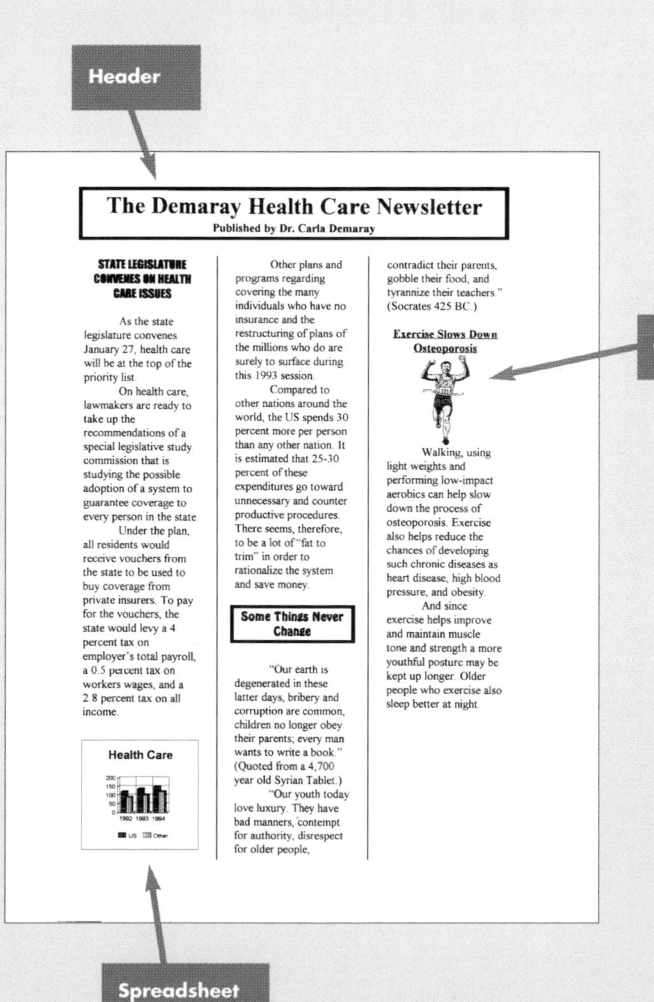


The Demaray Health Care Newsletter

Published by Dr. Carla Demaray

STATE LEGISLATURE CONVENES ON HEALTH CARE ISSUES

As the state legislature convenes January 27, health care will be at the top of the priority list.

On health care, lawmakers are ready to take up the recommendations of a special legislative study commission that is studying the possible adoption of a system to guarantee coverage to every person in the state.

Under the plan, all residents would receive vouchers from the state to be used to buy coverage from private insurers. To pay for the vouchers, the state would levy a 4 percent tax on employer's total payroll, a 0.5 percent tax on workers wages, and a 2.8 percent tax on all income.

Health Care

Other plans and programs regarding covering the many individuals who have no insurance and the restructuring of plans of the millions who do are surely to surface during this 1993 session.

Compared to other nations around the world, the US spends 30 percent more per person than any other nation. It is estimated that 25-30 percent of these expenditures go toward unnecessary and counter productive procedures. There seems, therefore, to be a lot of "fat to trim" in order to rationalize the system and save money.

Some Things Never Change

"Our earth is degenerated in these latter days, bribery and corruption are common, children no longer obey their parents; every man wants to write a book." (Quoted from a 4,700 year old Syrian Tablet.)

"Our youth today love luxury. They have bad manners, contempt for authority, disrespect for older people, contradict their parents, gobble their food, and tyrannize their teachers." (Socrates 425 BC.)

Exercise Slows Down Osteoporosis

Walking, using light weights and performing low-impact aerobics can help slow down the process of osteoporosis. Exercise also helps reduce the chances of developing such chronic diseases as heart disease, high blood pressure, and obesity.

And since exercise helps improve and maintain muscle tone and strength a more youthful posture may be kept up longer. Older people who exercise also sleep better at night.

Clip Art

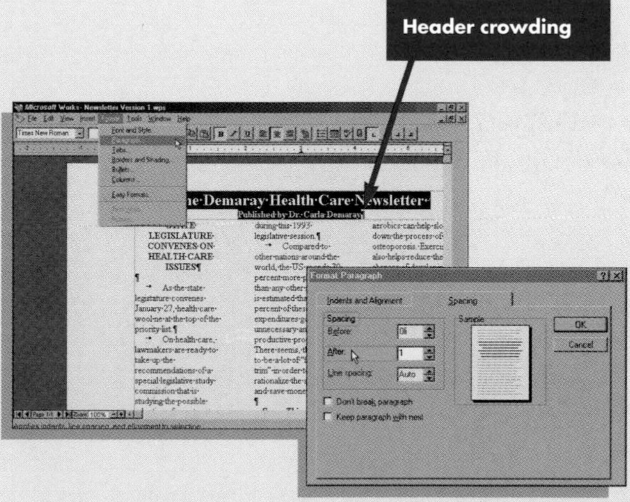


**4** To eliminate Header crowding, add a line after the header. Select the last paragraph in your header. From the Format menu select Paragraph. In the Format Paragraph window select the Spacing tab. In the After box enter the number of lines of spacing.

# How to Use the Spell Checker and Thesaurus

Don't let a misspelled word ruin the debut of your professionally formatted document. Works provides a spell checker that takes the guesswork out of proofing, and a thesaurus to help you find alternative words.

Or if you have another preferred dictionary on your computer, you can use it instead of the one that comes with Works. You can even create your own custom dictionary containing business jargon or special acronyms and abbreviations.

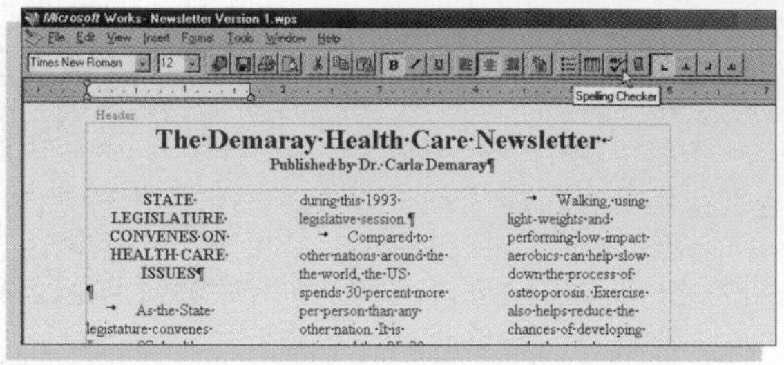


**1** Open the document you want to spell check. From the Toolbar, click on the Spelling Checker icon.

**TIP SHEET**

- To delete a word from your custom dictionary, start the spell checker, click on "Edit Custom Dictionary," select the word and click the Delete button. You can also add words to your dictionary by entering the word, then clicking the Add button.
- To change spelling dictionaries, open the Tools menu and click Options. Click the Proofing Tools tab, and in the Choose Dictionary list select the dictionary you want to use. Click OK to continue.
- Although Works' dictionary has thousands of words, it's not a complete source of all words. If the spell checker displays a word with no suggestions then check your regular dictionary for the proper spelling.

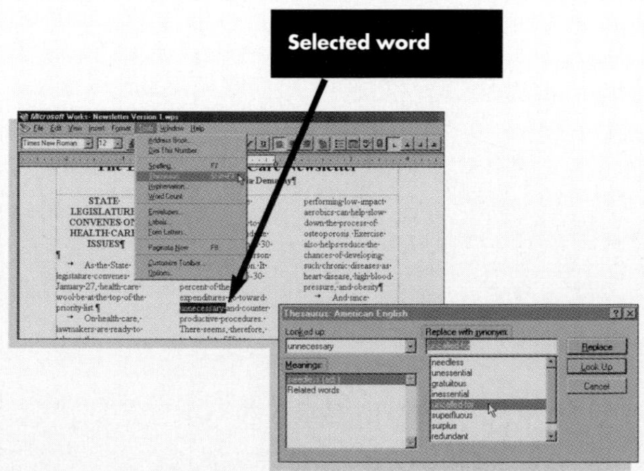


**6** Use the thesaurus to find alternative words (or synonyms). Select the word you wish to replace, then from the Tools menu select Thesaurus. From the Meanings list choose the proper meaning, then from the list of synonyms words pick a word to substitute and click Replace.

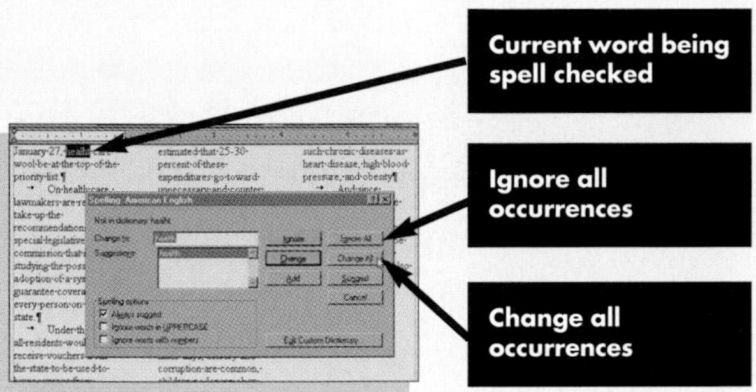


**2** As the spell checker encounters a word not in its dictionary, it displays the word in the Change To box. Suggested words appear in the Suggestions list box. You can change this word or change all occurrences of the word (Change All). On the other hand, if the word is correct, you can ignore the word or ignore all occurrences of the word (Ignore All).

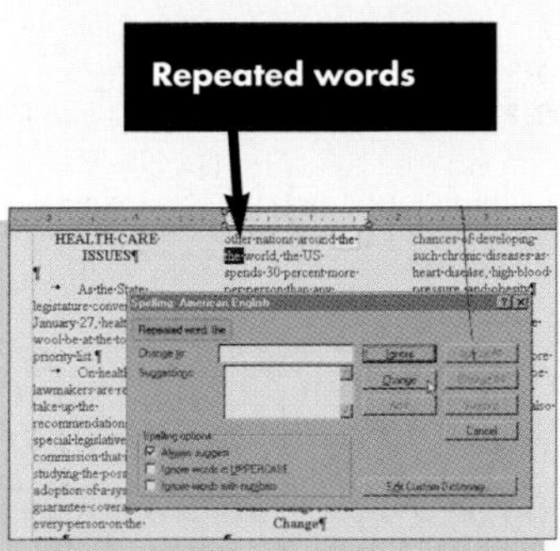


**3** The spell checker also finds words that are repeated, like "the the."

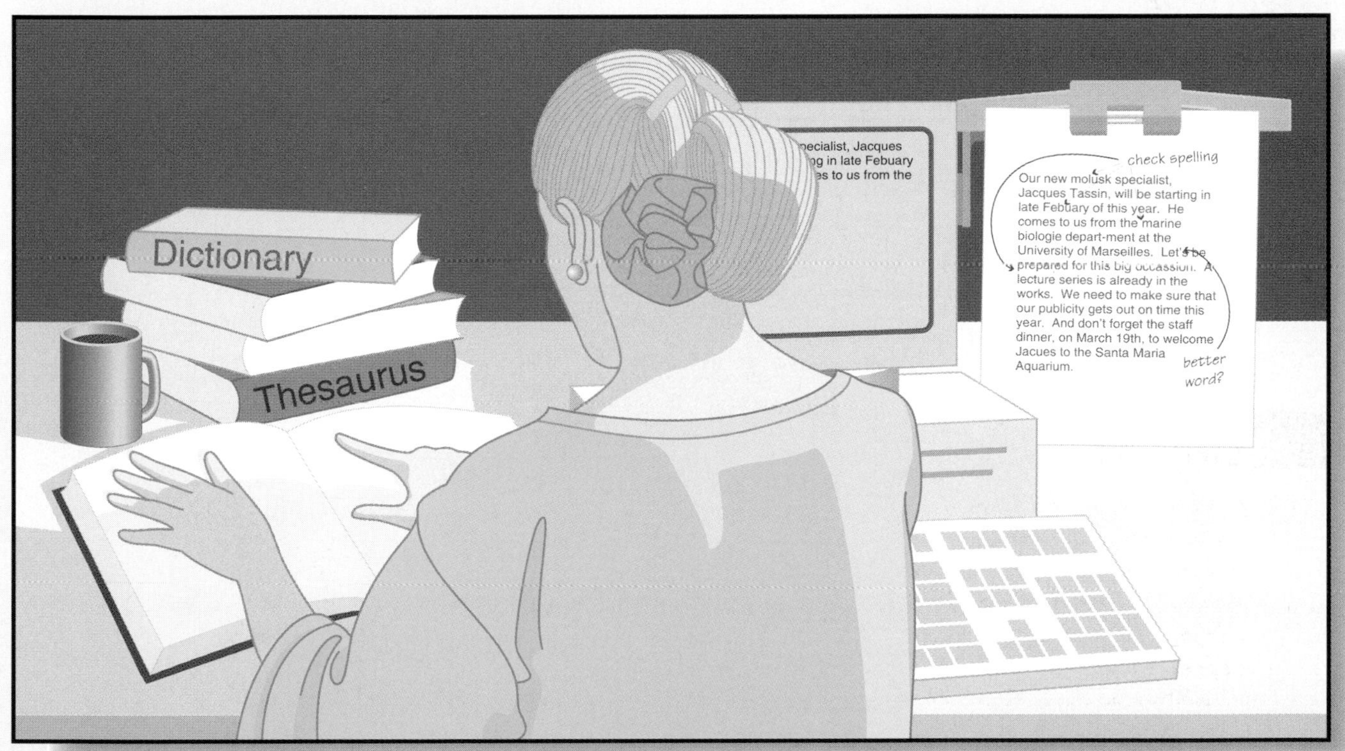


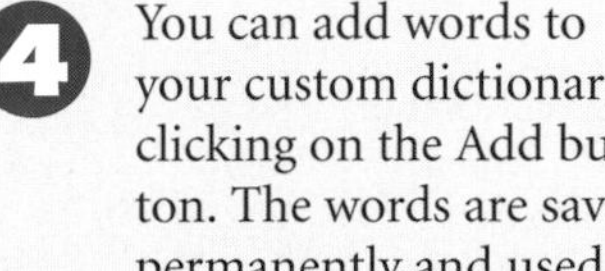

**4** You can add words to your custom dictionary by clicking on the Add button. The words are saved permanently and used in future spell checking.

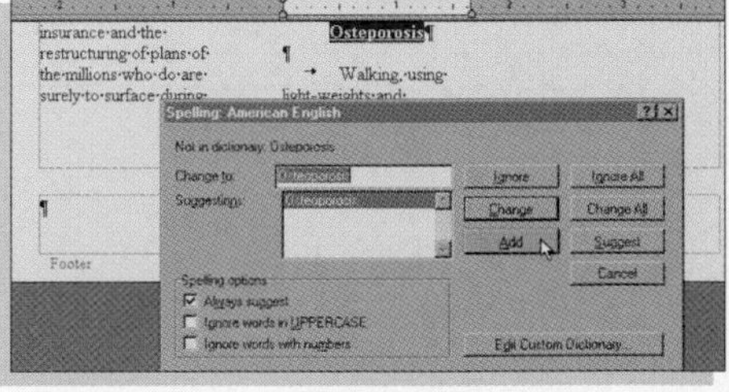

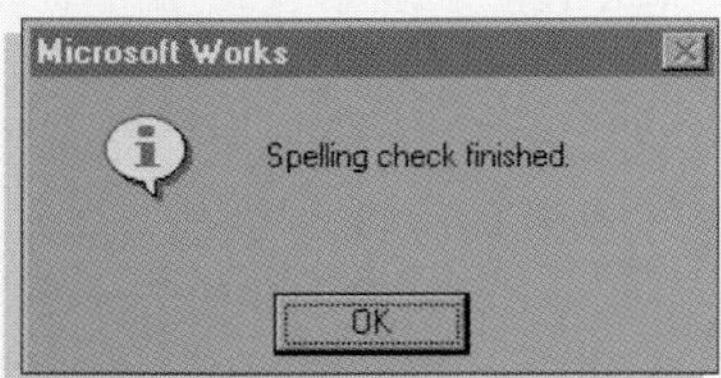


**5** A message box is displayed when the spelling check is finished.

# TRY IT!

Now it's time to practice your advanced word processing skills. First, you'll create a recipe card using custom tabs. Then, you'll use the Letterhead Wizard to create an invitation letter.

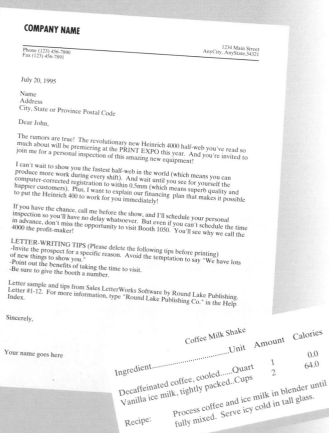

Open the Task Launcher window by selecting New from the file menu, select the Works Tools tab, and click the Word Processor.

COMPANY NAME

Phone (123) 456-7890
Fax (123) 456-7891

1234 Main Street
AnyCity, AnyState,54321

July 20, 1995

Name
Address
City, State or Province Postal Code

Dear John,

The rumors are true! The revolutionary new Heinrich 4000 half-web you've read so much about will be premiering at the PRINT EXPO this year. And you're invited to join me for a personal inspection of this amazing new equipment!

I can't wait to show you the fastest half-web in the world (which means you can produce more work during every shift). And wait until you see for yourself the computer-corrected registration to within 0.5mm (which means superb quality and happier customers). Plus, I want to explain our financing plan that makes it possible to put the Heinrich 400 to work for you immediately!

If you have the chance, call me before the show, and I'll schedule your personal inspection so you'll have no delay whatsoever. But even if you can't schedule the time in advance, don't miss the opportunity to visit Booth 1050. You'll see why we call the 4000 the profit-maker!

LETTER-WRITING TIPS (Please delete the following tips before printing)
-Invite the prospect for a specific reason. Avoid the temptation to say "We have lots of new things to show you."
-Point out the benefits of taking the time to visit.
-Be sure to give the booth a number.

Letter sample and tips from Sales LetterWorks Software by Round Lake Publishing. Letter #1-12. For more information, type "Round Lake Publishing Co." in the Help Index.

Sincerely,

Your name goes here

Coffee Milk Shake

| Ingredient.......................................Unit | Amount | Calories |
|---|---|---|
| Decaffeinated coffee, cooled......Quart | 1 | 0.0 |
| Vanilla ice milk, tightly packed..Cups | 2 | 64.0 |

Recipe: Process coffee and ice milk in blender until fully mixed. Serve icy cold in tall glass.

Display Tab marks and other nonprintable characters by enabling the All Characters option from the View menu.

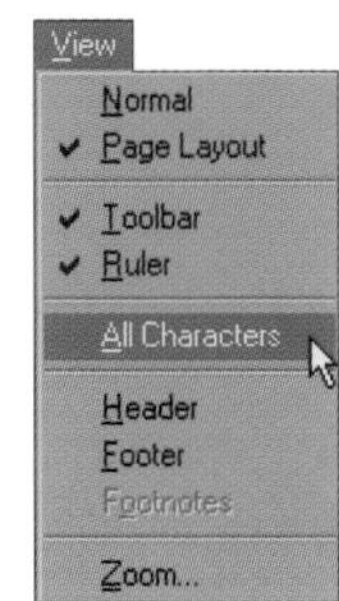

Type in the text of the recipe as shown. Each line containing text starts with a tab mark. Tab marks appear as right arrows (→) when you press the Tab key.

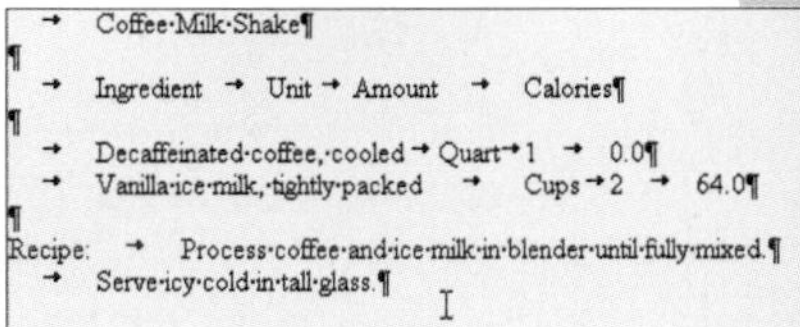

Select the text beginning with "Ingredient" through the line that begins with "Vanilla." Then from the Format menu, pick Tabs.

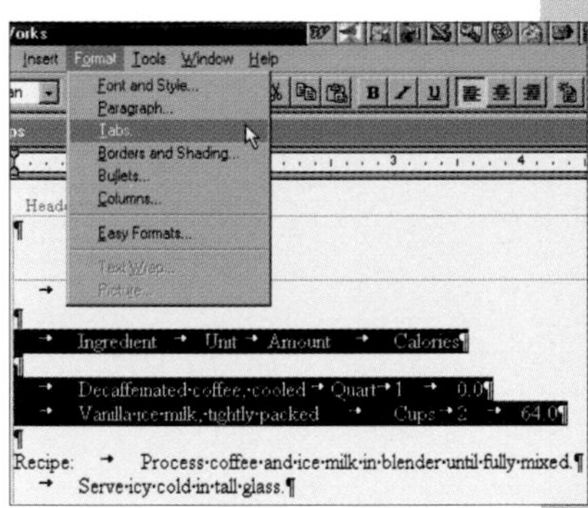

Enter the following four tab stop positions, alignments, and leader characteristics. Click the Set button after you enter each setting. Click OK after you've set all four tab stops.

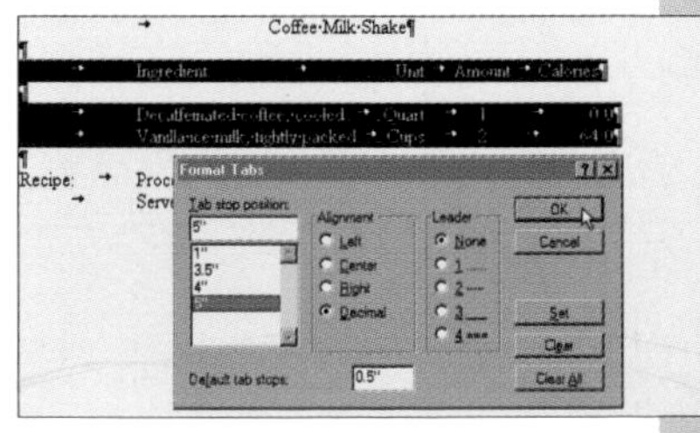


| Position | Alignment | Leader |
|---|---|---|
| 1˝ | Left | None |
| 3.5˝ | Right | 1... |
| 4˝ | Center | None |
| 5˝ | Decimal | None |

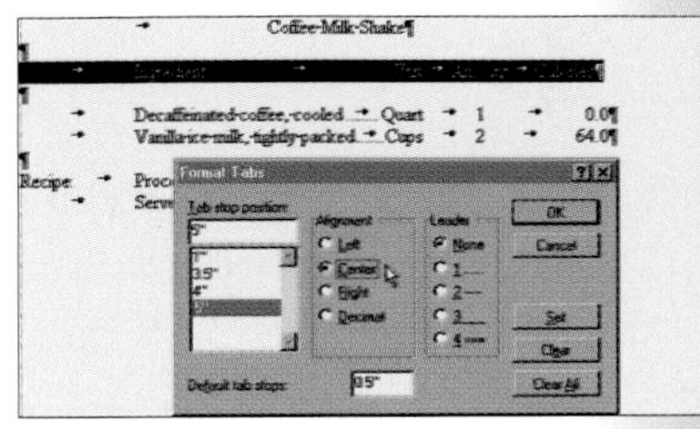


Notice how the word "Calories" aligns left of the decimal point. Don't align text with decimal alignment, instead use center alignment. To change this, select the line containing "Calories," open the Format menu and select Tabs, click on the 5" setting and change its alignment to Center.

Select the line "Coffee Milk Shake" and set one tab at 2.75", centered with no leaders. Then select the two lines at the bottom that begin with "Recipe." Set the tab for these lines at 1", left aligned, with no leader.

Close the recipe document. From the File menu select Close, then select Yes to save the document or No to continue.

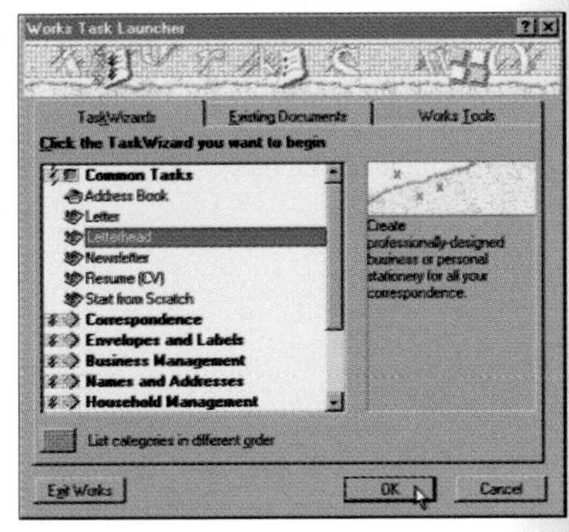


Now let's create a letter using a Wizard. The Task Launcher window should be open. If it's not, open the File menu and click New. Click on the TaskWizard tab, and from the Common Task category click Letterhead and then the OK button.

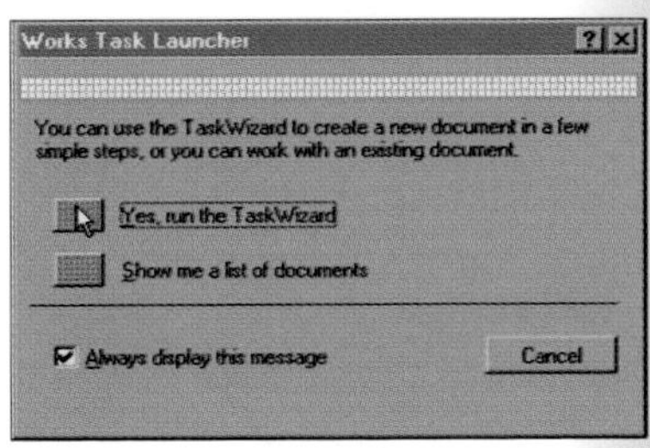


If this window is displayed, click "Yes, run the TaskWizard." Otherwise, continue to the next step.

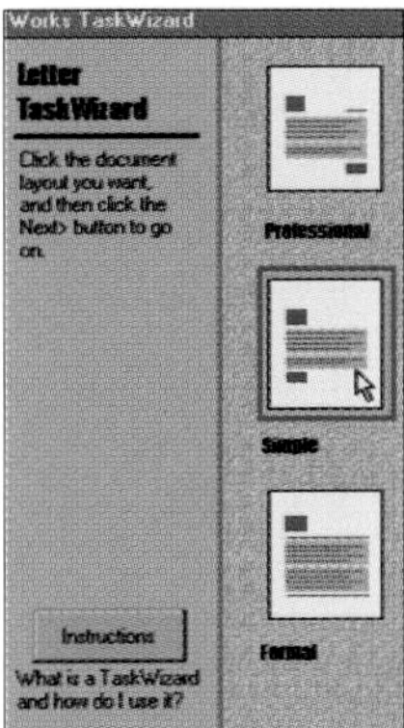


Select the Simple layout then click the Next button.

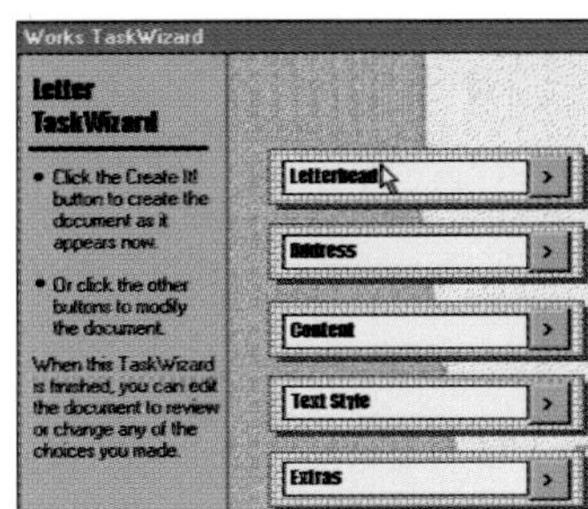


Select the Letterhead option.

Click "I want to design my own" and then click Next.

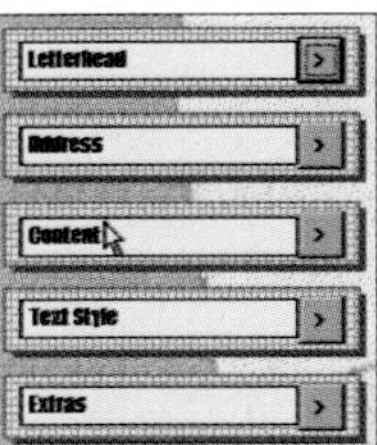


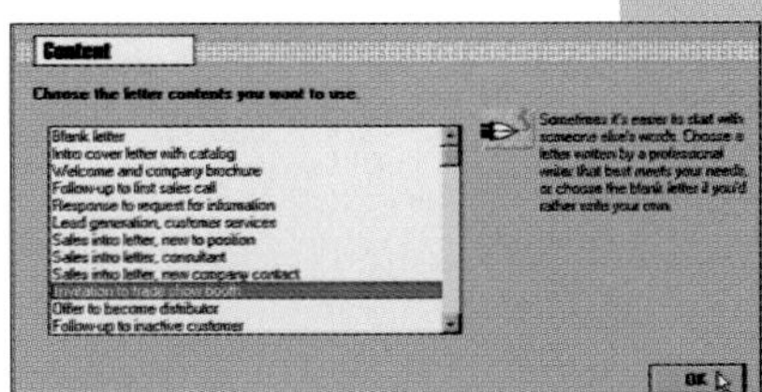


Select the Contents option to see the list of sample documents. For this exercise select "Invitation to trade show booth" and click OK.

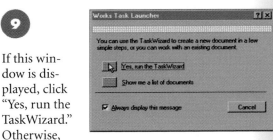

To complete the process, click on the "Create it!" button. In the next window displayed, click on the "Create Document" button.

# TRY IT!

Here's a chance to exercise your printing prowess. Follow the steps to print return and recipient addresses on an envelope. If you have access to a laser or ink-jet printer you shouldn't have any problems printing. Just check the printer reference manual for the "how-tos." If you're using a dot-matrix printer you may not have the capability to print an envelope. If that's the case, don't fret—you'll still be able to complete all the steps except the print step.

In the last exercise of this Try It, you'll create a two-column borchure with headers and footers from the letter you created in the previous Try It.

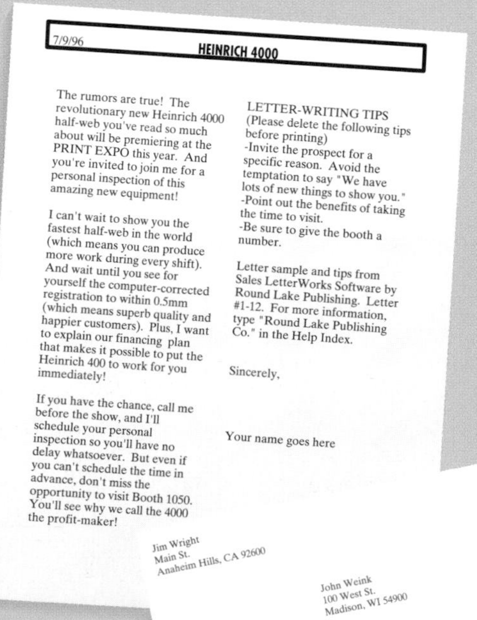
7/9/96

**HEINRICH 4000**

The rumors are true! The revolutionary new Heinrich 4000 half-web you've read so much about will be premiering at the PRINT EXPO this year. And you're invited to join me for a personal inspection of this amazing new equipment!

I can't wait to show you the fastest half-web in the world (which means you can produce more work during every shift). And wait until you see for yourself the computer-corrected registration to within 0.5mm (which means superb quality and happier customers). Plus, I want to explain our financing plan that makes it possible to put the Heinrich 400 to work for you immediately!

If you have the chance, call me before the show, and I'll schedule your personal inspection so you'll have no delay whatsoever. But even if you can't schedule the time in advance, don't miss the opportunity to visit Booth 1050. You'll see why we call the 4000 the profit-maker!

LETTER-WRITING TIPS
(Please delete the following tips before printing)
-Invite the prospect for a specific reason. Avoid the temptation to say "We have lots of new things to show you."
-Point out the benefits of taking the time to visit.
-Be sure to give the booth a number.

Letter sample and tips from Sales LetterWorks Software by Round Lake Publishing. Letter #1-12. For more information, type "Round Lake Publishing Co." in the Help Index.

Sincerely,

Your name goes here

Jim Wright
Main St.
Anaheim Hills, CA 92600

John Weink
100 West St.
Madison, WI 54900

If your printer prints envelopes, then you're in for a treat. You can quickly enter and print addresses on envelopes from Works. From the Tools menu select Envelopes.

Click on the Return Address tab and enter the return address.

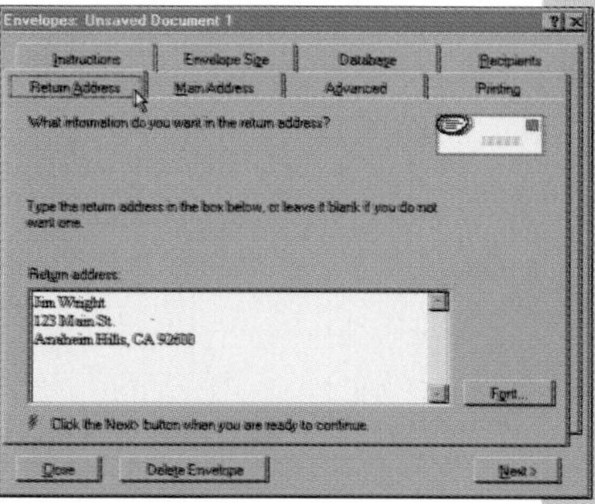

To enter the recipient address click on the Main Address tab, click into the text box and enter the address.

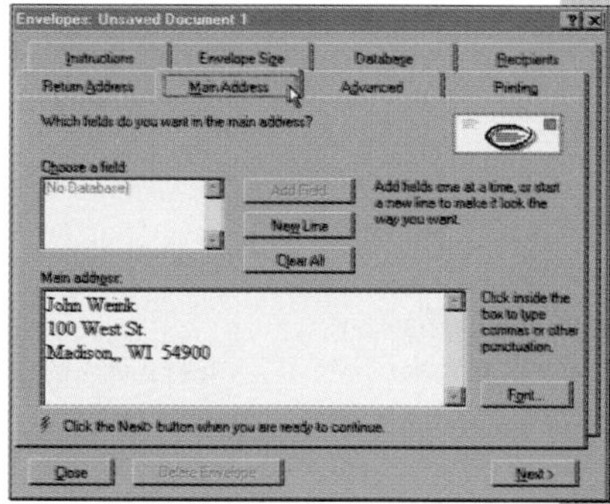

Works assumes you want to print a standard envelope size of 10 (4⅛" × 9½"). If you want something different, click on the Envelope Size tab and pick from the list of envelope sizes or click on the Custom button and specify a size.

Before you print the envelope, click on the Preview button to see how the envelope will appear when printed.

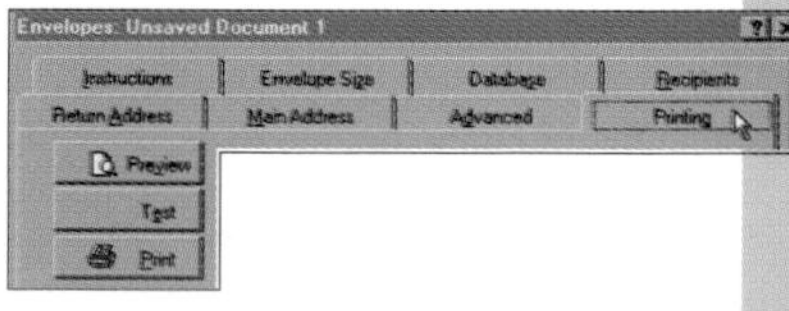

Insert an envelope into the printer. (Check the printer manual for instructions.) When you're ready to print, click on the Print button. To continue with the remaining Try It steps, press the Delete Envelope button in the bottom-left corner.

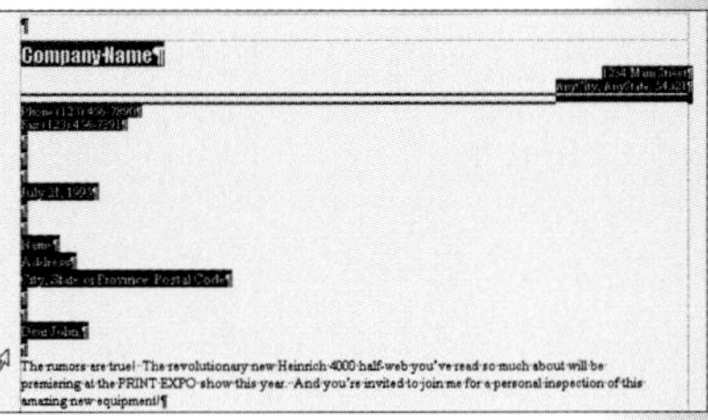

We'll use the text in the sample letter to create a multiple column brochure. Before we begin, let's do some clean up. From the top of the document select and delete the text down to (but not including) the first paragraph.

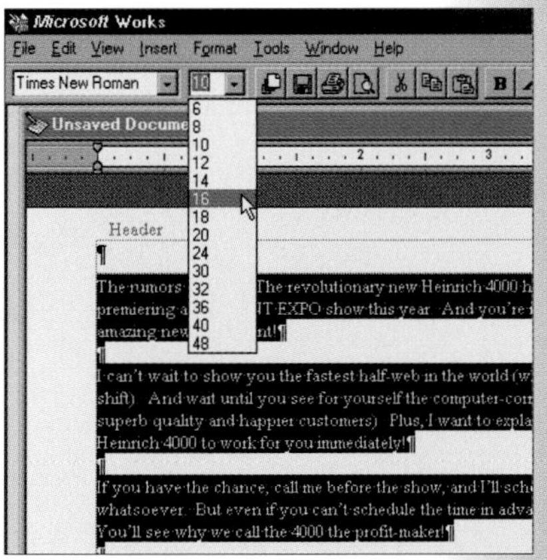


Change the font size of the brochure. Press Ctrl+A to select all the text in the document. Then click on the Size drop-down list and pick 16.

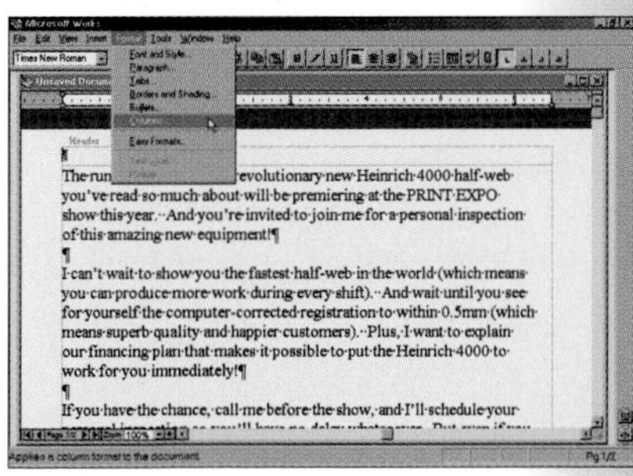

Now change the number of columns. From the Format menu select Columns. In the Number of Columns box enter 2, then click OK. Your document will now appear in two columns.

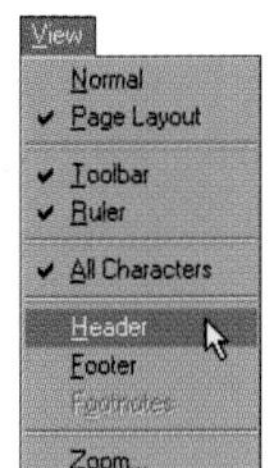


Finish the document by adding a header. From the View menu select Header. If you're not in Page View, go back to the View menu and select Page View.

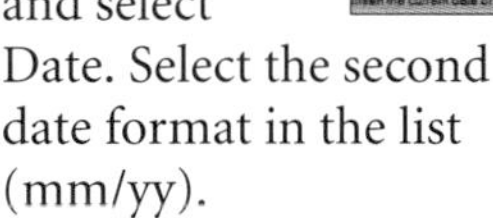

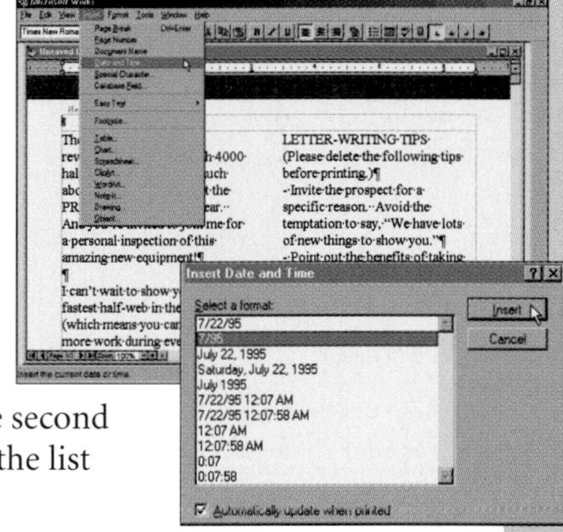


Insert the date in the left side of the header. Open the Insert menu and select Date. Select the second date format in the list (mm/yy).

Increase the size of the header text. Select the header and then from the size drop-down list pick size 16.

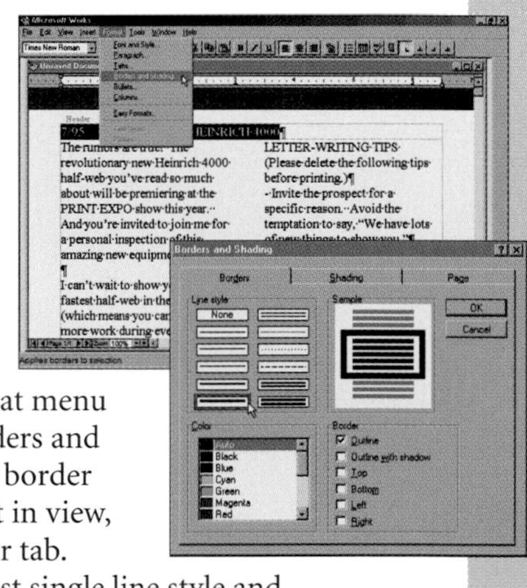


Add a border to the header to make it stand out. With the header still selected, open the Format menu and select Borders and Shading. If the border options are not in view, click the Border tab. Select the largest single line style and click OK. Use the Print Preview option to see your results.

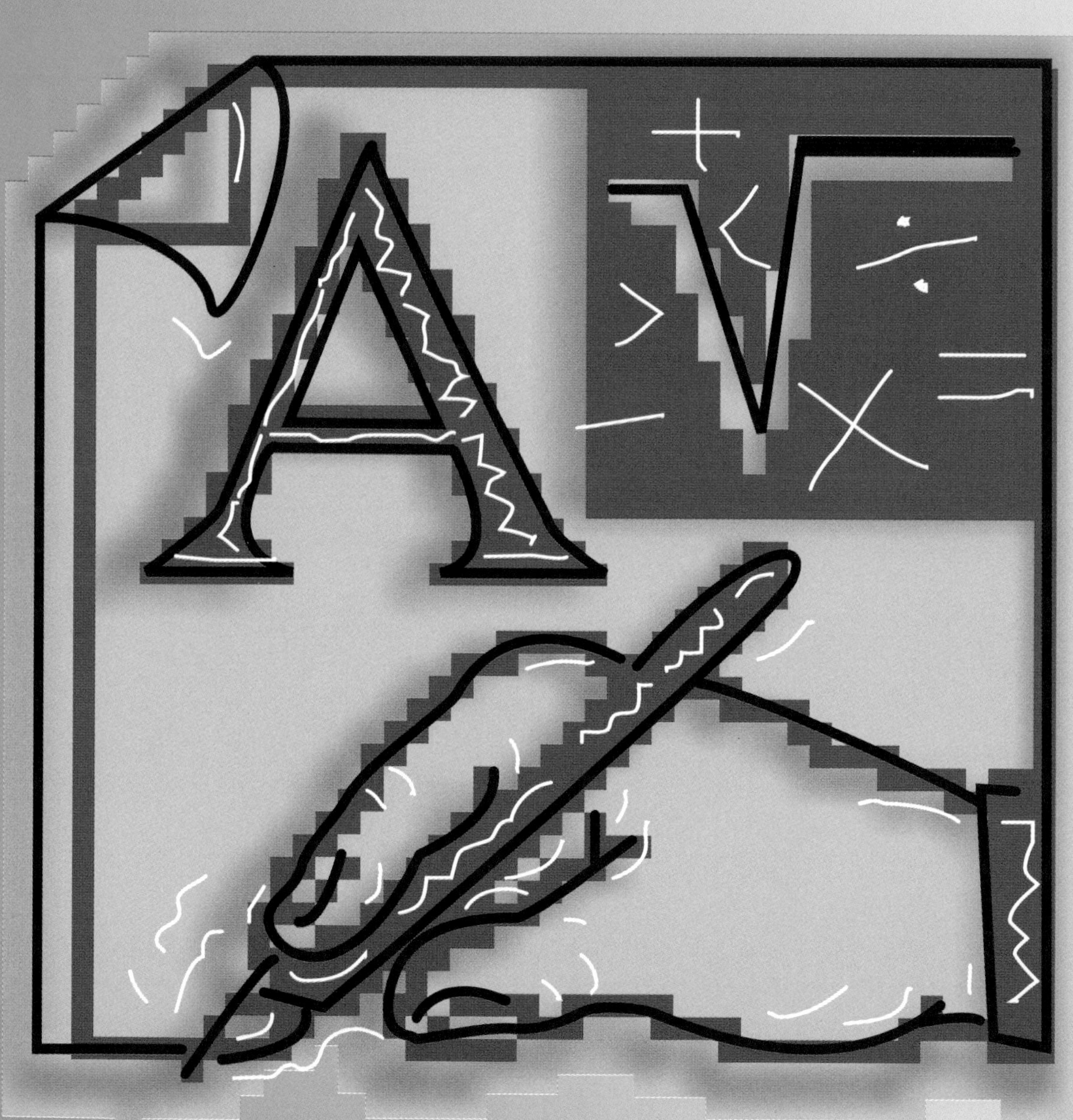

# CHAPTER 9

# Creating a Spreadsheet

A spreadsheet is a table of *cells*, laid out in rows and columns on your computer screen. Each cell is a rectangle where you can type in a number, a text label, or a mathematical formula. The entries "315," "March 15," and "=3*15" are all valid cell entries. (In Works, formulas don't end with "=," they begin with it—but you'll learn more about formulas in the next chapter.)

A spreadsheet program can help you perform repetitive calculations quickly, easily, and accurately. It can also let you check and change all of the numbers you've used in a calculation, even after showing you the result. A calculator, on the other hand, doesn't let you see all of the numbers you've used and lets you change only the last number you enter.

A spreadsheet program keeps all of the numbers, text, and formulas you enter in the computer's memory and displays them all on the screen so that it's easy to see them and understand how they're related. It performs calculations without error, showing you the numbers that went into the calculation, the numbers that came out, and the labels you chose to help you keep track of what all the numbers mean. It even lets you format everything you've entered to create professional-looking reports. If this sounds to you like a useful tool, it is. When most people learn how to use spreadsheets, they soon wonder how they ever got along without them.

# How to Create a New Spreadsheet Document

The word "spreadsheet" can be used to mean a computer document for performing calculations, or it can mean the program that creates those documents. Either meaning will be commonly understood, but for the purposes of this book, "spreadsheet" will mean the document.

To learn about spreadsheets, the first step is to create one. When you do, you'll see a grid of lines partitioning the document window into short, wide rectangles. Each of these rectangles is a cell, a place to store data. (You'll learn more about cells in the next chapter.)

If Works isn't currently open, open it now and select Works Tools from the Task Launcher as described in Chapter 3.

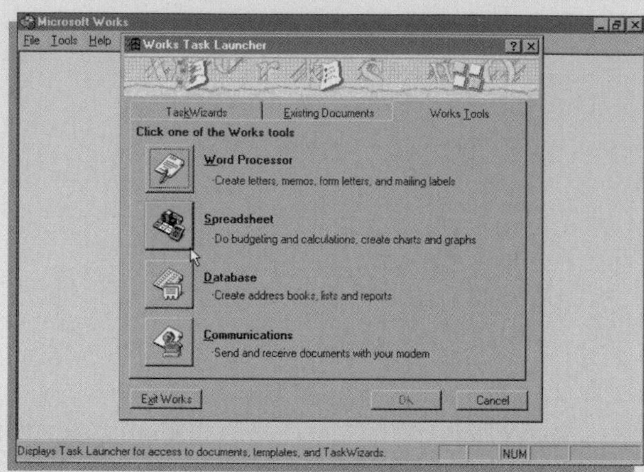


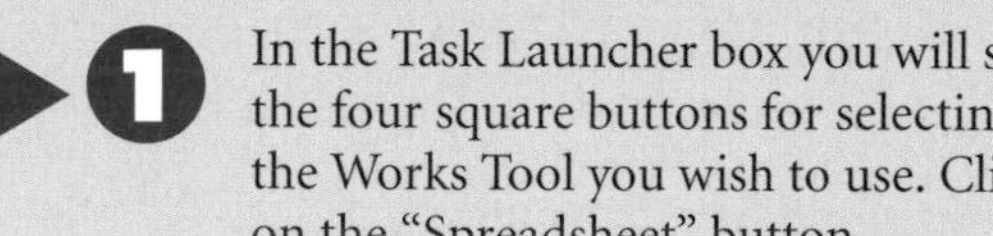

In the Task Launcher box you will see the four square buttons for selecting the Works Tool you wish to use. Click on the "Spreadsheet" button.

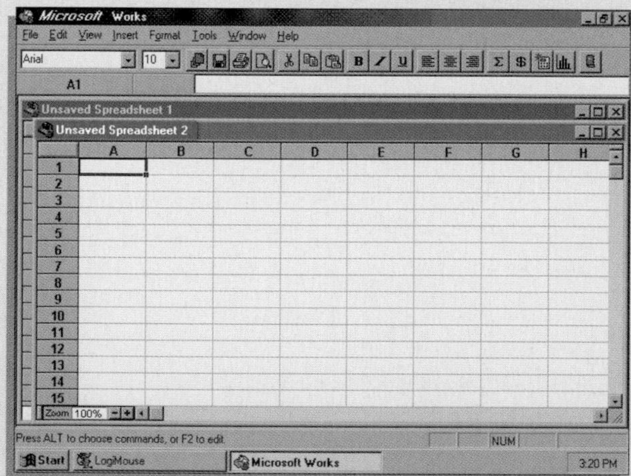

With your second document opened, your screen should look like this. Notice that the new active document is named *Unsaved Spreadsheet 2*, since it is the second new spreadsheet created in this session of Works. If you wish, you can maximize this second spreadsheet, which will also hide the first one.

**TIP SHEET**

- **Works lets you open as many as eight spreadsheets and other documents at a time. This might seem limiting, but in reality, eight is plenty for doing just about anything you can imagine. Besides, too many open windows can be confusing and may slow down your computer.**
- **You can open spreadsheet and word processor documents at the same time in Works. This can be a big help when you want to copy a table in your spreadsheet over to your word processor document (Chapter 20).**

**2** For a few extra cells in which to work, maximize the document window that appears inside the Microsoft Works application window. If the Microsoft Works application window isn't already maximized, maximize it. In the document title bar, you can see the current name of this new document, *Unsaved Spreadsheet 1*.

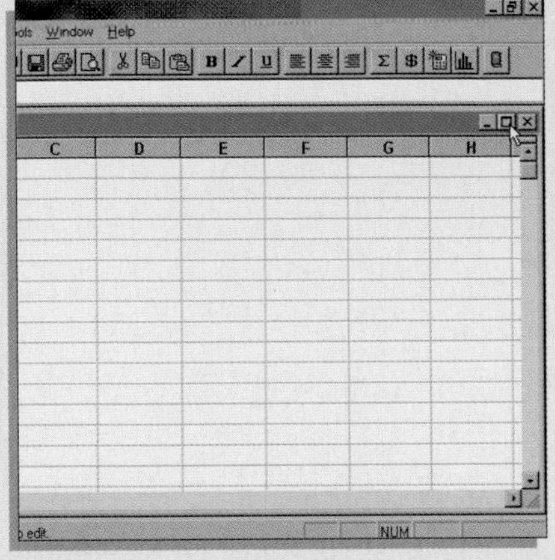

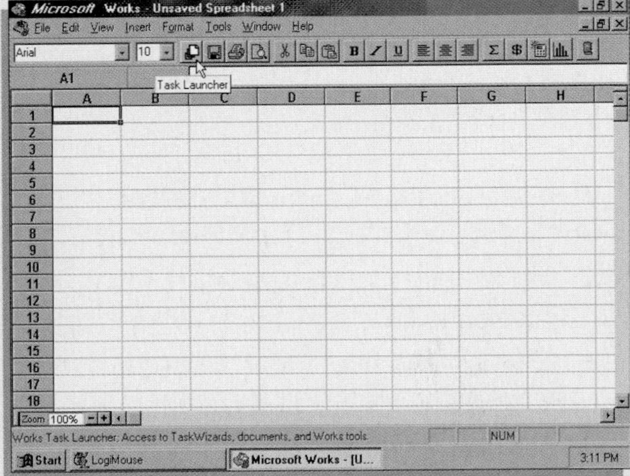


**3** Once you've created one document, try creating another. Just click on the Task Launcher button in the toolbar, and the Launcher dialog box will open without affecting your first document. Click on the spreadsheet button again to create a second spreadsheet.

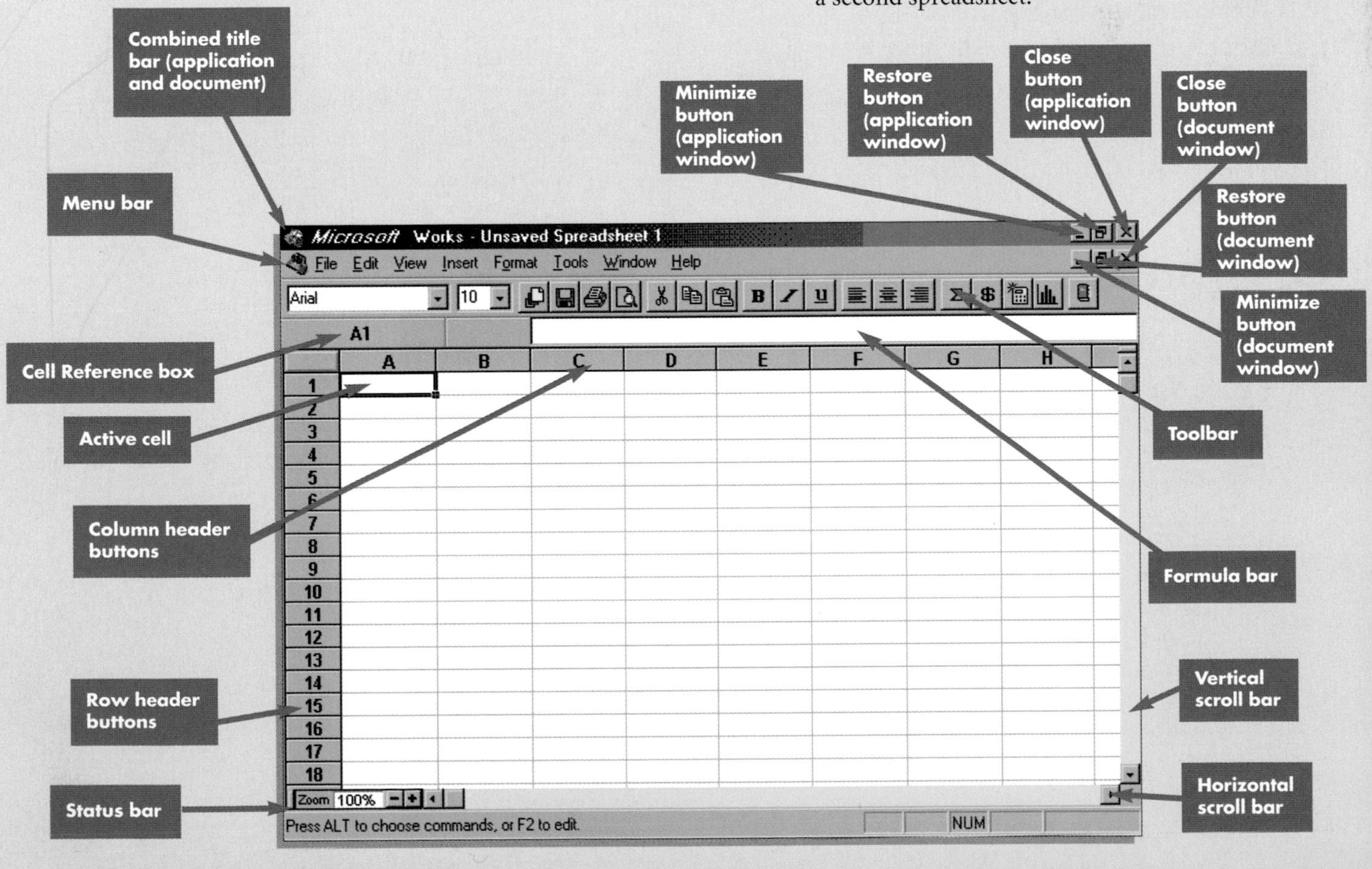

Combined title bar (application and document)

Menu bar

Minimize button (application window)

Restore button (application window)

Close button (application window)

Close button (document window)

Restore button (document window)

Minimize button (document window)

Cell Reference box

Active cell

Toolbar

Column header buttons

Formula bar

Row header buttons

Vertical scroll bar

Status bar

Horizontal scroll bar

# How to Enter Information into a Spreadsheet Cell

When you create a spreadsheet, you see a grid of lines partitioning the document window into short, wide rectangles. Each of these rectangles is a cell, a place to store data.

To help you tell the cells apart, each one has an address: a column letter followed by a row number. The first cell in a spreadsheet is always cell A1. That's just saying that it's the first cell in column A. The cell to its right is cell B1. Below that is cell B2.

Once you select a cell, there are two steps to entering information into it. First, you type data into the *Formula bar*, which serves as a temporary holding place. Next, you must tell Works to enter it into the cell, replacing what was there previously.

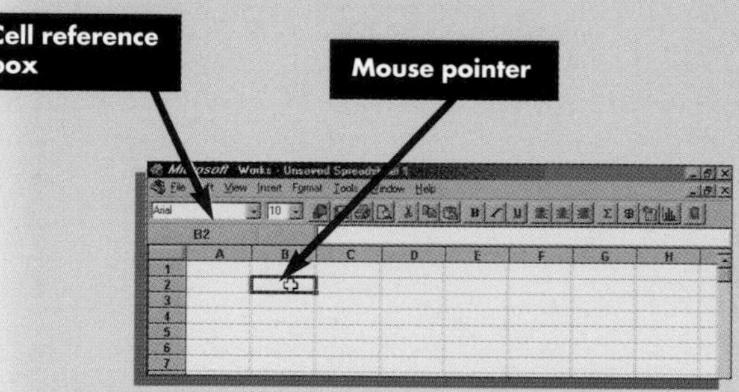


1. Choose a cell near the top of the spreadsheet and click on it. You'll see that the cell's address appears at the left end of the Formula bar in the Cell Reference box.

5. To cancel what you just typed and keep the cell's previous contents, press Esc.

## TIP SHEET

- **Works will let you type up to 255 characters into any cell, but it doesn't try to display all the text in a cell. If you type a lot of text into a cell, Works will display it across the empty cells to the right. If you type in a very long number, Works will display it in scientific notation, "1E+10," or as a string of pound signs, "########," depending on the cell's number format (formatting numbers is covered in Chapter 12).**
- **When you begin entering text into a cell, two buttons appear in the Formula bar. The button with an X is the Cancel button. Clicking this changes the cell contents to its previous contents. The button with a check mark is the Enter button. Clicking this works just like pressing the Enter key. The third button is the Help button. Clicking this will give you a menu of help topics to choose from.**

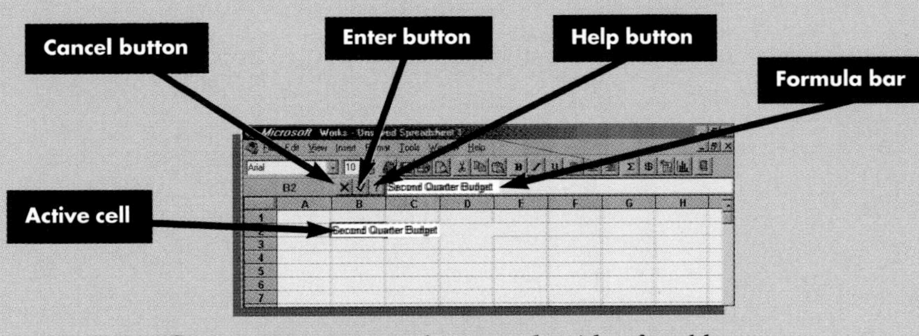


2 Type in text; in this case, the title of a table. As you begin, you'll see your text appear in two places: in the Formula bar and in the active cell (even though it isn't actually stored in the cell yet).

3 If you make a mistake typing, erase it with the Backspace key and retype the text.

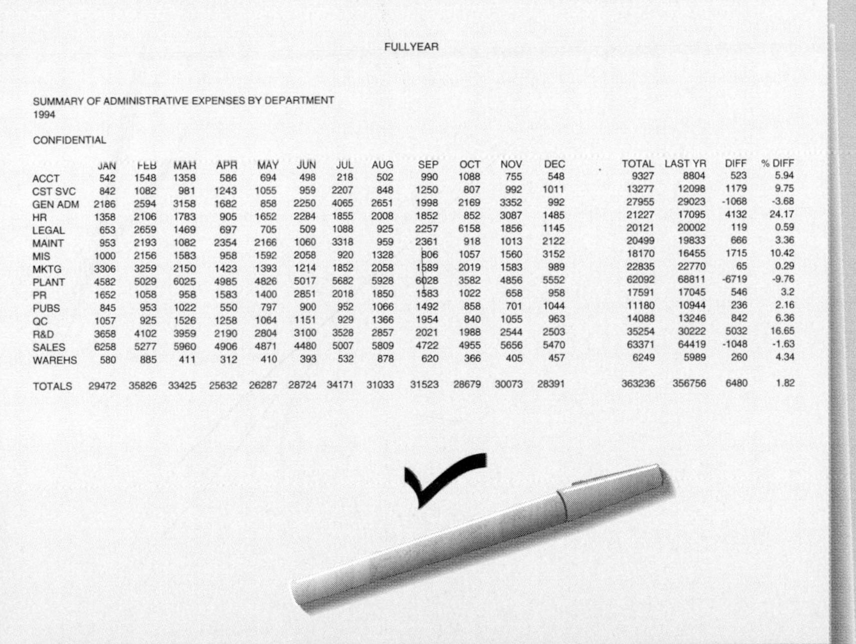

FULLYEAR

SUMMARY OF ADMINISTRATIVE EXPENSES BY DEPARTMENT
1994

CONFIDENTIAL

| | JAN | FEB | MAR | APR | MAY | JUN | JUL | AUG | SEP | OCT | NOV | DEC | TOTAL | LAST YR | DIFF | % DIFF |
|---|---|---|---|---|---|---|---|---|---|---|---|---|---|---|---|---|
| ACCT | 542 | 1548 | 1358 | 586 | 694 | 498 | 218 | 502 | 990 | 1088 | 755 | 548 | 9327 | 8804 | 523 | 5.94 |
| CST SVC | 842 | 1082 | 981 | 1243 | 1055 | 959 | 2207 | 848 | 1250 | 807 | 992 | 1011 | 13277 | 12098 | 1179 | 9.75 |
| GEN ADM | 2186 | 2594 | 3158 | 1682 | 858 | 2250 | 4065 | 2651 | 1998 | 2169 | 3352 | 992 | 27955 | 29023 | -1068 | -3.68 |
| HR | 1358 | 2106 | 1783 | 905 | 1652 | 2284 | 1855 | 2008 | 1852 | 852 | 3087 | 1485 | 21227 | 17095 | 4132 | 24.17 |
| LEGAL | 653 | 2659 | 1469 | 697 | 705 | 509 | 1088 | 925 | 2257 | 6158 | 1856 | 1145 | 20121 | 20002 | 119 | 0.59 |
| MAINT | 953 | 2193 | 1082 | 2354 | 2166 | 1060 | 3318 | 959 | 2361 | 918 | 1013 | 2122 | 20499 | 19833 | 666 | 3.36 |
| MIS | 1000 | 2156 | 1583 | 958 | 1592 | 2058 | 920 | 1328 | 806 | 1057 | 1560 | 3152 | 18170 | 16455 | 1715 | 10.42 |
| MKTG | 3306 | 3259 | 2150 | 1423 | 1393 | 1214 | 1852 | 2058 | 1589 | 2019 | 1583 | 989 | 22835 | 22770 | 65 | 0.29 |
| PLANT | 4582 | 5029 | 6025 | 4985 | 4826 | 5017 | 5682 | 5928 | 6028 | 3582 | 4856 | 5552 | 62092 | 68811 | -6719 | -9.76 |
| PR | 1652 | 1058 | 958 | 1583 | 1400 | 2851 | 2018 | 1850 | 1583 | 1022 | 658 | 958 | 17591 | 17045 | 546 | 3.2 |
| PUBS | 845 | 953 | 1022 | 550 | 797 | 900 | 952 | 1066 | 1492 | 858 | 701 | 1044 | 11180 | 10944 | 236 | 2.16 |
| QC | 1057 | 925 | 1526 | 1258 | 1064 | 1151 | 929 | 1366 | 1954 | 840 | 1055 | 963 | 14088 | 13246 | 842 | 6.36 |
| R&D | 3658 | 4102 | 3959 | 2190 | 2804 | 3100 | 3528 | 2857 | 2021 | 1988 | 2544 | 2503 | 35254 | 30222 | 5032 | 16.65 |
| SALES | 6258 | 5277 | 5960 | 4906 | 4871 | 4480 | 5007 | 5809 | 4722 | 4955 | 5656 | 5470 | 63371 | 64419 | -1048 | -1.63 |
| WAREHS | 580 | 885 | 411 | 312 | 410 | 393 | 532 | 878 | 620 | 366 | 405 | 457 | 6249 | 5989 | 260 | 4.34 |
| TOTALS | 29472 | 35826 | 33425 | 25632 | 26287 | 28724 | 34171 | 31033 | 31523 | 28679 | 30073 | 28391 | 363236 | 356756 | 6480 | 1.82 |

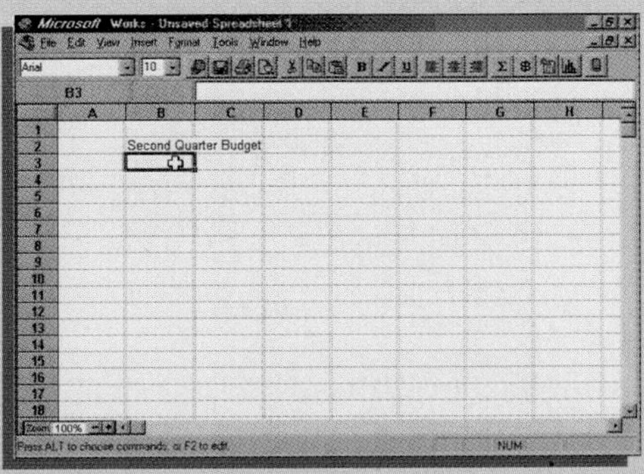

4 To store in the cell what you have typed into the Formula bar, press the Enter key or click on another cell.

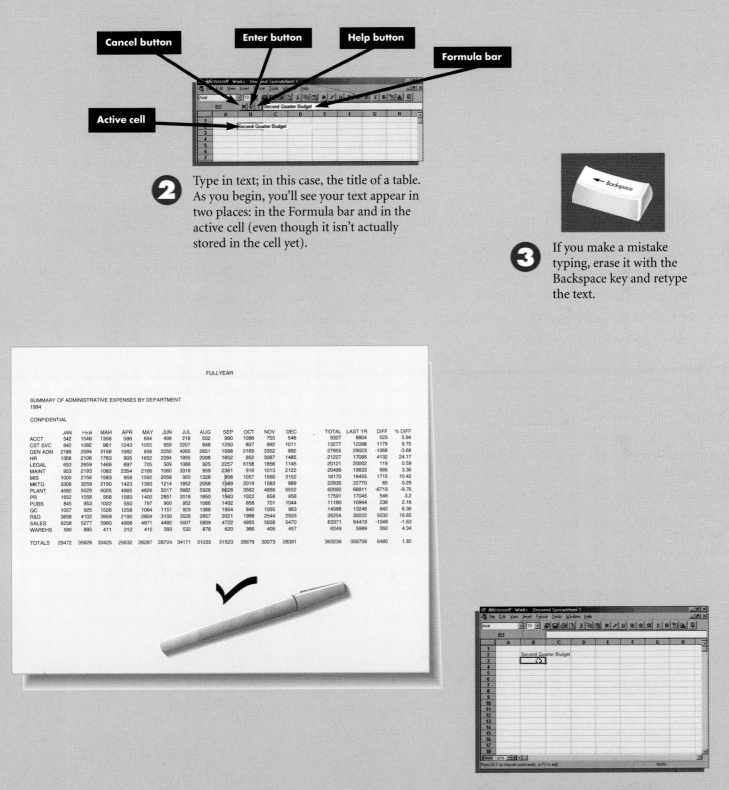

# How to Select Cells

Selecting cells is much like selecting text in the word processor. By selecting a group of cells you mark it for an action, like entering data in sequential cells, deleting data, copying it, formatting it, and so on. You've already selected a single cell by clicking on it. Now, selecting cells in blocks will let you work on all of them simultaneously, saving you time and effort.

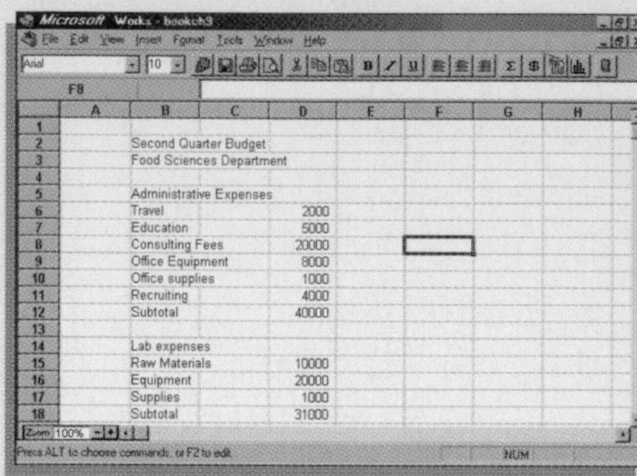


**1** Locate the cells you want to select. If possible, scroll the document so that the entire block to be selected is in view.

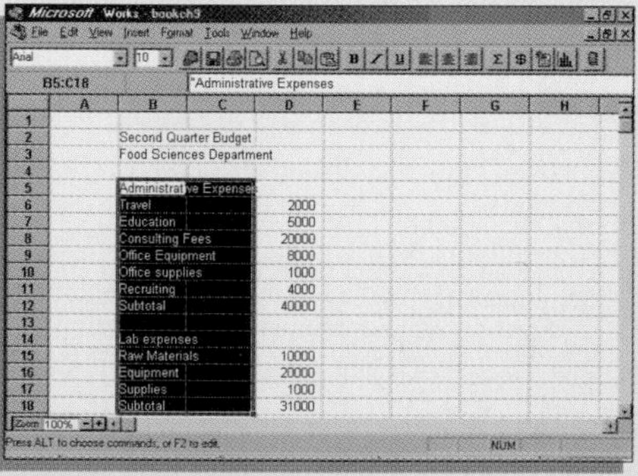


**5** Release the mouse button. The cells remain selected. Now you can issue commands that affect only the cells in this block.

## TIP SHEET

- **When you select a block of cells, all of the cells in the block except one are black. The one white cell is the *active cell*. It is the first cell you clicked on when you dragged to select the block.**
- **To select cells using the keyboard, first use the arrow keys to move to the cell at one corner of the block. Then, hold down the Shift key and use the arrow keys to move toward the opposite corner of the block, highlighting cells as you go. Release the Shift key when the complete block is selected.**
- **To select a complete row of cells, click on the row header button on the left side of the spreadsheet.**
- **To select a complete column of cells, click on the column header button at the top of the spreadsheet.**
- **To unselect a block of cells without performing an action on it, click anywhere outside the selection (but still in the spreadsheet). Or, if you're using the keyboard, release the Shift key and then press any arrow key.**

2 Position the mouse pointer at one corner of the block.

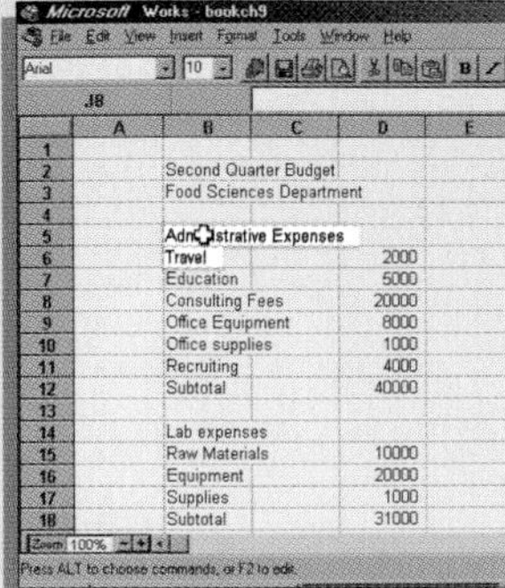


3 Holding down the left mouse button, drag the mouse toward the opposite corner of the block. As you drag over the cells, they become highlighted, indicating that they are selected.

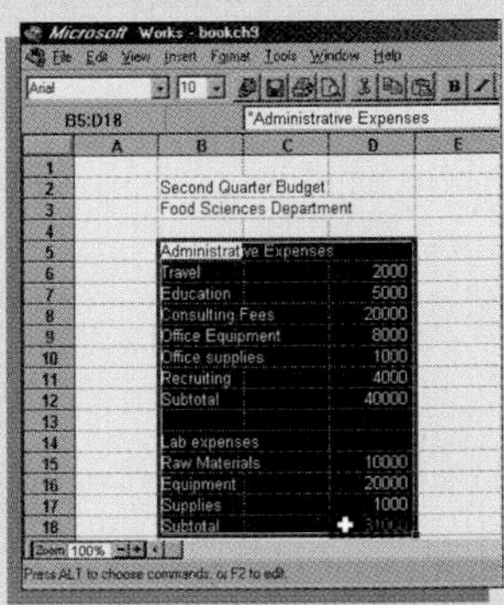


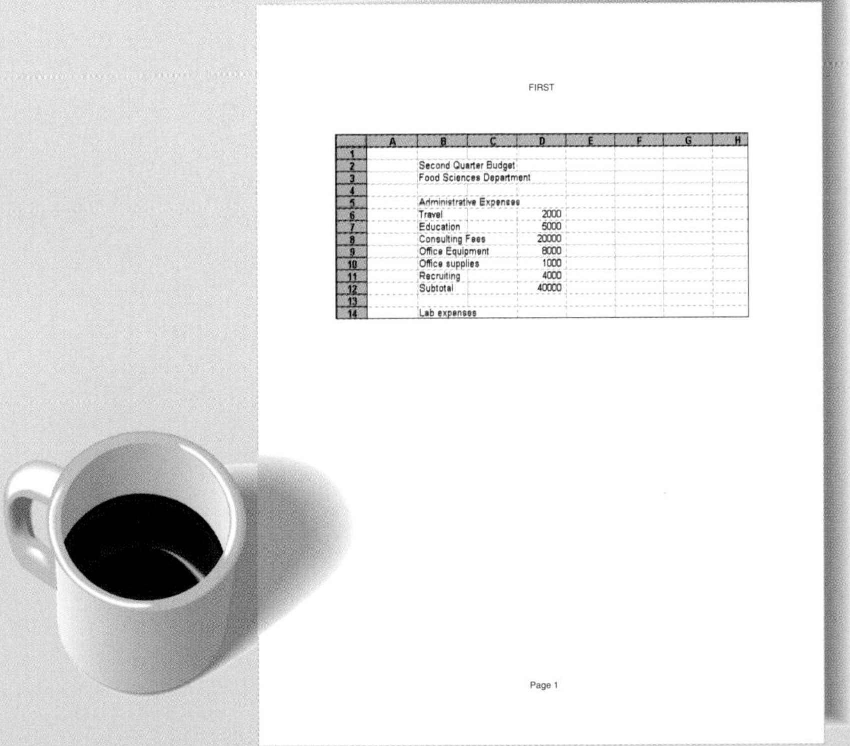

FIRST

| | A | B | C | D | E | F | G | H |
|---|---|---|---|---|---|---|---|---|
| 1 | | | | | | | | |
| 2 | | Second Quarter Budget | | | | | | |
| 3 | | Food Sciences Department | | | | | | |
| 4 | | | | | | | | |
| 5 | | Administrative Expenses | | | | | | |
| 6 | | Travel | | 2000 | | | | |
| 7 | | Education | | 5000 | | | | |
| 8 | | Consulting Fees | | 20000 | | | | |
| 9 | | Office Equipment | | 8000 | | | | |
| 10 | | Office supplies | | 1000 | | | | |
| 11 | | Recruiting | | 4000 | | | | |
| 12 | | Subtotal | | 40000 | | | | |
| 13 | | | | | | | | |
| 14 | | Lab expenses | | | | | | |

Page 1

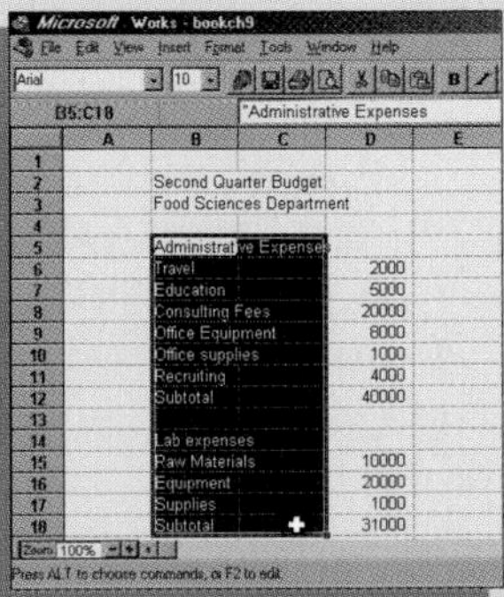

4 If you select too many cells, drag in the other direction to unselect them.

# How to Enter Blocks of Information into a Spreadsheet

When putting together a spreadsheet, you'll often want to enter data into sequential cells. Entering data in one cell, then selecting the next can be time-consuming. You have to move back and forth between the keyboard and either the mouse or arrow buttons, stopping to check your hand position with every move. To streamline the data-entry procedure, Works lets you select a block of cells and then enter data into those cells sequentially, without ever leaving the keyboard. This one-stop process makes typing data into a spreadsheet as efficient as typing in a word processor.

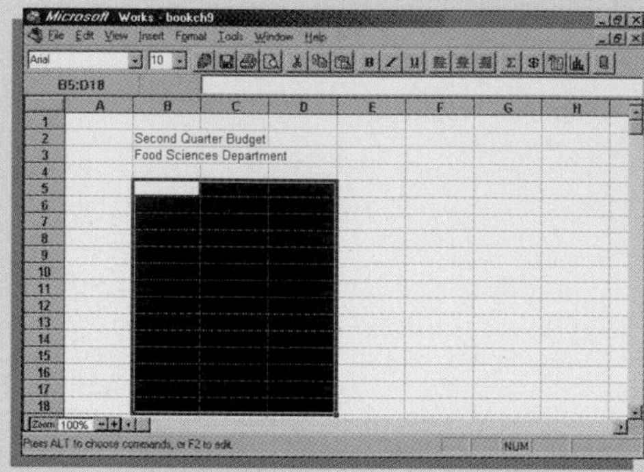


**1** Start by selecting the block of cells that you want to enter information into. In this case, drag from the upper-left corner to the lower-right corner of the block. You'll select the block and leave the upper-left cell active, or ready to receive data.

**Press Tab to move the active cell to the next column.**

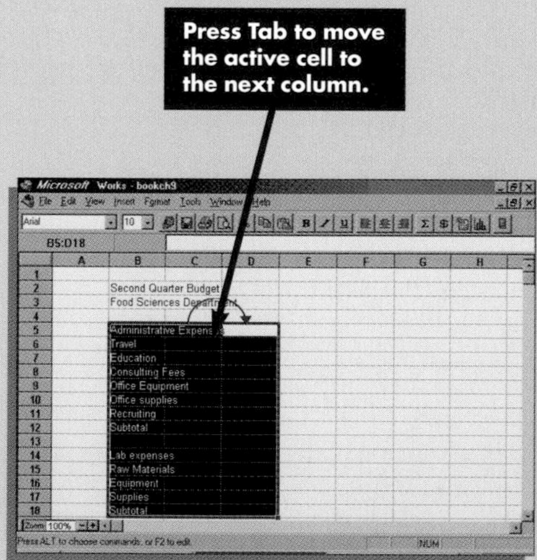


**5** To move the active cell horizontally across the block instead of vertically, press the Tab key instead of the Enter key. You'll enter your data in the currently active cell, and move the active cell one cell to the right instead of one cell down.

## TIP SHEET

- **The Enter and Tab keys move you to an adjacent cell only if you have a block selected. Make sure you do before you try to use them. If you don't have a block selected, you'll just replace the information in your currently active cell.**
- **The Enter and Tab keys move you down and to the right across a selected block. To move up and to the left, hold down the Shift key as you press Enter and Tab.**

2 Type the text into the upper-left cell as if it were the only cell selected.

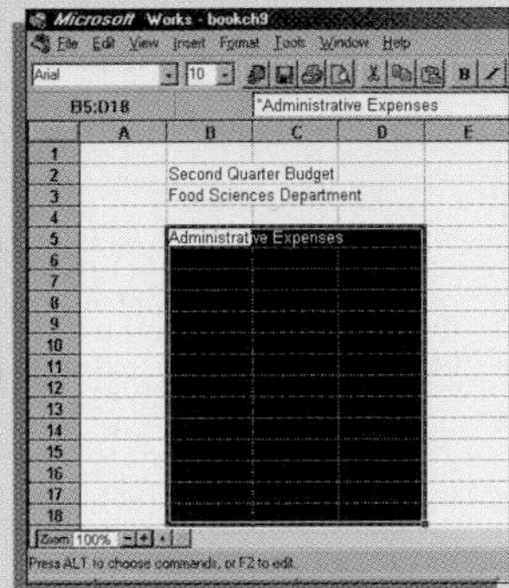

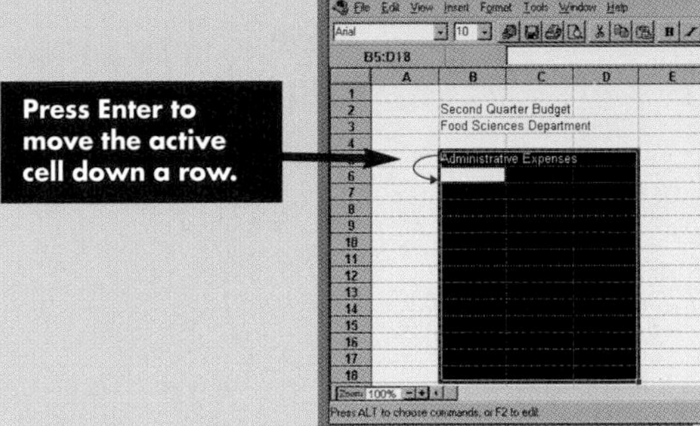
Press Enter to move the active cell down a row.

3 Press Enter. You'll enter your new data in that cell and make the next cell in the column active.

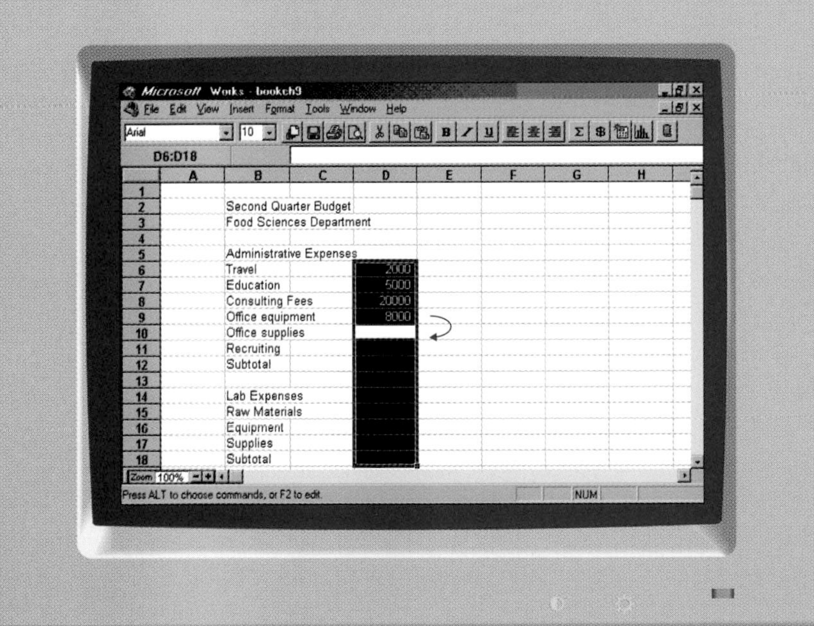

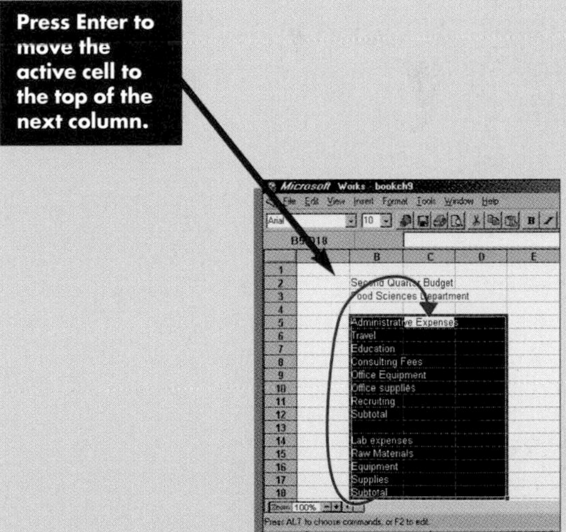
Press Enter to move the active cell to the top of the next column.

4 Continue entering data in this fashion. When you reach the end of the column of highlighted cells, press Enter to move the active cell to the top of the next column.

# How to Save a Spreadsheet

As you work on a spreadsheet, it is temporarily stored in your computer's memory, or RAM, just like a word processor document. And just as you did with your word processor document, you need to save your spreadsheet to your hard disk when you exit Works or turn off your computer.

It's a good idea to save your spreadsheet (or any document for that matter) just after you create it. Then, as you work on it, save it every few minutes. That way you won't lose much work if the unthinkable happens and your computer malfunctions before you can save.

The easiest way to save a spreadsheet is to click on the Save button on the toolbar.

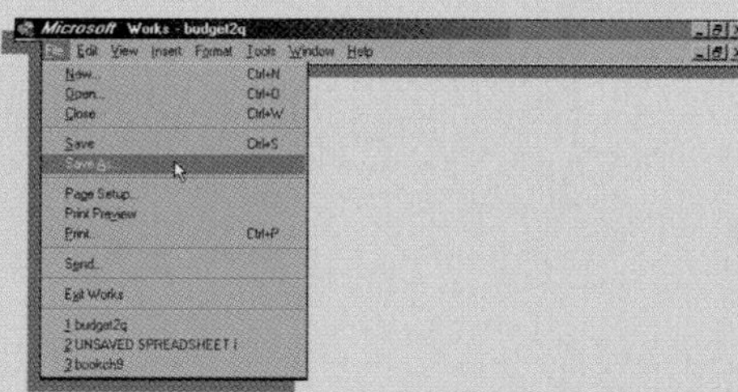

If you want to rename a spreadsheet after saving it, select the Save As command from the File menu. Works will open the Save As dialog box again so you can type in a new name.

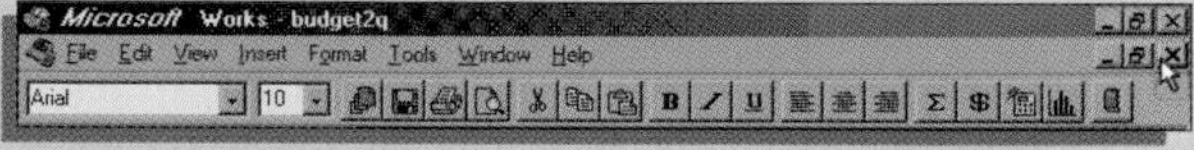

To close your spreadsheet, click on the Document Close button.

- **After you have saved a spreadsheet for the first time, you won't be asked to name it when you use the Save button again.**
- **Two alternatives to the Save button are to open the File menu and click on Save, or to press Ctrl+S.**
- **It's always a good idea to keep a backup copy of your work on a floppy disk. You never know when your hard drive might fail, or when someone may accidentally erase your file. To make a backup, select Save As from the File menu. Select the drive you wish to back up to in the Save In box and click on the Save button.**

**2** If this is the first time you're saving this spreadsheet, the Save As dialog box will open next. In the Save In box, make sure that the folder you want to save to is displayed. If the folder you want is not displayed, click the down arrow and click the folder you want. In the File Name box, type a name for the document.

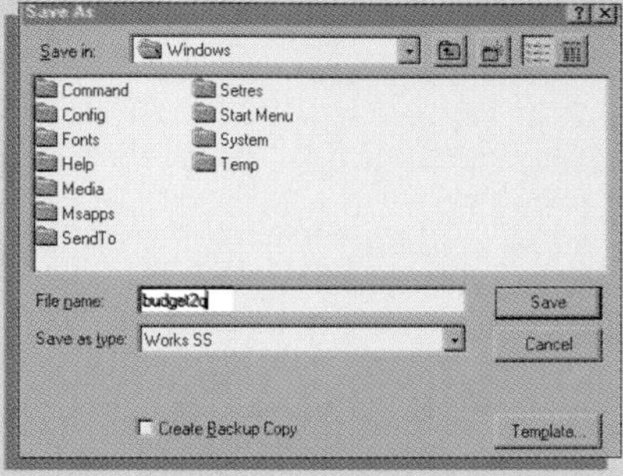


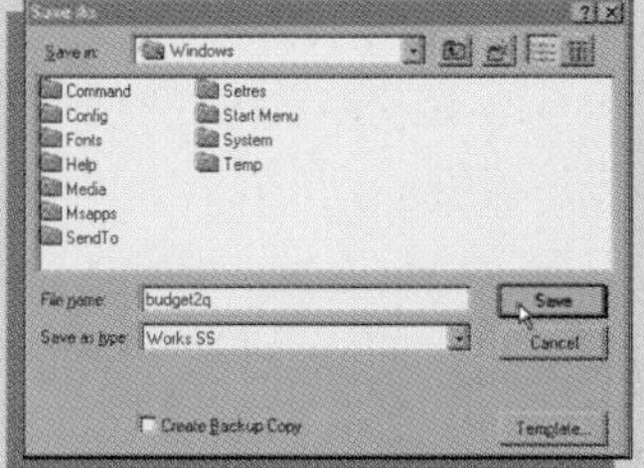

**3** Click on the Save button. Your spreadsheet will be saved to your hard disk where you can retrieve it whenever you want.

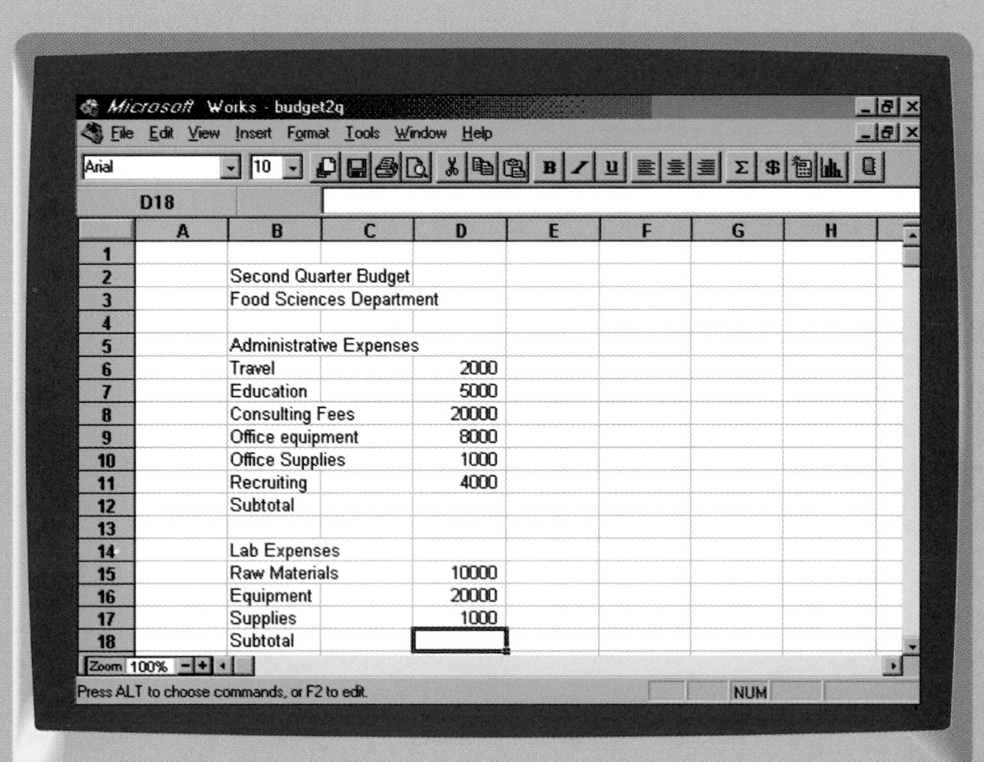

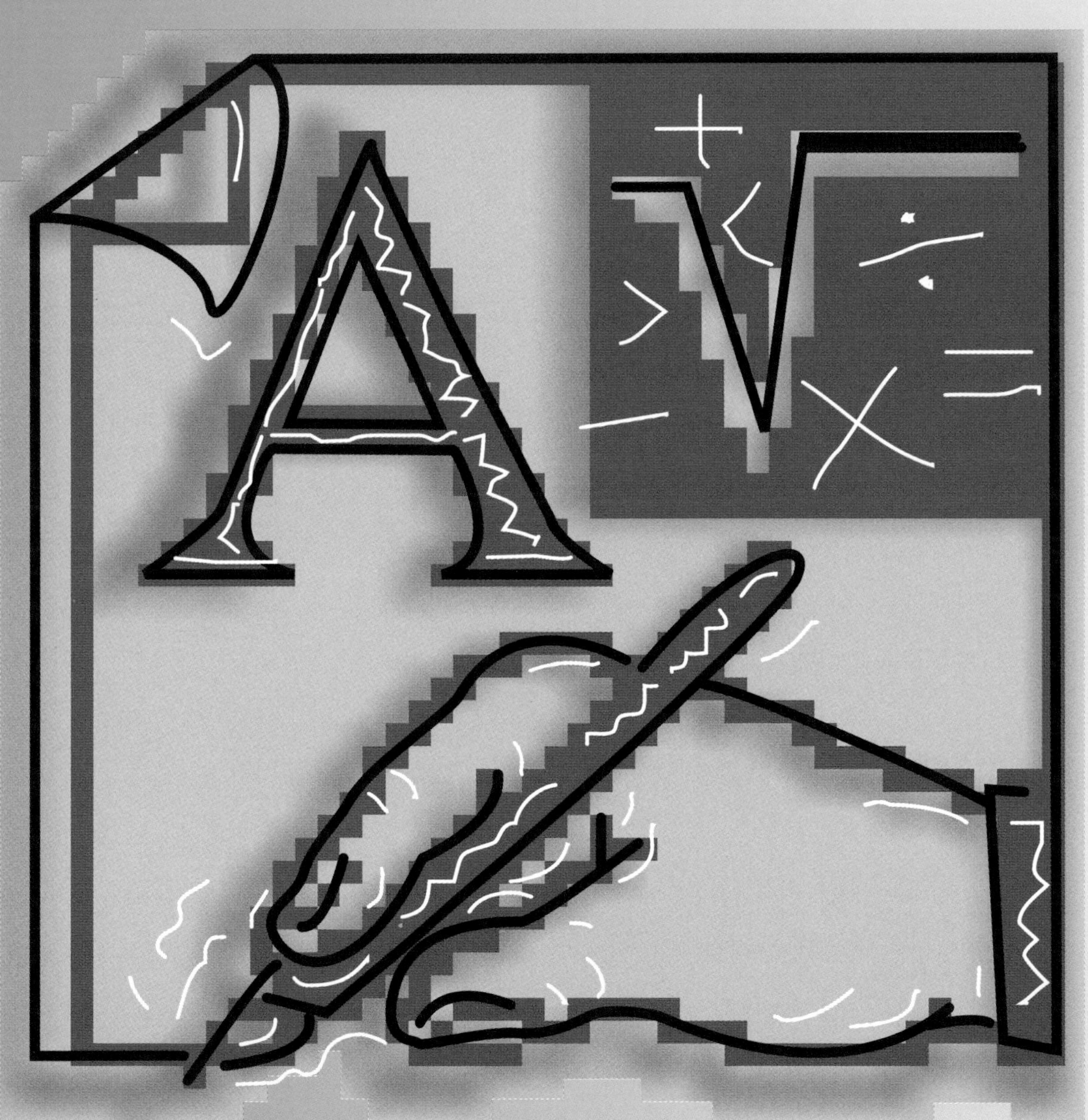

## CHAPTER 10

# Creating Formulas

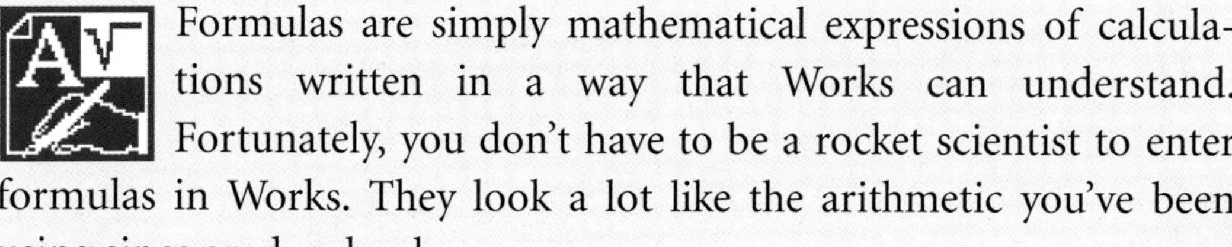

Formulas are simply mathematical expressions of calculations written in a way that Works can understand. Fortunately, you don't have to be a rocket scientist to enter formulas in Works. They look a lot like the arithmetic you've been using since grade school.

Formulas let you tell Works what math you want it to do. You might want to add up the cost of the items on your shopping list, or figure the gas mileage that your car is getting. You might even want to quantify the population changes in Alaskan caribou herds. You could do these things with a pocket calculator, but then you couldn't go back to make changes and correct mistakes. If you made a mistake with a calculator, you might not even know it. Formulas in Works let you make the calculations you want and see all the numbers that went into them. This way you can correct mistakes and change your assumptions as easily as entering new data into a cell.

# How to Add, Subtract, Multiply, and Divide Numbers

*Formulas* perform mathematical calculations with numbers. When you enter a formula into a cell, Works operates on the numbers contained in the cells referred to in the formula. The formula is then replaced by the result of the calculation.

When numbers in the formula's reference cells are changed, the result is automatically recomputed.

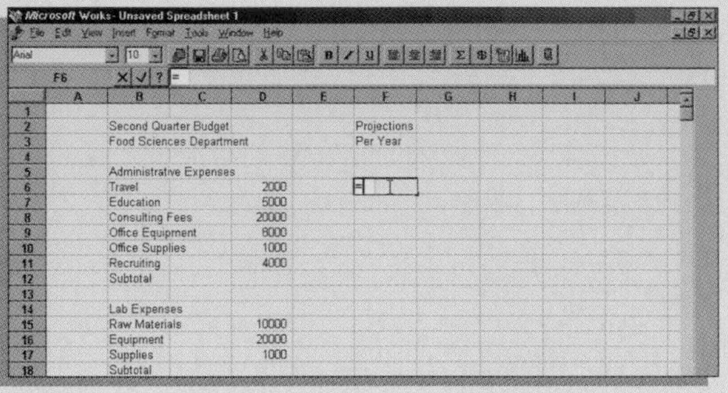


**1** In Works, every formula begins with an "=." Click on a cell to select it and press =.

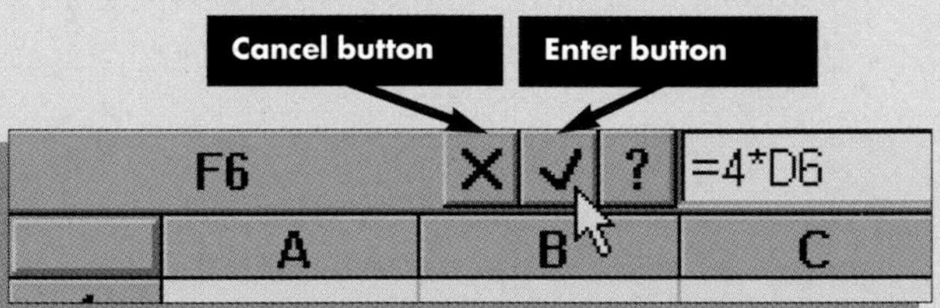


**6** When you are finished, press the Enter key or click the Enter button to store your formula in the current cell.

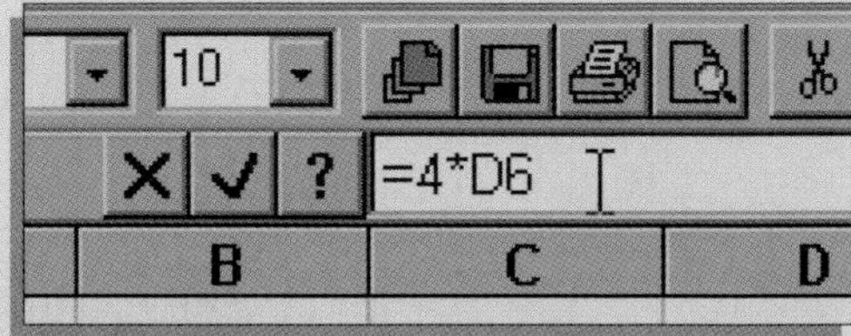


**5** After you click on a cell, its address appears in the Formula bar and in the active cell. To keep the address, click on the formula bar to the right of your equation to continue building the formula. To replace the address, click the cell whose address you want.

## TIP SHEET

- **Be sure to always enter your formulas according to standard rules of arithmetic. For example, Works won't know what to do if you put ** in the middle of your formula, or leave a + dangling at the end.**
- **Works ordinarily shows the results of your formulas in its spreadsheet cells. If you want to see the actual formulas displayed instead, click on the View menu then select Formulas.**
- **Whenever possible, arrange your spreadsheet so that similar items are grouped neatly together, and label your cells as if you won't remember what they are in 15 minutes. Later, you won't spend as much time figuring out what you did.**
- **If you're so inclined, Works lets you represent exponents with the ^ character and negative numbers by preceding them with a –. For example, Works reads =3*–1 as 3 times –1.**

Microsoft Works - Unsaved Spreadsheet 1

F6 =4

| | A | B | C | D | E | F | G | H | I | J |
|---|---|---|---|---|---|---|---|---|---|---|
| 1 | | | | | | | | | | |
| 2 | | Second Quarter Budget | | | | Projections | | | | |
| 3 | | Food Sciences Department | | | | Per Year | | | | |
| 4 | | | | | | | | | | |
| 5 | | Administrative Expenses | | | | | | | | |
| 6 | | Travel | | 2000 | | =4 | | | | |
| 7 | | Education | | 5000 | | | | | | |
| 8 | | Consulting Fees | | 20000 | | | | | | |
| 9 | | Office Equipment | | 8000 | | | | | | |
| 10 | | Office Supplies | | 1000 | | | | | | |
| 11 | | Recruiting | | 4000 | | | | | | |
| 12 | | Subtotal | | | | | | | | |
| 13 | | | | | | | | | | |
| 14 | | Lab Expenses | | | | | | | | |
| 15 | | Raw Materials | | 10000 | | | | | | |
| 16 | | Equipment | | 20000 | | | | | | |
| 17 | | Supplies | | 1000 | | | | | | |
| 18 | | Subtotal | | | | | | | | |

**2** To include a number in your formula, simply type it in.

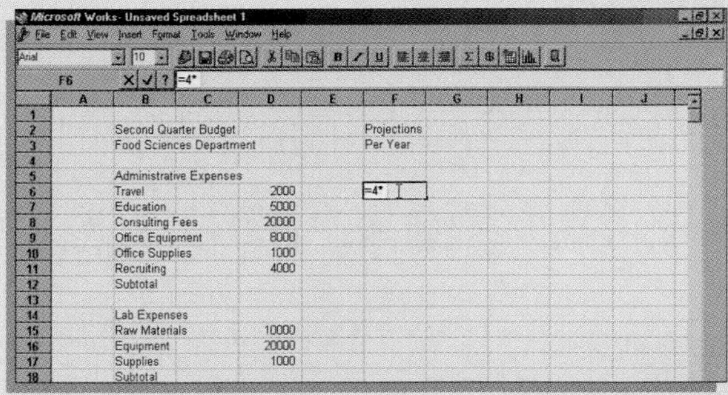

Microsoft Works - Unsaved Spreadsheet 1

F6 =4*

| | A | B | C | D | E | F | G | H | I | J |
|---|---|---|---|---|---|---|---|---|---|---|
| 1 | | | | | | | | | | |
| 2 | | Second Quarter Budget | | | | Projections | | | | |
| 3 | | Food Sciences Department | | | | Per Year | | | | |
| 4 | | | | | | | | | | |
| 5 | | Administrative Expenses | | | | | | | | |
| 6 | | Travel | | 2000 | | =4* | | | | |
| 7 | | Education | | 5000 | | | | | | |
| 8 | | Consulting Fees | | 20000 | | | | | | |
| 9 | | Office Equipment | | 8000 | | | | | | |
| 10 | | Office Supplies | | 1000 | | | | | | |
| 11 | | Recruiting | | 4000 | | | | | | |
| 12 | | Subtotal | | | | | | | | |
| 13 | | | | | | | | | | |
| 14 | | Lab Expenses | | | | | | | | |
| 15 | | Raw Materials | | 10000 | | | | | | |
| 16 | | Equipment | | 20000 | | | | | | |
| 17 | | Supplies | | 1000 | | | | | | |
| 18 | | Subtotal | | | | | | | | |

**3** Type in the mathematical operator you want to use. Common math operators Works uses are + (plus), – (minus), * (times), and / (divided by).

| | A | B | C | D | E | F | G |
|---|---|---|---|---|---|---|---|
| 1 | | | | | | | |
| 2 | | Second Quarter Budget | | | | Projections | |
| 3 | | Food Sciences Department | | | | Per Year | |
| 4 | | | | | | | |
| 5 | | Administrative Expenses | | | | | |
| 6 | | Travel | | 2000 | | 8000 | |
| 7 | | Education | | 5000 | | 20000 | |
| 8 | | Consulting Fees | | 20000 | | 80000 | |
| 9 | | Office Equipment | | 8000 | | 32000 | |
| 10 | | Office Supplies | | 1000 | | 4000 | |
| 11 | | Recruiting | | 4000 | | 16000 | |
| 12 | | Subtotal | | | | | |
| 13 | | | | | | | |
| 14 | | Lab Expenses | | | | | |
| 15 | | Raw Materials | | 10000 | | 40000 | |
| 16 | | Equipment | | 20000 | | 80000 | |
| 17 | | Supplies | | 1000 | | 4000 | |
| 18 | | Subtotal | | | | | |

**4** To include the contents of a cell in your calculation, click on that cell. Works will show the cell's address in your formula. Works accepts cell addresses as well as numbers in its formulas.

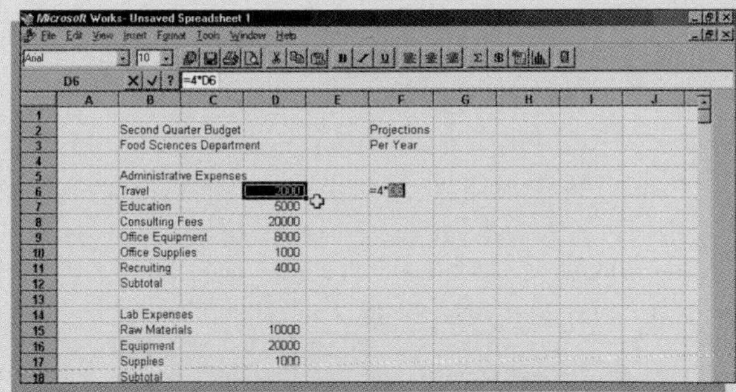

Microsoft Works - Unsaved Spreadsheet 1

D6 =4*D6

| | A | B | C | D | E | F | G | H | I | J |
|---|---|---|---|---|---|---|---|---|---|---|
| 1 | | | | | | | | | | |
| 2 | | Second Quarter Budget | | | | Projections | | | | |
| 3 | | Food Sciences Department | | | | Per Year | | | | |
| 4 | | | | | | | | | | |
| 5 | | Administrative Expenses | | | | | | | | |
| 6 | | Travel | | 2000 | | =4*D6 | | | | |
| 7 | | Education | | 5000 | | | | | | |
| 8 | | Consulting Fees | | 20000 | | | | | | |
| 9 | | Office Equipment | | 8000 | | | | | | |
| 10 | | Office Supplies | | 1000 | | | | | | |
| 11 | | Recruiting | | 4000 | | | | | | |
| 12 | | Subtotal | | | | | | | | |
| 13 | | | | | | | | | | |
| 14 | | Lab Expenses | | | | | | | | |
| 15 | | Raw Materials | | 10000 | | | | | | |
| 16 | | Equipment | | 20000 | | | | | | |
| 17 | | Supplies | | 1000 | | | | | | |
| 18 | | Subtotal | | | | | | | | |

# How to Sum a Column of Numbers

On the previous page you saw how to create mathematical formulas in spreadsheet cells. Suppose, however, that you had to total up several dozen items on a shopping list. If you tried to do this by clicking and adding each cell (=A1+A2+A3...), your mouse might need an oil change by the time you finished. What's more, it might be almost impossible to tell if you missed a cell.

Once again, Works has a solution to this dilemma: the SUM function. Beginners sometimes find functions a little hard to read at first, but they can make work so much easier and reliable that they will soon win your faith.

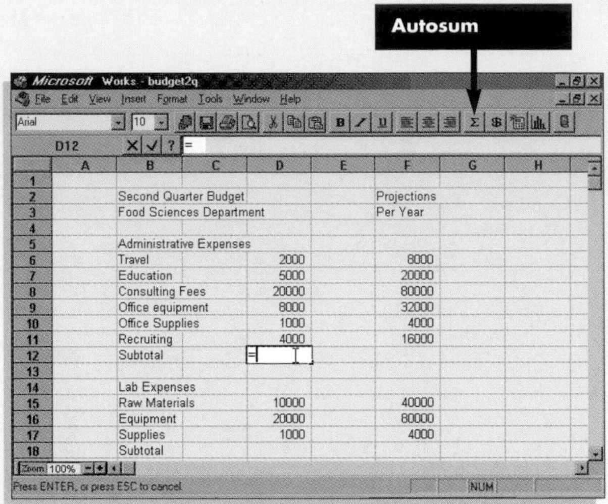


**1** To sum a column of numbers, click on the cell which is to contain the sum and type an = sign.

## TIP SHEET

- **In step 3 you saw a range of cells (D6:D11) in the Formula bar. This is the notation Works uses to describe blocks of cells. It consists of three parts: a starting cell address, a colon, and an ending cell address. The starting cell is always the upper-left cell in the selected block. The ending cell is always the lower-right cell in the selected block. You must use the colon to separate the two. You can type this notation directly into your formula if you like, but most people find it easier to use the mouse.**
- **Works has other functions to make working with blocks of cells easier. Open the Help menu, click on Index, and enter one of the following names: AVG, COUNT, MAX, MIN, STD, or VAR.**
- **If you want to sum a column of numbers that doesn't contain any blank cells, try the Autosum tool on the toolbar. (It shows the Greek letter Σ.) Click in the cell just below the column you want to sum, and double-click on the Autosum tool in the toolbar.**

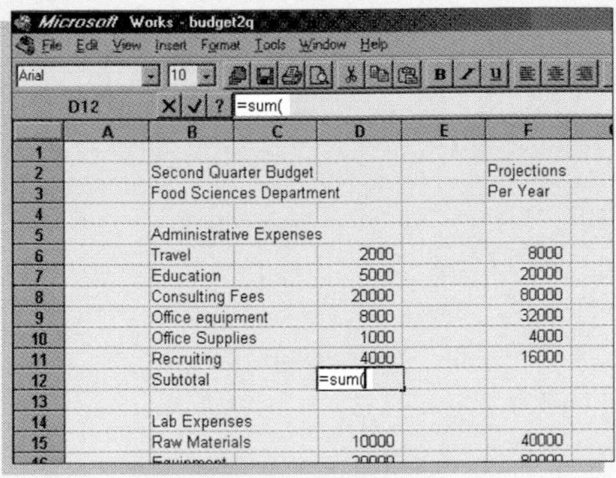


**2** Next, type in the characters **sum(**.

**3** Select the column of cells to add by clicking on the first cell and dragging down to the last cell. You'll see the *range* of cells you just selected appear in the Formula bar and in the active cell.

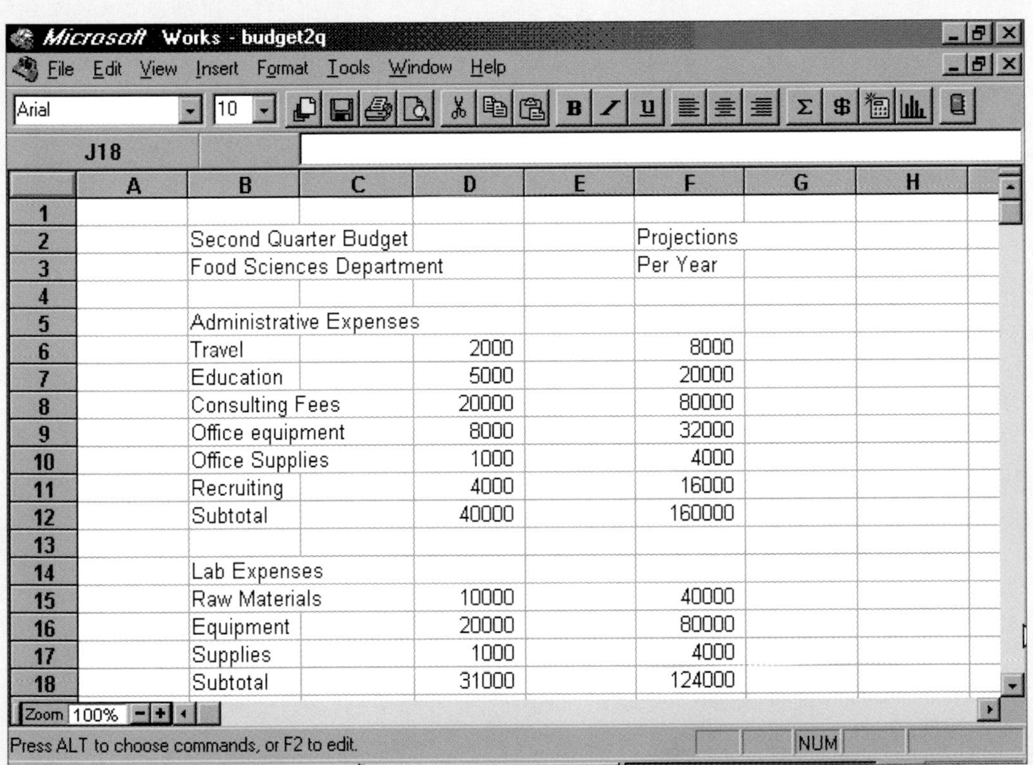


**4** Type ) to finish the formula and press Enter to place the new formula in the cell. Works will add all the cells in the block you selected and display the total in the cell containing the formula. If you selected any blank or text cells, works will count them as zero.

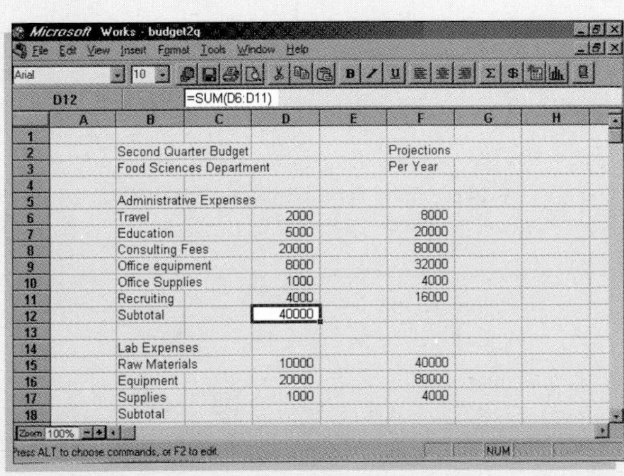

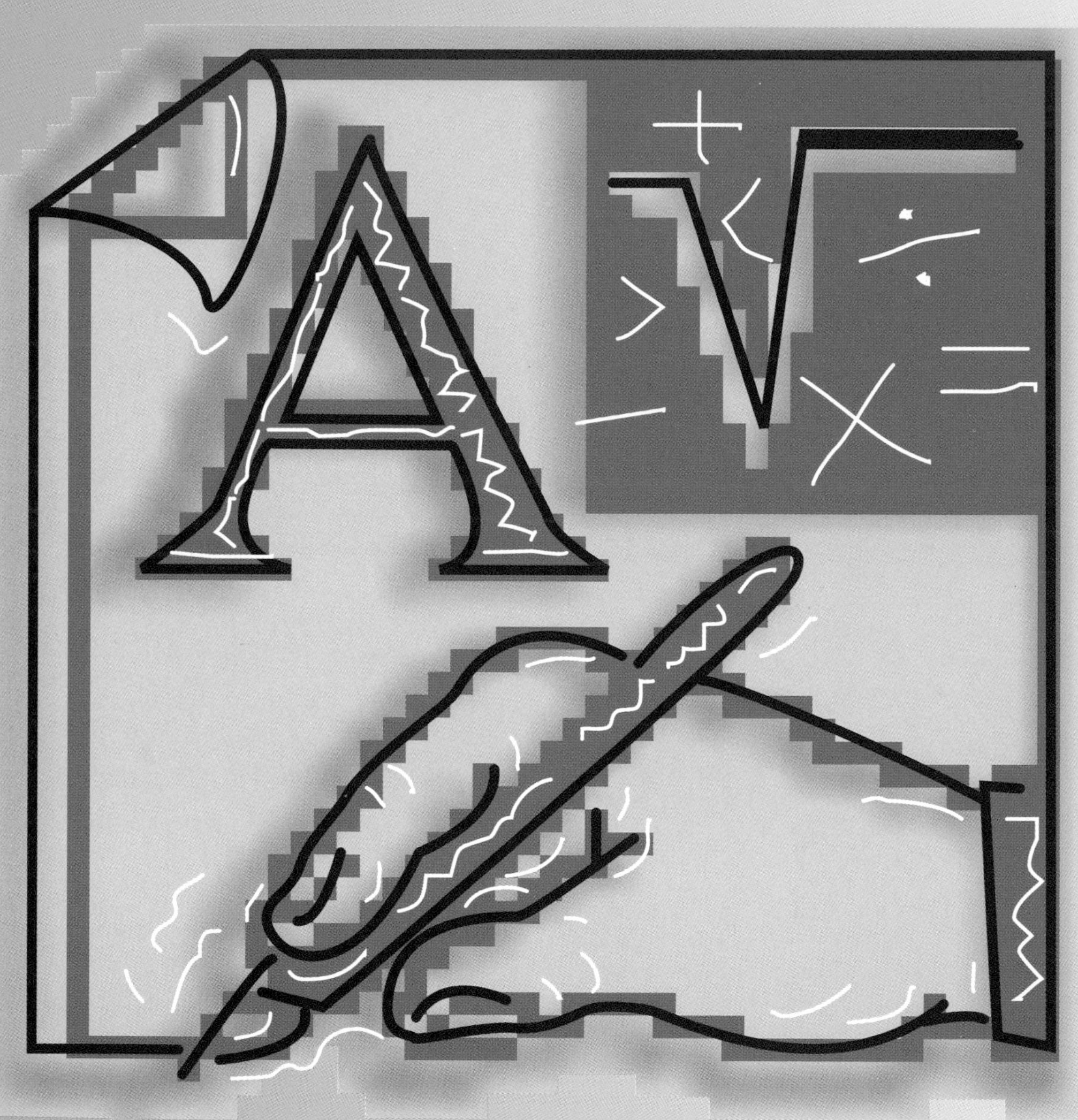

# CHAPTER 11

# Editing Cells in a Spreadsheet

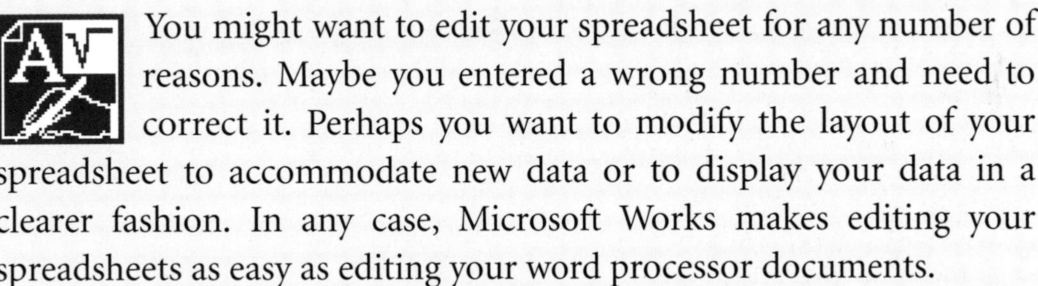

You might want to edit your spreadsheet for any number of reasons. Maybe you entered a wrong number and need to correct it. Perhaps you want to modify the layout of your spreadsheet to accommodate new data or to display your data in a clearer fashion. In any case, Microsoft Works makes editing your spreadsheets as easy as editing your word processor documents.

In Chapter 5 you learned several techniques for editing word processor documents. Most of these have direct equivalents for when you're editing spreadsheets. Navigation, insert and delete, copy and paste, drag and drop—Works brings all of these to the spreadsheet, slightly modified for working with cells instead of text.

# How to Navigate to Another Part of a Spreadsheet

With one exception, navigating through a spreadsheet is much the same as navigating through a word processor document. The exception arises because spreadsheets can be dozens of times wider than the window you see on your computer screen. Not only do you have to navigate spreadsheets vertically, you also have to navigate them horizontally.

Spreadsheets in Works can contain up to 16,384 rows and 256 columns. As you might guess, the rows are numbered 1 through 16,384, but with only 26 letters in the alphabet, you may wonder how Works keeps track of so many columns. The answer is straightforward. The first 26 columns are named columns A–Z; the second 26, AA–AZ; the third 26, BA–BZ; and so on. Few Works users ever venture out beyond the standard alphabet, but it's nice to know that there's room to spread out if you ever get claustrophobic.

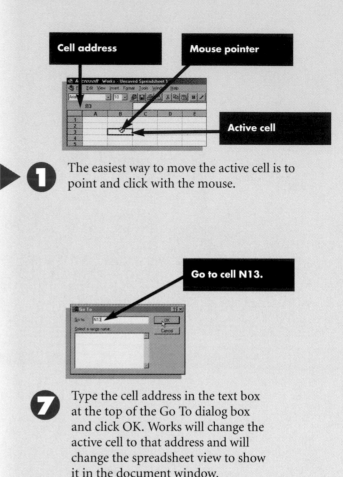

**TIP SHEET**

- **To navigate within the bounds of your past work, try the Home and End keys. The Home key will move the active cell and the spreadsheet view to column A in your current row. The End key will move you to the rightmost column in which you have worked.**
- **Press the Ctrl and Home keys together (Ctrl+Home) to move the active cell and the spreadsheet view to cell A1. Press Ctrl+End to move to the cell marking both the rightmost column and bottommost row in which you have worked.**

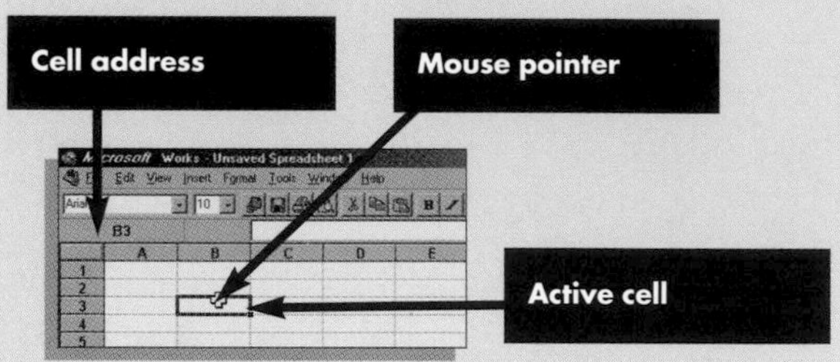


**1** The easiest way to move the active cell is to point and click with the mouse.

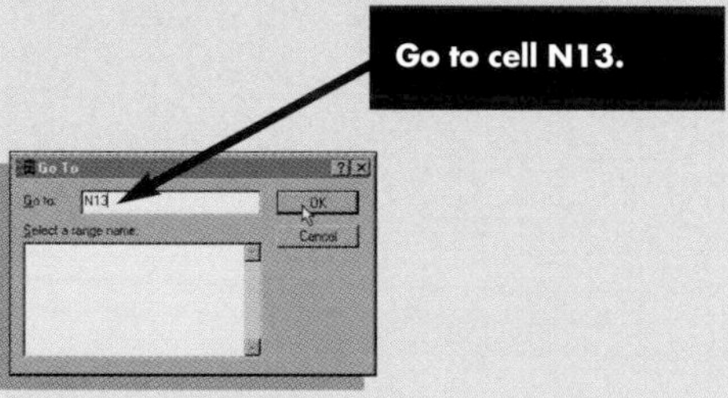


**7** Type the cell address in the text box at the top of the Go To dialog box and click OK. Works will change the active cell to that address and will change the spreadsheet view to show it in the document window.

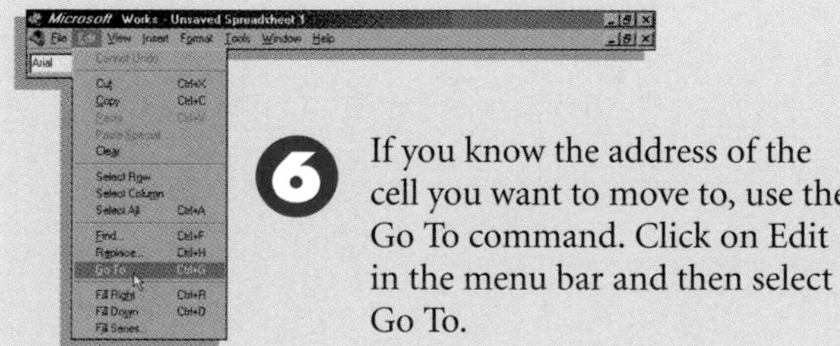

**6** If you know the address of the cell you want to move to, use the Go To command. Click on Edit in the menu bar and then select Go To.

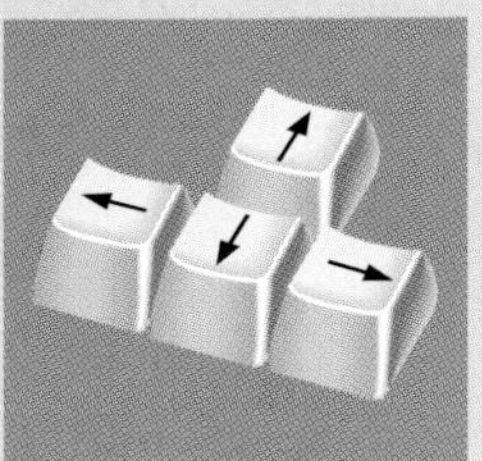

**2** The arrow keys on the keyboard let you move the insertion point one cell in any direction.

**3** The PgUp or PgDn key moves both the active cell and the spreadsheet view up or down by the amount you can see in the document window. Holding down the Ctrl key and then pressing the PgUp or PgDn key moves you respectively left or right by the amount you can see in the document window.

TO IV

TO 16,384

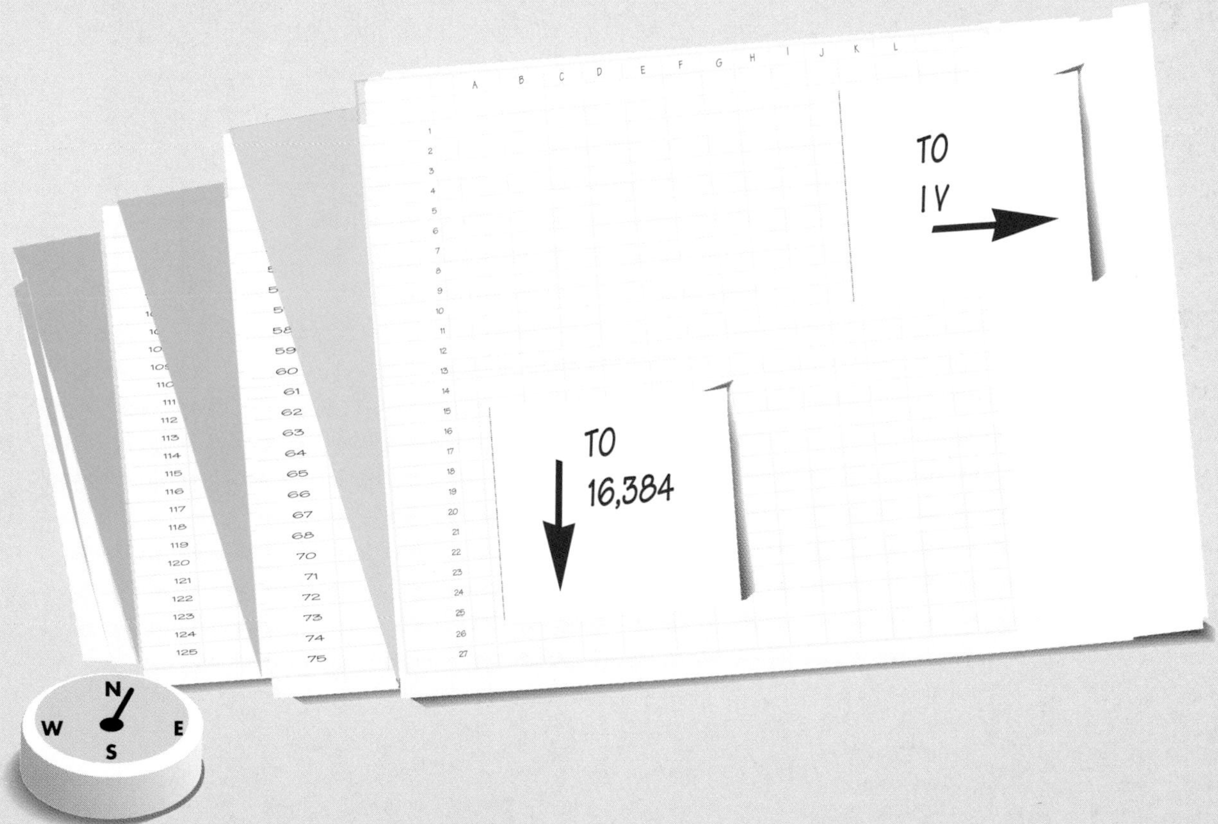

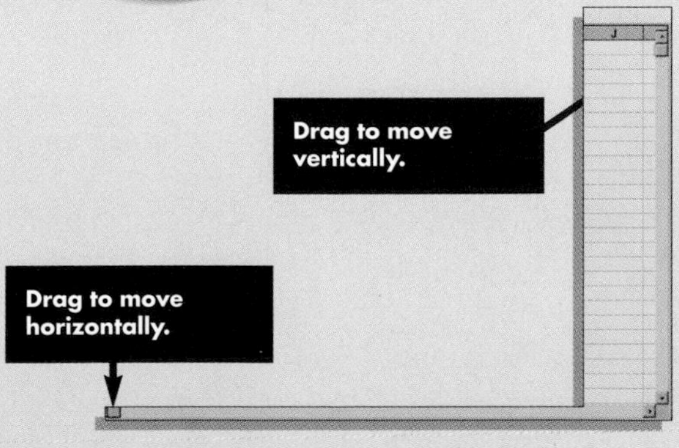

**5** Drag the scroll boxes in the vertical or horizontal scroll bar to move the spreadsheet view up and down, or left and right through the document.

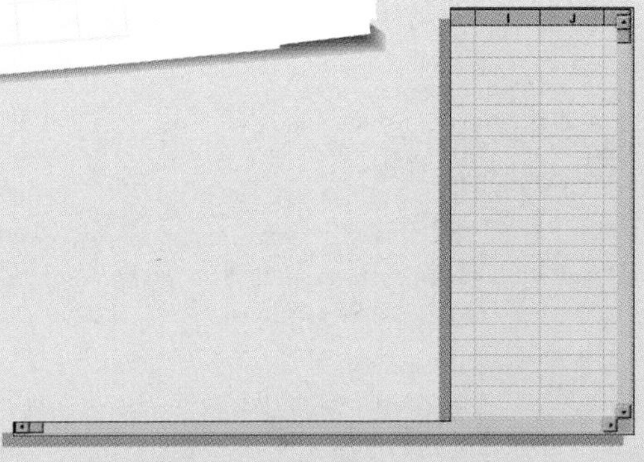

Drag to move vertically.

Drag to move horizontally.

**4** Click on the arrow buttons at the ends of the vertical scroll bars to move the spreadsheet up or down one cell at a time. Use the arrow buttons on the horizontal scroll bar to move the spreadsheet left or right one cell at a time.

# How to Move Cells

When working in spreadsheets, you'll frequently want to move the contents of cells from one location to another. You might do this to get old data out of the way of your new calculations, to bring numbers closer to the formulas that apply them, or to display information in a clearer and more concise fashion.

Moving cell contents brings up an important issue in addressing: What happens to the addresses contained in formulas that you move? As you might expect, Works automatically adjusts them.

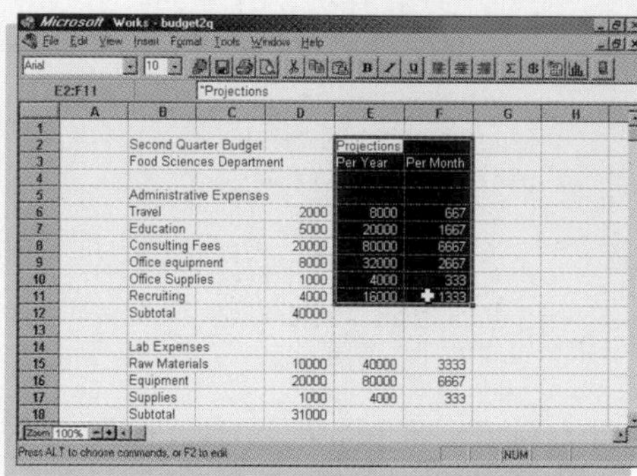

**1** As with the word processor, drag and drop is the easiest way to move the contents of a small group of cells a short distance. To select the cells to move, click and drag to highlight them.

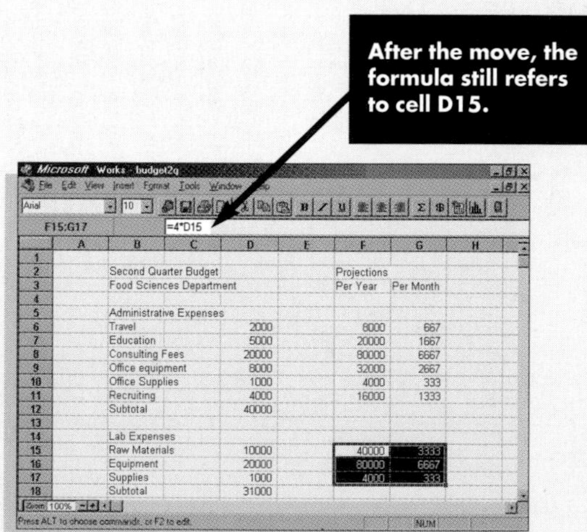

After the move, the formula still refers to cell D15.


**6** Select the top-left cell for the destination. This must be the same size and shape as the cut block of cells. Open the Edit menu again, and this time select Paste. Works will leave the cut cells' contents in the destination block.

**TIP SHEET**

- **If drag and drop isn't working on your computer, you can turn it on in the Options dialog box. Click once on the Tools menu, and then select Options. In the Options dialog box, select General and then click near the lower-left corner of the Options dialog box to place a check mark on the Drag and Drop check box. Click on OK to close the dialog box and activate drag and drop.**
- **When pasting a block of cells, you needn't select the full destination block. It's easier to select only the upper-left cell instead. The cut block will overwrite the cells below and to the right of the single destination cell you choose. Be careful when you do this, since you can easily overwrite cells unintentionally.**
- **If you want to cancel a drag and drop after you begin, simply drag the destination outline back over the selected block of cells and release the mouse button. Works will drop them right where it picked them up.**
- **Whether you use cut and paste or drag and drop, Works will move all the cell contents—text, numbers, formulas, and their formatting—to the new destination.**

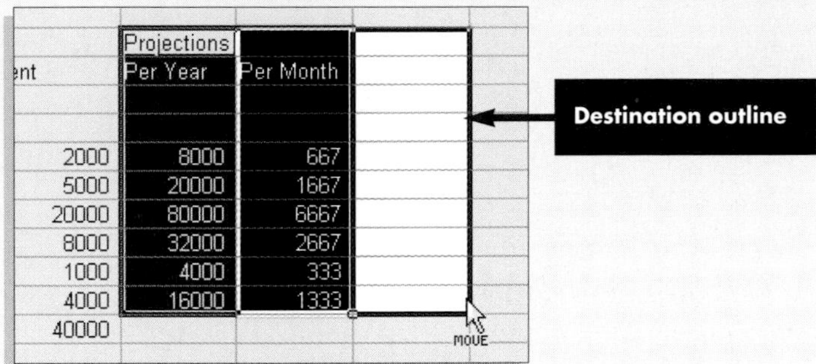
Destination outline

**2** To move the cell contents, position the mouse pointer over the border of the selection so that it changes to the DRAG pointer.

**3** Click the mouse button and drag the pointer to the desired location. As you drag, the pointer will change to read MOVE, and an outline of the selected cells will follow the pointer to show you their destination. Release the mouse button to place the cells in their new location.

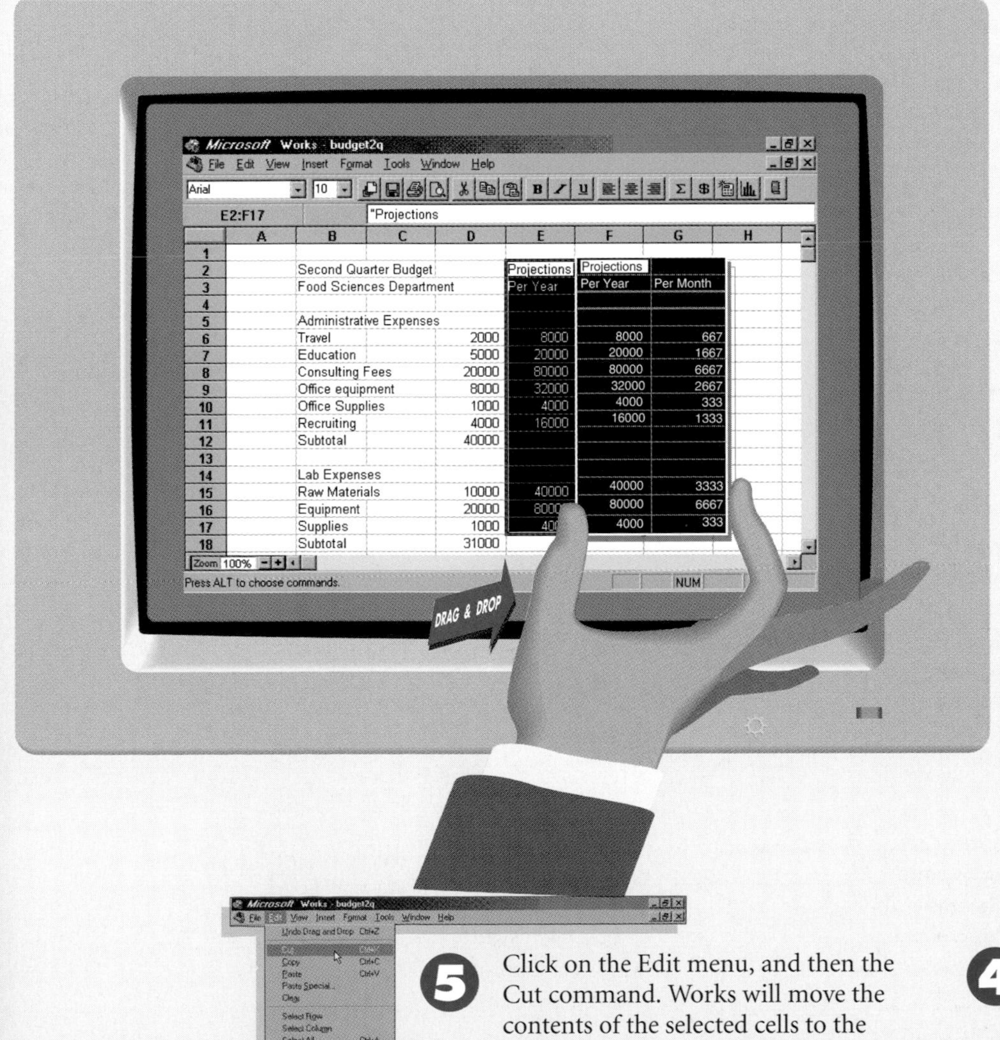
DRAG & DROP

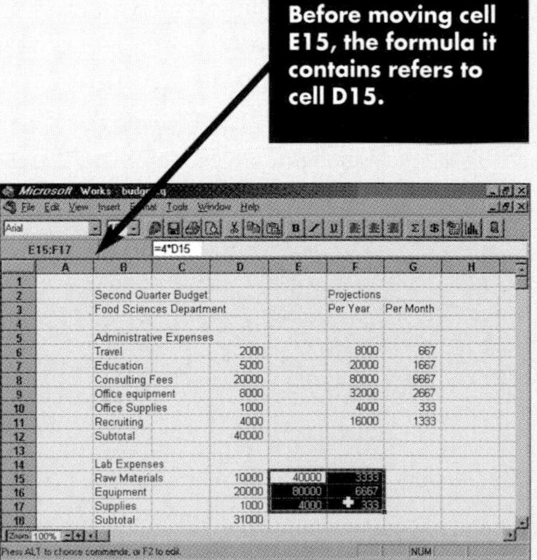
Before moving cell E15, the formula it contains refers to cell D15.

**4** Cut and paste is the easiest way to move the contents of a large block of cells any distance, or any block of cells a long distance. To move a block of text using cut and paste, start by selecting the block of text to move.

**5** Click on the Edit menu, and then the Cut command. Works will move the contents of the selected cells to the Windows Clipboard which, as you learned in Chapter 5, is a temporary holding place for data.

# How to Copy Cells

Copying cells is an easy way to fill out your spreadsheet. For example, you might want to repeat the same number several times. For saving time and improving accuracy, copying makes a lot of sense.

Copying formulas is another way to save time and improve accuracy. As you might expect, Works treats addresses contained in formulas the same when copying formulas as it does when moving them. When you copy a formula from one part of a spreadsheet to another, Works treats the addresses as relative to the cell you copy. A relative address is an address relative to another address. For example, "the house next door" and "the cell to the left" are both relative addresses. They both relate the address to your current location.

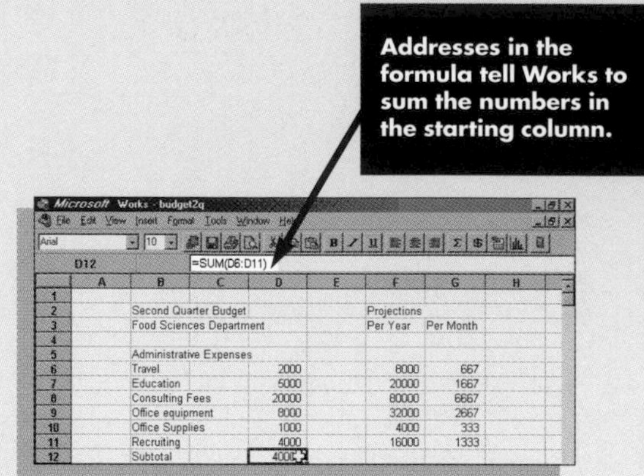
Addresses in the formula tell Works to sum the numbers in the starting column.
=SUM(D6:D11)

**1** Just as with moving cells, drag and drop is the easiest way to move a copy of a small group of cells a short distance. Use the mouse pointer to select the cells to copy.

## TIP SHEET

- **Works has a simple technique for copying the contents of one cell to many cells in a block. Copy the cell to the Clipboard as explained in step 5. Instead of selecting one cell as a destination, as you would in step 7, select a block of cells. Works will paste the contents of the one cell you copied to all the cells of the destination block. This is especially useful for filling columns or rows with repeating data or formulas.**
- **After you paste cells from the Clipboard, a copy remains there allowing you to paste them again and again. Windows will leave the cells there until you perform a new Cut or Copy command.**
- **Whenever you copy text, be sure to examine the destination to make sure that all of the data and formulas transferred correctly, and that nothing important was overwritten.**

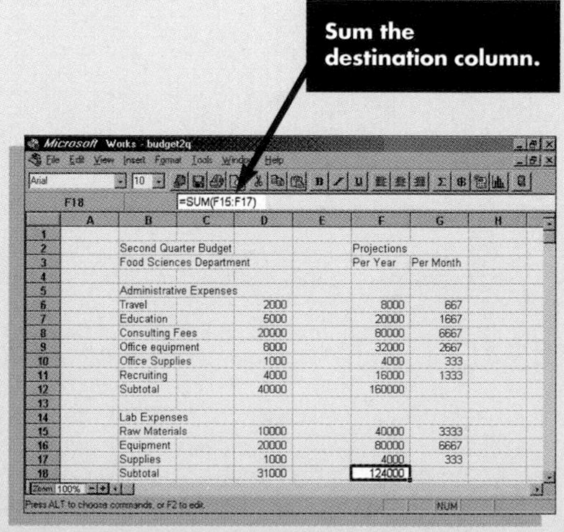
Sum the destination column.
=SUM(F15:F17)

**7** Select the top-left cell for the destination. Open the Edit menu again, and this time select Paste. Works will copy the selected cells to the destination block.

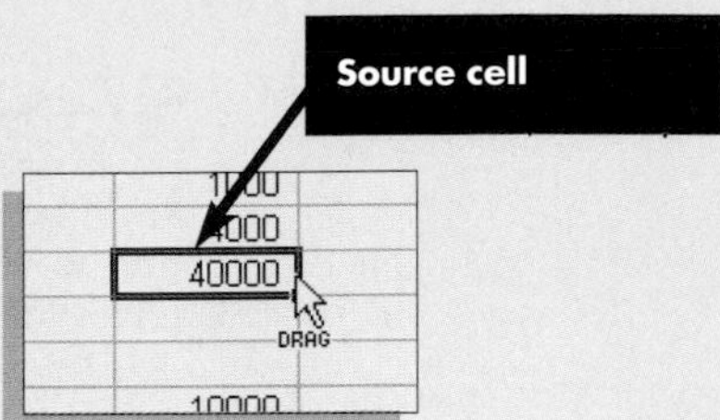


**2** To copy the cell's contents, position the mouse pointer over the border of the selection so that it changes to the DRAG pointer.

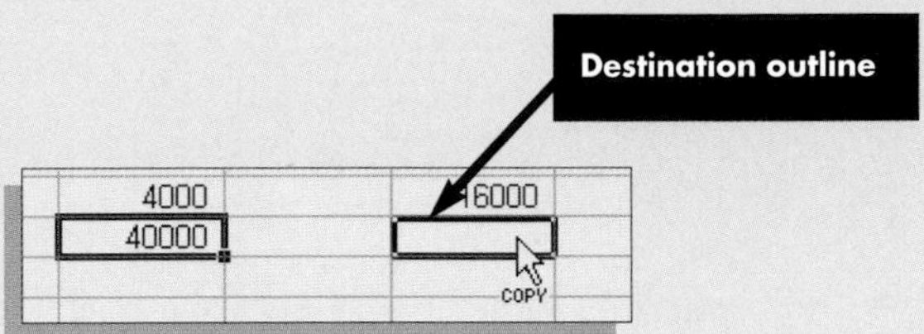


**3** Hold down the Ctrl key on the keyboard, and then click and drag the mouse button. As you drag, the pointer will change to COPY, and an outline of the selected cells will follow the pointer to show you the destination.

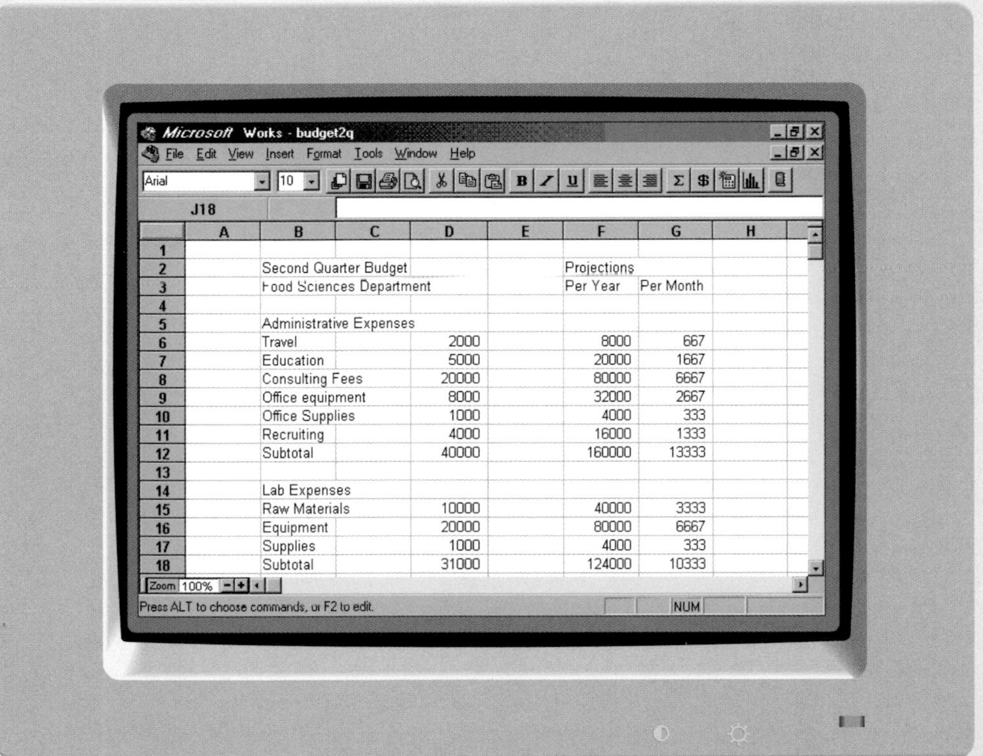


| | A | B | C | D | E | F | G | H |
|---|---|---|---|---|---|---|---|---|
| 1 | | | | | | | | |
| 2 | | Second Quarter Budget | | | | Projections | | |
| 3 | | Food Sciences Department | | | | Per Year | Per Month | |
| 4 | | | | | | | | |
| 5 | | Administrative Expenses | | | | | | |
| 6 | | Travel | | 2000 | | 8000 | 667 | |
| 7 | | Education | | 5000 | | 20000 | 1667 | |
| 8 | | Consulting Fees | | 20000 | | 80000 | 6667 | |
| 9 | | Office equipment | | 8000 | | 32000 | 2667 | |
| 10 | | Office Supplies | | 1000 | | 4000 | 333 | |
| 11 | | Recruiting | | 4000 | | 16000 | 1333 | |
| 12 | | Subtotal | | 40000 | | 160000 | 13333 | |
| 13 | | | | | | | | |
| 14 | | Lab Expenses | | | | | | |
| 15 | | Raw Materials | | 10000 | | 40000 | 3333 | |
| 16 | | Equipment | | 20000 | | 80000 | 6667 | |
| 17 | | Supplies | | 1000 | | 4000 | 333 | |
| 18 | | Subtotal | | 31000 | | 124000 | 10333 | |

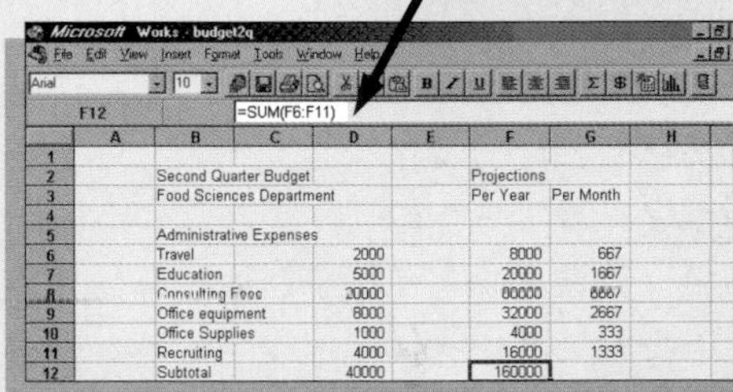


**4** When you finish the copying, the addresses from the original column change to addresses in the destination column.

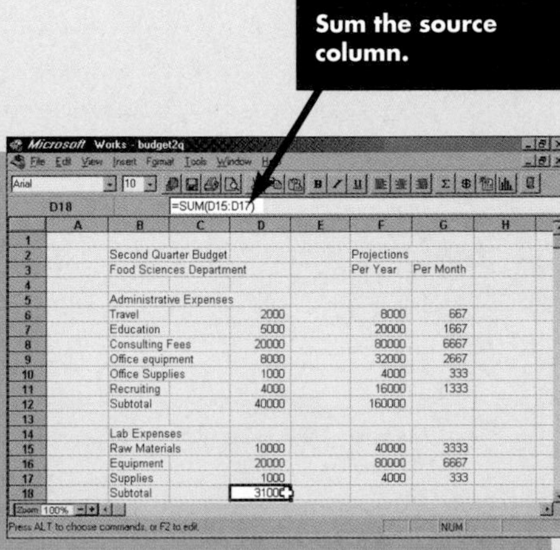


**5** To copy the contents of any block of cells a long distance or a large block of cells at all, use copy and paste. Start by selecting cells to copy.

**6** Click on the Edit menu, and then select Copy. Works will copy the contents of the selected cells to the Windows Clipboard.

# How to Remove Information from Cells

For some spreadsheet users, clearing cells can be like cleaning out the garbage. They keep unused or irrelevant data lying around their spreadsheets until they can't tell what's worth keeping and what's not.

The balance between showing too much on a spreadsheet and too little can be difficult to judge. When using a spreadsheet to perform complex calculations, it's generally best to delete information as soon as you know you won't need it again. Irrelevant data can easily be confused for the data you need to do your calculations. Of course, deleting formulas that you might need to justify your calculations might be going a little too far.

When using a spreadsheet for a presentation, it's generally best to show as little information as you can and still make your point. The simpler your spreadsheet appears, the easier it will be for your viewers to understand. If it looks too complex, it probably is. You might try breaking it down into two separate sheets.

Cells to delete

**1** To delete the contents of a single cell or a range of cells, select the cells with your mouse. When you select the cells, you'll be selecting all of their contents for deletion.

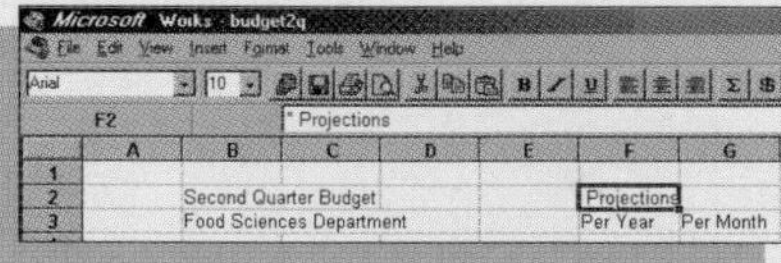


**6** Press Enter to keep the change you made to the cell. Press Esc to retain the cell's original contents.

## TIP SHEET

- **You can also use the Delete key to empty cells of their contents. Simply select the cells you want to clear and press the Delete key.**
- **When you clear cells using the techniques described in this chapter, you clear them of text, numbers, and formulas. Number and text formats (covered in Chapter 12), however, are left behind and will affect any new data you put in the cells.**

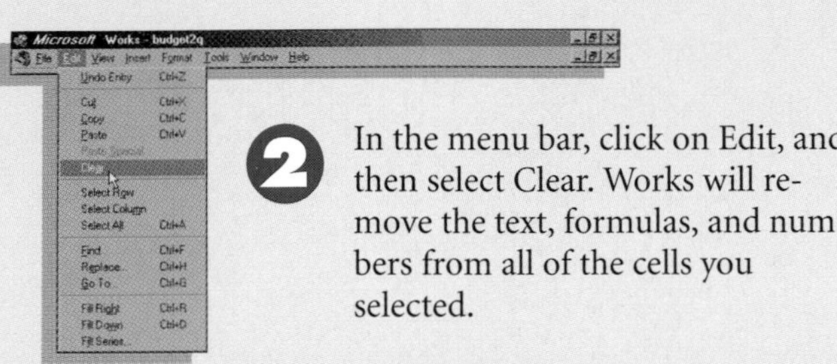

**2** In the menu bar, click on Edit, and then select Clear. Works will remove the text, formulas, and numbers from all of the cells you selected.

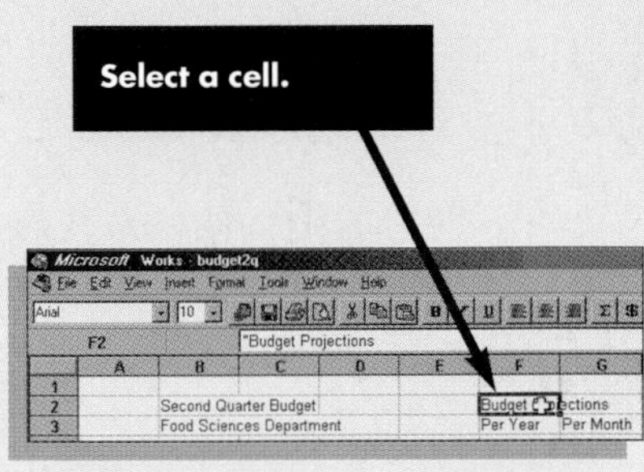


**3** To delete just a part of a cell's contents, start by selecting that cell.

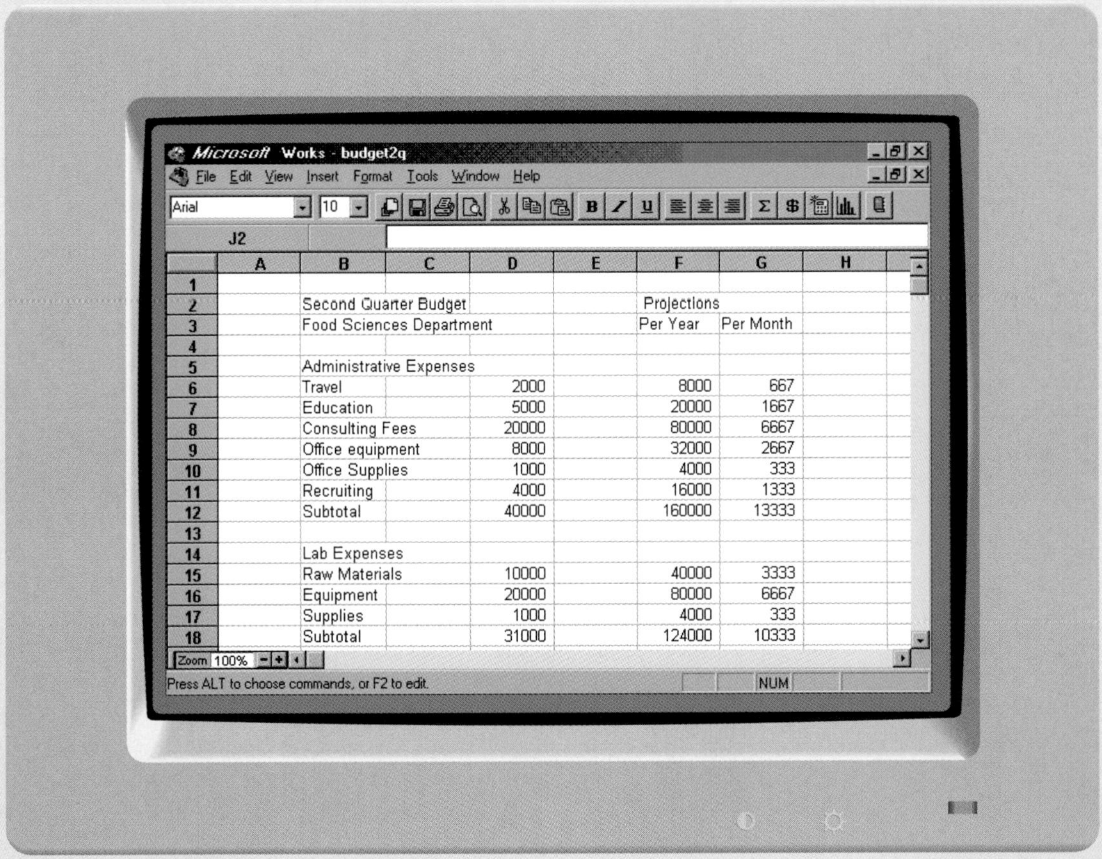


| | A | B | C | D | E | F | G | H |
|---|---|---|---|---|---|---|---|---|
| 1 | | | | | | | | |
| 2 | | Second Quarter Budget | | | | Projections | | |
| 3 | | Food Sciences Department | | | | Per Year | Per Month | |
| 4 | | | | | | | | |
| 5 | | Administrative Expenses | | | | | | |
| 6 | | Travel | | 2000 | | 8000 | 667 | |
| 7 | | Education | | 5000 | | 20000 | 1667 | |
| 8 | | Consulting Fees | | 20000 | | 80000 | 6667 | |
| 9 | | Office equipment | | 8000 | | 32000 | 2667 | |
| 10 | | Office Supplies | | 1000 | | 4000 | 333 | |
| 11 | | Recruiting | | 4000 | | 16000 | 1333 | |
| 12 | | Subtotal | | 40000 | | 160000 | 13333 | |
| 13 | | | | | | | | |
| 14 | | Lab Expenses | | | | | | |
| 15 | | Raw Materials | | 10000 | | 40000 | 3333 | |
| 16 | | Equipment | | 20000 | | 80000 | 6667 | |
| 17 | | Supplies | | 1000 | | 4000 | 333 | |
| 18 | | Subtotal | | 31000 | | 124000 | 10333 | |

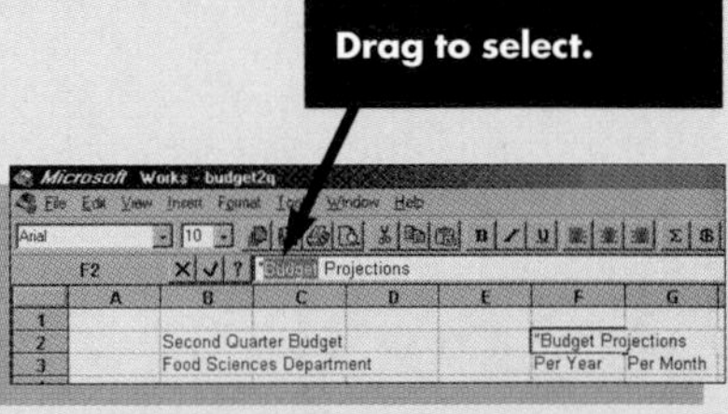


**4** In the Formula bar, click and drag with the mouse to select the portion of the cell's contents that you want to delete.

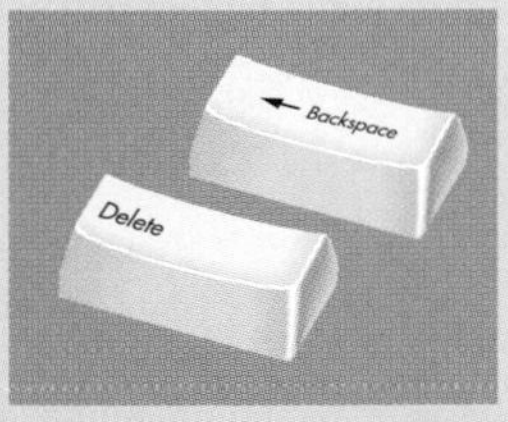


**5** Press either the Backspace or Delete key to remove the selection from the Formula bar.

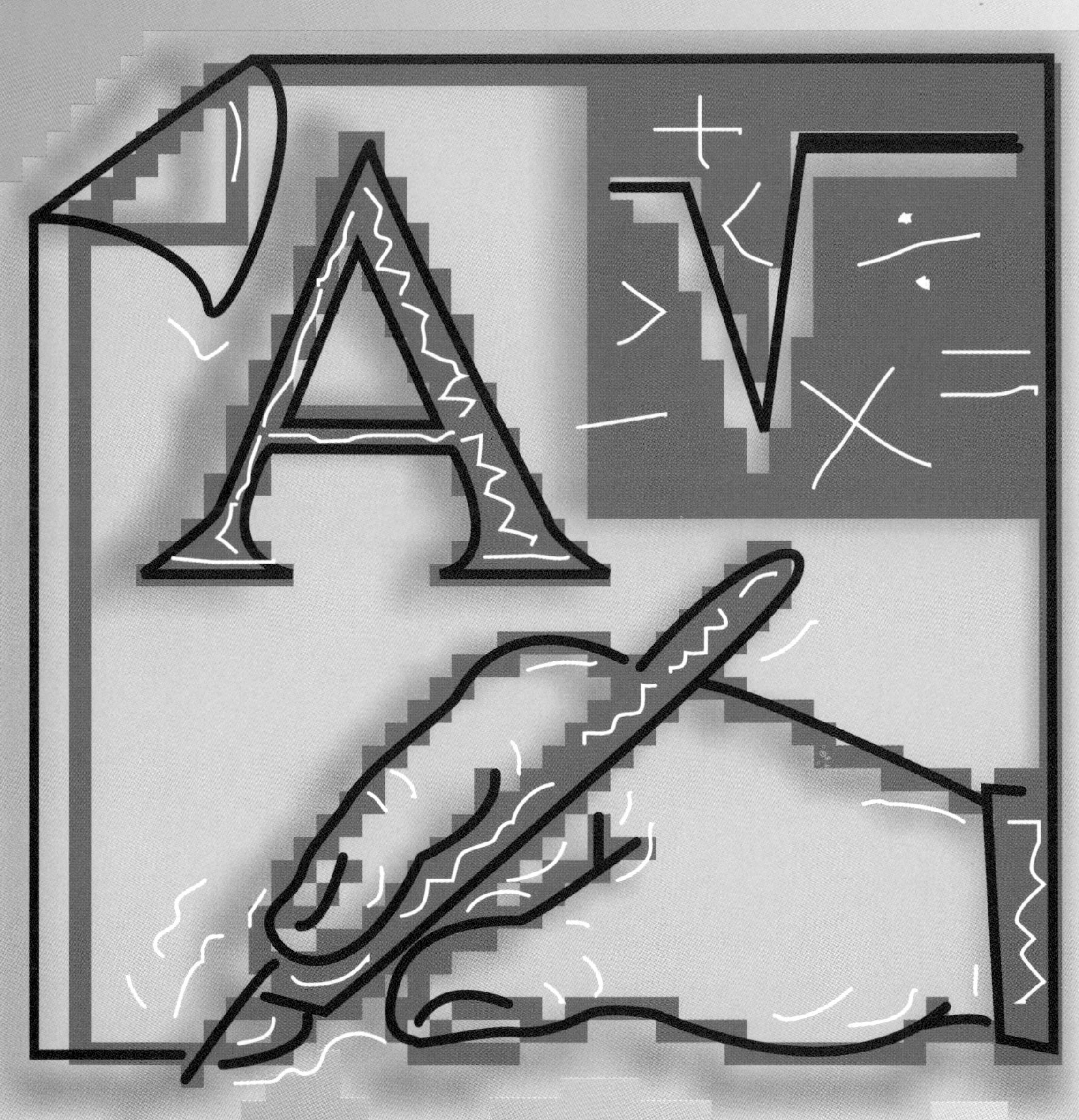

## CHAPTER 12

# Formatting and Printing a Spreadsheet

There are no hard-and-fast rules when it comes to formatting a spreadsheet, but you should still keep in mind a few basic goals.

The first goal of formatting a spreadsheet is neatness. You want your reader to realize that you've been careful and thorough in your calculations, and displaying your information neatly will create a good first impression.

After the first impression, you need to communicate as much information as possible to your reader. While much of this task is the reader's responsibility, there are steps you can take to make that task easier. Organize your spreadsheet so that its results, or conclusions, are easy to find. The data supporting the conclusions should be easily locatable, but it needs to take a backseat to the conclusions.

Aside from demonstrating these general ideas, the best spreadsheets also have a few similar the following features. Using the table format presents data neatly and suggests relationships among entries. Clear and concise labels tell the reader what every piece of data is. Finally, simplicity makes your conclusions clear by reducing reader distraction, so limit each table to one conclusion and its supporting data.

# How to Format Numbers

Number formatting is the easiest, and often the most important, way to make your spreadsheet clearer and easier to understand. Microsoft Works has 12 basic options for formatting numbers. They range from displaying numbers as fractions, to scientific notation, to times and dates.

**TIP SHEET**

- **If you apply a number format to an empty cell or to a cell containing a label, you won't see any changes there. If you later enter a number into the cell, however, Works will remember the number format and apply it to your new entry.**
- **The General format allows Works to guess what format you want based on the number you type in. For example, Works will display only as many decimal places as it needs to and will convert long numbers to scientific notation. Works will also judge whether a number is a special case, like a time, based on the format in which you type it.**
- **If you move or copy cells in a spreadsheet, you'll copy the number formats along with the cell contents.**
- **You can enhance the text in your spreadsheet just like you did in the word processor. The Font and Style dialog box in the spreadsheet is exactly the same as the one in the word processor, minus the options for superscript and subscript. (See Chapter 6 if you need help enhancing text.)**

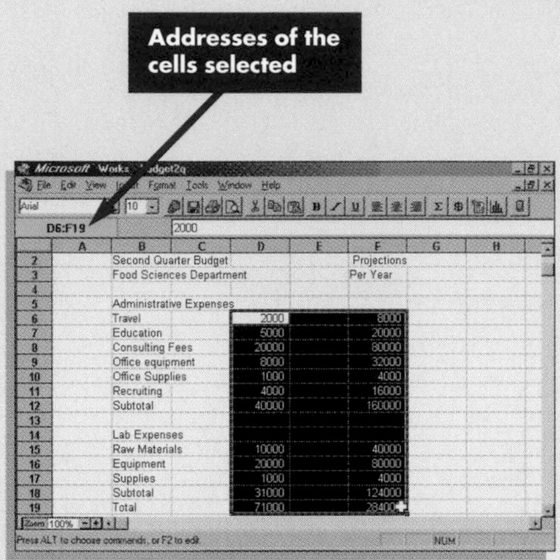


**1** Start by selecting the cell or cells containing the numbers you want to format. As usual, click and drag with the mouse to make a selection.

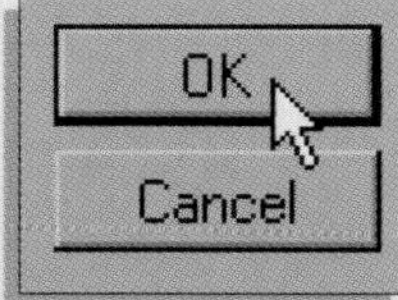


**5** When you have finished making your formatting choices, click the OK button to apply them to your cell selection.

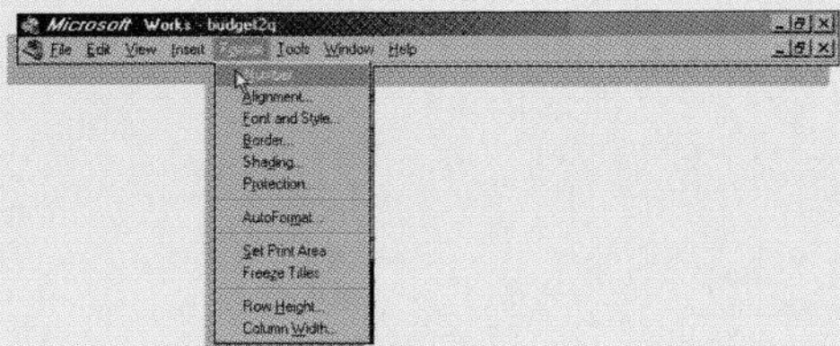

**2** Open the Format menu by clicking on it, and then select Number.

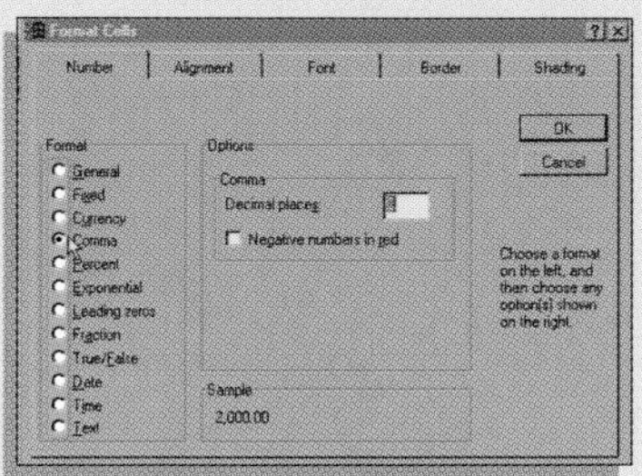

**3** In the Number dialog box, which opens next, click on one of the 12 formats. The sample at the bottom of the dialog box will change to reflect your selection.

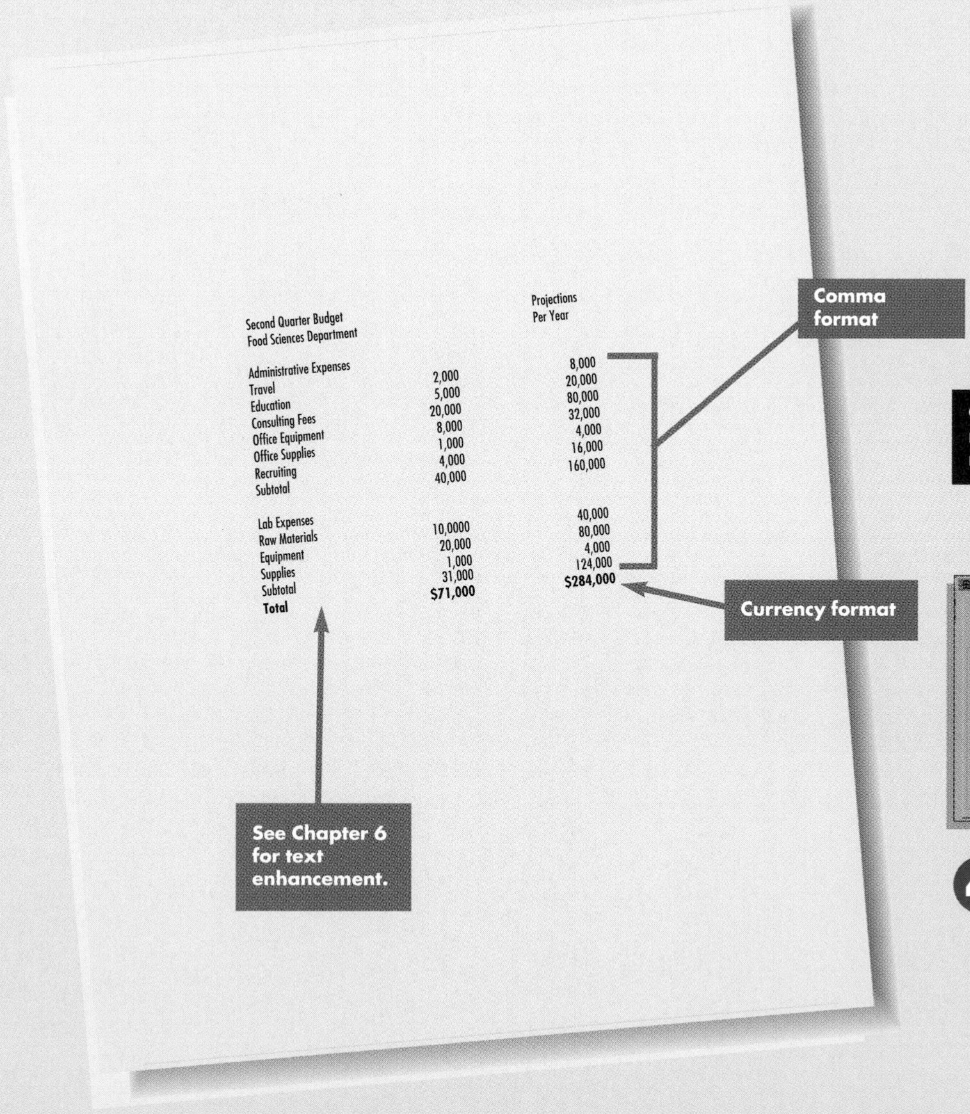

| Second Quarter Budget<br>Food Sciences Department | | Projections<br>Per Year |
|---|---|---|
| Administrative Expenses | | |
| Travel | 2,000 | 8,000 |
| Education | 5,000 | 20,000 |
| Consulting Fees | 20,000 | 80,000 |
| Office Equipment | 8,000 | 32,000 |
| Office Supplies | 1,000 | 4,000 |
| Recruiting | 4,000 | 16,000 |
| Subtotal | 40,000 | 160,000 |
| Lab Expenses | | |
| Raw Materials | 10,0000 | 40,000 |
| Equipment | 20,000 | 80,000 |
| Supplies | 1,000 | 4,000 |
| Subtotal | 31,000 | 124,000 |
| **Total** | **$71,000** | **$284,000** |

**Comma format**

**Currency format**

**See Chapter 6 for text enhancement.**

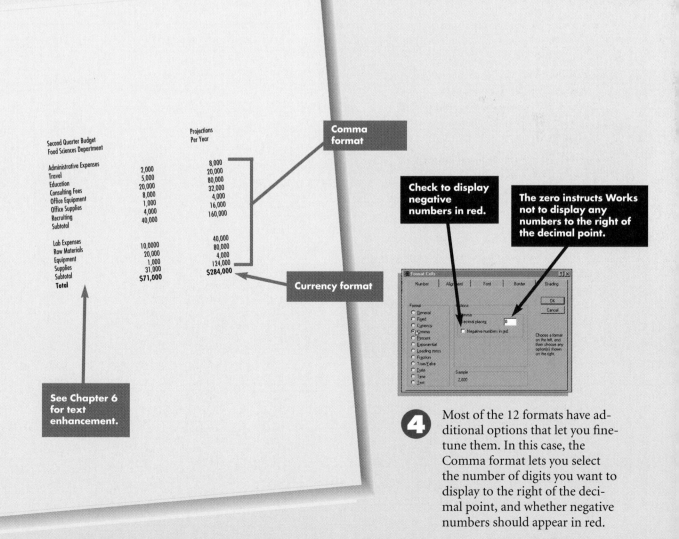

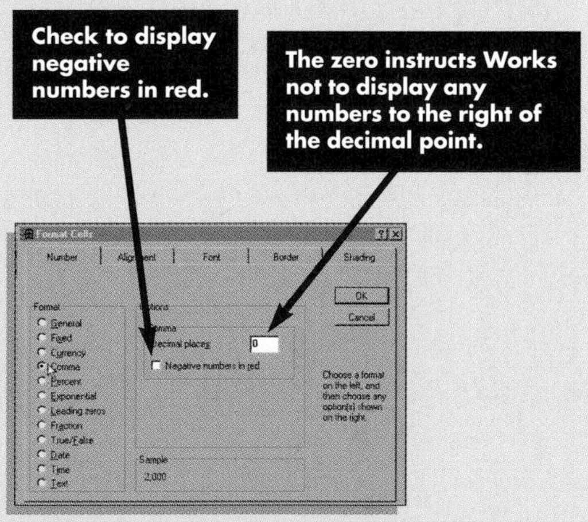

**Check to display negative numbers in red.**

**The zero instructs Works not to display any numbers to the right of the decimal point.**

**4** Most of the 12 formats have additional options that let you fine-tune them. In this case, the Comma format lets you select the number of digits you want to display to the right of the decimal point, and whether negative numbers should appear in red.

# How to Align Items in Cells

The alignment of information within cells can help your reader pick information out of your spreadsheet quickly and easily by providing subtle clues as to what that information is. For example, titles are often centered over the cells they describe, numbers are usually aligned on the right so that their decimal points coincide, and text labels describing individual cells are usually aligned on the left, like lines of text on a page. Of course, you can stray from these informal conventions, but always keep in mind how your changes will affect the readability of your spreadsheet.

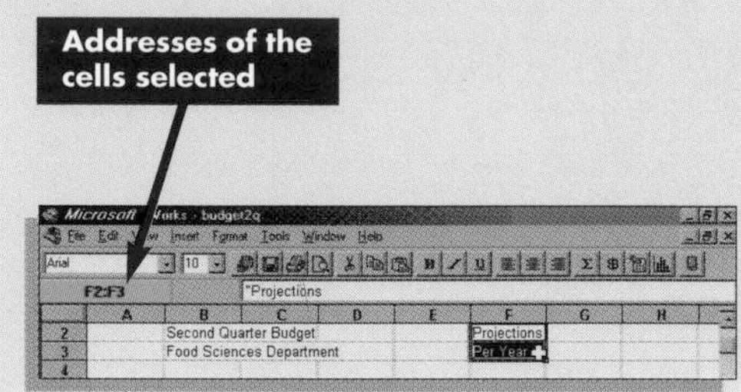


1. To set the alignment for a cell or group of cells, start by selecting the cells.

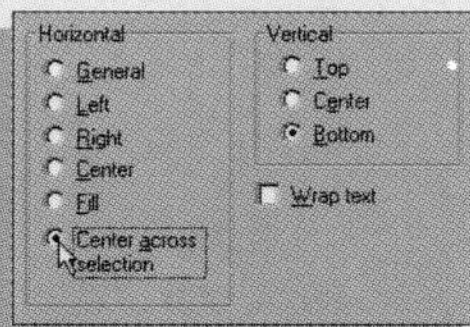


7. Follow steps 2 through 4 on this page. In step 3, select Center Across Selection in the Format Cells (Alignment) dialog box.

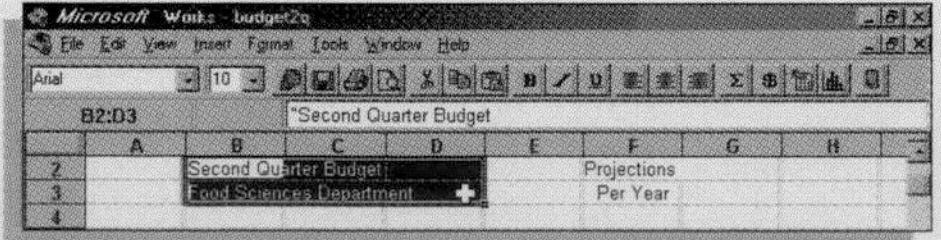


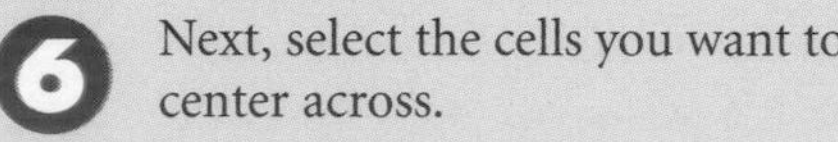

6. Next, select the cells you want to center across.

## TIP SHEET

- The General alignment option tells Works to guess what alignment you want based on the information you type in. For example, Works will left-align text labels and right-align numbers, dates, and times.
- The Fill alignment option tells Works to repeat the text in a cell from left to right. For example, you can create a simple border within your spreadsheet using a hyphen or asterisk with the Fill alignment option.
- The Wrap Text check box tells Works to break lines at the right edge of a cell to accommodate long text entries. The text will wrap to the next line, and the cell will automatically expand downward to fit it. This way, a long text label won't be covered up by the contents of the cell to the right.
- Besides fitting information to the cell that contains it, you can also change the cell to fit the information. To adjust column width to automatically fit the longest entry in the column, just double-click on the label at the top of the column (for example, A, B, C, and so on).

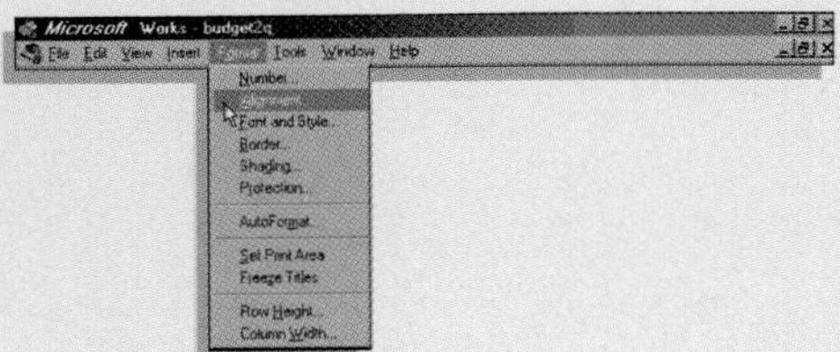

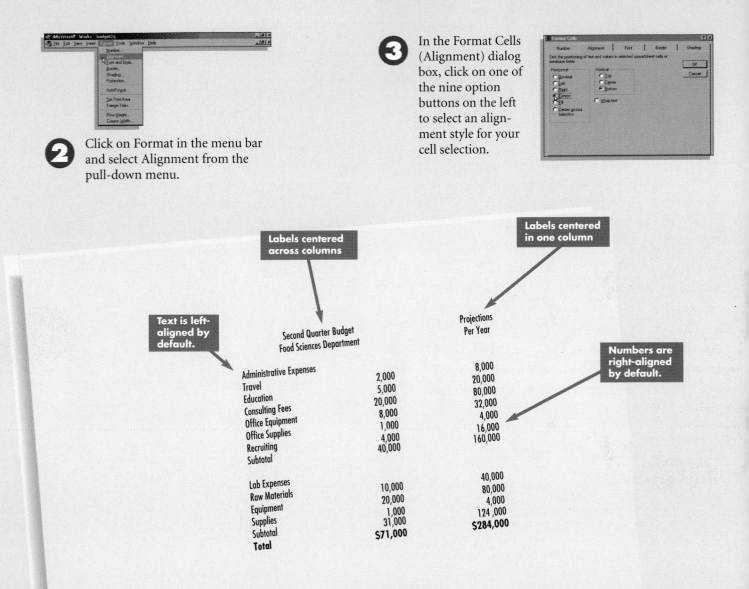

**2** Click on Format in the menu bar and select Alignment from the pull-down menu.

**3** In the Format Cells (Alignment) dialog box, click on one of the nine option buttons on the left to select an alignment style for your cell selection.

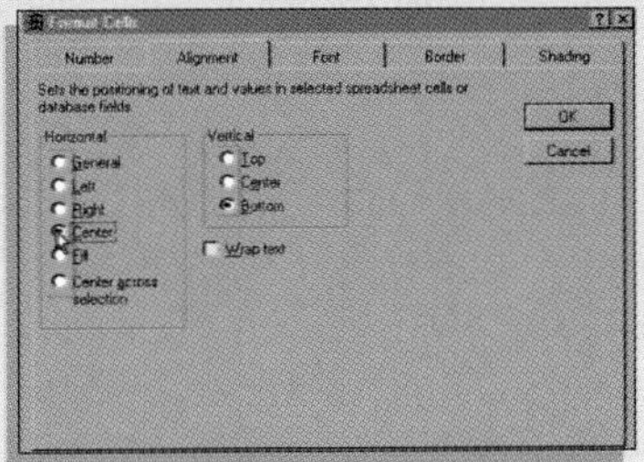


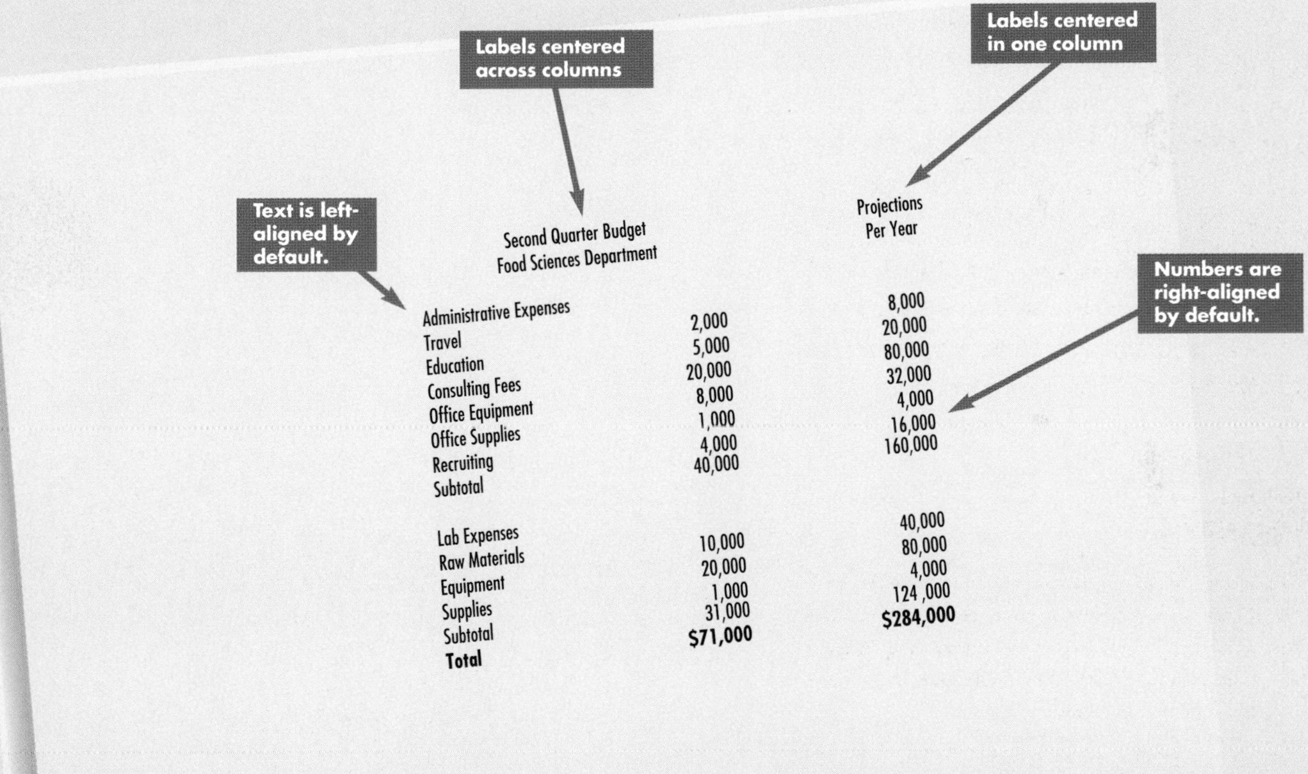


| Second Quarter Budget<br>Food Sciences Department | | Projections<br>Per Year |
|---|---|---|
| Administrative Expenses | | |
| Travel | 2,000 | 8,000 |
| Education | 5,000 | 20,000 |
| Consulting Fees | 20,000 | 80,000 |
| Office Equipment | 8,000 | 32,000 |
| Office Supplies | 1,000 | 4,000 |
| Recruiting | 4,000 | 16,000 |
| Subtotal | 40,000 | 160,000 |
| | | |
| Lab Expenses | | |
| Raw Materials | 10,000 | 40,000 |
| Equipment | 20,000 | 80,000 |
| Supplies | 1,000 | 4,000 |
| Subtotal | 31,000 | 124,000 |
| **Total** | **$71,000** | **$284,000** |

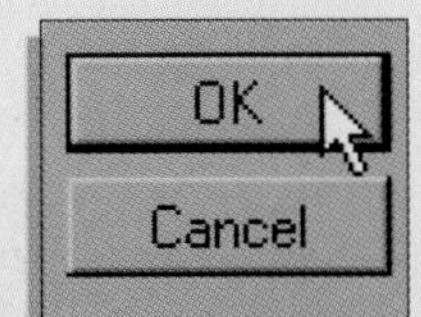


**4** Click on the OK button to align the items in the cells you selected.

**5** The Center Across Selection option is unique among alignment styles. It lets you take a cell entry in one column and center it across several columns. To start, you need to enter labels or numbers into cells in the leftmost column of the columns you want to center across.

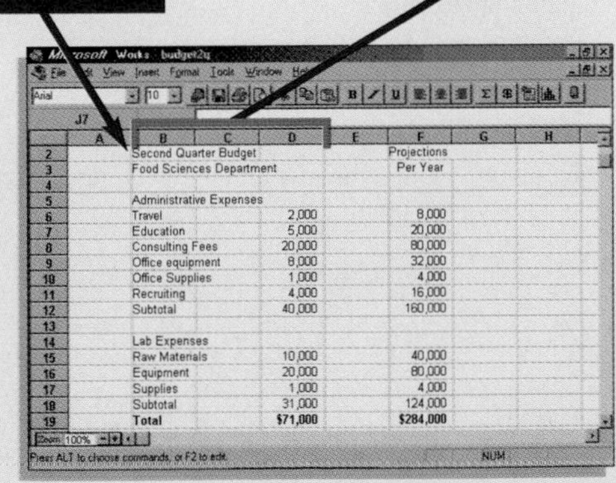


| | A | B | C | D | E | F |
|---|---|---|---|---|---|---|
| 2 | | Second Quarter Budget | | | | Projections |
| 3 | | Food Sciences Department | | | | Per Year |
| 4 | | | | | | |
| 5 | | Administrative Expenses | | | | |
| 6 | | Travel | | 2,000 | | 8,000 |
| 7 | | Education | | 5,000 | | 20,000 |
| 8 | | Consulting Fees | | 20,000 | | 80,000 |
| 9 | | Office equipment | | 8,000 | | 32,000 |
| 10 | | Office Supplies | | 1,000 | | 4,000 |
| 11 | | Recruiting | | 4,000 | | 16,000 |
| 12 | | Subtotal | | 40,000 | | 160,000 |
| 13 | | | | | | |
| 14 | | Lab Expenses | | | | |
| 15 | | Raw Materials | | 10,000 | | 40,000 |
| 16 | | Equipment | | 20,000 | | 80,000 |
| 17 | | Supplies | | 1,000 | | 4,000 |
| 18 | | Subtotal | | 31,000 | | 124,000 |
| 19 | | Total | | $71,000 | | $284,000 |

# How to Print a Spreadsheet

When you need to print your spreadsheet—maybe to impress the boss with your quantitative wizardry, maybe just to see all of your 15-page spreadsheet at one time—you'll find Works quite helpful. Printing spreadsheets is a little more complex than printing word processing documents, however, so you should know a few tricks to get just what you want.

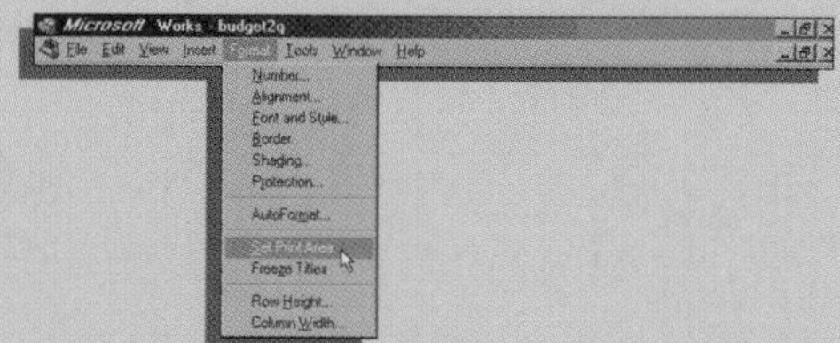

**1** Works will print your entire spreadsheet by default. If you want to print just a portion of it, select the portion you want to print, and then select Set Print Area from the Format menu.

**TIP SHEET**

- All of the changes you make in the Page Setup dialog box will apply to printing your entire spreadsheet.
- Because cells are so much wider than they are tall, you may want to print your spreadsheets in landscape mode (long edge of the paper horizontal). To do this, select the Source, Size, and Orientation tab in the Page Setup dialog box and click on the Landscape option button at the bottom of the dialog box. Click OK, and Works will print your spreadsheet in landscape mode from that time forward.
- Just as it did with the word processor, Works lets you print spreadsheets in the background. Once you start printing, you'll be able to continue using Works normally, while the computer takes care of the printing for you.

Type in the number of copies to print.

**7** To send your spreadsheet to the printer, select Print in the File menu to open the Print dialog box. Then, type in the number of copies you want to print and click OK.

**6** When you are through making selections in the Page Setup dialog box, click the OK button to apply your changes to the spreadsheet.

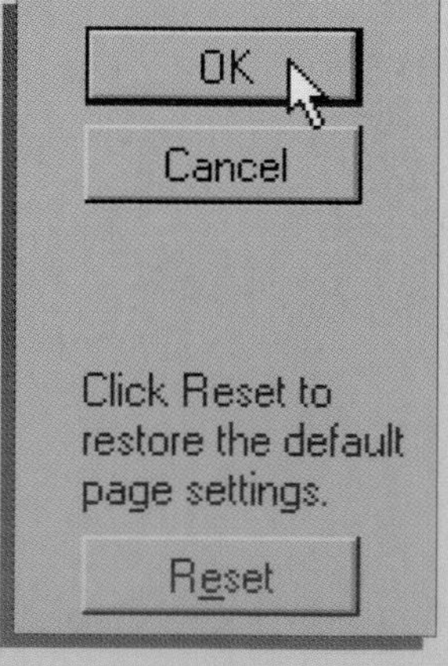
OK
Cancel
Click Reset to restore the default page settings.
Reset

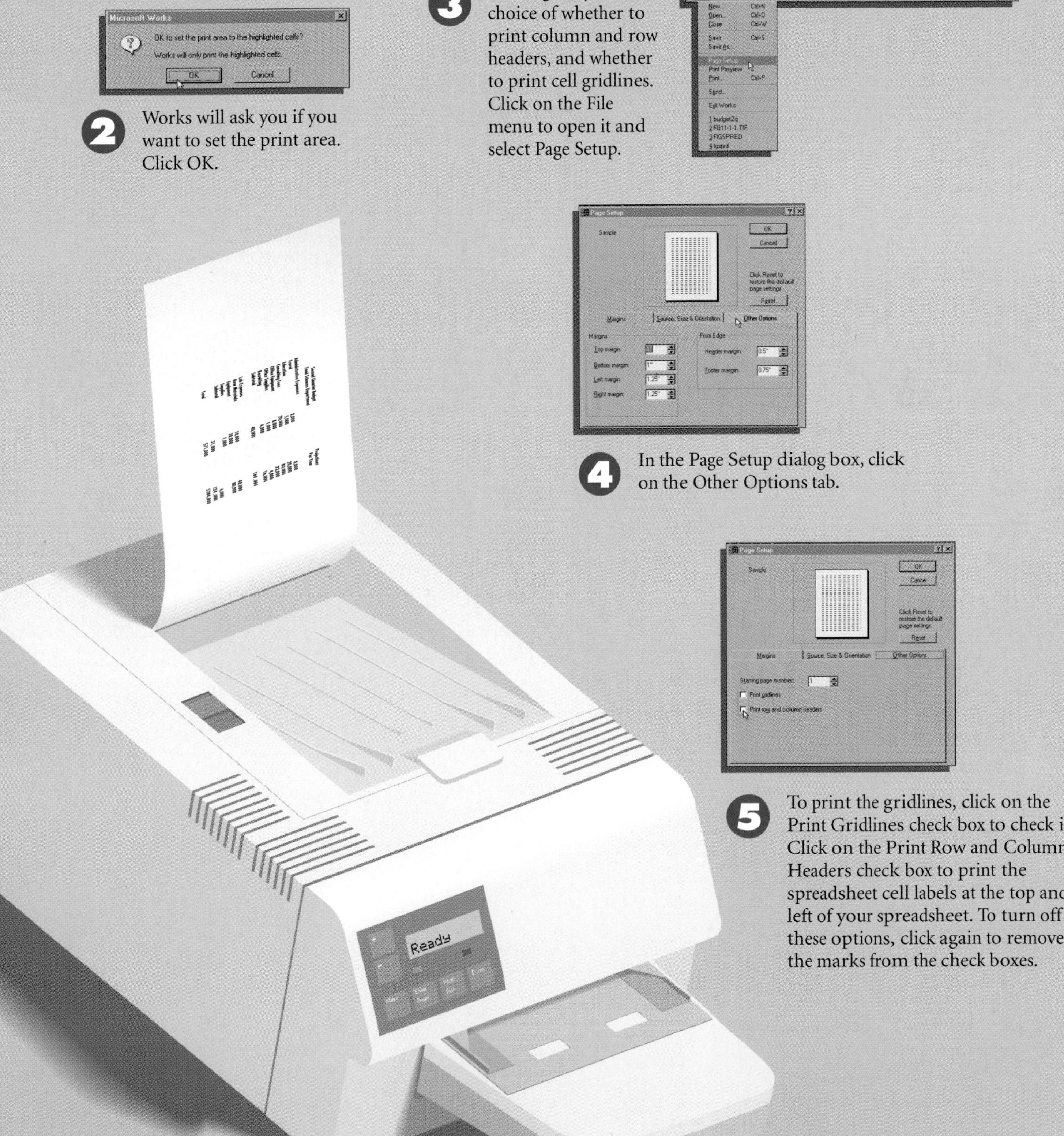

**2** Works will ask you if you want to set the print area. Click OK.

**3** Works gives you the choice of whether to print column and row headers, and whether to print cell gridlines. Click on the File menu to open it and select Page Setup.

**4** In the Page Setup dialog box, click on the Other Options tab.

**5** To print the gridlines, click on the Print Gridlines check box to check it. Click on the Print Row and Column Headers check box to print the spreadsheet cell labels at the top and left of your spreadsheet. To turn off these options, click again to remove the marks from the check boxes.

# TRY IT!

In the last four chapters, you assembled a solid collection of spreadsheet building and formatting techniques. Here is an opportunity to review these techniques and commit them to memory. Follow these steps to create this simple spreadsheet. All of the steps include chapter numbers in italics to help you review information on the skills required.

Start Works, and in the Task Launcher dialog box click on the Works Tools folder tab. *Chapter 9*

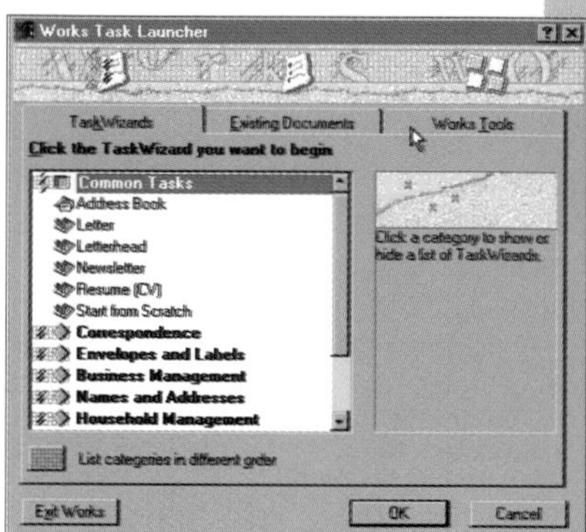


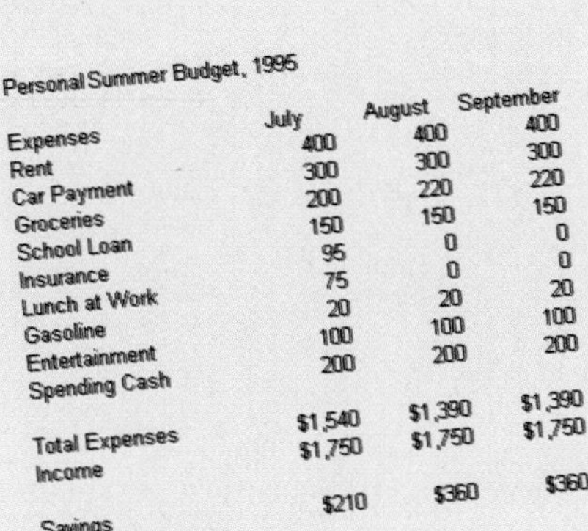

Personal Summer Budget, 1995

| Expenses | July | August | September |
|---|---|---|---|
| Rent | 400 | 400 | 400 |
| Car Payment | 300 | 300 | 300 |
| Groceries | 200 | 220 | 220 |
| School Loan | 150 | 150 | 150 |
| Insurance | 95 | 0 | 0 |
| Lunch at Work | 75 | 0 | 0 |
| Gasoline | 20 | 20 | 20 |
| Entertainment | 100 | 100 | 100 |
| Spending Cash | 200 | 200 | 200 |
| | | | |
| Total Expenses | $1,540 | $1,390 | $1,390 |
| Income | $1,750 | $1,750 | $1,750 |
| | | | |
| Savings | $210 | $360 | $360 |

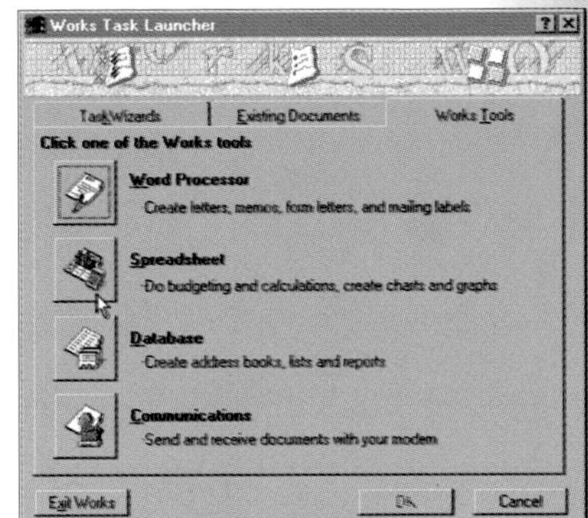


Click on the Spreadsheet button to create a new spreadsheet. *Chapter 9*

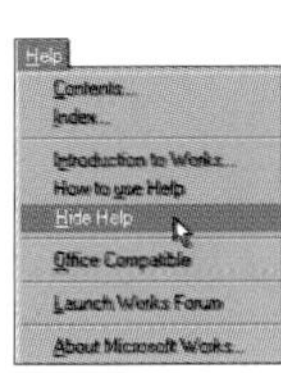


Remove the Help window by clicking on the Help menu. Then click on Hide Help. *Chapter 9*

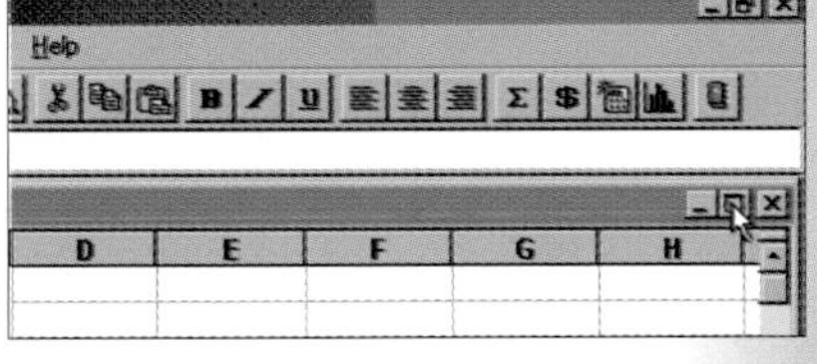


Maximize the document window by clicking on the Maximize button. *Chapter 9*

| Personal Summer Budget, 1995 | | | |
|---|---|---|---|
| Expenses | July | August | September |
| Rent | 400 | | |
| Car Payment | 300 | | |
| Groceries | 200 | | |
| School Loan | 150 | | |
| Insurance | 95 | | |
| Lunch at work | 75 | | |
| Gasoline | 20 | | |
| Entertainment | 100 | | |
| Spending Cash | 200 | | |
| Miscellaneous | | | |
| Total expenses | | | |
| Income | 1750 | | |
| Savings | | | |

This spreadsheet is a personal budget. Enter the preliminary data shown here. You may want to select block B2:D17 before you begin. *Chapter 9*

Get in the habit of saving your work early and often. Click on the Save button. *Chapter 9*

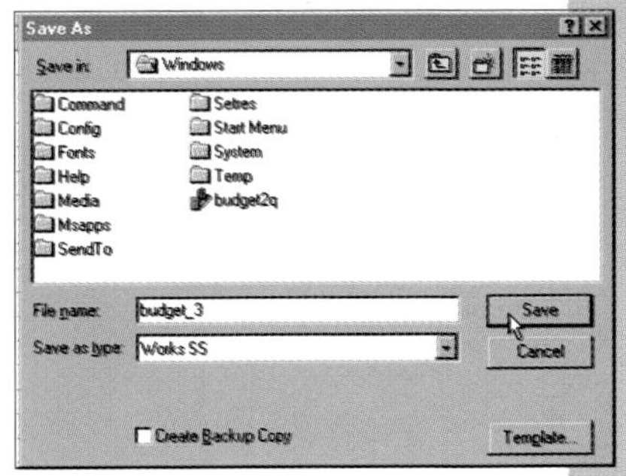


In the Save As dialog box, enter the name **budget_3** and click on Save. When you save your spreadsheet later, you won't have to enter the name again. *Chapter 9*

Click on cell D15, and double-click on the AutoSum button in the Toolbar. Works will write a formula in the cell to sum the column of numbers above. *Chapter 10*

Click on cell D17 and type the formula shown here into the formula bar. Press the Enter key on the keyboard when you are through. *Chapter 10*

|  | A | B | C | D |
|---|---|---|---|---|
| 1 | | | | |
| 2 | | Personal summer Budget, 1995 | | |
| 3 | | | | |
| 4 | | Expenses | | July |
| 5 | | Rent | | 400 |
| 6 | | Car Payment | | 300 |
| 7 | | Groceries | | 200 |
| 8 | | School Loan | | 150 |
| 9 | | Insurance | | 95 |
| 10 | | Lunch at Work | | 75 |
| 11 | | Gasoline | | 20 |
| 12 | | Entertainment | | 100 |
| 13 | | Spending Cash | | 200 |
| 14 | | Miscellaneous | | |
| 15 | | Total Expenses | | 1540 |
| 16 | | Income | | 1750 |
| 17 | | Savings | | |
| 18 | | | | |

Move the contents of row 17 down so that the information will stand out more. Select cells B17 through D17 (B17:D17) by clicking and dragging. *Chapter 10*

Continue to next page ▶

# TRY IT!

Continue below

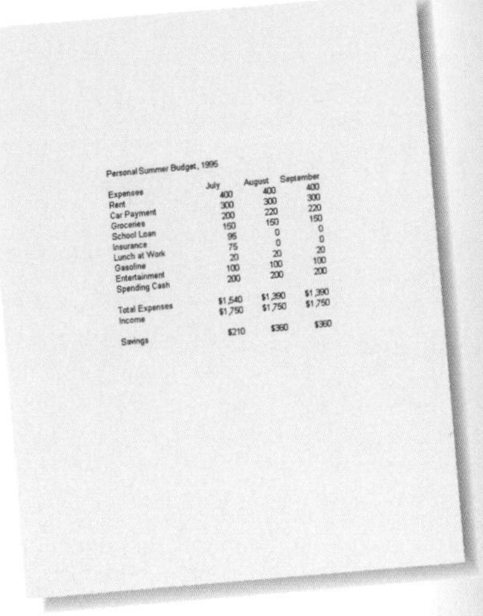

**15**

Click on Edit in the menu bar again, but this time select Paste. Works will copy the contents of column D to columns E and F simultaneously. *Chapter 11*

Move the mouse pointer over the border of the selection so that it changes to the DRAG pointer. *Chapter 11*

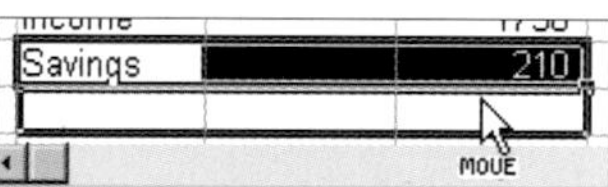


Drag straight down one row. Release the mouse button to drop the cells. *Chapter 11*

**13**

Select cells D5:D18. Click on Edit in the menu bar, and select Copy. *Chapter 11*

**14**

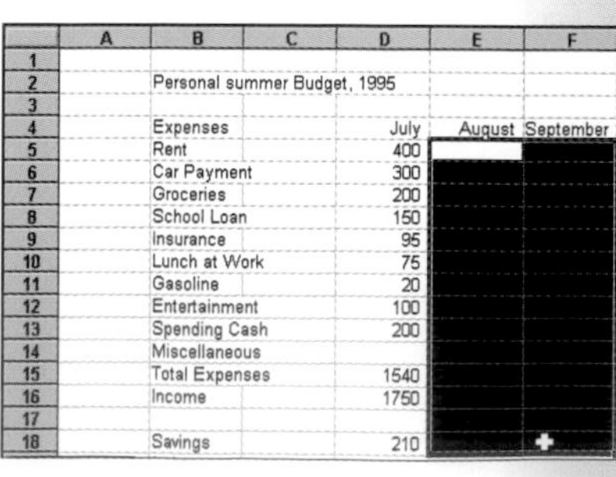

| | A | B | C | D | E | F |
|---|---|---|---|---|---|---|
| 1 | | | | | | |
| 2 | | Personal summer Budget, 1995 | | | | |
| 3 | | | | | | |
| 4 | | Expenses | | July | August | September |
| 5 | | Rent | | 400 | | |
| 6 | | Car Payment | | 300 | | |
| 7 | | Groceries | | 200 | | |
| 8 | | School Loan | | 150 | | |
| 9 | | Insurance | | 95 | | |
| 10 | | Lunch at Work | | 75 | | |
| 11 | | Gasoline | | 20 | | |
| 12 | | Entertainment | | 100 | | |
| 13 | | Spending Cash | | 200 | | |
| 14 | | Miscellaneous | | | | |
| 15 | | Total Expenses | | 1540 | | |
| 16 | | Income | | 1750 | | |
| 17 | | | | | | |
| 18 | | Savings | | 210 | | |

Select the destination by clicking and dragging over cells E5:F18. *Chapter 9*

**16**

| | A | B | C | D | E | F |
|---|---|---|---|---|---|---|
| 1 | | | | | | |
| 2 | | Personal summer Budget, 1995 | | | | |
| 3 | | | | | | |
| 4 | | Expenses | | July | August | September |
| 5 | | Rent | | 400 | 400 | 400 |
| 6 | | Car Payment | | 300 | 300 | 300 |
| 7 | | Groceries | | 200 | 220 | 220 |
| 8 | | School Loan | | 150 | 150 | 150 |
| 9 | | Insurance | | 95 | 0 | 0 |
| 10 | | Lunch at Work | | 75 | 0 | 0 |
| 11 | | Gasoline | | 20 | 20 | 20 |
| 12 | | Entertainment | | 100 | 100 | 100 |
| 13 | | Spending Cash | | 200 | 200 | 200 |
| 14 | | Miscellaneous | | | | |
| 15 | | Total Expenses | | 1540 | 1390 | 1390 |
| 16 | | Income | | 1750 | 1750 | 1750 |
| 17 | | | | | | |
| 18 | | Savings | | 210 | 360 | 360 |

Suppose your finances change in the months of August and September. (You finish paying for your insurance and start carrying lunch to work.) Change the data in columns E and F to reflect these changes as shown. Notice that the formulas at the bottom of the spreadsheet show new results. *Chapter 10*

**17**

Since there aren't any Miscellaneous expenses, clean up the spreadsheet by deleting the label. Click on cell B14 and press the Delete key. *Chapter 11*

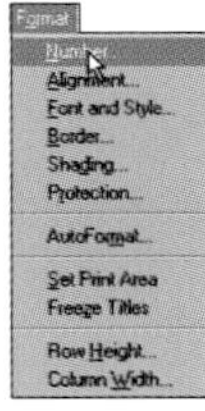


Format the totals at the bottom of the sheet. Select cells D15:F18, and then select Number from the Format menu. *Chapter 12*

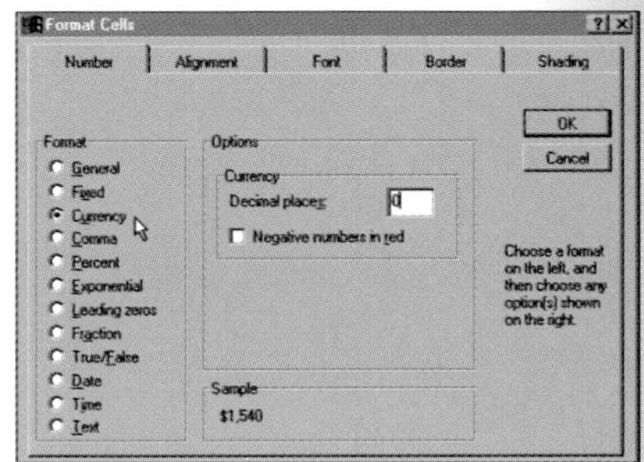


In the Number dialog box, click on the Currency option button, and set the number of decimal places to zero before clicking OK. *Chapter 12*

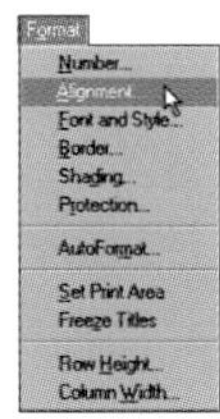


To center the column labels, select cells D4:F4. Next, click on Format in the menu bar and select Alignment. *Chapter 12*

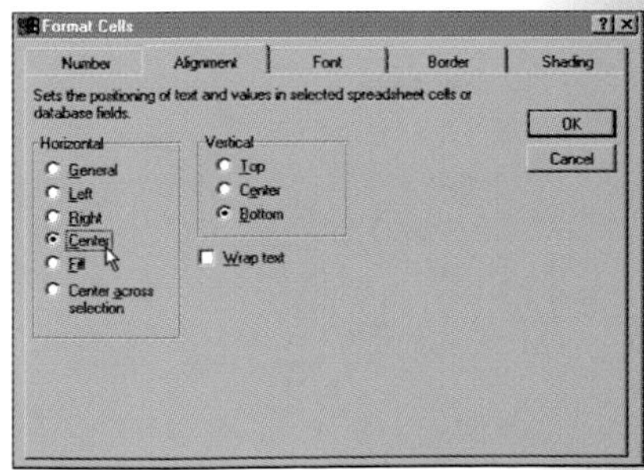


Select the Center alignment option button in the dialog box, and then click OK to center the labels. *Chapter 12*

Save all of your work by clicking on the Save button in the toolbar. *Chapter 9*

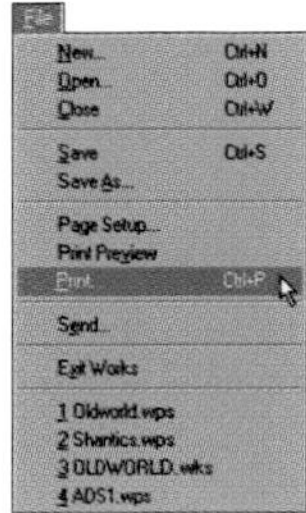


If you like, print the spreadsheet. First, select Print from the File menu. In the dialog box that opens next, click OK. *Chapter 12*

## CHAPTER 13

# More Advanced Spreadsheet Techniques

After learning and trying the basics of spreadsheets, you are ready to advance into the major leagues and discover the more powerful and convenient techniques which are available to you in Works.

Working with your formulas can be made simpler if you understand arithmetic operator precedence rules and if you can use names for pieces of information rather than cell reference numbers. Also, Works' library of pre-programmed functions will save you a great deal of time in creating complex formulas.

In addition to the basics of formatting, which you found can greatly enhance the appearance of your spreadsheet, you can will now add the capability to manipulate whole rows and columns at one time. You can also use the AutoFormat feature to give your spreadsheet a very professional look.

Finally, to help you resolve some commonly encountered problems, we'll describe some troubleshooting techniques.

# How to Insert or Delete Rows and Columns

After preparing a spreadsheet, you'll sometimes want to update it. This may be necessary to include additional information. If there is no empty row or column where you want to place this information, you can insert one.

You may also wish to improve the appearance of your spreadsheet by increasing or decreasing the space between certain parts of your work. This can be done by inserting or deleting rows or columns.

Although you may be inserting or deleting within your existing data, Works maintains the total number of columns and rows available at 256 and 16,384 respectively.

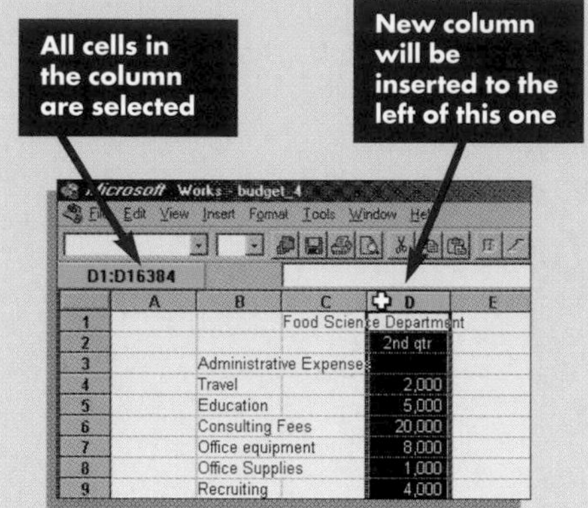
All cells in the column are selected
New column will be inserted to the left of this one

**1** Click on the header button of the column to the right of where you want the new information to go. All cells in that column will be highlighted.

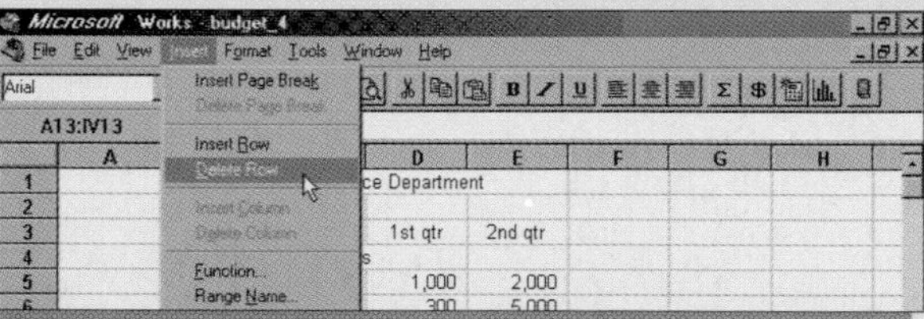

**7** Complete the deletion of the row by clicking on the Delete Row command in the Insert menu. To delete a column, select it, then choose Delete a Column from the Insert menu.

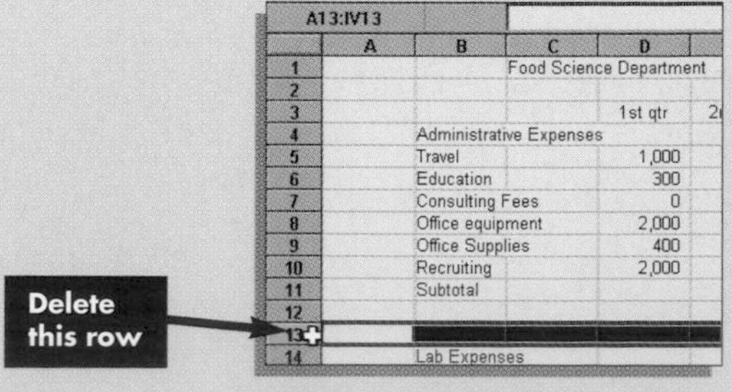
Delete this row

**6** Select a row to delete by clicking on its header button.

## TIP SHEET

- To insert more than one column or row, simply highlight the appropriate number of header buttons, beginning with the one to the right (for columns) or the one below (for rows).
- To delete more than one column or row, highlight their header buttons.
- Whenever you delete columns or rows, be certain that you are not inadvertently deleting data you want to keep. If this should happen, simply select the Undo Delete command from the Edit menu.
- The selection of a row or column for insertion or deletion is not restricted to the use of the header buttons. You may do the selection by simply clicking on any cell in the row or column.

**2** Click on the Insert menu and then the Insert Column command. Works will insert the new column to the left of the one you selected.

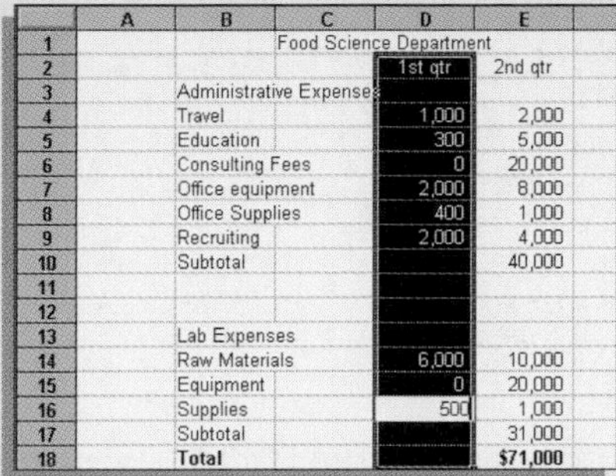

**3** You may now enter and format your data in the new column using the techniques you developed in previous chapters.

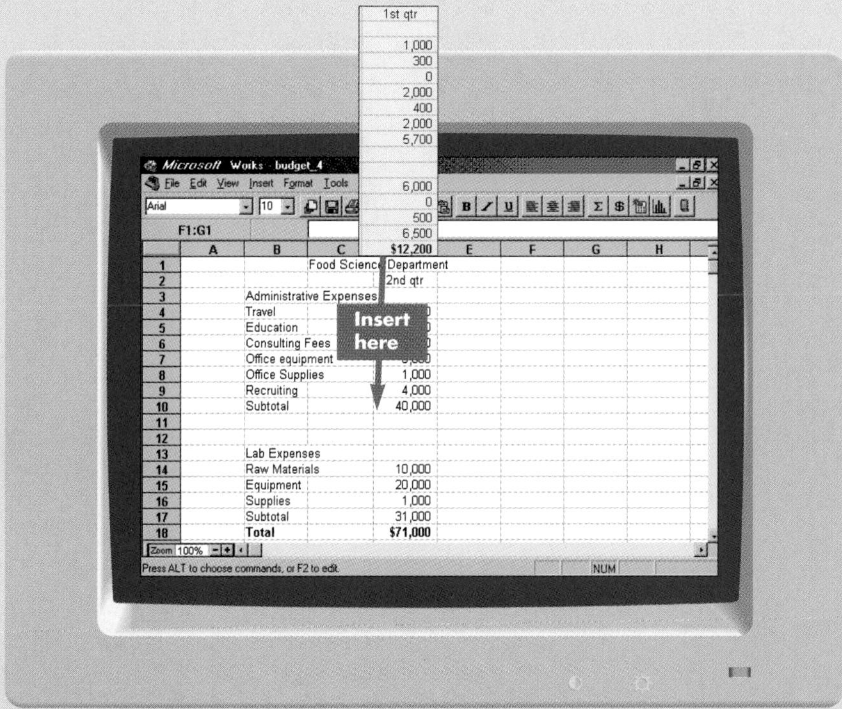
Insert here

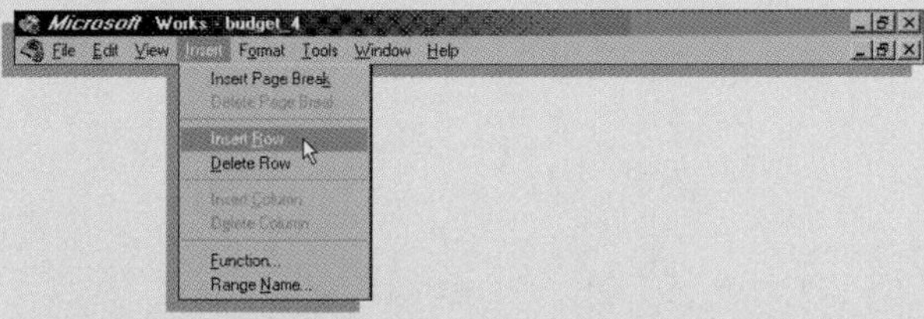

**5** Click on the Insert menu and then on the Insert Row command. Works will insert one new row above the one you have selected.

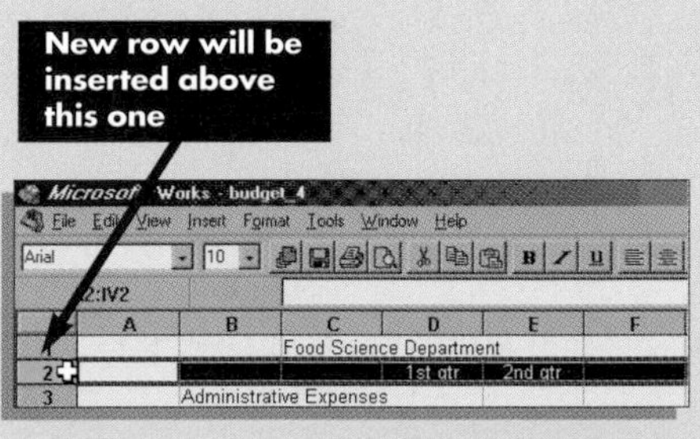
New row will be inserted above this one

**4** Click on the header button of the row below where you want to insert a new row. All cells in this row will be highlighted.

# How to Change the Width and Height of Columns and Rows

You may notice that sometimes very large values entered into a cell will be displayed as a series of number signs (#########). This is because Works initially sets the width of all columns to 10 characters, and numbers larger than this will not fit into the cell. Fortunately, you are able to adjust the width of columns to allow for more room. Similarly, you can adjust the height of rows to create more space where you want to "uncrowd" the lists of data.

Works allows you to decrease the width of columns or the height of rows to as much as you wish, all the way to zero. The result of decreasing to zero is that you will have a "hidden" column or row. This can be useful if you do not want to display certain information, but don't want to lose it by deleting the column or row.

## TIP SHEET

- **Works can save you time if you want to change column width or row height to "just fit" the size of your information. To do so, select Column Width or Row Height from the Format menu and click on Best Fit in the dialog box.**
- **By double-clicking on the column or row header button, Works automatically performs the Best Fit function.**
- **You can change the width or height of several columns or rows at one time by first dragging over and highlighting several column or row header buttons. Then, using the Format menu for Column Width or Row Height you can change them together.**

**1** To increase the column width, position the mouse pointer to the right boundary of the column header button. Observe that the "Adjust" pointer appears.

Number is too large for the column width

**7** Increase the width of the hidden column by selecting Column Width from the Format menu and entering any number larger than zero in the dialog box. Click OK to complete the action.

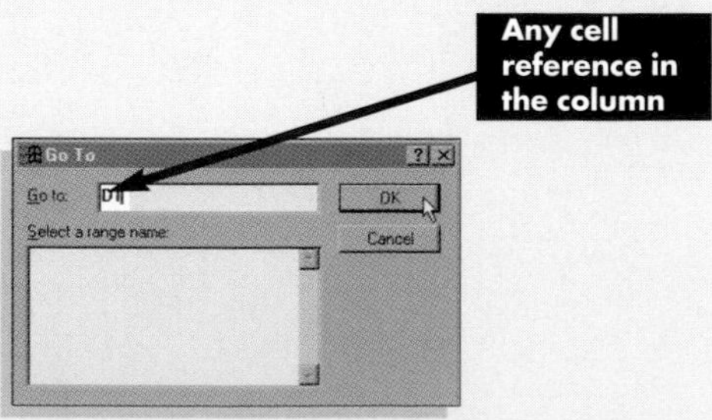


**6** In the Go To dialog box, enter any cell reference for the column you wish to unhide and click OK.

**2** Drag the pointer to the right and release it. You may need to do this more than once until the number appears or the width is to your liking.

**3** To increase the spacing between the column titles and the first row of data, a new empty row could be inserted. However, an equally good technique is to increase the height of the data row. Drag the Adjust pointer downward from the lower boundary of the row header button until you have the desired row height.

| Year | National Debt | Population | Debt Increase |
|---|---|---|---|
| 1900 | $12,479,008,290,000 | 60,000,000 | Base |
| 1910 | $12,610,711,950,900 | 70,000,000 | $131,703,660,900 |
| 1920 | $12,743,106,969,600 | 80,000,000 | $132,395,018,700 |
| 1930 | $12,876,193,346,100 | 90,000,000 | $133,086,376,500 |
| 1940 | $13,009,971,080,400 | 100,000,000 | $133,777,734,300 |
| 1950 | $13,144,440,172,500 | 110,000,000 | $134,469,092,100 |
| 1960 | $13,279,600,622,400 | 120,000,000 | $135,160,449,900 |
| 1970 | $13,415,452,430,100 | 130,000,000 | $135,851,807,700 |
| 1980 | $13,551,995,595,600 | 140,000,000 | $136,543,165,500 |

**4** Hide a column by reducing its width to zero. Drag the Adjust pointer from the right boundary to the left until it coincides with the boundary of the adjacent column and release. Observe that the header button for the hidden column is gone.

Column D is hidden

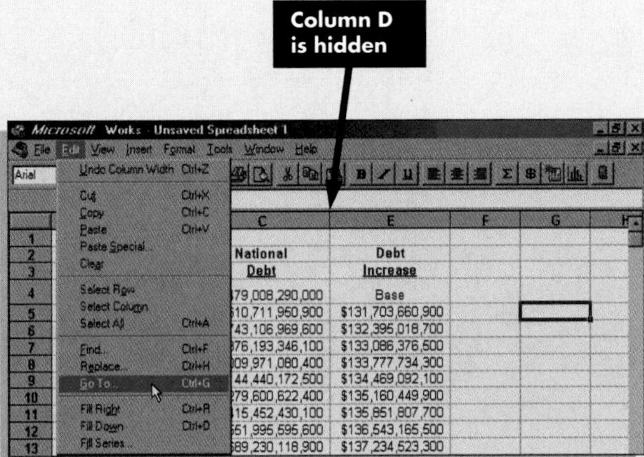

**5** To retrieve the hidden column, select Go To from the Edit menu.

# How to Create and Use Range Names

In making the most efficient use of spreadsheets, you'll be dealing with blocks of information contained in multiple cells. A block, or range, can be easily referenced and will have more meaning if it is given a unique name such as "expenses" instead of, for example, C5:G16. Navigating within your spreadsheet can be made easier by use of range names, but using them in formulas has an even greater advantage because you can verbalize the data to be operated on.

Works keeps the range names you select in a list just in case you should forget the exact name or the cells that the name refers to. One of the names you will want to use is Print Area for selecting only that part of your spreadsheet which you want on hard copy.

**TIP SHEET**

- **Range names must begin with a letter and should not contain spaces, arithmetic symbols such as +,=,-,/,*, or functions such as AVE, PMT, DATE.**
- **When using range names in formulas, Works can operate on blocks of data for addition or subtraction, but multiplication, division and exponentiation require names to reference a single cell.**
- **To see your list of range names, or display them for printing, move to an unused block of cells and from the Range Name dialog box select List.**

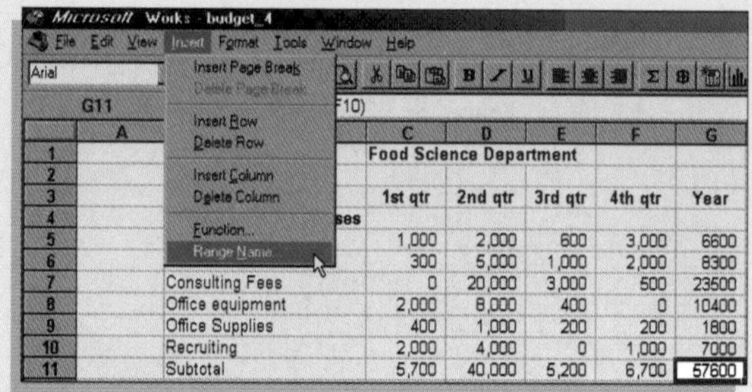


1 Select a cell to be named and from the Insert menu choose Range Name.

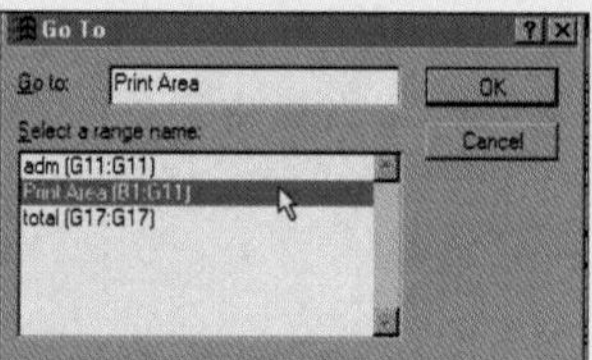


6 In the dialog box, select Print Area and click OK.

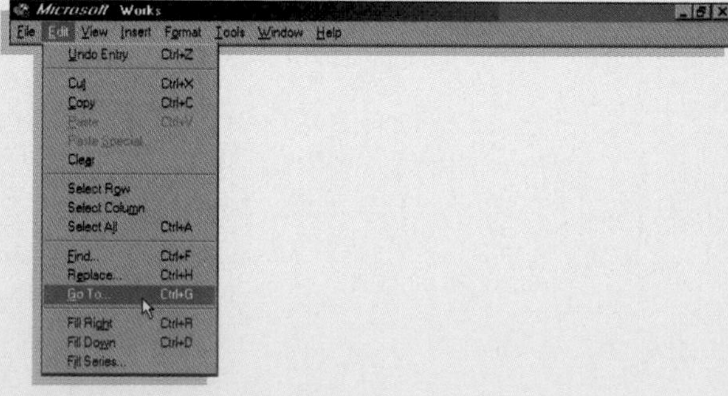


5 To locate or move to the block to be printed, open the Edit menu and choose Go To.

Range Name
Name: adm
Select a name:
Print Area (A1:A1)
OK
Cancel
List
Delete

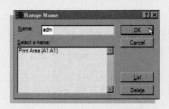

**2** In the dialog box type a meaningful name beginning with a letter (not a number) and click OK.

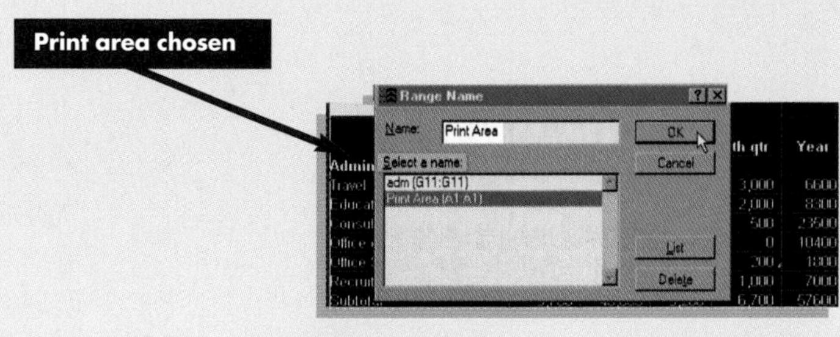


**3** Select any block of cells in your spreadsheet for printing later by highlighting the block and giving it the range name Print Area.

Name: Print Area

| | A | B | C | D | E | F | G | H |
|---|---|---|---|---|---|---|---|---|
| 1 | | | Food Science Department | | | | | |
| 2 | | | | | | | | % |
| 3 | | | 1st qtr | 2nd qtr | 3rd qtr | 4th qtr | Year | Total |
| 4 | | Administrative Expenses | | | | | | |
| 5 | | Travel | 1,000 | 2,000 | 600 | 3,000 | 6600 | |
| 6 | | Education | 300 | 5,000 | 1,000 | 2,000 | 8300 | |
| 7 | | Consulting Fees | 0 | 20,000 | 3,000 | 500 | 23500 | |
| 8 | | Office equipment | 2,000 | 8,000 | 400 | 0 | 10400 | |
| 9 | | Office Supplies | 400 | 1,000 | 200 | 200 | 1800 | |
| 10 | | Recruiting | 2,000 | 4,000 | 0 | 1,000 | 7000 | |
| 11 | | Subtotal | 5,700 | 40,000 | 5,200 | 6,700 | 57600 | 56% |
| 12 | | Lab Expenses | | | | | | |
| 13 | | Raw Materials | 6,000 | 10,000 | 2,000 | 4,000 | 22000 | |
| 14 | | Equipment | 0 | 20,000 | 0 | 1,000 | 21000 | |
| 15 | | Supplies | 500 | 1,000 | 400 | 700 | 2600 | |
| 16 | | Subtotal | 6,500 | 31,000 | 2,400 | 5,700 | 45600 | 44% |
| 17 | | Total | | | | | 103200 | |

Name: adm

Name: total

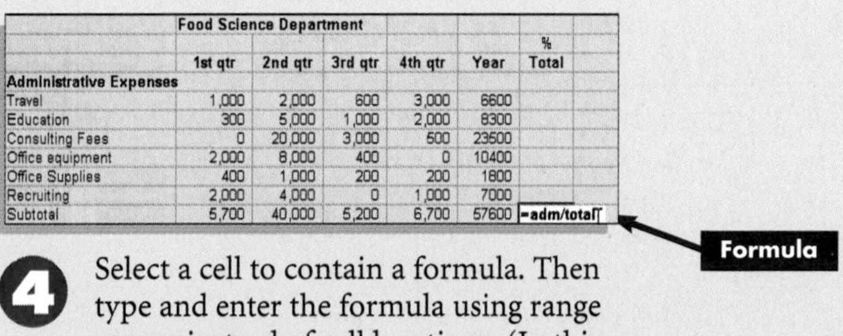

| | Food Science Department | | | | | |
|---|---|---|---|---|---|---|
| | | | | | | % |
| | 1st qtr | 2nd qtr | 3rd qtr | 4th qtr | Year | Total |
| Administrative Expenses | | | | | | |
| Travel | 1,000 | 2,000 | 600 | 3,000 | 6600 | |
| Education | 300 | 5,000 | 1,000 | 2,000 | 8300 | |
| Consulting Fees | 0 | 20,000 | 3,000 | 500 | 23500 | |
| Office equipment | 2,000 | 8,000 | 400 | 0 | 10400 | |
| Office Supplies | 400 | 1,000 | 200 | 200 | 1800 | |
| Recruiting | 2,000 | 4,000 | 0 | 1,000 | 7000 | |
| Subtotal | 5,700 | 40,000 | 5,200 | 6,700 | 57600 | =adm/total |



**4** Select a cell to contain a formula. Then type and enter the formula using range names instead of cell locations. (In this example cell F17 has been previously named "total.")

# How to Use the Fill Commands

To speed up the creation of your spreadsheet, Works can eliminate repetitive entry of the same or similar data through the use of three Fill commands.

Two commands, Fill Right and Fill Down, copy an entry you make in one cell to one or more cells.

The third command, Fill Series, fills your cells with consecutive numbers or dates in a series. You even get to choose the increment, or step value in your series.

| A | B | C | D | E |
|---|---|---|---|---|
| | | MONTHLY MISCELLANEOUS HARDWARE USAGE | | |
| | Hardware | Storage Bin | Part # | |
| | Nuts | Upper | | |
| | Bolts | | | |
| | Washers | | | |
| | Screws | | | |
| | Nails | | | |
| | Brackets | | | |
| | Handles | | | |

**1** To fill down (or right), first highlight the column or row of cells that you want to fill. Then type the number or word in the first cell.

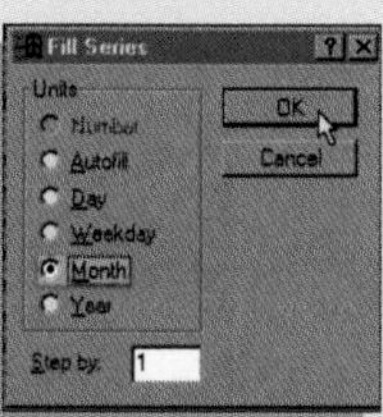


**5** To fill a row or column with dates, you may use days, weekdays, months, or years. Enter the starting date in the first cell of your highlighted block. In the Fill Series dialog box, choose the unit you want and the step value. Click OK to continue.

**TIP SHEET**

- **Fill commands can be used on several adjacent columns or rows. If a series is used, the step value for each will be the same.**
- **For a date series, you may use any of these formats: January; January 95; 1/95; 1/9/95; or January 9, 1995.**
- **Series step values can be any number including negative ones.**
- **If you fill cells with formulas, Works adjusts their cell references for you.**

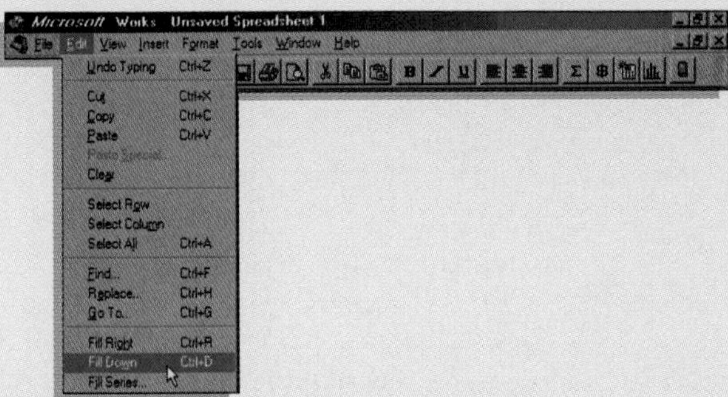

**2** From the Edit menu, choose the Fill Down command and click on it.

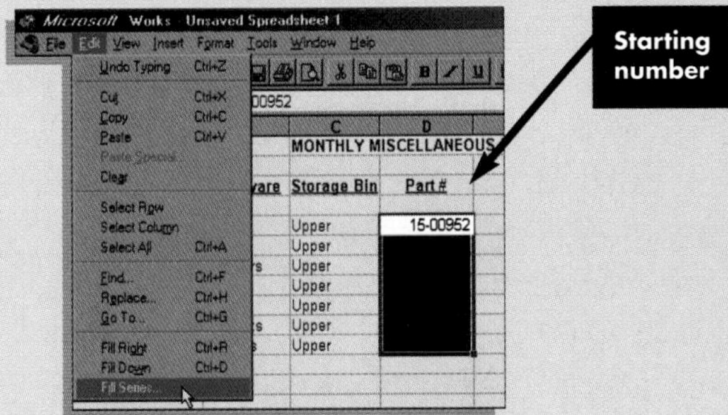


**3** To fill a number series, enter the starting number in the first cell of the block you have selected. From the edit menu choose the Fill Series command.

**MONTHLY MISCELLANEOUS HARDWARE USAGE**

| Hardware | Storage Bin | Part # | 1/95 | 2/95 | 3/95 | 4/95 | 5/95 |
|---|---|---|---|---|---|---|---|
| Nuts | Upper | 00524-10 | 468 | 936 | 1872 | 3744 | 7488 |
| Bolts | Upper | 00524-11 | 468 | 936 | 1872 | 3744 | 7488 |
| Washers | Upper | 00524-12 | 936 | 1872 | 3744 | 7488 | 14976 |
| Screws | Upper | 00524-13 | 120 | 240 | 480 | 960 | 1920 |
| Nails | Upper | 00524-14 | 88 | 176 | 352 | 704 | 1408 |
| Brackets | Upper | 00524-15 | 400 | 800 | 1600 | 3200 | 6400 |
| Handles | Upper | 00524-16 | 200 | 400 | 800 | 1600 | 3200 |

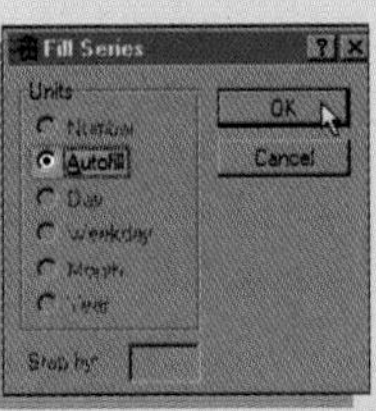

**4** In the Fill Series dialog box, Autofill will be designated. Click on OK to continue.

# How to Create Formulas with Multiple Operators

Some of the calculations you will want to have your spreadsheet perform for you may contain more than one type of mathematical operator (+,-,/,*,^). For these formulas, you'll need to be sure you have used the correct calculation precedence or order of evaluation.

Works uses the standard order of evaluation shown below unless instructed to do otherwise. In order to change this order, you will use parentheses () to enclose a part of your formula. Works will calculate the enclosed part first and then continue using the standard order. If parentheses are nested (one inside another) the calculation starts with the innermost one and proceeds outward.

**Standard Order of Evaluation**

*Order*

| | | |
|---|---|---|
| 1 | +,- | Negative or Positive |
| 2 | ^ | Exponentiation |
| 3 | *, / | Multiplication or Division |
| 4 | +, - | Addition or Subtraction |

**TIP SHEET**

- **You can use parentheses to enhance readability and still maintain the order of operation. Just make sure to pair your parentheses, that is, for every open parenthesis you have a close parenthesis. Then, of course, always test the results for the correct answer.**

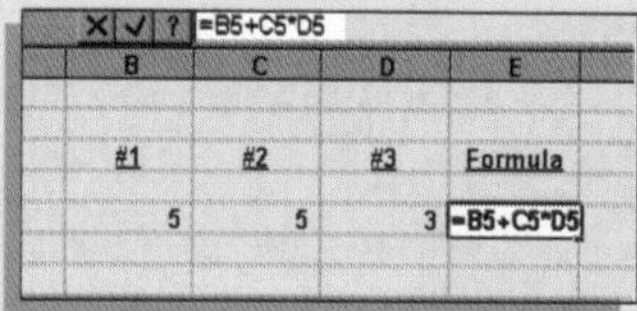


1 Enter your formula, always beginning with an equal sign. The formula appears in both the selected cell and in the Formula Bar.

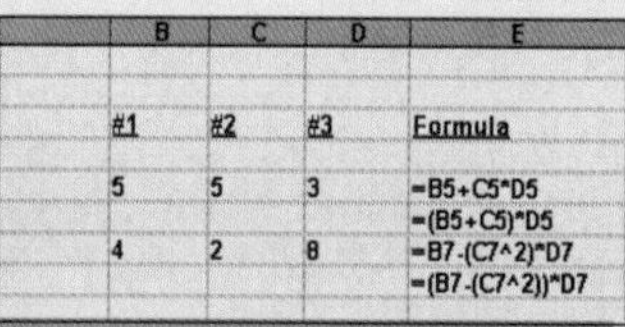


5 To review all the formulas contained in your entire spreadsheet, select Formulas from the View menu. A new screen appears with the formulas showing instead of the results. To return to the spreadsheet containing results, click on Formulas in the View menu again

Added parentheses

=(B5+C5)*D5

| B | C | D | E |
|---|---|---|---|
| #1 | #2 | #3 | Formula |
| 5 | 5 | 3 | 20 |
| | | | 30 |

**2** After entering the formula, if the result is different than what you expected, check the order of evaluation and modify it using parentheses as necessary. The new result here is 30 instead of 20 because the addition is done before the multiplication.

=B7-(C7^2)*D7

| B | C | D | E |
|---|---|---|---|
| #1 | #2 | #3 | Formula |
| 5 | 5 | 3 | 20 |
| | | | 30 |
| 4 | 2 | 8 | -28 |

**3** A formula containing one set of parentheses will be calculated by first evaluating the part in the parentheses.

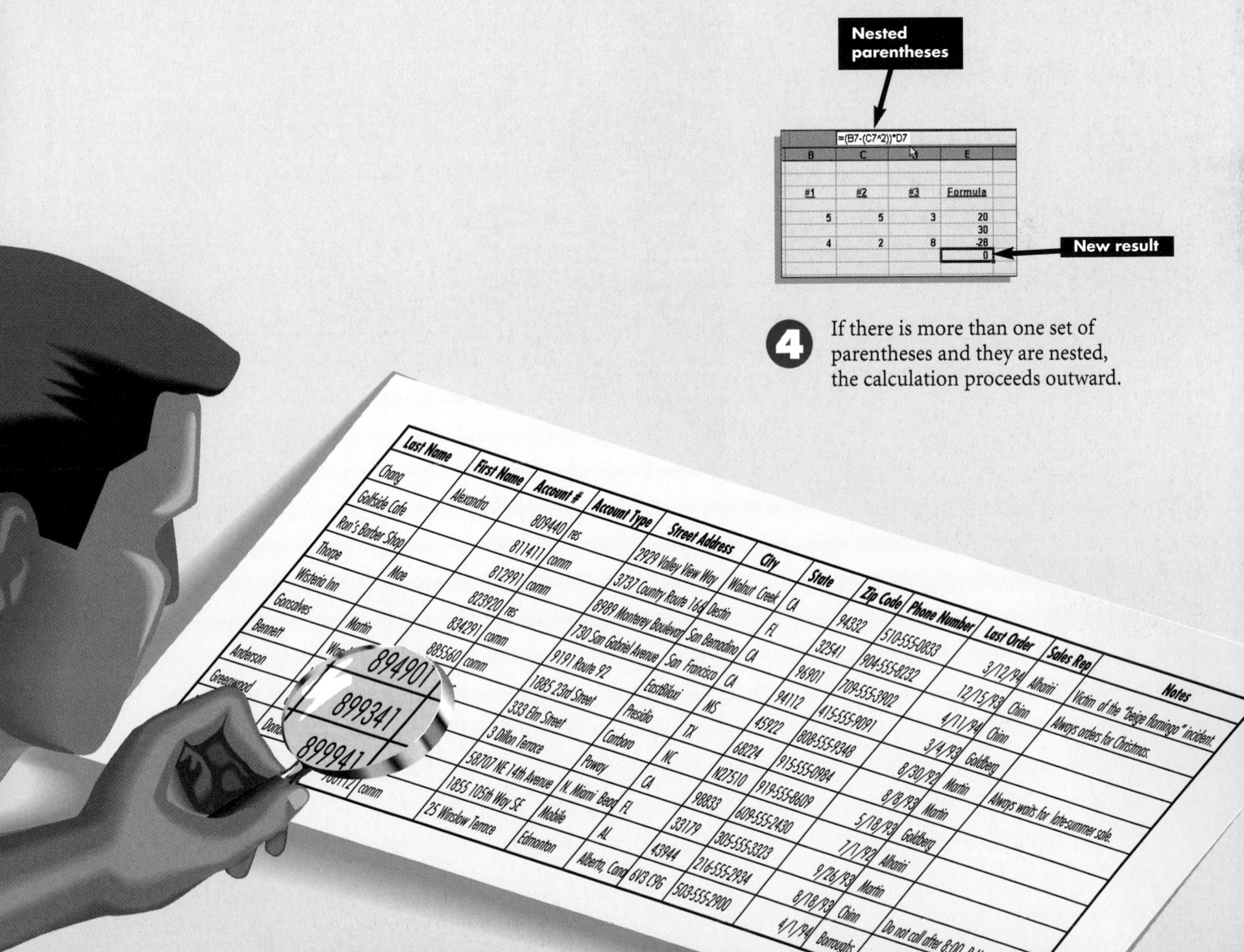


**4** If there is more than one set of parentheses and they are nested, the calculation proceeds outward.

# How to Work with Relative, Absolute, and Mixed Cell References

As you learned in a previous chapter, when you move or copy a formula containing the more common type of cell reference, Works automatically adjusts the references so that they are relative to the new location. Thus, if you move a formula "down one and right one," the row and column references in the formula will be incremented by one.

It will be necessary in some calculations to have one or more cell references remain absolutely unchanged. In this case, you will have to tell Works which cell reference you want to be absolute. You do this by using two $ signs in the reference.

Another cell-referencing scheme combines both relative and absolute values. These mixed references can hold either the row or the column absolute while the other is allowed to be relative. This saves wear and tear on the $ sign because only one is needed.

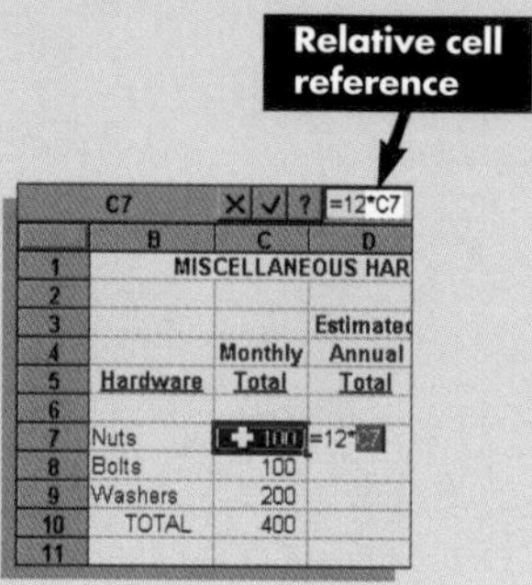


**1** When entering a formula and selecting the cell to be referenced by clicking on it, Works assumes you intend it to be a relative reference.

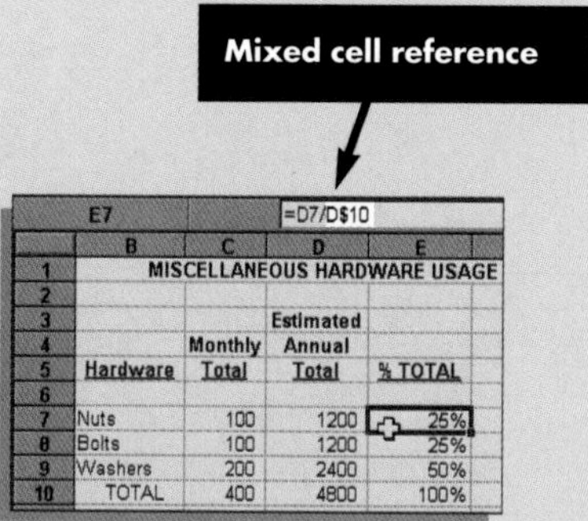


**6** If it is necessary to hold only the column or row identifier fixed, type the $ sign in front of the one you wish to remain absolute.

**TIP SHEET**

- **Works will insert the $ sign for you if, after highlighting the cell during formula entry, you depress the F4 function key. You will need to depress the key until the $ sign appears in front of the absolute part of the address you wish.**

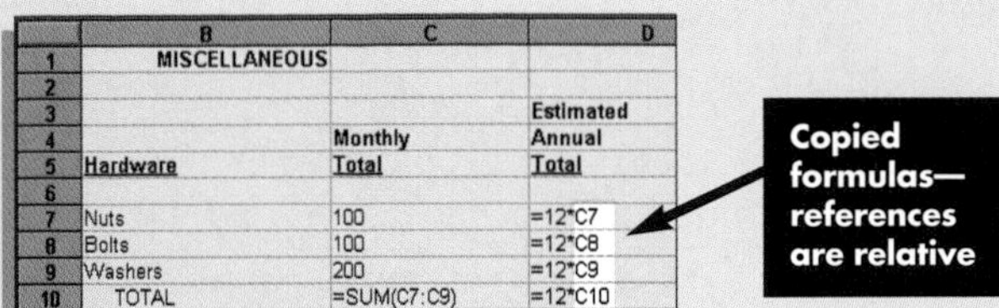

| | B | C | D |
|---|---|---|---|
| 1 | MISCELLANEOUS | | |
| 2 | | | |
| 3 | | | Estimated |
| 4 | | Monthly | Annual |
| 5 | Hardware | Total | Total |
| 6 | | | |
| 7 | Nuts | 100 | =12*C7 |
| 8 | Bolts | 100 | =12*C8 |
| 9 | Washers | 200 | =12*C9 |
| 10 | TOTAL | =SUM(C7:C9) | =12*C10 |
| 11 | | | |

Copied formulas—references are relative

**2** After moving or copying the formula to other locations, the references are adjusted to be relative to the new location.

E8 =D8/D11

| | B | C | D | E |
|---|---|---|---|---|
| 1 | MISCELLANEOUS HARDWARE USAGE | | | |
| 2 | | | | |
| 3 | | | Estimated | |
| 4 | | Monthly | Annual | |
| 5 | Hardware | Total | Total | % TOTAL |
| 6 | | | | |
| 7 | Nuts | 100 | 1200 | 25% |
| 8 | Bolts | 100 | 1200 | ERR |
| 9 | Washers | 200 | 2400 | ERR |
| 10 | TOTAL | 400 | 4800 | ERR |
| 11 | | | | |
| 12 | | | | |

**3** If the cell reference is relative, but should be absolute, errors will occur. These errors will not always be flagged by Works if the relative location contains a valid number.

Absolute cell reference

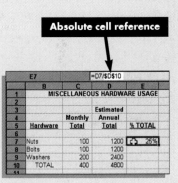

E7 =D7/$D$10

| | B | C | D | E |
|---|---|---|---|---|
| 1 | MISCELLANEOUS HARDWARE USAGE | | | |
| 2 | | | | |
| 3 | | | Estimated | |
| 4 | | Monthly | Annual | |
| 5 | Hardware | Total | Total | % TOTAL |
| 6 | | | | |
| 7 | Nuts | 100 | 1200 | 25% |
| 8 | Bolts | 100 | 1200 | |
| 9 | Washers | 200 | 2400 | |
| 10 | TOTAL | 400 | 4800 | |

**4** To enter an Absolute cell reference, type a $ sign before the column and row identifiers.

| | B | C | D | E |
|---|---|---|---|---|
| 1 | MISCEL | | | |
| 2 | | | | |
| 3 | | | Estimated | |
| 4 | | Monthly | Annual | |
| 5 | Hardware | Total | Total | % TOTAL |
| 6 | | | | |
| 7 | Nuts | 100 | =12*C7 | =D7/$D$10 |
| 8 | Bolts | 100 | =12*C8 | =D8/$D$10 |
| 9 | Washers | 200 | =12*C9 | =D9/$D$10 |
| 10 | TOTAL | =SUM(C7:C9) | =12*C10 | =D10/$D$10 |

Copied formulas—references are absolute

**5** When the formula containing an absolute reference is copied to other locations, the absolute reference part remains unchanged.

# How to Create Formulas Using More Advanced Functions

Although your spreadsheet know-how is already well advanced, you will appreciate the additional ways Works helps to make complex calculations simple. Through the use of pre-programmed functions, your formulas can now contain statistics, math and trigonometry calculations, financial calculations, logical functions, and many other useful operations, with very little effort on your part.

Instead of your creating the steps in the calculations and then typing all of them into several related cells, you can now select the function you want and only type in the data or cell locations to be used.

## TIP SHEET

- **Normally, your spreadsheet will be displaying the results of your formulas. If, however, your answers appear to be incorrect and the spreadsheet contains many calculations, you may want to examine your formulas for errors. To do this, select Formulas from the View menu.**
- **Works Help can assist you in recalling how the functions are selected and how to enter the required information in them.**
- **If a spreadsheet contains a fixed table of data, you need to be careful when adding or deleting rows when you are working in the other areas of the spreadsheet. It is generally a good idea to use absolute cell references when referring to locations in a fixed table.**

| | A | B | C | D | E | F | G | H | I |
|---|---|---|---|---|---|---|---|---|---|
| 1 | | INDIVIDUAL BUDGET PLAN | | | | | | | |
| 2 | | | | | Gross Pay | | Withhold | | |
| 3 | Monthly Gross | $3,000 | | | | | Federal | State | |
| 4 | Medicare & SS | $230 | | | | | | | |
| 5 | Fed W/H Tax | $206 | | | Min | Max | | | |
| 6 | State W/H Tax | | | | 0 | ....... | ... | ... | |
| 7 | Discretionary expense | $1,000 | | | 2940 | 2980 | 200 | 60 | |
| 8 | Loans | $300 | | | 2980 | 3020 | 206 | 62 | |
| 9 | Mortgage | | | | 3020 | 3060 | 212 | 64 | |
| 10 | Property Tax & Ins. | $250 | | | 3060 | 3100 | 210 | 66 | |
| 11 | Total Expense | $1,986 | | | 3100 | 3140 | 216 | 68 | |
| 12 | SAVINGS | $1,015 | | | 3140 | 3120 | 222 | 70 | |

**1** In the spreadsheet which contains the basic information your new formula needs, move to the cell you want it to appear in.

**7** Logical functions require you to type a "condition" in the first part of the function.

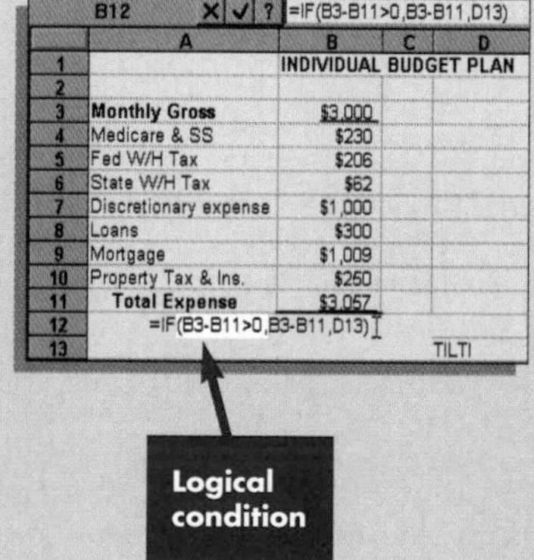

B12 =IF(B3-B11>0,B3-B11,D13)

| | A | B | C | D |
|---|---|---|---|---|
| 1 | | INDIVIDUAL BUDGET PLAN | | |
| 2 | | | | |
| 3 | Monthly Gross | $3,000 | | |
| 4 | Medicare & SS | $230 | | |
| 5 | Fed W/H Tax | $206 | | |
| 6 | State W/H Tax | $62 | | |
| 7 | Discretionary expense | $1,000 | | |
| 8 | Loans | $300 | | |
| 9 | Mortgage | $1,009 | | |
| 10 | Property Tax & Ins. | $250 | | |
| 11 | Total Expense | $3,057 | | |
| 12 | =IF(B3-B11>0,B3-B11,D13) | | | |
| 13 | | | | TILTI |

Microsoft Works - functions
File Edit View Insert Format Tools Window Help
Insert Page Break
Delete Page Break
Insert Row
Delete Row
Insert Column
Delete Column
Function...
Range Name...

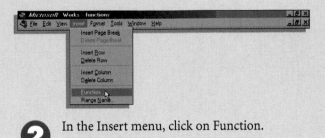

**2** In the Insert menu, click on Function.

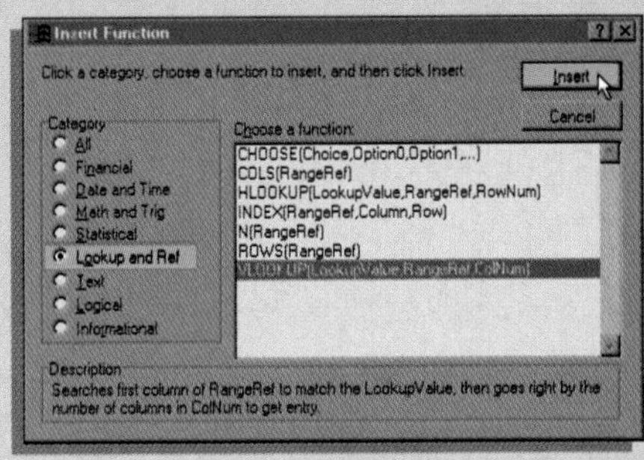


**3** In the Insert Function dialog box, choose the category and the specific function you need and click on Insert.

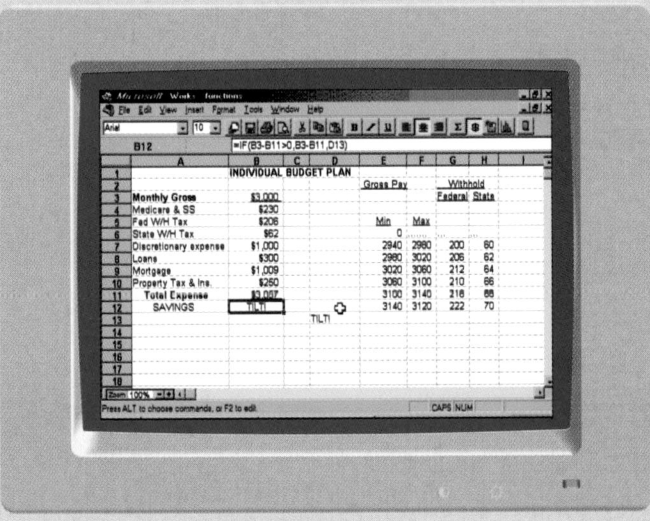

B6 =VLOOKUP(LookupValue,RangeRef,ColNum)

| | A | B | C | D | E | F | G | H |
|---|---|---|---|---|---|---|---|---|
| 1 | | INDIVIDUAL BUDGET PLAN | | | | | | |
| 2 | | | | | Gross Pay | | Withhold | |
| 3 | Monthly Gross | $3,000 | | | | | Federal | State |
| 4 | Medicare & SS | $230 | | | | | | |
| 5 | Fed W/H Tax | $206 | | | Min | Max | | |
| 6 | State W/H Tax | =VLOOKUP(LookupValue,RangeRef,ColNum) | | | | | | |
| 7 | Discretionary expense | $1,000 | | | 2940 | 2980 | 200 | 60 |
| 8 | Loans | $300 | | | 2980 | 3020 | 206 | 62 |
| 9 | Mortgage | | | | 3020 | 3060 | 212 | 64 |
| 10 | Property Tax & Ins. | $250 | | | 3060 | 3100 | 210 | 66 |
| 11 | Total Expense | $1,986 | | | 3100 | 3140 | 216 | 68 |
| 12 | SAVINGS | $1,015 | | | 3140 | 3120 | 222 | 70 |

**4** The selected function is displayed in both the cell and Formula bar. Works tells you what information you need to supply.

| | A | B | C | D | E | F | G | H |
|---|---|---|---|---|---|---|---|---|
| 1 | | INDIVIDUAL BUDGET PLAN | | | | | | |
| 2 | | | | | Gross Pay | | Withhold | |
| 3 | Monthly Gross | $3,000 | | | | | Federal | State |
| 4 | Medicare & SS | $230 | | | | | | |
| 5 | Fed W/H Tax | $206 | | | Min | Max | | |
| 6 | State W/H Tax | =VLOOKUP(B3,E7:H12,3 | | | | | | |
| 7 | Discretionary expense | $1,000 | | | 2940 | 2980 | 200 | 60 |
| 8 | Loans | $300 | | | 2980 | 3020 | 206 | 62 |
| 9 | Mortgage | | | | 3020 | 3060 | 212 | 64 |
| 10 | Property Tax & Ins. | $250 | | | 3060 | 3100 | 210 | 66 |
| 11 | Total Expense | $1,986 | | | 3100 | 3140 | 216 | 68 |
| 12 | SAVINGS | $1,015 | | | 3140 | 3120 | 222 | 70 |

**5** Type in the cell references or numbers that are to be used and press Enter.

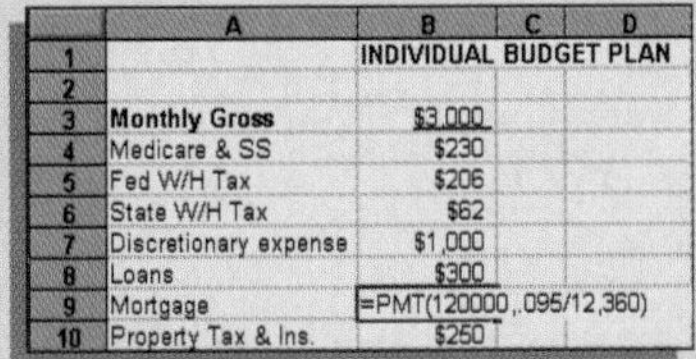

| | A | B | C | D |
|---|---|---|---|---|
| 1 | | INDIVIDUAL BUDGET PLAN | | |
| 2 | | | | |
| 3 | Monthly Gross | $3,000 | | |
| 4 | Medicare & SS | $230 | | |
| 5 | Fed W/H Tax | $206 | | |
| 6 | State W/H Tax | $62 | | |
| 7 | Discretionary expense | $1,000 | | |
| 8 | Loans | $300 | | |
| 9 | Mortgage | =PMT(120000,.095/12,360) | | |
| 10 | Property Tax & Ins. | $250 | | |

**6** If other functions are needed to complete your spreadsheet, repeat steps 1 through 5.

# How to Protect Spreadsheet Data

Although you have seen how easy it is to enter or change data in your spreadsheet, you may not want it to be that easy for someone else to do it. It might be necessary for someone else to have access to your spreadsheet, but you may choose to limit that access to just a part of it. You may even wish to prevent yourself from accidentally overwriting some complicated formula which is your pride and joy.

Earlier in this chapter you learned one method of protection, which is hiding columns or rows. The second method actually protects the contents of designated cells from being easily modified. This feature involves two functions, namely Protection and Locking.

To protect cells, they must be locked and the Protection feature must be on. Works automatically sets all cells to the locked condition initially. Therefore, when you select Protection, all cells are protected. To remove protection from designated cells, you should unlock them.

## TIP SHEET

- **The contents of a protected cell will change automatically if it contains a formula which references another cell whose contents have changed.**
- **Should you wish to leave all but a few special cells in your spreadsheet unprotected, simply highlight the entire spreadsheet and unlock all cells using step number 5. Then reverse the process by highlighting your special cells and lock only those. For overall data safety reasons this choice should be carefully considered.**

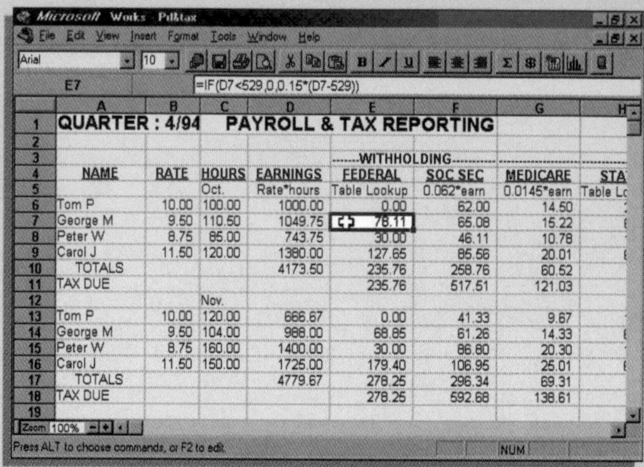

Microsoft Works - Pilltax

E7 =IF(D7<529,0,0.15*(D7-529))

| | A | B | C | D | E | F | G | H |
|---|---|---|---|---|---|---|---|---|
| 1 | QUARTER : 4/94 | | PAYROLL & TAX REPORTING | | | | | |
| 2 | | | | | | | | |
| 3 | | | | | -------WITHHOLDING---------- | | | |
| 4 | NAME | RATE | HOURS | EARNINGS | FEDERAL | SOC SEC | MEDICARE | STA |
| 5 | | | Oct. | Rate*hours | Table Lookup | 0.062*earn | 0.0145*earn | Table Lo |
| 6 | Tom P | 10.00 | 100.00 | 1000.00 | 0.00 | 62.00 | 14.50 | |
| 7 | George M | 9.50 | 110.50 | 1049.75 | 78.11 | 65.08 | 15.22 | |
| 8 | Peter W | 8.75 | 85.00 | 743.75 | 30.00 | 46.11 | 10.78 | |
| 9 | Carol J | 11.50 | 120.00 | 1380.00 | 127.65 | 85.56 | 20.01 | |
| 10 | TOTALS | | | 4173.50 | 235.76 | 258.76 | 60.52 | |
| 11 | TAX DUE | | | | 235.76 | 517.51 | 121.03 | |
| 12 | | | Nov. | | | | | |
| 13 | Tom P | 10.00 | 120.00 | 666.67 | 0.00 | 41.33 | 9.67 | |
| 14 | George M | 9.50 | 104.00 | 988.00 | 68.85 | 61.26 | 14.33 | |
| 15 | Peter W | 8.75 | 160.00 | 1400.00 | 30.00 | 86.80 | 20.30 | |
| 16 | Carol J | 11.50 | 150.00 | 1725.00 | 179.40 | 106.95 | 25.01 | |
| 17 | TOTALS | | | 4779.67 | 278.25 | 296.34 | 69.31 | |
| 18 | TAX DUE | | | | 278.25 | 592.68 | 138.61 | |
| 19 | | | | | | | | |

Press ALT to choose commands, or F2 to edit.

**1** Open a spreadsheet and highlight any cell of interest by clicking on it.

E7 12345

| | A | B | C | D | E | F | G | H |
|---|---|---|---|---|---|---|---|---|
| 1 | QUARTER : 4/94 | | PAYROLL & TAX REPORTING | | | | | |
| 2 | | | | | | | | |
| 3 | | | | | -------WITHHOLDING---------- | | | |
| 4 | NAME | RATE | HOURS | EARNINGS | FEDERAL | SOC SEC | MEDICARE | STA |
| 5 | | | Oct. | Rate*hours | Table Lookup | 0.062*earn | 0.0145*earn | Table L |
| 6 | Tom P | 10.00 | 100.00 | 1000.00 | 0.00 | 62.00 | 14.50 | |
| 7 | George M | 9.50 | 110.50 | 1049.75 | 12345.00 | 65.08 | 15.22 | |
| 8 | Peter W | 8.75 | 85.00 | 743.75 | 30.00 | 46.11 | 10.78 | |
| 9 | Carol J | 11.50 | 120.00 | 1380.00 | 127.65 | 85.56 | 20.01 | |

Type in any new data and press enter. Note that the contents of this cell is allowed to change.

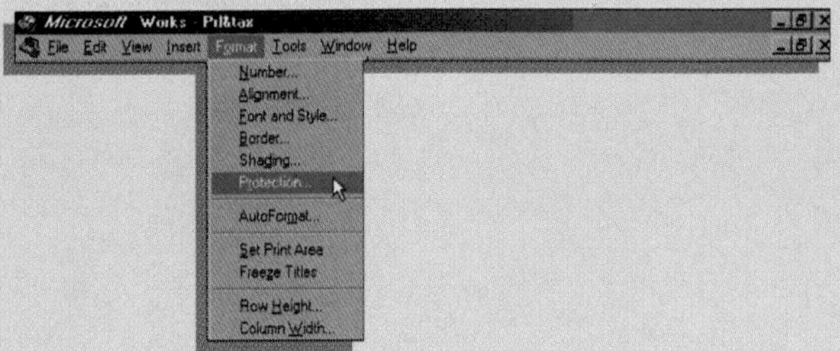


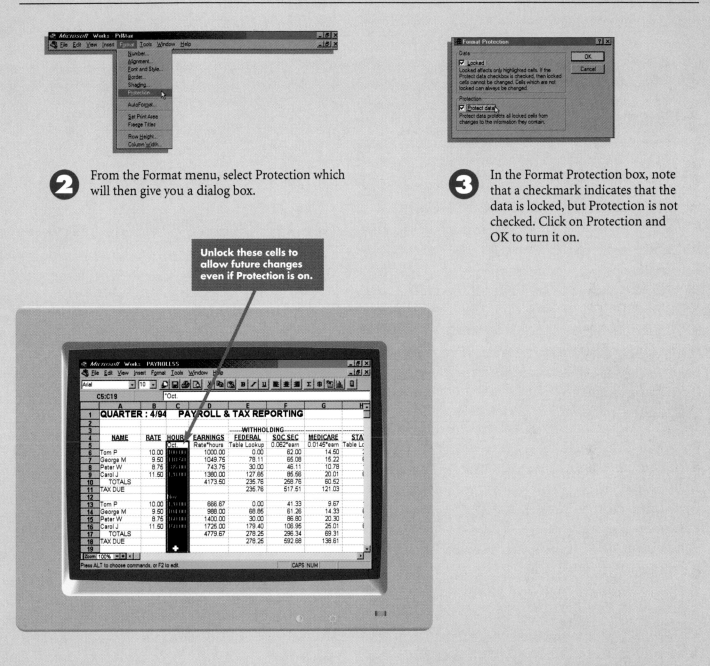

**2** From the Format menu, select Protection which will then give you a dialog box.

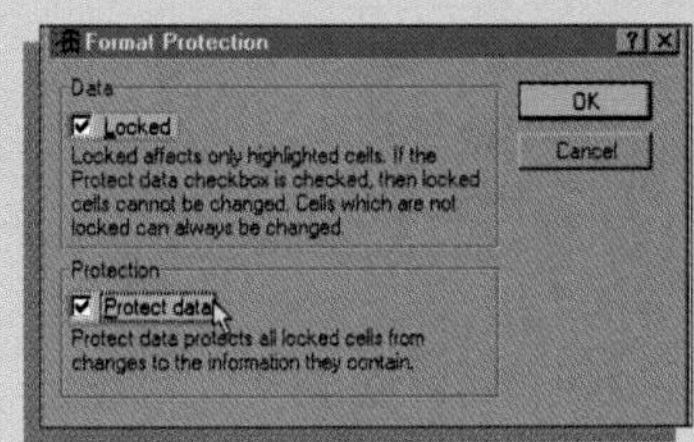


**3** In the Format Protection box, note that a checkmark indicates that the data is locked, but Protection is not checked. Click on Protection and OK to turn it on.

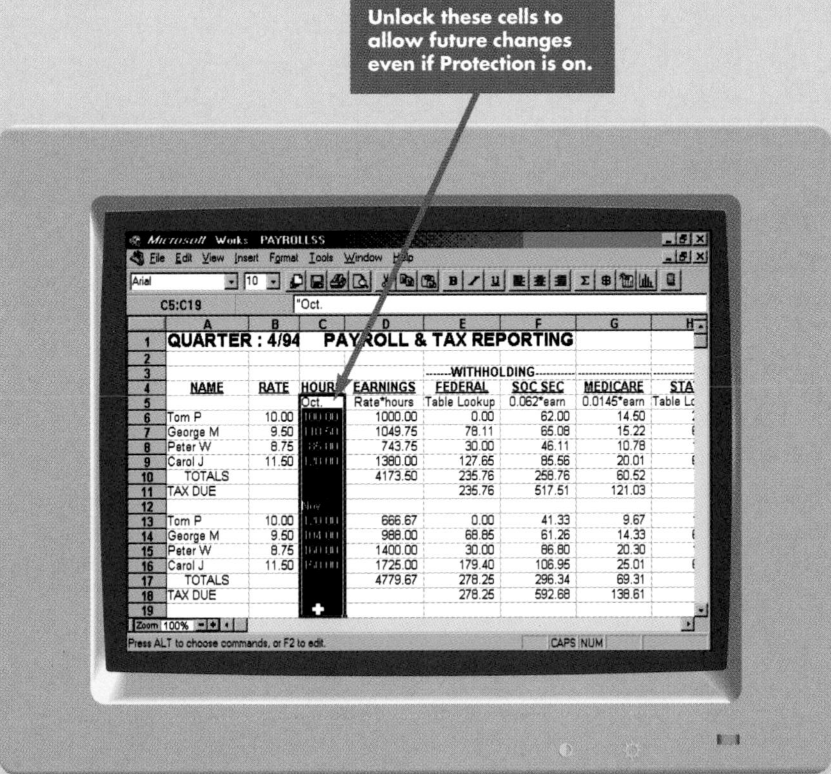


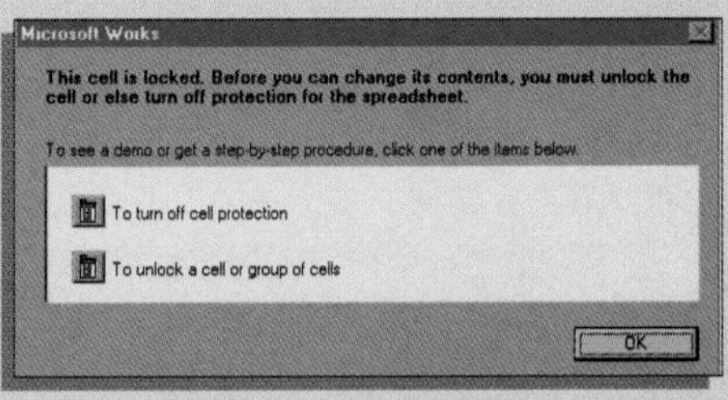

Microsoft Works
This cell is locked. Before you can change its contents, you must unlock the cell or else turn off protection for the spreadsheet.
To see a demo or get a step-by-step procedure, click one of the items below.
To turn off cell protection
To unlock a cell or group of cells
OK


**4** Type any new data in any cell and press Enter. Works will now give you a help dialog box from which you may choose to see a detailed procedure for "un-protecting" the cell. Click on OK to skip the help.

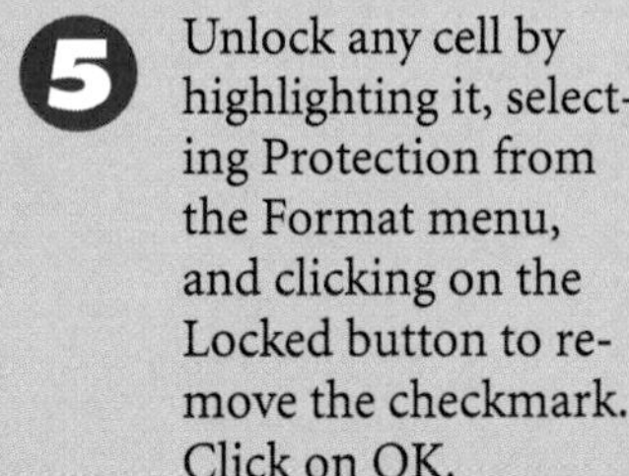

**5** Unlock any cell by highlighting it, selecting Protection from the Format menu, and clicking on the Locked button to remove the checkmark. Click on OK.

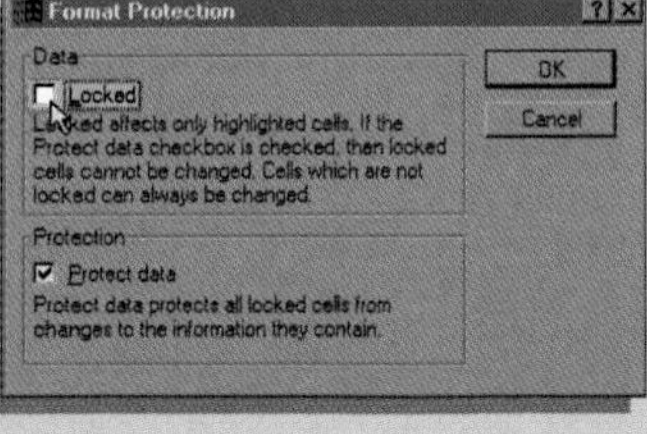

# How to Use the AutoFormat Feature

After all that hard work creating your spreadsheet, certainly you'll want to show it to someone special (like your boss). In addition to showing your mastery of the material contained in the spreadsheet, wouldn't it be great if it looked good too? Works comes to your rescue again, by allowing you to select from 16 different preset formats.

The AutoFormat feature sets your column widths, font, cell height, alignments, numbers, borders, patterns, and colors—all for the best presentation-quality look.

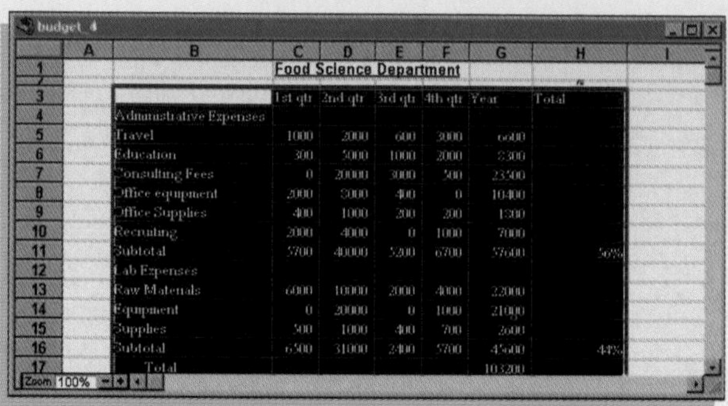

In your spreadsheet, highlight the group of cells you want formatted.

**TIP SHEET**

- **Since AutoFormat formats your numbers, you may need to go back and reset some of your cells. Do this by highlighting the affected ones, and choosing Number from the Format menu.**
- **You may use several different formats within your spreadsheet by highlighting and AutoFormatting separate, non-overlapping areas.**

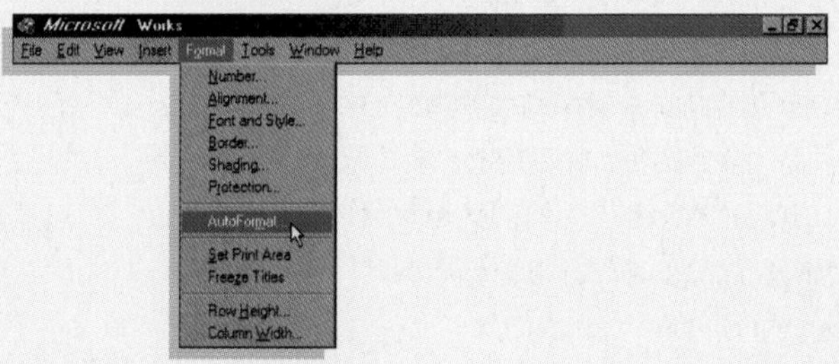


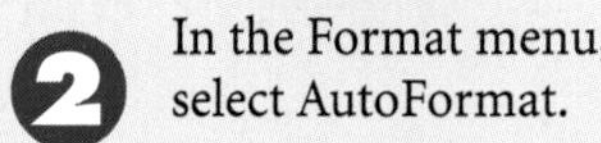
**2** In the Format menu, select AutoFormat.

| Food Science Department | | | | | | |
|---|---|---|---|---|---|---|
| | 1st qtr | 2nd qtr | 3rd qtr | 4th qtr | Year | Total |
| **Administrative Expenses** | | | | | | |
| **Travel** | 1000 | 2000 | 600 | 3000 | 6600 | |
| **Education** | 300 | 5000 | 1000 | 2000 | 8300 | |
| **Consulting Fees** | 0 | 20000 | 3000 | 500 | 23500 | |
| **Office equipment** | 2000 | 8000 | 400 | 0 | 10400 | |
| **Office Supplies** | 400 | 1000 | 200 | 200 | 1800 | |
| **Recruiting** | 2000 | 4000 | 0 | 1000 | 7000 | |
| **Subtotal** | 5700 | 40000 | 5200 | 6700 | 57600 | 56% |
| **Lab Expenses** | | | | | | |
| **Raw Materials** | 6000 | 10000 | 2000 | 4000 | 22000 | |
| **Equipment** | 0 | 20000 | 0 | 1000 | 21000 | |
| **Supplies** | 500 | 1000 | 400 | 700 | 2600 | |
| **Subtotal** | 6500 | 31000 | 2400 | 5700 | 45600 | 44% |
| **Total** | | | | | 103200 | |

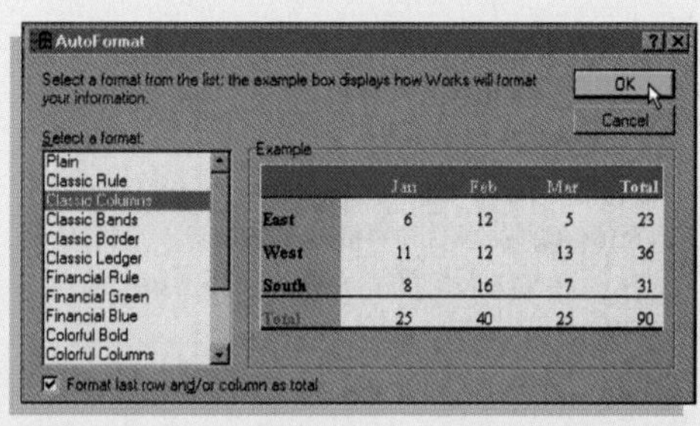

**3** In the AutoFormat dialog box, select a format. Works displays an example of the selected format. Click on OK.

# Troubleshooting Spreadsheet Problems

Despite your grasp of all the spreadsheet techniques, it is just possible that problems may occur. Fortunately, in many cases, Works will recognize that fact and will display a dialog box with helpful information. In those cases, simply follow the prompts.

In this section topic and the next, you will learn how to deal with problems in formatting and in calculations that Works will not detect. These are common problems which you will soon learn to avoid when constructing your spreadsheets.

The Tip Sheet tells you which steps apply to a given problem.

When you type text that overflows a cell, and the cell to the right of the current cell contains information, your text will be truncated to fit the cell. You can correct this by widening the column as described in the second topic of this chapter.

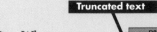

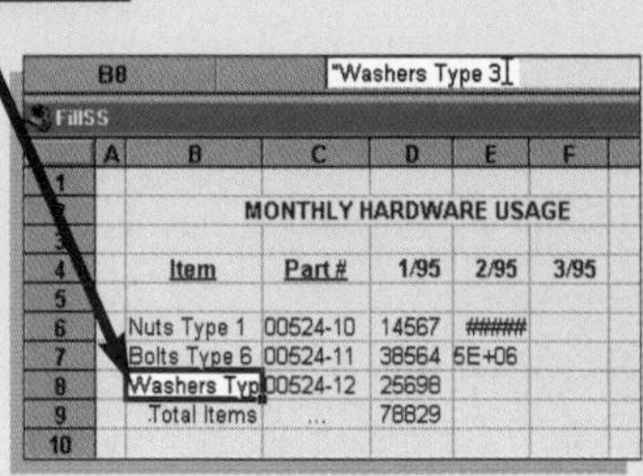


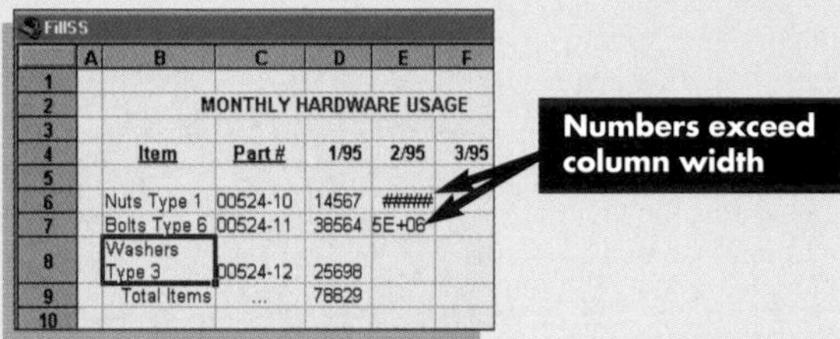

If, when entering numbers, you exceed the column width, Works will enter in the cell either pound (#) signs or an exponential format for the number.

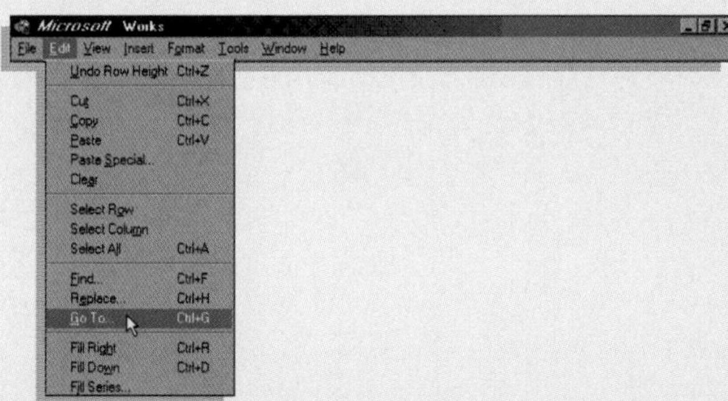

To recover the hidden row or column, first select Go To in the Edit menu.

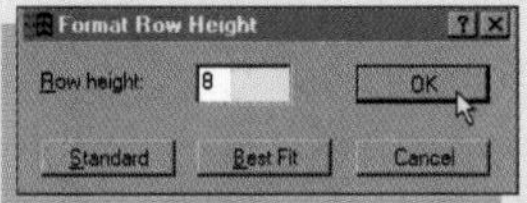

In the Format Row Height dialog box, type in any number greater than zero. Click on OK.

**TIP SHEET**

- **Truncated text: steps 1—3**
- **Numbers overflow cell: steps 4 and 5**
- **Missing row or column: steps 6—10**
- **Gridlines missing in printout: steps 11 and 12**

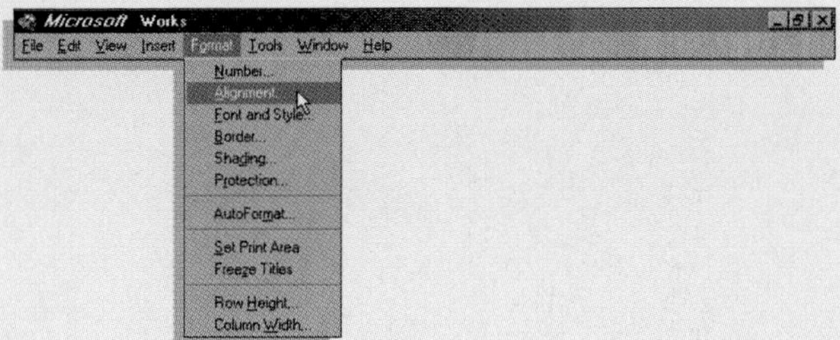


**2** In a second approach to truncation problems, first choose Alignment from the Format menu.

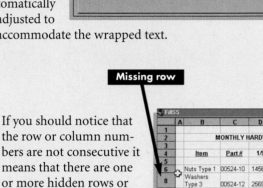

**3** In the Format Cells dialog box, select Wrap text and click on OK. The row height will be automatically adjusted to accommodate the wrapped text.

**5** To remedy this problem, widen the column by either dragging the column header right border or by double-clicking on the header.

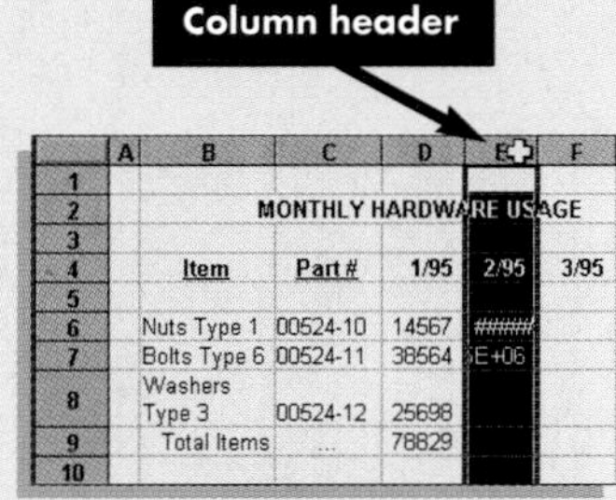


**6** If you should notice that the row or column numbers are not consecutive it means that there are one or more hidden rows or columns. These were discussed in the second topic of this chapter.

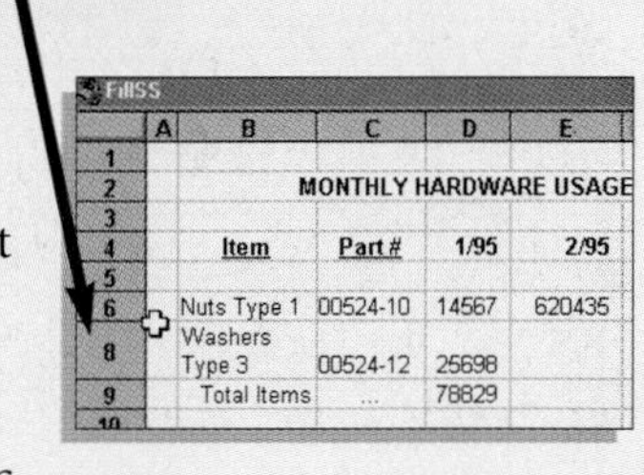


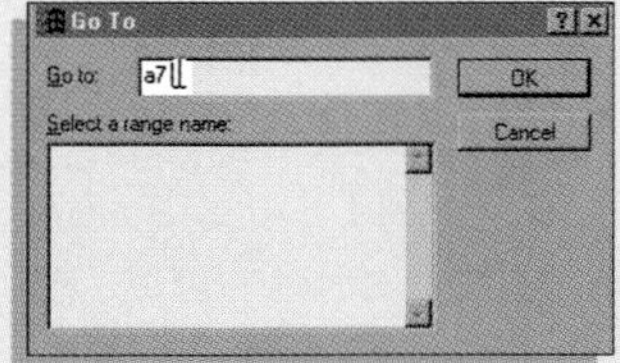


**8** In the Go To dialog box, type any cell reference in the row or column of interest and click on OK.

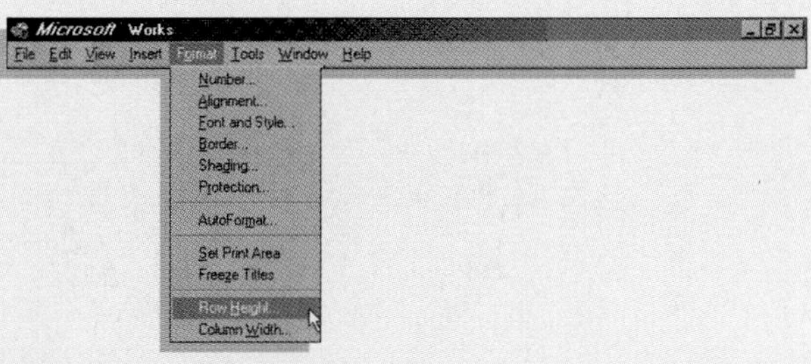


**9** In the Format menu, choose Row Height or Column Width. as appropriate.

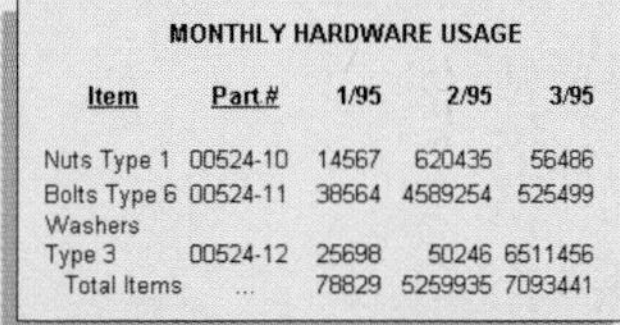

MONTHLY HARDWARE USAGE

| Item | Part # | 1/95 | 2/95 | 3/95 |
|---|---|---|---|---|
| Nuts Type 1 | 00524-10 | 14567 | 620435 | 56486 |
| Bolts Type 6 | 00524-11 | 38564 | 4589254 | 525499 |
| Washers Type 3 | 00524-12 | 25698 | 50246 | 6511456 |
| Total Items | ... | 78829 | 5259935 | 7093441 |

**11** If, when printing your spreadsheet, there are no gridlines as shown here, but you wish them to be printed, first select Page Setup in the File menu.

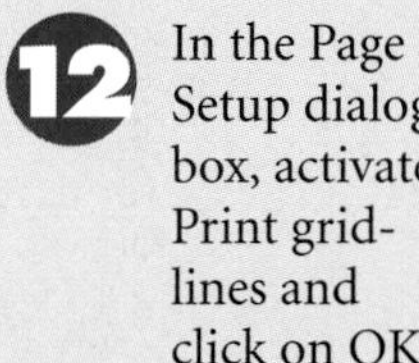

**12** In the Page Setup dialog box, activate Print gridlines and click on OK.

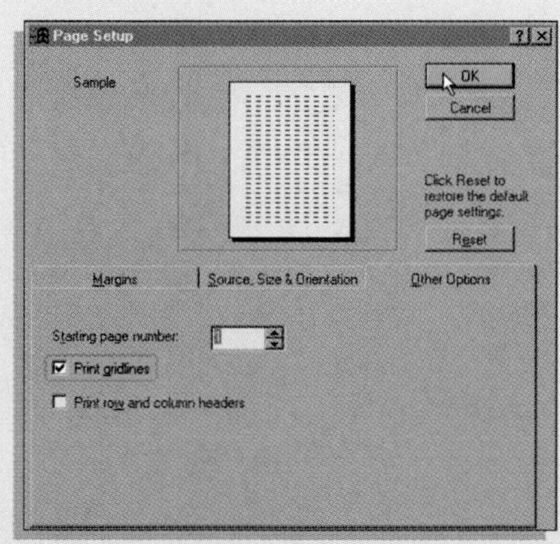

# Troubleshooting Spreadsheet Problems (Continued)

Aside from format problems, you may occasionally encounter unexpected results from your spreadsheet formulas. Generally, Works gives you a warning notice if a formula is incorrectly entered and will often highlight the specific part which is in error. The following are common problems which will give you unexpected results, but cannot be detected by Works. Plan your formulas carefully to avoid these.

Improper ("rocky") range name

E11 =admin94/1994

| | A | B | C | D | E | F |
|---|---|---|---|---|---|---|
| 1 | | Food Science Department | | | | |
| 2 | | | | | % OF TOTAL: | |
| 3 | | | 1994 | 1995 | '94 | |
| 4 | | Administrative Expenses | | | | |
| 5 | | Travel | 6,600 | 1,800 | | |
| 6 | | Education | 8,300 | 6,200 | | |
| 7 | | Consulting Fees | 23,500 | 20,000 | | |
| 8 | | Office equipment | 10,400 | 8,000 | | |
| 9 | | Office Supplies | 1,800 | 1,000 | | |
| 10 | | Recruiting | 7,000 | 4,000 | | |
| 11 | | Subtotal | 57,600 | 41,000 | 2888.7% | |

If your result appears to be incorrect, check the formula in the Formula Bar. In this example, notice that the number 1994, which was intended to be a range name, appears as a divisor. Improper or "rocky" range names containing numbers, cell references, or function names (1994, B1, AVG) can create problems.

Alphanumeric name

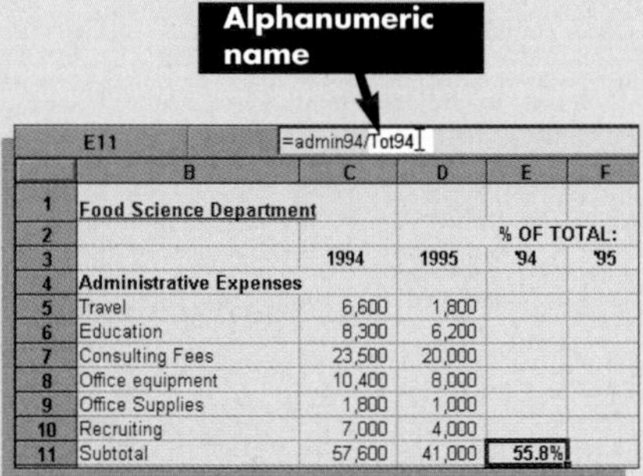

E11 =admin94/Tot94

| | B | C | D | E | F |
|---|---|---|---|---|---|
| 1 | Food Science Department | | | | |
| 2 | | | | % OF TOTAL: | |
| 3 | | 1994 | 1995 | '94 | '95 |
| 4 | Administrative Expenses | | | | |
| 5 | Travel | 6,600 | 1,800 | | |
| 6 | Education | 8,300 | 6,200 | | |
| 7 | Consulting Fees | 23,500 | 20,000 | | |
| 8 | Office equipment | 10,400 | 8,000 | | |
| 9 | Office Supplies | 1,800 | 1,000 | | |
| 10 | Recruiting | 7,000 | 4,000 | | |
| 11 | Subtotal | 57,600 | 41,000 | 55.8% | |

Click on the cell containing the formula and change its contents to use the new range name.

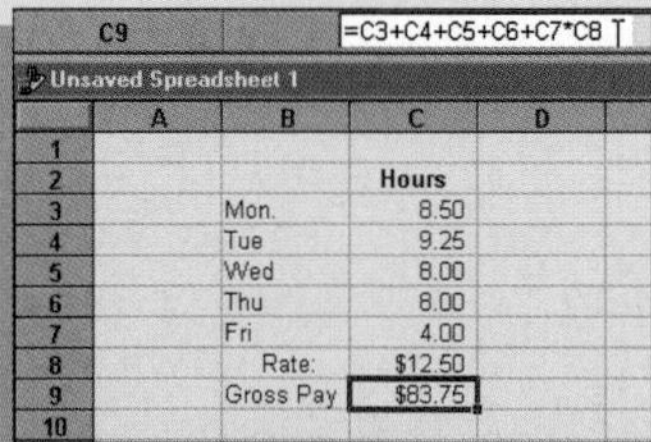

C9 =C3+C4+C5+C6+C7*C8

Unsaved Spreadsheet 1

| | A | B | C | D |
|---|---|---|---|---|
| 1 | | | | |
| 2 | | | Hours | |
| 3 | | Mon. | 8.50 | |
| 4 | | Tue | 9.25 | |
| 5 | | Wed | 8.00 | |
| 6 | | Thu | 8.00 | |
| 7 | | Fri | 4.00 | |
| 8 | | Rate: | $12.50 | |
| 9 | | Gross Pay | $83.75 | |
| 10 | | | | |

If there are multiple operators in your formula, failure to follow the rules of precedence can cause unexpected results as shown here. Review the formula structure in the Formula bar.

**TIP SHEET**

- **Improper range names: steps 13—16. Also refer to "How to Create and Use Range Names."**
- **Copied cell references are normally relative: steps 17 and 18. Also refer to "How to Work with Absolute, Relative, and Mixed Cell References."**
- **Failure to follow calculation operator precedence rules: steps 19 and 20. Also refer to "How to Create Formulas with Multiple Operators."**

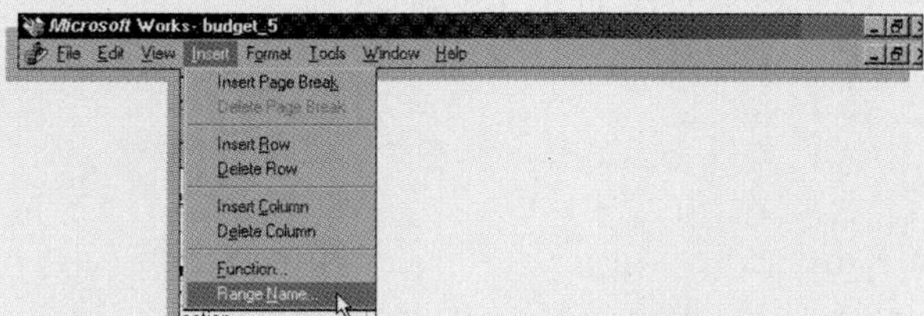

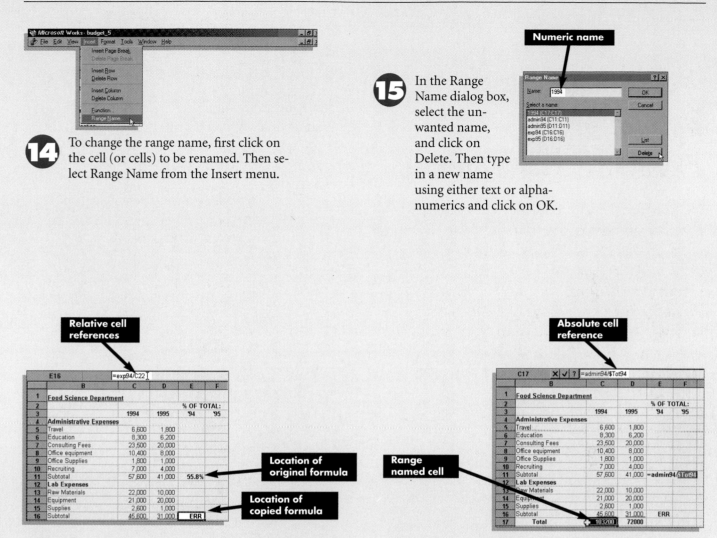

To change the range name, first click on the cell (or cells) to be renamed. Then select Range Name from the Insert menu.

15 In the Range Name dialog box, select the unwanted name, and click on Delete. Then type in a new name using either text or alphanumerics and click on OK.

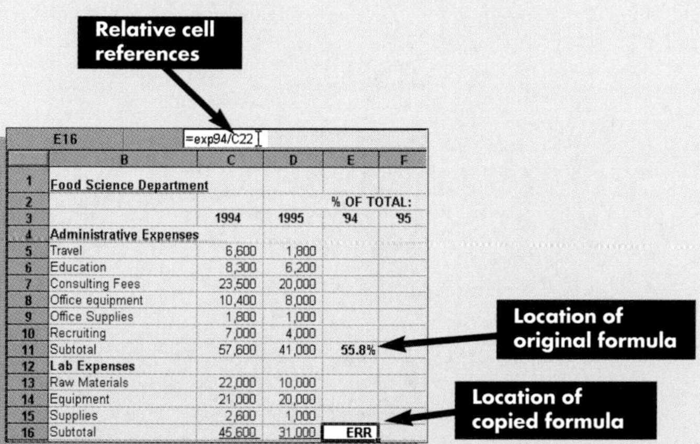


| E16 | =exp94/C22 | | | | |
|---|---|---|---|---|---|
| | B | C | D | E | F |
| 1 | Food Science Department | | | | |
| 2 | | | | % OF TOTAL: | |
| 3 | | 1994 | 1995 | '94 | '95 |
| 4 | Administrative Expenses | | | | |
| 5 | Travel | 6,600 | 1,800 | | |
| 6 | Education | 8,300 | 6,200 | | |
| 7 | Consulting Fees | 23,500 | 20,000 | | |
| 8 | Office equipment | 10,400 | 8,000 | | |
| 9 | Office Supplies | 1,800 | 1,000 | | |
| 10 | Recruiting | 7,000 | 4,000 | | |
| 11 | Subtotal | 57,600 | 41,000 | 55.8% | |
| 12 | Lab Expenses | | | | |
| 13 | Raw Materials | 22,000 | 10,000 | | |
| 14 | Equipment | 21,000 | 20,000 | | |
| 15 | Supplies | 2,600 | 1,000 | | |
| 16 | Subtotal | 45,600 | 31,000 | ERR | |

If a formula is copied from one cell to another, the cell references will normally change relatively. This can introduce undesired results as shown here where cell C22 is referenced instead of Tot94.

18 It may be necessary to change the original formula to contain either an absolute or mixed cell reference. Highlight the incorrect cell reference in the formula and also the range named cell. Then press the function key F4 until $ signs appear to create an absolute or mixed cell reference. Copying and pasting the new formula to the second location will then correct the problem.

Use parentheses to change the order of calculations so that the operations are performed in the correct sequence.

# TRY IT!

All of your rehearsals in the last chapter lead to this, the grand finale of…Works Spreadsheets Made Easy! This production will demonstrate the ease with which you are now able to create a modest little spreadsheet containing some of the more advanced techniques. You will get rave reviews!

As you proceed through the following steps, you may find it convenient to use the Zoom control at the bottom of the screen to reduce the size of the spreadsheet, thereby saving you from scrolling to observe off-screen columns.

Start Works and create a new spreadsheet by clicking on the Spreadsheet button under the Works Tool tab. *Chapter 9*

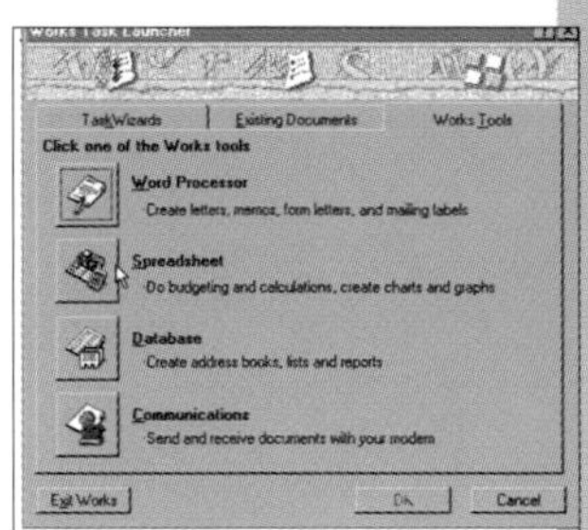


**Weekly Payroll**

| NAME | RATE | HOURS | EARNINGS | FEDERAL | STATE | CHECK AMT |
|---|---|---|---|---|---|---|
| Stacy R | 15.50 | 48.00 | 1116.00 | 84.00 | 18.00 | 928.63 |
| Brandon V | 12.25 | 50.00 | 918.75 | 60.00 | 14.00 | 831.43 |
| Paige E | 9.75 | 24.00 | 234.00 | 0.00 | 0.00 | 234.00 |
| John G | 8.50 | 32.00 | 272.00 | 0.00 | 0.00 | 272.00 |

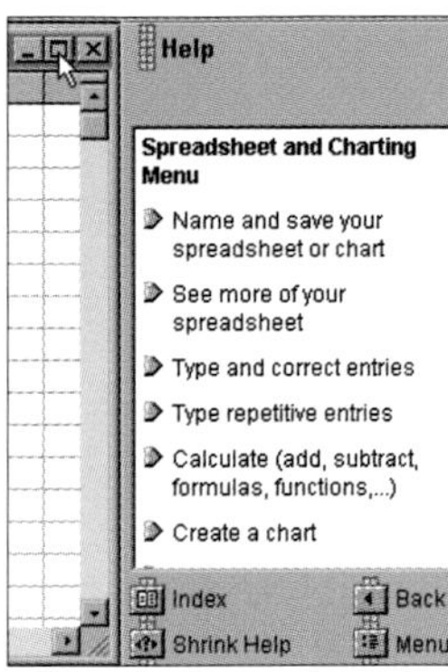


Minimize Help by clicking on the Shrink Help icon below the Help window. Also maximize the document by clicking on the Maximize button on the Toolbar. *Chapter 9*

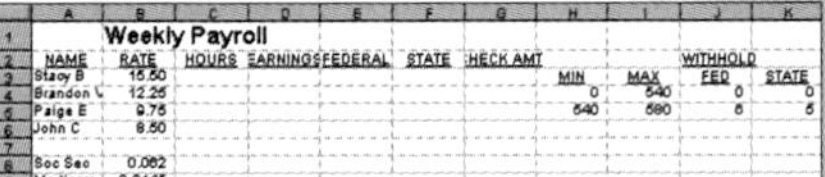

This will be a payroll spreadsheet. Enter the information shown. Choose your own font style and size for title and headings and use centering or bold as necessary. *Chapter 9*

Get in the habit of saving your work early and often. Click on the Save icon in the Toolbar and save the spreadsheet as **Payroll**. *Chapter 9*

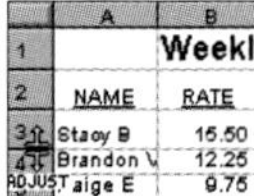

To improve the appearance of the spreadsheet, increase the height of row 2 by adjusting the lower boundary of its header button. Repeat the process for row 3. *Chapter 13*

Adjust column widths by double-clicking on each column header button. For columns B and J, adjust the widths by dragging the right boundary of the header button. *Chaptesr 13*

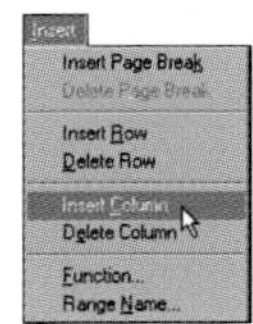


To separate the table of withholding from the rest of the spreadsheet, insert a column by clicking anywhere in column H and then selecting Insert Column from the Insert menu. *Chapter 13*

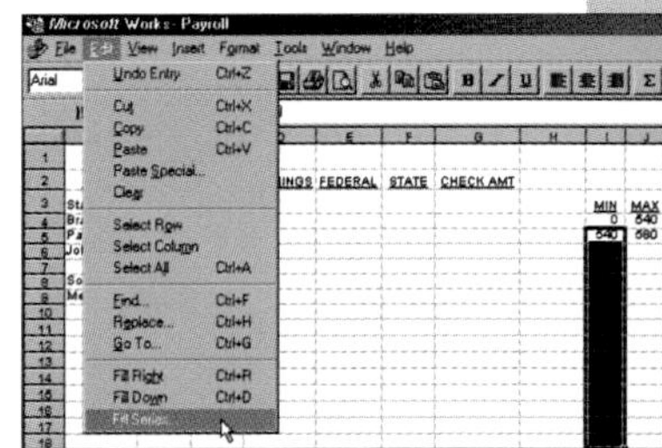

To add necessary values to the withholding table, highlight cells I4 through I18 and choose Fill Series from the Edit menu. *Chapter 13*

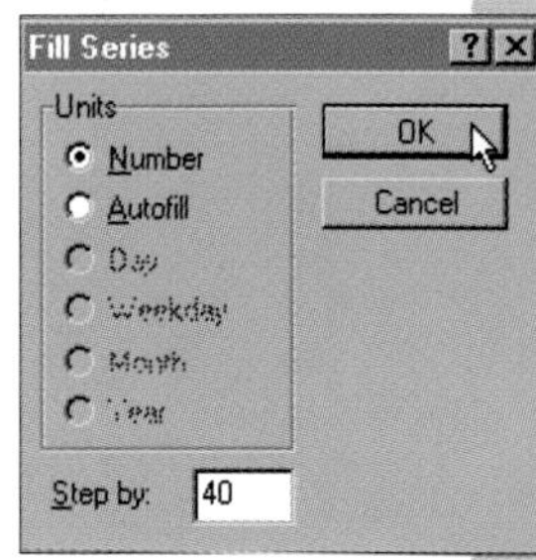


In the Fill Series dialog box, make sure that Number is selected. Then enter the number **40** in the Step By box and click OK. *Chapter 13*

10

Continue filling in the withholding table as in the previous step. Use increment values of **40**, **6**, and **1** for columns J, K, and L. *Chapter 13*

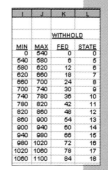

| I | J | K | L |
|---|---|---|---|
| | | WITHHOLD | |
| MIN | MAX | FED | STATE |
| 0 | 540 | 0 | 0 |
| 540 | 580 | 6 | 5 |
| 580 | 620 | 12 | 6 |
| 620 | 660 | 18 | 7 |
| 660 | 700 | 24 | 8 |
| 700 | 740 | 30 | 9 |
| 740 | 780 | 36 | 10 |
| 780 | 820 | 42 | 11 |
| 820 | 860 | 48 | 12 |
| 860 | 900 | 54 | 13 |
| 900 | 940 | 60 | 14 |
| 940 | 980 | 66 | 15 |
| 980 | 1020 | 72 | 16 |
| 1020 | 1060 | 78 | 17 |
| 1060 | 1100 | 84 | 18 |

Continue to next page ▶

# TRY IT!

Continue below

To create range names to be used in your formulas, begin by highlighting cells B3:B6 in the Rate column and selecting Range Name from the Insert menu. *Chapter 13*

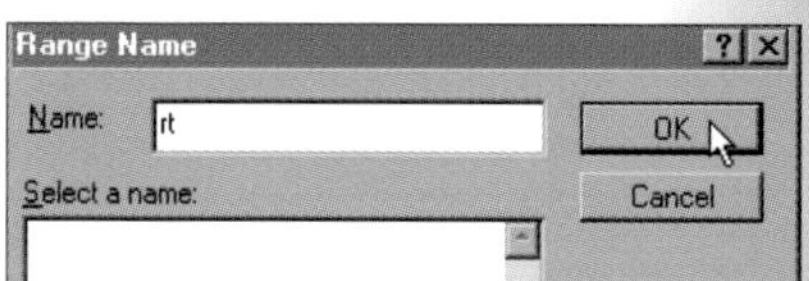


In the Range Name dialog box note that Rate is suggested as the range name. To reduce the amount of typing in your formulas, use abbreviations where possible. In this example, type **rt** and click OK. *Chapter 13*

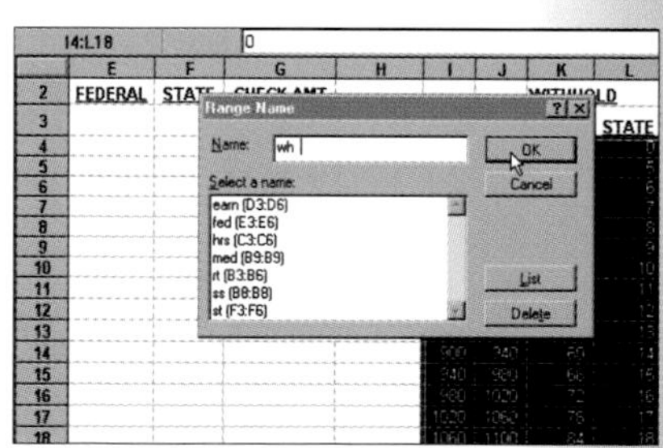

Repeat the step 12 process to create range names for cells C3:C6, D3:D6, E3:E6, F3:F6, I4:L18, B8, and B9 as shown in this dialog box. Use the names **hrs**, **earn**, **fed**, **st**, **wh**, **ss**, and **med** respectively. *Chapter 13*

=IF(hrs>40,rt*(1.5*hrs),rt*hrs)

In cell D3, enter the EARNINGS formula shown. This formula allows for overtime at time-and-a-half. *Chapter 13*

Copy the formula in cell D3 to cells D4:D6 using the copy-and-paste technique.

=vlookup(earn,wh,2)

In cell E3 enter the Federal withholding table lookup formula shown. Copy the formula to cells E4:E6. *Chapter 13*

=VLOOKUP(D4,I5:L19,2)

An error indication appears because the copied formula contains relative cell references for the range name "wh" part, namely I5:L19. *Chapter 13*

=VLOOKUP(D3,$wh,2)

To correct the problem, go back to the original formula in cell E3 and insert a $ sign before "wh" to make the cell range reference absolute. Copy the corrected formula into cells E4:E6. *Chapter 13*

=vlookup(earn,$wh,3)

In cell F3 enter the State withholding lookup formula shown here. Remember to make "**wh**" absolute and note that desired withholding is in the third offset column of the table. Copy the formula into cells F4:F6. *Chapter 13*

**20**

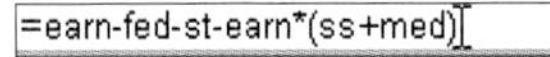


In cell G3, enter the Check Amt formula shown here. Copy the formula into cells G4:G6.

Protect all of the data in your spreadsheet except in the column of Hours which will changed weekly. Highlight cells C3:C63 and choose Protection in the Format menu. *Chapter 13*

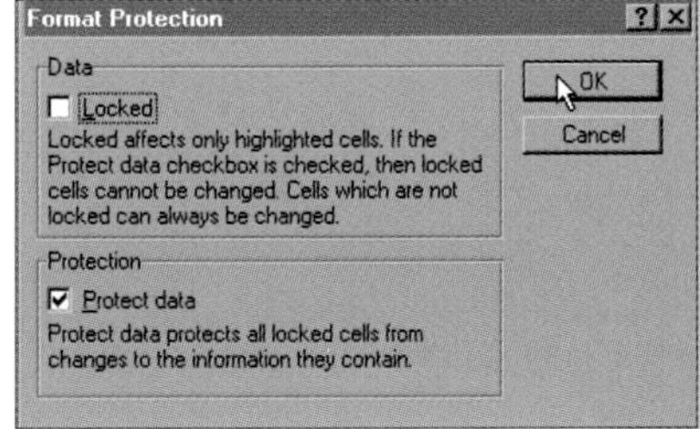


In the Format Protection dialog box, click on the Protect Data box and clear the Locked box. *Chapter 13*

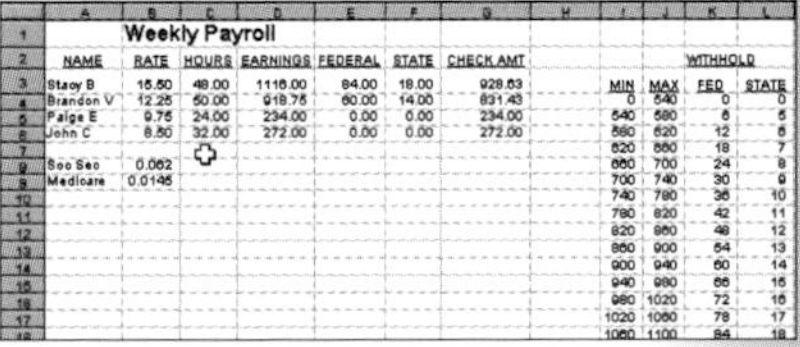


Enter the number of hours in cell C3:C6 and observe the formula results for Earnings, Federal & State withholding, and Check Amt. Try to enter any number into any other cell and notice that they are protected. *Chapter 13*

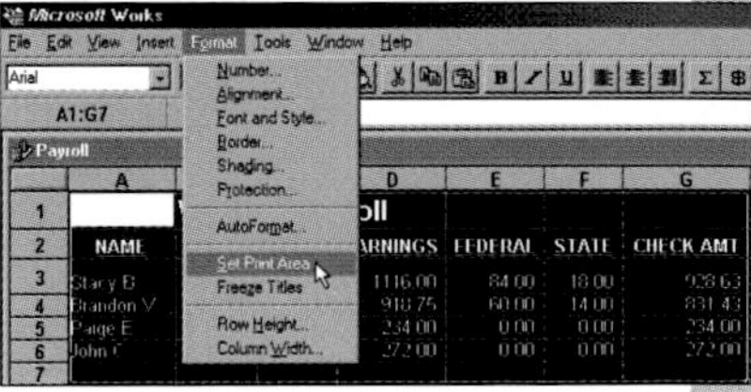

To select only a part of the total spreadsheet for printing, you must first turn off protection by deselecting Protect Data in the Format Protection dialog box. (Refer to steps 21 and 22.) Then highlight the cells to be printed and click on Set Print Area in the Format menu.

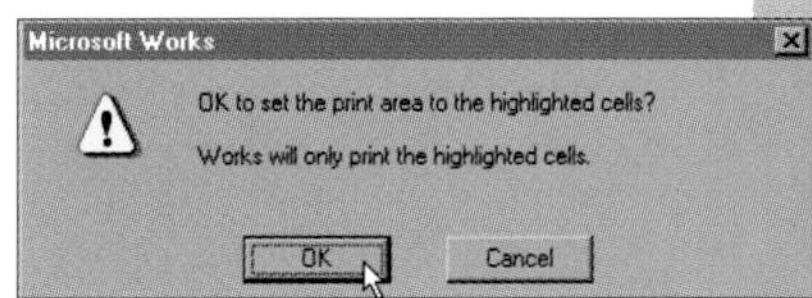


In the Works verification box, click on OK.

**26**

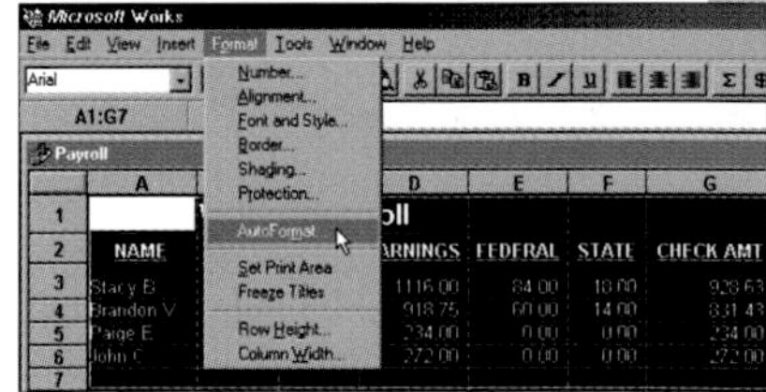

To create a special effect in your spreadsheet, select AutoFormat from the Format menu. *Chapter 13*

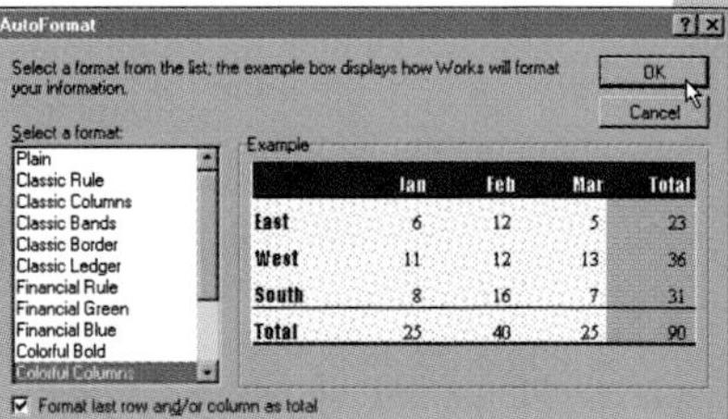


Select a format from the list and click OK. *Chapter 13*

If you wish to keep your spreadsheet protected, repeat steps 21 and 22.

## CHAPTER 14

# Creating Charts in a Spreadsheet

Although spreadsheets are useful for organizing and analyzing your data, their usefulness can be greatly enhanced by adding charts. Charts of various types display the relationships of spreadsheet numbers in graphic form. They allow you to quickly visualize and easily identify trends as well as maximum and minimum values. Charts can be created in various types: bar, line, pie, scatter, combination, area, 3-D bar, 3-D area, and 3-D line.

The simplest chart can be created from your spreadsheet by just selecting the type of chart you want. Up to eight charts of the same or different types can be created using the data from one spreadsheet.

You may choose to chart all or just a part of the spreadsheet, and each chart can represent different portions of your overall spreadsheet. You can tailor the chart's appearance to your liking by adding titles, labels, and legends, and by changing fonts, color, and patterns.

# Chart Basics

As you will see throughout this chapter, Works provides you with a great degree of flexibility in the preparation of your charts with very little effort on your part. Also, as you select chart types and add text to them, Works displays a reduced version of the chart so you can see the results of your selections.

## TIP SHEET

- **If you do not have a color printer, Works detects this and selects patterns to apply to the chart instead of colors.**
- **You may switch your view between charts and spreadsheets by selecting the applicable chart or spreadsheet name in the Window menu.**
- **The fastest way to switch from the chart to the spreadsheet is to click on the Go To 1st Series icon in the toolbar. This action will also highlight your first series.**
- **For a pie chart, the Edit: Data Labels command enables you to apply percentage labels or numbers (1,2,3...) to the slices.**

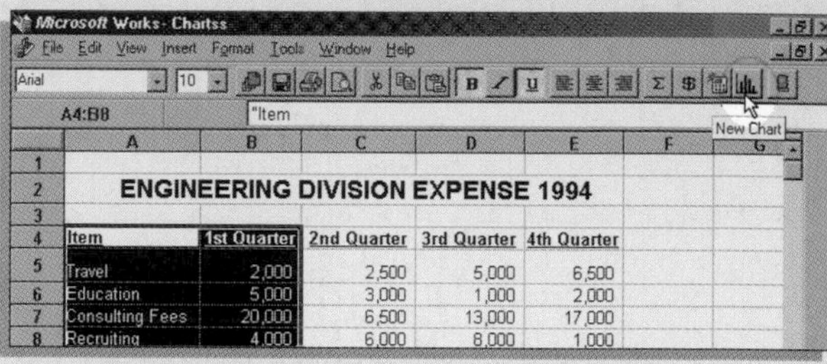

Microsoft Works - Chartss
File Edit View Insert Format Tools Window Help
Arial
10
A4:B8
"Item
New Chart
A B C D E F G
ENGINEERING DIVISION EXPENSE 1994
Item 1st Quarter 2nd Quarter 3rd Quarter 4th Quarter
Travel 2,000 2,500 5,000 6,500
Education 5,000 3,000 1,000 2,000
Consulting Fees 20,000 6,500 13,000 17,000
Recruiting 4,000 6,000 8,000 1,000

1. Highlight the data in the spreadsheet that you wish to have charted, including the legend and category cells, and click on the New Chart icon in the toolbar.

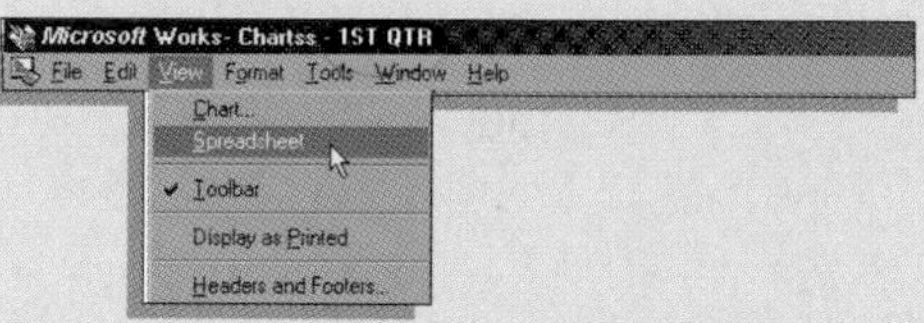


6. To return to the spreadsheet, click on Spreadsheet in the View menu.

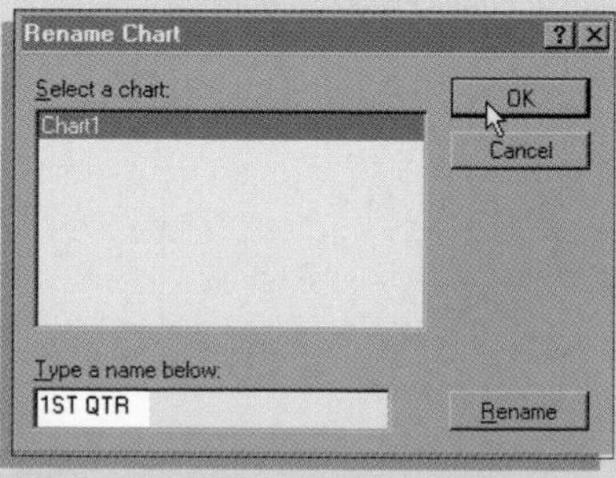


5. Type in a descriptive name and click OK.

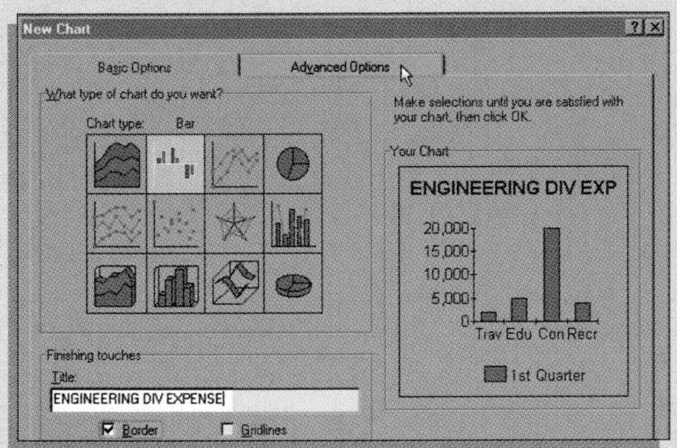


**2** In the Basic Options folder of the New Chart dialog box, click on the chart type you wish. You may also type in a title and select gridlines and a border. Open the Advanced Options folder by clicking on its tab. (If the First Time Help dialog box appears after clicking on New Chart, you may choose to take a quick tour of charting. If not, simply click on OK to skip Help.)

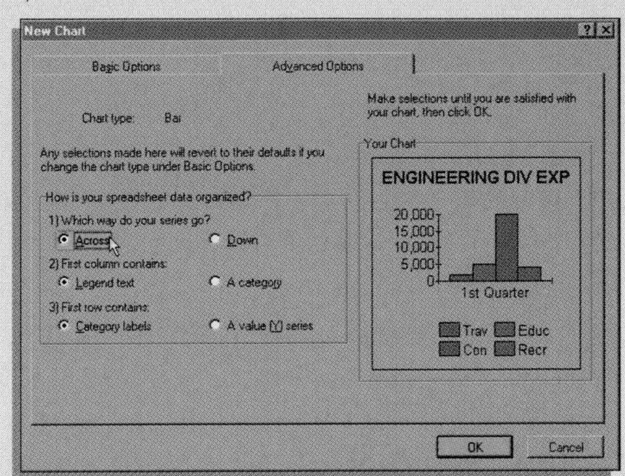


**3** You may select different ways of organizing your spreadsheet data to obtain other chart orientations which are displayed for you. When you are satisfied with your selections, click OK.

**4** After the chart is in your window, you can give it a name by choosing Rename Chart from the Tools menu.

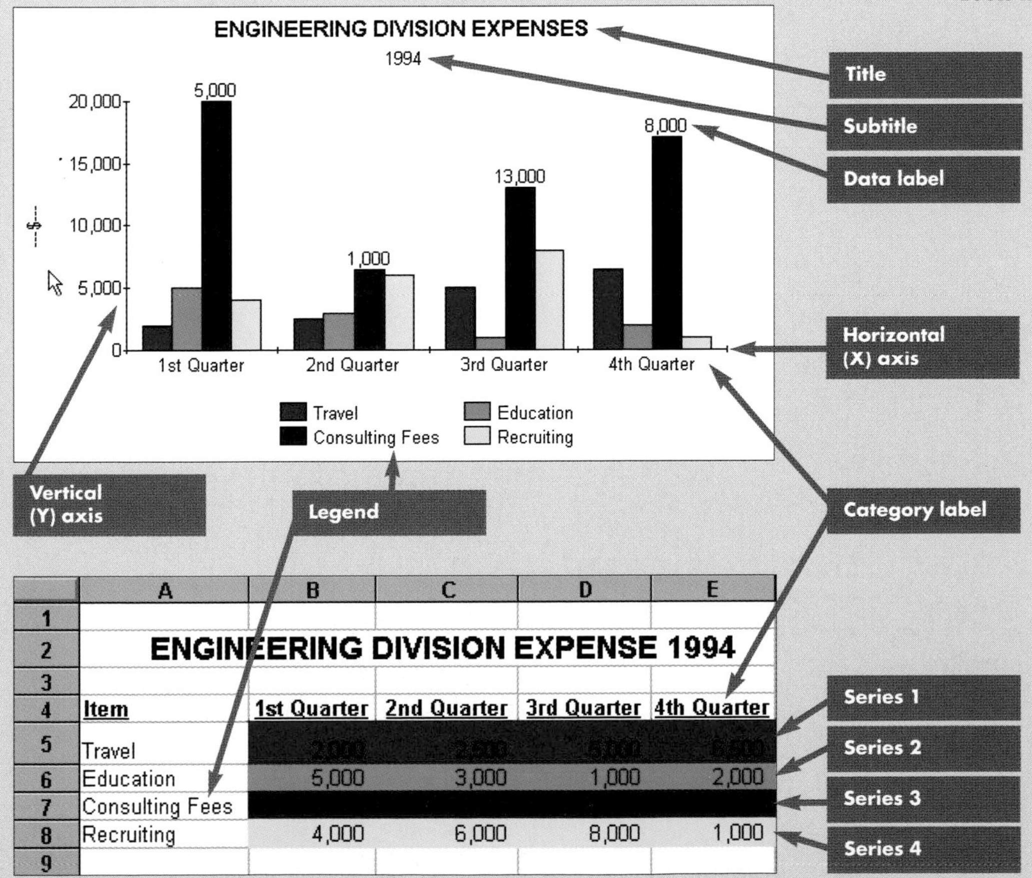

# Chart Basics (Continued)

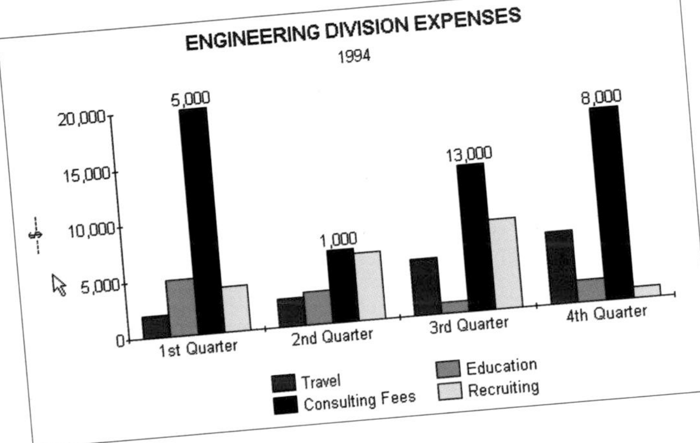


The sets of numbers in either columns or rows are the *series* which are plotted against the Y axis in the chart. Works can plot as many as six series on a chart. The *legend* series is usually the set of text with which the numbers are associated. The *categories* are also associated with the numbers and typically are the X axis scale. Categories and legends are interchangeable depending on the number of columns versus the number of rows you have selected. Fortunately, Works detects the column-to-row relationship and sets up the chart accordingly.

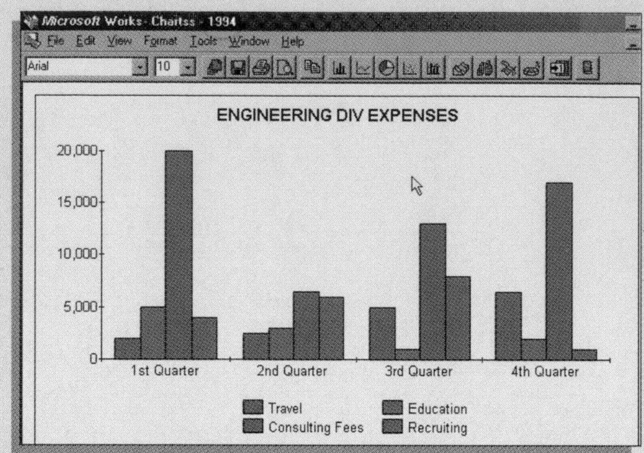


7 To create additional charts, highlight the range of cells to be charted and repeat steps 1 through 5. Be sure to give the new chart a different name.

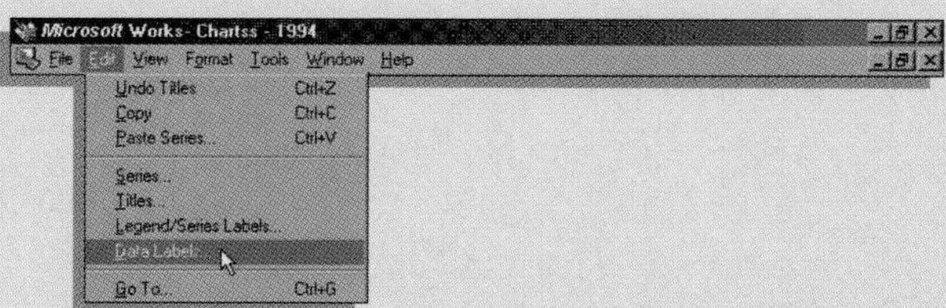


10 If you wish to have specific data values shown on one or more of your chart series, select Data Labels from the Edit menu.

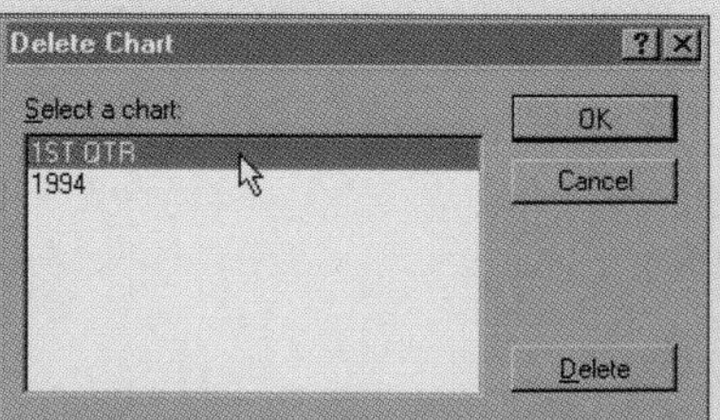


13 In the Delete Chart dialog box, click on the chart name and click OK.

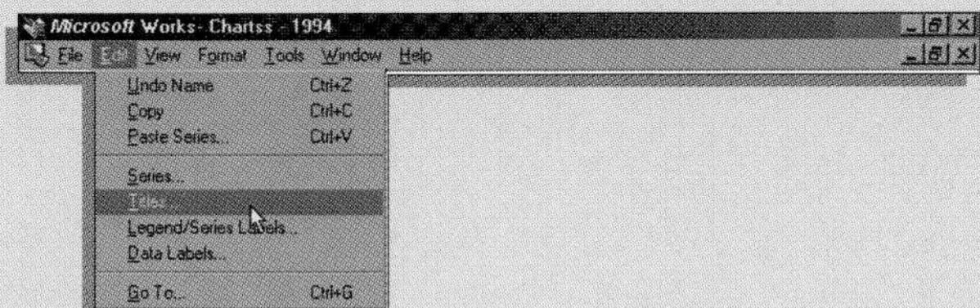


**8** To add or change titles, select Titles from the Edit menu.

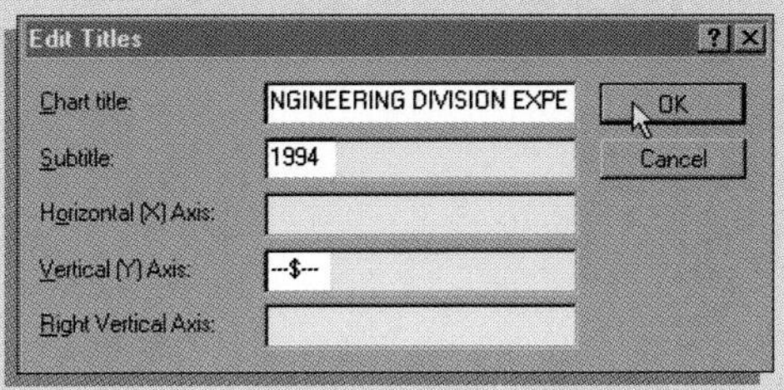


**9** In the Edit Titles dialog box type the information you wish displayed for the main chart titles and for the axes.

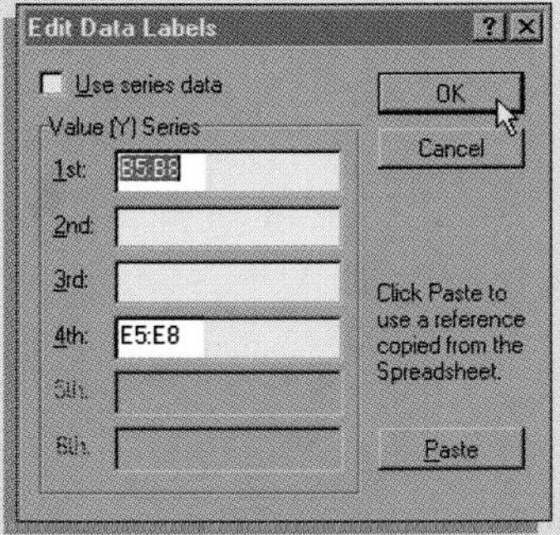


**11** In the Edit Data Labels dialog box, enter the cell location of the specific values you wish displayed. You may display all data values by checking the Use Series Data box.

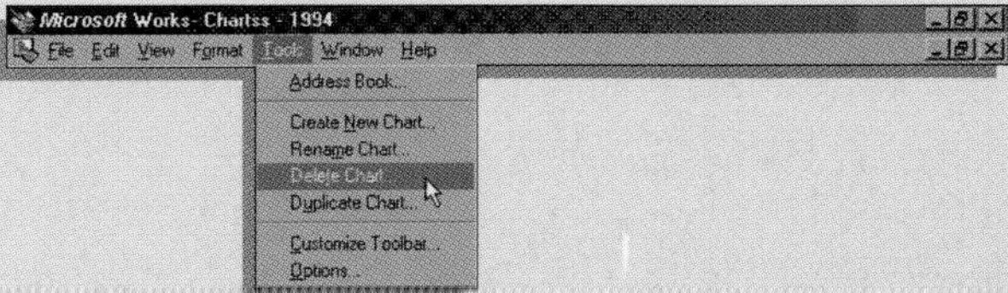


**12** To delete one of your charts, select Delete Chart from the Tools menu

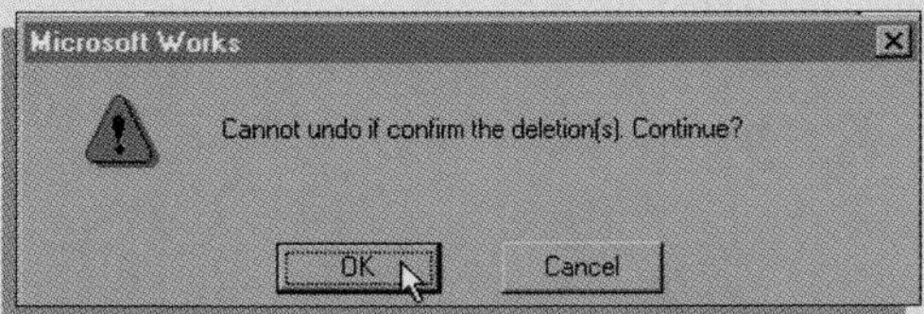


**14** Works gives a deletion warning because you cannot undo this action once it is taken. Click OK.

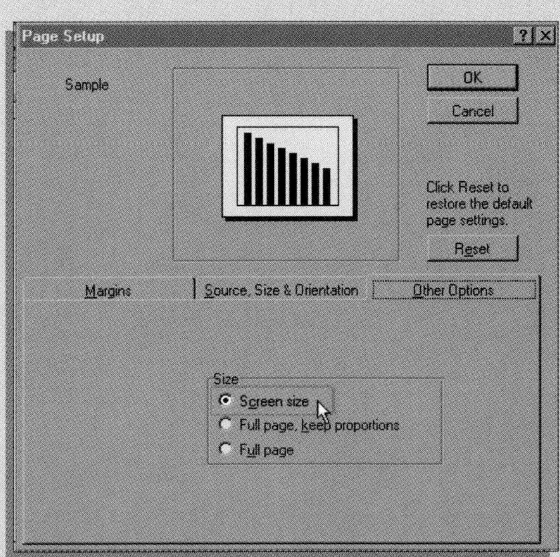


**15** To prepare to print your chart, select Page Setup from the File menu and choose the size and orientation you wish. Use the Print Preview to verify your selection.

# Formatting Chart Objects

After creating your basic chart, you will want to spruce it up to give it a professional presentation quality. Some of the things you can do include selecting text fonts, styles, colors, and patterns, adding a second vertical axis, changing the axis scaling, and adding borders and gridlines.

To start any of these actions in the following steps, you will first click on the Format menu and then choose the specific command indicated in each step given here. The one exception to this rule is step 1.

If you wish to show gridlines, they can be selected using the Horizontal and Vertical Axis commands in the Format menu.

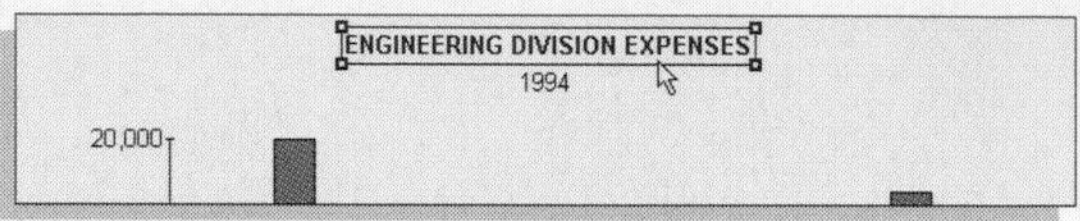

Font and Style: To change the appearance of the text in your titles, click on the title itself to obtain the control box surrounding it and then go to the Format menu. For all other text, start with the Format menu.

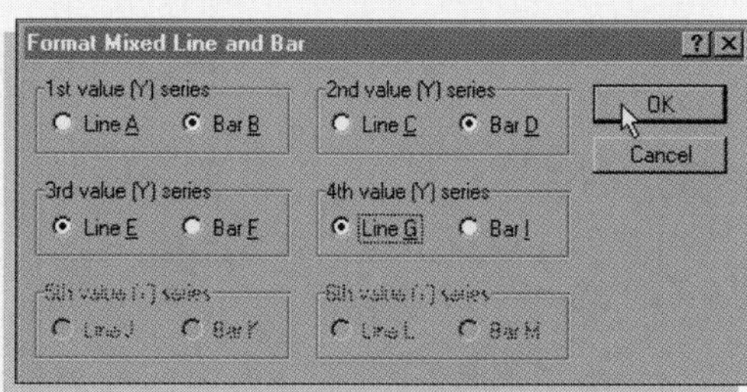

Mixed Line and Bar: For each series choose whether it should be plotted as a line or a bar.

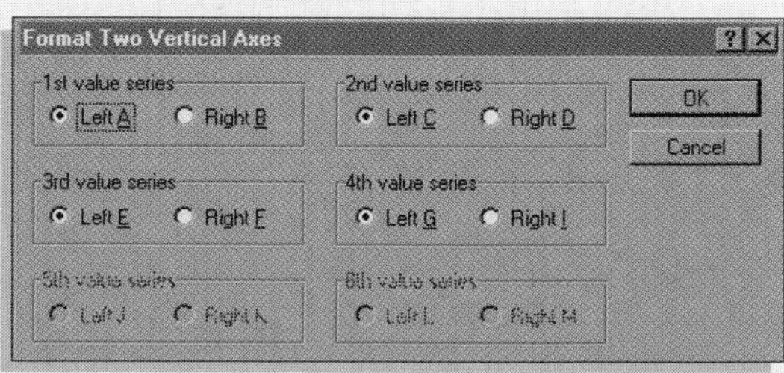

Two Vertical Axes: If you wish some of your series to be plotted against a second (right) axis, designate which ones will use the right scale versus the left.

**TIP SHEET**

- **For line charts you can choose the type of data point marker you wish by using the Format Shading and Color command.**
- **For pie charts, the Shading and Color command also allows you to explode slices away from the rest of the pie.**
- **For scatter charts, the Horizontal Axis command allows you to select the minimum, maximum, and interval scale values and to choose a logarithmic scale.**
- **For area and 3-D area charts, the Horizontal Axis command gives an option to display droplines from the breakpoints in the chart.**

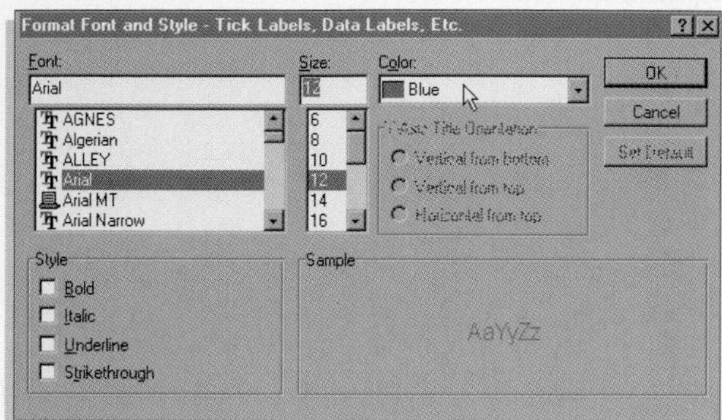


**2** Make your selections in the dialog box and click OK.

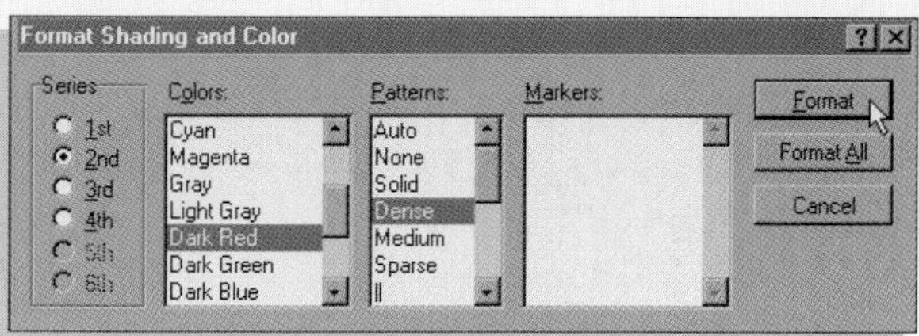


**3** Shading and Color: In the dialog box, choose the color and pattern for each or all of the series. Click Format or Format All, as applicable.

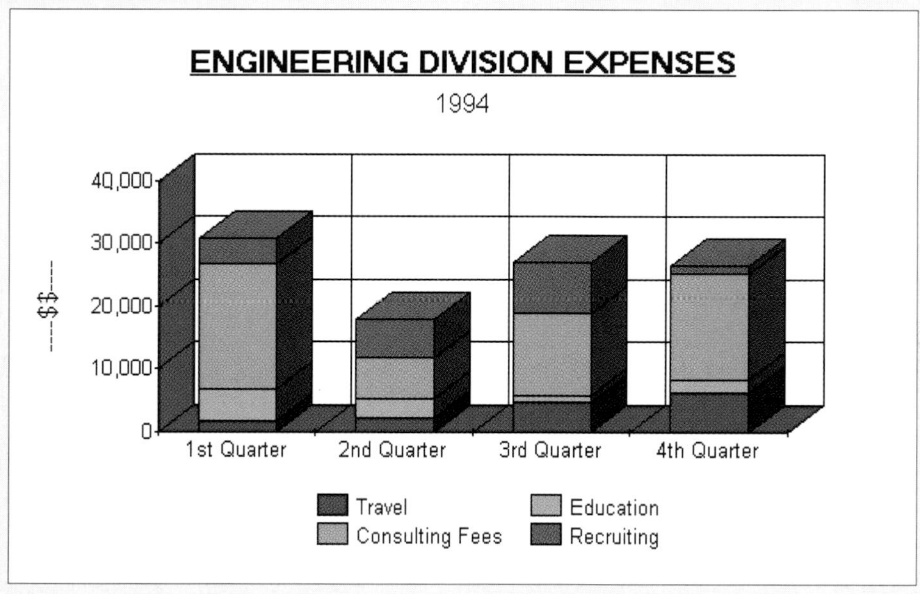


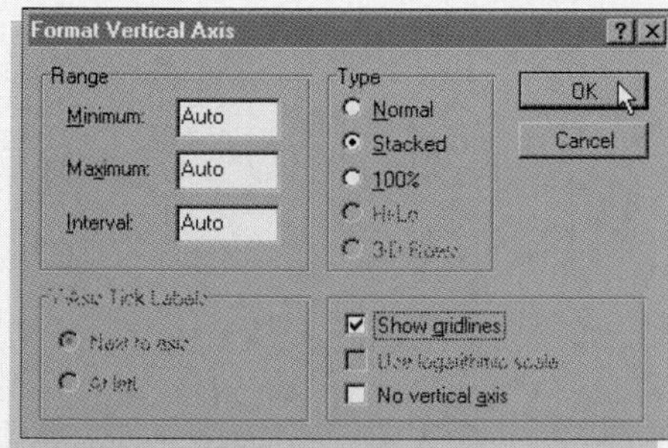


**5** Vertical (Y) Axis: The Minimum, Maximum, and Interval boxes allow you to alter the scale of the Y axis. The axis type "Stacked" will show the series values stacked on one another, while "100%" stacks the values and uses a percent scale. "Logarithmic" scale uses axis increments that are a power of 10.

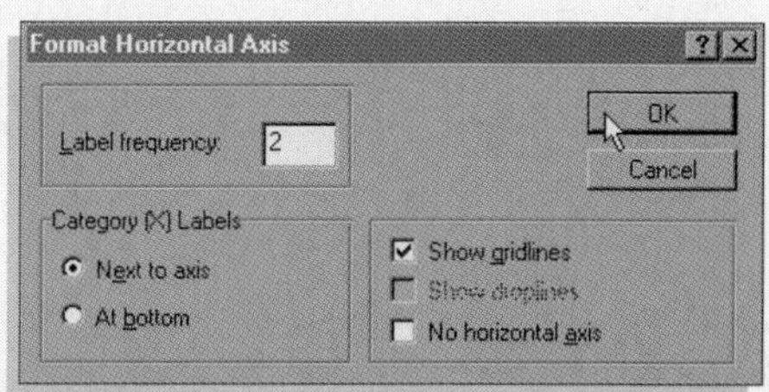


**4** Horizontal (X) Axis: Make your selection for Category labels, Gridlines, or No axis. In the Label Frequency box, value 1 labels each category, value 2 labels every other category, and so forth. Using these values can reduce clutter or overlapping labels.

# Changing the Chart Type

If you believe your current chart type isn't giving the graphic picture you think will convey your information, Works has a few alternatives available to you. The library of charts contains 12 basic types and 65 variations. Choosing which one is best is easy because the Chart Type dialog box provides a preview each time you select a type and variation.

Experimenting with different types can be a gratifying experience. Try it…you might like it!

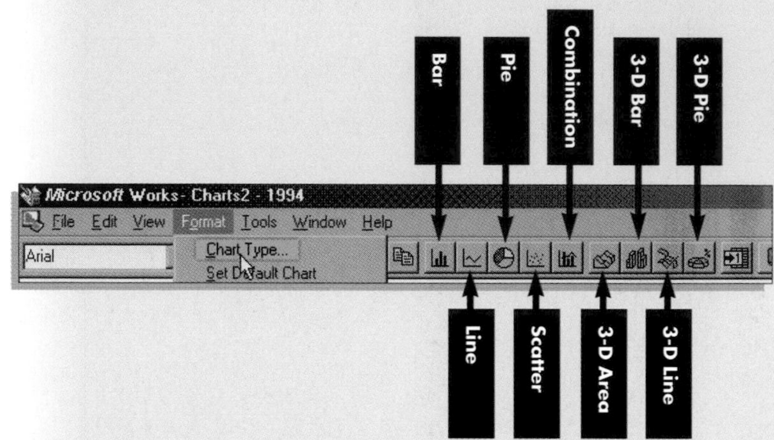


1. With your chart in view, select Chart Type from the Format menu or click on any of the chart type icons on the toolbar.

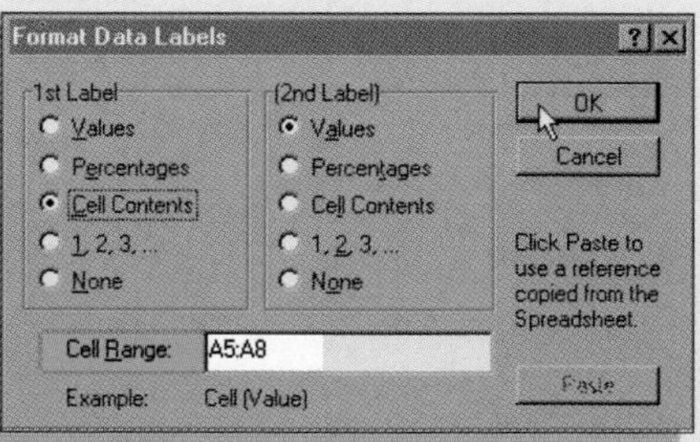

Format Data Labels

1st Label: Values / Percentages / Cell Contents / 1, 2, 3, ... / None

2nd Label: Values / Percentages / Cell Contents / 1, 2, 3, ... / None

OK | Cancel

Click Paste to use a reference copied from the Spreadsheet.

Cell Range: A5:A8

Example: Cell (Value)

Paste

6. To recover data labels for your pie chart, choose Data Labels in the Edit menu and select from the choices for the 1st and 2nd Labels in the dialog box. Also, enter the cell range which contains the text labels if you wish to use them.

**TIP SHEET**

- **As an alternative to steps 5 and 6, you may want to create a whole new pie chart by switching back to the spreadsheet, highlighting the cell ranges for labels and data values, and proceeding to create the new chart to your design.**

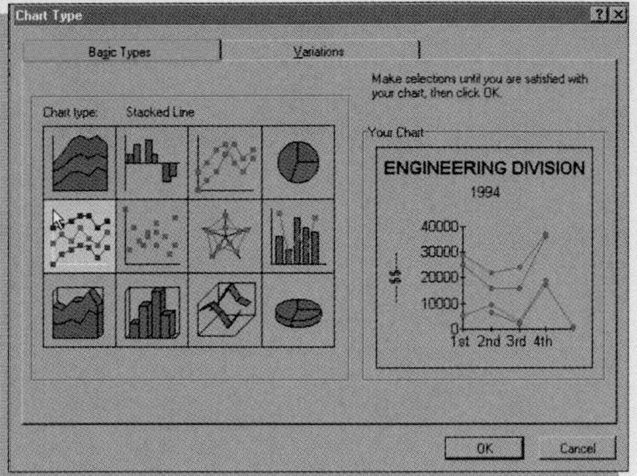


2 In the Basic Types folder, click on one of the types and observe the preview of your chart.

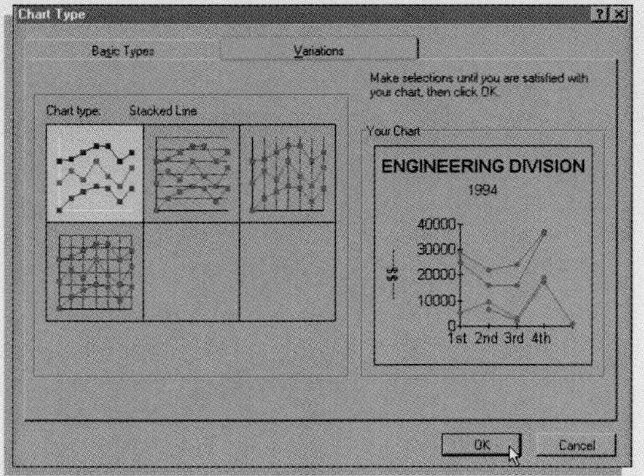


3 Before clicking OK, if you wish to look at a change to the basic chart type, open the Variations folder and click on your choice. When finished, click on OK.

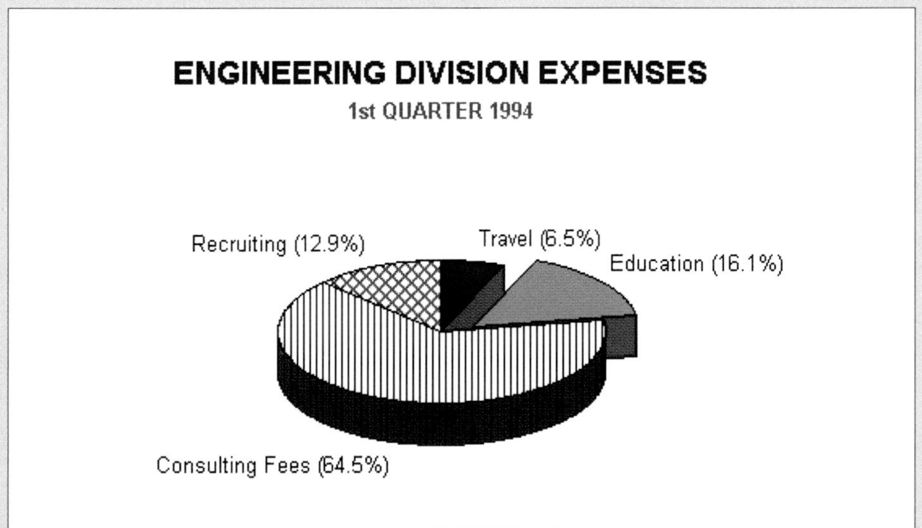


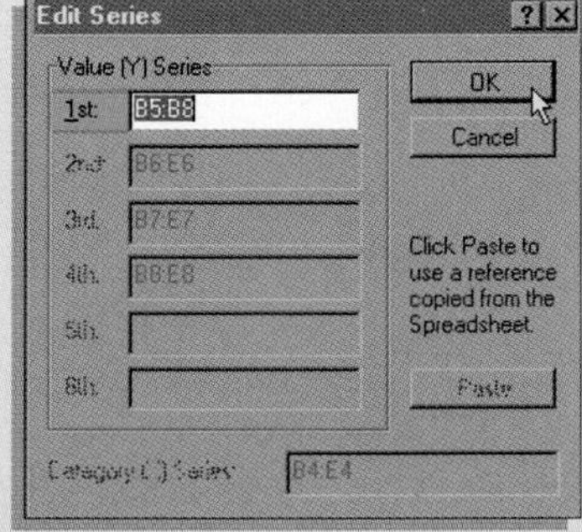


5 If your chart has more than one series and you wish to change to a pie chart type, Works can use only one of them. To select the one series of interest, click on Series in the Edit menu and enter the cell range of the data series.

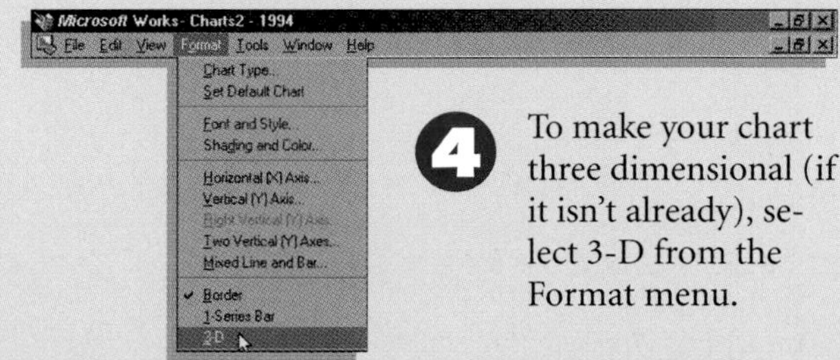


4 To make your chart three dimensional (if it isn't already), select 3-D from the Format menu.

# Adding a Series to a Chart

Works allows you to create as many as eight charts associated with one spreadsheet. There may be a time when, instead of creating a whole new chart, you simply want to just add another series to an existing chart. For example, a new item has been added to the inventory or a new employee added to the payroll.

If you recall your copy-and-paste skills, this will be a breeze.

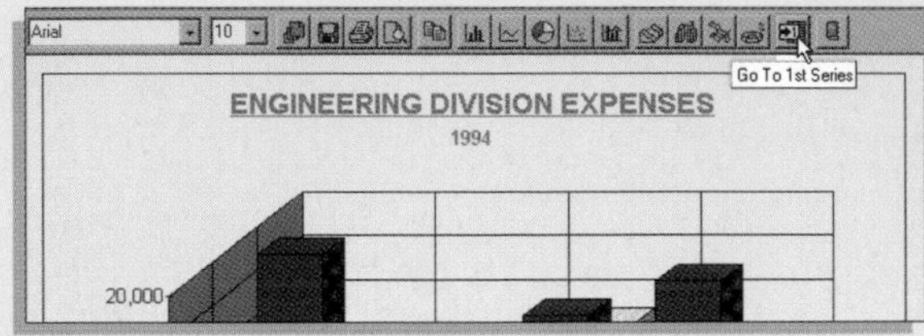


**1** With your existing chart in view, switch to the spreadsheet by clicking on the Go To 1st Series in the toolbar.

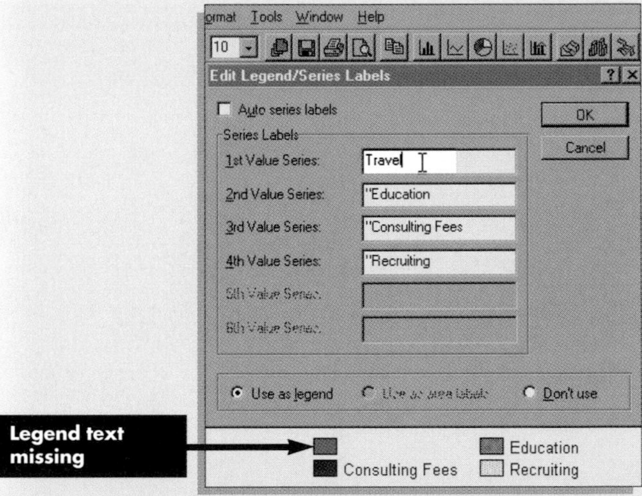


**6** If the legend text for the new series is missing, click on Legend/Series in the Edit menu and in the dialog box type in the text.

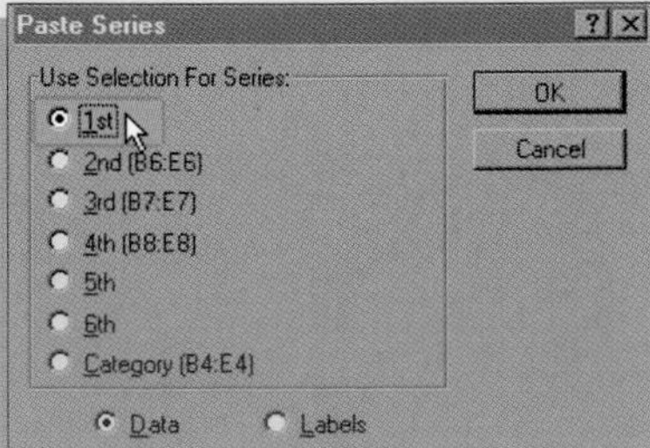


**5** Select the series sequence number and click OK.

**TIP SHEET**

- **If you know the cell range references of the series to be added, use the Edit:Series command and enter the reference in the Edit Series dialog box.**
- **The length (number of cells) of a series can be modified or the whole series deleted by simply changing its cell references in the Edit Series dialog box.**

| | A | B | C | D | E |
|---|---|---|---|---|---|
| 1 | | | | | |
| 2 | ENGINEERING DIVISION EXPENSE 1994 | | | | |
| 3 | | | | | |
| 4 | Item | 1st Quarter | 2nd Quarter | 3rd Quarter | 4th Quarter |
| 5 | Travel | 2,000 | 2,500 | 5,000 | 6,500 |
| 6 | Education | 5,000 | 3,000 | 1,000 | 2,000 |

2 Highlight the range of cells to be used as the new series and click on the Copy icon on the toolbar.

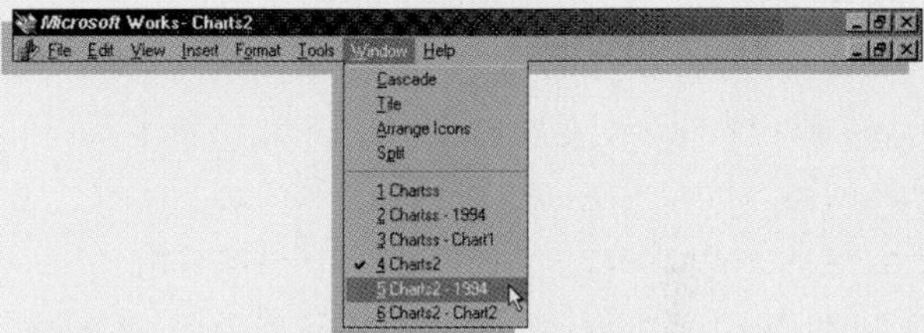


3 Return to the chart by clicking on its name in the Window menu.

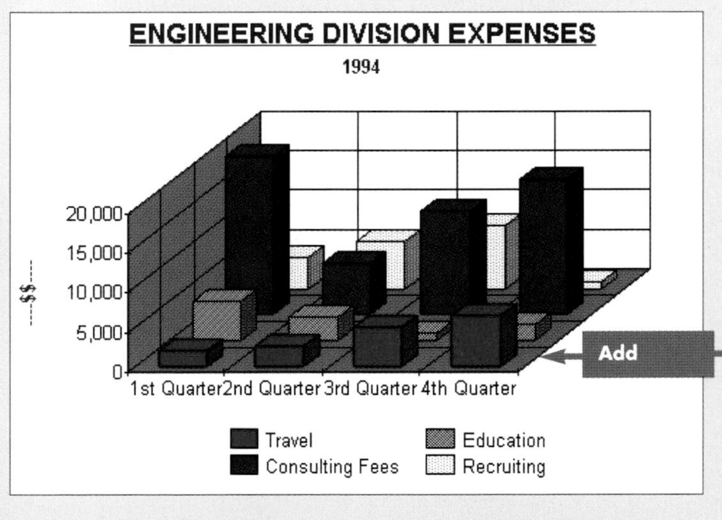


| | | | | |
|---|---|---|---|---|
| ENGINEERING DIVISION EXPENSE 1994 | | | | |
| Item | 1st Quarter | 2nd Quarter | 3rd Quarter | 4th Quarter |
| Travel | 2,000 | 2,500 | 5,000 | 6,500 |
| Education | 5,000 | 3,000 | 1,000 | 2,000 |
| Consulting Fees | 20,000 | 6,500 | 13,000 | 17,000 |
| Recruiting | 4,000 | 6,000 | 8,000 | 1,000 |

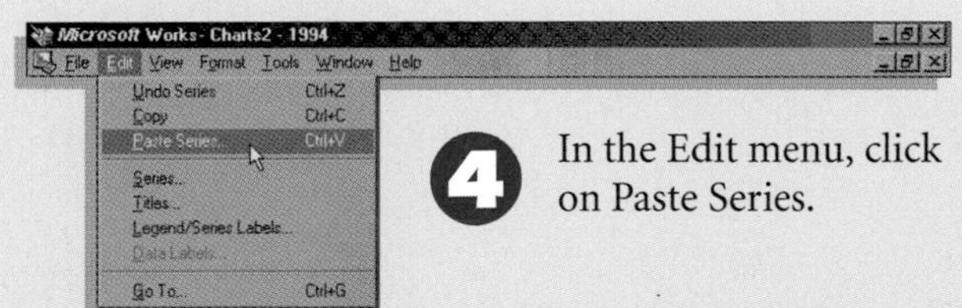


4 In the Edit menu, click on Paste Series.

# TRY IT!

To try the charting techniques described in the previous chapter, you will need a spreadsheet to work from. Create the one that is presented here as the example, then follow the steps to develop a chart. All of the procedures used here are also described in Chapter 14.

A
B
C
D
E
F
MONTHLY FINANCES '95
Budget
September
October
November
December
Rent
500
500
Car loan
200
200
Food
200
290
Insurance
150
150
Gasoline
50
40
Entertainment
100
150


FINANCES
'95
$$$
500
400
300
200
100
0
Rent
Car loan
Food
Insurance
Gasoline
Entertainm
Budget
September
October


**1**

A2:C8
MONTHLY FINANCES '95
Budget
September
October
November
December


Highlight the cell range A2:C8 and click on the New Chart icon on the Toolbar.

**2**

New Chart
Basic Options
Advanced Options
What type of chart do you want?
Chart type: 3-D Bar
Make selections until you are satisfied with your chart, then click OK.
Your Chart
FINANCES
Finishing touches
Title:
FINANCES
Border
Gridlines
OK
Cancel


Click on a 3-D bar chart type. Type in the title, and select Gridlines and Border. Click on the Advanced Options tab.

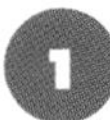

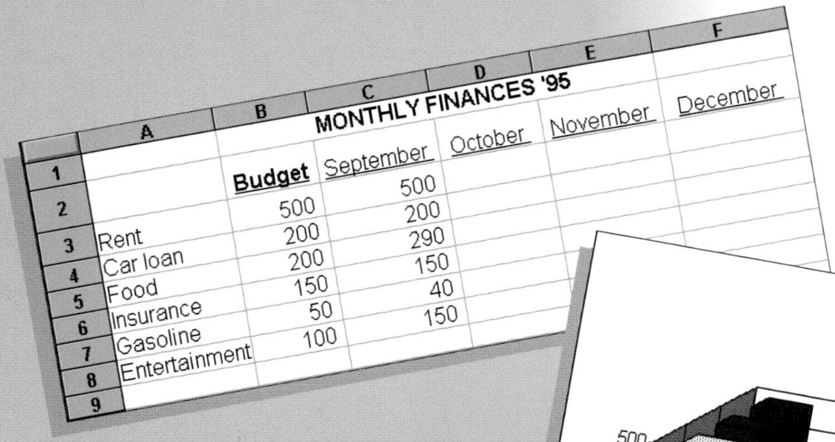

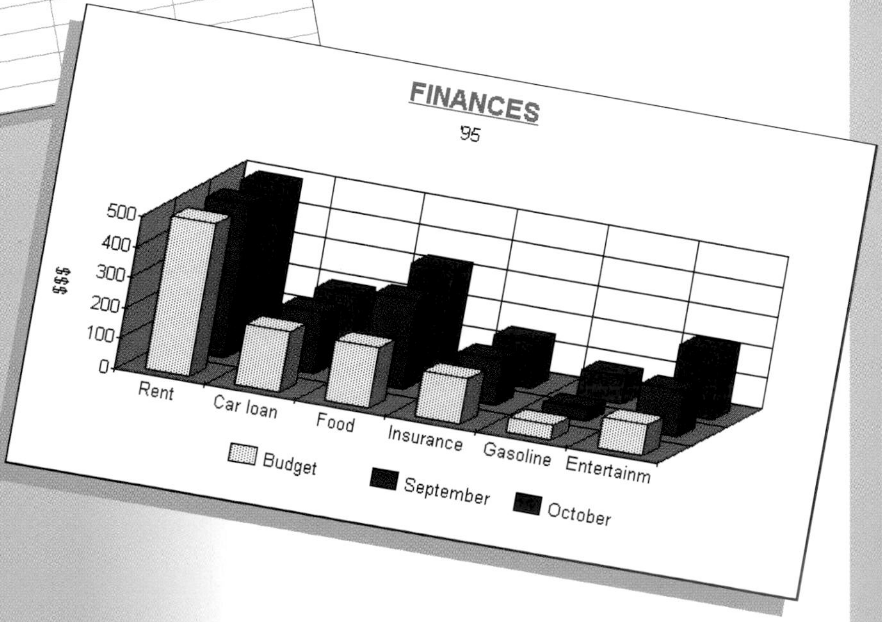

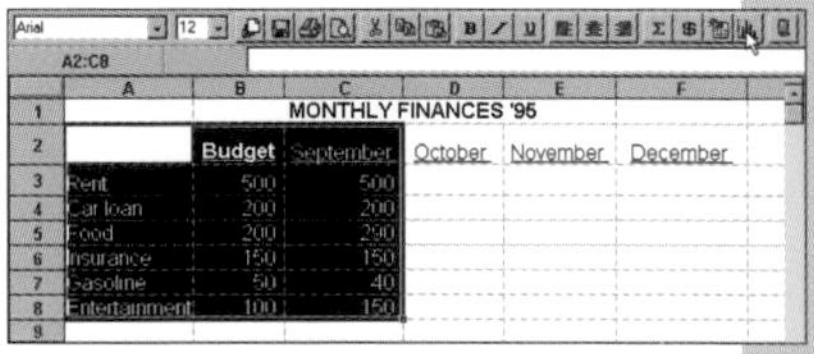

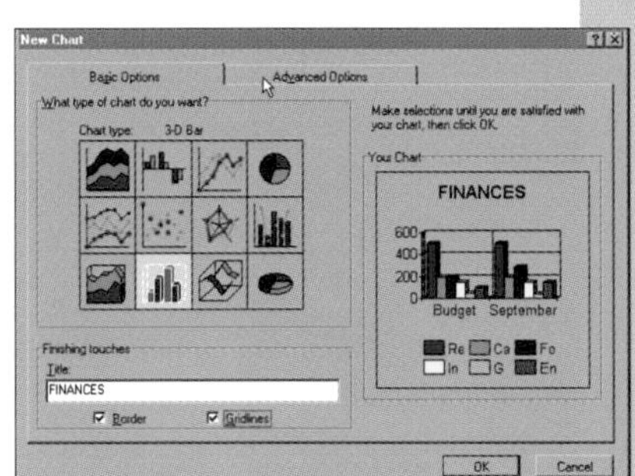

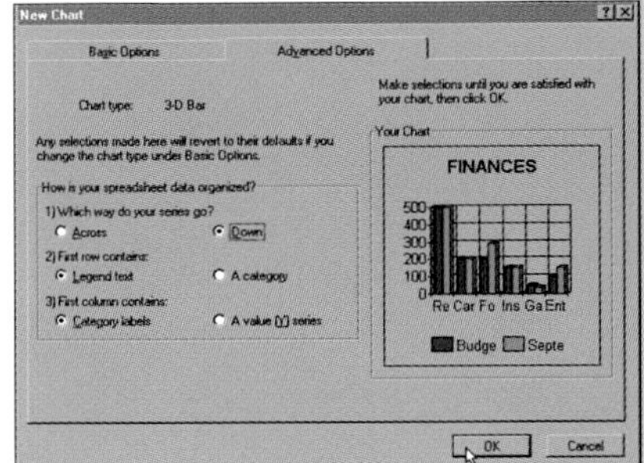


In the selections for data organization, change the way the series goes from Across to Down. The other selections are correct as given.

In the Tools menu, click on Rename Chart.

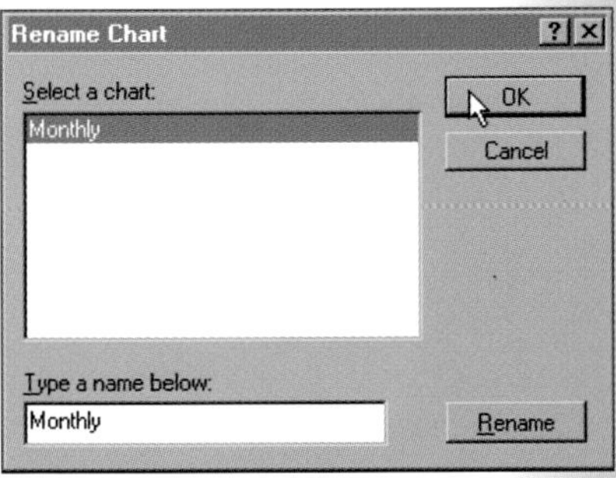


In the dialog box type in a name.

In the Format menu, select Horizontal (X) Axis.

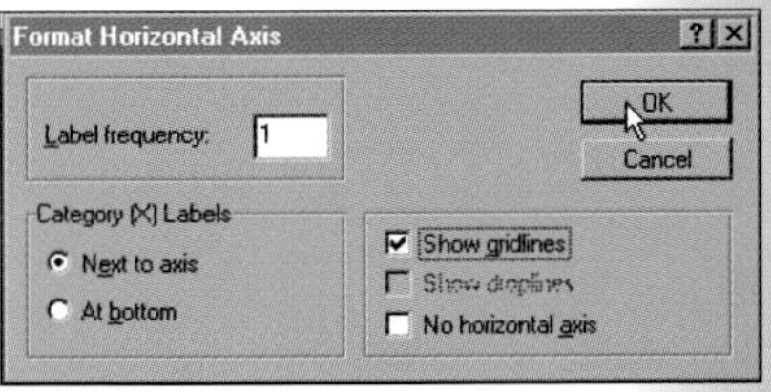


In the dialog box, click on Show Gridlines.

In the Format menu, select Vertical (Y) Axis.

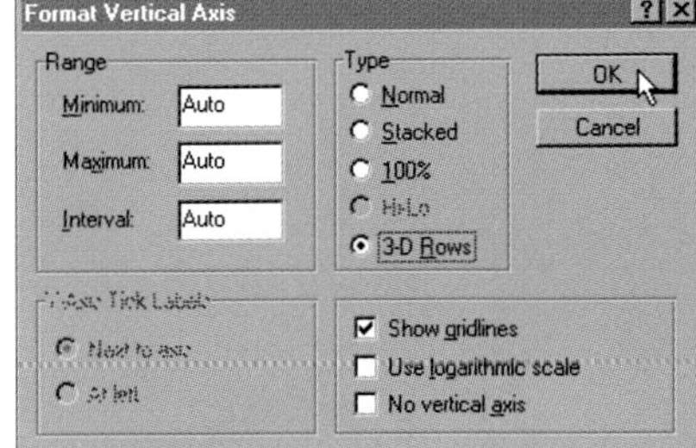


In the dialog box, click on 3-D Rows and on Show Gridlines.





In the Format menu, select Shading and Color.

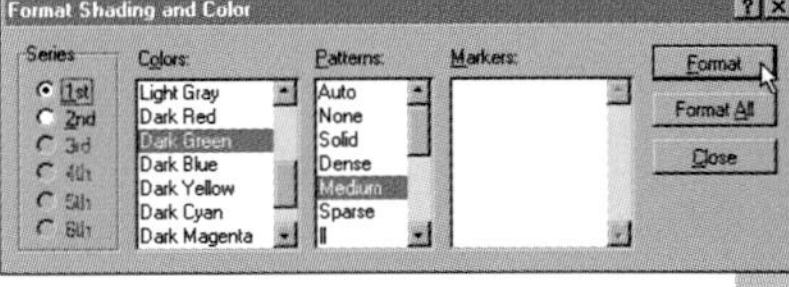


In the selection box, for the 1st Series, choose a color and a pattern. Click on Format.

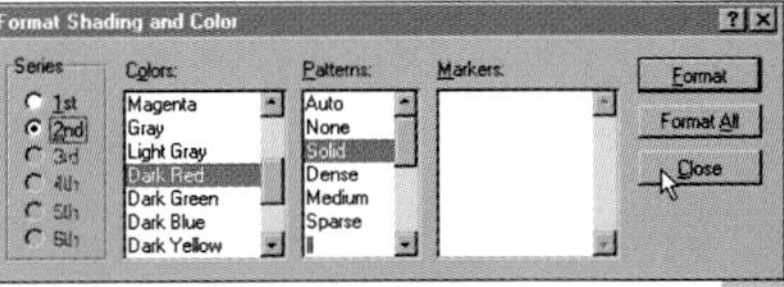


Repeat the selection process for the 2nd Series.

Continue to next page ▶

# TRY IT!

Continue below

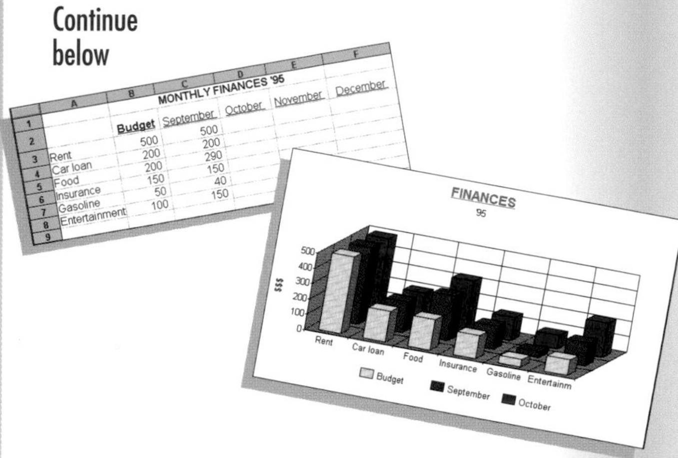


**13**

In the Edit menu, select Titles.

**14**

In the dialog box, enter a Subtitle and a title for the Vertical (Y) axis.

Edit Titles

| | |
|---|---|
| Chart title: | "FINANCES |
| Subtitle: | '95 |
| Horizontal (X) Axis: | |
| Vertical (Y) Axis: | $$$ |
| Right Vertical Axis: | |

OK · Cancel

**15**

Click on the main title and observe the control box surrounding it.

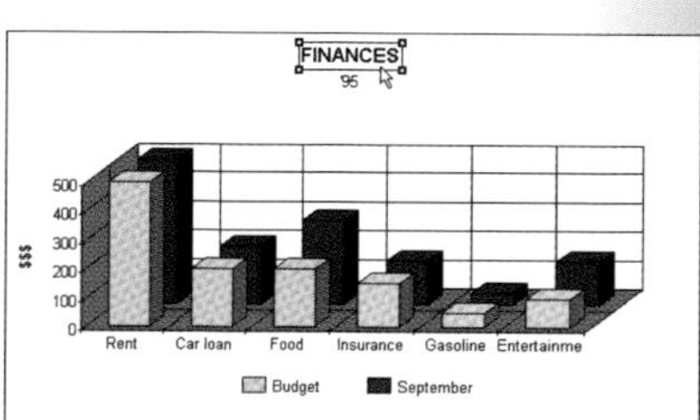

**16**

In the Format menu, select Font and Style.

**17**

Choose a font, a size, a color, and the Bold style. Click OK.

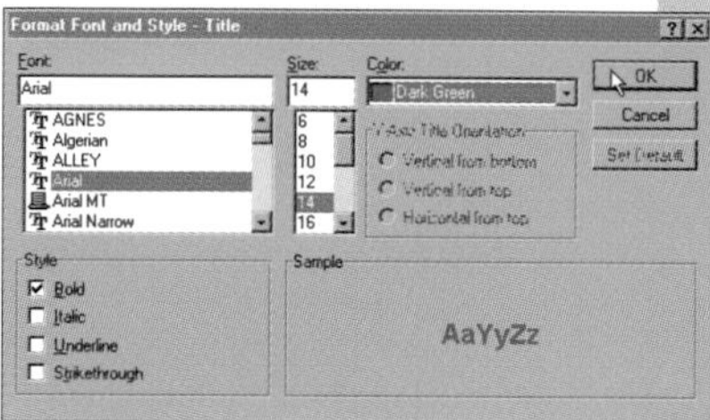

**18**

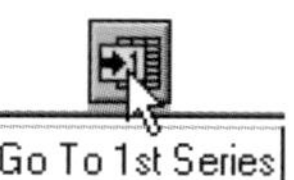


To return to the spreadsheet, click on the Go To 1st Series icon in the toolbar.

**19**

In the October column, highlight cells D3:D8 and enter a set of values as shown here. Then click on Copy on the toolbar.

| | A | B | C | D |
|---|---|---|---|---|
| 1 | | | MONTHLY FINANCES ' | |
| 2 | | Budget | September | October |
| 3 | Rent | 500 | 500 | 500 |
| 4 | Car loan | 200 | 200 | 200 |
| 5 | Food | 200 | 290 | 330 |
| 6 | Insurance | 150 | 150 | 150 |
| 7 | Gasoline | 50 | 40 | 90 |
| 8 | Entertainment | 100 | 150 | 220 |

**20**

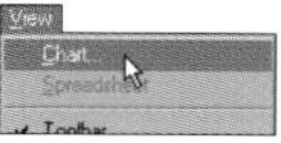


To return to the chart, click on Chart in the View menu.

In the selection box, choose your chart and click OK.

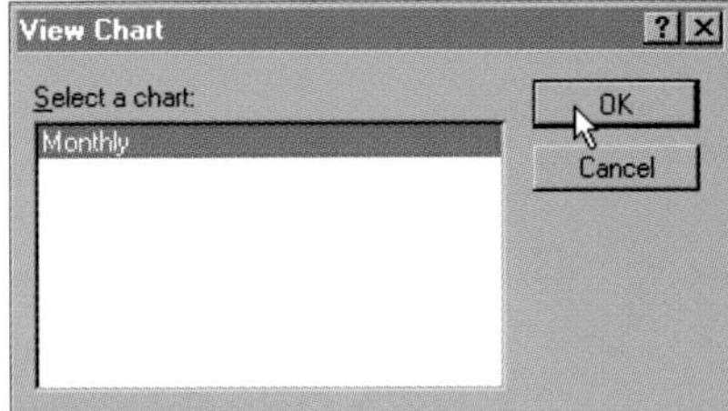

In the Edit menu, click on Paste Series.

In the selection box, choose the 3rd Series and click OK.

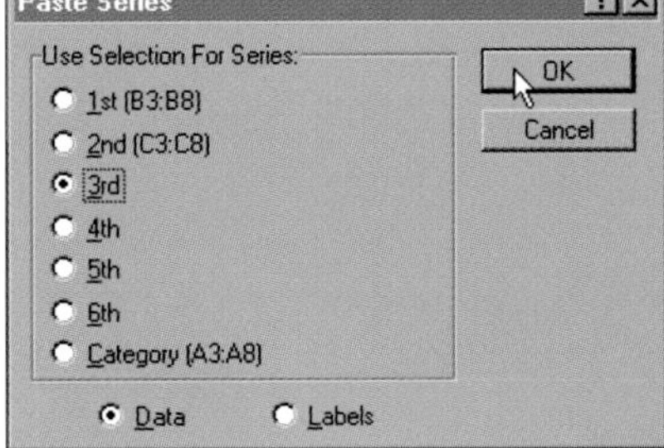

In the edit menu, select Legend/Series Labels.

In the 3rd Value Series box, type cell location D2. Click OK to view the results.

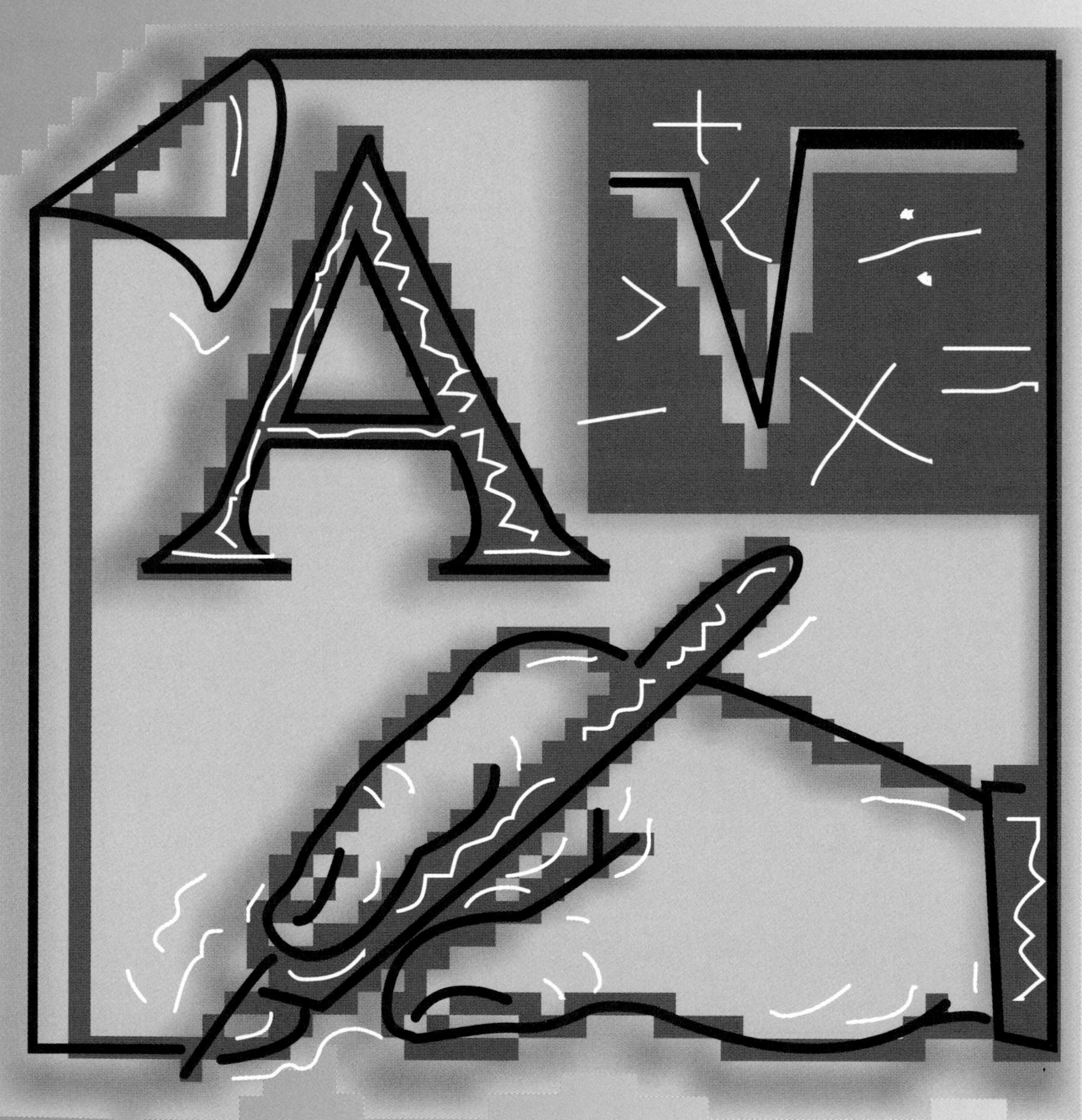

# CHAPTER 15

# Creating a Database

A database is simply any collection of information. It could be an address book, a library card catalog, or a filing cabinet. It could even be a shoe box full of receipts.

In addition to stashing away information, databases perform several other functions. They make it easy to store information in a compact and organized manner. They make retrieval of their information fast and efficient. While a shoe box may perform some of these functions well, it might disappoint you if you had to dig through lots of odd slips of paper to unearth some important information.

The database program in Microsoft Works performs all of these tasks well. Information storage is as easy as typing in text and can be as compact as a floppy disk. Just as important, information retrieval can be as easy as reading a name from a list.

Works also lets you apply the power of your computer to automate common uses of database information. You can create reports, or summaries, of your database's contents. You can even merge, or combine, the names and addresses in your database with a word processor document to automate and personalize your next mailing. Don't try that with a shoe box.

# How to Create a Database

The first step in creating a database is to define the types or individual pieces of data you will be entering into it. These pieces are called fields. You will then be entering groups of associated data. These groups are called records. For example, if you wanted to create a database phone book of your friends, Name and Phone Number would be the two fields. The data for each friend would be a record. An unlimited number of records can be entered: one for each friend who likes you enough to give you his or her number.

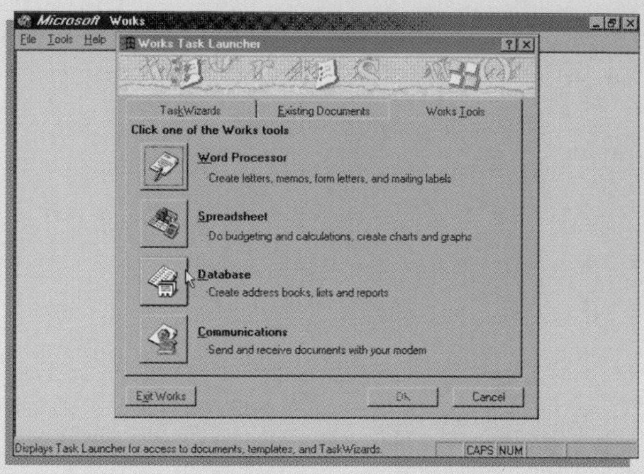


**1** Start by creating a new database document. Start Works, and in the Works Task Launcher, click on the Database button.

Plaza Heights Residents

**Name:** __________

**Number:** ___

9000 Brush Street

San Francisco, CA 94109

**Phone:** __________

## TIP SHEET

- **You can format the text in a database just as you would in a spreadsheet or word processor document. Switch to the view you want to modify, select the text, and use the formatting options on the Toolbar or Format menu. Bear in mind that the formatting will apply across all records.**
- **In List View, you can adjust column width in the same way as in a spreadsheet. Either double-click on the column header button for automatic setting, or adjust the width by dragging the Adjust pointer on the header button border.**
- **To simplify the entry of repeating data, use the Fill commands from the Edit menu as explained in Chapter 13. This must be done in the List View.**
- **In the Form View window you can move rapidly from one record to another by using the arrows adjacent to the record number at the bottom-left of the window.**

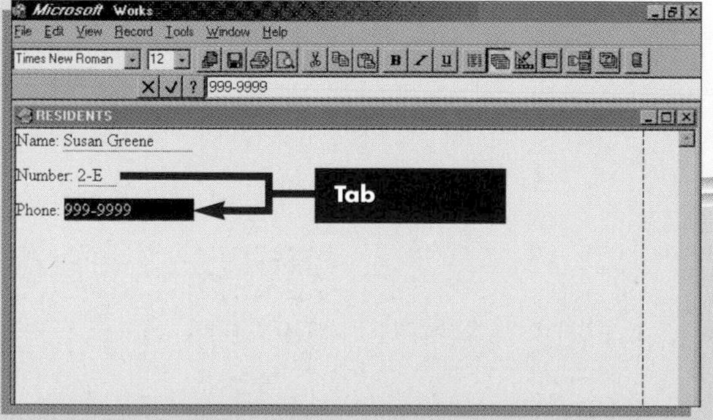


**6** After highlighting the first field and typing in the information, you can move to the next field by pressing Tab. After the last field has been entered, Works will move you to the next blank record.

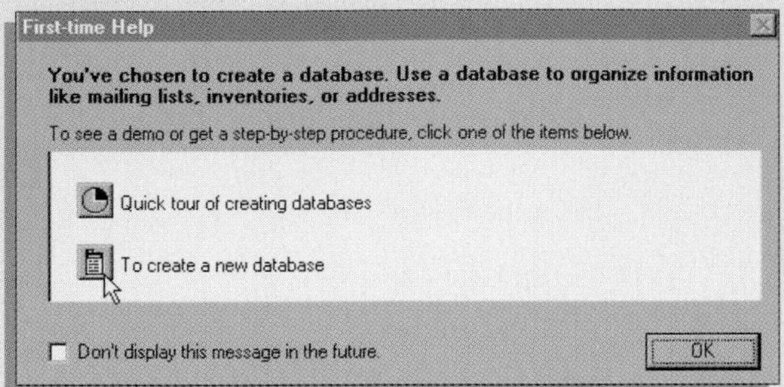

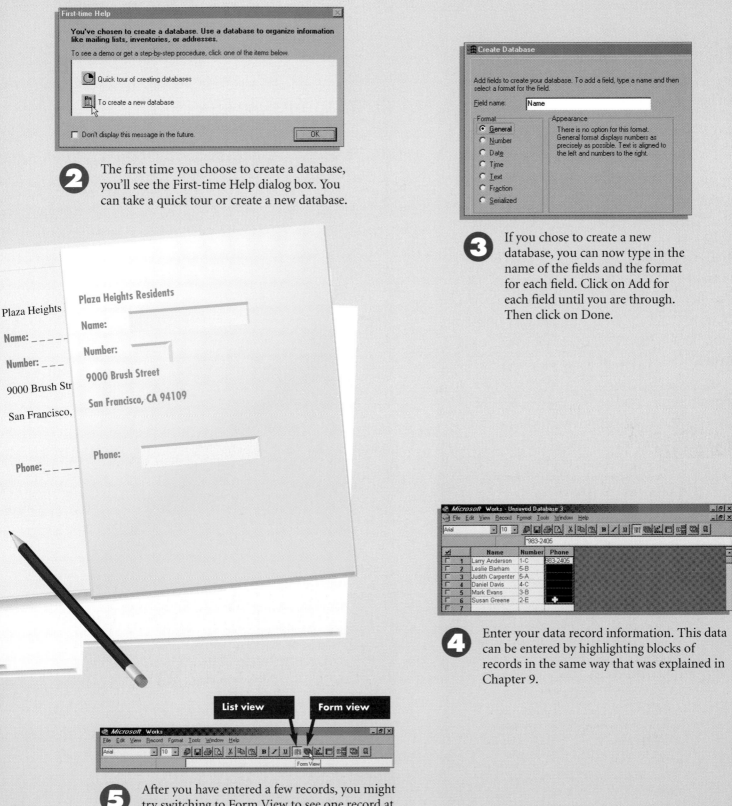

**2** The first time you choose to create a database, you'll see the First-time Help dialog box. You can take a quick tour or create a new database.

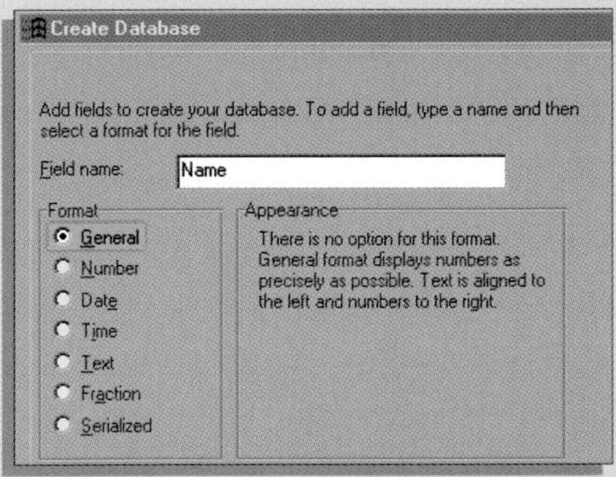


**3** If you chose to create a new database, you can now type in the name of the fields and the format for each field. Click on Add for each field until you are through. Then click on Done.

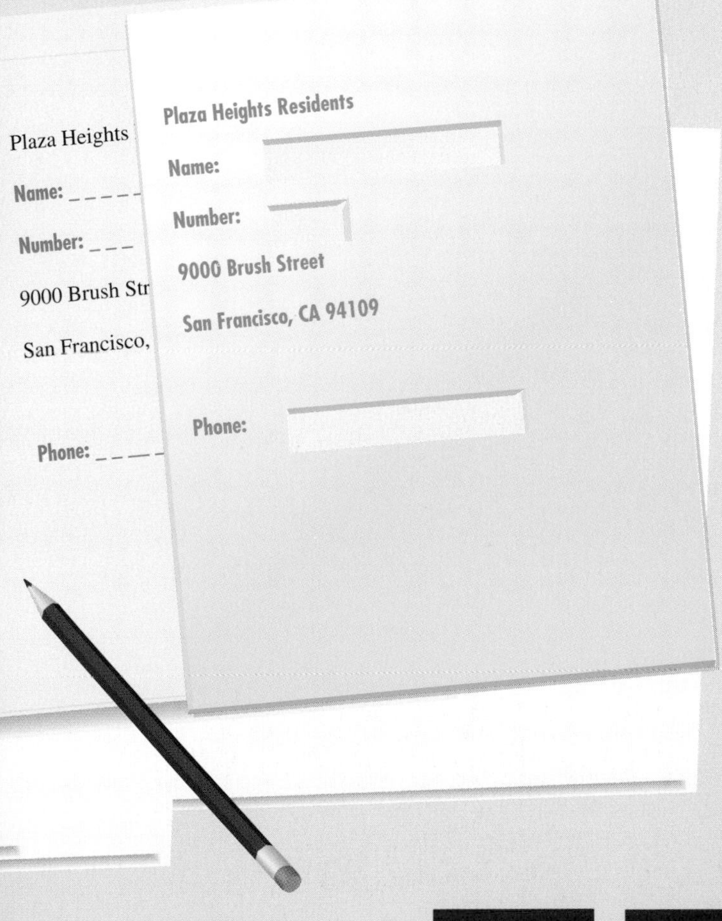


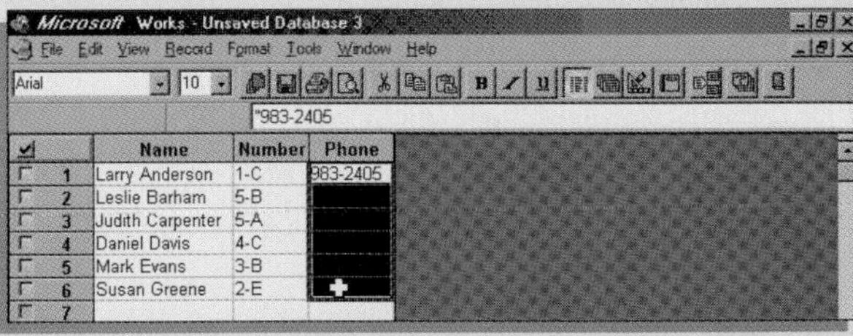


**4** Enter your data record information. This data can be entered by highlighting blocks of records in the same way that was explained in Chapter 9.

List view

Form view

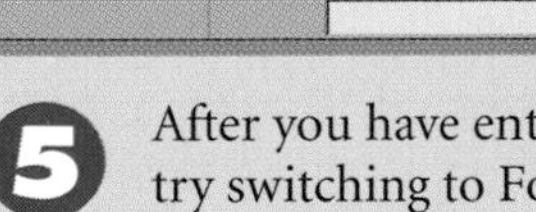


**5** After you have entered a few records, you might try switching to Form View to see one record at a time. You make this selection by clicking on Form from the View menu or by clicking on the Form View button on the toolbar.

# How to Design a Form

Having created your database, you'll now want to design the way it will look as a form or template from which further record entries can be made.

The form is like a stencil for entering information. The field boxes are the windows for entering that information.

Works enables you to position the fields in any order and wherever you wish them to appear on the page. You can add text information such as instructions or headings which are different from the records and are called labels.

If you are concerned that someone might accidentally change some of your data, not to worry! Works can keep your data safe by protecting it from misbehaving fingers.

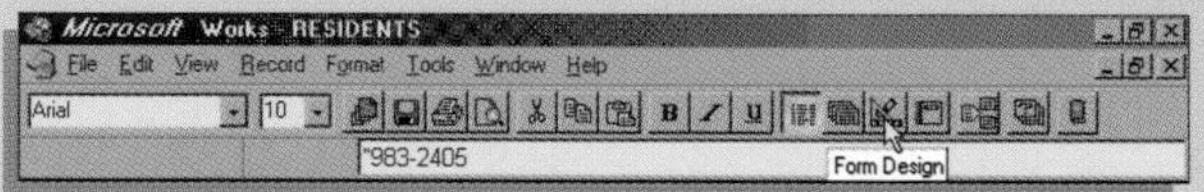

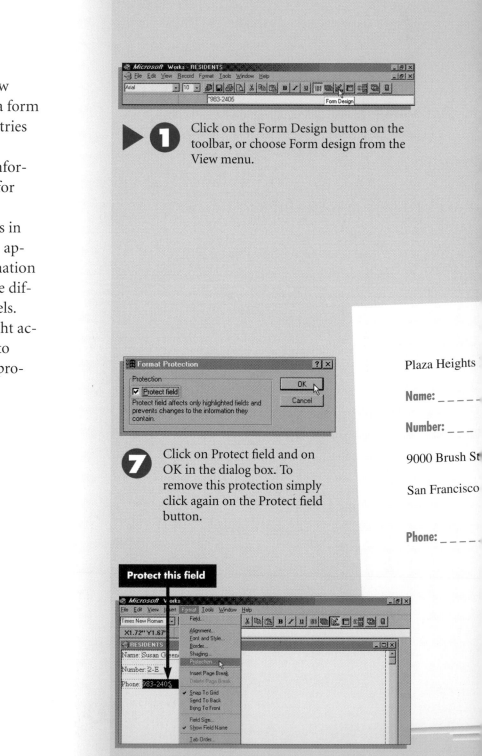

Click on the Form Design button on the toolbar, or choose Form design from the View menu.

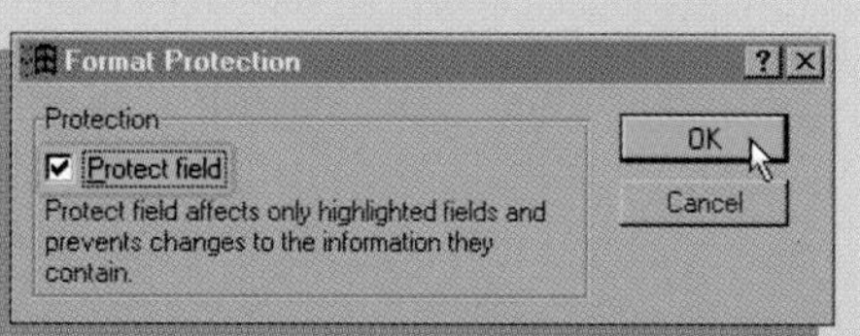

Click on Protect field and on OK in the dialog box. To remove this protection simply click again on the Protect field button.

Plaza Heights

**Name:** _ _ _ _

**Number:** _ _ _

9000 Brush St

San Francisco

**Phone:** _ _ _ _

**Protect this field**

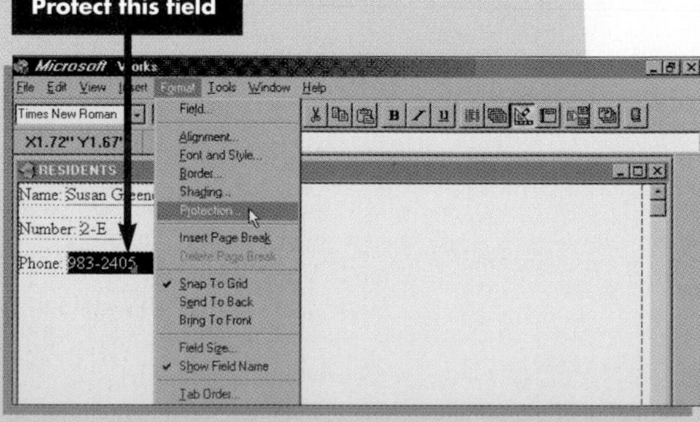

To protect a field, highlight it and select Protection from the Format menu.

## TIP SHEET

- **To find information in any record, use the Find command in the Edit menu. In the Find dialog box, type in the text or numbers you're looking for. Works will search for exact matches in all the fields of all the records in the database.**
- **To precisely align your fields both vertically and horizontally in the form view, choose Snap to Grid from the Format menu. Without this selection you can position fields with an accuracy of 0.01 inch.**

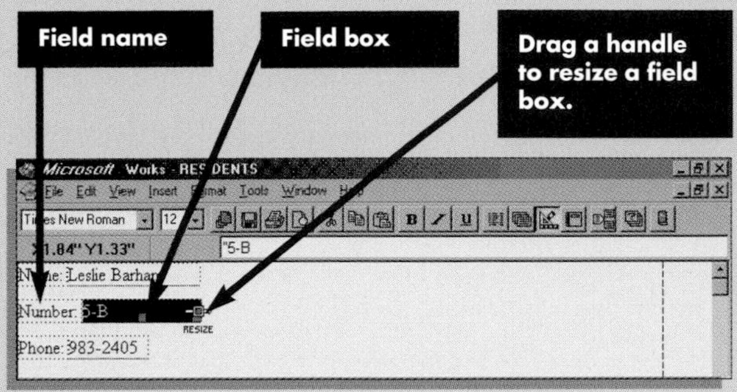


**2** Click and drag the square handles on the field box to resize it. Drag to the left or right to adjust the box length, and up or down to adjust the number of rows.

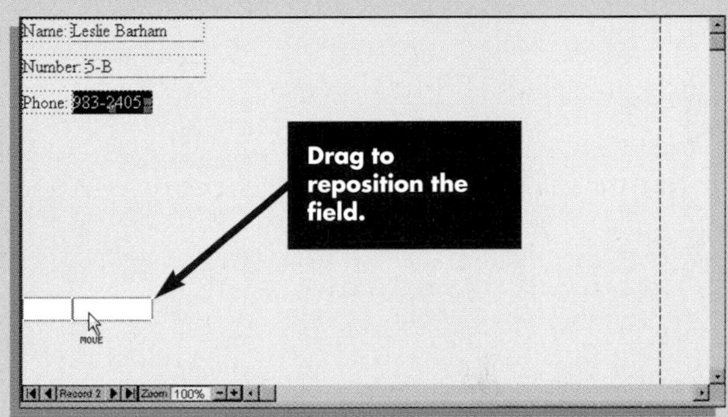


**3** Click and hold on the highlighted field box until the Drag pointer appears. Then drag and move the box to the new location.

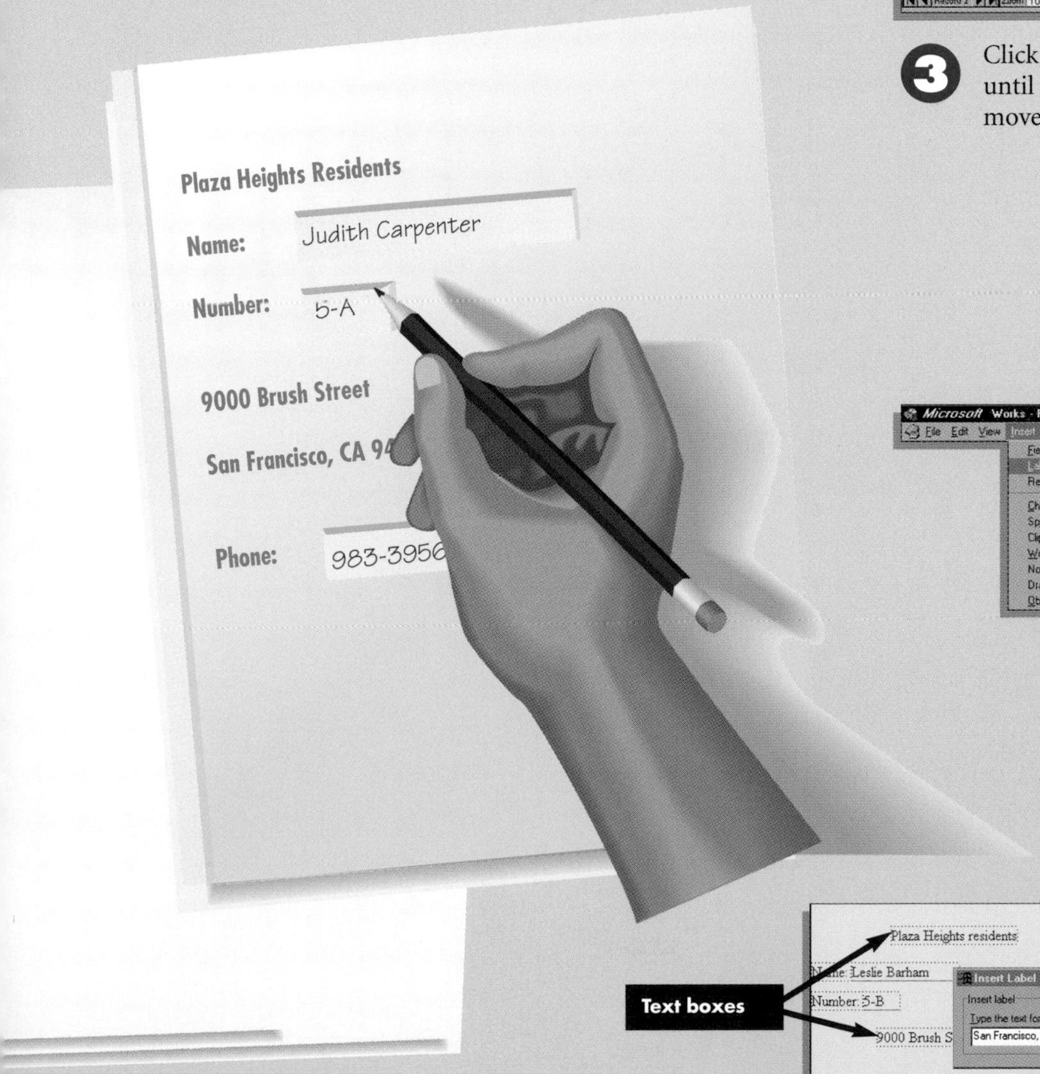

**4** Move the cursor to a blank area of the screen. Then to insert additional text information, position the cursor and select Label from the Insert menu.

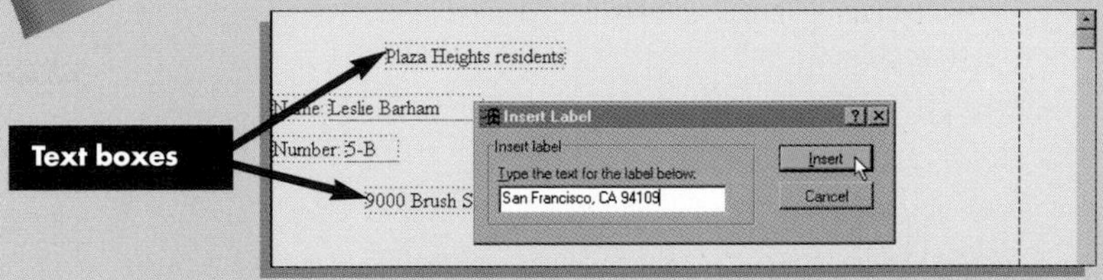

**5** In the Insert Label dialog box, type the information.

# How to Edit a Database

Even if you have flawless information, errors will still find their way into your database. Friends move, contacts change, objects in your inventory grow legs and move to a sunnier climate. Sooner or later, you'll need to modify the database you've worked hard to develop. When that time comes, you'll find some of the same techniques available that you used to modify your word processor and spreadsheet documents.

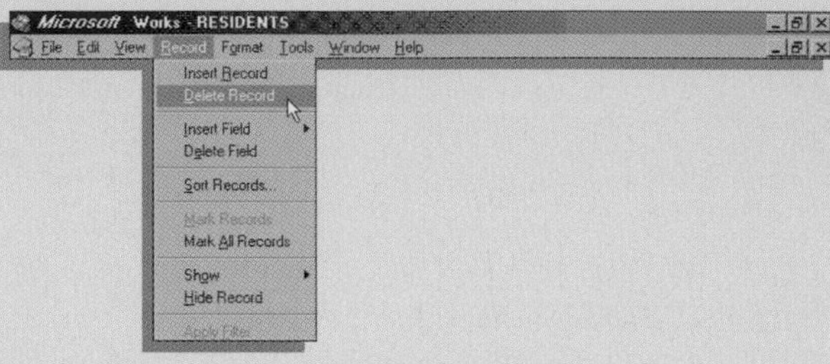


**1** To delete a record in either Form or List View, click anywhere in that record and choose the Delete Record command from the Insert menu.

Plaza Heights R
Daniel Davis
4-C
9000 Brush Str
San Francisco,
1(415)983-456

| | | Name | Number | Phone | Age |
|---|---|---|---|---|---|
| | 1 | Larry Anderson | 1-C | 983-2405 | |
| | 2 | Leslie Barham | 5-B | 983-4433 | |
| | 3 | Judith Carpenter | 5-A | 983-5533 | |
| | 4 | Daniel Davis | 4-C | 983-6622 | |
| | 5 | Mark Evans | 3-B | 983-5687 | |
| | 6 | Susan Greene | 2-E | 999-999 | |
| | 7 | | | | |

**6** You can always overwrite the contents of a field. Simply click on the field box and type in the new data. Press Enter when you are done to record the changes.

- **To navigate more easily in a large database, use the Go To command in the Edit menu. In the dialog box type the record number if you want a specific record. If you want to move to a particular field, highlight the field name in the Names box and click OK.**
- **To locate a certain set of characters within the database records, use the Find command from the Edit menu. In the dialog box enter enough characters to make your selection unique. Choose Match: All Records to display every record that contains the selected characters. Choosing Match: Next Record will only move you to the next record containing the selection.**

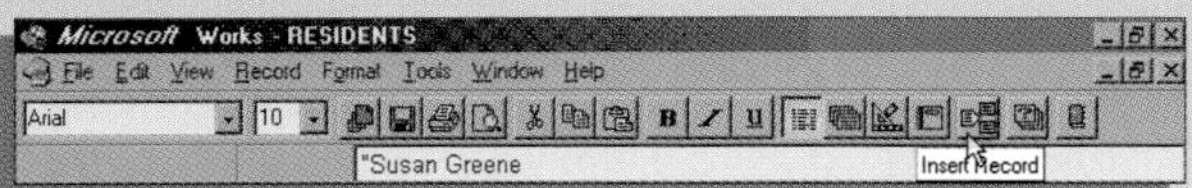


**2** To insert a record in Form or List View, move to the record that will come after the new record, and then click on the Insert Record icon in the toolbar.

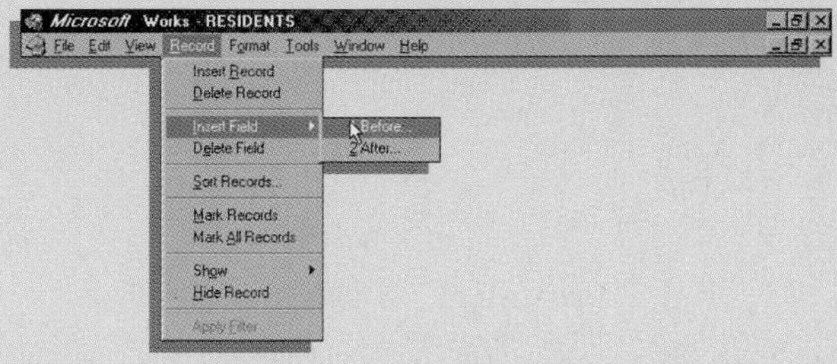


**3** To insert a new field, you must be in List View. Click anywhere in the field next to where you want to insert and select the Insert Field command from the Record menu. In the add-on box, select either Before or After.

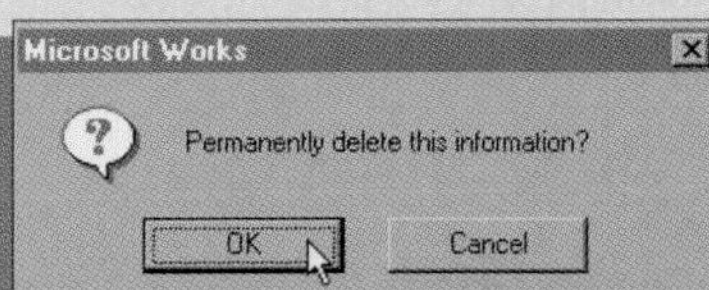


**4** To remove a field and all its contents, you must be in List View. Highlight any data in the field and from the Record menu, select Delete Field. You will be given a confirmation dialog box, because if you choose to delete, you cannot undo this operation.

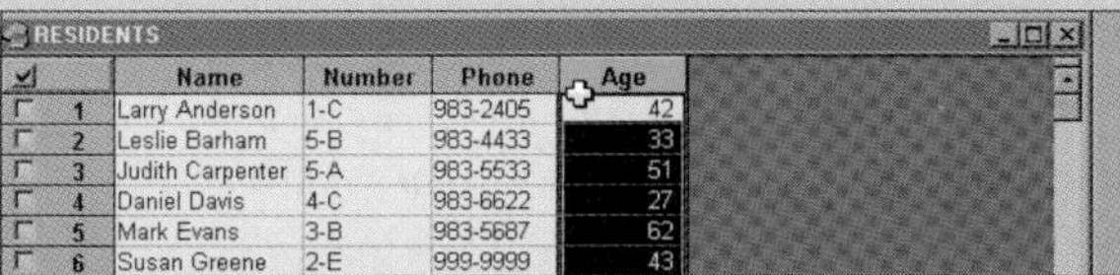

RESIDENTS

| | | Name | Number | Phone | Age |
|---|---|---|---|---|---|
| | 1 | Larry Anderson | 1-C | 983-2405 | 42 |
| | 2 | Leslie Barham | 5-B | 983-4433 | 33 |
| | 3 | Judith Carpenter | 5-A | 983-5533 | 51 |
| | 4 | Daniel Davis | 4-C | 983-6622 | 27 |
| | 5 | Mark Evans | 3-B | 983-5687 | 62 |
| | 6 | Susan Greene | 2-E | 999-9999 | 43 |

**5** To delete only the contents of the entire field, click on its header button which will highlight all the data. Then press the Delete key.

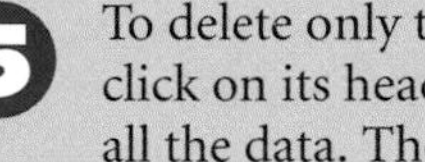

# How to Print a Report

Reports are a convenient way to tabulate, summarize, and print the information in your database. They have four parts: title, column headings, records, and summaries. You specify the title that Works prints at the top of your report. You can also choose the column headings, but Works suggests the field names by default. As for the records, Works prints every record on its own line below the column headings, while the fields chosen for the column headings determine which fields appear on each line. Finally, you select what data summaries, or report statistics, you want Works to display for each field at the bottom of the report.

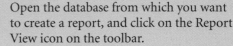

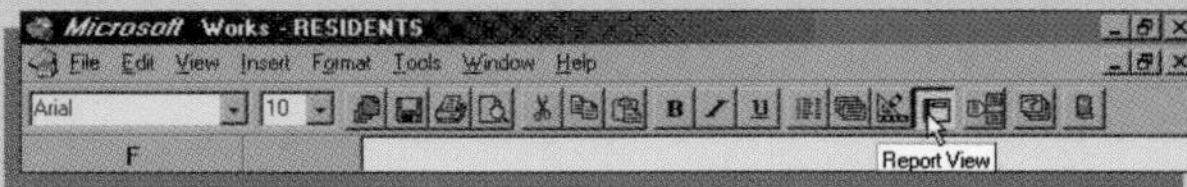

Open the database from which you want to create a report, and click on the Report View icon on the toolbar.

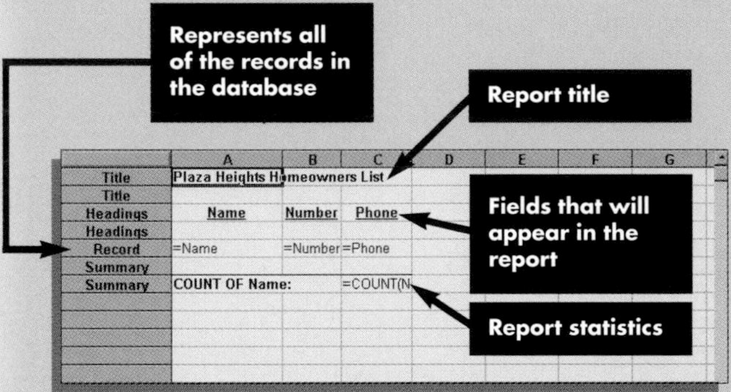


**8** Works will display an outline of the report without any data, but showing all of the selections you have made.

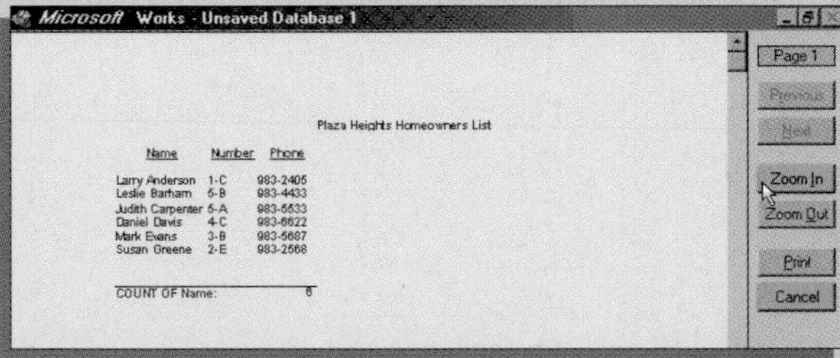


**7** To see your report without printing it in hard copy, you would have selected Preview in the previous step. When the report is displayed you may need to zoom in to see the data more clearly. You may now choose to either print the report or cancel to return to view the report setup. Click on Cancel.

**TIP SHEET**

- To print a hard copy, select Print from the File menu or click on the Print icon on the toolbar.
- You can edit your report once you've created it. In Report View, click on and type over the title or headings to change them; or if you want, click on and delete fields and summary information with the Delete key.

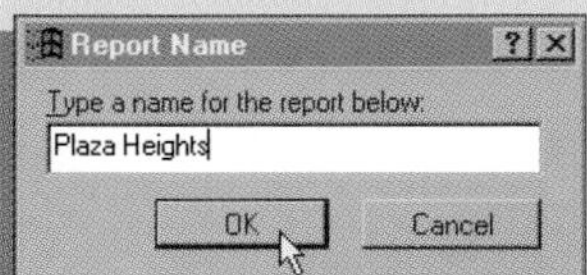


2 Type a name for your report in the Report Name dialog box. You may use up to 15 characters.

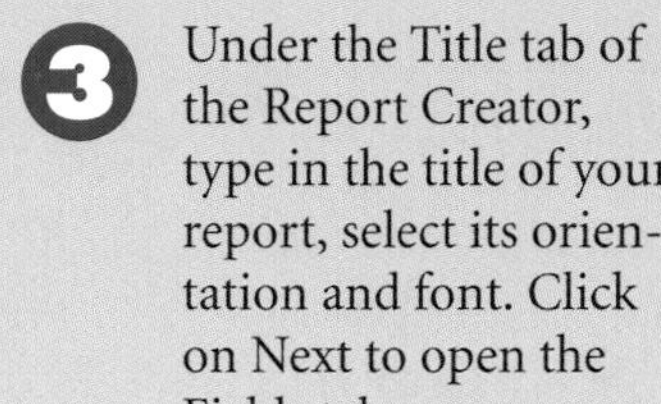

3 Under the Title tab of the Report Creator, type in the title of your report, select its orientation and font. Click on Next to open the Fields tab.

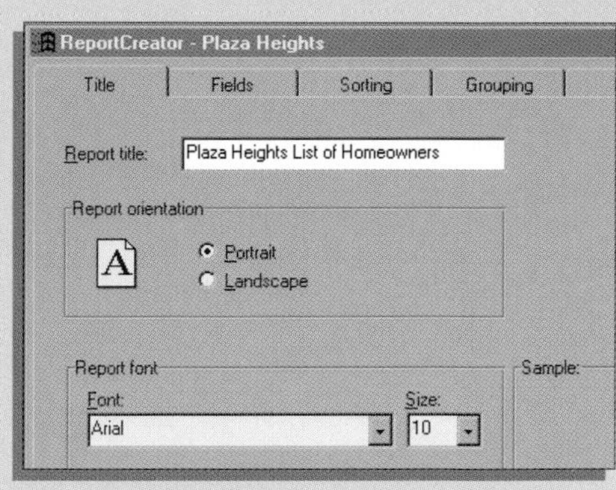


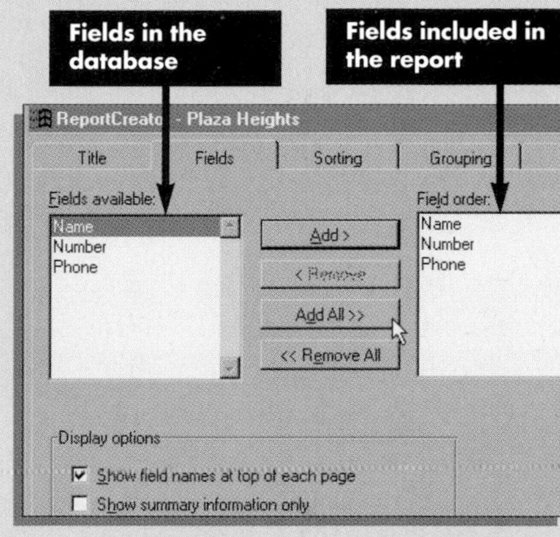


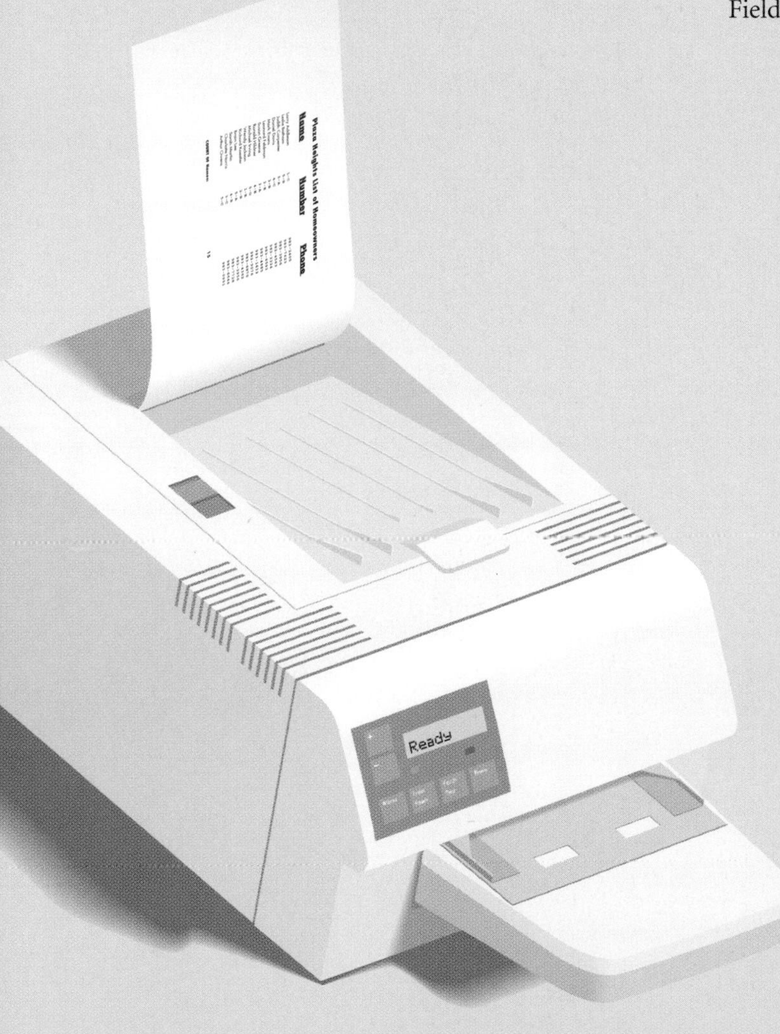


4 For each field that you want to appear as a column in your report, click on the field name, then on the Add button. When you are through, choose Next to open any of the remaining tabs or Done to complete the report.

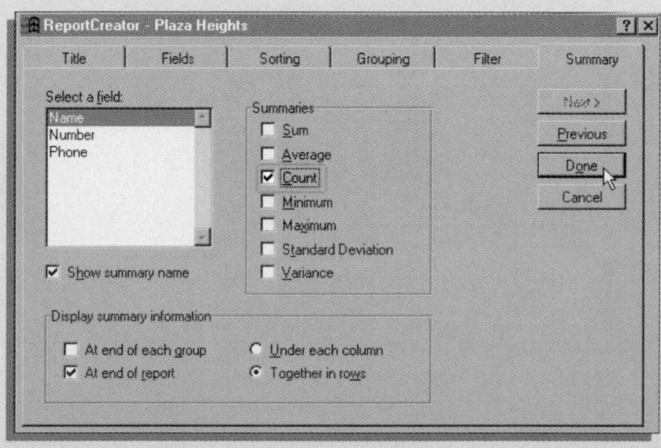


5 To include statistics in your report, click on the Summary tab and select the field and summary calculation you want. Then, in the Display Summary Information selection box, tell Works where to locate the information in your report. When you're finished, click on Done.

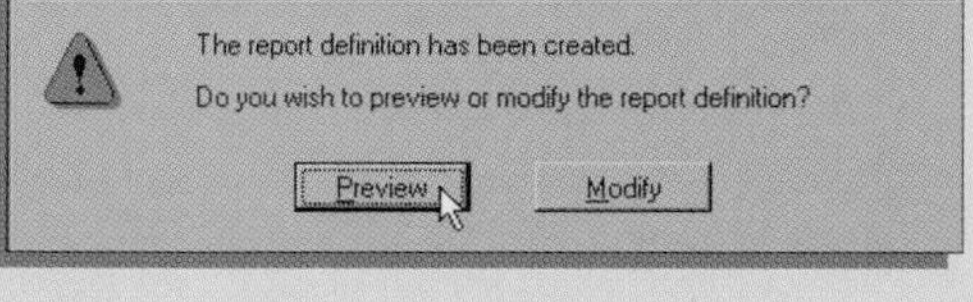


6 At this point Works asks if you wish to preview the report or to modify it. Click on the button of your choice.

# CHAPTER 16

# More Advanced Database Techniques

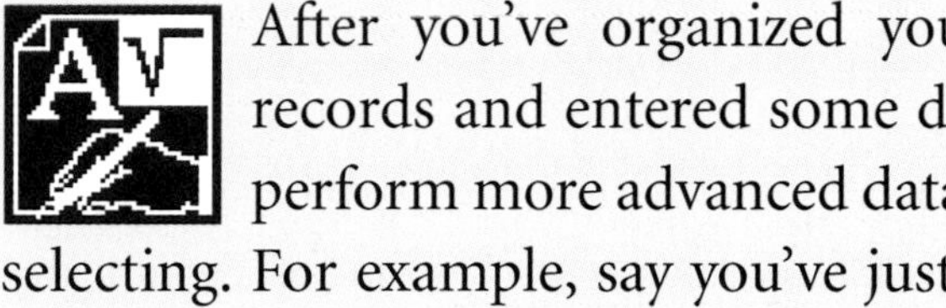

After you've organized your information into fields and records and entered some data, you'll soon find the need to perform more advanced database techniques like sorting and selecting. For example, say you've just created a database of employee records, and want a report of employees sorted by name. Or maybe you need to select and print a list of part-time employees for a particular department. Works provides a convenient way to sort and select information from your database. All you do is fill out an electronic form to tell Works how you want the data ordered or what records you want to extract. In moments Works completes your requests and displays the results.

The sections in this chapter assume that Works is running and the database is open.

# How to Sort Records

Sorting records in your database is a snap. Just tell Works what fields you want to sort by and how you want the information ordered. Works allows you to sort up to three fields at one time. Each sort field can be sorted in either ascending or descending order. Ascending order sorts text from A to Z, numbers from smallest to highest, dates from earliest to latest. Descending order is the opposite of ascending order.

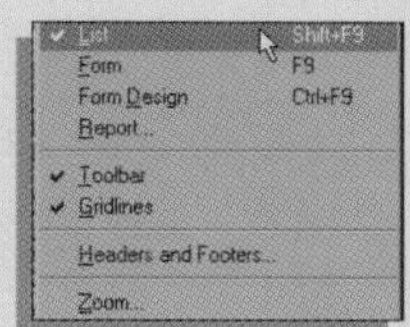

**1** Your database should be in list view for sorting. To switch views, open the View menu and click List.

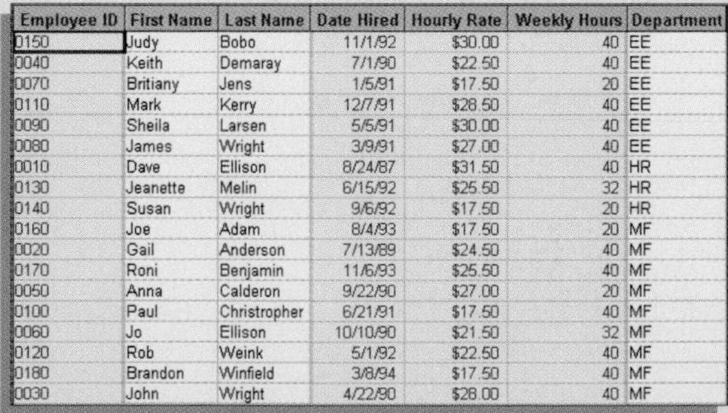

| Employee ID | First Name | Last Name | Date Hired | Hourly Rate | Weekly Hours | Department |
|---|---|---|---|---|---|---|
| 0150 | Judy | Bobo | 11/1/92 | $30.00 | 40 | EE |
| 0040 | Keith | Demaray | 7/1/90 | $22.50 | 40 | EE |
| 0070 | Britiany | Jens | 1/5/91 | $17.50 | 20 | EE |
| 0110 | Mark | Kerry | 12/7/91 | $28.50 | 40 | EE |
| 0090 | Sheila | Larsen | 5/5/91 | $30.00 | 40 | EE |
| 0080 | James | Wright | 3/9/91 | $27.00 | 40 | EE |
| 0010 | Dave | Ellison | 8/24/87 | $31.50 | 40 | HR |
| 0130 | Jeanette | Melin | 6/15/92 | $25.50 | 32 | HR |
| 0140 | Susan | Wright | 9/6/92 | $17.50 | 20 | HR |
| 0160 | Joe | Adam | 8/4/93 | $17.50 | 20 | MF |
| 0020 | Gail | Anderson | 7/13/89 | $24.50 | 40 | MF |
| 0170 | Roni | Benjamin | 11/6/93 | $25.50 | 40 | MF |
| 0050 | Anna | Calderon | 9/22/90 | $27.00 | 20 | MF |
| 0100 | Paul | Christropher | 6/21/91 | $17.50 | 40 | MF |
| 0060 | Jo | Ellison | 10/10/90 | $21.50 | 32 | MF |
| 0120 | Rob | Weink | 5/1/92 | $22.50 | 40 | MF |
| 0180 | Brandon | Winfield | 3/8/94 | $17.50 | 40 | MF |
| 0030 | John | Wright | 4/22/90 | $28.00 | 40 | MF |

**7** The records are now properly sorted by department. By the way, if you just want a list of company employees sorted by name, then remove the department field from the sort specifications.

## TIP SHEET

- **You can sort data in reports and preserve the original order of your database records. For more information, open the Help menu, select Index, and enter "sorting database reports."**
- **You can undo a sort by selecting Undo Sort from the Edit menu immediately after performing the sort.**
- **Blank fields are always sorted last.**
- **If you plan to sort names, create two fields—one for the first name and one for the last name. Then sort the last name first.**

One sort field

2 To sort your records by one sort field, open the Record menu and select Sort Records. In the "Sort by" box, click the down arrow and select a field name. Now move to the right and choose ascending (A–Z) or descending (Z–A).

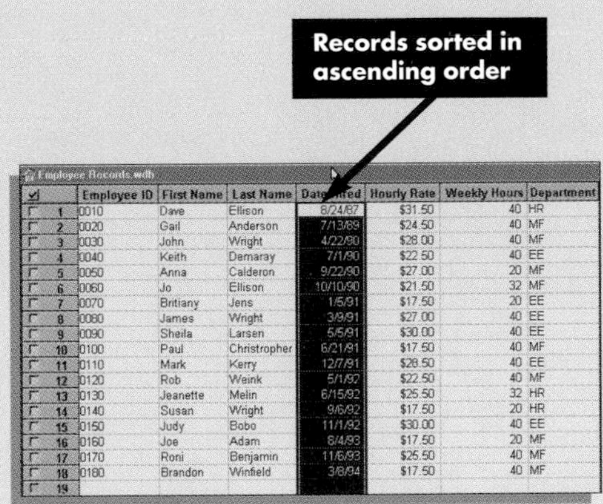


| | Employee ID | First Name | Last Name | Date Hired | Hourly Rate | Weekly Hours | Department |
|---|---|---|---|---|---|---|---|
| 1 | 0010 | Dave | Ellison | 8/24/87 | $31.50 | 40 | HR |
| 2 | 0020 | Gail | Anderson | 7/13/89 | $24.50 | 40 | MF |
| 3 | 0030 | John | Wright | 4/22/90 | $28.00 | 40 | MF |
| 4 | 0040 | Keith | Demaray | 7/1/90 | $22.50 | 40 | EE |
| 5 | 0050 | Anna | Calderon | 9/22/90 | $27.00 | 20 | MF |
| 6 | 0060 | Jo | Ellison | 10/10/90 | $21.50 | 32 | MF |
| 7 | 0070 | Britiany | Jens | 1/5/91 | $17.50 | 20 | EE |
| 8 | 0080 | James | Wright | 3/9/91 | $27.00 | 40 | EE |
| 9 | 0090 | Sheila | Larsen | 5/5/91 | $30.00 | 40 | EE |
| 10 | 0100 | Paul | Christopher | 6/21/91 | $17.50 | 40 | MF |
| 11 | 0110 | Mark | Kerry | 12/7/91 | $28.50 | 40 | EE |
| 12 | 0120 | Rob | Weink | 5/1/92 | $22.50 | 40 | MF |
| 13 | 0130 | Jeanette | Melin | 6/15/92 | $25.50 | 32 | HR |
| 14 | 0140 | Susan | Wright | 9/6/92 | $17.50 | 20 | HR |
| 15 | 0150 | Judy | Bobo | 11/1/92 | $30.00 | 40 | EE |
| 16 | 0160 | Joe | Adam | 8/4/93 | $17.50 | 20 | MF |
| 17 | 0170 | Roni | Benjamin | 11/6/93 | $25.50 | 40 | MF |
| 18 | 0180 | Brandon | Winfield | 3/8/94 | $17.50 | 40 | MF |
| 19 | | | | | | | |

3 Our records are sorted by hire date in ascending order (first hired to last hired).

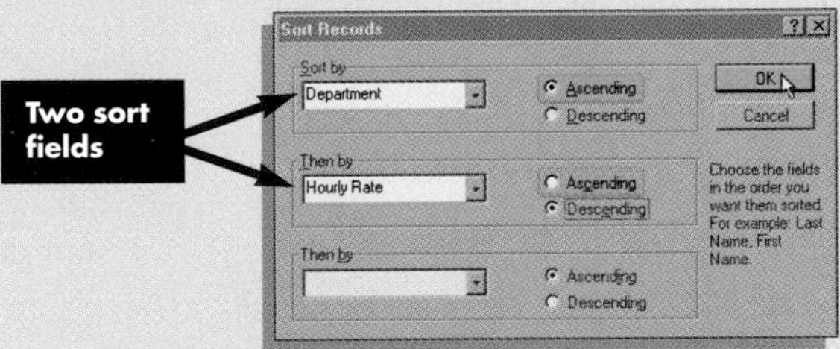


4 Let's create a list of the highest paid employees in each department. To do this we'll use two sort fields. Because we want the employees grouped by department, we'll choose the Department field as the first sort field. The Hourly Rate field is our second sort field and because we want the highest paid employee at the top of the list, we'll choose descending order.

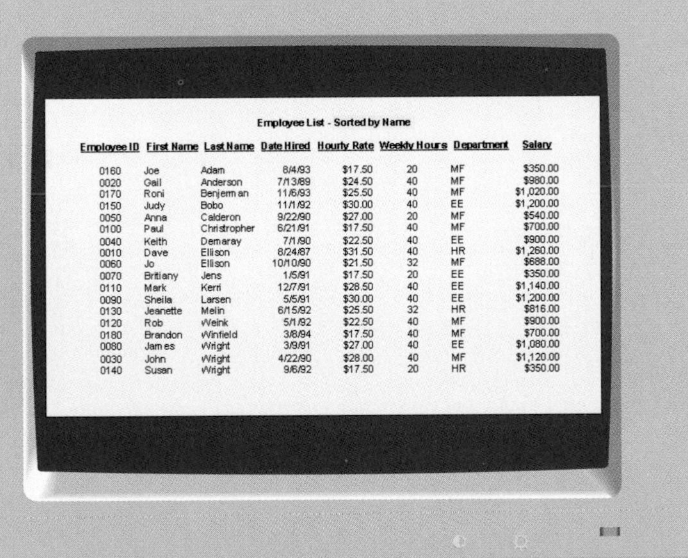

Employee List - Sorted by Name

| Employee ID | First Name | Last Name | Date Hired | Hourly Rate | Weekly Hours | Department | Salary |
|---|---|---|---|---|---|---|---|
| 0160 | Joe | Adam | 8/4/93 | $17.50 | 20 | MF | $350.00 |
| 0020 | Gail | Anderson | 7/13/89 | $24.50 | 40 | MF | $980.00 |
| 0170 | Roni | Benjem an | 11/6/93 | $25.50 | 40 | MF | $1,020.00 |
| 0150 | Judy | Bobo | 11/1/92 | $30.00 | 40 | EE | $1,200.00 |
| 0050 | Anna | Calderon | 9/22/90 | $27.00 | 20 | MF | $540.00 |
| 0100 | Paul | Christropher | 6/21/91 | $17.50 | 40 | MF | $700.00 |
| 0040 | Keith | Demaray | 7/1/90 | $22.50 | 40 | EE | $900.00 |
| 0010 | Dave | Ellison | 8/24/87 | $31.50 | 40 | HR | $1,260.00 |
| 0060 | Jo | Ellison | 10/10/90 | $21.50 | 32 | MF | $688.00 |
| 0070 | Britiany | Jens | 1/5/91 | $17.50 | 20 | EE | $350.00 |
| 0110 | Mark | Kerri | 12/7/91 | $28.50 | 40 | EE | $1,140.00 |
| 0090 | Sheila | Larsen | 5/5/91 | $30.00 | 40 | EE | $1,200.00 |
| 0130 | Jeanette | Melin | 6/15/92 | $25.50 | 32 | HR | $816.00 |
| 0120 | Rob | Weink | 5/1/92 | $22.50 | 40 | MF | $900.00 |
| 0180 | Brandon | Winfield | 3/8/94 | $17.50 | 40 | MF | $700.00 |
| 0080 | Jam es | Wright | 3/9/91 | $27.00 | 40 | EE | $1,080.00 |
| 0030 | John | Wright | 4/22/90 | $28.00 | 40 | MF | $1,120.00 |
| 0140 | Susan | Wright | 9/6/92 | $17.50 | 20 | HR | $350.00 |

| Employee ID | First Name | Last Name | Date Hired | Hourly Rate | Weekly Hours | Department |
|---|---|---|---|---|---|---|
| 0090 | Sheila | Larsen | 5/5/91 | $30.00 | 40 | EE |
| 0150 | Judy | Bobo | 11/1/92 | $30.00 | 40 | EE |
| 0110 | Mark | Kerry | 12/7/91 | $28.50 | 40 | EE |
| 0080 | James | Wright | 3/9/91 | $27.00 | 40 | EE |
| 0040 | Keith | Demaray | 7/1/90 | $22.50 | 40 | EE |
| 0070 | Britiany | Jens | 1/5/91 | $17.50 | 20 | EE |
| 0010 | Dave | Ellison | 8/24/87 | $31.50 | 40 | HR |
| 0130 | Jeanette | Melin | 6/15/92 | $25.50 | 32 | HR |
| 0140 | Susan | Wright | 9/6/92 | $17.50 | 20 | HR |
| 0030 | John | Wright | 4/22/90 | $28.00 | 40 | MF |
| 0050 | Anna | Calderon | 9/22/90 | $27.00 | 20 | MF |
| 0170 | Roni | Benjamin | 11/6/93 | $25.50 | 40 | MF |
| 0020 | Gail | Anderson | 7/13/89 | $24.50 | 40 | MF |
| 0120 | Rob | Weink | 5/1/92 | $22.50 | 40 | MF |
| 0060 | Jo | Ellison | 10/10/90 | $21.50 | 32 | MF |
| 0100 | Paul | Christopher | 6/21/91 | $17.50 | 40 | MF |
| 0160 | Joe | Adam | 8/4/93 | $17.50 | 20 | MF |
| 0180 | Brandon | Winfield | 3/8/94 | $17.50 | 40 | MF |

5 Notice that our records are sorted first by department then by hire date—perfect!

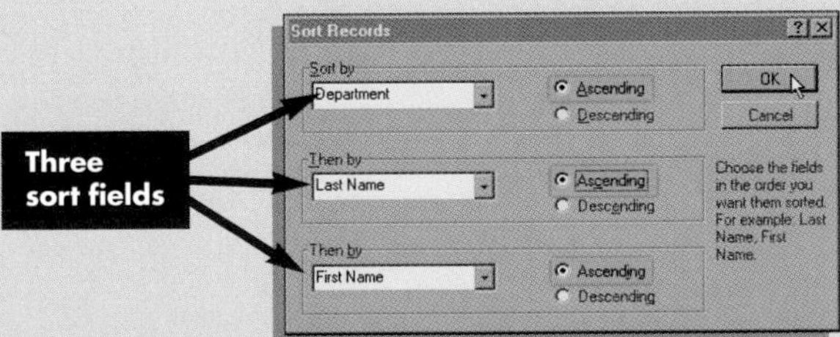


6 Our last example will produce an alphabetized list of employees by department. As in the previous sort we'll specify Department as the first sort field. Just in case we have several employees with the same last name, we'll sort the Last name field next and then sort the first name field.

# How to Query a Database

Commonly, records in a database number in the hundreds or even thousands. When this is the case you'll need the ability to query (or select) only certain records that meet one or more conditions. For example, you may want a list of employees who are in the engineering department, or you may want to print a list of all the employees hired in 1993.

Works allows you to query records from your database using a feature called a *filter*. As the name implies, filters allow only records that meet the selection criteria to pass through to the results list thus eliminating unneeded information.

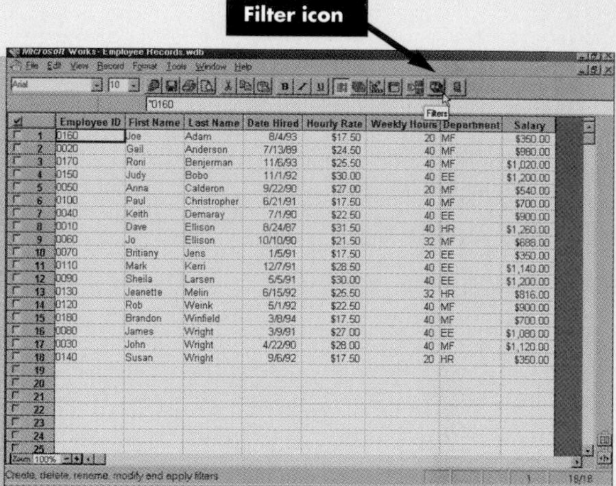


**1** To create a filter click on the Filter icon in the toolbar.

**7** To redisplay all the records in your database, click on the Record menu, select Show, then choose All Records.

EE department employees

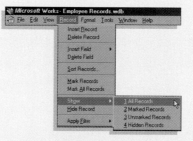

| | Employee ID | First Name | Last Name | Date Hired | Hourly Rate | Weekly Hours | Department | Sa |
|---|---|---|---|---|---|---|---|---|
| 4 | 0150 | Judy | Bobo | 11/1/92 | $30.00 | 40 | EE | $1,2 |
| 7 | 0040 | Keith | Demaray | 7/1/90 | $22.50 | 40 | EE | $9 |
| 10 | 0070 | Britiany | Jens | 1/5/91 | $17.50 | 20 | EE | $3 |
| 11 | 0110 | Mark | Kerri | 12/7/91 | $28.50 | 40 | EE | $1,1 |
| 12 | 0090 | Sheila | Larsen | 5/5/91 | $30.00 | 40 | EE | $1,2 |
| 16 | 0080 | James | Wright | 3/9/91 | $27.00 | 40 | EE | $1,0 |
| 19 | | | | | | | | |

**6** The records shown are those which match the selection criteria. In this example they are the employee records from the "EE" department.

**TIP SHEET**

- You can also access filters from the Tools menu. Open the Tools menu and click on Filters.
- Filter names can be up to 15 character with embedded spaces.
- You can enter text, numbers, or formulas in the Compare To box in the Filter window.

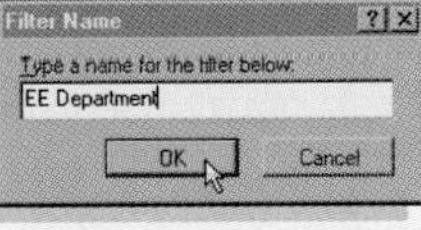


**2** For a new database, Works displays the Filter Name window. Type the name of the new filter, then click OK. If you have previously created one or more filters, then Click on the New Filters button.

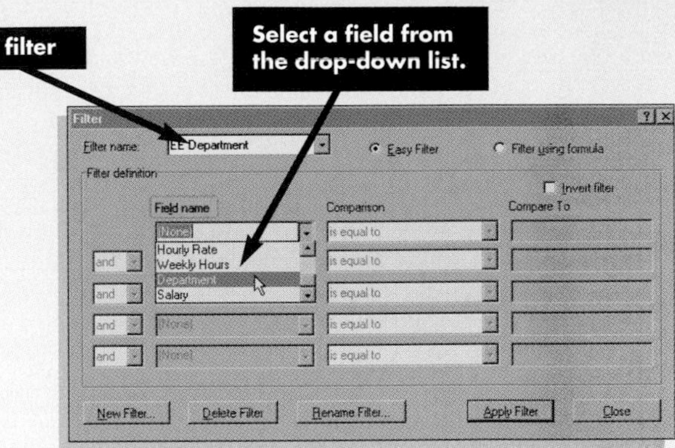


**3** In the Filter window specify your selection criteria. In this first example we'll create a list of employees from the engineering (EE) department. Select the department field name.

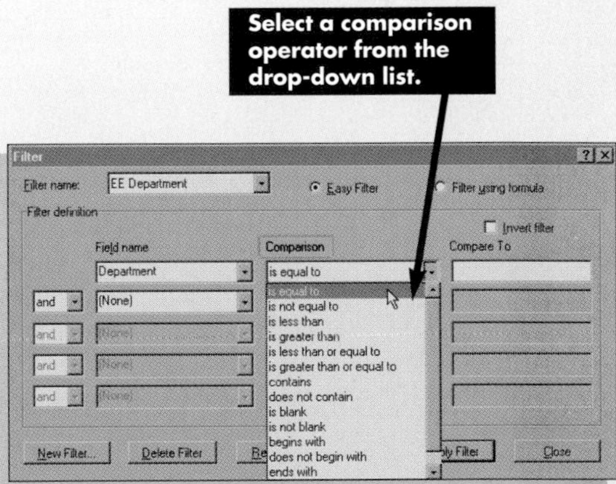


**4** Pick a comparison term. If you want to match a value exactly, use "is equal to."

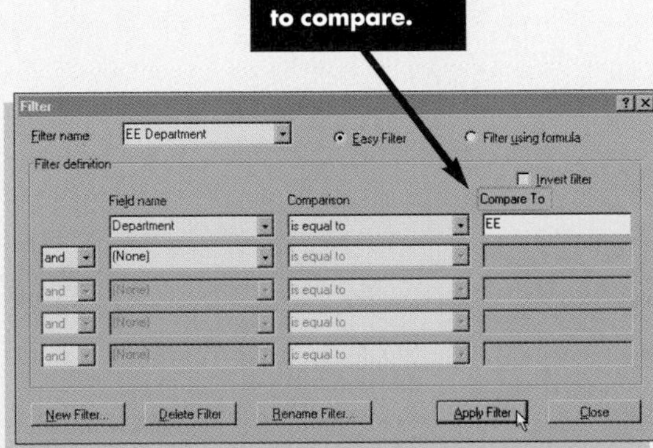


**5** Enter a value to compare. In our example we want to select records whose department field is equal to "EE." Therefore, in the Compare To field enter "EE." Click Apply Filter to select and display the matching records.

# How to Create Multiple Criteria Queries

So far, we've created queries with one criterion, for example, "List the employees in the EE department." The ability to select records that meet multiple criteria will be essential as your sophistication of databases grows.

In this spread we'll show you how to construct criteria using the "and" and "or" operators. In no time you'll be able to answer questions like "Which manufacturing employees where hired before 1991."

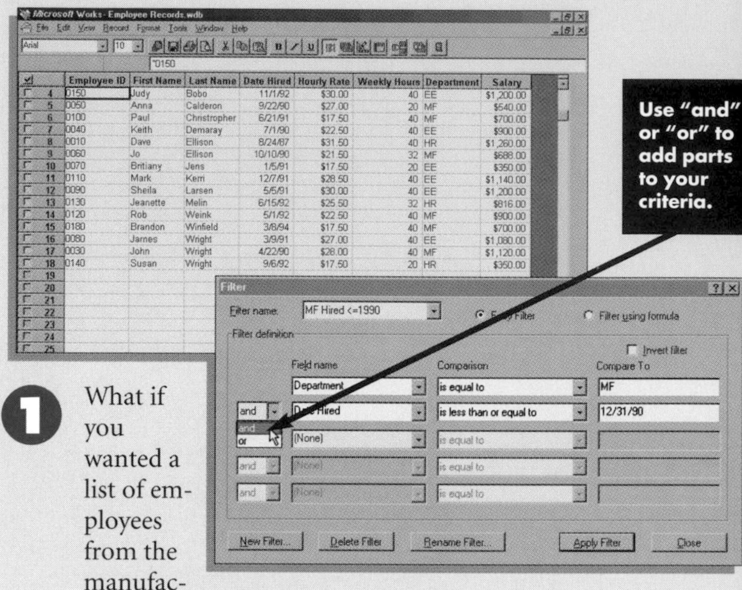


1 What if you wanted a list of employees from the manufacturing (MF) department who were hired before 1991. This selection criteria has two parts, that is, records whose department field is equal to "MF" and whose hire date field is less than or equal to 12/31/90.

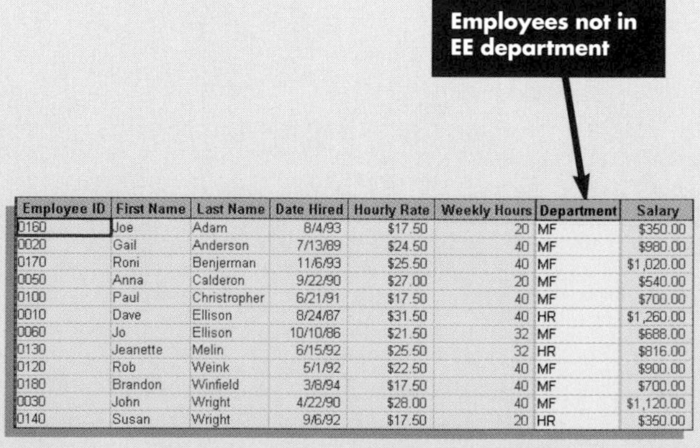


| Employee ID | First Name | Last Name | Date Hired | Hourly Rate | Weekly Hours | Department | Salary |
|---|---|---|---|---|---|---|---|
| 0160 | Joe | Adam | 8/4/93 | $17.50 | 20 | MF | $350.00 |
| 0020 | Gail | Anderson | 7/13/89 | $24.50 | 40 | MF | $980.00 |
| 0170 | Roni | Benjerman | 11/6/93 | $25.50 | 40 | MF | $1,020.00 |
| 0050 | Anna | Calderon | 9/22/90 | $27.00 | 20 | MF | $540.00 |
| 0100 | Paul | Christopher | 6/21/91 | $17.50 | 40 | MF | $700.00 |
| 0010 | Dave | Ellison | 8/24/87 | $31.50 | 40 | HR | $1,260.00 |
| 0060 | Jo | Ellison | 10/10/86 | $21.50 | 32 | MF | $688.00 |
| 0130 | Jeanette | Melin | 6/15/92 | $25.50 | 32 | HR | $816.00 |
| 0120 | Rob | Weink | 5/1/92 | $22.50 | 40 | MF | $900.00 |
| 0180 | Brandon | Winfield | 3/8/94 | $17.50 | 40 | MF | $700.00 |
| 0030 | John | Wright | 4/22/90 | $28.00 | 40 | MF | $1,120.00 |
| 0140 | Susan | Wright | 9/6/92 | $17.50 | 20 | HR | $350.00 |

Notice the results. The "EE" department employees records are not included in the results.

## TIP SHEET

- **Verify the results of all multiple criteria queries before using the results.**
- **You can create a complex filter that requires a formula. In the right corner of the Filter Dialog box click on Filter Using Formula.**
- **You can rename or delete filters. From the Filter Dialog box click the Rename or Delete button.**

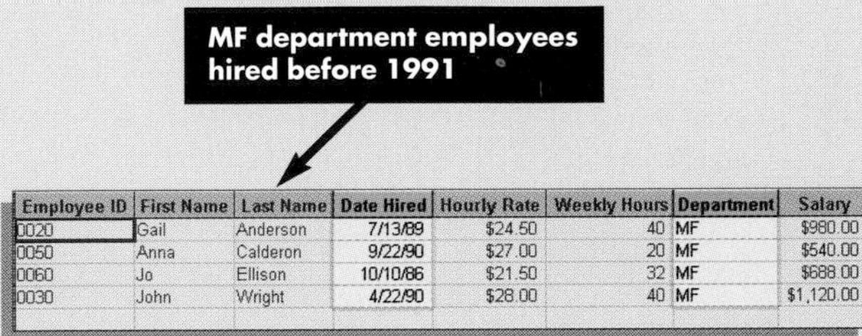


| Employee ID | First Name | Last Name | Date Hired | Hourly Rate | Weekly Hours | Department | Salary |
|---|---|---|---|---|---|---|---|
| 0020 | Gail | Anderson | 7/13/89 | $24.50 | 40 | MF | $980.00 |
| 0050 | Anna | Calderon | 9/22/90 | $27.00 | 20 | MF | $540.00 |
| 0060 | Jo | Ellison | 10/10/86 | $21.50 | 32 | MF | $688.00 |
| 0030 | John | Wright | 4/22/90 | $28.00 | 40 | MF | $1,120.00 |

**2** The selected records meet both parts of the criteria; that is, employees from the "MF" department hired on or before 12/31/90.

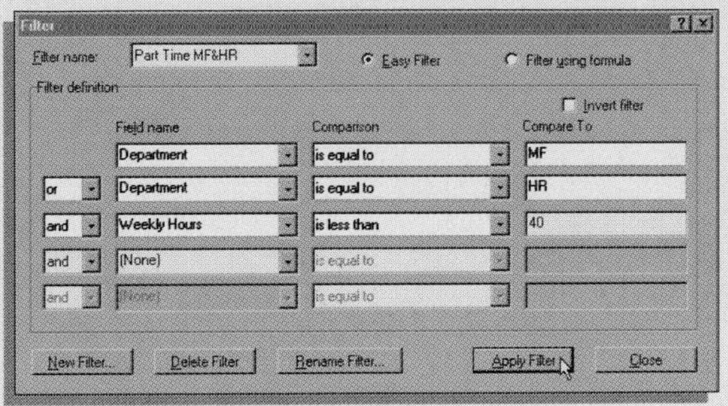


**3** You can have up to five parts to your selection criteria, making it easy to select records that match several criteria. For example, say you want a list of employees from either the manufacturing (MF) department or the human resources (HR) department who work less than 40 hours a week (part timers). Notice how the second and third lines contain the "or" and "and" parts of the criteria.

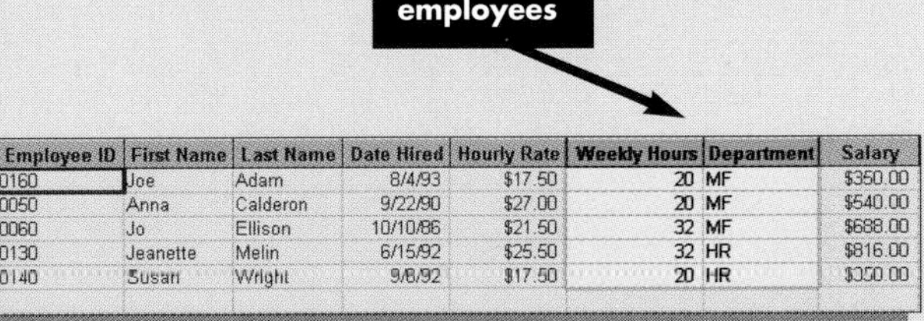


| Employee ID | First Name | Last Name | Date Hired | Hourly Rate | Weekly Hours | Department | Salary |
|---|---|---|---|---|---|---|---|
| 0160 | Joe | Adam | 8/4/93 | $17.50 | 20 | MF | $350.00 |
| 0050 | Anna | Calderon | 9/22/90 | $27.00 | 20 | MF | $540.00 |
| 0060 | Jo | Ellison | 10/10/86 | $21.50 | 32 | MF | $688.00 |
| 0130 | Jeanette | Melin | 6/15/92 | $25.50 | 32 | HR | $816.00 |
| 0140 | Susan | Wright | 9/6/92 | $17.50 | 20 | HR | $350.00 |

**4** Your criteria must be ordered carefully or the results of the query could be incorrect. For example, if you switch the "or" and "and" parts in the previous query, you'll get a list of part-time employees from the "MF" department and all of the employees from the "HR" department.

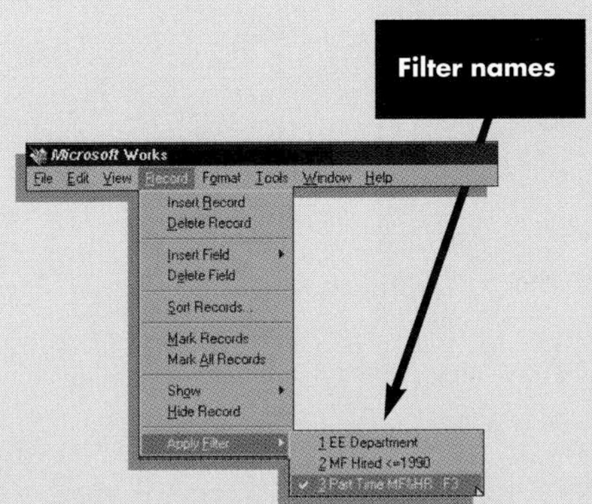


**5** To display and apply your filters click on the Record menu, select Apply Filters, and then pick a filter from the list.

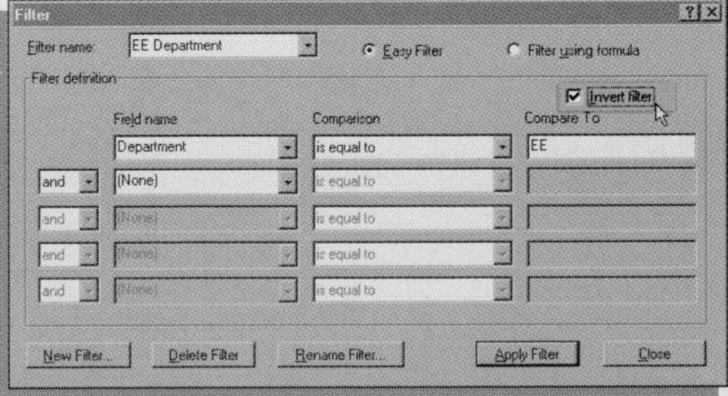


**6** Let's say you want a list of all the employees not in the "EE" department. Works has a solution—and you don't have to use "and" parts to include all the other departments. Try this little trick. Create a query to select "EE" employees and then enable the Invert Filter option to give you everything but!

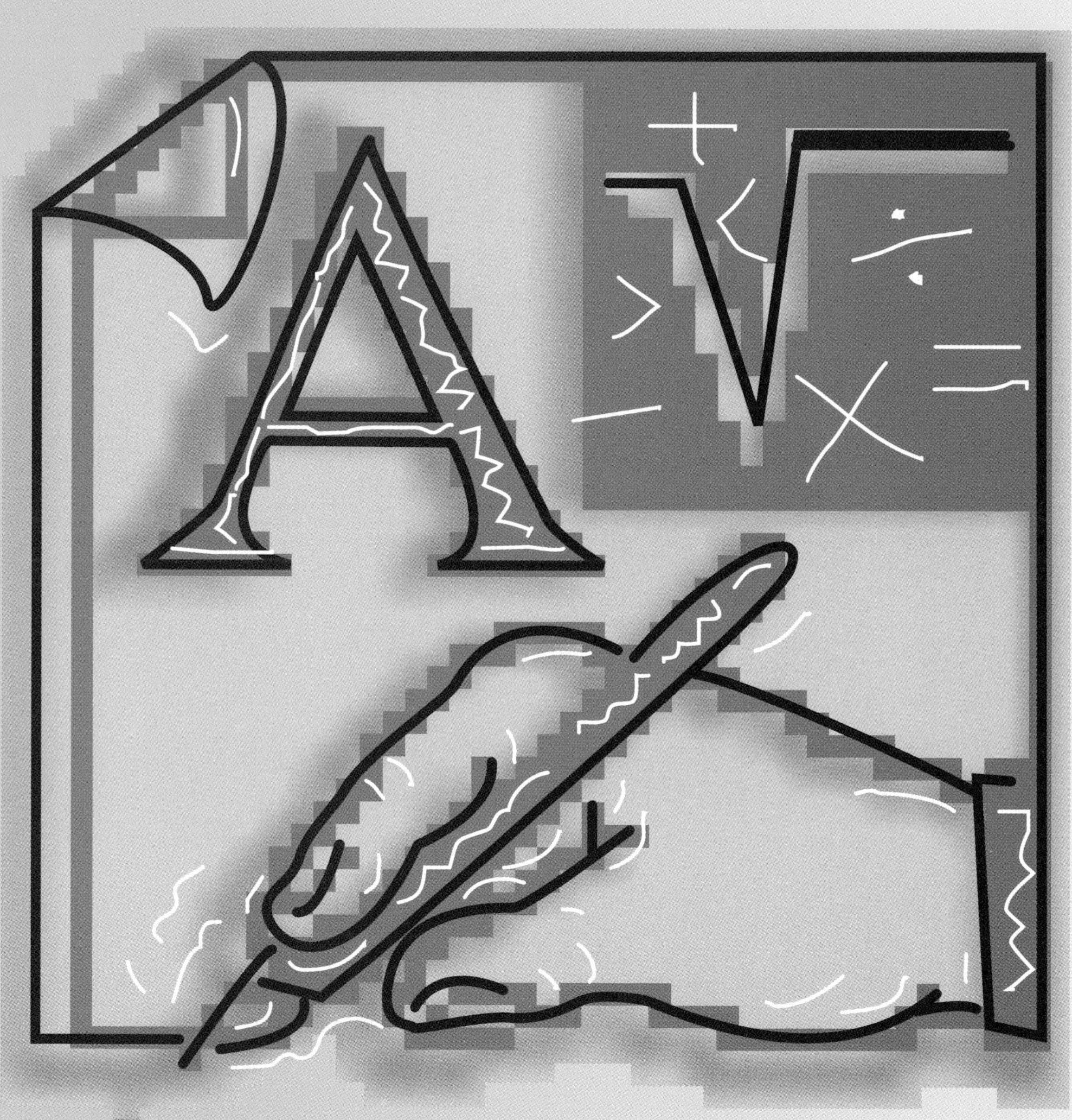

# CHAPTER 17

# Creating a Mass Mailing

Are you intrigued by getting personal mail from people you've never met? Do you collect those little cards that fall out of magazines? If so, you're about to find your calling. You can stop waiting by the mailbox for the next clearinghouse giveaway and turn instead to creating your own mailings. With Works, you can turn out personal letters faster than your recipients can read them.

But seriously, you may have a real need for mass mailings. Maybe you need to send bills to all of your customers with outstanding balances. Perhaps you just want revenge for all those photocopied holiday card inserts you received last year. No matter what your purpose, mass mailings can be a time- and cost-efficient method for delivering your message.

The key to creating a mass mailing is a technique called *merging*. Merging is simply the process of taking personal information from your database, one record at a time, and inserting it into your word processor document, one copy at a time. That way, you get one copy of your letter for each record in your database, each with its own database information. If you can create a letter and create a database, you're well on your way to merging the two for your next mailing.

# How to Create a Form Letter

You learned in the previous chapter how to create a database. Once you complete your database, the next step in preparing a mailing is to create the form letter.

Form letters are much like ordinary letters, but with one major difference: They have special *placeholders* for personal information. Placeholders are word processor objects that mark on each form letter the location where you want to print the contents of a database field.

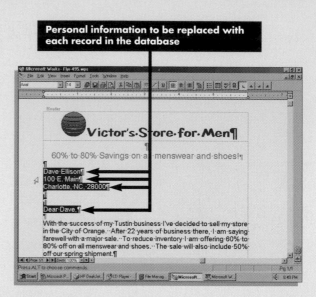

Personal information to be replaced with each record in the database

**1** With the word processor, create, and save the letter you want to send to several people. Type in personal information as you go, just as a reminder of where you want to place the information in the database fields when you perform the merge.

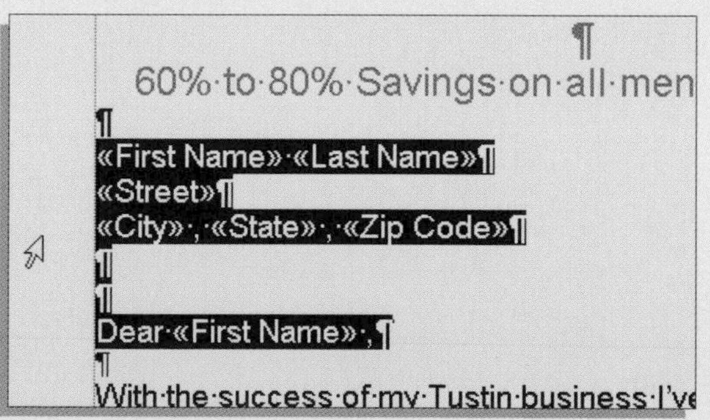


**7** To insert additional fields, one by one, into your document, you'll need to repeat steps 2, 3, and 6. (If you repeat steps 4 and 5, you could end up selecting another database, which may not contain the information you need.) As needed, include spaces and commas between field placeholders; otherwise your field values with run together when Works prints the form letters.

## TIP SHEET

- **You can create form letters of varying levels of sophistication by inserting different fields. For example, if you have separate database fields for a person's title, first name, and last name, you can generate a personalized greeting by combining those fields: Dear <<Title>> <<Last Name>>:**
- **You're not limited to address information when you merge. You can include any relevant information that you keep in your database. For example, you may want to send letters to all of your credit customers with outstanding balances. If you have created a database containing information about amount owed, you can insert a placeholder for that information into your document, and Works will merge the data in automatically at the same time as the address.**

**2** Select the text in your word processor document that you want to replace with your first database field.

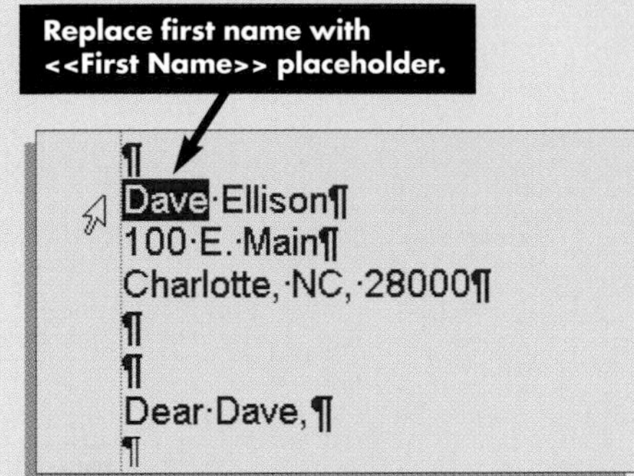


**3** To insert a placeholder for a database field, start by clicking on the Insert menu and selecting Database Field.

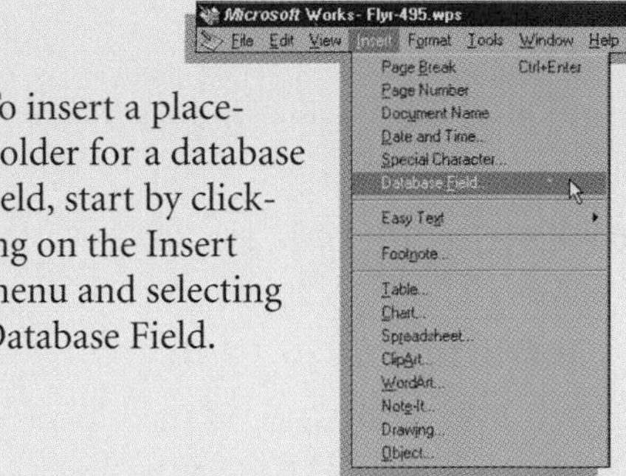


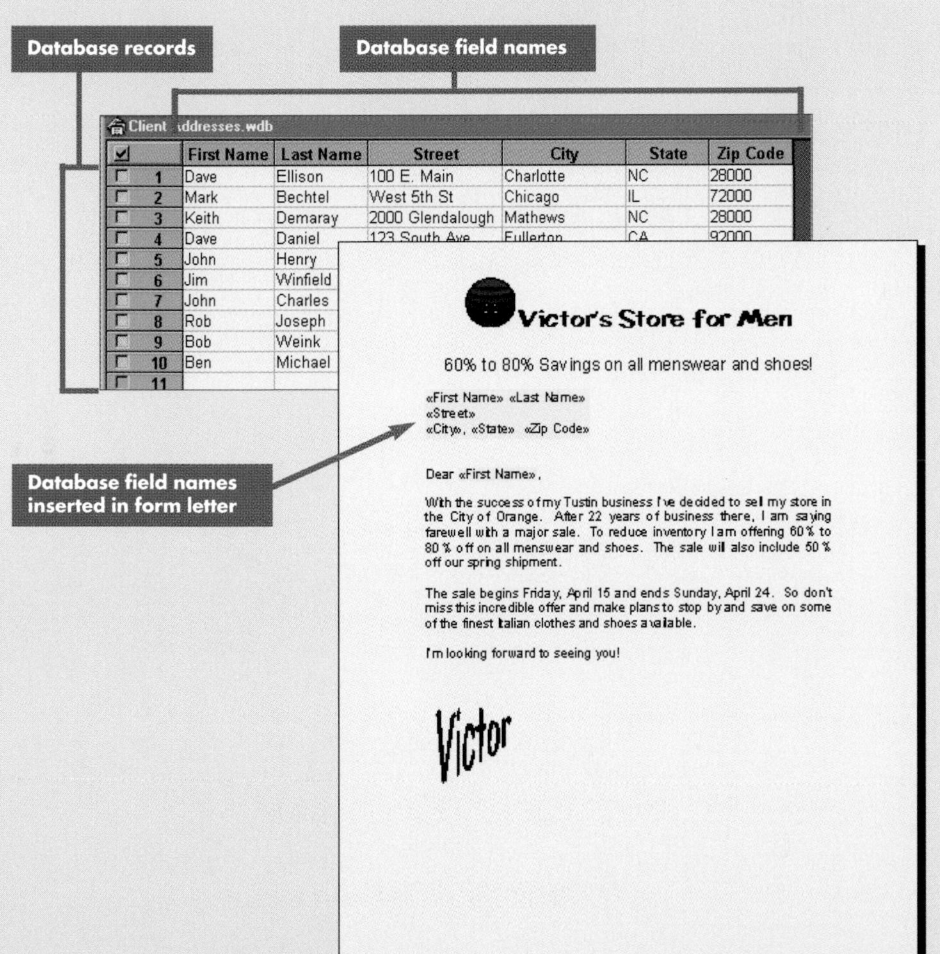


| | First Name | Last Name | Street | City | State | Zip Code |
|---|---|---|---|---|---|---|
| 1 | Dave | Ellison | 100 E. Main | Charlotte | NC | 28000 |
| 2 | Mark | Bechtel | West 5th St | Chicago | IL | 72000 |
| 3 | Keith | Demaray | 2000 Glendalough | Mathews | NC | 28000 |
| 4 | Dave | Daniel | 123 South Ave | Fullerton | CA | 92000 |
| 5 | John | Henry | | | | |
| 6 | Jim | Winfield | | | | |
| 7 | John | Charles | | | | |
| 8 | Rob | Joseph | | | | |
| 9 | Bob | Weink | | | | |
| 10 | Ben | Michael | | | | |
| 11 | | | | | | |

Victor's Store for Men

60% to 80% Savings on all menswear and shoes!

«First Name» «Last Name»
«Street»
«City», «State» «Zip Code»

Dear «First Name»,

With the success of my Tustin business I've decided to sell my store in the City of Orange. After 22 years of business there, I am saying farewell with a major sale. To reduce inventory I am offering 60% to 80% off on all menswear and shoes. The sale will also include 50% off our spring shipment.

The sale begins Friday, April 15 and ends Sunday, April 24. So don't miss this incredible offer and make plans to stop by and save on some of the finest Italian clothes and shoes available.

I'm looking forward to seeing you!

Victor

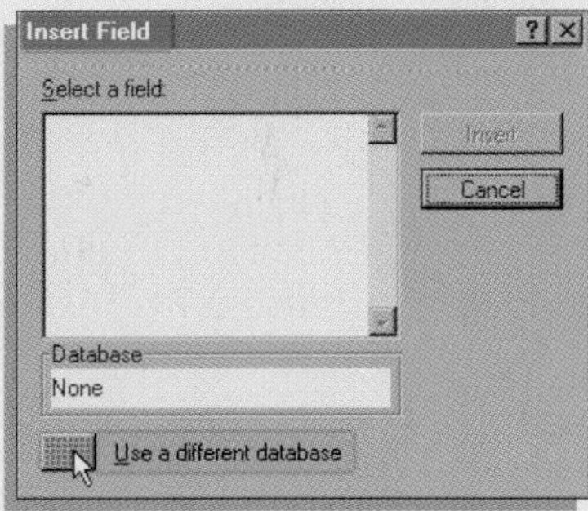


**4** Click on the "Use a different database" button in the lower-left corner of the Insert Field dialog box to choose from a list of available databases.

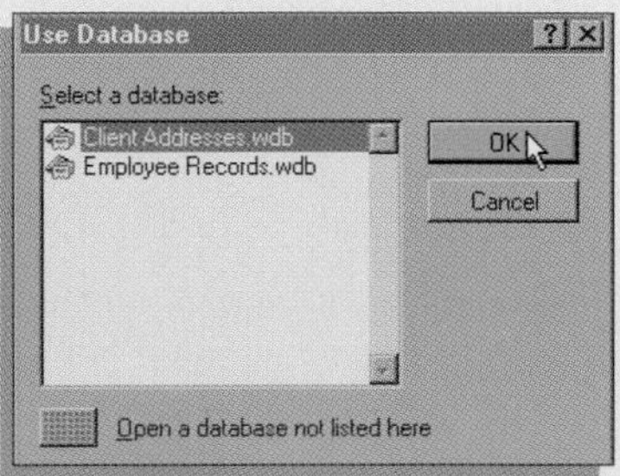


**5** In the Use Database dialog box, click on the Works database file name you want to use in the "Select a database" list and then click OK. Your selection will appear in the Database box when the Insert Field dialog box returns to your screen.

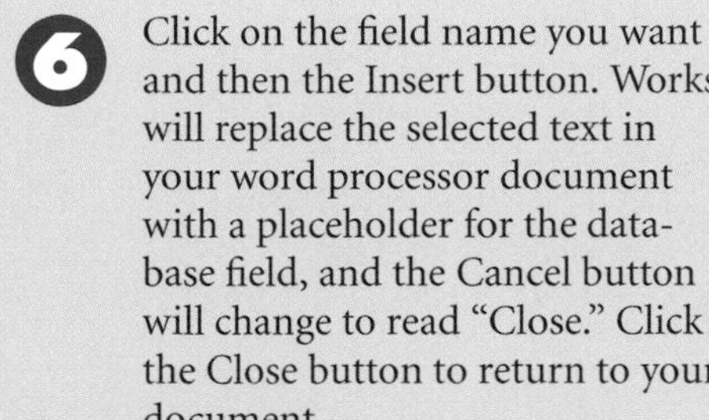

**6** Click on the field name you want and then the Insert button. Works will replace the selected text in your word processor document with a placeholder for the database field, and the Cancel button will change to read "Close." Click the Close button to return to your document.

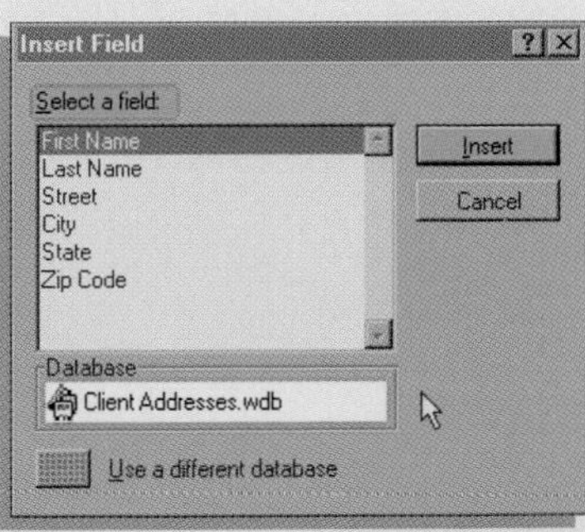

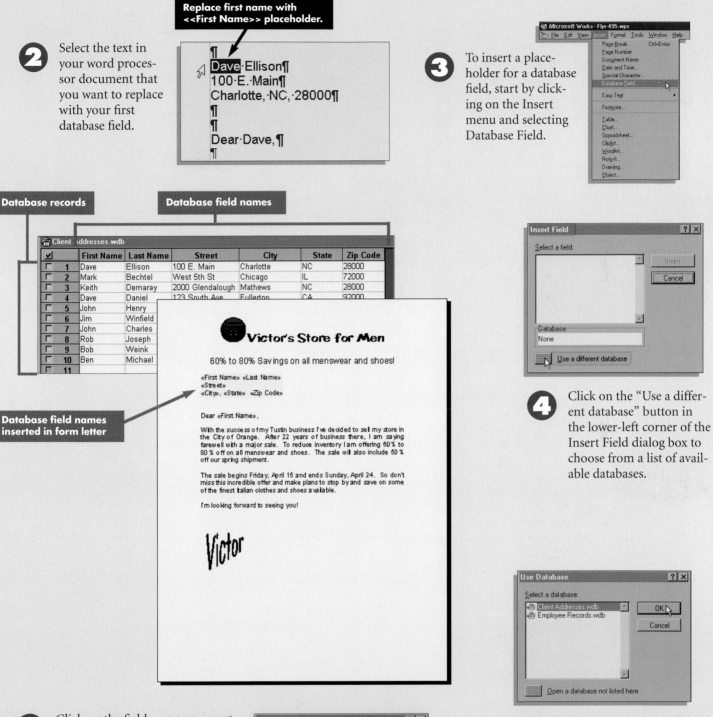

# How to Merge a Letter and a Mailing List

In the previous spread you learned how to prepare a word processor document to become a form letter. With the database ready, merging these two is the final step in creating your mailing.

Works performs your merge as part of the printing process. You've already used the Print command to output your documents, but taking just a few extra steps along the way will allow you to electronically generate a unique printout for each record, or person, in your database.

## TIP SHEET

- **Because print merges can use large quantities of paper, make sure you have everything in order before you begin printing. Check your document for spelling, grammar, and syntax, and check that you're merging the correct database.**
- **If you sort your database before you print your letters and mailing labels (our next topic) then when it's time to stuff and label envelopes it will be easy to keep the right letter with the right label.**
- **If you leave a field in your database blank, during the merge Works will treat it like it doesn't exist. If the field is on a line with other text, Works will close up the text around it. If the field is on a line by itself, Works will delete the line.**
- **When you merge the document with the database, make sure the font used for the field text matches the font used for the rest of the document. Any benefit gained from personalizing your document will be lost if it looks like a ransom note.**

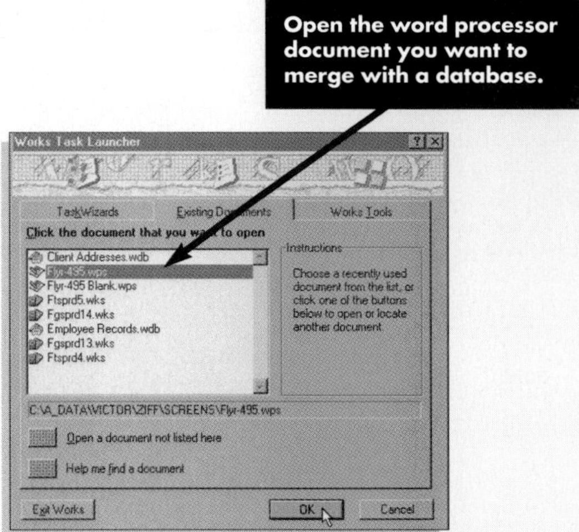


1. Start Works if you haven't already done so, and open the word processor document that you want to merge. (To merge with a database, you'll need field placeholders in your document. See the previous spread if you need help with this.) Click OK to continue.

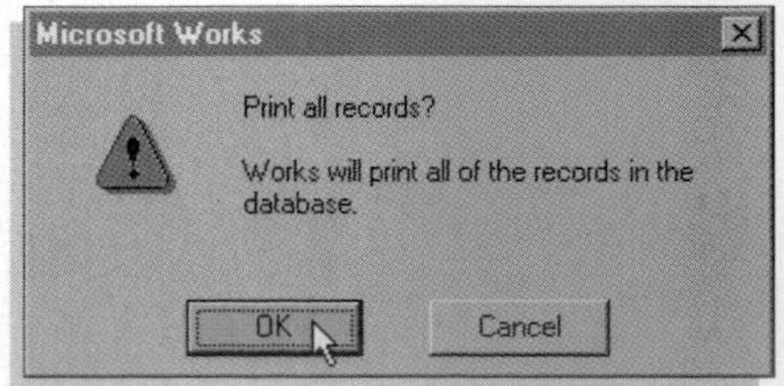


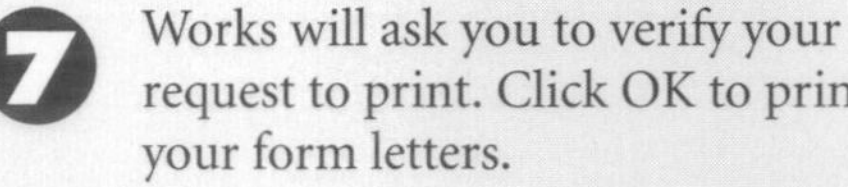

7. Works will ask you to verify your request to print. Click OK to print your form letters.

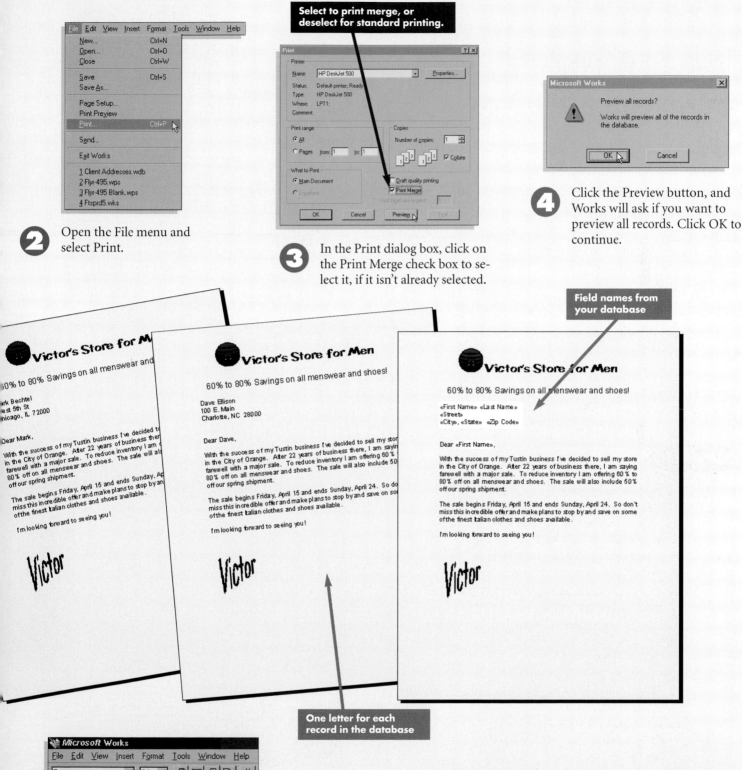

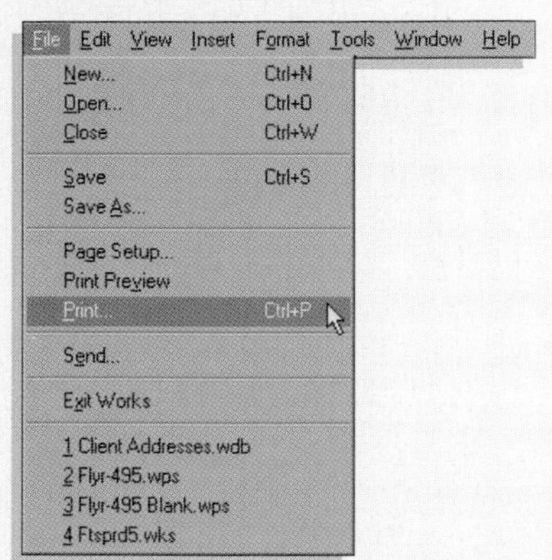


**2** Open the File menu and select Print.

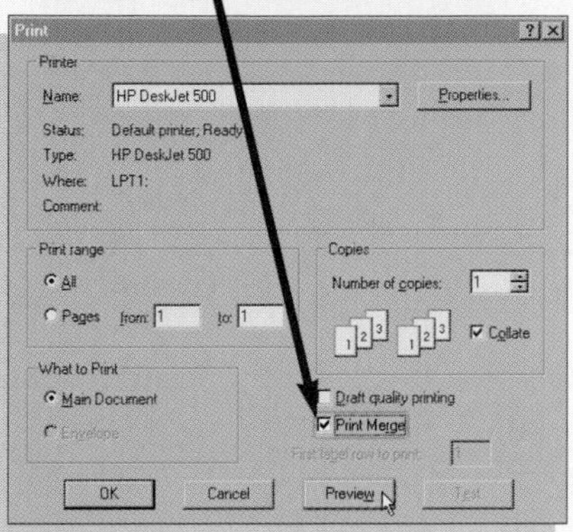


**3** In the Print dialog box, click on the Print Merge check box to select it, if it isn't already selected.

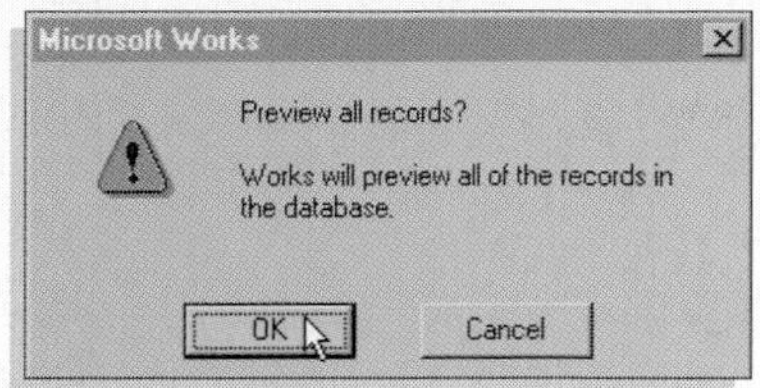


**4** Click the Preview button, and Works will ask if you want to preview all records. Click OK to continue.

Field names from your database

One letter for each record in the database

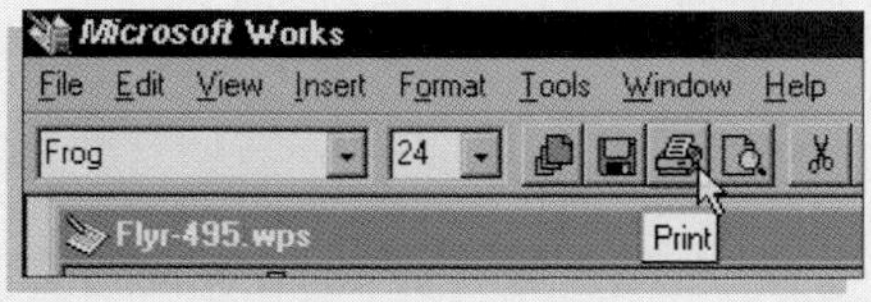

**5** Works will display the first form letter in the preview window. Use the Previous and Next buttons to move between form letters. Notice that the field placeholders (<<First Name>>, <<Last Name>>, etc.) are replaced with field values from your database.

**6** You can print the form letter from the Preview window or you can leave the Preview window by clicking the Cancel button and then select the Print icon from the Toolbar.

# How to Print the Mailing Labels

With your print merge finished, there are only a few tasks separating your stack of printouts and the post office. Works can't stuff the envelopes or lick the stamps, but it can automate the most tedious and time-consuming job remaining: printing the mailing labels.

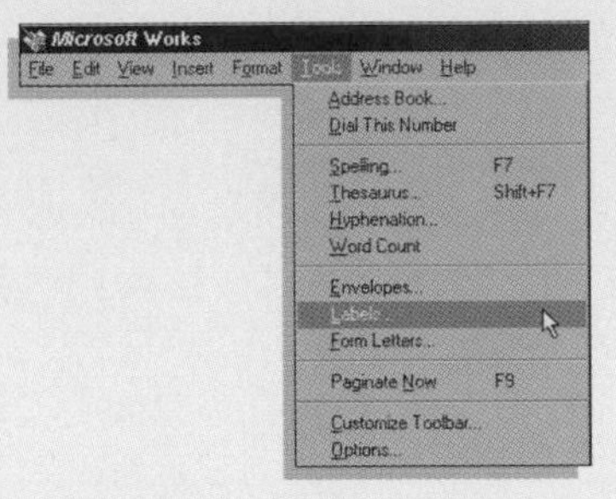


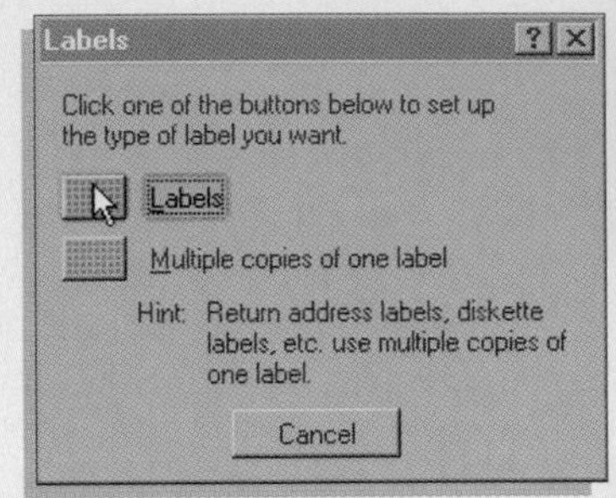


**1** Open a new word processor document and select Labels from the Tools menu. In the Labels dialog box, select the Labels button.

**9** Next click on the Printing tab, and in the Number of Labels box enter the number of labels per sheet. Check the label box: The number of labels per sheet is usually printed on it. Preview your return labels before you print them.

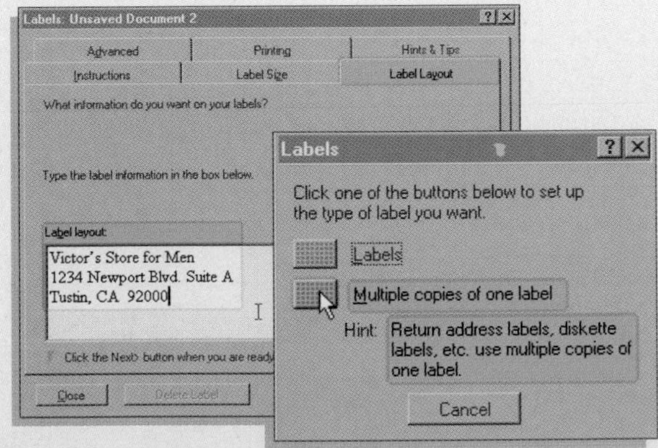


**8** If you don't have return address labels, let Works print those, too! From the Tools menu select Labels again, but this time click the "Multiple copies of one label" button. Click on the Label Layout tab and enter your return address.

**TIP SHEET**

- **If your printer permits, you can print envelopes as easily as printing labels. Just click on Envelopes instead of Labels from the Tools menu and follow the instructions.**

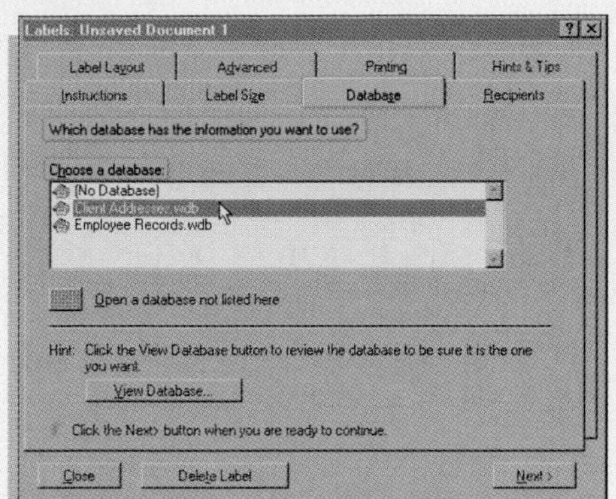


**2** Choose a database by clicking on the Database Tab, then from the list of databases select the database that has the information you want to use.

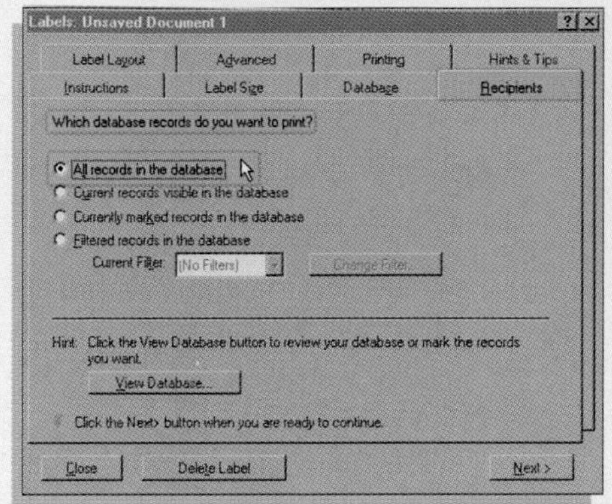


**3** Specify which records you want to print. Click on the Recipients Tab, then select which database records you want to print.

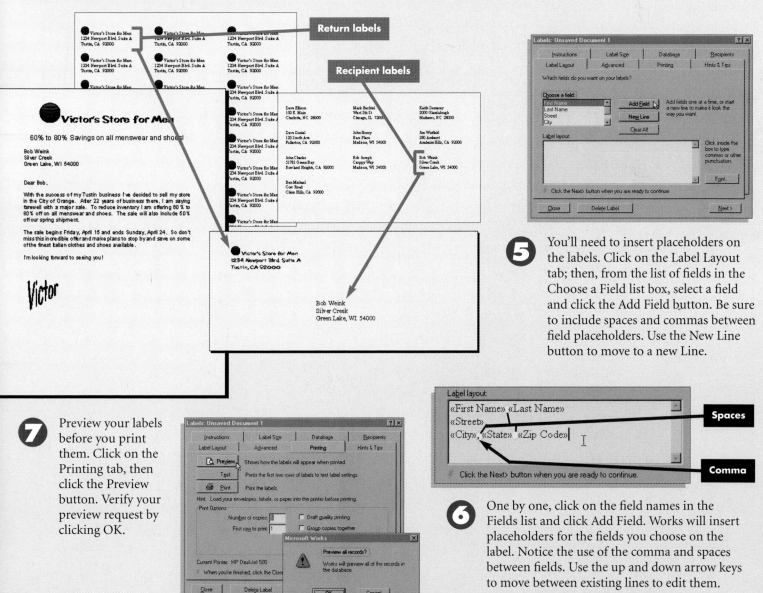

**4** Select the size of the labels you're using. Click on the Label Size tab. Works has the printer settings of the 44 most popular labels already programmed in. Use the scroll bar to select the label type from the list.

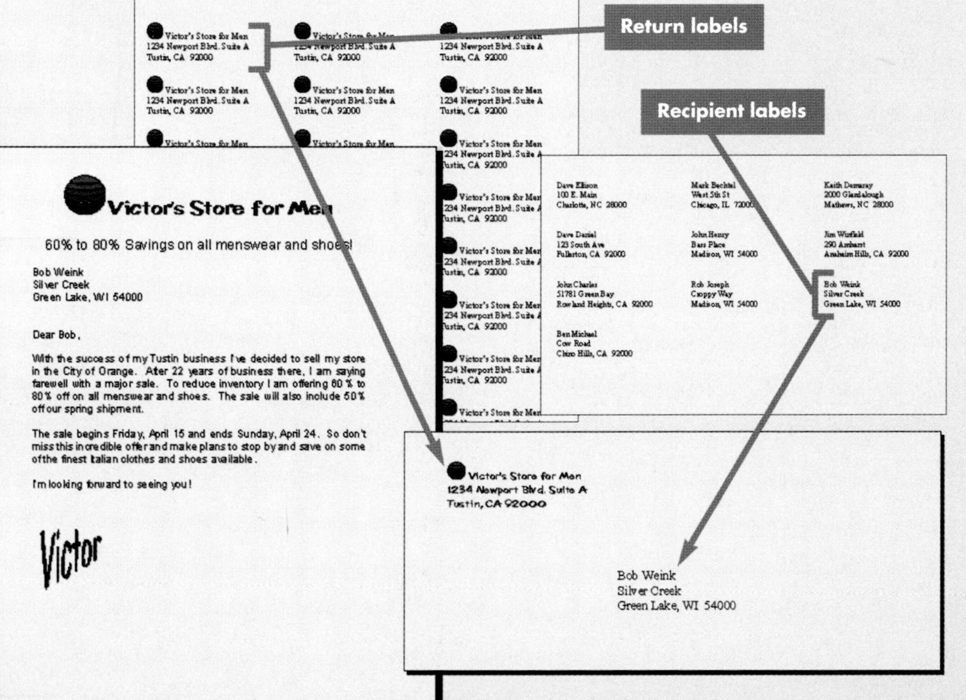


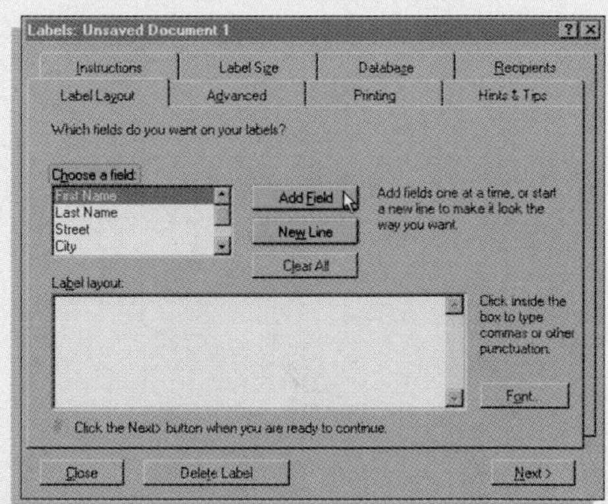


**5** You'll need to insert placeholders on the labels. Click on the Label Layout tab; then, from the list of fields in the Choose a Field list box, select a field and click the Add Field button. Be sure to include spaces and commas between field placeholders. Use the New Line button to move to a new Line.

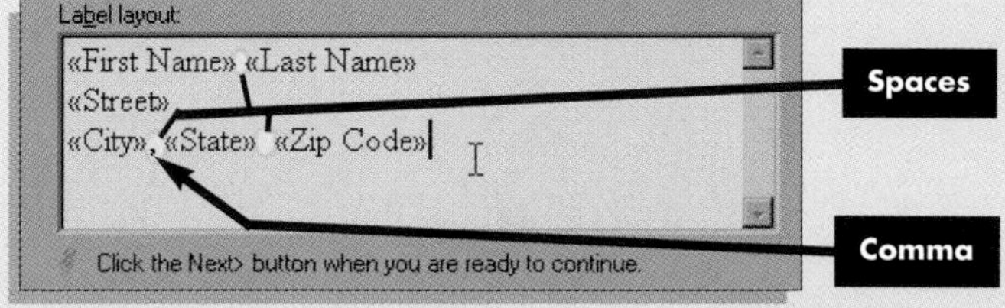


**6** One by one, click on the field names in the Fields list and click Add Field. Works will insert placeholders for the fields you choose on the label. Notice the use of the comma and spaces between fields. Use the up and down arrow keys to move between existing lines to edit them.

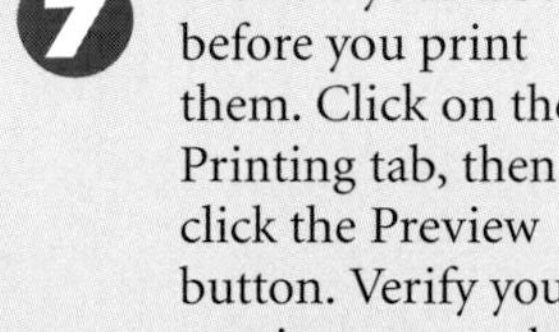

**7** Preview your labels before you print them. Click on the Printing tab, then click the Preview button. Verify your preview request by clicking OK.

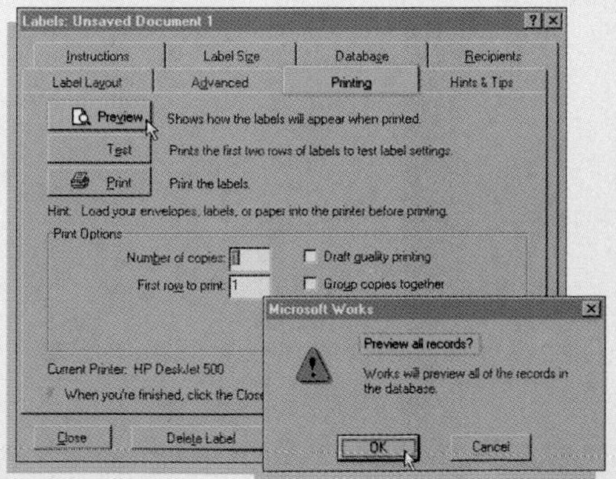

## CHAPTER 18

# Working with AutoStart Templates

If you need to use forms over and over again, Works has a feature just for you—it's called an AutoStart Template. A template is like a form. Templates can be used to process memos, invoices, credit card accounts, and newsletters—and much more. AutoStart means that Works *auto*matically opens a *template* file each time you *start* a program (like the word processor).

To begin, you'll learn template basics. Then we'll show you the steps for creating templates for the spreadsheet, database, and word processor. Now turn the page and get ready for template basics.

# Template Basics

First we'll show you how to create an AutoStart or default template by creating a memo template for the word processor. Next you'll see how to create memos using the template. We'll also show you how to stop an AutoStart template, and how to rename or delete a template file.

Before you start, check to see that Works is running and that the Task Launcher window is open.

**TIP SHEET**

- **If you don't want an AutoStart template then don't check the "Use this template for new... documents" check box (see step 4).**
- **If you want to clear all AutoStart templates, click the Clear All button in the Save As Template dialog box (see step 7).**
- **Include the word *template* in your file name. That way you won't inadvertently use it as a regular file and destroy your hard work.**

From the Task Launcher window click on the Works Tools tab, then select Word Processor.

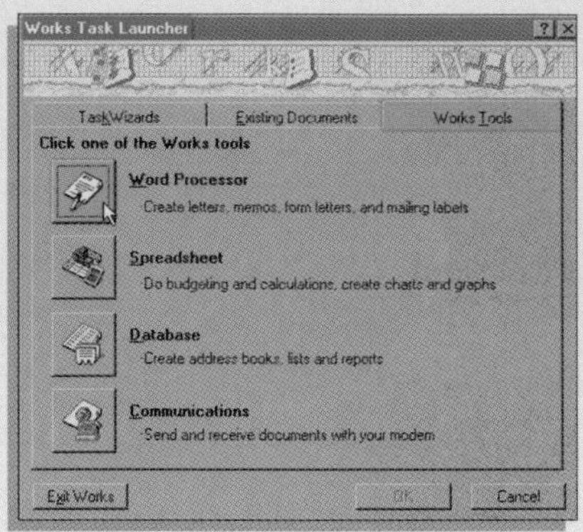


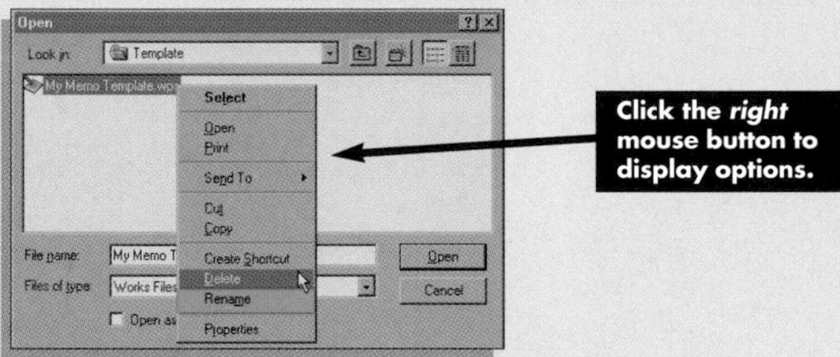


8 To delete or rename a template file, open the File menu and select Open. From the Open dialog box, open the MS Works folder and then open the Template folder. Select a template file and click the right mouse button to choose Delete or Rename.

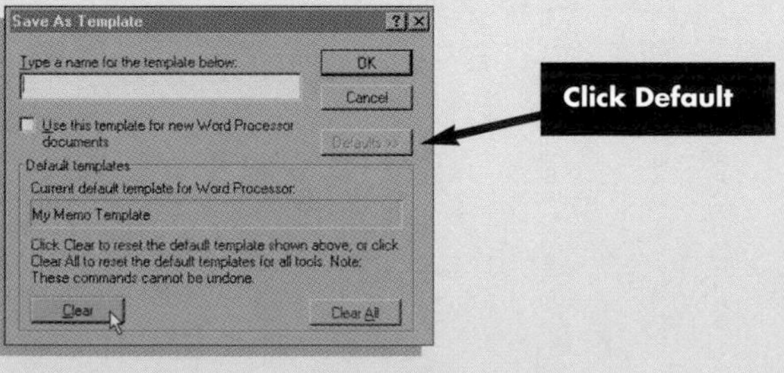


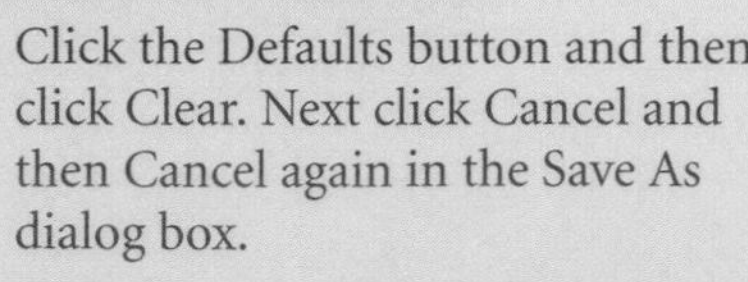

7 Click the Defaults button and then click Clear. Next click Cancel and then Cancel again in the Save As dialog box.

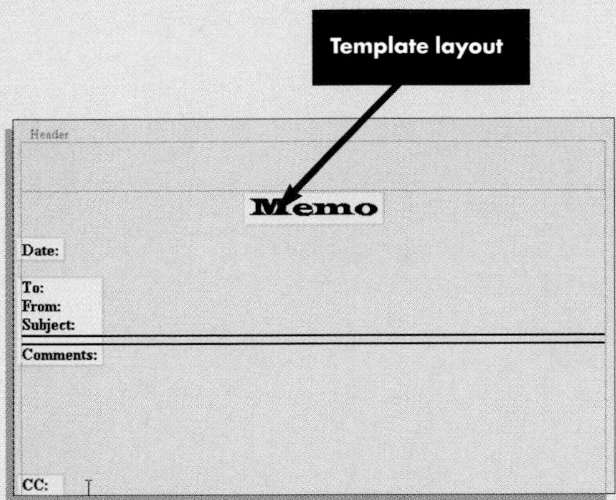

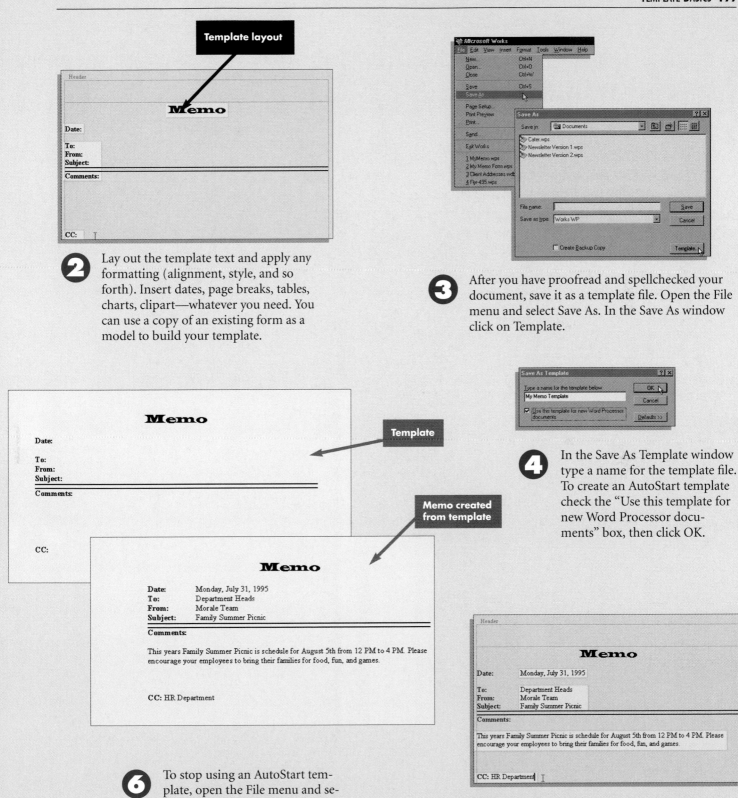

2 Lay out the template text and apply any formatting (alignment, style, and so forth). Insert dates, page breaks, tables, charts, clipart—whatever you need. You can use a copy of an existing form as a model to build your template.

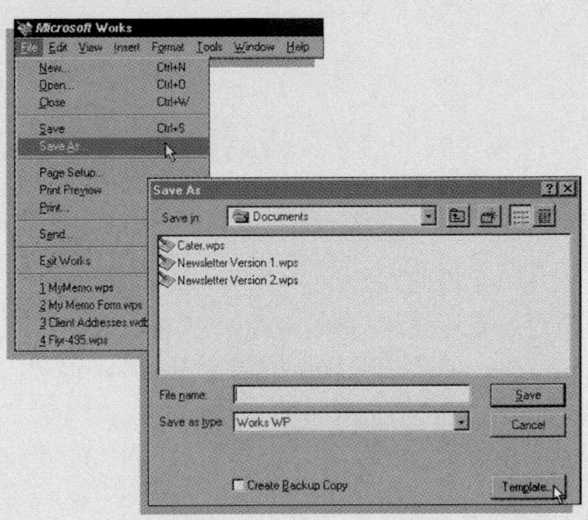


3 After you have proofread and spellchecked your document, save it as a template file. Open the File menu and select Save As. In the Save As window click on Template.

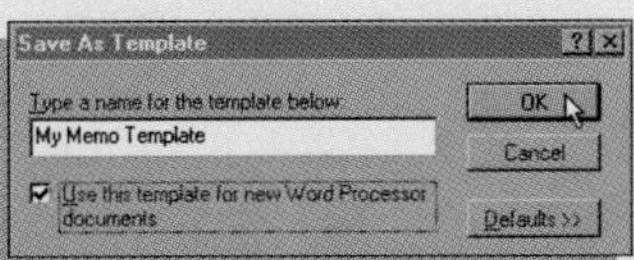


4 In the Save As Template window type a name for the template file. To create an AutoStart template check the "Use this template for new Word Processor documents" box, then click OK.

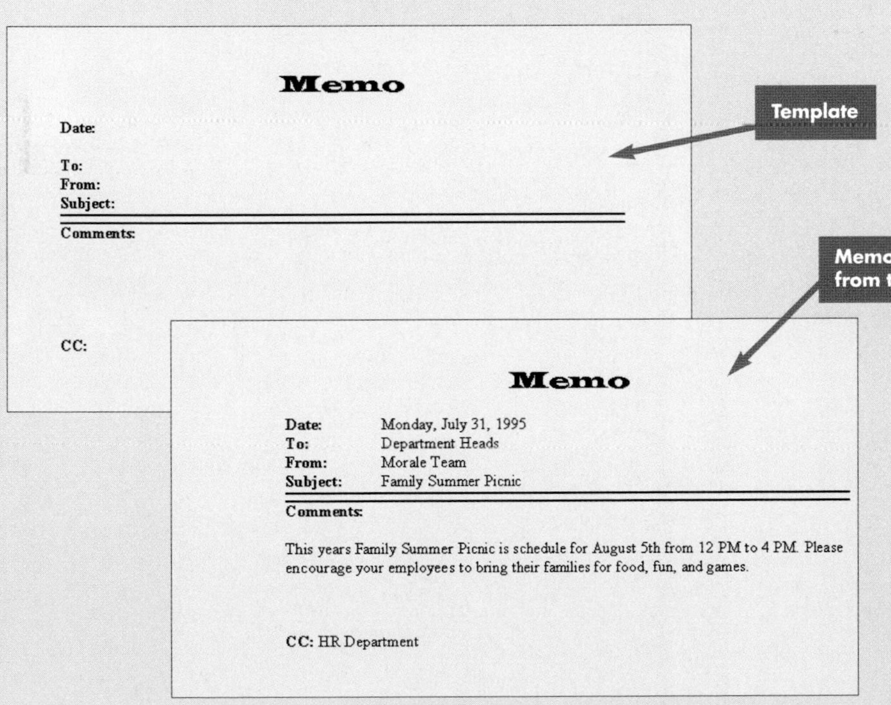


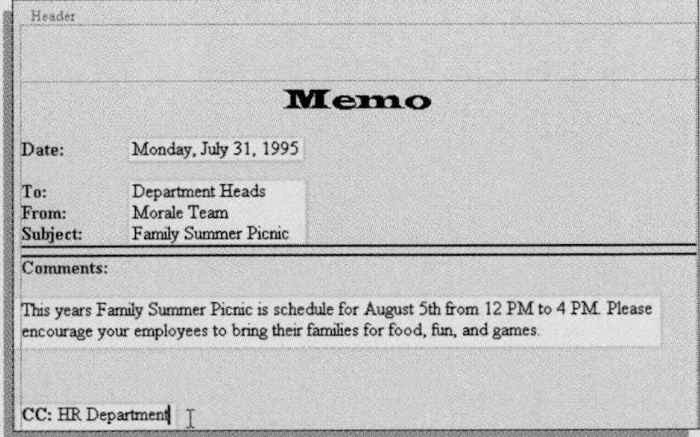


5 Use your new template to create a memo. Open a new word processor document. A copy of your template file will appear—not the original. Fill in the missing information and then save the memo as you normally would.

6 To stop using an AutoStart template, open the File menu and select Save As. In the Save As dialog box click Template.

# Invoice Template

Of all the common business documents, an invoice is the perfect candidate for using a template. Invoices have a predefined format and are usually processed on a daily basis. As you probably already know, the best program to create an invoice is the spreadsheet. And as you'll learn in the next chapter, Works can help you build a variety of documents using a feature called a TaskWizard. As a matter of fact, the template invoice you see in the middle of the page was create by a TaskWizard. But let's not get ahead of ourselves—just remember that if you don't want to create an invoice from scratch, let Works create it for you.

**TIP SHEET**

- **Save time by inserting the NOW() date formula in the invoice date field. Each time the template file loads the current date will appear automatically so you don't have to enter it.**
- **Give your files descriptive names. With Windows 95, long file names are no problem. You are not limited to eight characters with a three-character extension. You can even use spaces!**

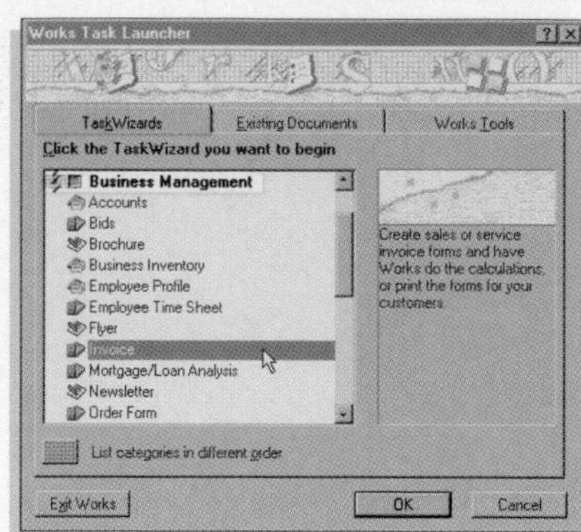

1. From the Task Launcher window, select TaskWizards. Then select Invoice from the Business Management category.

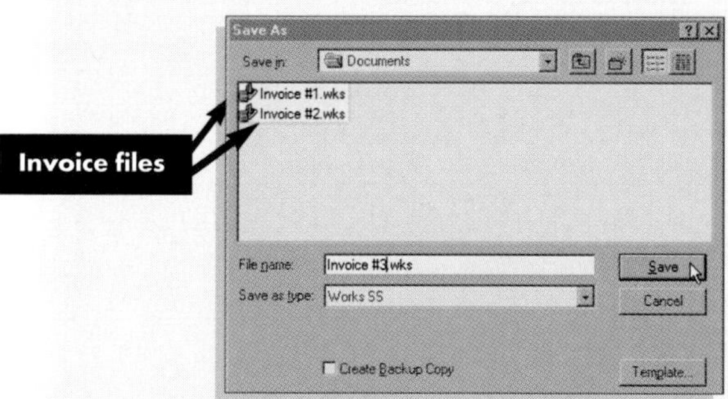

7. After you have processed the invoice, save it with a suitable name so that you can easily find and retrieve it later. Remember, you haven't changed the original template file—you've just saved a copy of it!

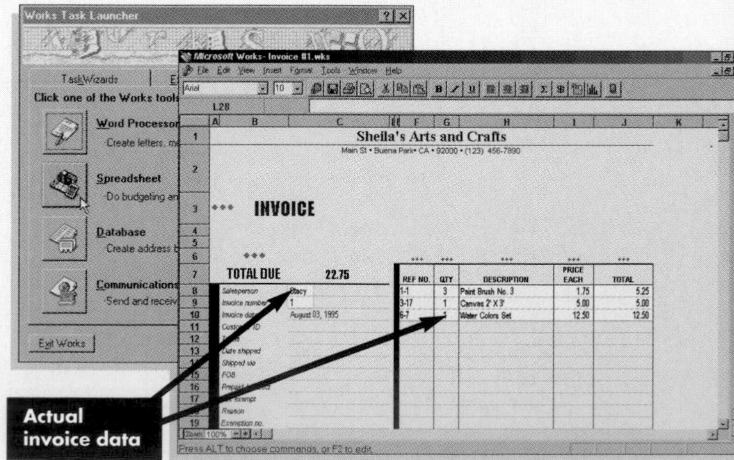

6. Each time you start the spreadsheet program your AutoStart template will load. Fill out the invoice and print a copy for your customer.

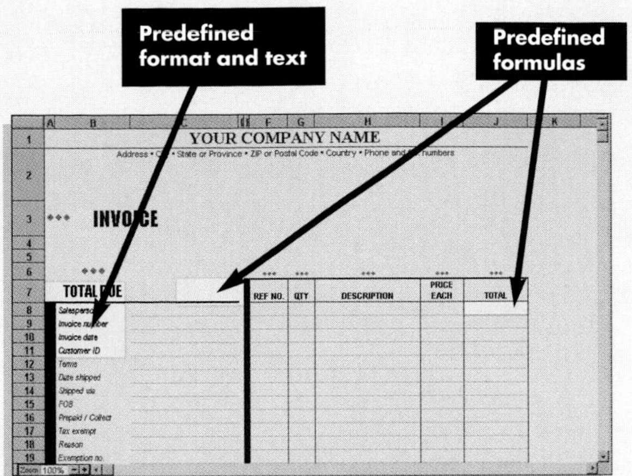

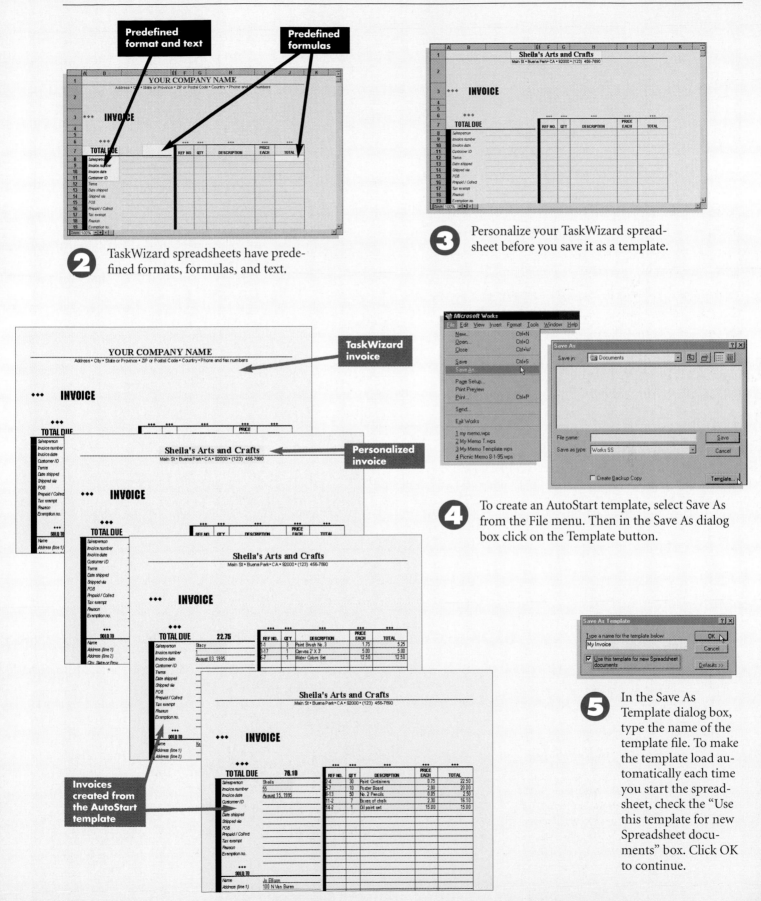

**2** TaskWizard spreadsheets have predefined formats, formulas, and text.

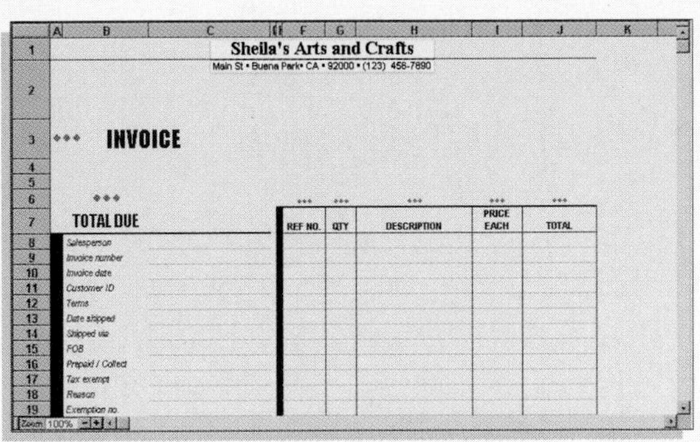


**3** Personalize your TaskWizard spreadsheet before you save it as a template.

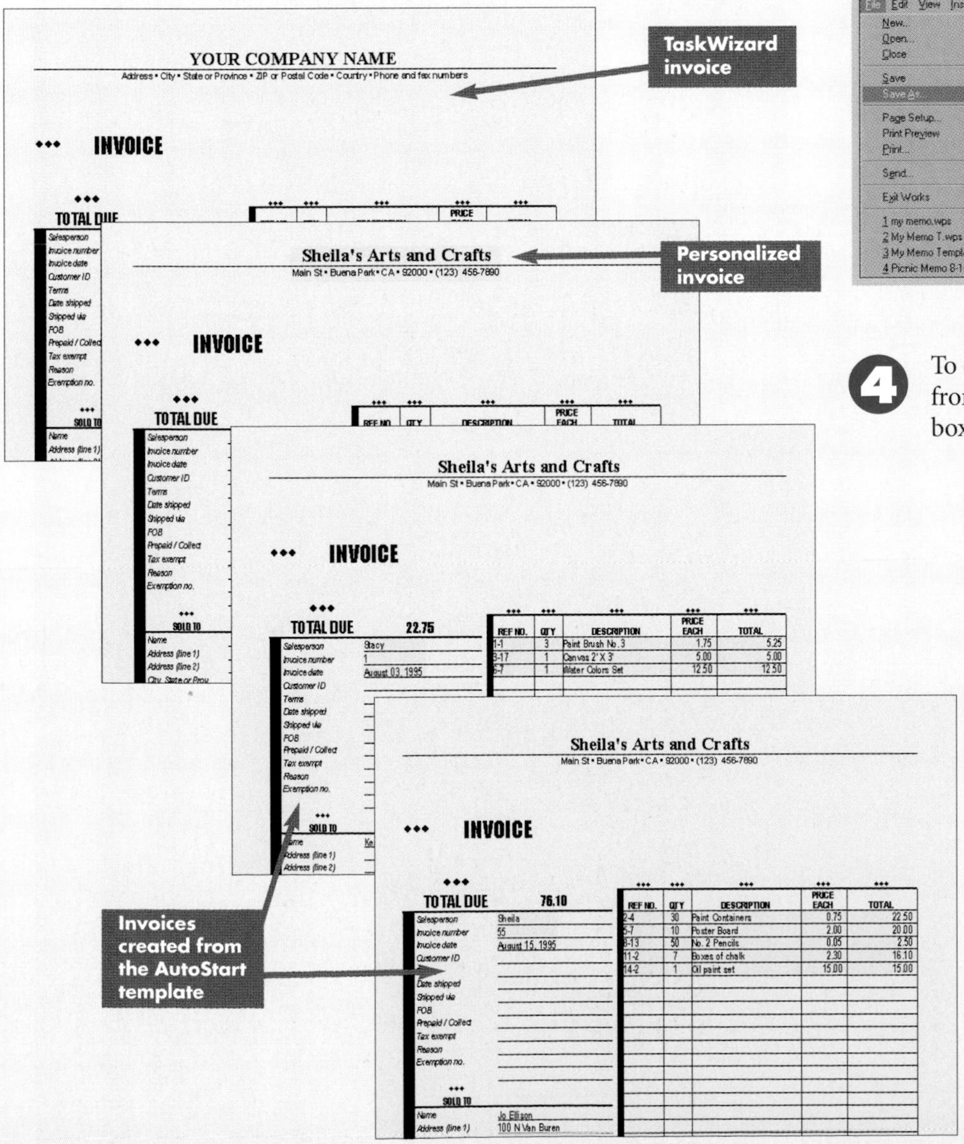

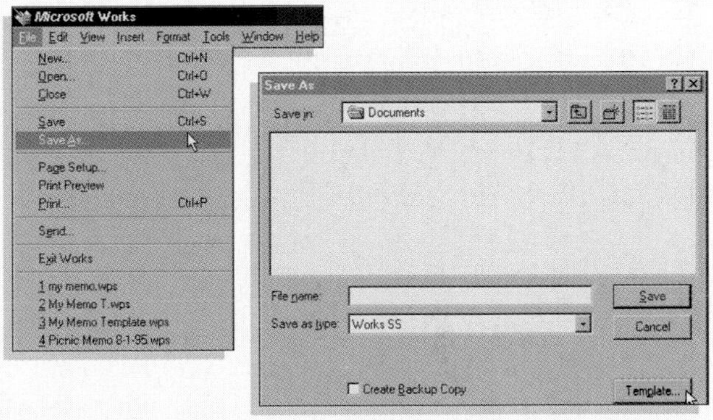

TaskWizard invoice

Personalized invoice

Invoices created from the AutoStart template

**4** To create an AutoStart template, select Save As from the File menu. Then in the Save As dialog box click on the Template button.

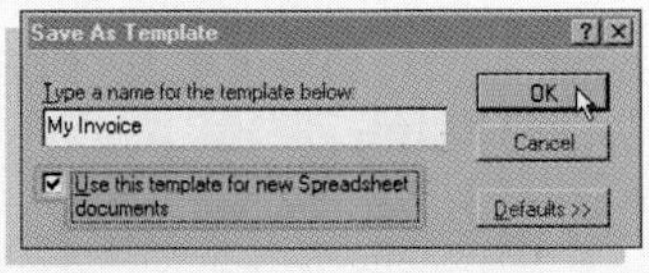

**5** In the Save As Template dialog box, type the name of the template file. To make the template load automatically each time you start the spreadsheet, check the "Use this template for new Spreadsheet documents" box. Click OK to continue.

# Credit Card Template

Suppose you operate a credit card protection business. To track individual accounts you create a template database with fields, forms, and reports. Each time you start the database your template file is loaded, ready for you to process a new account. Sounds too good to be true—but it isn't!

In this example we'll provide the basic steps for creating a database template. Use the example to create your own database templates for whatever business need you happen to have.

We assume you know how to define fields, forms, and reports. If you need a refresher on those skills, return to Chapter 15.

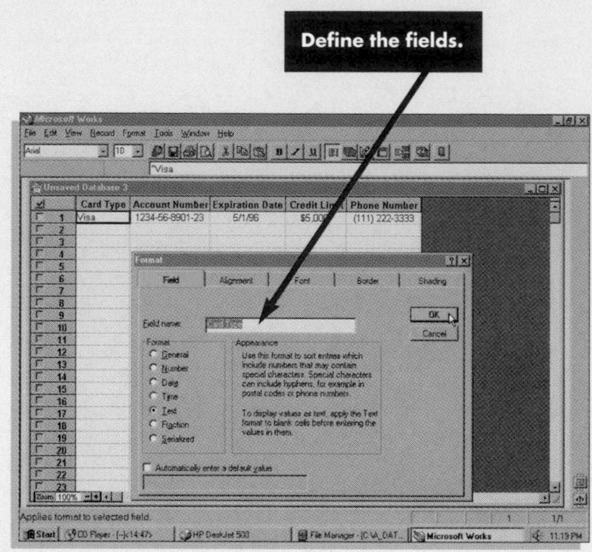


1. After launching the database tool from the Task Launcher window, define the database fields.

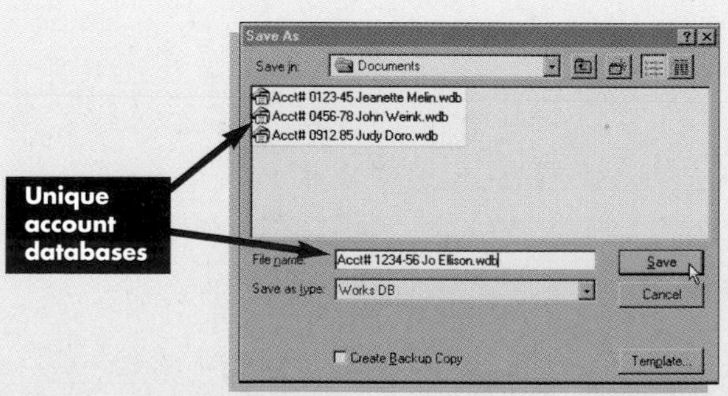


6. Save the database with a unique file name. When you want to retrieve a particular account database open the File menu, select Open, and select the appropriate file.

**TIP SHEET**

- **Normally, you'll want your database to open in Form View so that it opens ready for you to enter data. Before saving your database, switch to Form View, then from the toolbar click the Form View icon and then save your database.**

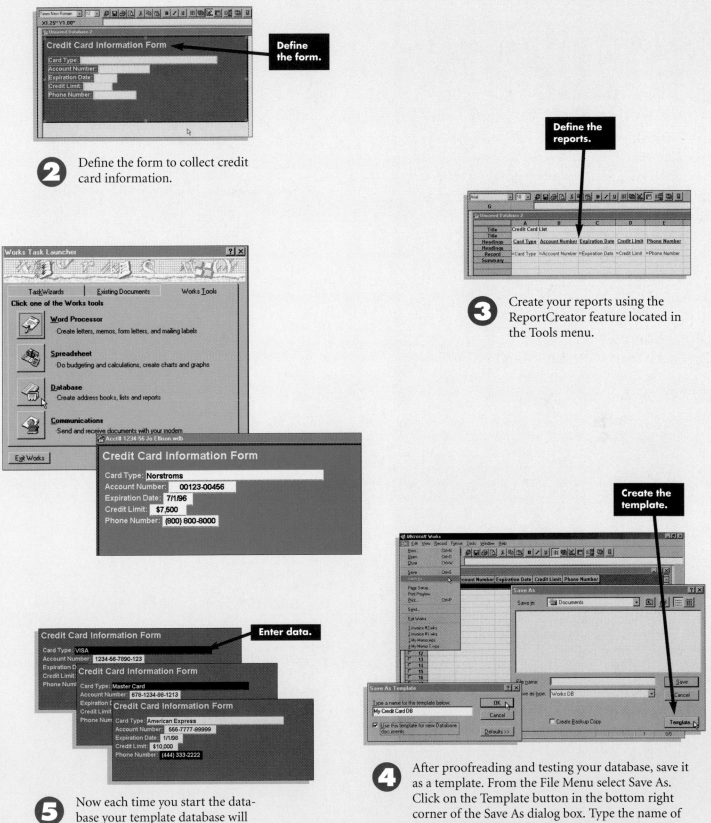

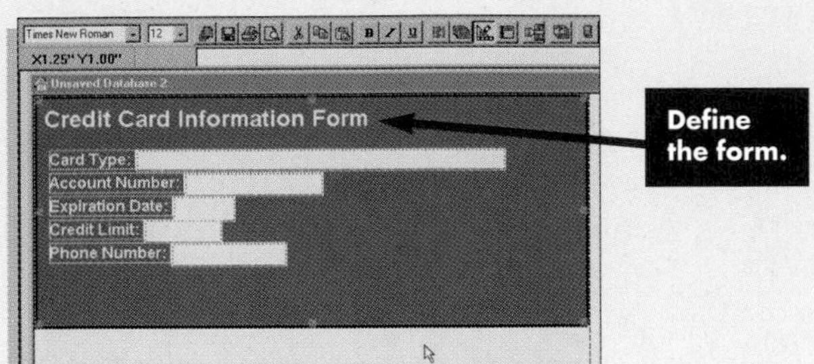


**2** Define the form to collect credit card information.

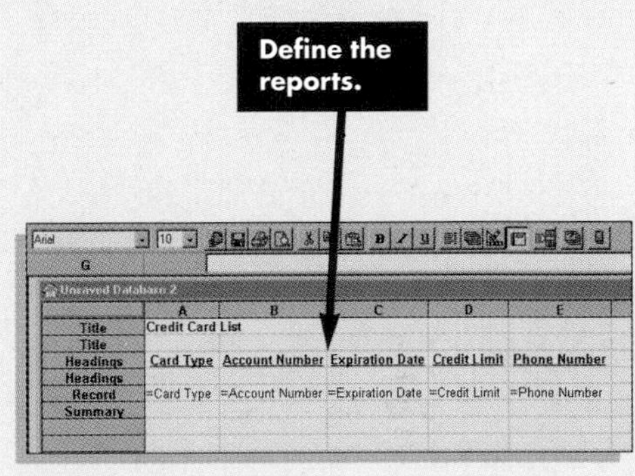


**3** Create your reports using the ReportCreator feature located in the Tools menu.

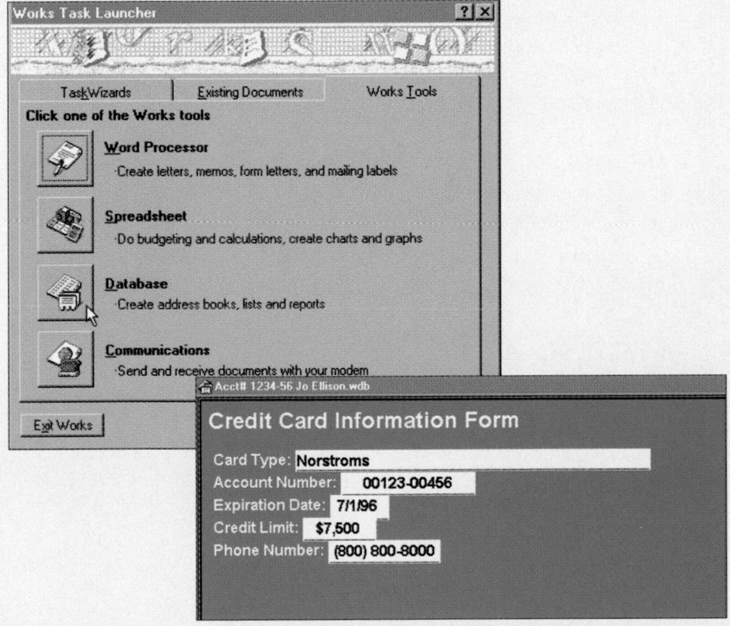


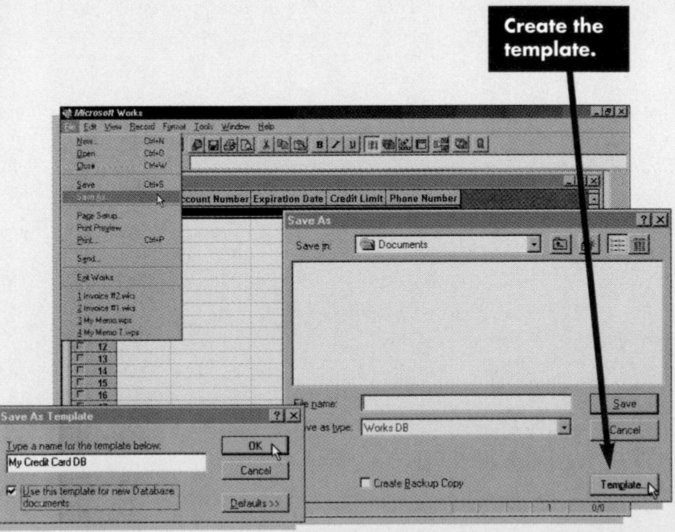


**4** After proofreading and testing your database, save it as a template. From the File Menu select Save As. Click on the Template button in the bottom right corner of the Save As dialog box. Type the name of your template, check the "Use this template…" box, and click OK. Click Cancel in the Save As dialog box.

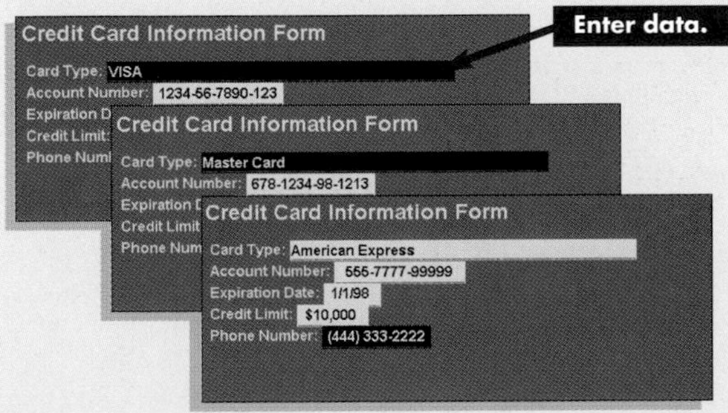


**5** Now each time you start the database your template database will load. Enter and validate the account information.

# Newsletter Template (The Basics)

Looking for a clever way to get the word out? A newsletter could be the solution. A template can save you the hassle of building a newsletter from scratch. Using a template also guarantees a consistent professional look sure to impress your readers.

In this spread we'll show you the ABC's of creating a basic newsletter: making headers, footers, and the body. In the next spread, we'll show you some tips, tricks, and techniques for enhancing your newsletter.

The word processor should be running in Page View. To switch to Page View open the View menu and click on Page View.

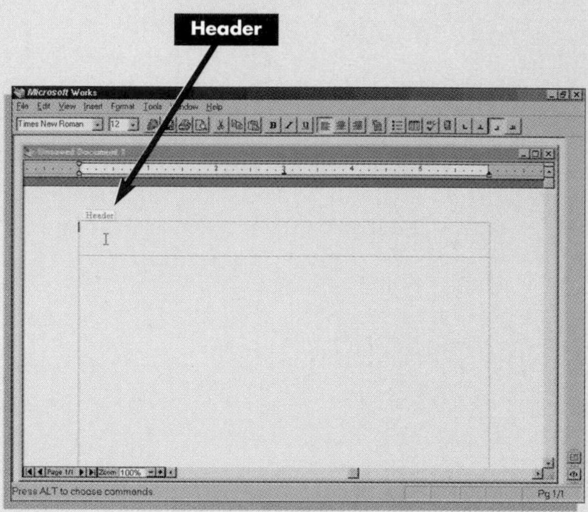


**1** The first step in preparing a newsletter is to create the header. Open a new word processor document and click into the header section (or from the View menu select Header).

**7** When you enter the newsletter articles the text will appear in column format. Using the steps outlined in the first spread of this chapter, save your newsletter as a template.

**TIP SHEET**

- **If you're going to include an existing article, don't retype it. Open the file containing the article and then use the copy and paste technique to add it.**
- **If you have a printer that prints in color, change the color of your fonts to highlight titles and important text.**

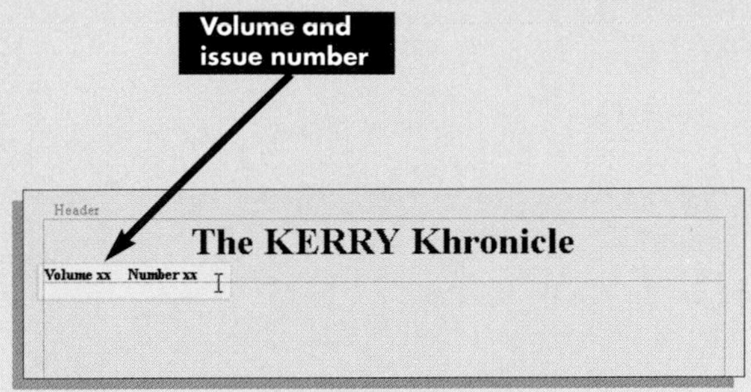

**2** Enter the title of your newsletter. Apply whatever font, size, and style you want to highlight your title.

**3** Periodic newsletters frequently include volume and issue numbers. Space down a few lines from the header and enter a placeholder for the volume and issue number (Volume xx Number xx).

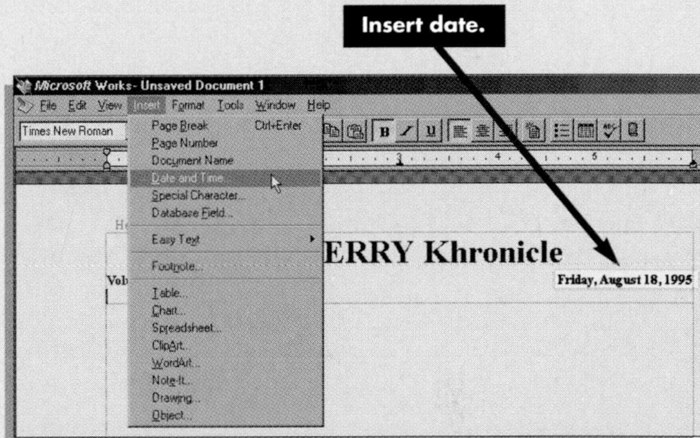

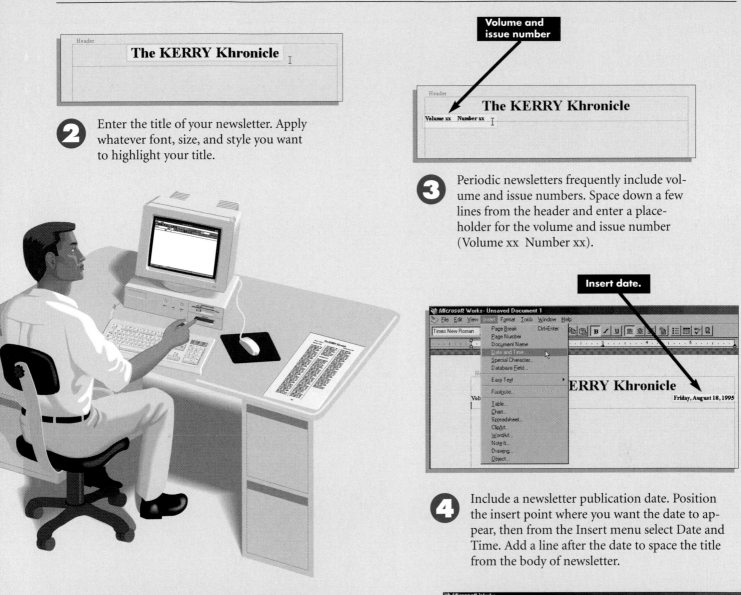

**4** Include a newsletter publication date. Position the insert point where you want the date to appear, then from the Insert menu select Date and Time. Add a line after the date to space the title from the body of newsletter.

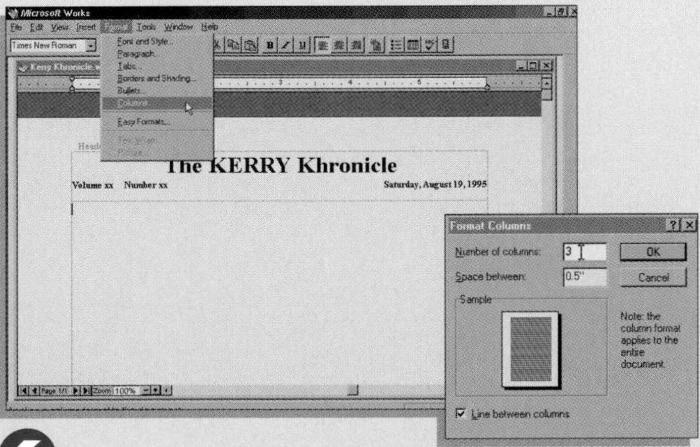


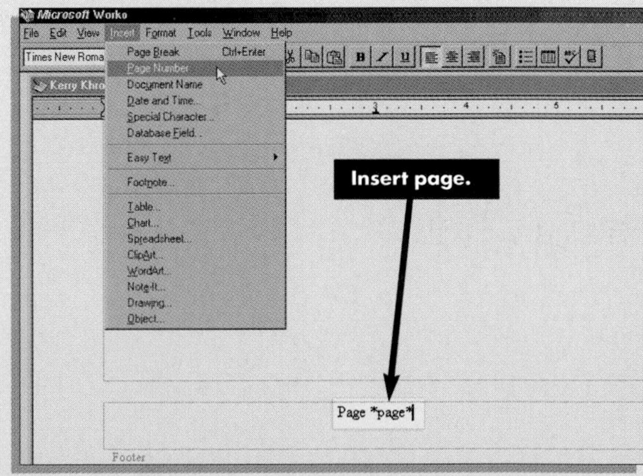


**6** Most newsletters appear in multiple column format. Click anywhere in the body of your newsletter. From the Format menu select Columns. In the Number of Columns box enter the number of columns and click OK.

**5** Now add a footer. Click into the footer or from the View menu select Footer. Type the word **Page** and then a space. Next, open the Insert menu and select Page Number.

# Newsletter Template (Enhancing the Look)

Now you are ready to learn how to turn your basic newsletter into something special. Works offers many features that will enhance the look of your newsletter. In this spread we'll show you how to do just that by adding borders, WordArt, and ClipArt. As you'll see, enhancing your newsletter is easy and fun. But more important, you increase your readers' satisfaction and enjoyment.

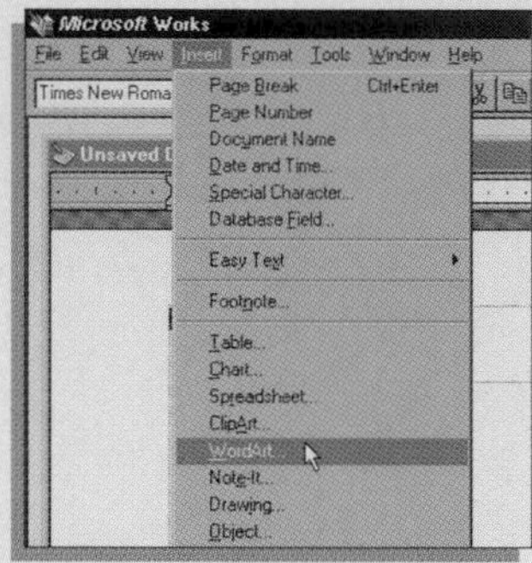


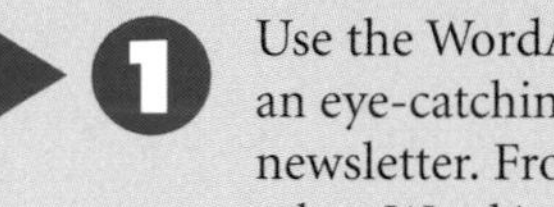

Use the WordArt feature to create an eye-catching title for your newsletter. From the Insert menu select WordArt.

## TIP SHEET

- Using the header of a document is the simplest way to include a newsletter title. However, you may want the title to appear on the first page only. If this is the case, you will need to do two things. First, open the File menu and select Page Setup. In the Page Setup dialog box click on the Other Options tab and place a check in the No Header on First Page box. Second, create your newsletter title using WordArt. Position the insertion point at the top of the first page. From the Insert menu select WordArt. Enter your text. To fit the WordArt across multiple columns you'll need to select the WordArt text box (click once). Then from the Format menu select Text Wrap and choose the absolute setting. Now size the WordArt text box across the columns.
- You can buy and install more ClipArt from your local computer store. Ask the retailer to show you what's available.

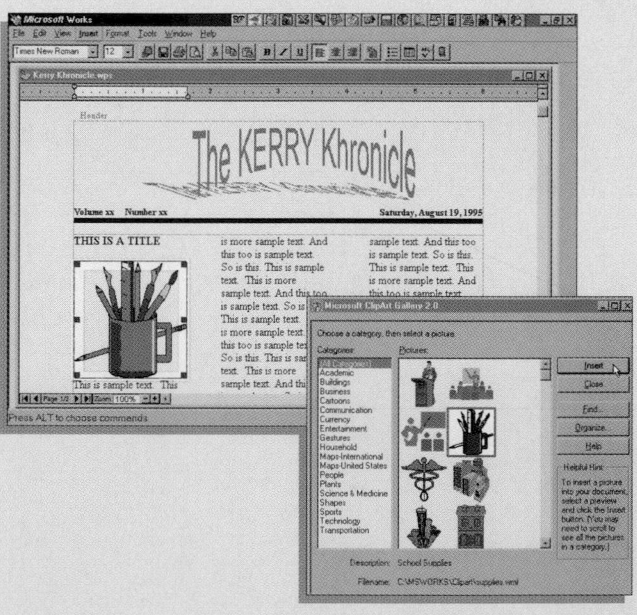


**6** Works comes with a gallery of art that you can insert into your newsletter. Position the insertion point where you want the art, then from the Insert menu select ClipArt. Select an art piece from the list that appears in the ClipArt dialog box. Click Insert to continue.

2 Enter the title of the newsletter in the text box then click the X button. You can use the resize handles to adjust the size of your title.

3 Add style and panache to WordArt by applying one of several WordArt shapes. Double-click on the WordArt text box then click on the drop-down list to view the various shapes.

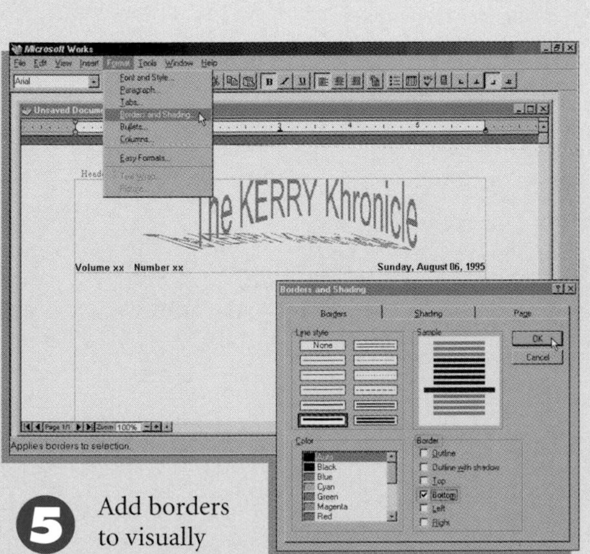

5 Add borders to visually separate the body of the newsletter from the header and footer. Click into the header or the footer, then from the Format menu select Borders and Shading. Select a line style, color, and border type then click OK.

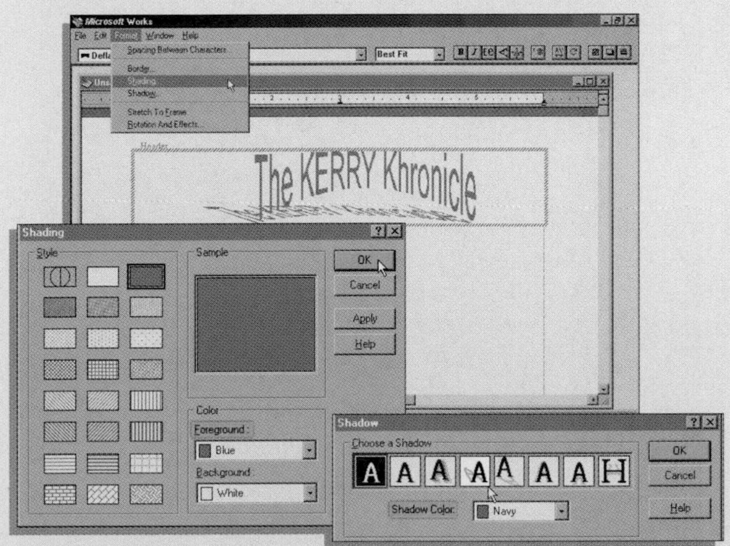

4 You can also apply shading and shadows to your WordArt. Both shading and shadow options are located in the WordArt Format menu.

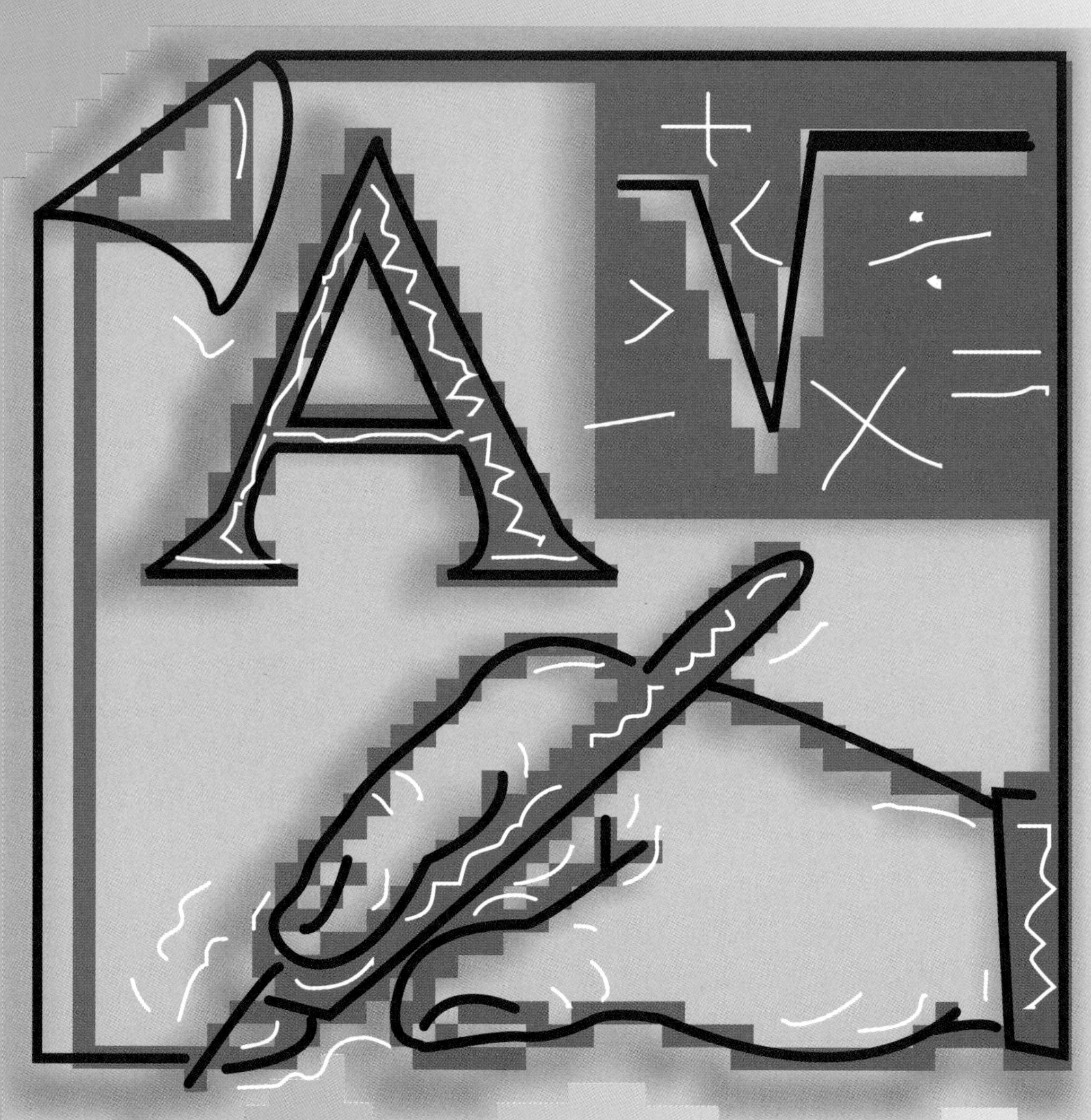

## CHAPTER 19

# How to Use TaskWizards

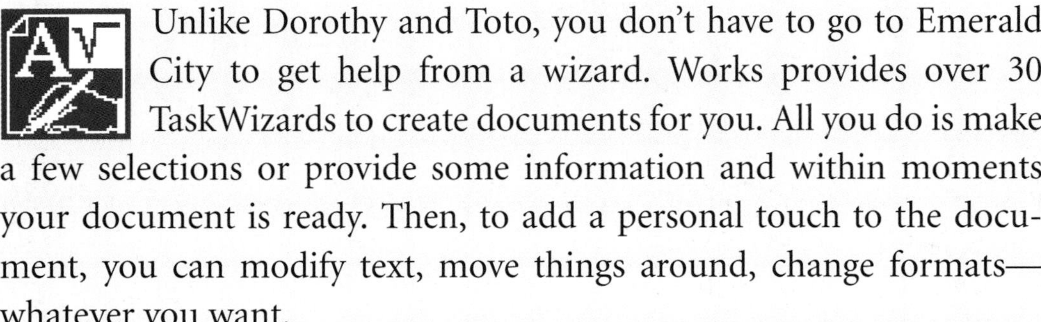

Unlike Dorothy and Toto, you don't have to go to Emerald City to get help from a wizard. Works provides over 30 TaskWizards to create documents for you. All you do is make a few selections or provide some information and within moments your document is ready. Then, to add a personal touch to the document, you can modify text, move things around, change formats—whatever you want.

Whether you're an accountant looking for a database to track accounts payable or a zookeeper who needs an order form to order food from a supplier, you'll find just what you need in a TaskWizard. Just click the TaskWizards tab from the Works Task Launcher window and you'll see a list of categories and documents that a Wizard can create for you. You'll never want to create a document from scratch again after you see what these little guys can do for you.

# How to Create a Resume

Keeping a record of your employment history and job skills is simply a smart thing to do—and a resume does just that. A resume, of course, is also the document we use to tout our experience and expertise to prospective employers. But to most of us, the thought of putting together a resume falls somewhere between paying taxes and pulling your bottom lip over your head.

Works has a solution that even the most proficient procrastinators will appreciate. It's called the Resume TaskWizard. In just minutes you'll be on your way to creating a professional looking resume. Just make a few selections and fill out some personal information and the Wizard will do the rest.

Before you start make sure Works is running and that the Task Launcher window is open. If it isn't, open the File menu and select New.

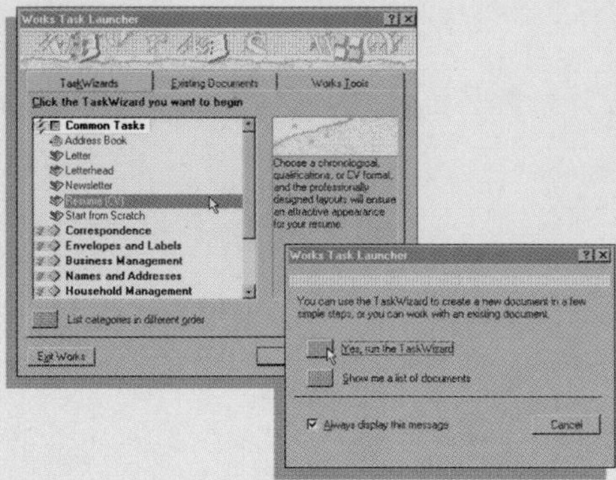

1. From the Task Launcher window click on the Common Tasks category and select Resume. If a second Task Launcher window appears, click on Yes run the task Wizard.

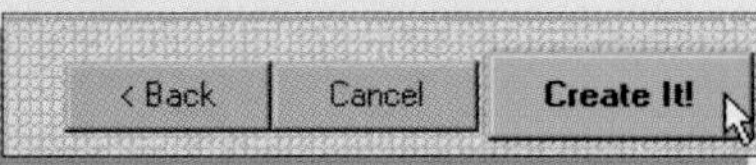


8. When you're satisfied with your selections, click the Create It! button. The resume you see in the central graphic was created by the Resume TaskWizard.

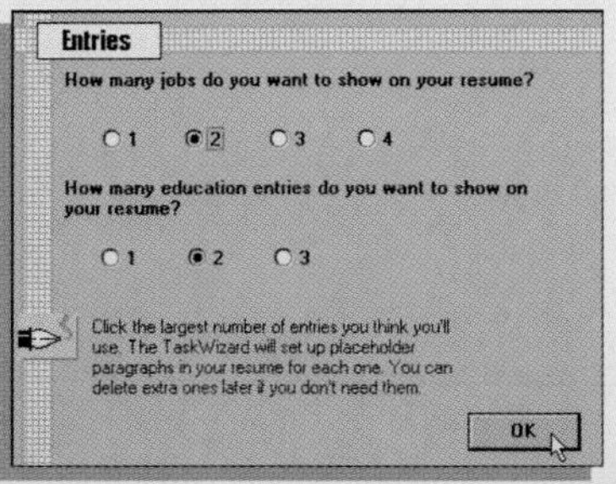


7. Select the number of jobs and education entries you want to show on your resume.

**TIP SHEET**

- **When you save your resume, include the date in the name (My Resume Aug 95) for easy reference.**
- **Keep backup copies of all your resume files for future reference. The Save As option has a "Create backup" feature. See the Help option for more information.**
- **If you're looking for ideas on how to write the details for your resume try your local bookstore. There are several good books on writing resumes—good luck.**

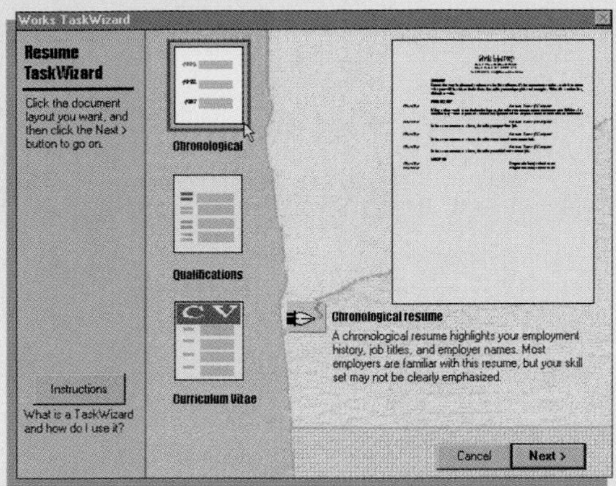


**2** Works offers three basic resume layouts. Click on each and read the description that appears. Click Next after you've made your selection.

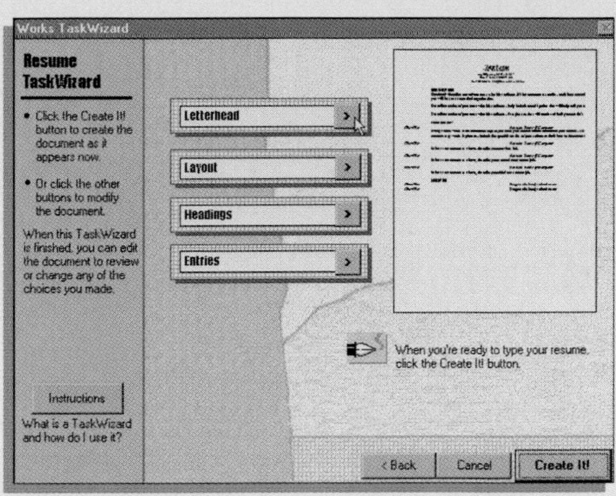


**3** Before you create your resume, add a personal touch by clicking on one of the other Resume TaskWizard buttons.

**Your Name**
1234 Main Street
AnyCity, AnyState, 54321
Home Phone (123) 456-7890
Email 73302,403@CompuServe.com

QUALIFICATIONS

Succinctly describe one of your most valuable attributes. Using concrete examples, explain to potential employers precisely why you will be an asset to their organization.

Describe another of your most valuable attributes. Only include crucial points that will help sell you to a potential employer.

Describe another of your most valuable attributes. Use phrases that will catch and hold your reader's attention.

WORK HISTORY

***Position, Name of Company*** ***19xx- 19xx***

Using action words to maximize the impact, describe your current or most recent responsibilities. Be concise; remove all unnecessary words & phrases. Include the specific results of your actions or decisions to demonstrate your contribution.

***Position, Name of Company*** ***19xx- 19xx***

In the same manner as above, describe your previous job.

EDUCATION

Degree obtained, school name, year of graduation
Degree obtained, school name, year of graduation

COMPUTER SKILLS

- List software applications, operating systems, and pertinent hardware information.
- Include years of experience, or describe your level of knowledge.

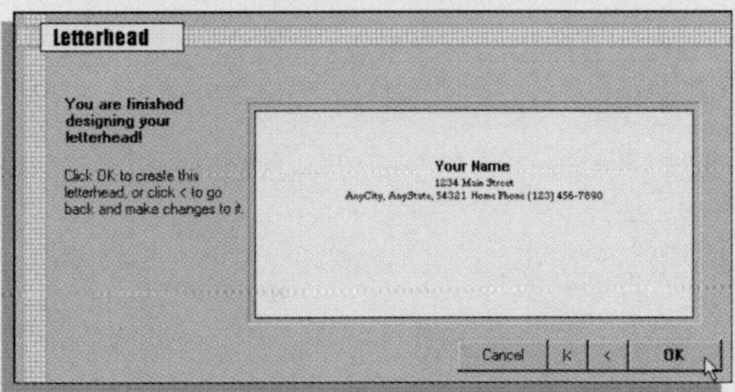


**4** The Letterhead option allows you to pick the style and content (name, address, and so forth) of the resume letterhead. When you finish Works will return you to the screen shown in step 3. Click OK to continue.

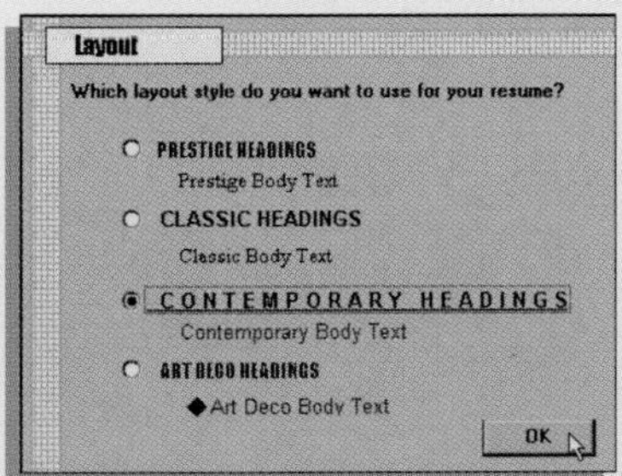


**5** Choose Layout to pick from four layout options. Click OK to continue.

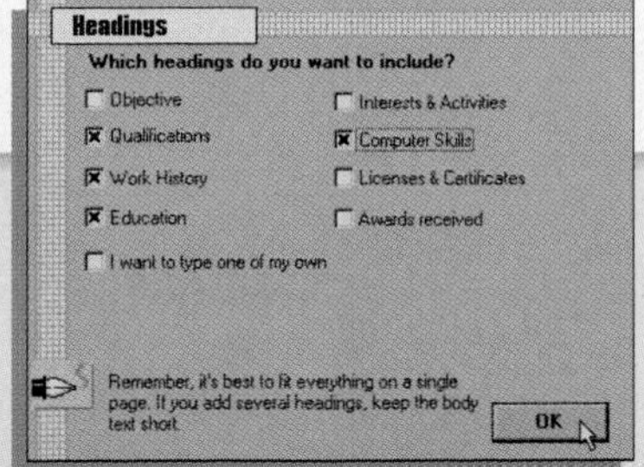


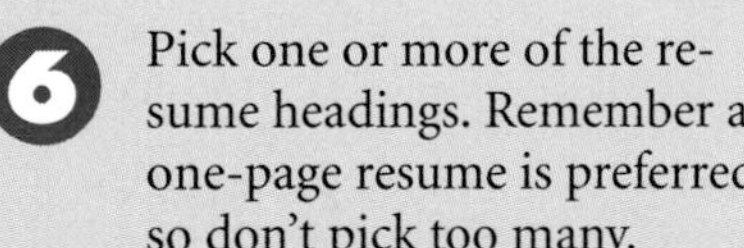

**6** Pick one or more of the resume headings. Remember a one-page resume is preferred, so don't pick too many.

# How to Use the Membership Tracker

Looking for a way to record names, addresses, emergency phone numbers, and medical information for your students, club members, or teammates? Look no further. There's a TaskWizard that will create a membership tracking database for you.

Gather your membership information, because shortly after you finish this spread you could be entering member data and printing a team roster. But first check to see that Works is running and that the Task Launcher window is open. If the Task Launcher window isn't open, select New from the File menu.

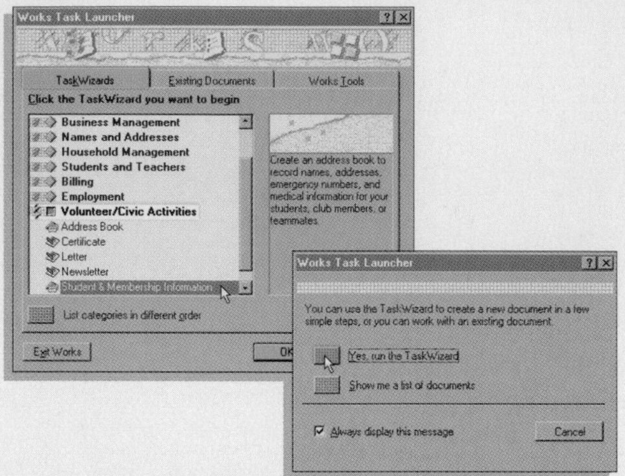


**1** Click on the TaskWizards tab and then using the scroll bar, find the Volunteer/Civic Activities category. Select the Student & Membership Information option and then click OK. If a second Task Launcher dialog box opens, click on Yes, run the TaskWizard, otherwise continue to the next step.

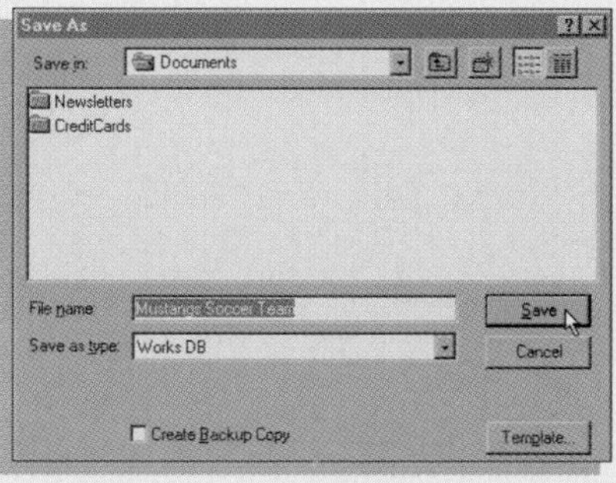


**7** Be sure to save your database. Note the folder that you're storing it in so you can easily retrieve it later.

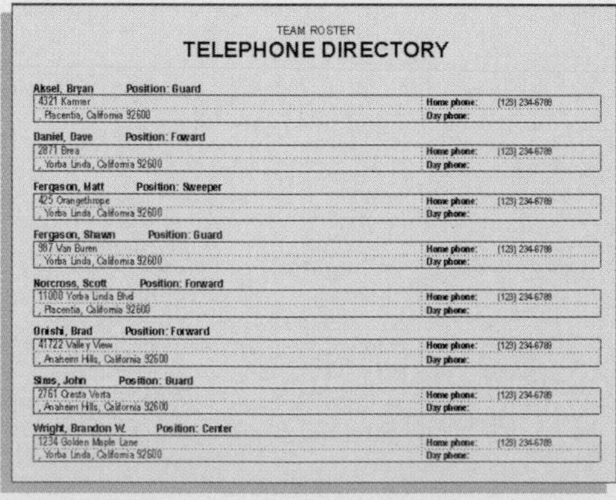


**6** Your new database comes with predefined reports as well. The default report for the Team Roster database is a Telephone Directory.

**TIP SHEET**

- There are three other reports available in the Team Roster database (Birthday list, Event report, and Addresses). Use the Reports option in the View menu to preview them.
- Create additional reports using the ReportCreator option found in the Tools menu.
- Member information is automatically stored and displayed in alphabetic order by name—the order you entered the data in doesn't matter.

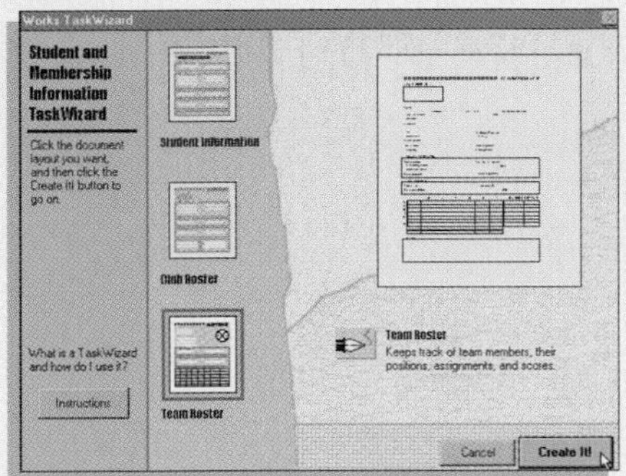

**2** Select one of three document layouts (Student Information, Club Roster, or Team Roster). Click the Create It! button to continue.

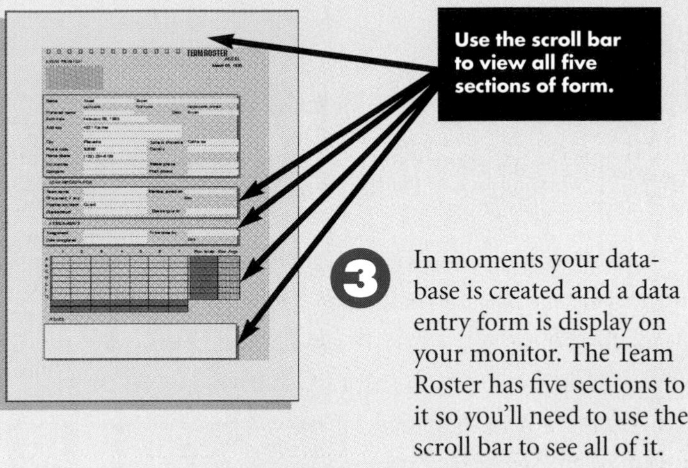


**3** In moments your database is created and a data entry form is display on your monitor. The Team Roster has five sections to it so you'll need to use the scroll bar to see all of it.

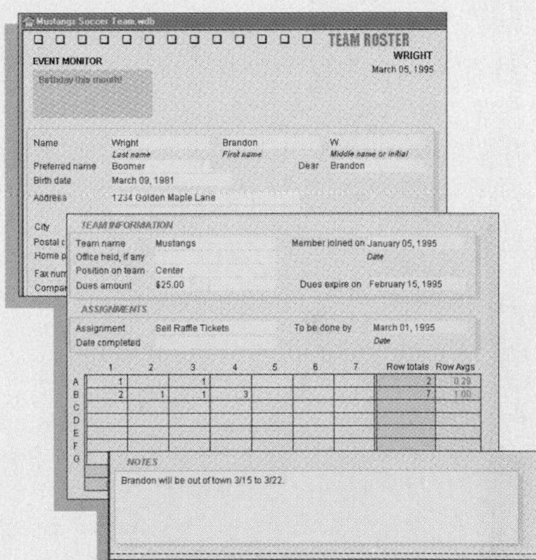

**4** Fill out the membership information for each member. Use the record navigation buttons at the bottom left corner of the screen to add a new record or move between existing records.

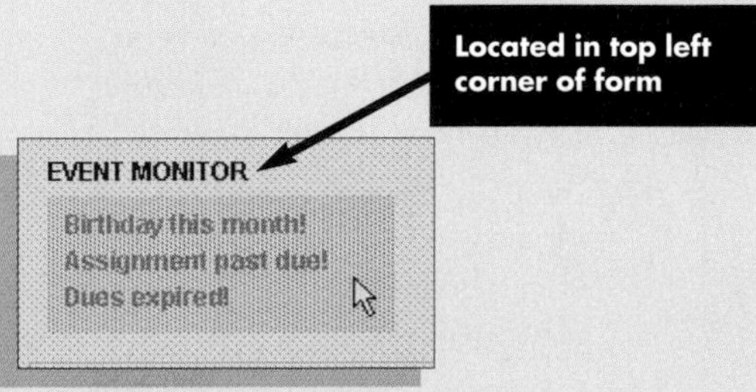


**5** If you enter birth dates, assignments (like "Sell raffle tickets by 3/15/95," and dues information, the Event Monitor box will display messages to help monitor these events.

# How to Create a Home Inventory

Don't wait until it's too late to take inventory of your home. Let a TaskWizard take set you up with your very own database. It's easy, it's quick, and it's fun! So get started now and you'll have peace of mind knowing that your possessions are accounted for.

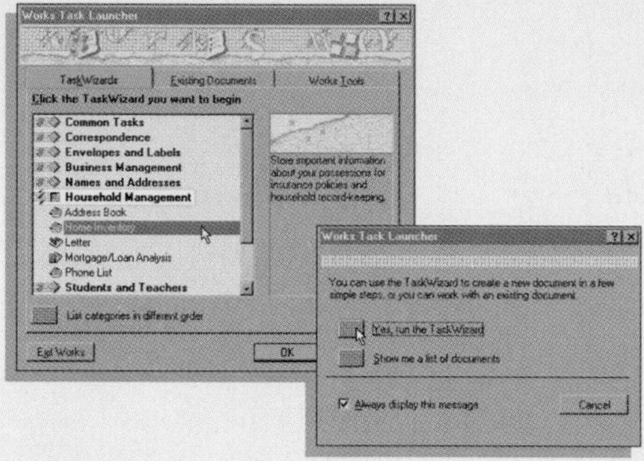


1. From the Task Launcher window click on the TaskWizards tab. Use the scroll bar to locate the Household Management category. Select Home Inventory and then click OK. If a second Task Launcher window appears, click the Yes, run the TaskWizard button.

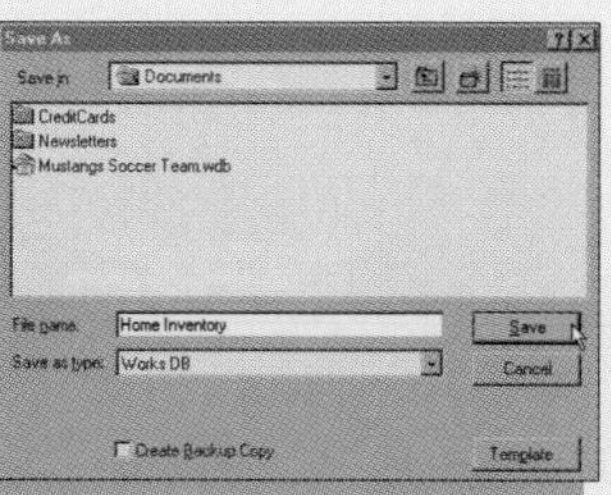


6. Before you exit Works, save your database.

## TIP SHEET

- Use the Reports option in the View menu to preview the reports that come with the inventory database. The reports include inventory listed by location, category, and supplier.
- Create your own reports by using the ReportCreator feature located in the Tools menu.
- Always print a copy of your inventory report and then keep it in a fire-safe place—a bank deposit box is ideal.

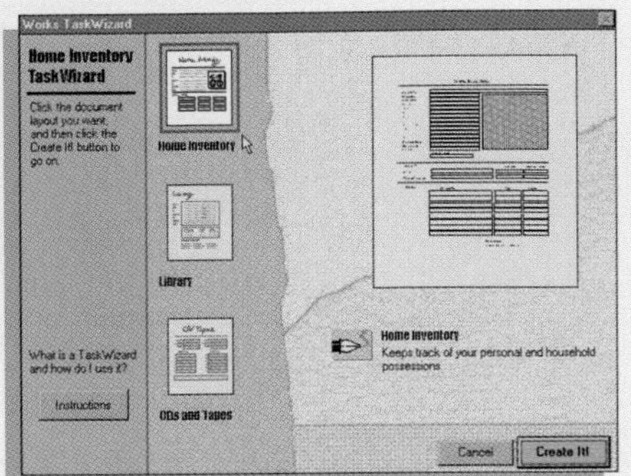


**2** Select Home Inventory and click Create It!

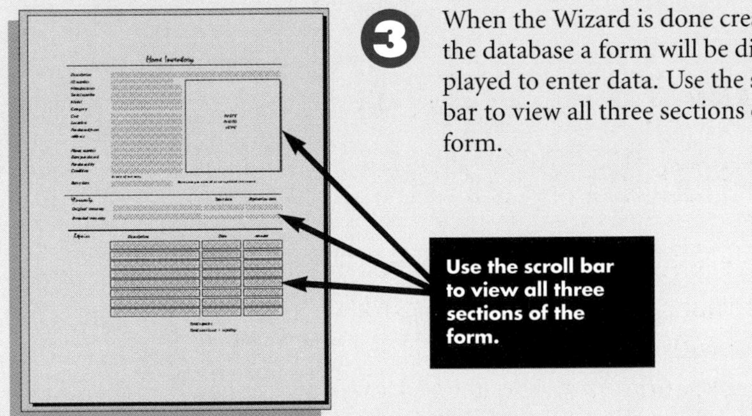


**3** When the Wizard is done creating the database a form will be displayed to enter data. Use the scroll bar to view all three sections of the form.

Unsaved Database 2

Home Inventory

| | |
|---|---|
| Description | PC |
| ID number | VW-0001 |
| Manufacturer | Gateway |
| Serial number | 123-456-789 |
| Model | P5-100XL |
| Category | Office Equipment |
| Cost | $3900 |
| Location | Study |
| Purchased from | Gateway |
| Address | |
| Phone number | (800) 123-4567 |
| Date purchased | March 01, 1995 |
| Purchased by | Victor |
| Condition | New |
| Entry date | August 04, 1995 |

| Warranty | | Start date | Expiration date |
|---|---|---|---|
| Original warranty | 3 Years Parts & Labor | 3/1/95 | 3/1/98 |
| Extended warranty | | | |

| Repairs | Description | Date | Amount |
|---|---|---|---|
| | Add 8 MB of memory | 5/15/95 | 400.00 |
| | Total repairs | | 400.00 |
| | Total cost (cost + repairs) | | 400.00 |

**4** Enter the inventory description, warranty information, and repair history. Use the record navigation buttons in the bottom-left corner of the screen to add new records or move through existing records.

**HOME INVENTORY LISTED BY LOCATION**

| Dinning Room | MANUFACTURER | SERIAL NUMBER | CATEGORY | COST |
|---|---|---|---|---|
| Table and Chairs | Chadvey | NA | Furniture | 4,400.00 |
| Hutch | Chadvey | NA | Furniture | 2,500.00 |
| | | Subtotal | Total items | 2 |
| | | | Total cost value | 6,900.00 |

| Kitchen | MANUFACTURER | SERIAL NUMBER | CATEGORY | COST |
|---|---|---|---|---|
| Toaster | Ashton | 1234-11 | Kitchen Appliance | 25.00 |
| Microwave | Cookmaster | 11-222-3333-44 | Kitchen Appliance | 200.00 |
| Refrigerator | GE | ABC-1000 | Kitchen Appliance | 1,700.00 |
| Blender | Oster | 123-123 | Kitchen Appliance | 30.00 |
| | | Subtotal | Total items | 4 |
| | | | Total cost value | 1,955.00 |

SUMMARY OF ALL ITEMS

| | |
|---|---|
| Total items | 6 |
| Total cost value | 8,855.00 |

**5** Switch to the report view to preview your inventory list by location.

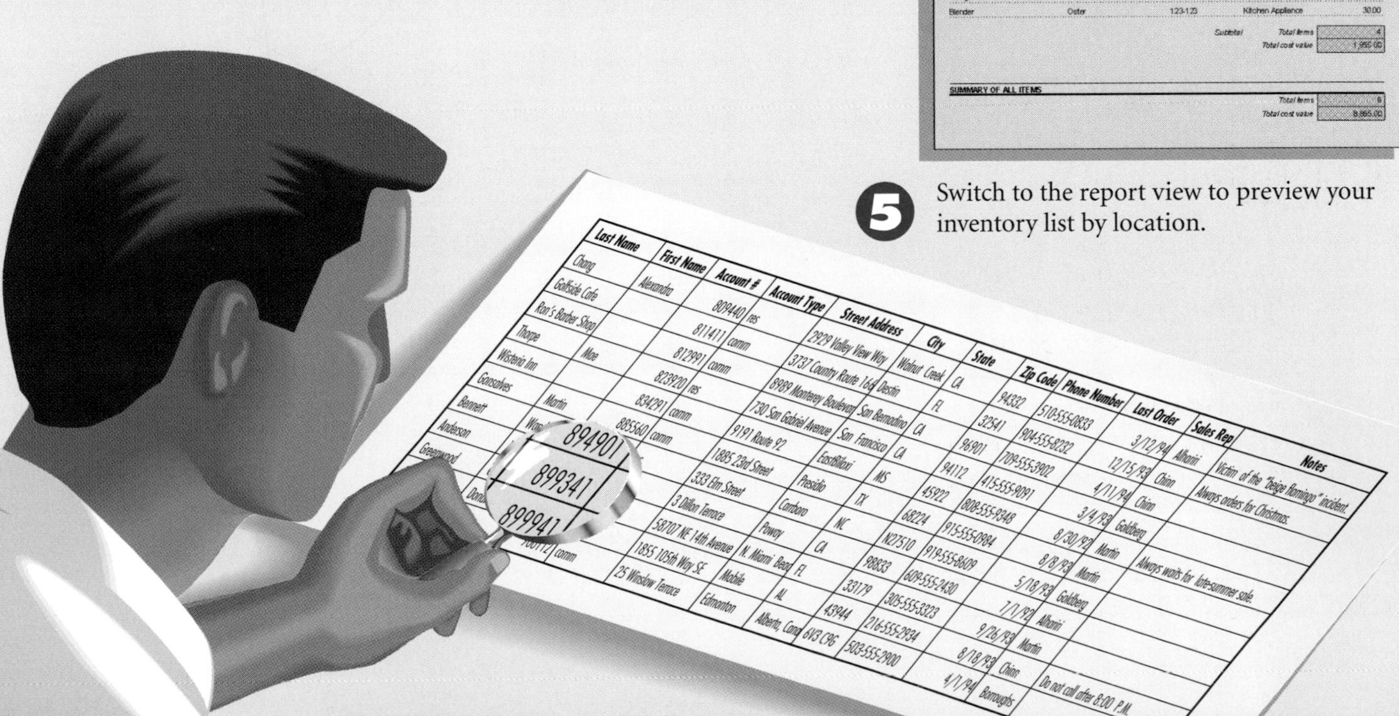

# How to Create a True/False Test

If you're reading this then there's a good chance you're involved in education. And as you know, creating a test is an important part of teaching. It can also be tedious and time consuming as well. Works has a teaching assistant that will help you create true or false, multiple choice, and essay exams. Sound interesting? Then follow along as we walk you through the steps.

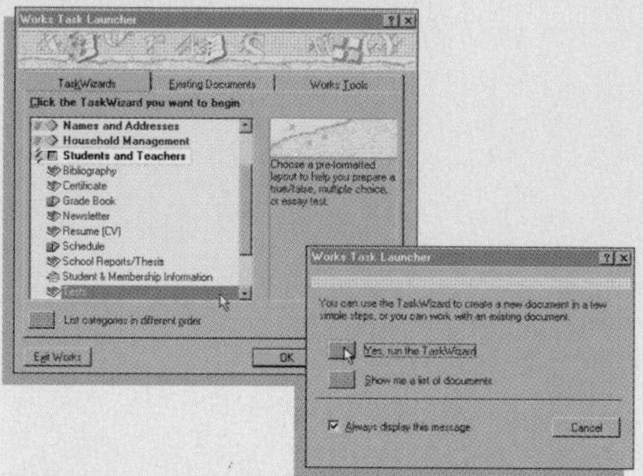

**1** From the Task Launcher window click on the TaskWizards tab. Using the scroll bar locate the Students and Teachers category. Select Tests and click OK. If a second Task Launcher window appears click on Yes, run the TaskWizard.

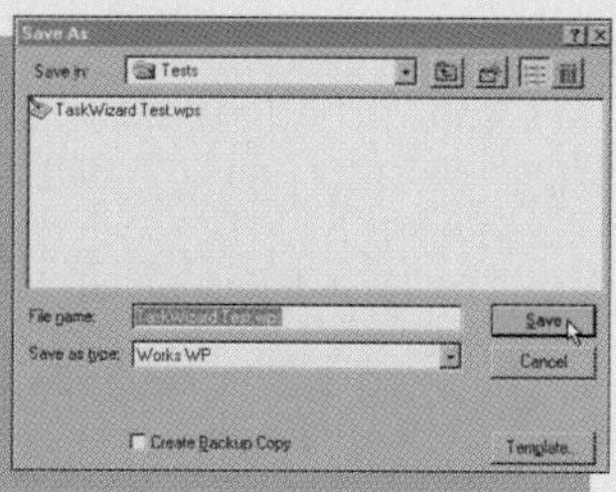

**6** Save your test for later use.

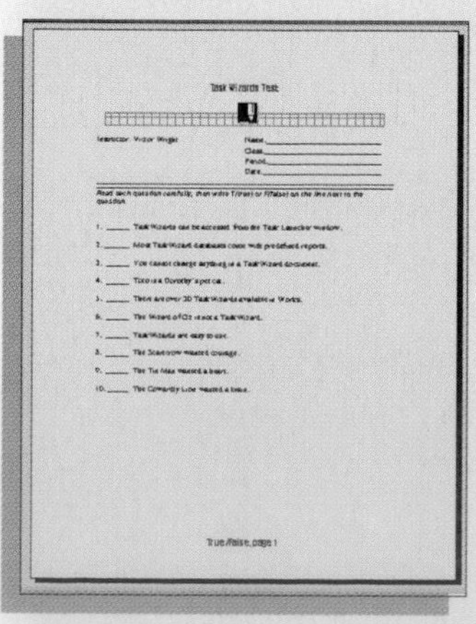

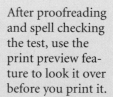

**5** After proofreading and spell checking the test, use the print preview feature to look it over before you print it.

TIP SHEET

- **You can make a copy of your test containing the correct answers. After you've saved the test, fill in the correct answers and use the Save As option in the File Menu to create a second file with the answers. In our example we would create a second file named TaskWizards Test - Answers.**

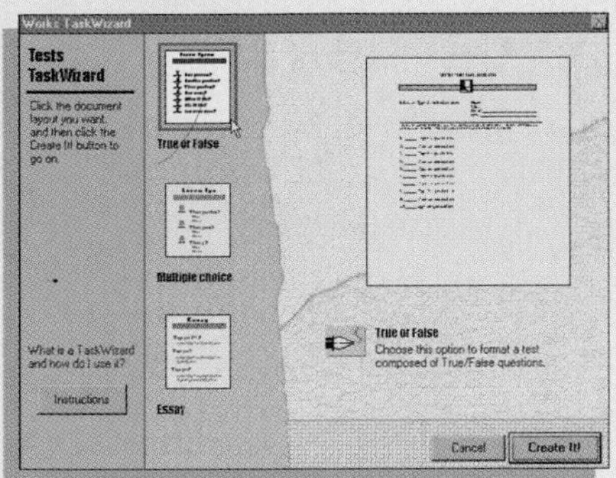

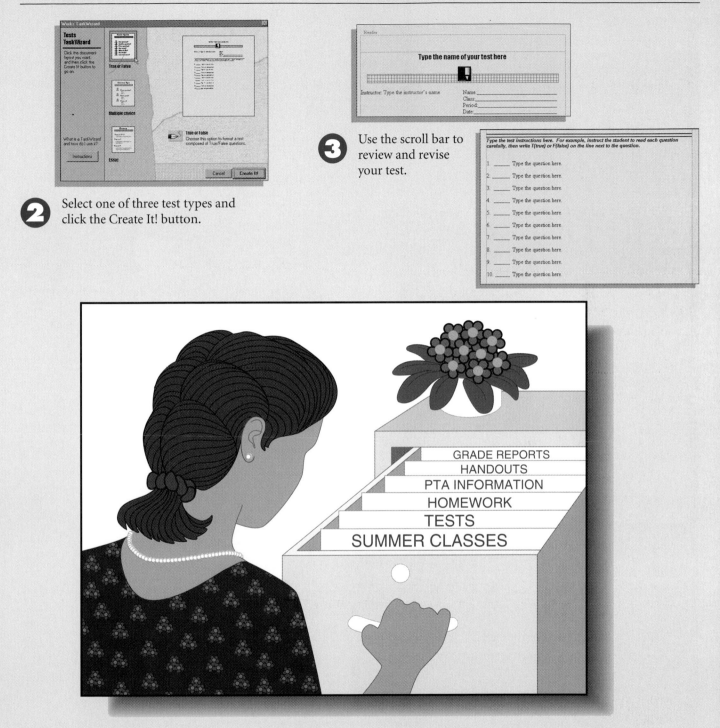

**2** Select one of three test types and click the Create It! button.

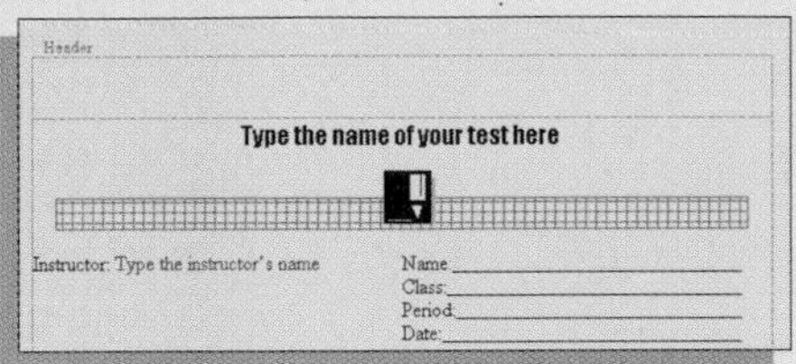

Header

**Type the name of your test here**

Instructor: Type the instructor's name

Name:__________
Class:__________
Period:__________
Date:__________

**3** Use the scroll bar to review and revise your test.

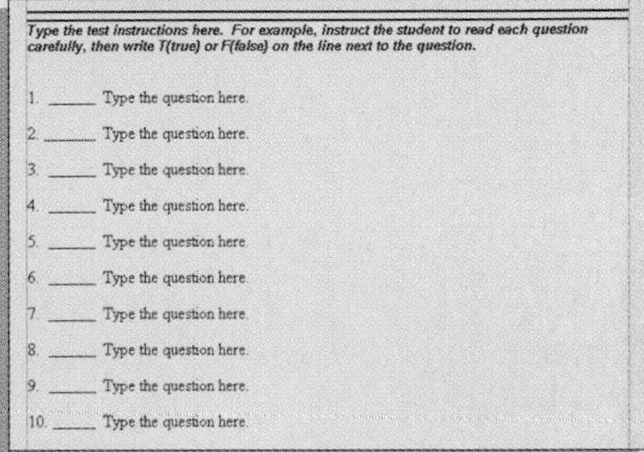

*Type the test instructions here. For example, instruct the student to read each question carefully, then write T(true) or F(false) on the line next to the question.*

1\. _____ Type the question here.
2\. _____ Type the question here.
3\. _____ Type the question here.
4\. _____ Type the question here.
5\. _____ Type the question here.
6\. _____ Type the question here.
7\. _____ Type the question here.
8\. _____ Type the question here.
9\. _____ Type the question here.
10\. _____ Type the question here.

**TaskWizards Test**

Instructor: Victor Wright

Name:__________
Class:__________
Period:__________
Date:__________

*Type the test instructions here. For example, instruct the student to read each question carefully, then write T(true) or F(false) on the line next to the question.*

1\. _____ Type the question here.
2\. _____ Type the question here.
3\. _____ Type the question here.
4\. _____ Type the question here.
5\. _____ Type the question here.
6\. _____ Type the question here.
7\. _____ Type the question here.
8\. _____ Type the question here.
9\. _____ Type the question here.
10\. _____ Type the question here.

**4** In the top part of the document enter the test title and instructor's name. In the body of the document enter the test instructions and questions.

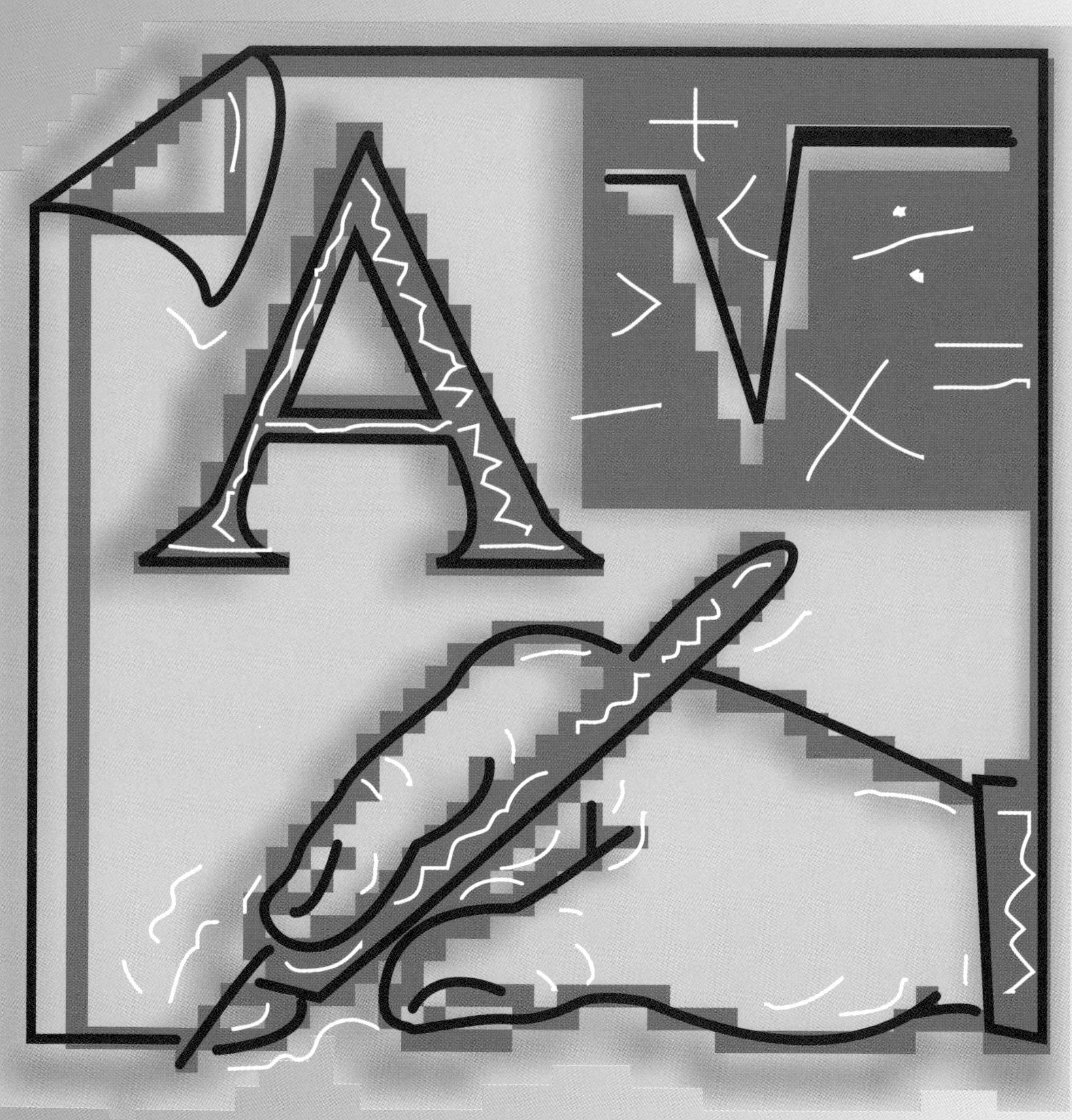

## CHAPTER 20

# Combining the Features of Microsoft Works

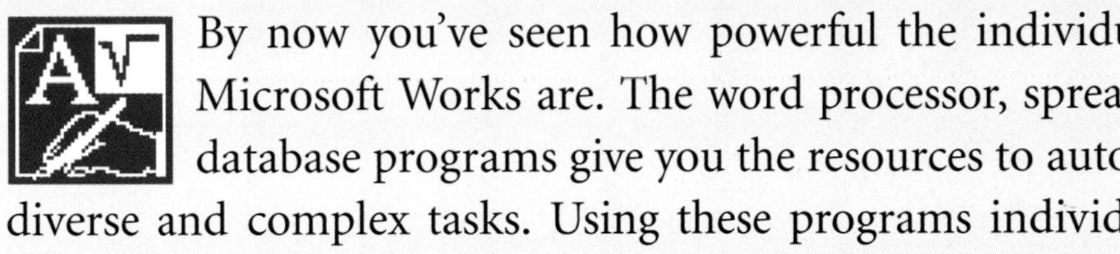

By now you've seen how powerful the individual parts of Microsoft Works are. The word processor, spreadsheet, and database programs give you the resources to automate many diverse and complex tasks. Using these programs individually, however, applies only a fraction of the power of Works.

In this chapter, you'll learn how to combine information from your spreadsheet with your word processor document. You will also learn how to use ready-made artwork, called ClipArt, to add special effects to your documents. Then to further enhance your Rembrandt-like talents, you'll learn about a feature called WordArt. When you're through with this chapter, you'll be able to create documents with stylish flair.

# How to Combine Objects by Using the Clipboard

You've used the Windows Clipboard to copy text and spreadsheet information from one location and paste it in another location within a document. What you may not know is that you can also apply these techniques to copy blocks of information, or objects, from one type of document to another.

For example, you may want to place a table from your quarterly budget spreadsheet in the memo you're drafting in the word processor. You might instead want to copy a table of outstanding balances from a spreadsheet to your customer information database, and then merge that data with a bill you've set up with the word processor. While the possibilities of objects to copy and paste are endless, the techniques stay the same.

## TIP SHEET

- **The Windows Clipboard can transfer objects, not only within Works, but between programs as well. You can copy objects in other programs and paste them into Works. You can also copy objects in Works and paste them into other programs.**
- **When you're working with more than one Works document open at a time, use the Ctrl+Tab key combination to switch between them rapidly.**

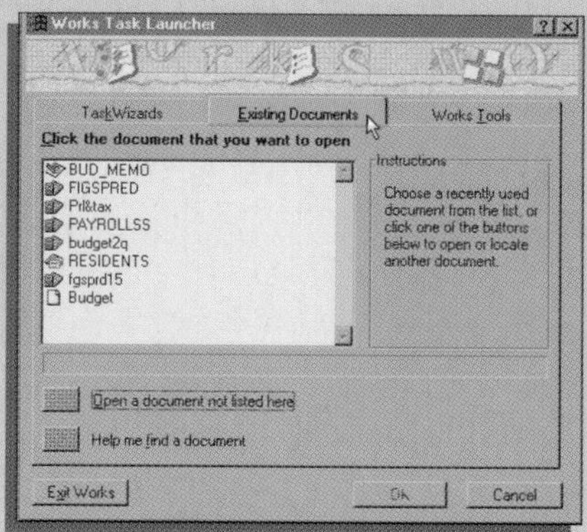

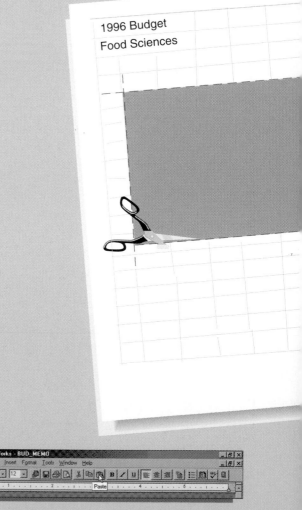

1 To speed data transfer, start by opening both of the documents you want to work with: the document containing the object you want to copy, and the document in which you want to paste the object.

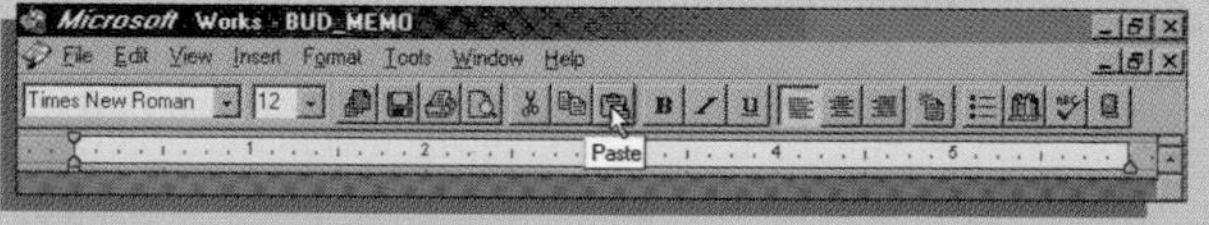

6 On the Toolbar, click on the Paste icon. Works will place the copied object in the location you selected.

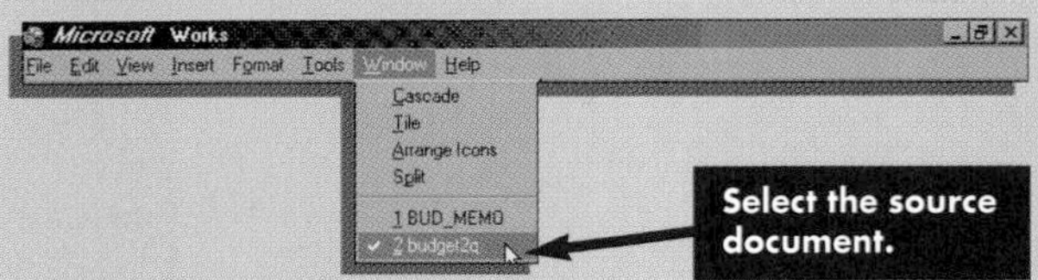

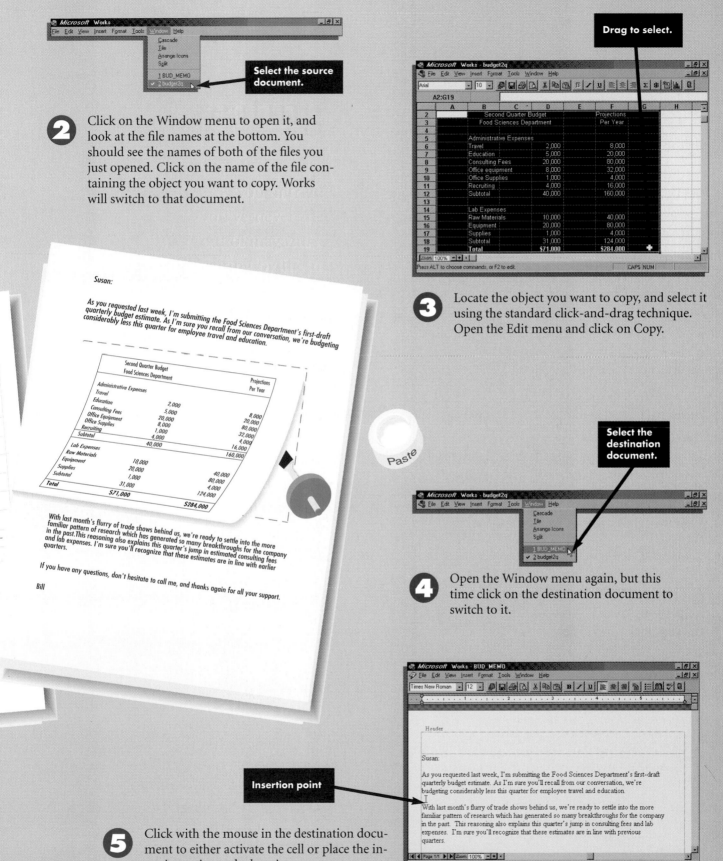

**2** Click on the Window menu to open it, and look at the file names at the bottom. You should see the names of both of the files you just opened. Click on the name of the file containing the object you want to copy. Works will switch to that document.

Drag to select.

**3** Locate the object you want to copy, and select it using the standard click-and-drag technique. Open the Edit menu and click on Copy.

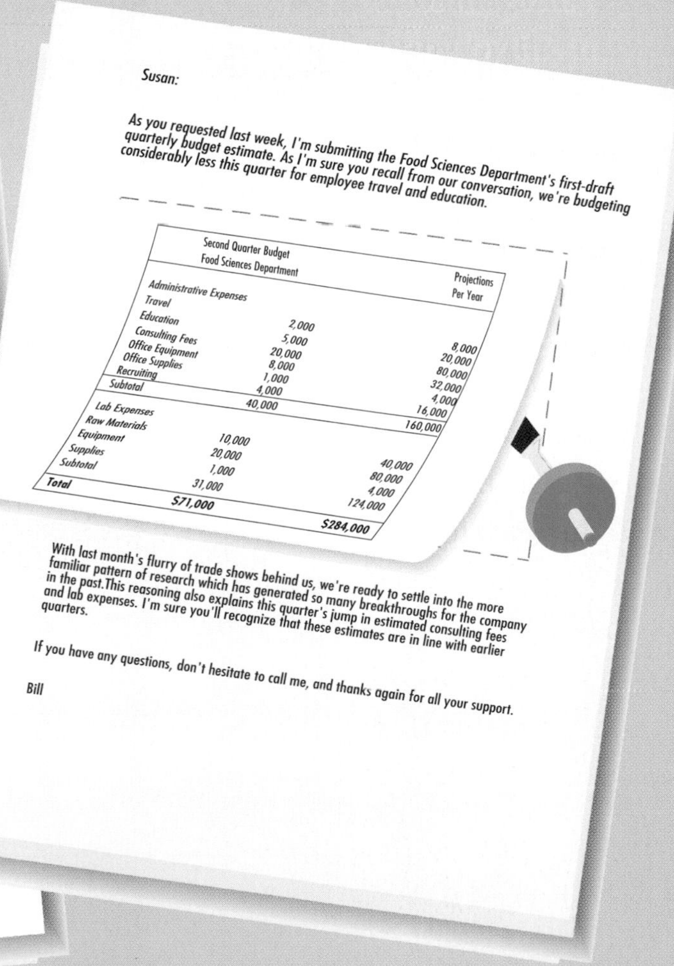

Susan:

As you requested last week, I'm submitting the Food Sciences Department's first-draft quarterly budget estimate. As I'm sure you recall from our conversation, we're budgeting considerably less this quarter for employee travel and education.

| Second Quarter Budget<br>Food Sciences Department | | Projections<br>Per Year |
|---|---|---|
| Administrative Expenses | | |
| Travel | 2,000 | 8,000 |
| Education | 5,000 | 20,000 |
| Consulting Fees | 20,000 | 80,000 |
| Office Equipment | 8,000 | 32,000 |
| Office Supplies | 1,000 | 4,000 |
| Recruiting | 4,000 | 16,000 |
| Subtotal | 40,000 | 160,000 |
| Lab Expenses | | |
| Raw Materials | 10,000 | 40,000 |
| Equipment | 20,000 | 80,000 |
| Supplies | 1,000 | 4,000 |
| Subtotal | 31,000 | 124,000 |
| Total | $71,000 | $284,000 |

With last month's flurry of trade shows behind us, we're ready to settle into the more familiar pattern of research which has generated so many breakthroughs for the company in the past. This reasoning also explains this quarter's jump in estimated consulting fees and lab expenses. I'm sure you'll recognize that these estimates are in line with earlier quarters.

If you have any questions, don't hesitate to call me, and thanks again for all your support.

Bill

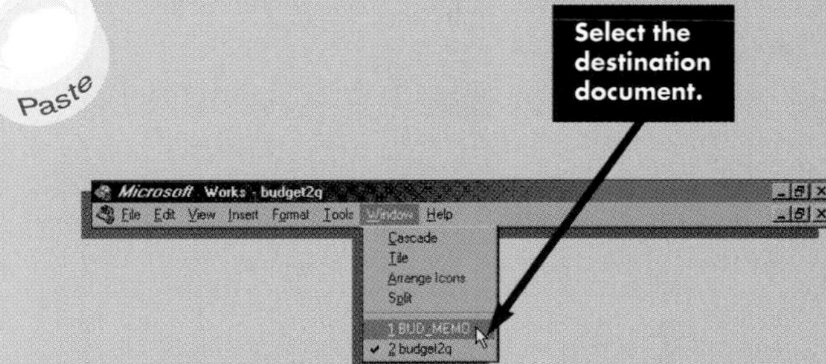


**4** Open the Window menu again, but this time click on the destination document to switch to it.

Insertion point

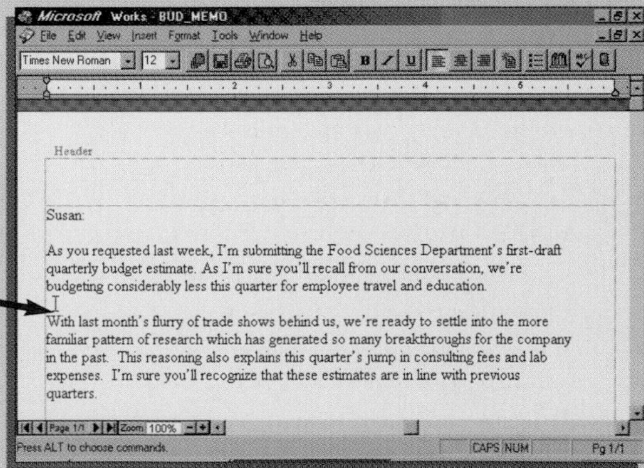


**5** Click with the mouse in the destination document to either activate the cell or place the insertion point at the location you want to paste.

# How to Use the Insert Commands

Using the Insert commands, you can place a wide variety of objects in your word processor documents. These objects can originate in other parts of Works or in entirely different programs. The Insert commands work somewhat like the Clipboard with one major exception: Rather than copy an existing object from an open application, you open an application to create an object of the type you specify.

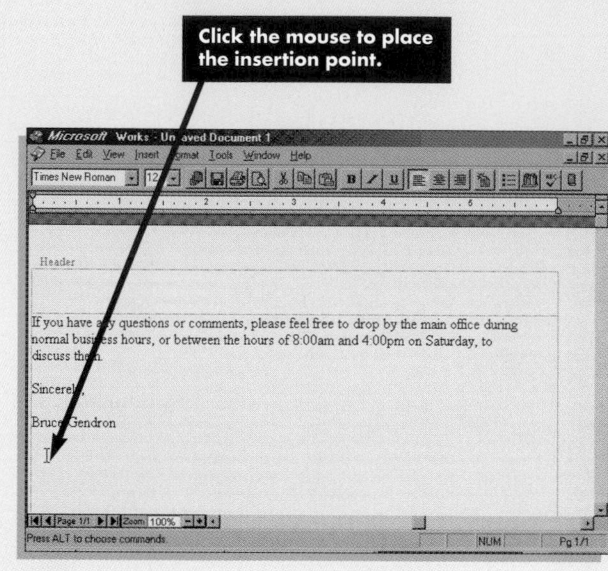
Click the mouse to place the insertion point.

**1** Click in your document at the location you want to insert an object.

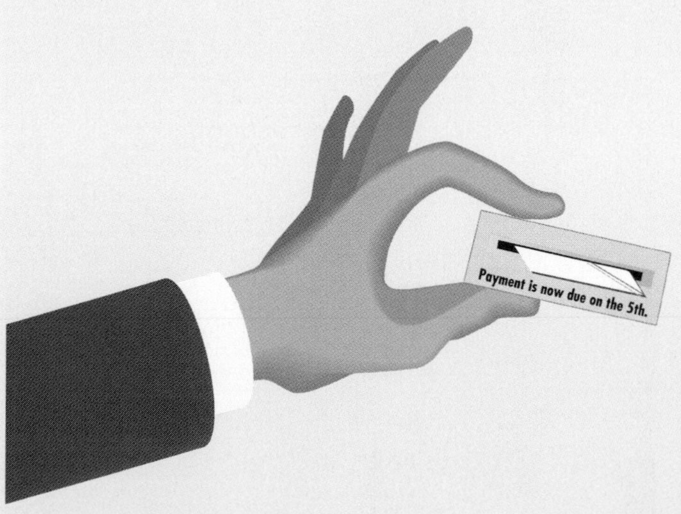
Payment is now due on the 5th.

**TIP SHEET**

- **The object types available in the Insert Object dialog box depend on the applications you have installed on your computer. For example, if you have Microsoft Excel installed, you will be able to select Excel Chart, Worksheet, and Macrosheet objects.**
- **The Insert menu contains shortcuts for inserting several kinds of objects. Select from these menu items to skip the Insert Object dialog box.**
- **The Insert commands, along with the general nature of the word processor, make the word processor the best place to assemble documents from objects of different types.**

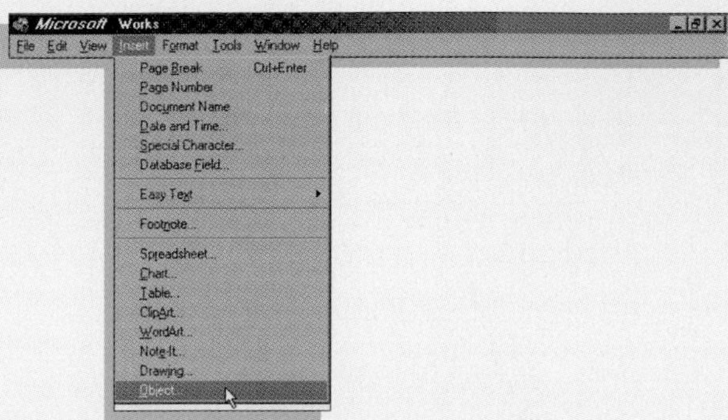

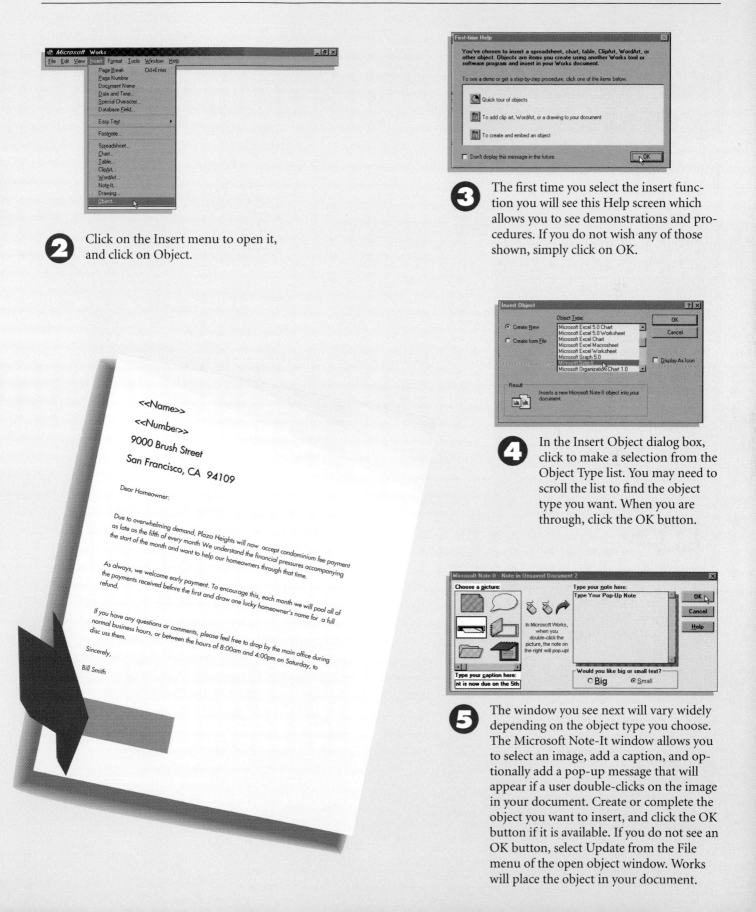

**2** Click on the Insert menu to open it, and click on Object.

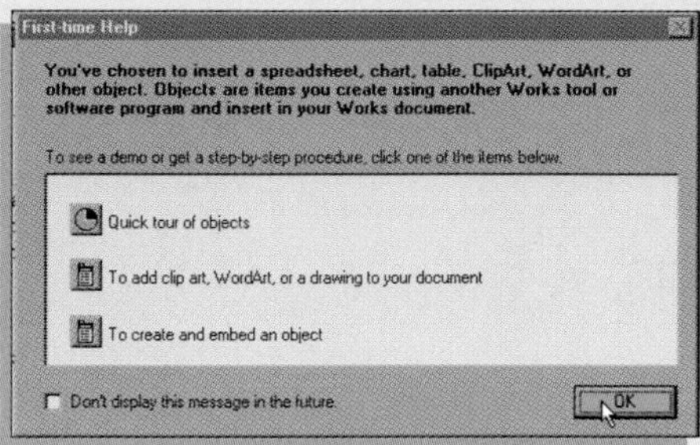


**3** The first time you select the insert function you will see this Help screen which allows you to see demonstrations and procedures. If you do not wish any of those shown, simply click on OK.

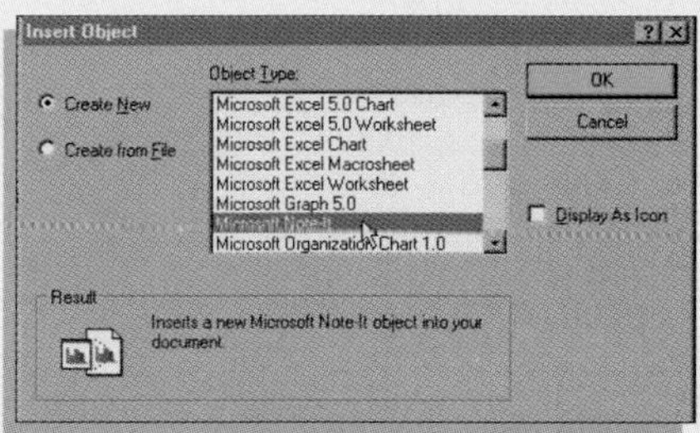


**4** In the Insert Object dialog box, click to make a selection from the Object Type list. You may need to scroll the list to find the object type you want. When you are through, click the OK button.

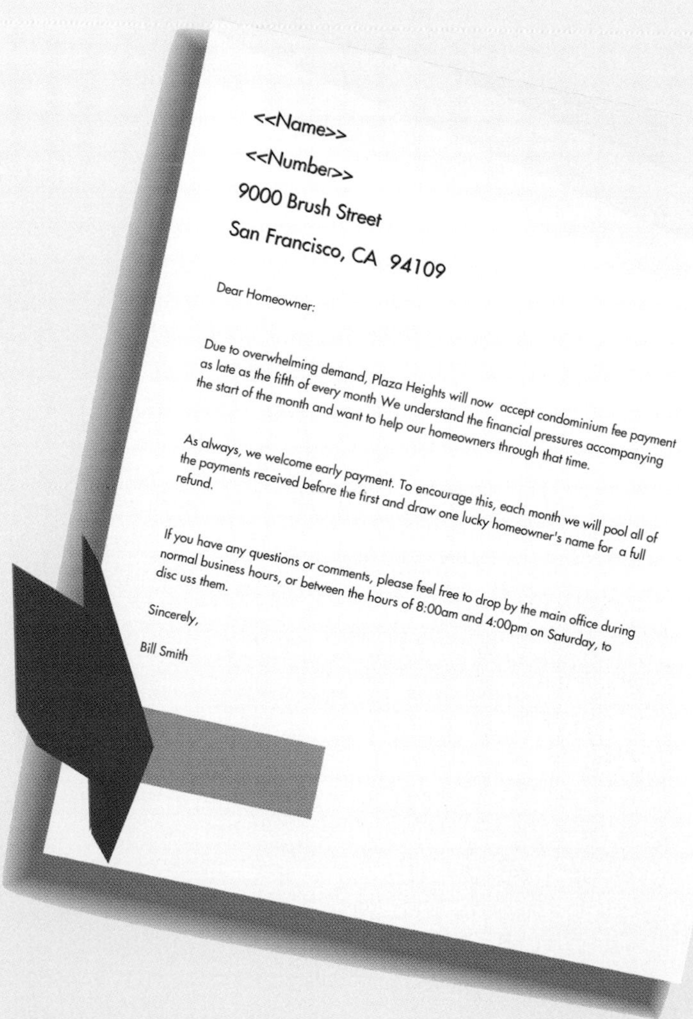
<<Name>>

<<Number>>

9000 Brush Street

San Francisco, CA 94109

Dear Homeowner:

Due to overwhelming demand, Plaza Heights will now accept condominium fee payment as late as the fifth of every month We understand the financial pressures accompanying the start of the month and want to help our homeowners through that time.

As always, we welcome early payment. To encourage this, each month we will pool all of the payments received before the first and draw one lucky homeowner's name for a full refund.

If you have any questions or comments, please feel free to drop by the main office during normal business hours, or between the hours of 8:00am and 4:00pm on Saturday, to disc uss them.

Sincerely,

Bill Smith

**5** The window you see next will vary widely depending on the object type you choose. The Microsoft Note-It window allows you to select an image, add a caption, and optionally add a pop-up message that will appear if a user double-clicks on the image in your document. Create or complete the object you want to insert, and click the OK button if it is available. If you do not see an OK button, select Update from the File menu of the open object window. Works will place the object in your document.

# How to Insert a ClipArt Image

To give your letters, notes, or reports a professional look, Works helps you to insert any piece of ClipArt that is stored on your disk. This process applies to either a database form or a word processing document.

The artwork is stored in the ClipArt Gallery, which is organized in categories such as Business or Borders & Banners to simplify your search for that "just right" piece of art.

1. To start, either create or open an existing database form or word processing document.

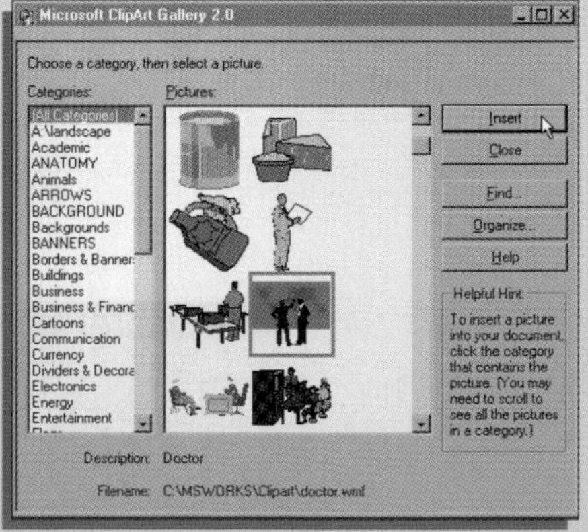


6. Click on the Insert button.

- **Once you've added the ClipArt to your document, you can resize, move, or copy the art.**
- **ClipArt can be edited to your liking by using MSDraw.**

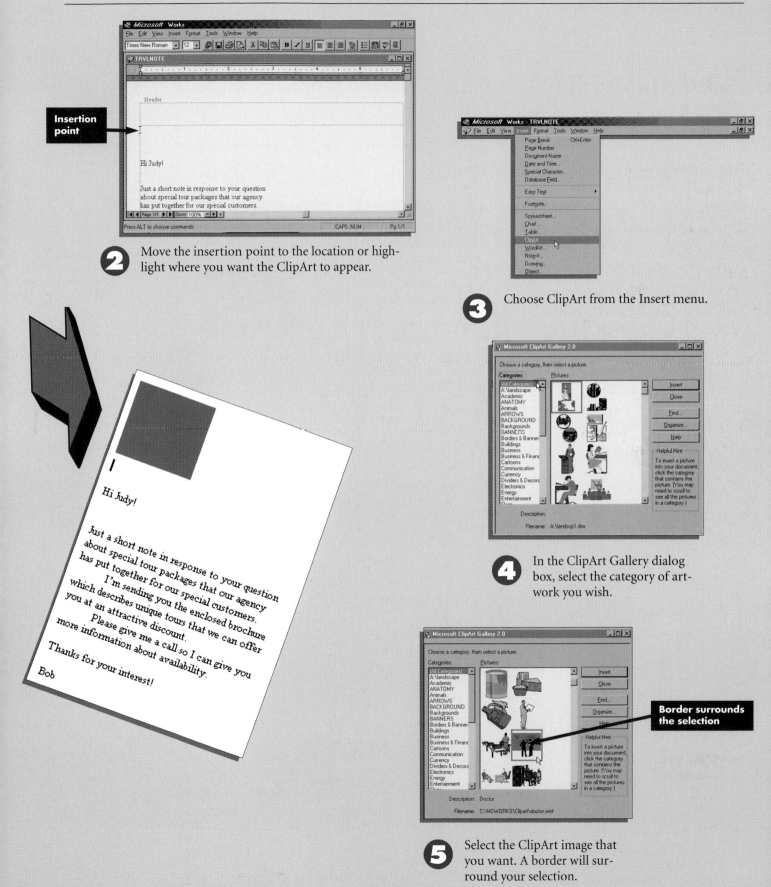

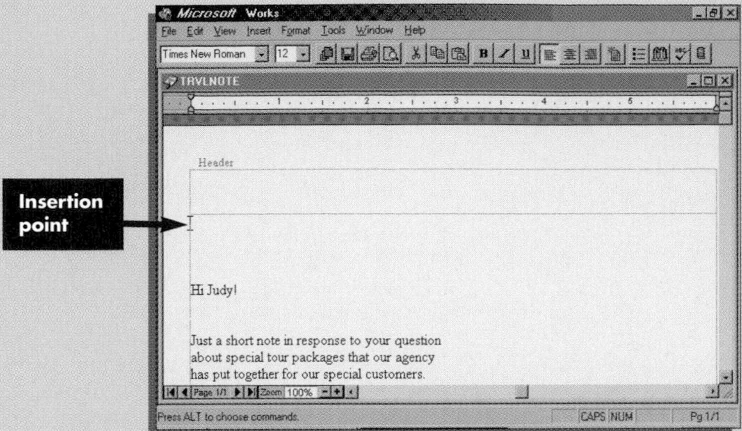


**2** Move the insertion point to the location or highlight where you want the ClipArt to appear.

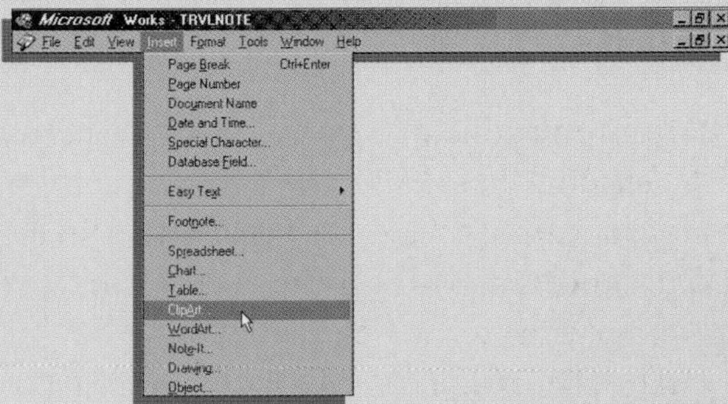


**3** Choose ClipArt from the Insert menu.

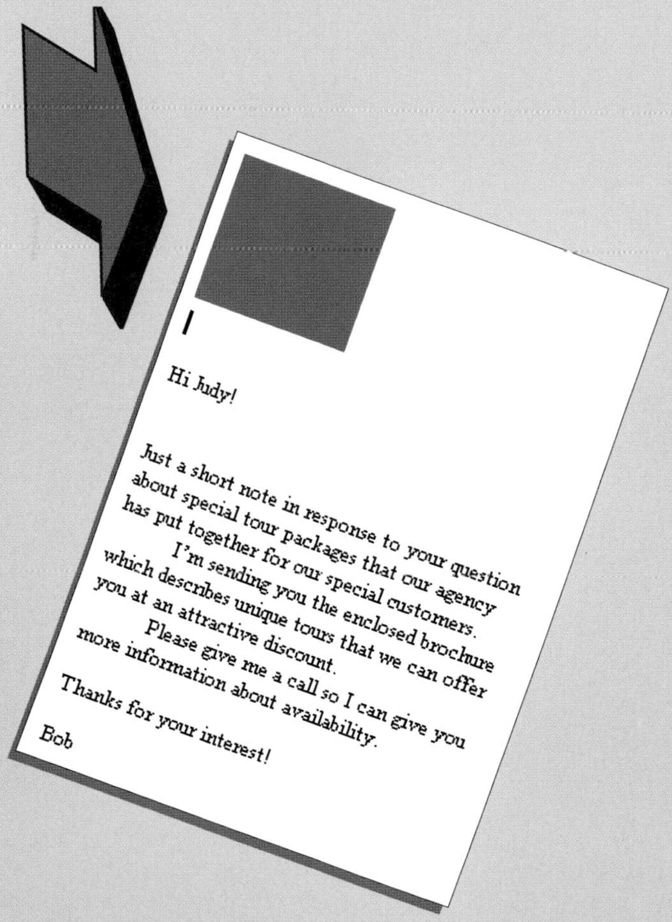

Hi Judy!

Just a short note in response to your question about special tour packages that our agency has put together for our special customers.
I'm sending you the enclosed brochure which describes unique tours that we can offer you at an attractive discount.
Please give me a call so I can give you more information about availability.

Thanks for your interest!

Bob

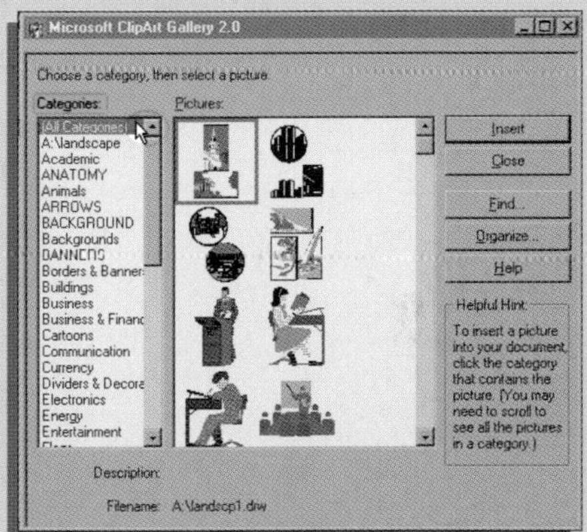


**4** In the ClipArt Gallery dialog box, select the category of artwork you wish.

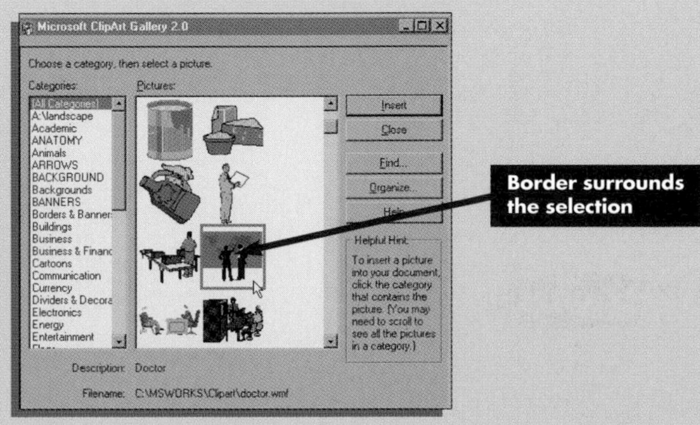


**5** Select the ClipArt image that you want. A border will surround your selection.

# How to Insert WordArt

In addition to using ClipArt, you can create special effects in your Works documents by making your own logos, titles, headlines, and fancy first letters in paragraphs. The effects can include vertical text, circular text, wavy text, and many more.

WordArt allows these effects to be added to your database forms or your word processor documents.

You may also edit, move, and resize the WordArt to obtain the most pleasing effect.

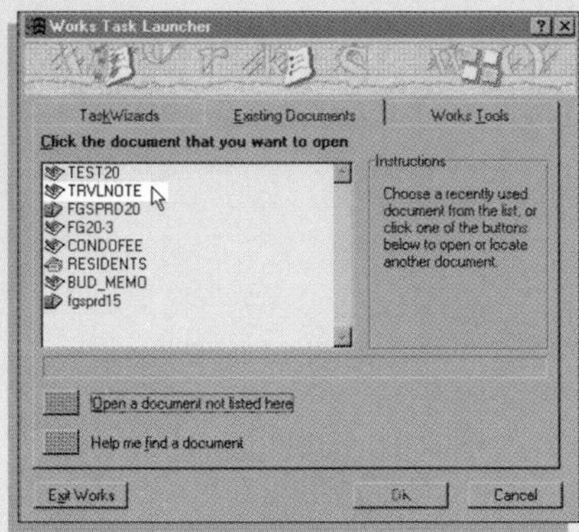

**1** To insert WordArt, begin by either creating a new document or opening an existing one. Click on an existing document and on OK.

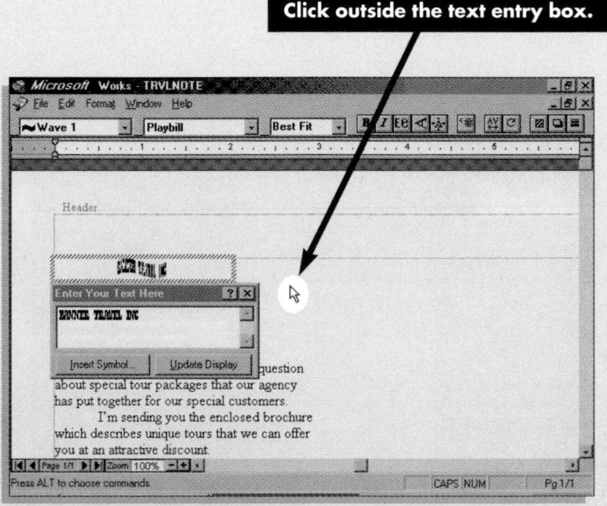
Click outside the text entry box.

**6** After the selection is complete, click anywhere outside the Enter Your Text Here box to insert the new WordArt in your document

## TIP SHEET

- **After inserting the WordArt, you can move or resize it by first clicking on it. Resizing is done by using the square handles in the box. Moving is done by the now familiar drag-and-drop method.**
- **If you wish to edit the WordArt or change the special effects, begin by double-clicking on the WordArt and proceeding as in steps 4 through 6.**

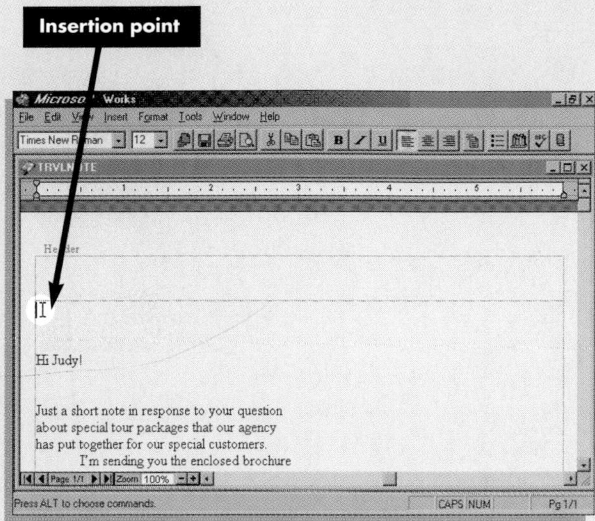


**2** Position the insertion point to the location you want to add the WordArt.

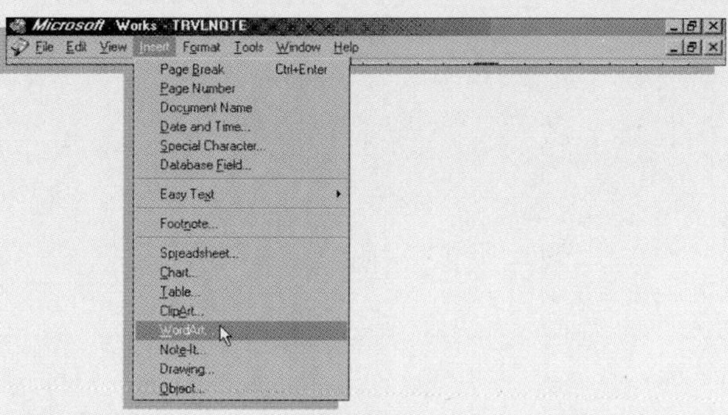


**3** From the Insert menu, select WordArt.

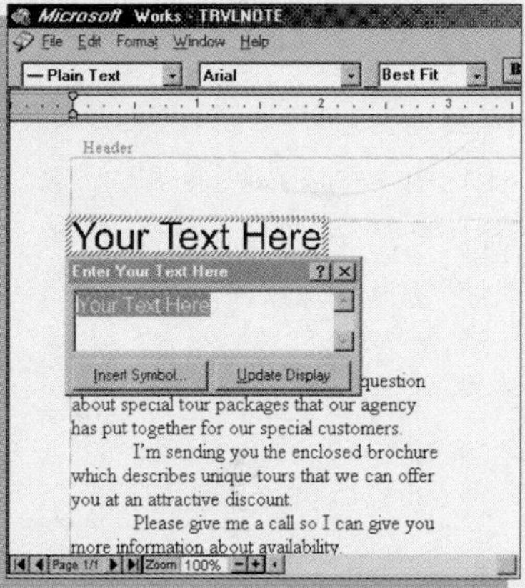


**4** In the Enter Your Text Here box, type your text.

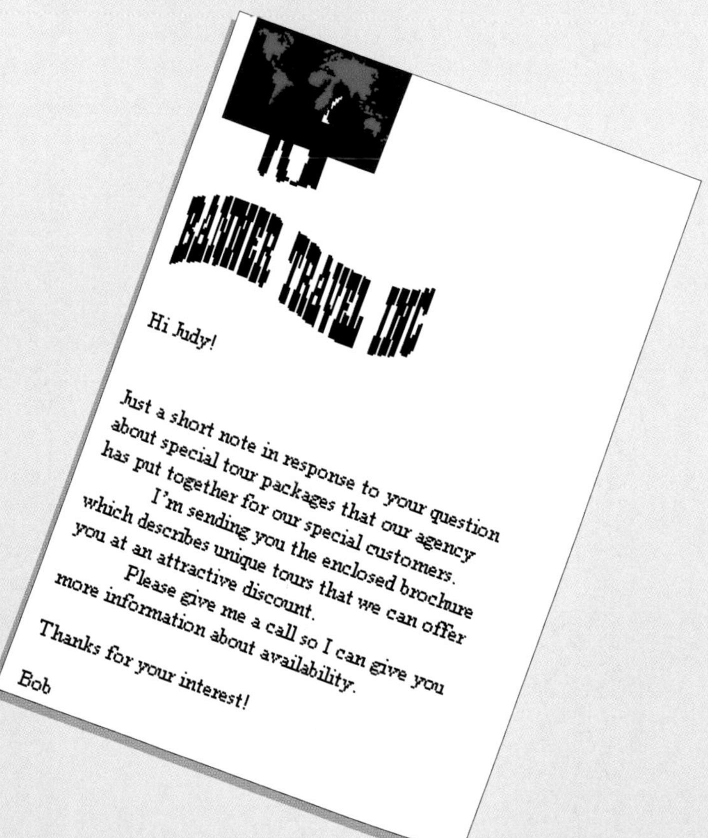
BANNER TRAVEL INC

Hi Judy!

Just a short note in response to your question about special tour packages that our agency has put together for our special customers.

I'm sending you the enclosed brochure which describes unique tours that we can offer you at an attractive discount.

Please give me a call so I can give you more information about availability.

Thanks for your interest!

Bob

**5** Using the Toolbar, click on the special effects you would like to use.

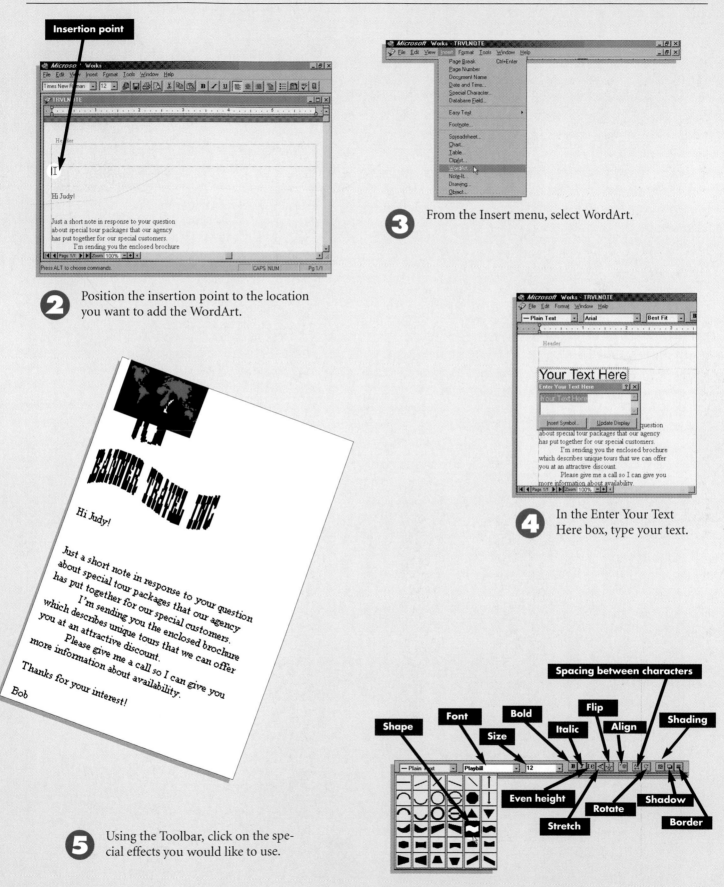

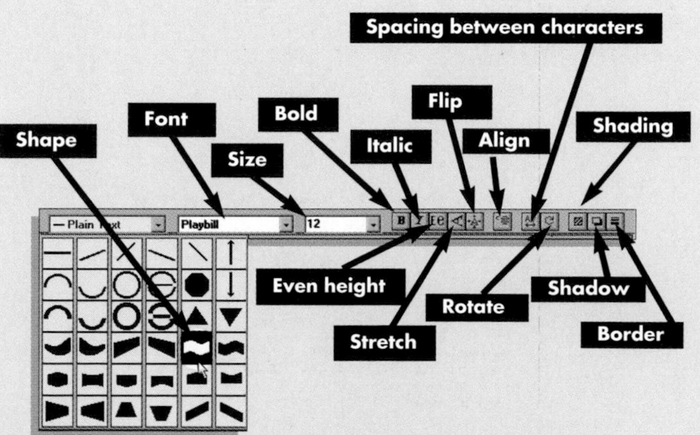

# TRY IT!

With your new database and object inserting skills still fresh in your mind, it's time to give them a short workout to bring them to peak condition. Follow these steps to gather information from a variety of sources, create a database and billing statement, and then merge the two. In addition, create a special letterhead using ClipArt and WordArt. Many of the steps include a chapter reference in case you need to go back and refresh your memory.

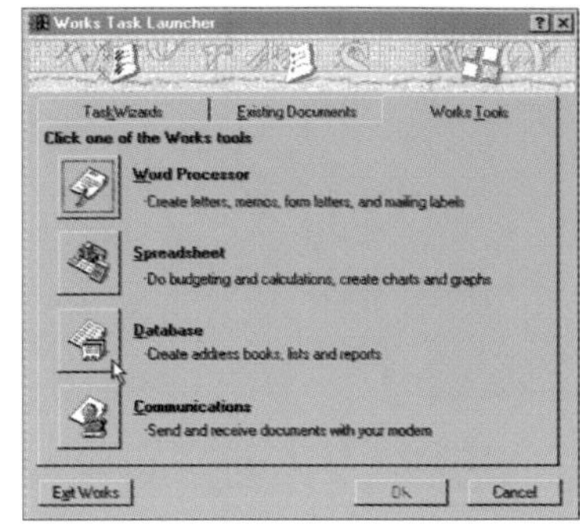


Start Works and open a new database document by first clicking on the Works Tools tab in Task Launcher. Then click on the Database button. *Chapter 15*

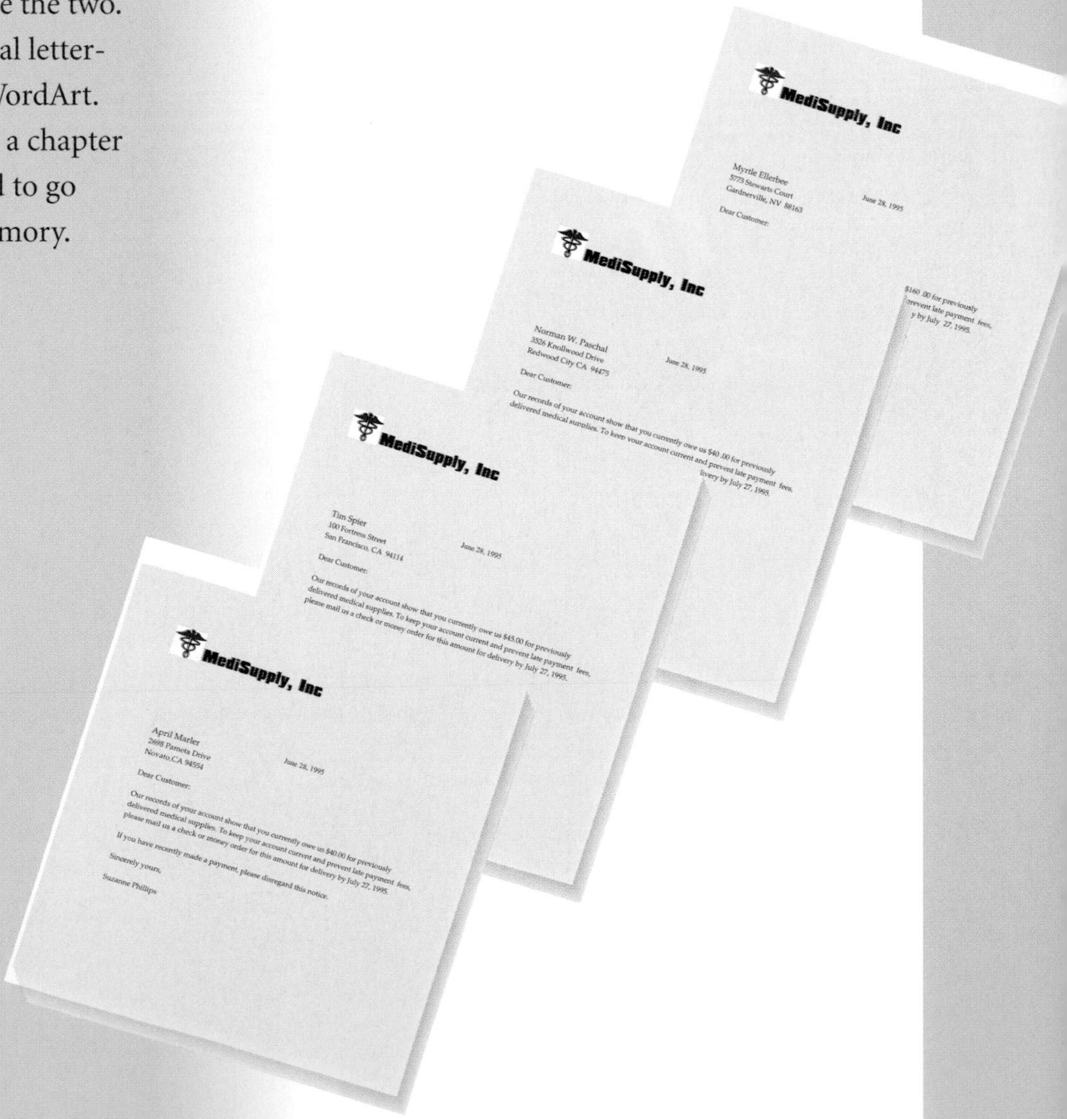

In the Create Database dialog box, type the name of the field, **Customer Name**, and click on Add. *Chapter 15*

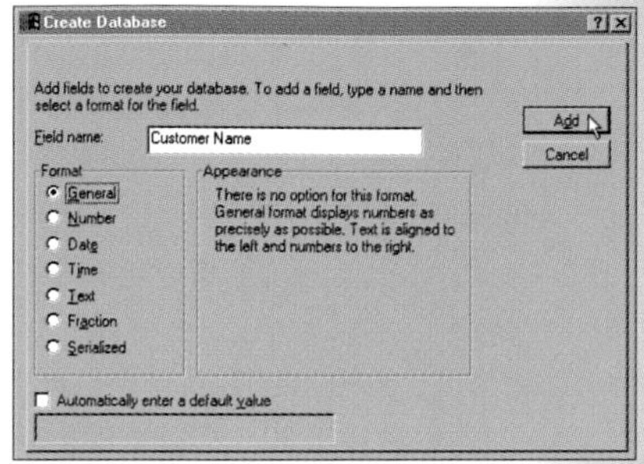


3

Repeat step 2 for the **Address** and **Account Balance** fields. When finished, click on Done. *Chapter 15*

4

Click on Hide Help in the Help menu. *Chapter 15*

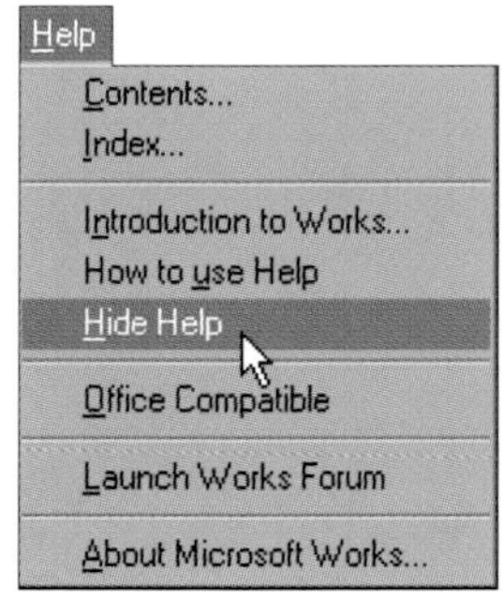

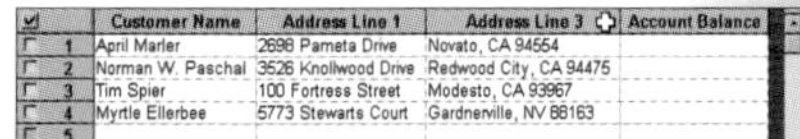

Enter the information shown into the database. When you are through, double-click on the field names at the top of the columns to resize the column widths. *Chapter 15*

In the View menu, select Form Design. *Chapter 15*

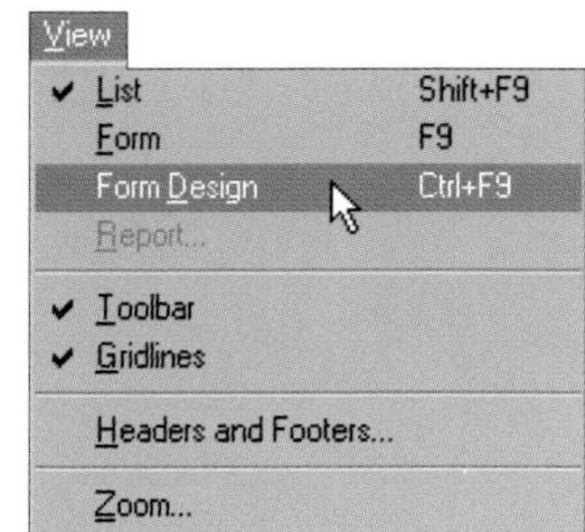

Drag the field names down to make room for a title above them, and with the insertion point at the top of the form, click on Label in the Insert menu. *Chapter 15*

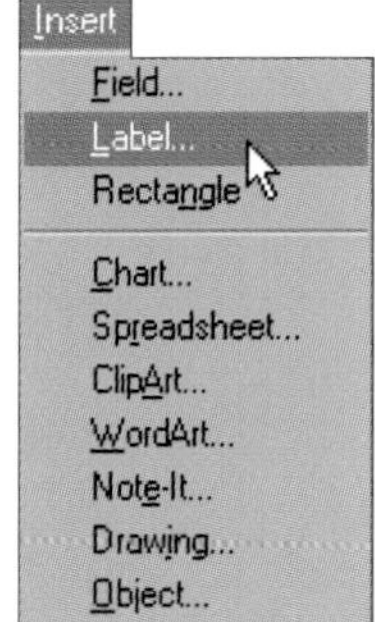

In the Insert Label dialog box, type in the title of the form. *Chapter 15*

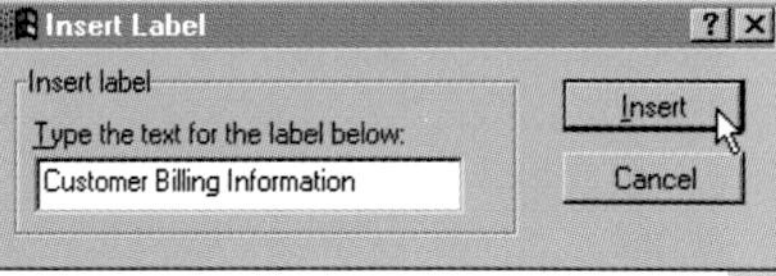

Drag the field names to align the colons vertically, then drag on the handles on the right side of the fields to lengthen them uniformly. *Chapter 15*

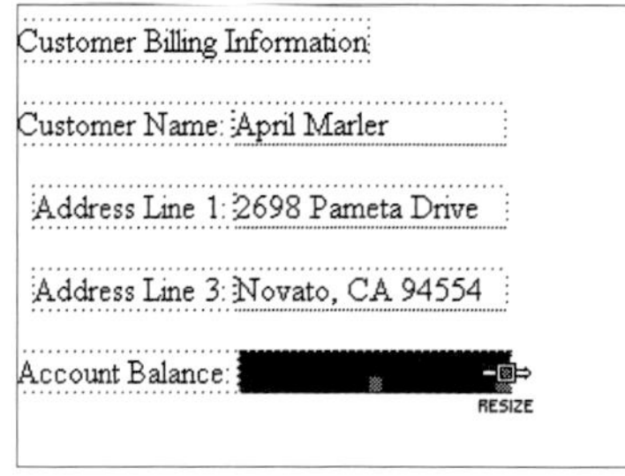


Continue to next page ►

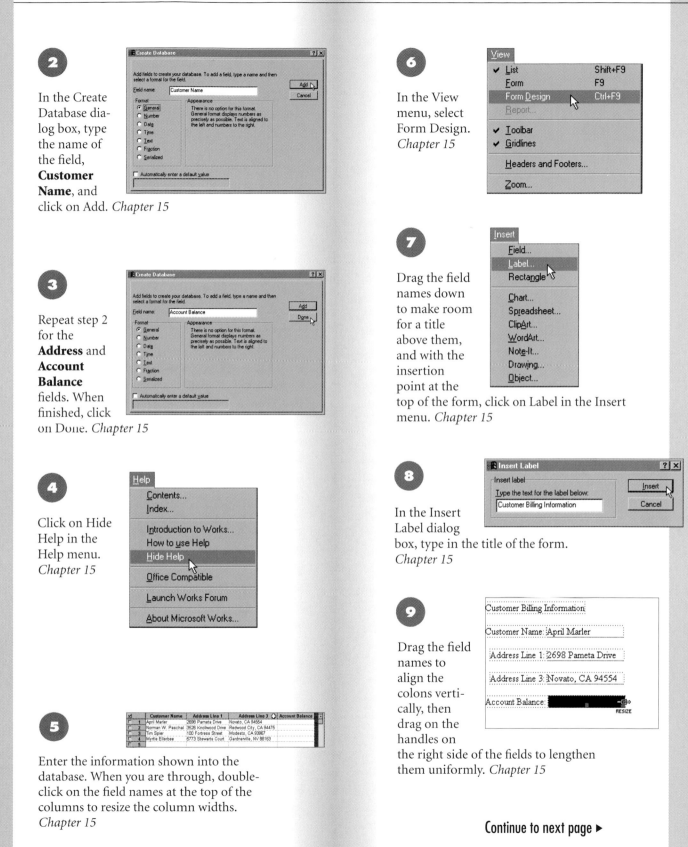

# TRY IT!

Continue below

10

Save the database by clicking on the Save icon on the Toolbar. Do not close the file yet. *Chapter 4*

In the Save As dialog box, type in the name of the file as **Billing1** and click on Save. *Chapter 4*

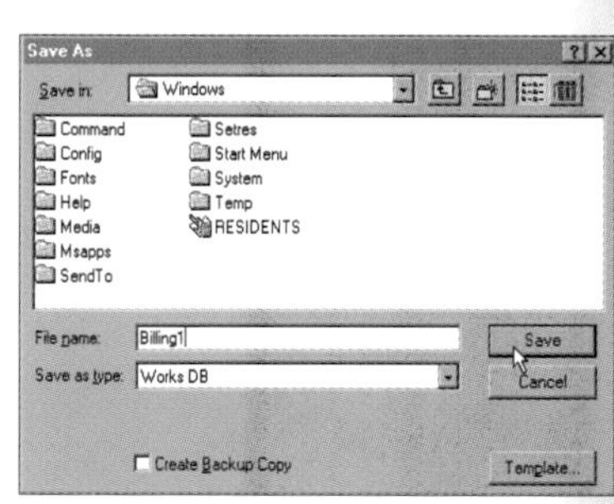

Click on the Task Launcher icon on the Toolbar. *Chapter 4*

Under the Works Tools tab, click on the Word Processor button to create a new document. *Chapter 4*

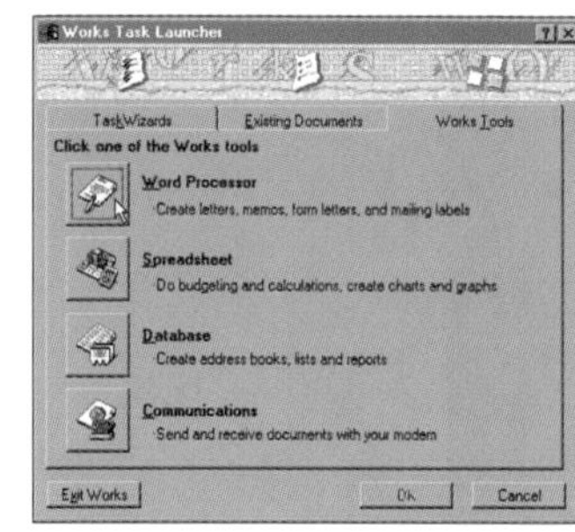

To create a logo, begin by inserting a piece of artwork. From the Insert menu, select ClipArt. (If the First Time Help box appears, click on OK.) *Chapter 20*

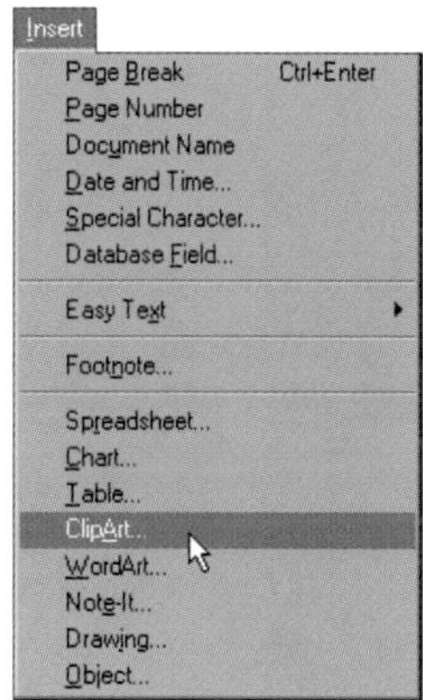

In the ClipArt Gallery, select a category and a piece of ClipArt. Click on Insert. *Chapter 20*

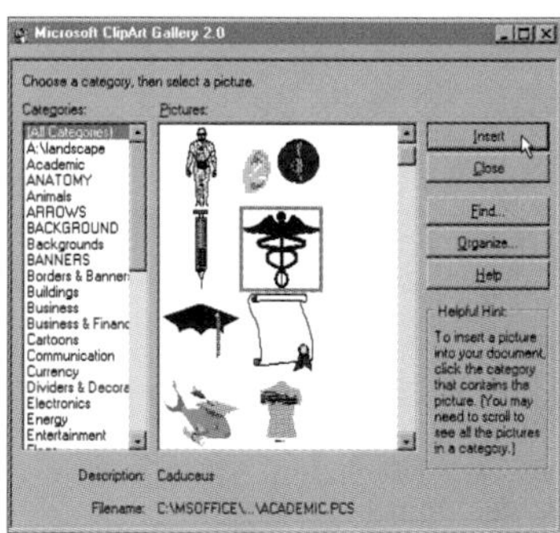

Resize the ClipArt by clicking and dragging on one of the corner handles. *Chapter 20*

With the insertion point to the right of the ClipArt, select WordArt from the Insert menu. *Chapter 20*

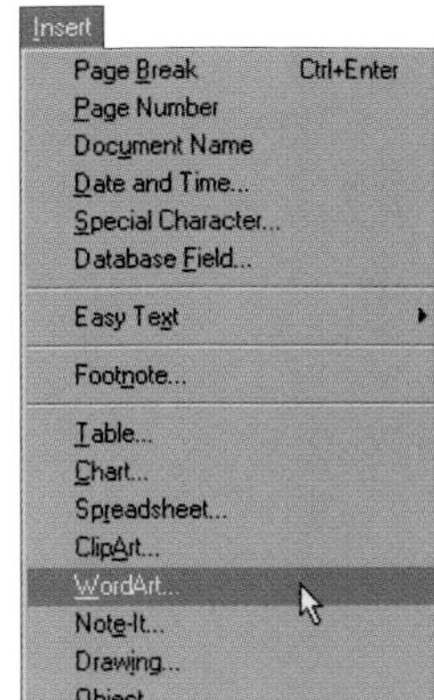

In the Enter Your Text Here box, type in a name. Then, to create special effects, choose your selections from the Toolbar. When you're finished, click anywhere outside the Enter Your Text Here box. *Chapter 20*

Type in this text. *Chapter 20*

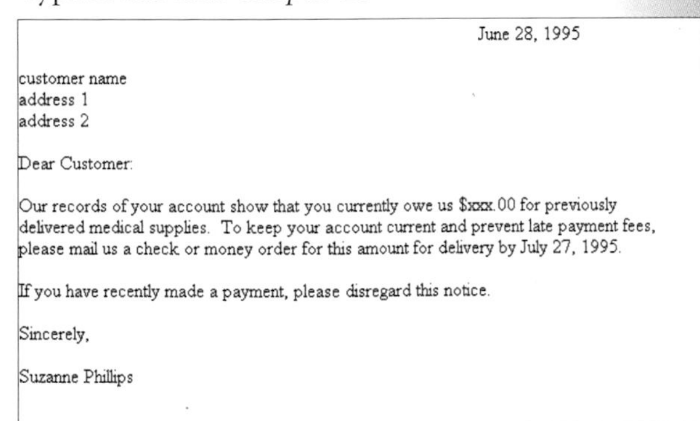

June 28, 1995

customer name
address 1
address 2

Dear Customer:

Our records of your account show that you currently owe us $xxx.00 for previously delivered medical supplies. To keep your account current and prevent late payment fees, please mail us a check or money order for this amount for delivery by July 27, 1995.

If you have recently made a payment, please disregard this notice.

Sincerely,

Suzanne Phillips

Select the text Customer Name at the top of the document, and then click on the Database Field command in the Insert menu. *Chapter 17*

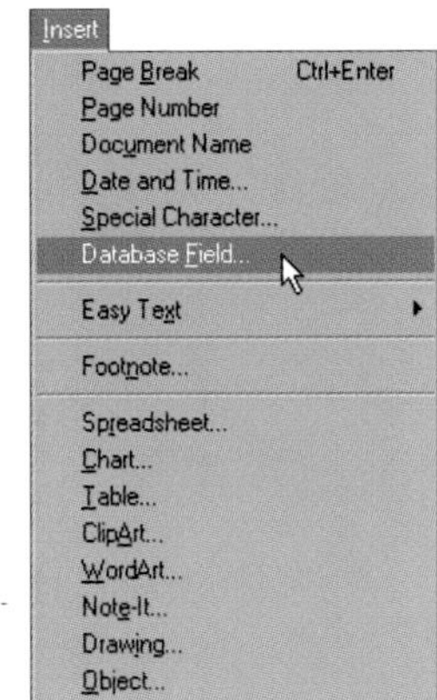

In the Insert Field dialog box, if the name of your database is not shown in the Database block, click on the Use a Different Database button. *Chapter 17*

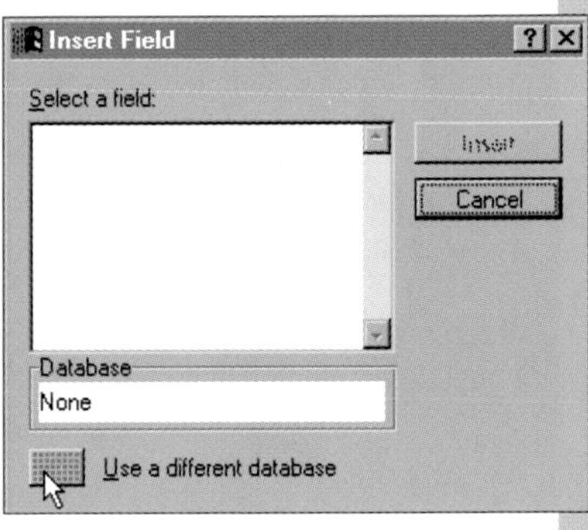

Your open database file should appear at the top of the list in the Use Database dialog box. Click on it and on the OK button. *Chapter 17*

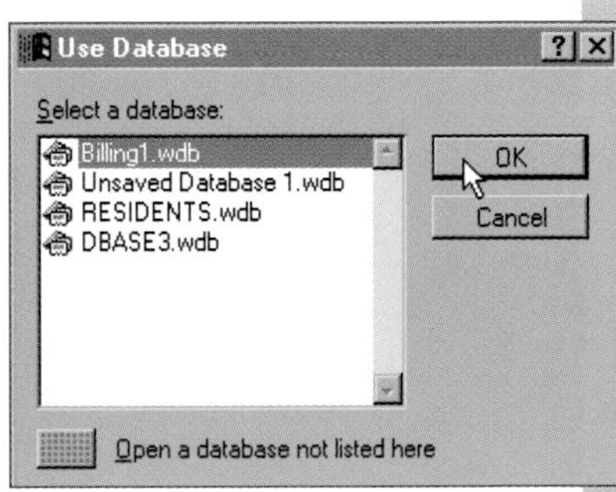


**Continue to next page ▸**

## TRY IT!

Continue below

23

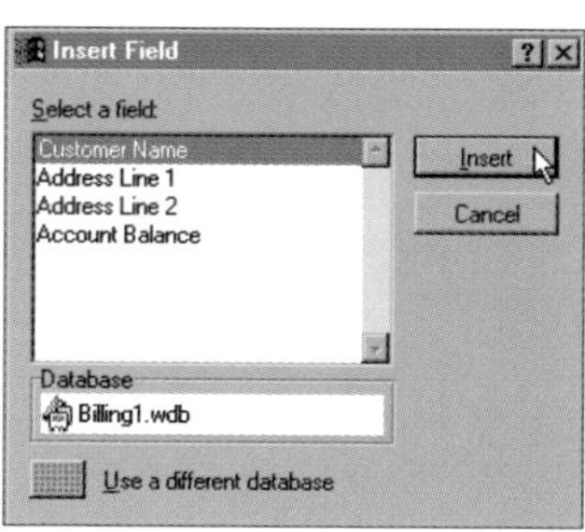


Back in the Insert Field dialog box, click on the Customer Name field and then the Insert button. Works will replace the selected text with a field placeholder, and the Cancel button will change to Close. Click on the Close button to return to the document. Chapter 17

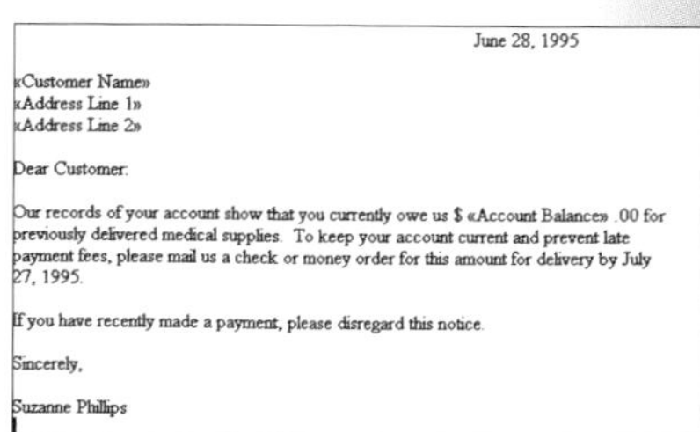

June 28, 1995

«Customer Name»
«Address Line 1»
«Address Line 2»

Dear Customer:

Our records of your account show that you currently owe us $ «Account Balance» .00 for previously delivered medical supplies. To keep your account current and prevent late payment fees, please mail us a check or money order for this amount for delivery by July 27, 1995.

If you have recently made a payment, please disregard this notice.

Sincerely,

Suzanne Phillips

Repeat steps 20 and 23 to replace *address 1, address 2, and xxx* (the account balance) with the appropriate fields from the open database. When you are finished, save the file as **Billing2**. Do not close the word processor document. *Chapter 4*

Click on the Task Launcher icon. Then click on the square spreadsheet button to create a new spreadsheet document. *Chapter 9*

| | A | B | C | D | E | F |
|---|---|---|---|---|---|---|
| 1 | | | | | | |
| 2 | | Status of New Accounts. June 28, 1995 | | | | |
| 3 | | | | | | |
| 4 | Customer | Previous Balance | Payments | Purchases | Additional Fees | New Balance |
| 5 | | | | | | |
| 6 | April Marler | 120 | 80 | | | 40 |
| 7 | Norman W. Paschall | 80 | 80 | 40 | | 40 |
| 8 | Tim Spier | 40 | | | 5 | 45 |
| 9 | Myrtle Ellerbee | | | 160 | | 160 |

Type in the text and numbers shown in the illustration. For cell F6, enter the contents of the formula bar shown here, and then copy that formula to the three cells below it. Remember both that you can select a block of cells to speed up data entry, and that you can double-click on the column headers to adjust their width to fit the data within them. *Chapters 10–12*

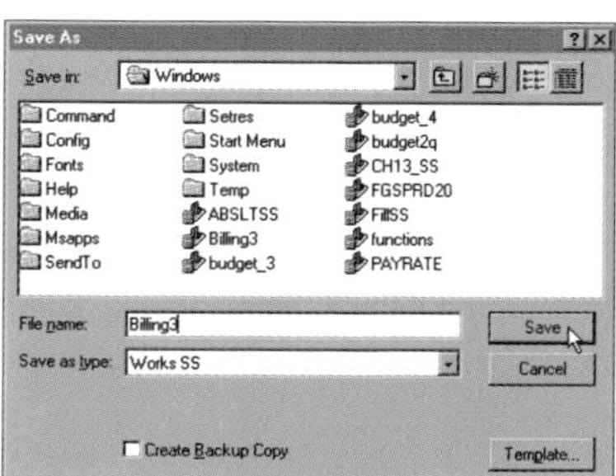


When you have completed the spreadsheet, save it as **Billing3**, but don't close it. *Chapter 9*

Next, transfer the account balances from the spreadsheet where they are calculated to the database where they can merge with the word-processed billing statement. Click and drag to select cells F6:F9, the numbers representing new balances, and then select Copy from the Toolbar. *Chapter 11*

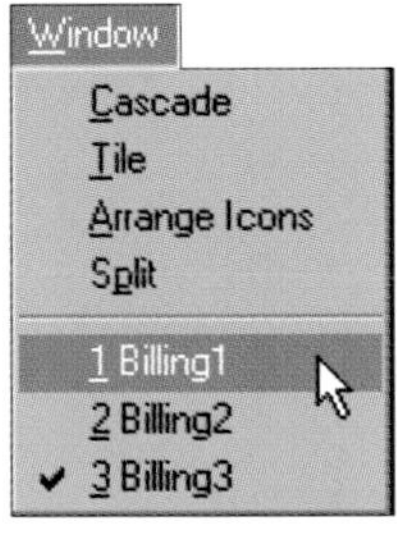


Click on the Window menu to pull it down, and click on the name of the database file you saved in step 11. *Chapter 20*

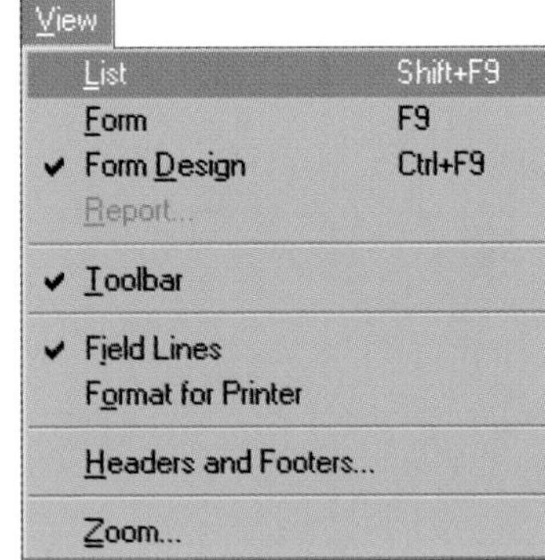


In the database document, switch to the list by clicking on List in the View menu. *Chapter 20*

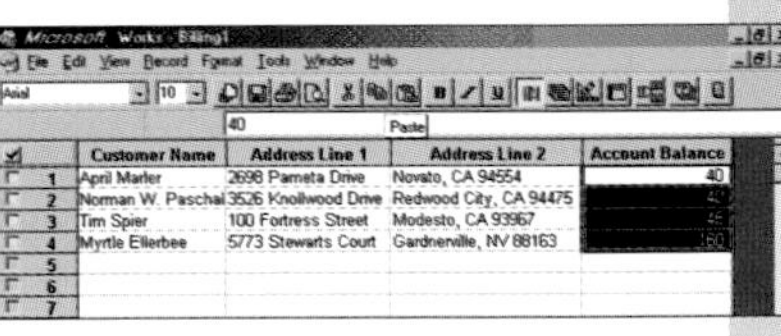


In the database document, click in the top row of the Account Balance column and then click on the Paste icon on the Toolbar. Works will paste the balance numbers from the spreadsheet into the database where they can merge with the billing statement. *Chapter 17*

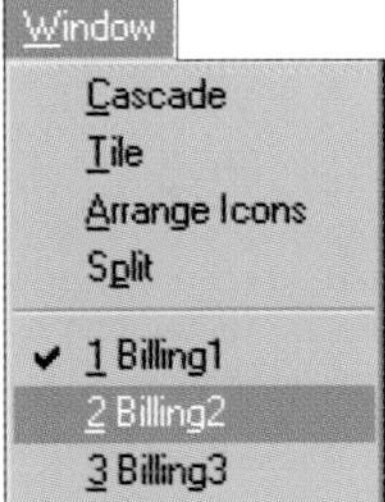


Click on the Window menu again, but this time switch to the word processor file you saved in step 24. *Chapter 17*

Get set to print the word processor file by clicking on the Print icon on the Toolbar. *Chapter 17*

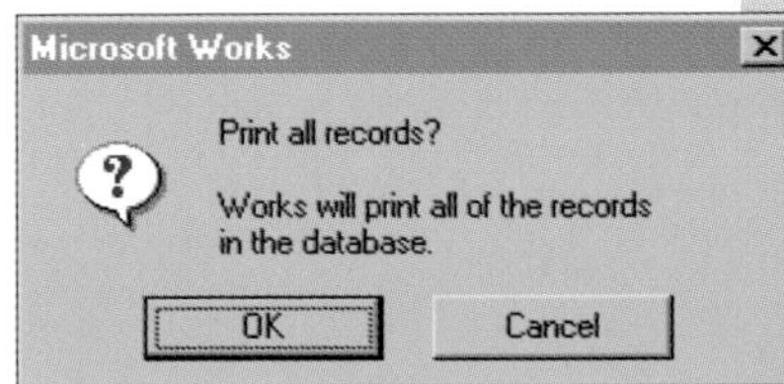


In the Microsoft Works dialog box, respond to the question "Print all records?" by clicking on OK. *Chapter 17*

## CHAPTER 21

# Connecting with Other Computers

Communication can be described as the exchange of information. You've long understood the value of communication between people, but you may wonder how you can benefit from communication between computers. The answer is simple. You probably store much of the information you use every day in your computer, and the same is true for millions of other people. When your computer can communicate directly with other computers, you have easier and more direct access to all that information.

The possible sources of information are limitless: E-mail can connect you quickly and inexpensively to friends and associates all over the world. You might have a special interest like beer brewing or whale watching and want to exchange ideas through a computer forum. You could take advantage of an unbelievable range of public domain data files ranging from recent space photographs to press releases from the White House. Maybe you're in the Bahamas and want to send a file to your boss at work so she'll think you're working at home.

Hitchhiking on the information superhighway is discouraged, so you'll need to gather a few things before you can travel there: First, you'll need an access road—any but the noisiest telephone line will work. Next, you'll need a vehicle. You already have a computer, but you'll also need a modem, a small device for connecting your computer to a telephone line. Finally, to go in style, you'll need a driver. This is where Microsoft Works becomes your best friend.

# How to Set Up Your Modem in Microsoft Works

Before you begin your travels, you'll need to get your affairs in order. Just like you had to set up Works when you got it, you'll need to take a few steps to ensure that Works, your modem, and all of the other parts of your computer are ready to work together.

**1** If you have an external modem, first make sure that it is connected to both your computer and the telephone line, and check that it is plugged in and turned on. If you have an internal modem, check that it is connected to the telephone line, and in the case of some notebook computers, that it is inserted properly and turned on.

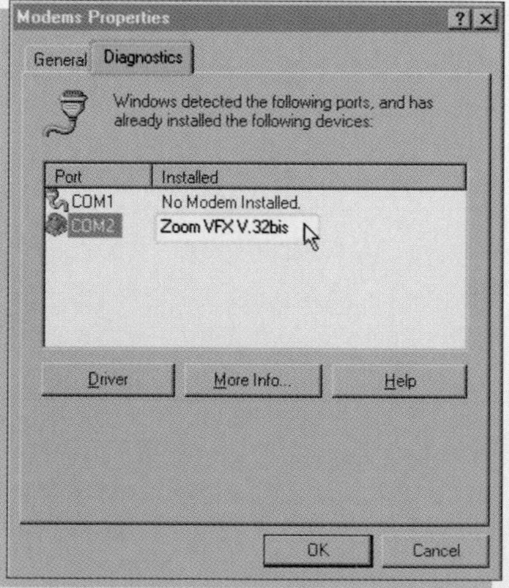


**5** Your modem is connected to your computer through a data channel called COM port. ("COM" is short for "communication.") This port may be an external connector on the back of your computer, or it may be an internal card. To see what port your modem is connected to, click on the Diagnostic tab. Works displays a list of available ports and any devices assigned to those ports.

**TIP SHEET**

- **Nine times out of ten, connecting an external modem is just a matter of fitting cables to your modem and computer. If you connect your modem and Works can't find it, you may need some technical help from your vendor, modem manufacturer, or in-house technician.**
- **If you're not absolutely sure how to install an internal modem, get help. Many vendors will install it for you if you bring in your machine.**

**2** Start Works. In the Works Task Launcher Dialog box, click on the Communications button to begin a new communications session.

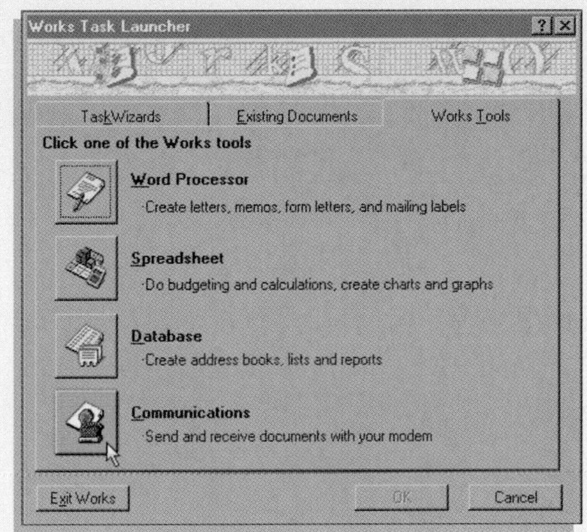

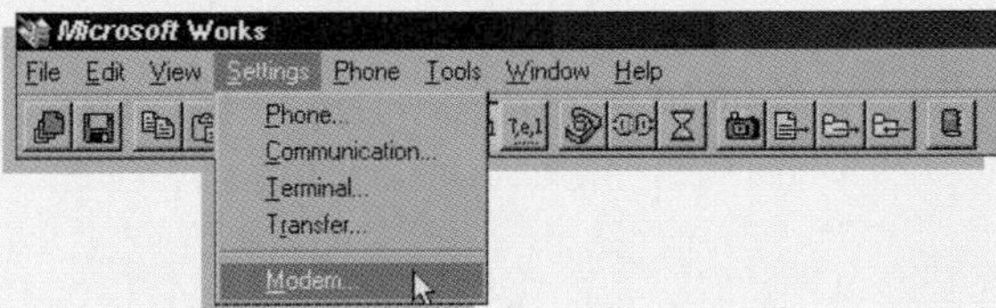


**3** The first time you run the communications program, Works will display the Modem Setup dialog box. If you see the Easy Connect dialog box instead, click the Cancel button. Next select Modem from the Settings menu. Works will then display the Modem Setup dialog box.

**4** With Windows 95's new Plug and Play feature Works can automatically detect whether your computer has a modem installed.

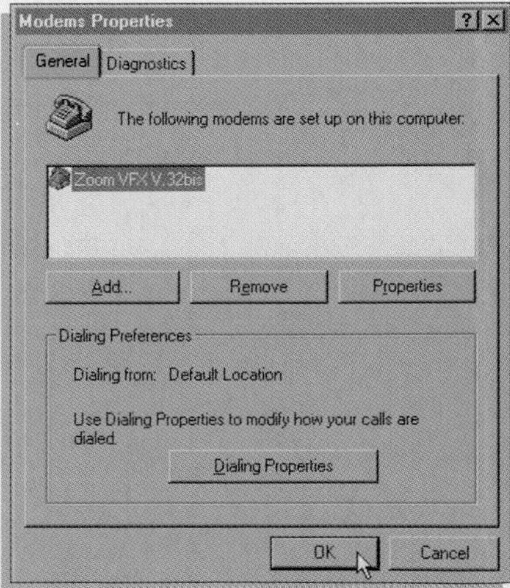

# How to Change Communication Settings

When you talk to another person, you generally know ahead of time what language you will speak and what rules of grammar you will use. Unfortunately, when you set up your computer to "talk" to another computer, you generally can't assume what protocols, or rules of communication, the other computer will be set up to use.

This means a little legwork on your part. Before you dial with your modem, you'll need to find someone familiar with the other computer (the one you want to communicate with) and ask a few questions about protocols. Once you know what protocols the other computer is using, you'll want to change your Microsoft Works communication settings to use the same ones.

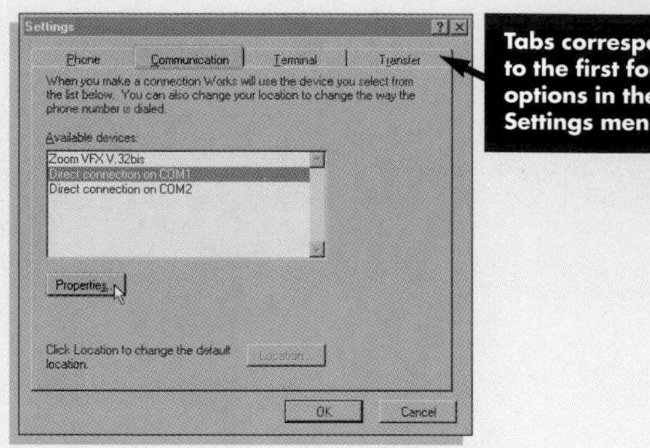


**Tabs correspond to the first four options in the Settings menu.**

**1** Open the Settings menu and click on Communication. Works will respond by opening the Settings dialog box. To view connection properties, click on the Properties button.

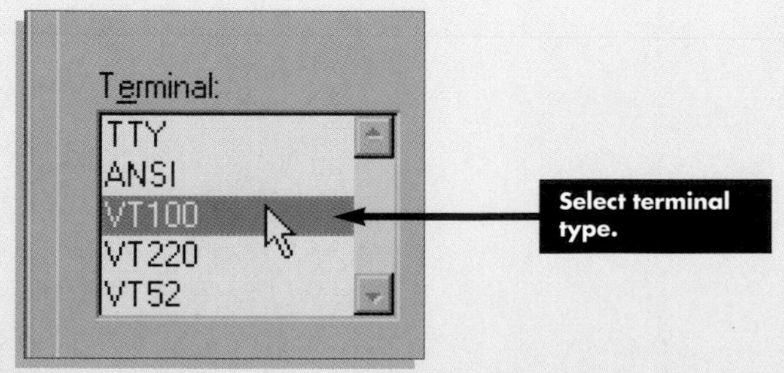


**Select terminal type.**

**7** You may need to find out ahead of time what terminal types are supported by the computer you're connecting to. Often, however, many different types are available, and you can select one for Works to emulate after you connect.

**TIP SHEET**

- **If you have trouble transferring files, or get random characters when sending and receiving text, you may have a noisy line. Try a lower baud rate.**
- **If you connect to another computer and the text on your display writes repeatedly on the same line, try different End of Lines options on the Terminal page of the Settings dialog box. The other computer may not be sending CR (carriage return) or LF (line feed) signals to your computer. If you select these options and click the OK button, Works will add them.**
- **If you connect to another computer and can't see the text you type, mark the Local Echo check box.**

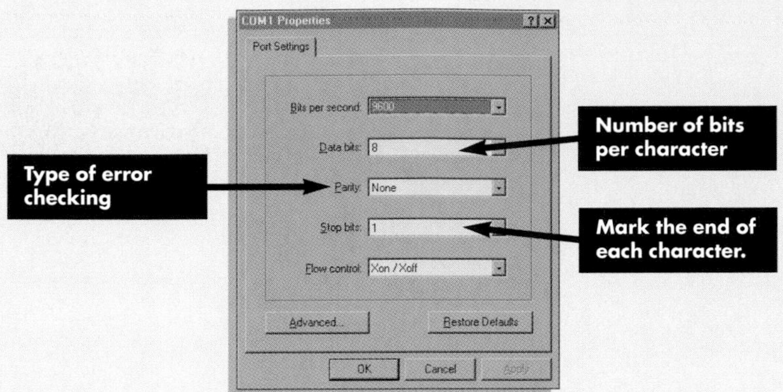

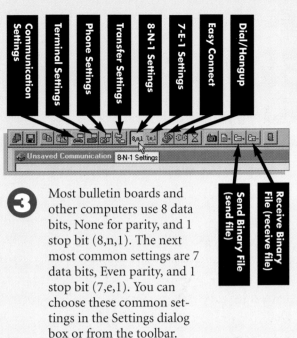


Communication Settings
Terminal Settings
Phone Settings
Transfer Settings
8-N-1 Settings
7-E-1 Settings
Easy Connect
Dial/Hangup
Unsaved Communication
8-N-1 Settings
Send Binary File (send file)
Receive Binary File (receive file)

**2** The most important options in this dialog box are Data Bits, Parity, and Stop Bits. The Data Bits setting is the number of bits in each character that you send and receive. The Parity setting describes how your computer will check each character for accuracy. The Stop Bits setting tells how to mark the end of each character. Before you can connect computers, you must match the settings the other computer will use.

**3** Most bulletin boards and other computers use 8 data bits, None for parity, and 1 stop bit (8,n,1). The next most common settings are 7 data bits, Even parity, and 1 stop bit (7,e,1). You can choose these common settings in the Settings dialog box or from the toolbar.

**4** Set the Port setting for your modem. From the list of available devices select your modem. Then click the Properties button

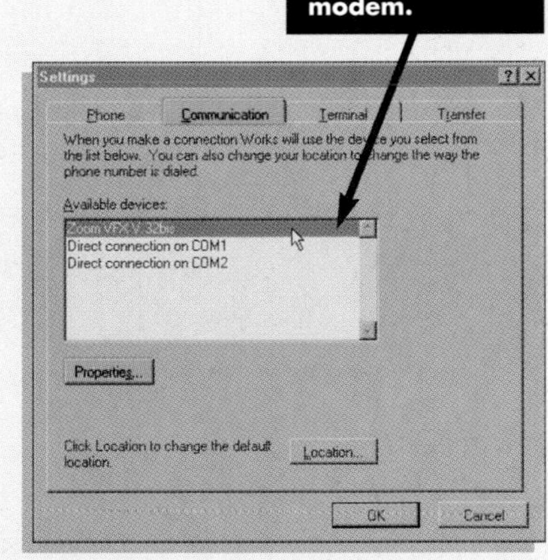


**6** To check your terminal settings, click on the Terminal tab at the top of the Settings dialog box, or select Terminal from the Settings menu.

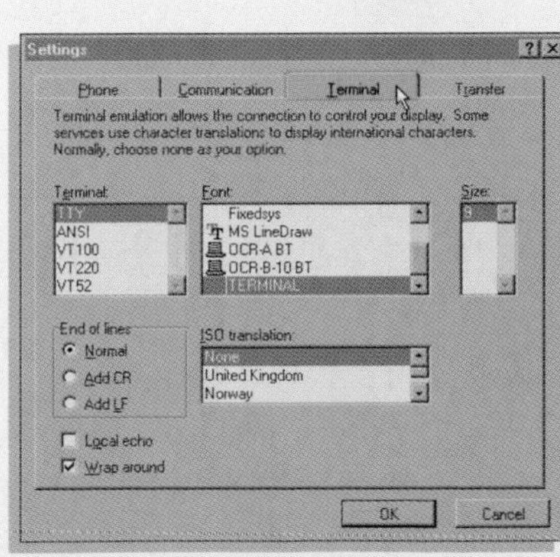


**5** *Baud rate* is the speed, in bits per second, at which data will travel between computers (higher numbers mean faster communication). Select the fastest setting that your modem will support (it's in the modem documentation).

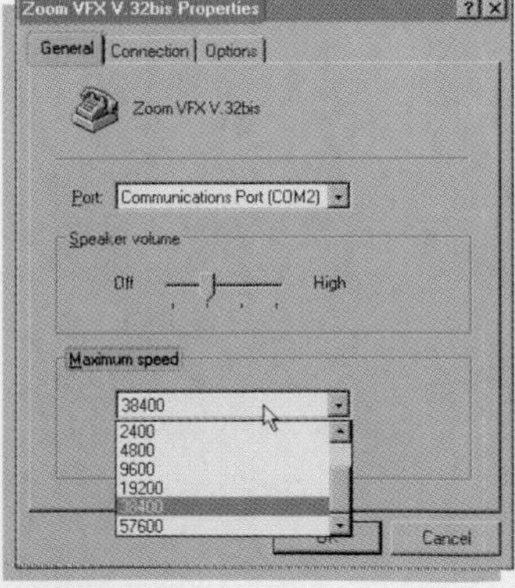

# How to Connect to Another Computer

Once you know and establish the communications settings, you can connect to a wide assortment of computer services. The example here connects to Microsoft Download Service. This service is a computer bulletin board that lets you download files (transfer them from a large central computer to yours) for updating Microsoft products that you already license or own. The communication settings for the service are 8,n,1; and it supports baud rates of 1,200; 2,400; 9,600; and 14,400 bits per second.

The example on this page includes a telephone call to Washington State. If you want to follow along with the example, you may want to look over this and the next spread first, so that you don't spend unnecessary time on a long-distance call.

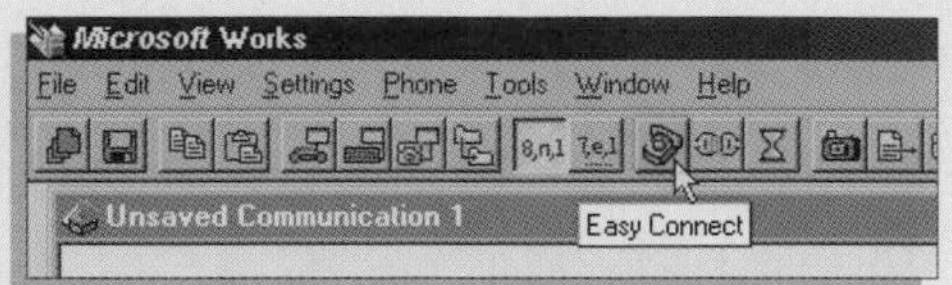

1. Double-check that the settings you chose in the previous two spreads are correct. Then, click on the Easy Connect icon on the toolbar.

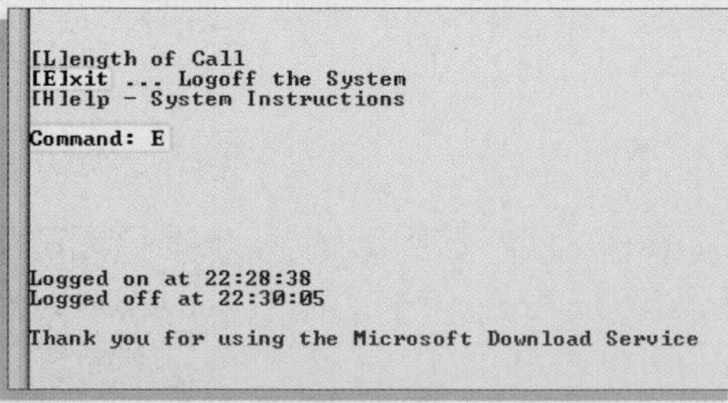

7. When you're finished with your business, follow the instructions on the screen to return to the Main menu, and press E to exit.

## TIP SHEET

- **Works ignores the hyphens you put in telephone numbers. If you need a short pause between numbers while dialing a telephone number, add a comma where you want the pause. If you need a longer pause, add more than one comma.**
- **To save all your settings in a file so you don't have to reenter them the next time you connect, select Save from the File menu. Later, you can reuse them by opening the file you saved, or you can select the service by name from the Easy Connect dialog box.**
- **Some computer services have online charges. That means they charge you for the time you spend connected to them. Always ask if you will be billed before you make a connection. (Microsoft Download Service does not have an online charge.)**

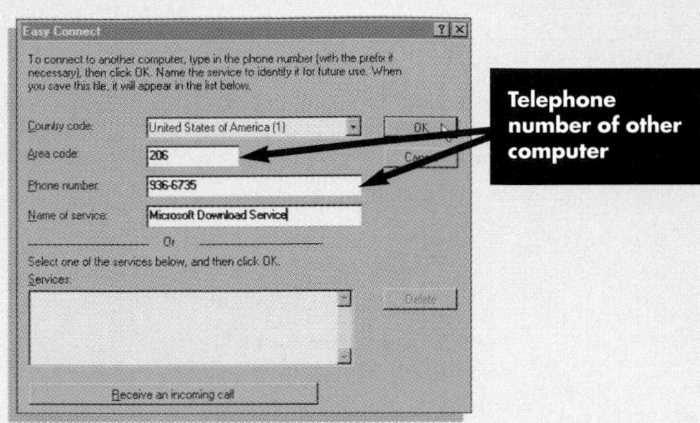


**2** Type in the telephone number of the computer you want to call. Next type in a descriptive name for the service. This name will appear in the Easy Connect dialog box the next time you start the communications program.

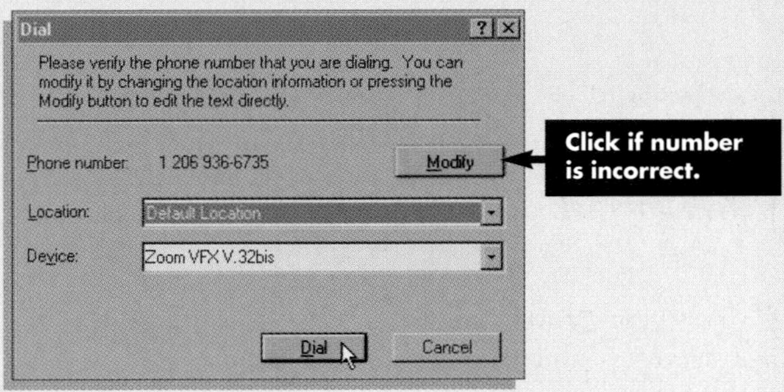


**3** Check the phone number once more and if it is correct click the Dial button. If the number is incorrect click the Modify button instead.

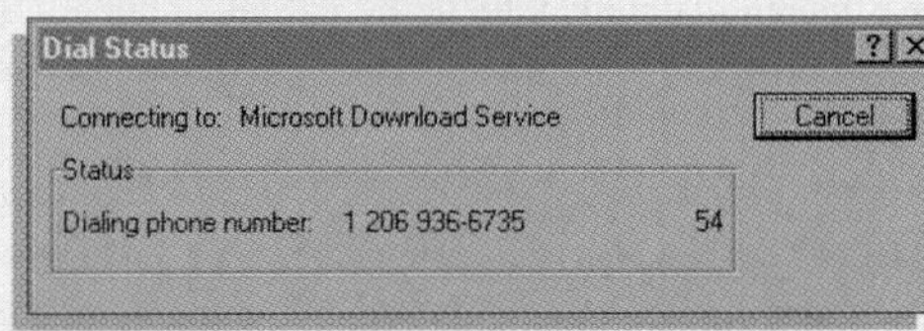


**4** The Dial Status dialog box will appear while Works connects to the service. Listen closely and you'll hear the dial tone, the number being entered, and then the distinctive connect tones—it's an electronic symphony.

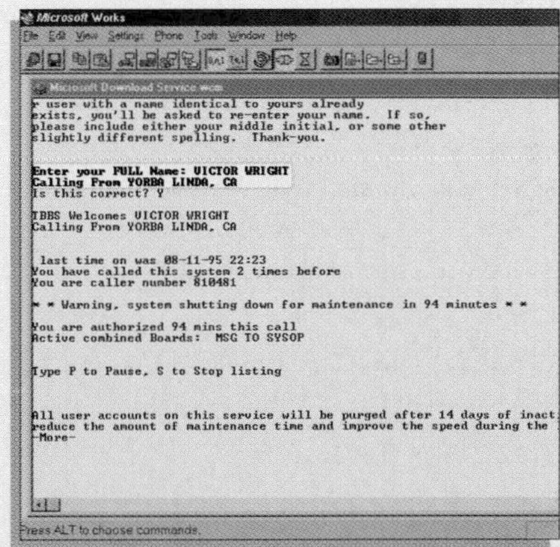


**5** Every information service offers different features, but many computer bulletin boards have a look and feel similar to the Microsoft Download Service. The first time you connect, the service will ask you for your name and location. It then greets you, shows service news summaries, and shows you to its Main menu.

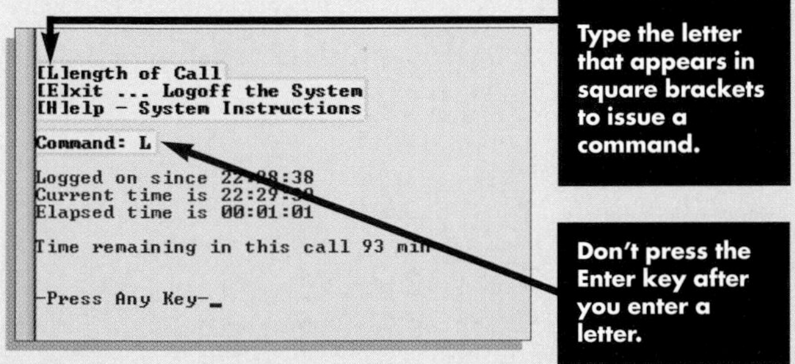


**6** To execute a command in any menu, type the letter that appears in square brackets. You don't need to press Enter afterward. For example, to find out how long you've been connected, press L on your keyboard. (Downloading files is covered in the next spread.)

# How to Send and Receive Files

Transferring files is a highly specialized form of communicating with another computer. Because of this, many transfer protocols, or languages, have evolved for doing nothing but transferring files. Four of the best transfer protocols are provided for your use in Microsoft Works.

## TIP SHEET

- **Sending a file to another computer is much the same as receiving one. Instead of selecting Receive File from the Tools menu, however, select Send File. You'll need to locate the file for Works to send. It's a good idea to know where it is before you connect to the other computer. If possible, put it in the same folder as Works for easy access.**
- **If you know what transfer protocol you will be using for your transfer, save money by selecting it before you connect to the other computer.**
- **The four transfer protocols all have unique characteristics. XMODEM is the most commonly used, and is quite reliable for transferring data accurately. YMODEM is faster than XMODEM, but does not work well with a noisy telephone line. ZMODEM is faster than YMODEM and as reliable as XMODEM, but is not quite as commonly used. Use it when you can. Kermit, the slowest of the four, is also the most reliable, working well with noisy telephone lines. Use it only when necessary.**

1. Following the procedures explained earlier in this chapter, connect Works to another computer that will let you receive, or download, a file.

8. Wait for an indicator that the transfer is complete. Once you see it, you are free to interact with the other computer exactly as you did before the transfer.

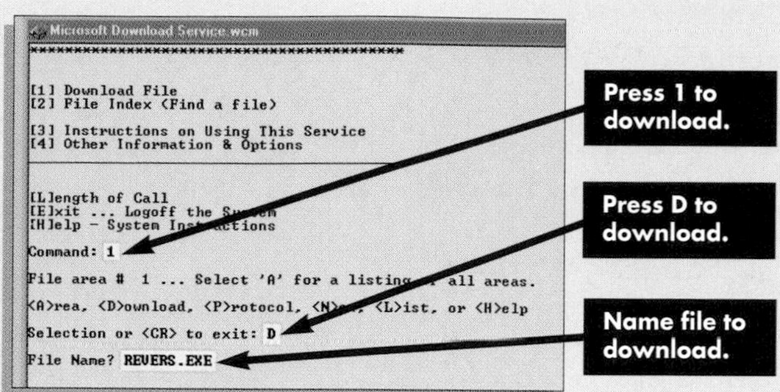


**2** Send the other computer the signal that you want to download a file. (In this case, press D.) Once you tell it the file you want (in this case, REVERS.EXE), the other computer will ask you what transfer protocol to use.

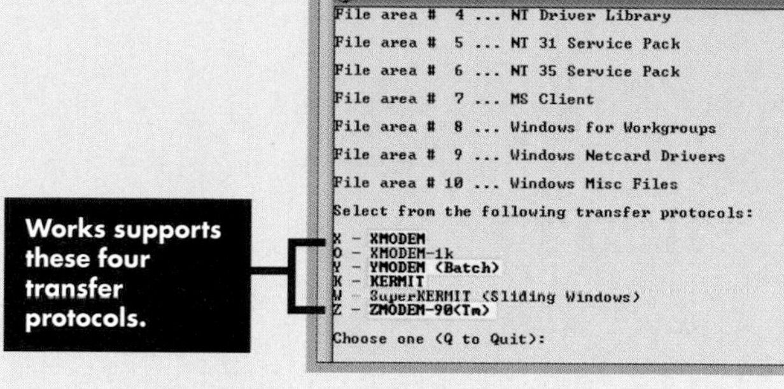

Microsoft Download Service.wcm
File area # 4 ... NT Driver Library
File area # 5 ... NT 31 Service Pack
File area # 6 ... NT 35 Service Pack
File area # 7 ... MS Client
File area # 8 ... Windows for Workgroups
File area # 9 ... Windows Netcard Drivers
File area # 10 ... Windows Misc Files
Select from the following transfer protocols:
X - XMODEM
O - XMODEM-1k
Y - YMODEM (Batch)
K - KERMIT
W - SuperKERMIT (Sliding Windows)
Z - ZMODEM-90(Tm)
Choose one (Q to Quit):
Works supports these four transfer protocols.


**3** Works offers four file-transfer protocols: XMODEM, YMODEM, ZMODEM, and Kermit. Select one of them.

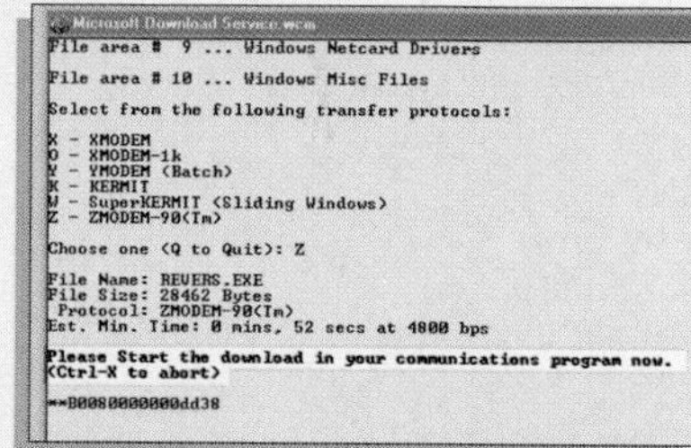

File area # 9 ... Windows Netcard Drivers
File area # 10 ... Windows Misc Files
Select from the following transfer protocols:
X - XMODEM
O - XMODEM-1k
Y - YMODEM (Batch)
K - KERMIT
W - SuperKERMIT (Sliding Windows)
Z - ZMODEM-90(Tm)
Choose one (Q to Quit): Z
File Name: REVERS.EXE
File Size: 28462 Bytes
Protocol: ZMODEM-90(Tm)
Est. Min. Time: 0 mins, 52 secs at 4800 bps
Please Start the download in your communications program now.
(Ctrl-X to abort)


**4** The other computer will tell you to initiate the download in your communications software.

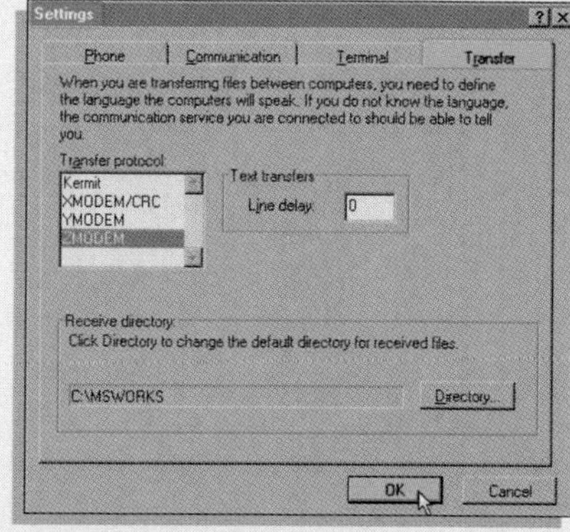


**5** Select Transfer from the Settings menu and select the same transfer protocol as you did in step 3. Then click the OK button.

Receive File

| | |
|---|---|
| Receiving File: | revers.exe |
| Saved As: | C:\MSWORKS\revers.e |
| Bytes received: | 3072 |
| Percent complete: | 11% |
| Error count: | 0 |

Status: Receiving in progress...

Cancel

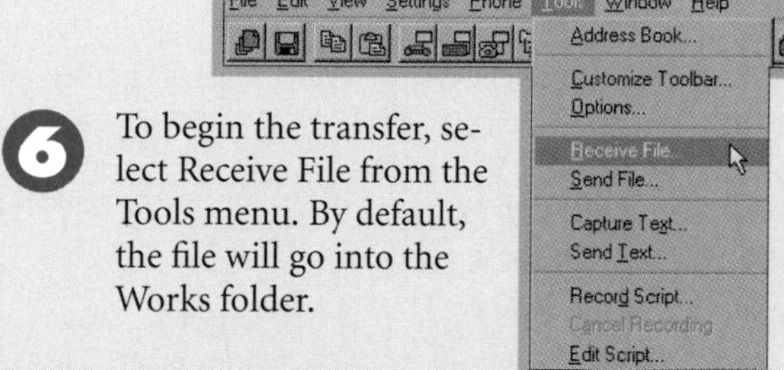


**6** To begin the transfer, select Receive File from the Tools menu. By default, the file will go into the Works folder.

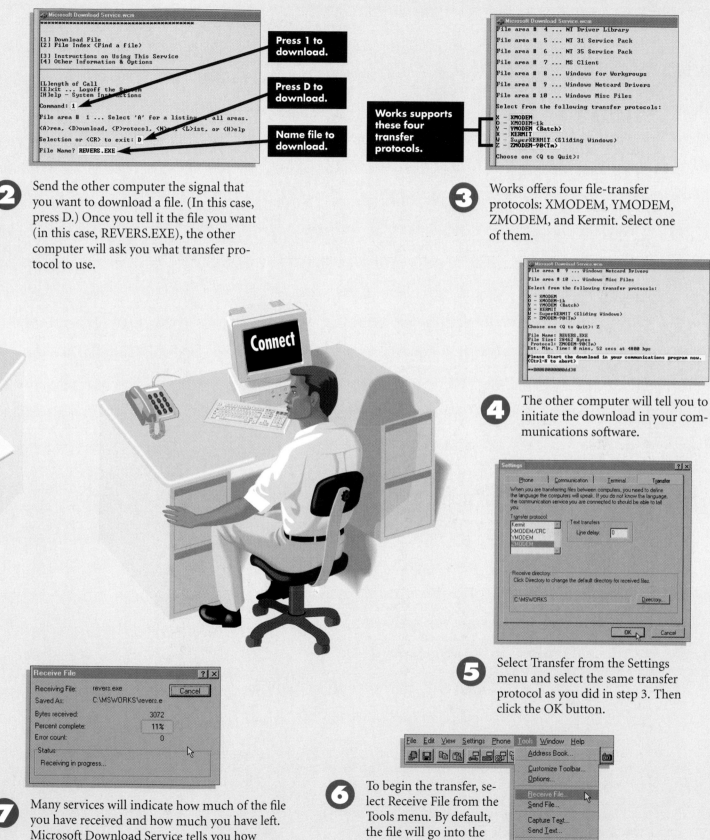

**7** Many services will indicate how much of the file you have received and how much you have left. Microsoft Download Service tells you how many bytes and what percentage of the file you have received.

# INDEX

## J



## K



## L



## M



## N



## O



## P



## Q



## R

*Cut Here*

*Cut Here*

## Ziff-Davis Press Survey of Readers

Please help us in our effort to produce the best books on personal computing. For your assistance, we would be pleased to send you a FREE catalog featuring the complete line of Ziff-Davis Press books.

1. How did you first learn about this book?

- Recommended by a friend . . . . . . . . . . . . . . . ☐ -1 (5)
- Recommended by store personnel . . . . . . . . . ☐ -2
- Saw in Ziff-Davis Press catalog . . . . . . . . . . . ☐ -3
- Received advertisement in the mail . . . . . . . . ☐ -4
- Saw the book on bookshelf at store . . . . . . . . ☐ -5
- Read book review in: ________________ ☐ -6
- Saw an advertisement in: ________________ ☐ -7
- Other (Please specify): ________________ ☐ -8

2. Which THREE of the following factors most influenced your decision to purchase this book? (Please check up to THREE.)

- Front or back cover information on book . . . ☐ -1 (6)
- Logo of magazine affiliated with book . . . . . ☐ -2
- Special approach to the content . . . . . . . . . . ☐ -3
- Completeness of content . . . . . . . . . . . . . . . . ☐ -4
- Author's reputation. . . . . . . . . . . . . . . . . . . . ☐ -5
- Publisher's reputation . . . . . . . . . . . . . . . . . ☐ -6
- Book cover design or layout . . . . . . . . . . . . . ☐ -7
- Index or table of contents of book . . . . . . . . . ☐ -8
- Price of book . . . . . . . . . . . . . . . . . . . . . . . . ☐ -9
- Special effects, graphics, illustrations . . . . . . ☐ -0
- Other (Please specify): ________________ ☐ -x

3. How many computer books have you purchased in the last six months? _____ (7-10)

4. On a scale of 1 to 5, where 5 is excellent, 4 is above average, 3 is average, 2 is below average, and 1 is poor, please rate each of the following aspects of this book below. (Please circle your answer.)

| | | | | | | |
|---|---|---|---|---|---|---|
| Depth/completeness of coverage | 5 | 4 | 3 | 2 | 1 | (11) |
| Organization of material | 5 | 4 | 3 | 2 | 1 | (12) |
| Ease of finding topic | 5 | 4 | 3 | 2 | 1 | (13) |
| Special features/time saving tips | 5 | 4 | 3 | 2 | 1 | (14) |
| Appropriate level of writing | 5 | 4 | 3 | 2 | 1 | (15) |
| Usefulness of table of contents | 5 | 4 | 3 | 2 | 1 | (16) |
| Usefulness of index | 5 | 4 | 3 | 2 | 1 | (17) |
| Usefulness of accompanying disk | 5 | 4 | 3 | 2 | 1 | (18) |
| Usefulness of illustrations/graphics | 5 | 4 | 3 | 2 | 1 | (19) |
| Cover design and attractiveness | 5 | 4 | 3 | 2 | 1 | (20) |
| Overall design and layout of book | 5 | 4 | 3 | 2 | 1 | (21) |
| Overall satisfaction with book | 5 | 4 | 3 | 2 | 1 | (22) |

5. Which of the following computer publications do you read regularly; that is, 3 out of 4 issues?

- Byte . . . . . . . . . . . . . . . . . . . . . . . . . . . . . . . . ☐ -1 (23)
- Computer Shopper . . . . . . . . . . . . . . . . . . . . ☐ -2
- Corporate Computing . . . . . . . . . . . . . . . . . . ☐ -3
- Dr. Dobb's Journal . . . . . . . . . . . . . . . . . . . . ☐ -4
- LAN Magazine . . . . . . . . . . . . . . . . . . . . . . . ☐ -5
- MacWEEK . . . . . . . . . . . . . . . . . . . . . . . . . . ☐ -6
- MacUser . . . . . . . . . . . . . . . . . . . . . . . . . . . ☐ -7
- PC Computing . . . . . . . . . . . . . . . . . . . . . . . ☐ -8
- PC Magazine . . . . . . . . . . . . . . . . . . . . . . . . ☐ -9
- PC WEEK . . . . . . . . . . . . . . . . . . . . . . . . . . ☐ -0
- Windows Sources . . . . . . . . . . . . . . . . . . . . . ☐ -x
- Other (Please specify): ________________ ☐ -y

**Please turn page.**

Cut Here

Cut Here

PLEASE TAPE HERE ONLY—DO NOT STAPLE

6. What is your level of experience with personal computers? With the subject of this book?

| | With PCs | | With subject of book | |
|---|---|---|---|---|
| Beginner. . . . . . . . . . . . . . . | ☐ | -1 (24) | ☐ | -1 (25) |
| Intermediate. . . . . . . . . . . | ☐ | -2 | ☐ | -2 |
| Advanced. . . . . . . . . . . . . . | ☐ | -3 | ☐ | -3 |

7. Which of the following best describes your job title?

Officer (CEO/President/VP/owner). . . . . . . . ☐ -1 (26)
Director/head. . . . . . . . . . . . . . . . . . . . . . . . . ☐ -2
Manager/supervisor. . . . . . . . . . . . . . . . . . . . . ☐ -3
Administration/staff. . . . . . . . . . . . . . . . . . . . ☐ -4
Teacher/educator/trainer. . . . . . . . . . . . . . . . . ☐ -5
Lawyer/doctor/medical professional. . . . . . . . ☐ -6
Engineer/technician. . . . . . . . . . . . . . . . . . . . ☐ -7
Consultant. . . . . . . . . . . . . . . . . . . . . . . . . . . ☐ -8
Not employed/student/retired. . . . . . . . . . . . ☐ -9
Other (Please specify): ________________ ☐ -0

8. What is your age?

Under 20. . . . . . . . . . . . . . . . . . . . . . . . . . . . . ☐ -1 (27)
21-29. . . . . . . . . . . . . . . . . . . . . . . . . . . . . . . . ☐ -2
30-39. . . . . . . . . . . . . . . . . . . . . . . . . . . . . . . . ☐ -3
40-49. . . . . . . . . . . . . . . . . . . . . . . . . . . . . . . . ☐ -4
50-59. . . . . . . . . . . . . . . . . . . . . . . . . . . . . . . . ☐ -5
60 or over. . . . . . . . . . . . . . . . . . . . . . . . . . . ☐ -6

9. Are you:

Male. . . . . . . . . . . . . . . . . . . . . . . . . . . . . . . . . ☐ -1 (28)
Female. . . . . . . . . . . . . . . . . . . . . . . . . . . . . . . ☐ -2

Thank you for your assistance with this important information! Please write your address below to receive our free catalog.

Name: ______________________________

Address: ____________________________

City/State/Zip: _______________________

**Fold here to mail.**

3504-13-14

NO POSTAGE NECESSARY IF MAILED IN THE UNITED STATES

**BUSINESS REPLY MAIL**

FIRST CLASS MAIL PERMIT NO. 1612 OAKLAND, CA

POSTAGE WILL BE PAID BY ADDRESSEE

**Ziff-Davis Press**
5903 Christie Avenue
Emeryville, CA 94608-1925
Attn: Marketing